Documents of American Broadcasting

Third Edition

Edited by
Frank J. Kahn

Herbert H. Lehman College
City University of New York

PRENTICE-HALL, Inc. Englewood Cliffs, New Jersey 07632

Library of Congress Cataloging in Publication Data

Kahn, Frank J comp.
    Documents of American broadcasting.

    Bibliography: p.
    Includes index.
        1. Television—Law and legislation—United States.
        2. Radio—United States—Laws and regulations.
    I. Title.
    KF2804.K3 1978   343'.73'0994   77–17387
    ISBN 0–13–217067–1

© 1978 by Prentice-Hall, Inc., Englewood Cliffs, N.J. 07632

Printed in the United States of America

10 9 8 7 6 5 4 3

Prentice-Hall International, Inc., *London*
Prentice-Hall of Australia Pty. Limited, *Sydney*
Prentice-Hall of Canada, Ltd., *Toronto*
Prentice-Hall of India Private Limited, *New Delhi*
Prentice-Hall of Japan, Inc., *Tokyo*
Prentice-Hall of Southeast Asia Pte. Ltd., *Singapore*
Whitehall Books Limited, *Wellington, New Zealand*

For Abby, Julie, and Leora

Contents

Thematic Contents

FREEDOM OF EXPRESSION: BROADCAST JOURNALISM

REGULATION OF COMPETITION

Preface

This third edition of *Documents of American Broadcasting* should continue to serve the need for a collection of primary source materials in the field of broadcasting history, regulation, and public policy. Every attempt has been made to strike the best balance between timelessness and timeliness. Some of the documents carried over from earlier editions have undergone modifications which are reflected in this current edition.

Documents of American Broadcasting is a source book that can be used in many ways. It can serve as the main text in undergraduate and graduate level broadcasting courses such as the foundations course, regulation, and others. It is also intended as a supplementary ready reference for various non-studio courses, especially programming, history, management, and broadcast journalism. In addition, the book will be helpful to professional broadcasters and general readers who simply want to know more about this fascinating and challenging field.

Aside from the addition and deletion of certain documents, a number of major changes mark this edition. First of all, I have expanded my introductions to the documents to provide more background, explanation, and interpretation. I hope the added material enhances the meaning and value of the documents themselves. Secondly, the present edition includes two new features: a concise glossary of legal terms and an index. Thirdly, all bibliographic entries are assembled at the end of the volume. The entries are numbered to correspond to the numbered Related Reading suggestions appearing after the introductions to individual documents.

Users of the first two editions will note that I have abandoned the thematic pattern of organization used in the past. A chronological arrangement is followed in this edition. Temporal ordering sharpens the historical—developmental focus of the book for readers who proceed from cover to cover. It invites other users to read the contents in whatever versatile sequence their needs dictate. An alternate thematic table of contents, based on the organizational patterns of the earlier editions of this book, augments the main table of contents. The index, together with the references to other documents that are included in the introductions, will suggest many relationships among documents separated in time.

I have endeavored to include as much of each document as readers are likely to find useful. While some materials have been abridged to minimize the redundant and irrelevant, most documents appear in their entirety, including the frequently lengthy footnotes that accompany legal opinions. If I have erred on the side of plenitude, the reader can rectify this by skipping over what he deems of little consequence. Variant footnote styles and forms of legal citation have not been brought into conformity. Such an attempt at consistency would modify documents whose formal and substantive integrity it is this book's intention to preserve.

Undoubtedly, had this work been edited by someone else its contents would have been somewhat different. The selections are functions of my particular orientation to broadcasting and broadcasting education, as well as the era during which the choices were made. No work can include everything, and this one is no exception. Given the practical limitations of size and cost, I have chosen those materials I deem most important for most readers. I realize that importance, like beauty, is in the eye of the beholder, and I regret excluding many valuable documents from this collection. Cutting back on the completeness of the included documents would have provided space for excerpts from additional materials, but at the expense of vitiating the underlying concept of *Documents of American Broadcasting,* namely, to make accessible essential source materials *in their entirety* whenever useful and practical.

I am indebted to more people than I can mention, including the scores who commented on the concept, contents, and organization of this book during its genesis and decade-long metamorphosis. I especially acknowledge the contribution of my two most influential broadcasting teachers, Bob Crawford and Charles Siepmann, who taught me better than I can thank them for. Martin Stanford, my original editor at Appleton-Century-Crofts, has my gratitude for seeing merit in this book in the first place, and for giving me seasoned guidance that has left its mark on all subsequent editions. My appreciation also goes to Lydia Bloom, who provided valued secretarial assistance during the preparation of the manuscript. I, of course, am solely responsible for any of this work's shortcomings.

November, 1977   *F.J.K.*

Introduction

Broadcasting in America is a major force. There are more radio receivers than people in the nation. Only 3 percent of all households lack a television set. We get most of our entertainment and news from a TV screen that is turned on more than 6 hours a day in the typical home. Cable television, the rising star among broadcast-related media, reaches more than 15 percent of the public. Businesses spend approximately $10 billion a year for broadcast advertising. Many people freely confess they wouldn't know what to do with themselves if broadcasting suddenly disappeared. We are very dependent on the broadcast media—perhaps *too* dependent. Nevertheless, whether radio and television are stimulants or soporifics, beneficial or harmful, servants or masters, undeniably they are popular entertainment sources as well as powerful social, educational, economic, journalistic, and political instruments in the United States.

The basic system of American broadcasting is an amalgam of commercial free enterprise and limited governmental regulation. This structure is augmented by a similarly regulated noncommercial system called "public broadcasting." (The name is somewhat ironic since public television, which accounts for about one-quarter of licensed TV stations, attracts only 1 percent of the audience on the average.) Most of the programming attended by most of the public most of the time is frivolous, passive entertainment that provides diversion, relaxation, and a type of companionship. Yet the licenses required to operate broadcasting stations are issued to serve the "public interest, convenience, and necessity." This state of affairs seems anomalous to some and perfectly consistent to others.

The present organization and accepted institutional status of broadcasting in the United States did not simply "happen." Rather, radio and television evolved as products of particular values and needs. The documents in this volume cast light on shifting values and needs and on unique democratic methods of applying values to implement needs. They are fundamental to an understanding of the development, operation, and significance of broadcasting in America.

A chronological arrangement has been followed except for periodically amended documents such as the Communications Act of 1934 and the Television Code of the National Association of Broadcasters. These living documents are among the last entries in the book.

If the past is indeed prologue to the future, then readers of this work will be well prepared to greet coming developments in broadcasting and related media with realistic expectations and insight, for they will know where we have been and how we got where we are. "Just as the twig is bent the tree's inclined."

1

The U.S. Constitution

1787–1868

The Constitution is the wellspring of all federal law, and broadcasting is no exception. The "commerce clause" of Article I,
Section 8, assigns to Congress the responsibility for regulating
interstate and foreign commerce. But what is "commerce"? The
Supreme Court of the United States has determined that "commerce" includes communication. Because radio waves are physically incapable of staying within the political boundaries of states
and nations, broadcasting is inherently a form of interstate and
foreign "commerce" over which Congress has jurisdiction. Note
the Constitution gives Congress authority over the mails. Another
portion of Section 8 lays down the constitutional basis for copyright and patent law.

The First Amendment to the Constitution is echoed by Section 29 of the Radio Act of 1927 and Section 326 of the Communications Act of 1934. But free expression is not an absolute
right. The Fifth, Sixth, and Fourteenth Amendments present one
area in which the rights of free speech and press might conflict
with other values, i.e., the rights of a defendant under the American system of criminal justice. See Document 33, pp. 316–328.

Related Reading: 131, 138, 164, 187, 196.

Article 1, Section 8. The Congress shall have Power . . . to regulate Commerce with foreign Nations, and among the several States, and with the Indian
Tribes; . . . To establish Post Offices and post Roads; To promote the Progress
of Science and useful Arts, by securing for limited Times to Authors and In-
ventors the exclusive Right to their respective Writings and Discoveries . . .

First Amendment. Congress shall make no law respecting an establishment of religion, or prohibiting the free exercise thereof; or abridging the

1

freedom of speech, or of the press; or the right of the people peaceably to assemble, and to petition the government for a redress of grievances.

Fifth Amendment.   No person shall ... be deprived of life, liberty, or property, without due process of law; nor shall private property be taken for public use, without just compensation.

Sixth Amendment.   In all criminal prosecutions, the accused shall enjoy the right to a speedy and public trial, by an impartial jury of the State and district wherein the crime shall have been committed, which district shall have been previously ascertained by law, and to be informed of the nature and cause of the accusation; to be confronted with the witnesses against him; to have compulsory process for obtaining witnesses in his favor, and to have the Assistance of Counsel for his defence.

Fourteenth Amendment. Sec. 1.   ... No State shall make or enforce any law which shall abridge the privileges or immunities of citizens of the United States; nor shall any State deprive any person of life, liberty, or property, without due process of law; nor deny to any person within its jurisdiction the equal protection of the laws. ...

2
The Wireless Ship Act
of 1910

Public Law 262, 61st Congress
June 24, 1910

During the first decade of this century wireless telegraphy and telephony emerged as a technical marvel that fascinated hobbyists and was without equal as a lifesaving device at sea. This first American radio law, enacted 10 years before the advent of broadcasting, was limited to the uses of radio for point-to-point maritime communication.

Following the *Titanic* disaster of April, 1912, the 62d Congress passed Public Law 238 (approved July 23, 1912, a month before the Radio Act of 1912), which strengthened the provisions of the Wireless Ship Act by requiring vessels to have auxiliary power supplies for their transmitters and to have at least two skilled radio operators, one of whom would have to be on duty at all times the ship was moving.

Related Reading: 2, 220.

Be it enacted by the Senate and House of Representatives of the United States of America in Congress assembled, That from and after the first day of July, nineteen hundred and eleven, it shall be unlawful for any ocean-going steamer of the United States, or of any foreign country, carrying passengers and carrying fifty or more persons, including passengers and crew, to leave or attempt to leave any port of the United States unless such steamer shall be equipped with an efficient apparatus for radio-communication, in good working order, in charge of a person skilled in the use of such apparatus, which apparatus shall be capable of

3

transmitting and receiving messages over a distance of at least one hundred miles, night or day: *Provided,* That the provisions of this act shall not apply to steamers plying only between ports less than two hundred miles apart.

Sec. 2.   That for the purpose of this act apparatus for radio-communication shall not be deemed to be efficient unless the company installing it shall contract in writing to exchange, and shall, in fact, exchange, as far as may be physically practicable, to be determined by the master of the vessel, messages with shore or ship stations using other systems of radio-communication.

Sec. 3.   That the master or other person being in charge of any such vessel which leaves or attempts to leave any port of the United States in violation of any of the provisions of this act shall, upon conviction, be fined in a sum not more than five thousand dollars, and any such fine shall be a lien upon such vessel, and such vessel may be libeled therefor in any district court of the United States within the jurisdiction of which such vessel shall arrive or depart, and the leaving or attempting to leave each and every port of the United States shall constitute a separate offense.

Sec. 4.   That the Secretary of Commerce and Labor shall make such regulations as may be necessary to secure the proper execution of this act by collectors of customs and other officers of the Government.

3

The Radio Act of 1912

Public Law 264, 62d Congress
August 13, 1912

International wireless conferences were held in Berlin in 1903 and 1906 and in London in 1912 in order to establish a degree of uniformity in the use of radio. The Radio Act of 1912 was enacted to honor America's treaty obligations with respect to these international radio agreements.

    This first comprehensive piece of radio legislation made it illegal to operate a radio station without a license from the Secretary of Commerce, but it failed to provide sufficient discretionary standards for the effective regulation of broadcasting, which was still not envisioned at this early stage of radio's development.

Related Reading: 18, 111, 123, 191, 220.

Be it enacted by the Senate and House of Representatives of the United States of America in Congress assembled, That a person, company, or corporation within the jurisdiction of the United States shall not use or operate any apparatus for radio communication as a means of commercial intercourse among the several States, or with foreign nations, or upon any vessel of the United States engaged in interstate or foreign commerce, or for the transmission of radiograms or signals the effect of which extends beyond the jurisdiction of the State or Territory in which the same are made, or where interference would be caused thereby with the receipt of messages or signals from beyond the jurisdiction of the said State or Territory, except under and in accordance with a license, revocable for cause, in that behalf granted by the Secretary of Commerce and Labor upon application therefor; but nothing in this Act shall be construed to apply to the transmission and exchange of radiograms or signals between points situated in the same State: *Provided,* That the effect thereof shall not extend beyond the jurisdiction of the said State or interfere with the reception of radiograms or signals from beyond said jurisdiction; and a license shall not be required for the transmission or exchange of radiograms or signals by or on behalf of the Government of the United States, but every Government station on land or sea shall have special call letters designated and published in the list of radio stations of the United States by the Department of Commerce and Labor. Any person, company, or corporation that shall use or operate any apparatus for radio communication in violation of this section, or knowingly aid or abet another person, company, or corporation in so doing, shall be deemed guilty of a misdemeanor, and on conviction thereof shall be punished by a fine not exceeding five hundred dollars, and the apparatus or device so unlawfully used and operated may be adjudged forfeited to the United States.

Sec. 2.   That every such license shall be in such form as the Secretary of Commerce and Labor shall determine and shall contain the restrictions, pursuant to this Act, on and subject to which the license is granted; that every such license shall be issued only to citizens of the United States or Porto Rico or to a company incorporated under the laws of some State or Territory or of the United States or Porto Rico, and shall specify the ownership and location of the station in which said apparatus shall be used and other particulars for its identification and to enable its range to be estimated; shall state the purpose of the station, and, in case of a station in actual operation at the date of passage of this Act, shall contain the statement that satisfactory proof has been furnished that it was actually operating on the above-mentioned date; shall state the wave length or the wave lengths authorized for use by the station for the prevention of interference and the hours for which the station is licensed for work; and shall not be construed to authorize the use of any apparatus for radio communication in any other station than that specified. Every such license shall be subject to the regulations contained herein, and such regulations as may be established from time to time by authority of this act or subsequent acts and treaties of the United States. Every such license shall provide that the President of the United States in time of war or public peril or disaster may cause the closing of any station for radio communication and the removal therefrom of all radio apparatus, or may authorize the use or control of any such station or apparatus by any department of the Government, upon just compensation to the owners.

Sec. 3.   That every such apparatus shall at all times while in use and operation as aforesaid be in charge or under the supervision of a person or persons licensed for that purpose by the Secretary of Commerce and Labor. Every person so licensed who in the operation of any radio apparatus shall fail to observe and obey regulations contained in or made pursuant to this act or subsequent acts or treaties of the United States, or any one of them, or who shall fail to enforce obedience thereto by an unlicensed person while serving under his supervision, in addition to the punishments and penalties herein prescribed, may suffer the suspension of the said license for a period to be fixed by the Secretary of

Commerce and Labor not exceeding one year. It shall be unlawful to employ any unlicensed person or for any unlicensed person to serve in charge or in supervision of the use and operation of such apparatus, and any person violating this provision shall be guilty of a misdemeanor, and on conviction thereof shall be punished by a fine of not more than one hundred dollars or imprisonment for not more than two months; or both, in the discretion of the court, for each and every such offense: *Provided*, That in case of emergency the Secretary of Commerce and Labor may authorize a collector of customs to issue a temporary permit, in lieu of a license, to the operator on a vessel subject to the radio ship act of June twenty-fourth, nineteen hundred and ten.

Sec. 4.   That for the purpose of preventing or minimizing interference with communication between stations in which such apparatus is operated, to facilitate radio communication, and to further the prompt receipt of distress signals, said private and commercial stations shall be subject to the regulations of this section. These regulations shall be enforced by the Secretary of Commerce and Labor through the collectors of customs and other officers of the Government as other regulations herein provided for.

The Secretary of Commerce and Labor may, in his discretion, waive the provisions of any or all of these regulations when no interference of the character above mentioned can ensue.

The Secretary of Commerce and Labor may grant special temporary licenses to stations actually engaged in conducting experiments for the development of the science of radio communication, or the apparatus pertaining thereto, to carry on special tests, using any amount of power or any wave lengths, at such hours and under such conditions as will insure the least interference with the sending or receipt of commercial or Government radiograms, of distress signals and radiograms, or with the work of other stations.

In these regulations the naval and military stations shall be understood to be stations on land.

REGULATIONS

Normal wave length

First.   Every station shall be required to designate a certain definite wave length as the normal sending and receiving wave length of the station. This wave length shall not exceed six hundred meters or it shall exceed one thousand six hundred meters. Every coastal station open to general public service shall at all times be ready to receive messages of such wave lengths as are required by the

Berlin convention. Every ship station, except as hereinafter provided, and every coast station open to general public service shall be prepared to use two sending wave lengths, one of three hundred meters and one of six hundred meters, as required by the international convention in force: *Provided*, That the Secretary of Commerce and Labor may, in his discretion, change the limit of wave length reservation made by regulations first and second to accord with any international agreement to which the United States is a party.

Other wave lengths

Second.   In addition to the normal sending wave length all stations, except as provided hereinafter in these regulations, may use other sending wave lengths: *Provided*, That they do not exceed six hundred meters or that they do exceed one thousand six hundred meters: *Provided further*, That the character of the waves emitted conforms to the requirements of regulations third and fourth following.

Use of a "pure wave"

Third.   At all stations if the sending apparatus, to be referred to hereinafter as the "transmitter," is of such a character that the energy is radiated in two or more wave lengths, more or less sharply defined, as indicated by a sensitive wave meter, the energy in no one of the lesser waves shall exceed ten per centum of that in the greatest.

Use of a "sharp wave"

Fourth.   At all stations the logarithmic decreement per complete oscillation in the wave trains emitted by the transmitter shall not exceed two-tenths, except when sending distress signals or signals and messages relating thereto.

Use of "standard distress wave"

Fifth.   Every station on shipboard shall be prepared to send distress calls on the normal wave length designated by the international convention in force, except on vessels of small tonnage unable to have plants insuring that wave length.

Signal of distress

Sixth.   The distress call used shall be the international signal of distress
. . . — — — . . .

Use of "broad interfering wave" for distress signals

Seventh.   When sending distress signals, the transmitter of a station on shipboard may be tuned in such a manner as to create a maximum of interference with a maximum of radiation.

Distance requirements for distress signals

Eighth.   Every station on shipboard, wherever practicable, shall be prepared to send distress signals of the character specified in regulations fifth and sixth with sufficient power to enable them to be received by day over sea a distance of one hundred nautical miles by a shipboard station equipped with apparatus for both sending and receiving equal in all essential particulars to that of the station first mentioned.

"Right of way" for distress signals

Ninth.   All stations are required to give absolute priority to signals and radiograms relating to ships in distress; to cease all sending on hearing a distress signal; and, except when engaged in answering or aiding the ship in distress, to refrain from sending until all signals and radiograms relating thereto are completed.

Reduced power for ships near a government station

Tenth.   No station on shipboard, when within fifteen nautical miles of a naval or military station, shall use a transformer input exceeding one kilowatt, nor, when within five nautical miles of such a station, a transformer input exceeding one-half kilowatt, except for sending signals of distress, or signals or radiograms relating thereto.

Intercommunication

Eleventh.   Each shore station open to general public service between the coast and vessels at sea shall be bound to exchange radiograms with any similar shore station and with any ship station without distinction of the radio system adopted by such stations, respectively, and each station on shipboard shall be bound to exchange radiograms with any other station on shipboard without distinction of the radio systems adopted by each station, respectively.

It shall be the duty of each such shore station, during the hours it is in operation, to listen in at intervals of not less than fifteen minutes and for a period not less than two minutes, with the receiver tuned to receive messages of three hundred-meter wave lengths.

Division of time

Twelfth.   At important seaports and at all other places where naval or military and private commercial shore stations operate in such close proximity that interference with the work of naval and military stations can not be avoided by the enforcement of the regulations contained in the foregoing regulations concerning wave lengths and character of signals emitted, such private or commercial shore stations as do interfere with the reception of signals by the naval and military stations concerned shall not use their transmitters during the first fifteen minutes of each hour, local standard time. The Secretary of Commerce and Labor may, on the recommendation of the department concerned, designate the station or stations which may be required to observe this division of time.

Government stations to observe division of time

Thirteenth.   The naval or military stations for which the above-mentioned division of time may be established shall transmit signals or radiograms only during the first fifteen minutes of each hour, local standard time, except in case of signals or radiograms relating to vessels in distress, as hereinbefore provided.

Use of unnecessary power

Fourteenth.   In all circumstances, except in case of signals or radiograms relating to vessels in distress, all stations shall use the minimum amount of energy necessary to carry out any communication desired.

General restrictions on private stations

Fifteenth. No private or commercial station not engaged in the transaction of bona fide commercial business by radio communication or in experimentation in connection with the development and manufacture of radio apparatus for commercial purposes shall use a transmitting wave length exceeding two hundred meters, or a transformer input exceeding one kilowatt, except by special authority of the Secretary of Commerce and Labor contained in the license of the station: *Provided*, That the owner or operator of a station of the character mentioned in this regulation shall not be liable for a violation of the requirements of the third or fourth regulations to the penalties of one hundred dollars or twenty-five dollars, respectively, provided in this section unless the person maintaining or operating such station shall have been notified in writing that the said transmitter has been found, upon tests conducted by the Government, to be so adjusted as to violate the third and fourth regulations, and opportunity has been given to said owner or operator to adjust said transmitter in conformity with said regulations.

Special restrictions in the vicinities of government stations

Sixteenth. No station of the character mentioned in regulation fifteenth situated within five nautical miles of a naval or military station shall use a transmitting wave length exceeding two hundred meters or a transformer input exceeding one-half kilowatt.

Ship stations to communicate with nearest shore stations

Seventeenth. In general, the shipboard stations shall transmit their radiograms to the nearest shore station. A sender on board a vessel shall, however, have the right to designate the shore station through which he desires to have his radiograms transmitted. If this can not be done, the wishes of the sender are to be complied with only if the transmission can be effected without interfering with the service of other stations.

Limitations for future installations in vicinities of government stations

Eighteenth. No station on shore not in actual operation at the date of the passage of this act shall be licensed for the transaction of commercial business by radio communication within fifteen nautical miles of the following naval or military stations, to wit: Arlington, Virginia; Key West, Florida; San Juan, Porto Rico; North Head and Tatoosh Island, Washington; San Diego, California; and those established or which may be established in Alaska and in the Canal Zone; and the head of the department having control of such Government stations shall, so far as is consistent with the transaction of governmental business, arrange for the transmission and receipt of commercial radiograms under the provisions of the Berlin convention of nineteen hundred and six and future international conventions or treaties to which the United States may be a party, at each of the stations above referred to, and shall fix the rates therefor, subject to control of such rates by Congress. At such stations and wherever and whenever shore stations open for general public business between the coast and vessels at sea under the provisions of the Berlin convention of nineteen hundred and six and future international conventions and treaties to which the United States may be a party shall not be so established as to insure a constant service day and night without interruption, and in all localities wherever or whenever such service shall not be maintained by a commercial shore station within one hundred nautical miles of a naval radio station, the Secretary of the Navy shall, so far as is consistent with the transaction of Government business, open naval radio stations to the general public business described above, and shall fix rates for such service, subject to control of such rates by Congress. The receipts from such radiograms shall be covered into the Treasury as miscellaneous receipts.

Secrecy of messages

Nineteenth.   No person or persons engaged in or having knowledge of the operation of any station or stations shall divulge or publish the contents of any messages transmitted or received by such station, except to the person or persons to whom the same may be directed, or their authorized agent, or to another station employed to forward such message to its destination, unless legally required so to do by the court of competent jurisdiction or other competent authority. Any person guilty of divulging or publishing any message, except as herein provided, shall, on conviction thereof, be punishable by a fine of not more than two hundred and fifty dollars or imprisonment for a period of not exceeding three months, or both fine and imprisonment, in the discretion of the court.

Penalties

For violation of any of these regulations, subject to which a license under sections one and two of this act may be issued, the owner of the apparatus shall be liable to a penalty of one hundred dollars, which may be reduced or remitted by the Secretary of Commerce and Labor, and for repeated violations of any of such regulations the license may be revoked.

For violation of any of these regulations, except as provided in regulation nineteenth, subject to which a license under section three of this act may be issued, the operator shall be subject to a penalty of twenty-five dollars, which may be reduced or remitted by the Secretary of Commerce and Labor, and for repeated violations of any such regulations, the license shall be suspended or revoked.

Sec. 5.   That every license granted under the provisions of this act for the operation or use of apparatus for radio communication shall prescribe that the operator thereof shall not willfully or maliciously interfere with any other radio communication. Such interference shall be deemed a misdemeanor, and upon conviction thereof the owner or operator, or both, shall be punishable by a fine of not to exceed five hundred dollars or imprisonment for not to exceed one year, or both.

Sec. 6.   That the expression "radio communication" as used in this act means any system of electrical communication by telegraphy or telephony without the aid of any wire connecting the points from and at which the radiograms, signals, or other communications are sent or received.

Sec. 7.   That a person, company, or corporation within the jurisdiction of the United States shall not knowingly utter or transmit, or cause to be uttered or transmitted, any false or fraudulent distress signal or call or false or fraudulent signal, call, or other radiogram of any kind. The penalty for so uttering or transmitting a false or fraudulent distress signal or call shall be a fine of not more than two thousand five hundred dollars or imprisonment for not more than five years, or both, in the discretion of the court, for each and every such offense, and the penalty for so uttering or transmitting, or causing to be uttered or transmitted, any other false or fraudulent signal, call, or other radiogram shall be a fine of not more than one thousand dollars or imprisonment for not more than two years, or both, in the discretion of the court, for each and every such offense.

Sec. 8.   That a person, company, or corporation shall not use or operate any apparatus for radio communication on a foreign ship in territorial waters of the United States otherwise than in accordance with the provisions of sections four and seven of this act and so much of section five as imposes a penalty for interference. Save as aforesaid, nothing in this act shall apply to apparatus for radio communication on any foreign ship.

Sec. 9.   That the trial of any offense under this act shall be in the district in which it is committed, or if the offense is committed upon the high seas or out of the jurisdiction of any particular State or district the trial shall be in the district where the offender may be found or into which he shall be first brought.

Sec. 10.   That this act shall not apply to the Philippine Islands.

Sec. 11.   That this act shall take effect and be in force on and after four months from its passage.

4

The Vision
of David Sarnoff

Memorandum to E. J. Nally*
1915-1916

The British controlled Marconi Wireless Telegraph Company of America was formed in 1899 to develop the commercial potential of the radio patents of Italian inventor Guglielmo Marconi. Transatlantic radio signals (Morse code dots and dashes) were first transmitted in 1901, and wireless telephony (voices and music) was achieved in 1906, the same year David Sarnoff (1891-1971) joined American Marconi as an office boy.

An expert telegrapher with an agile mind and great ambition, Sarnoff quickly rose through the organization's ranks. It was Sarnoff, assigned to a Marconi station in New York City in 1912, who spent three solid days relaying wireless messages to the press telling of the survivors of the tragic *Titanic* disaster. A year later he was promoted to the position of Assistant Traffic Manager of the growing company. In 1915 or 1916, sensing a way to exploit an attribute of radiotelephony that many considered to be a liability—its lack of privacy—Sarnoff accurately prophesied the coming of broadcasting in the following memorandum to Edward J. Nally, Vice-President and General Manager of American Marconi.

World War I brought a temporary lull to the commercial (but not technical) development of radio, and Sarnoff's idea was put

*Reprinted with permission from "Radio and David Sarnoff," unpublished manuscript by Elmer E. Bucher deposited in the David Sarnoff Research Center Library, Princeton, New Jersey.

15

aside. When the assets of American Marconi were acquired by the newly formed Radio Corporation of America in 1919, Sarnoff stayed with the nascent organization as Commercial Manager. He was instrumental in forming the National Broadcasting Company, an RCA subsidiary, in 1926. Sarnoff fostered the emergence of monochrome and color television from laboratory to market-place. He headed RCA from 1930 until his retirement in 1969. More than any other person, David Sarnoff influenced the pattern of growth of broadcasting in America.

Related Reading: 2, 4, 10, 142, 192.

I have in mind a plan of development which would make radio a "household utility" in the same sense as the piano or phonograph. The idea is to bring music into the home by wireless.

While this has been tried in the past by wires, it has been a failure because wires do not lend themselves to this scheme. With radio, however, it would be entirely feasible. For example, a radio telephone transmitter having a range of say 25 to 50 miles can be installed at a fixed point where instrumental or vocal music or both are produced. The problem of transmitting music has already been solved in principle and therefore all the receivers attuned to the transmitting wave length should be capable of receiving such music. The receiver can be de-signed in the form of a simple "Radio Music Box" and arranged for several dif-ferent wave lengths, which should be changeable with throwing of a single switch or pressing of a single button.

The "Radio Music Box" can be supplied with amplifying tubes and a loud-speaking telephone, all of which can be neatly mounted in one box. The box can be placed on a table in the parlor or living room, the switch set accordingly and the transmitted music received. There should be no difficulty in receiving music perfectly when transmitted within a radius of 25 to 50 miles. Within such a radius there reside hundreds of thousands of families; and as all can simultaneously receive from a single transmitter, there would be no question of obtaining suf-ficiently loud signals to make the performance enjoyable. The power of the transmitter can be made 5 K. W., if necessary, to cover even a short radius of 25 to 50 miles; thereby giving extra loud signals in the home if desired. The use of head telephones would be obviated by this method. The development of a small loop antenna to go with each "Radio Music Box" would likewise solve the antennae problem.

The same principle can be extended to numerous other fields as, for example, receiving lectures at home which can be made perfectly audible; also events of national importance can be simultaneously announced and received. Baseball scores can be transmitted in the air by the use of one set installed at the Polo

Grounds. The same would be true of other cities. This proposition would be especially interesting to farmers and others living in outlying districts removed from cities. By the purchase of a "Radio Music Box" they could enjoy concerts, lectures, music, recitals, etc., which may be going on in the nearest city within their radius. While I have indicated a few of the most probable fields of usefulness for such a device, yet there are numerous other fields to which the principle can be extended. . . .

The manufacture of the "Radio Music Box" including antenna, in large quantities, would make possible their sale at a moderate figure of perhaps $75.00 per outfit. The main revenue to be derived will be from the sale of "Radio Music Boxes" which if manufactured in quantities of one hundred thousand or so could yield a handsome profit when sold at the price mentioned above. Secondary sources of revenue would be from the sale of transmitters and from increased advertising and circulation of the "Wireless Age." The Company would have to undertake the arrangements, I am sure, for music recitals, lectures, etc., which arrangements can be satisfactorily worked out. It is not possible to estimate the total amount of business obtainable with this plan until it has been developed and actually tried out but there are about 15,000,000 families in the United States alone, and if only one million or 7% of the total families thought well of the idea it would, at the figure mentioned, mean a gross business of about $75,000,000 which should yield considerable revenue.

Aside from the profit to be derived from this proposition the possibilities for advertising for the Company are tremendous, for its name would ultimately be brought into the household and wireless would receive national and universal attention.

5

Emergence of Broadcast Advertising

Queensboro Corporation Sales Talk

Transmitted by Radio Station WEAF,

New York City*

August 28, 1922, 5:15–5:30 p.m.

It can be said that broadcasting in the United States began on November 2, 1920, when the Westinghouse Electric and Manufacturing Corporation inaugurated station KDKA in Pittsburgh, Pennsylvania, with reports of the Harding–Cox presidential election returns. Fewer than 50 pioneering radio stations had joined KDKA by the end of 1921, but the number swelled to more than 500 a year later. Some of the early radio stations were built and operated by equipment manufacturers like Westinghouse that were interested in increasing the market for radio receivers and parts. Department stores, educational institutions, and newspapers became prevalent among station licensees during these formative years as the public's investment in receiving apparatus increased by leaps and bounds.

But was there a more permanent way to finance station operation than through sales of equipment to audience members? The American Telephone and Telegraph Company (AT&T) built station WEAF in New York City in the summer of 1922 for the

*Reprinted from Gleason L. Archer, *History of Radio to 1926* (New York: American Historical Society, Inc., 1938), pp. 397–399.

express purpose of experimenting with what they called "toll broadcasting"—making radio facilities available to anybody who wanted to transmit something to the general public provided one could pay the price. The following radio talk was the first paid program aired on WEAF. It cost the sponsor $50.00.

AT&T attempted to prevent other broadcasters from accepting commercially sponsored matter, but by the mid-1920's more and more stations carried advertising. By 1930 commercial advertising had become institutionalized as the way to support America's broadcast system. AT&T gave up station and network operation, selling WEAF to RCA in 1926 for $1 million. The telephone company, however, reserved the right to provide radio networks with the lines needed for station interconnection.

Related Reading: 2, 6, 10, 64, 100, 155, 179, 208.

BROADCASTING PROGRAM HAWTHORNE COURT INTRODUCTION

This afternoon the radio audience is to be addressed by Mr. Blackwell of the Queensboro Corporation, who through arrangements made by the Griffin Radio Service, Inc., will say a few words concerning Nathaniel Hawthorne and the desirability of fostering the helpful community spirit and the healthful, unconfined home life that were Hawthorne ideals. Ladies and Gentlemen: Mr. Blackwell.

BROADCASTING PROGRAM HAWTHORNE COURT

It is fifty-eight years since Nathaniel Hawthorne, the greatest of American fictionists, passed away. To honor his memory the Queensboro Corporation, creator and operator of the tenant-owned system of apartment homes at Jackson Heights, New York City, has named its latest group of high-grade dwellings "Hawthorne Court."

I wish to thank those within sound of my voice for the broadcasting opportunity afforded me to urge this vast radio audience to seek the recreation and the daily comfort of the home removed from the congested part of the city, right at the boundaries of God's great outdoors, and within a few minutes by subway from the business section of Manhattan. This sort of residential environment strongly influenced Hawthorne, America's greatest writer of fiction. He analyzed with charming keenness the social spirit of those who had thus happily selected their homes, and he painted the people inhabiting those homes with good-natured relish.

There should be more Hawthorne sermons preached about the utter inadequacy and the general hopelessness of the congested city home. The cry of the heart is for more living room, more chance to unfold, more opportunity to get near to Mother Earth, to play, to romp, to plant and to dig.

Let me enjoin upon you as you value your health and your hopes and your home happiness, get away from the solid masses of brick, where the meagre opening admitting a slant of sunlight is mockingly called a light shaft, and where children grow up starved for a run over a patch of grass and the sight of a tree.

Apartments in congested parts of the city have proven failures. The word neighbor is an expression of peculiar irony—a daily joke.

Thousands of dwellers in the congested district apartments want to remove to healthier and happier sections but they don't know and they can't seem to get into the belief that their living situation and home environment can be improved. Many of them balk at buying a home in the country or the suburbs and becoming a commuter. They have visions of toiling down in a cellar with a sullen furnace, or shoveling snow, or of blistering palms pushing a clanking lawn mower. They can't seem to overcome the pessimistic inertia that keeps pounding into their brains that their crowded, unhealthy, unhappy living conditions cannot be improved.

The fact is, however, that apartment homes on the tenant-ownership plan can be secured by these city martyrs merely for the deciding to pick them—merely for the devoting of an hour or so to preliminary verification of the living advantages that are within their grasp. And this too within twenty minutes of New York's business center by subway transit.

Those who balk at building a house or buying one already built need not remain deprived of the blessings of the home within the ideal residential environment, or the home surrounded by social advantages and the community benefits where neighbor means more than a word of eight letters.

In these better days of more opportunities, it is possible under the tenant-ownership plan to possess an apartment-home that is equal in every way to the house-home and superior to it in numberless respects.

In these same better days, the purchaser of an apartment-home can enjoy all the latest conveniences and contrivances demanded by the housewife and yet have all of the outdoor life that the city dweller yearns for but has deludedly supposed could only be obtained through purchase of a house in the country.

Imagine a congested city apartment lifted bodily to the middle of a large garden within twenty minutes travel of the city's business center. Imagine the interior of a group of such apartments traversed by a garden court stretching a block, with beautiful flower beds and rich sward, so that the present jaded congested section dweller on looking out of his windows is not chilled with the brick and mortar vista, but gladdened and enthused by colors and scents that make life worth living once more. Imagine an apartment to live in at a place where you and your neighbor join the same community clubs, organizations and activities, where you golf with your neighbor, tennis with your neighbor, bowl with your neighbor and join him in a long list of outdoor and indoor pleasure-giving health-giving activities.

And finally imagine such a tenant-owned apartment, where you own a floor in a house the same as you can own an entire house with a proportionate owner-ship of the ground the same as the ground attached to an entire house but where you have great spaces for planting and growing the flowers you love, and raising the vegetables of which you are fond.

Right at your door is such an opportunity. It only requires the will to take advantage of it all. You owe it to yourself and you owe it to your family to leave the hemmed-in, sombre-hued, artificial apartment life of the congested city section and enjoy what nature intended you should enjoy.

Dr. Royal S. Copeland, Health Commissioner of New York, recently de-clared that any person who preached leaving the crowded city for the open country was a public-spirited citizen and a benefactor to the race. Shall we not follow this advice and become the benefactors he praises? Let us resolve to do so. Let me close by urging that you hurry to the apartment home near the green fields and the neighborly atmosphere right on the subway without the expense and the trouble of a commuter, where health and community happiness beckon—the community life and friendly environment that Hawthorne advocated.

6
Breakdown of the Act of 1912

35 Ops. Att'y Gen 126

July 8, 1926

From its beginning broadcasting was a medium characterized by a scarcity of frequencies. All broadcast stations operated on no more than two or three wave lengths during broadcasting's first two years, necessitating shared-time arrangements among the early stations.

Herbert Hoover became Secretary of Commerce in 1921. He convened the first of four annual National Radio Conferences in Washington in 1922. All those attending agreed that the Radio Act of 1912 was inadequate to regulate recent radio developments, including broadcasting; new legislation was introduced that year by Congressman Wallace White, Jr., but Congress was slow to act.

In 1923 a federal appeals court held that the Secretary of Commerce had no discretionary power to refuse a radio license to anyone who was qualified under the 1912 Act [*Hoover* v. *Intercity Radio Co., Inc.*, 286 F. 1003 (D.C. Cir. 1923)]. The same decision opined that the Secretary did possess authority to select the frequency "which, in his judgment, will result in the least possible interference." Hoover thereupon opened up many more frequencies to broadcasting, and the congestion was temporarily relieved as the broadcasting industry cooperated with government attempts to minimize interference. This worked reasonably well, and Congress paid little heed to repeated requests for a new law.

But by 1925, as new stations came on the air and broadcasting schedules expanded, the congestion became intolerable, and Hoover decided in November to refuse to grant any new authorizations to operate on the 89 frequencies then available for broadcasting. The penultimate crack in the regulatory structure appeared on April 16, 1926, when a federal district court ruled that Hoover was powerless to require a licensee to broadcast only at specified times and only on designated channels, for the Radio Act of 1912 gave the Secretary of Commerce no authority to issue regulations [*United States* v. *Zenith Radio Corporation et al.,* 12 F.2d 614 (N.D. Ill. 1926)].

Hoover's request for clarification of his lawful authority was answered in the Attorney General's opinion, below, which pointed out the crying need for more effective broadcast legislation.

Related Reading: 2, 10, 18, 19, 107, 111, 123, 155, 191.

Department of Justice
July 8, 1926.

Sir: Receipt is acknowledged of your letter of June 4, 1926, in which you ask for a definition of your powers and duties with respect to the regulation of radio broadcasting under the Act of August 13, 1912, c. 287 (37 Stat. 302). Specifically, you request my opinion upon the following five questions:

(1)   Does the 1912 Act require broadcasting stations to obtain licenses, and is the operation of such a station without a license an offense under that Act?

(2)   Has the Secretary of Commerce authority under the 1912 Act to assign wave lengths and times of operation and limit the power of stations?

(3)   Has a station, whose license stipulates a wave length for its use, the right to use any other wave length, and if it does operate on a different wave length, is it in violation of the law and does it become subject to the penalties of the Act?

(4)   If a station, whose license stipulates a period during which only the station may operate and limits its power, transmits at different times, or with excessive power, is it in violation of the Act and does it become subject to the penalties of the Act?

(5)   Has the Secretary of Commerce power to fix the duration of the licenses which he issues or should they be indeterminate, continuing in effect until revoked or until Congress otherwise provides?

With respect to the first question, my answer to both its parts is in the affirmative. Section 1 of the Act of 1912 provides—

That a person, company, or corporation within the jurisdiction of the United States shall not use or operate any apparatus for radio communication as a means of commercial intercourse among the several States, or with foreign nations, or upon any vessel of the United States engaged in interstate or foreign commerce, or for the transmission of radiograms or signals the effect of which extends beyond the jurisdiction of the State or Territory in which the same are made, or where interference would be caused thereby with the receipt of messages or signals from beyond the jurisdiction of the said State or Territory, except under and in accordance with a license, revocable for cause, in that behalf granted by the Secretary of Commerce (and Labor) upon application therefor; but nothing in this Act shall be construed to apply to the transmission and exchange of radiograms or signals between points situated in the same State: *Provided*, That the effect thereof shall not extend beyond the jurisdiction of the said State or interfere with the reception of radiograms or signals from beyond said jurisdiction. . . .

Violation of this section is declared to be a misdemeano..

There is no doubt whatever that radio communication is a proper subject for Federal regulation under the commerce clause of the Constitution. *Pensacola Telegraph Company* v. *Western Union Telegraph Company*, 96 U.S. 1, 9, 24 Op. 100. And it may be noticed in passing that even purely intrastate transmission of radio waves may fall within the scope of Federal power when it disturbs the air in such a manner as to interfere with interstate communication, a situation recognized and provided for in the Act. Cf. *Minnesota Rate Cases*, 230 U.S. 352.

While the Act of 1912 was originally drafted to apply primarily to wireless telegraphy, its language is broad enough to cover wireless telephony as well; and this was clearly the intention of its framers (62nd Cong., 2nd Sess., S. Rept. 698). Whether the transmission is for profit is immaterial so far as the commerce clause is concerned. *American Express Company* v. *United States*, 212 U.S. 522; *Caminetti* v. *United States*, 242 U.S. 470.

For these reasons I am of the opinion that broadcasting is within the terms of the 1912 Act; that a license must be obtained before a broadcasting station may be lawfully operated; and that the penalties of section 1 of the Act may be imposed upon any person or corporation who operates such a station without a license.

Your second question involves three separate problems:

    (a)   The assignment of wave lengths.

    (b)   The assignment of hours of operation.

    (c)   The limitation of power.

(a)   As to the assignment of wave lengths, section 2 of the Act provides—

That every such license shall be in such form as the Secretary of Commerce (and Labor) shall determine and shall contain the restrictions, pursuant to this Act, on and subject to which the license is granted; . . . shall state the wave length or the wave lengths authorized for use by the station for the prevention of interference and the hours for which the station is licensed for work. . . . Every such license shall be subject to the regulations contained herein and such regulations as may be established from time to time by authority of this Act or subsequent Acts and treaties of the United States.

The power to make general regulations is nowhere granted by specific language to the Secretary. On the contrary, it seems clear from section 4 of the Act that Congress intended to cover the entire field itself, and that, with minor exceptions, Congress left very little to the discretion of any administrative officer. This fact is made additionally plain by the reports which accompanied the Act in both Houses. 62d Cong. 2d Sess., S. Rept. 698; *ibid.*, H.R. Rept. 582. Cf. 29 Op. 579.

The first regulation in section 4 provides that the station shall be required to designate a definite wave length, outside of the band between 600 and 1,600 meters (reserved for Government stations), and that ship stations shall be prepared to use 300 and 600 meters.

The second regulation provides that in addition to the normal sending wave length, all stations, except as otherwise provided in the regulations, may use "other sending wave lengths," again excluding the band from 600 to 1,600 meters.

These two regulations constitute a direct legislative regulation of the use of wave lengths. They preclude the possibility of administrative discretion in the same field. In *Hoover* v. *Intercity Radio Company*, 286 Fed. 1003, it was held that it was mandatory upon the Secretary under the Act to grant licenses to all applicants complying with its provisions. The court added in that case these remarks:

In the present case the duty of naming a wave length is mandatory upon the Secretary. The only discretionary act is in selecting a wave length, within the limitations prescribed in the statute, which, in his judgment, will result in the least possible interference. The issuing of a license is not dependent upon the fixing of a wave length. It is a restriction entering into the license. The wave length named by the Secretary merely measures the extent of the privilege granted to the licensee.

You have advised me that following this decision you have assumed that you had discretionary authority in assigning wave lengths for the use of particular stations, and have made such assignments to the individual broad-casting stations.

However, in my opinion, these remarks of the Court of Appeals are to be construed as applying only to the *normal* sending and receiving wave length which every station is required to designate under the first regulation. But under the second regulation, any station is at liberty to use "other wave lengths" at will, provided only that they do not trespass upon the band from 600 to 1,600 meters. This conclusion appears to be in accord with the opinion of the District Court for the Northern District of Illinois in the case . . . of *United States* v. *Zenith Radio Corporation*.

But it is suggested that under the fifteenth regulation broadcasting stations may not, without special authority from the Secretary, use wave lengths over 200 meters or power exceeding one kilowatt. This regulation is applicable only to "private and commercial stations not engaged in the transaction of bona fide commercial business by radio communication." I am of opinion that broadcasting is "the transaction of bona fide commercial business" (*Witmark* v. *Bamberger*, 291 Fed. 776; *Remick* v. *American Automobile Accessories Co.*, 298 Fed. 628), and that it is conducted "by radio communication." Broadcasting stations, therefore, do not fall within the scope of the fifteenth regulation; and the Secretary is without power to impose on them the restrictions provided therein.

From the foregoing consideration I am forced to conclude that you have no general authority under the Act to assign wave lengths to broadcasting stations, except for the purpose of designating normal wave lengths under regulation 1.

(b)   As to the assignment of hours of operation:

The second section of the Act, already quoted, provides that the license shall state "the hours for which the station is licensed for work." By the twelfth and thirteenth regulations the Secretary, on the recommendation of the Department concerned, may designate stations which must refrain from operating during the first 15 minutes of each hour — a period to be reserved in designated localities for Government stations. These two regulations are the only ones in which a division of time is mentioned; and it is to them that the second section of the Act refers. I therefore conclude that you have no general authority to fix the times at which broadcasting stations may operate, apart from the limitations of regulations 12 and 13.

(c)   As to the limitation of power:

The only provisions concerning this are to be found in regulation 14, which requires all stations to use "the minimum amount of energy necessary to carry out any communication desired." It does not appear that the Secretary is given power to determine in advance what this minimum amount shall be for every case; and I therefore conclude that you have no authority to insert such a determination as a part of any license.

What I have said above with respect to your second question necessarily serves also as an answer to your third. While a station may not lawfully operate without a license, yet under the decision in the *Intercity Co.* case and under 29 Op. 579 you are required to issue such a license on request. And while a normal wave length must be designated under regulation 1, any station is free to operate on other wave lengths under regulation 2.

The same considerations cover your fourth question. Since the Act confers upon you no general authority to fix hours of operation or to limit power, any station may with impunity operate at hours and with powers other than those fixed in its license, subject only to regulations 12 and 13 and to the penalties against malicious interference contained in section 5.

With respect to your fifth question, I can find no authority in the Act for the issuance of licenses of limited duration.

It is apparent from the answers contained in this opinion that the present legislation is inadequate to cover the art of broadcasting, which has been almost entirely developed since the passage of the 1912 Act. If the present situation requires control, I can only suggest that it be sought in new legislation, carefully adapted to meet the needs of both the present and the future.

Respectfully,

William J. Donovan,
Acting Attorney General.

To the Secretary of Commerce.

7

President Coolidge's Message to Congress

H.R. Doc. 483, 69th Congress, 2d Session

December 7, 1926

Following the Attorney General's Opinion of July 8, 1926, Secretary Hoover abandoned his valiant efforts to maintain a semblance of order on the airwaves and urged the radio industry to regulate itself. Chaos ensued as stations switched frequencies and locations and increased their power at will. In short order some 200 new stations crowded on the air. Broadcast reception became jumbled and sporadic.

The general public and the radio industry both clamored for effective regulation. When Congress reconvened they found that even President Calvin Coolidge had joined the chorus as illustrated in the following excerpt from his Congressional message recommending the enactment of new radio legislation.

RADIO LEGISLATION

The Department of Commerce has for some years urgently presented the necessity for further legislation in order to protect radio listeners from interference between broadcasting stations and to carry out other regulatory functions. Both branches of Congress at the last session passed enactments intended to effect such regulation, but the two bills yet remain to be brought into agreement and final passage.

Due to decisions of the courts, the authority of the department under the law of 1912 has broken down; many more stations have been operating than can be accommodated within the limited number of wave lengths available; further stations are in course of construction; many stations have departed from the scheme of allocation set down by the department, and the whole service of this most important public function has drifted into such chaos as seems likely, if not remedied, to destroy its great value. I most urgently recommend that this legislation should be speedily enacted.

I do not believe it is desirable to set up further independent agencies in the Government. Rather I believe it advisable to entrust the important functions of deciding who shall exercise the privilege of radio transmission and under what conditions, the assigning of wave lengths and determination of power, to a board to be assembled whenever action on such questions becomes necessary. There should be right of appeal to the courts from the decisions of such board. The administration of the decisions of the board and the other features of regulation and promotion of radio in the public interest, together with scientific research, should remain in the Department of Commerce. Such an arrangement makes for more expert, more efficient, and more economical administration than an independent agency or board, whose duties, after initial stages, require but little attention, in which administrative functions are confused with semijudicial functions and from which of necessity there must be greatly increased personnel and expenditure.

8

Senate
Joint Resolution 125

Public Resolution 47, 69th Congress
December 8, 1926

On March 15, 1926, the House of Representatives passed a radio
bill introduced by Congressman Wallace White, Jr., and based on
recommendations of the Fourth National Radio Conference. On
July 2, 1926, the Senate passed a similar bill introduced by
Senator Clarence Dill. Senate-House conferees reported one day
later that they could not reconcile the differences in the two
versions prior to the session's end. They suggested passage of a
Senate Joint Resolution that would preserve the status quo of all
radio by limiting licensing periods and by requiring licensees to
sign a waiver of claim to ownership of frequencies. This Resolution, although swiftly passed by the Senate and House, was delayed by the impending close of the session and was thus not
signed by the President until December 8, 1926.

*Resolved by the Senate and House of Representatives of the United States of
America in Congress assembled,*   That until otherwise provided by law, no
original license for the operation of any radio broadcasting station and no
renewal of a license of an existing broadcasting station, shall be granted for
longer periods than ninety days and no original license for the operation of any
other class of radio station and no renewal of the license for an existing station
of any other class than a broadcasting station, shall be granted for longer periods
than two years; and that no original radio license or the renewal of an existing
license shall be granted after the date of the passage of this resolution unless the
applicant therefor shall execute in writing a waiver of any right or of any claim

to any right, as against the United States, to any wave length or to the use of the ether in radio transmission because of previous license to use the same or because of the use thereof.

9
The Radio Act of 1927

Public Law 632, 69th Congress
February 23, 1927

The Senate–House conferees presented their compromise bill on January 27, 1927. It was passed by the House on January 29; the Senate approved it on February 18. Five days later President Coolidge signed the Dill–White Radio Act of 1927 into law.

The five-member Federal Radio Commission, created as a temporary body by the Act, remained in power from year to year and "until otherwise provided" through various acts of Congress until the 1927 law was supplanted by the Communications Act of 1934 that gave rise to a permanent body, the seven-member Federal Communications Commission.

Communications law, while generally paralleling technological development, has never been able to keep pace with entrepreneurial innovation in the broadcast field. This was certainly true of the Radio Act of 1927, which owed much to the original White bill of 1922. But between then and 1927 broadcasting first assumed its now familiar form as a network distributed and advertiser supported mass medium under the inadequate provisions of the 1912 Radio Act. The 1927 Act remedied the deficiencies of the earlier law by establishing a discretionary licensing standard ("public interest, convenience, or necessity") and by granting broad rule-making powers to the licensing authority. Sections 13 and 15 made it clear that monopoly in the radio field would not be condoned, and Section 18 required broadcast stations to treat political candidates without favoritism. As a statement of public policy, however, the new Radio Act was curiously vague about radio networks and advertising, the two dominant elements of the unfolding broadcasting industry.

These examples of "regulatory lag" were to manifest themselves again when the major features of the Radio Act of 1927 were re-enacted as Title III of the Dill-Rayburn Communications Act of 1934 (Document 47, pp. 511-573). The 1927 law is thus the basis of current broadcast regulation.

Related Reading: 36, 61, 106, 107, 111, 123, 131, 136, 155, 191, 195, 199.

Be it enacted by the Senate and House of Representatives of the United States of America in Congress assembled, That this Act is intended to regulate all forms of interstate and foreign radio transmissions and communications within the United States, its Territories and possessions; to maintain the control of the United States over all the channels of interstate and foreign radio transmission; and to provide for the use of such channels, but not the ownership thereof, by individuals, firms, or corporations, for limited periods of time, under licenses granted by Federal authority, and no such license shall be construed to create any right, beyond the terms, conditions, and periods of the license. That no person, firm, company, or corporation shall use or operate any apparatus for the transmission of energy or communications or signals by radio (a) from one place in any Territory or possession of the United States or in the District of Columbia to another place in the same Territory, possession, or District; or (b) from any State, Territory, or possession of the United States, or from the District of Columbia to any other State, Territory, or possession of the United States; or (c) from any place in any State, Territory, or possession of the United States, or in the District of Columbia, to any place in any foreign country or to any vessel; or (d) within any State when the effects of such use extend beyond the borders of said State, or when interference is caused by such use or operation with the transmission of such energy, communications, or signals from within said State to any place beyond its borders, or from any place beyond its borders to any place within said State, or with the transmission or reception of such energy, communications, or signals from and/or to places beyond the borders of said State; or (e) upon any vessel of the United States; or (f) upon any aircraft or other mobile stations within the United States, except under and in accordance with this Act and with a license in that behalf granted under the provisions of this Act.

Sec. 2. For the purposes of this Act, the United States is divided into five zones, as follows: The first zone shall embrace the States of Maine, New Hampshire, Vermont, Massachusetts, Connecticut, Rhode Island, New York, New Jersey, Delaware, Maryland, the District of Columbia, Porto Rico, and the Virgin Islands; the second zone shall embrace the States of Pennsylvania, Virginia, West Virginia, Ohio, Michigan, and Kentucky; the third zone shall embrace the States of North Carolina, South Carolina, Georgia, Florida,

Alabama, Tennessee, Mississippi, Arkansas, Louisiana, Texas, and Oklahoma; the fourth zone shall embrace the States of Indiana, Illinois, Wisconsin, Minnesota, North Dakota, South Dakota, Iowa, Nebraska, Kansas, and Missouri; and the fifth zone shall embrace the States of Montana, Idaho, Wyoming, Colorado, New Mexico, Arizona, Utah, Nevada, Washington, Oregon, California, the Territory of Hawaii, and Alaska.

Sec. 3.   That a commission is hereby created and established to be known as the Federal Radio Commission, hereinafter referred to as the commission, which shall be composed of five commissioners appointed by the President, by and with the advice and consent of the Senate, and one of whom the President shall designate as chairman: *Provided*, That chairmen thereafter elected shall be chosen by the commission itself.

Each member of the commission shall be a citizen of the United States and an actual resident citizen of a State within the zone from which appointed at the time of said appointment. Not more than one commissioner shall be appointed from any zone. No member of the commission shall be financially interested in the manufacture or sale of radio apparatus or in the transmission or operation of radiotelegraphy, radiotelephony, or radio broadcasting. Not more than three commissioners shall be members of the same political party.

The first commissioners shall be appointed for the terms of two, three, four, five, and six years, respectively, from the date of the taking effect of this Act, the term of each to be designated by the President, but their successors shall be appointed for terms of six years, except that any person chosen to fill a vacancy shall be appointed only for the unexpired term of the commissioner whom he shall succeed.

The first meeting of the commission shall be held in the city of Washington at such time and place as the chairman of the commission may fix. The commission shall convene thereafter at such times and places as a majority of the commission may determine, or upon call of the chairman thereof.

The commission may appoint a secretary, and such clerks, special counsel, experts, examiners, and other employees as it may from time to time find necessary for the proper performance of its duties and as from time to time may be appropriated for by Congress.

The commission shall have an official seal and shall annually make a full report of its operations to the Congress.

The members of the commission shall receive a compensation of $10,000 for the first year of their service, said year to date from the first meeting of said commission, and thereafter a compensation of $30 per day for each day's attendance upon sessions of the commission or while engaged upon work of the commission and while traveling to and from such sessions, and also their necessary traveling expenses.

Sec. 4.   Except as otherwise provided in this Act, the commission, from time to time, as public convenience, interest, or necessity requires, shall—

(a)   Classify radio stations;

(b)   Prescribe the nature of the service to be rendered by each class of licensed stations and each station within any class;

(c)   Assign bands of frequencies or wave lengths to the various classes of stations, and assign frequencies or wave lengths for each individual station and determine the power which each station shall use and the time during which it may operate;

(d)   Determine the location of classes of stations or individual stations;

(e)   Regulate the kind of apparatus to be used with respect to its external effects and the purity and sharpness of the emissions from each station and from the apparatus therein;

(f)   Make such regulations not inconsistent with law as it may deem necessary to prevent interference between stations and to carry out the provisions of this Act: *Provided, however,* That changes in the wave lengths, authorized power, in the character of emitted signals, or in the times of operation of any station, shall not be made without the consent of the station licensee unless, in the judgment of the commission, such changes will promote public convenience or interest or will serve public necessity or the provisions of this Act will be more fully complied with;

(g)   Have authority to establish areas or zones to be served by any station;

(h)   Have authority to make special regulations applicable to radio stations engaged in chain broadcasting;

(i)   Have authority to make general rules and regulations requiring stations to keep such records of programs, transmissions of energy, communications, or signals as it may deem desirable;

(j)   Have authority to exclude from the requirements of any regulations in whole or in part any radio station upon railroad rolling stock, or to modify such regulations in its discretion;

(k)   Have authority to hold hearings, summon witnesses, administer oaths, compel the production of books, documents, and papers and to make such investigations as may be necessary in the performance of its duties. The commission may make such expenditures (including expenditures for rent and personal services at the seat of government and elsewhere, for law books, periodicals, and books of reference, and for printing and binding) as may be necessary for the execution of the functions vested in the commission and, as from time to time may be appropriated for by Congress. All expenditures of the commission shall be allowed and paid upon the presentation of itemized vouchers therefor approved by the chairman.

Sec. 5.   From and after one year after the first meeting of the commission created by this Act, all the powers and authority vested in the commission under the terms of this Act, except as to the revocation of licenses, shall be vested in and exercised by the Secretary of Commerce; except that thereafter the commission shall have power and jurisdiction to act upon and determine any and all matters brought before it under the terms of this section.

It shall also be the duty of the Secretary of Commerce—

(A)   For and during a period of one year from the first meeting of the commission created by this Act, to immediately refer to the commission all applications for station licenses or for the renewal or modification of existing station licenses.

(B)   From and after one year from the first meeting of the commission created by this Act, to refer to the commission for its action any application for a station license or for the renewal or modification of any existing station license as to the granting of which dispute, controversy, or conflict arises or against the granting of which protest is filed within ten days after the date of filing said application by any party in interest and any application as to which such reference is requested by the applicant at the time of filing said application.

(C)   To prescribe the qualifications of station operators, to classify them according to the duties to be performed, to fix the forms of such licenses, and to issue them to such persons as he finds qualified.

(D)   To suspend the license of any operator for a period not exceeding two years upon proof sufficient to satisfy him that the licensee (a) has violated any provision of any Act or treaty binding on the United States which the Secretary of Commerce or the commission is authorized by this Act to administer or by any regulation made by the commission or the Secretary of Commerce under any such Act or treaty; or (b) has failed to carry out the lawful orders of the master of the vessel on which he is employed; or (c) has willfully damaged or permitted radio apparatus to be damaged; or (d) has transmitted superfluous radio communications or signals or radio communications containing profane or obscene words or language; or (e) has willfully or maliciously interfered with any other radio communications or signals.

(E)   To inspect all transmitting apparatus to ascertain whether in construction and operation it conforms to the requirements of this Act, the rules and regulations of the licensing authority, and the license under which it is constructed or operated.

(F)   To report to the commission from time to time any violations of this Act, the rules, regulations, or orders of the commission, or of the terms or conditions of any license.

(G)   To designate call letters of all stations.

(H)   To cause to be published such call letters and such other announcements and data as in his judgment may be required for the efficient operation of radio stations subject to the jurisdiction of the United States and for the proper enforcement of this Act.

The Secretary may refer to the commission at any time any matter the determination of which is vested in him by the terms of this Act.

Any person, firm, company, or corporation, any State or political division thereof aggrieved or whose interests are adversely affected by any decision, determination, or regulation of the Secretary of Commerce may appeal therefrom to the commission by filing with the Secretary of Commerce notice of such appeal within thirty days after such decision or determination or promulgation of such regulation. All papers, documents, and other records pertaining to such application on file with the Secretary shall thereupon be transferred by him to the commission. The commission shall hear such appeal de novo under such rules and regulations as it may determine.

Decisions by the commission as to matters so appealed and as to all other matters over which it has jurisdiction shall be final, subject to the right of appeal herein given.

No station license shall be granted by the commission or the Secretary of Commerce until the applicant therefor shall have signed a waiver of any claim to the use of any particular frequency or wave length or of the ether as against the regulatory power of the United States because of the previous use of the same, whether by license or otherwise.

Sec. 6.   Radio stations belonging to and operated by the United States shall not be subject to the provisions of sections 1, 4, and 5 of this Act. All such Government stations shall use such frequencies or wave lengths as shall be assigned to each or to each class by the President. All such stations, except stations on board naval and other Government vessels while at sea or beyond the limits of the continental United States, when transmitting any radio communication or signal other than a communication or signal relating to Government business shall conform to such rules and regulations designed to prevent interference with other radio stations and the rights of others as the licensing authority may prescribe. Upon proclamation by the President that there exists war or a threat of war or a state of public peril or disaster or other national emergency, or in order to preserve the neutrality of the United States, the President may suspend or amend, for such time as he may see fit, the rules and regulations applicable to any or all stations within the jurisdiction of the United States as prescribed by the licensing authority, and may cause the closing of any station for radio communication and the removal therefrom of its apparatus and equipment, or he may authorize the use or control of any such station and/or its apparatus and equipment by any department of the Government under such regulations as he may prescribe, upon just compensation to the owners. Radio stations on board vessels of the United States Shipping Board or the United States Shipping Board Emergency Fleet Corporation or the Inland and Coastwise Waterways Service shall be subject to the provisions of this Act.

Sec. 7.   The President shall ascertain the just compensation for such use or control and certify the amount ascertained to Congress for appropriation and payment to the person entitled thereto. If the amount so certified is unsatisfactory to the person entitled thereto, such person shall be paid only 75 per centum of the amount and shall be entitled to sue the United States to recover such further sum as added to such payment of 75 per centum which will make such amount as will be just compensation for the use and control. Such suit shall be brought in the manner provided by paragraph 20 of section 24, or by section 145 of the Judicial Code, as amended.

Sec. 8.   All stations owned and operated by the United States, except mobile stations of the Army of the United States, and all other stations on land and sea, shall have special call letters designated by the Secretary of Commerce.

Section 1 of this Act shall not apply to any person, firm, company, or corporation sending radio communications or signals on a foreign ship while the same is within the jurisdiction of the United States, but such communications or signals shall be transmitted only in accordance with such regulations designed to prevent interference as may be promulgated under the authority of this Act.

Sec. 9.   The licensing authority, if public convenience, interest, or necessity will be served thereby, subject to the limitations of this Act, shall grant to any applicant therefor a station license provided for by this Act.

In considering applications for licenses and renewals of licenses, when and in so far as there is a demand for the same, the licensing authority shall make such a distribution of licenses, bands of frequency of wave lengths, periods of time for operation, and of power among the different States and communities as to give fair, efficient, and equitable radio service to each of the same.

No license granted for the operation of a broadcasting station shall be for a longer term than three years and no license so granted for any other class of station shall be for a longer term than five years, and any license granted may be revoked as hereinafter provided. Upon the expiration of any license, upon application therefor, a renewal of such license may be granted from time to time for a term of not to exceed three years in the case of broadcasting licenses and not to exceed five years in the case of other licenses.

No renewal of an existing station license shall be granted more than thirty days prior to the expiration of the original license.

Sec. 10.   The licensing authority may grant station licenses only upon written application therefor addressed to it. All applications shall be filed with the Secretary of Commerce. All such applications shall set forth such facts as the licensing authority by regulation may prescribe as to the citizenship, character, and financial, technical, and other qualifications of the applicant to operate the station; the ownership and location of the proposed station and of the stations, if any, with which it is proposed to communicate; the frequencies or wave lengths and the power desired to be used; the hours of the day or other periods of time during which it is proposed to operate the station; the purposes for which the station is to be used; and such other information as it may require. The licensing authority at any time after the filing of such original application and during the term of any such license may require from an applicant or licensee further written statements of fact to enable it to determine whether such original application should be granted or denied or such license revoked. Such application and/or such statement of fact shall be signed by the applicant and/or licensee under oath or affirmation.

The licensing authority in granting any license for a station intended or used for commercial communication between the United States or any Territory or possession, continental or insular, subject to the jurisdiction of the United States, and any foreign country, may impose any terms, conditions, or restrictions authorized to be imposed with respect to submarine-cable licenses by section 2 of an Act entitled "An Act relating to the landing and the operation of submarine cables in the United States," approved May 24, 1921.

Sec. 11.   If upon examination of any application for a station license or for the renewal or modification of a station license the licensing authority shall determine that public interest, convenience, or necessity would be served by the granting thereof, it shall authorize the issuance, renewal, or modification thereof in accordance with said finding. In the event the licensing authority upon examination of any such application does not reach such decision with respect thereto, it shall notify the applicant thereof, shall fix and give notice of a time and place for hearing thereon, and shall afford such applicant an opportunity to be heard under such rules and regulations as it may prescribe.

Such station licenses as the licensing authority may grant shall be in such general form as it may prescribe, but each license shall contain, in addition to other provisions, a statement of the following conditions to which such license shall be subject:

(A)   The station license shall not vest in the licensee any right to operate the station nor any right in the use of the frequencies or wave length designated in the license beyond the term thereof nor in any other manner than authorized therein.

(B)   Neither the license nor the right granted thereunder shall be assigned or otherwise transferred in violation of this Act.

(C)   Every license issued under this Act shall be subject in terms to the right of use or control conferred by section 6 hereof.

In cases of emergency arising during the period of one year from and after the first meeting of the commission created hereby, or on applications filed during said time for temporary changes in terms of licenses when the commission is not in session and prompt action is deemed necessary, the Secretary of Commerce shall have authority to exercise the powers and duties of the commission, except as to revocation of licenses, but all such exercise of powers shall be promptly reported to the members of the commission, and any action by the Secretary authorized under this paragraph shall continue in force and have effect only until such time as the commission shall act thereon.

Sec. 12.   The station license required hereby shall not be granted to, or after the granting thereof such license shall not be transferred in any manner, either voluntarily or involuntarily, to (a) any alien or the representative of any alien; (b) to any foreign government, or the representative thereof; (c) to any company, corporation, or association organized under the laws of any foreign government; (d) to any company, corporation, or association of which any officer or director is an alien, or of which more than one-fifth of the capital stock may be voted by aliens or their representatives or by a foreign government or representative thereof, or by any company, corporation, or association organized under the laws of a foreign country.

The station license required hereby, the frequencies or wave length or lengths authorized to be used by the licensee, and the rights therein granted shall not be transferred, assigned, or in any manner, either voluntarily or involuntarily, disposed of to any person, firm, company, or corporation without the consent in writing of the licensing authority.

Sec. 13.   The licensing authority is hereby directed to refuse a station license and/or the permit hereinafter required for the construction of a station to any person, firm, company, or corporation, or any subsidiary thereof, which has been finally adjudged guilty by a Federal court of unlawfully monopolizing or attempting unlawfully to monopolize, after this Act takes effect, radio communication, directly or indirectly, through the control of the manufacture or sale of radio apparatus, through exclusive traffic arrangements, or by any other means or to have been using unfair methods of competition. The granting of a license shall not estop the United States or any person aggrieved from proceeding against such person, firm, company, or corporation for violating the law against unfair methods of competition or for a violation of the law against unlawful restraints and monopolies and/or combinations, contracts, or agreements in restraint of trade, or from instituting proceedings for the dissolution of such firm, company, or corporation.

Sec. 14.   Any station license shall be revocable by the commission for false statements either in the application or in the statement of fact which may be required by section 10 hereof, or because of conditions revealed by such statements of fact as may be required from time to time which would warrant the licensing authority in refusing to grant a license on an original application, or for failure to operate substantially as set forth in the license, for violation of or failure to observe any of the restrictions and conditions of this Act, or of any regulation of the licensing authority authorized by this Act or by a treaty ratified by the United States, or whenever the Interstate Commerce Commission, or any other Federal body in the exercise of authority conferred upon it by law, shall find and shall certify to the commission that any licensee bound so to do, has failed to provide reasonable facilities for the transmission of radio communications, or that any licensee has made any unjust and unreasonable charge, or has been guilty of any discrimination, either as to charge or as to service or has made or prescribed any unjust and unreasonable classification, regulation, or practice with respect to the transmission of radio communications or service: *Provided*, That no such order of revocation shall take effect until thirty days' notice in writing thereof, stating the cause for the proposed revocation, has been given to the parties known by the commission to be interested in such license. Any person in interest aggrieved by said order may make written application to the commission at any time within said thirty days for a hearing upon such order, and upon the filing of such written application said order of revocation shall stand suspended until the conclusion of the hearing herein directed. Notice in writing of said hearing shall be given by the commission to all the parties known to it to be interested in such license twenty days prior to the time of said hearing. Said hearing shall be conducted under such rules and in such manner as the commission may prescribe. Upon the conclusion hereof the commission may affirm. modify, or revoke said orders of revocation.

Sec. 15.   All laws of the United States relating to unlawful restraints and monopolies and to combinations, contracts, or agreements in restraint of trade are hereby declared to be applicable to the manufacture and sale of and to trade in radio apparatus and devices entering into or affecting interstate or foreign commerce and to interstate or foreign radio communications. Whenever in any suit, action, or proceeding, civil or criminal, brought under the provisions of any of said laws or in any proceeding brought to enforce or to review findings and orders of the Federal Trade Commission or other governmental agency in respect of any matters as to which said commission or other governmental agency is by law authorized to act, any licensee shall be found guilty of the violation of the provisions of such laws or any of them, the court, in addition to the penalties imposed by said laws, may adjudge, order, and/or decree that the license of such licensee shall, as of the date the decree or judgment becomes finally effective or as of such other date as the said decree shall fix, be revoked and that all rights under such license shall thereupon cease: *Provided, however.* That such licensee shall have the same right of appeal or review as is provided by law in respect of other decrees and judgments of said court.

Sec. 16.   Any applicant for a construction permit, for a station license, or for the renewal or modification of an existing station license whose application is refused by the licensing authority shall have the right to appeal from said decision to the Court of Appeals of the District of Columbia; and any licensee whose license is revoked by the commission shall have the right to appeal from such decision of revocation to said Court of Appeals of the District of Columbia or to the district court of the United States in which the apparatus licensed is operated, by filing with said court, within twenty days after the decision complained of is effective, notice in writing of said appeal and of the reasons therefor.

The licensing authority from whose decision an appeal is taken shall be notified of said appeal by service upon it, prior to the filing thereof, of a certified copy of said appeal and of the reasons therefor. Within twenty days after the filing of said appeal the licensing authority shall file with the court the originals or certified copies of all papers and evidence presented to it upon the original application for a permit or license or in the hearing upon said order of revocation, and also a like copy of its decision thereon and a full statement in writing of the facts and the grounds for its decision as found and given by it.

Within twenty days after the filing of said statement by the licensing authority either party may give notice to the court of his desire to adduce additional evidence. Said notice shall be in the form of a verified petition stating the nature and character of said additional evidence, and the court may thereupon order such evidence to be taken in such manner and upon such terms and conditions as it may deem proper.

At the earliest convenient time the court shall hear, review, and determine the appeal upon said record and evidence, and may alter or revise the decision appealed from and enter such judgment as to it may seem just. The revision by the court shall be confined to the points set forth in the reasons of appeal.

Sec. 17.   After the passage of this Act no person, firm, company, or corporation now or hereafter directly or indirectly through any subsidiary, associated, or affiliated person, firm, company, corporation, or agent, or otherwise, in the business of transmitting and/or receiving for hire energy, communications, or signals by radio in accordance with the terms of the license issued under this Act, shall by purchase, lease, construction, or otherwise, directly or indirectly, acquire, own, control, or operate any cable or wire telegraph or telephone line or system between any place in any State, Territory, or possession of the United States or in the District of Columbia, and any place in any foreign country, or shall acquire, own, or control any part of the stock or other capital share of any interest in the physical property and/or other assets of any such cable, wire, telegraph, or telephone line or system, if in either case the purpose is and/or the effect thereof may be to substantially lessen competition or to restrain commerce between any place in any State, Territory, or possession of the United States or in the District of Columbia and any place in any foreign country, or unlawfully to create monopoly in any line of commerce; nor shall any person, firm, company, or corporation now or hereafter engaged directly or indirectly through any subsidiary, associated, or affiliated person, company, corporation, or agent, or otherwise, in the business of transmitting and/or receiving for hire messages by any cable, wire, telegraph, or telephone line or system (a) between any place in any State, Territory, or possession of the United States or in the District of Columbia, and any place in any other State, Territory, or possession of the United States; or (b) between any place in any State, Territory, or possession of the United States, or the District of Columbia, and any place in any foreign country, by purchase, lease, construction, or otherwise, directly or indirectly acquire, own, control, or operate any station or the apparatus therein, or any system for transmitting and/or receiving radio communications or signals between any place in any State, Territory, or possession of the United States or in the District of Columbia, and any place in any foreign country, or shall acquire, own, or control any part of the stock or other capital share or any interest in the physical property and/or other assets of any such radio station, apparatus, or system, if in either case the purpose is and/or the effect thereof may be to substantially lessen competition or to restrain commerce between any place in any State, Territory, or possession of the United States or in the District of Columbia, and any place in any foreign country, or unlawfully to create monopoly in any line of commerce.

Sec. 18. If any licensee shall permit any person who is a legally qualified candidate for any public office to use a broadcasting station, he shall afford equal opportunities to all other such candidates for that office in the use of such broadcasting station, and the licensing authority shall make rules and regulations to carry this provision into effect: *Provided*, That such licensee shall have no power of censorship over the material broadcast under the provisions of this paragraph. No obligation is hereby imposed upon any licensee to allow the use of its station by any such candidate.

Sec. 19. All matter broadcast by any radio station for which service, money, or any other valuable consideration is directly or indirectly paid, or promised to or charged or accepted by, the station so broadcasting, from any person, firm, company, or corporation, shall, at the time the same is so broadcast, be announced as paid for or furnished, as the case may be, by such person, firm, company, or corporation.

Sec. 20. The actual operation of all transmitting apparatus in any radio station for which a station license is required by this Act shall be carried on only by a person holding an operator's license issued hereunder. No person shall operate any such apparatus in such station except under and in accordance with an operator's license issued to him by the Secretary of Commerce.

Sec. 21. No license shall be issued under the authority of this Act for the operation of any station the construction of which is begun or is continued after this Act takes effect, unless a permit for its construction has been granted by the licensing authority upon written application therefor. The licensing authority may grant such permit if public convenience, interest, or necessity will be served by the construction of the station. This application shall set forth such facts as the licensing authority by regulation may prescribe as to the citizenship, character, and the financial, technical, and other ability of the applicant to construct and operate the station, the ownership and location of the proposed station and of the station or stations with which it is proposed to communicate, the frequencies and wave length or wave lengths desired to be used, the hours of the day or other periods of time during which it is proposed to operate the station, the purpose for which the station is to be used, the type of transmitting apparatus to be used, the power to be used, the date upon which the station is expected to be completed and in operation, and such other information as the licensing authority may require. Such application shall be signed by the applicant under oath or affirmation.

Such permit for construction shall show specifically the earliest and latest dates between which the actual operation of such station is expected to begin, and shall provide that said permit will be automatically forfeited if the station is not ready for operation within the time specified or within such further time as the licensing authority may allow, unless prevented by causes not under the control of the grantee. The rights under any such permit shall not be assigned or otherwise transferred to any person, firm, company, or corporation without the approval of the licensing authority. A permit for construction shall not be required for Government stations, amateur stations, or stations upon mobile vessels, railroad rolling stock, or aircraft. Upon the completion of any station for the construction or continued construction for which a permit has been granted, and upon it being made to appear to the licensing authority that all the terms, conditions, and obligations set forth in the application and permit have been fully met, and that no cause or circumstance arising or first coming to the knowledge of the licensing authority since the granting of the permit would, in the judgment of the licensing authority, make the operation of such station against the public interest, the licensing authority shall issue a license to the lawful holder of said permit for the operation of said station. Said license shall conform generally to the terms of said permit.

Sec. 22.   The licensing authority is authorized to designate from time to time radio stations the communications or signals of which, in its opinion, are liable to interfere with the transmission or with respect thereto which the Commission may by order require, to keep a licensed radio operator listening in on the wave lengths designated for signals of distress and radio communications relating thereto during the entire period the transmitter of such station is in operation.

Sec. 23.   Every radio station on shipboard shall be equipped to transmit radio communications or signals of distress on the frequency or wave length specified by the licensing authority, with apparatus capable of transmitting and receiving messages over a distance of at least one hundred miles by day or night. When sending radio communications or signals of distress and radio communications relating thereto the transmitting set may be adjusted in such a manner as to produce a maximum of radiation irrespective of the amount of interference which may thus be caused.

All radio stations, including Government stations and stations on board foreign vessels when within the territorial waters of the United States, shall give absolute priority to radio communications or signals relating to ships in distress; shall cease all sending on frequencies or wave lengths which will interfere with hearing a radio communication or signal of distress, and, except when engaged in answering or aiding the ship in distress, shall refrain from sending any radio communications or signals until there is assurance that no interference will be caused with the radio communications or signals relating thereto, and shall assist the vessel in distress, so far as possible, by complying with its instructions.

Sec. 24.   Every shore station open to general public service between the coast and vessels at sea shall be bound to exchange radio communications or signals with any ship station without distinction as to radio systems or instruments adopted by such stations, respectively, and each station on shipboard shall be bound to exchange radio communications or signals with any other station on shipboard without distinction as to radio systems or instruments adopted by each station.

Sec. 25. At all places where Government and private or commercial radio stations on land operate in such close proximity that interference with the work of Government stations can not be avoided when they are operating simultaneously such private or commercial stations as do interfere with the transmission or reception of radio communications or signals by the Government stations concerned shall not use their transmitters during the first fifteen minutes of each hour, local standard time.

The Government stations for which the above-mentioned division of time is established shall transmit radio communications or signals only during the first fifteen minutes of each hour, local standard time, except in case of signals or radio communications relating to vessels in distress and vessel requests for information as to course, location, or compass direction.

Sec. 26. In all circumstances, except in case of radio communications or signals relating to vessels in distress, all radio stations, including those owned and operated by the United States, shall use the minimum amount of power necessary to carry out the communication desired.

Sec. 27. No person receiving or assisting in receiving any radio communication shall divulge or publish the contents, substance, purport, effect, or meaning thereof except through authorized channels of transmission or reception to any person other than the addressee, his agent, or attorney, or to a telephone, telegraph, cable, or radio station employed or authorized to forward such radio communication to its destination, or to proper accounting or distributing officers of the various communicating centers over which the radio communication may be passed, or to the master of a ship under whom he is serving, or in response to a subpoena issued by a court of competent jurisdiction, or on demand of other lawful authority; and no person not being authorized by the sender shall intercept any message and divulge or publish the contents, substance, purport, effect, or meaning of such intercepted message to any person; and no person not being entitled thereto shall receive or assist in receiving any radio communication and use the same or any information therein contained for his own benefit or for the benefit of another not entitled thereto; and no person having received such intercepted radio communication or having become acquainted with the contents, substance, purport, effect, or meaning of the same or any part thereof, knowing that such information was so obtained, shall divulge or publish the contents, substance, purport, effect, or meaning of the same or any part thereof, or use the same or any information therein contained for his own benefit or for the benefit of another not entitled thereto: *Provided,* That this section shall not apply to the receiving, divulging, publishing, or utilizing the contents of any radio communication broadcasted or transmitted by amateurs or others for the use of the general public or relating to ships in distress.

Sec. 28.   No person, firm, company, or corporation within the jurisdiction of the United States shall knowingly utter or transmit, or cause to be uttered or transmitted, any false or fraudulent signal of distress, or communication relating thereto, nor shall any broadcasting station rebroadcast the program or any part thereof of another broadcasting station without the express authority of the originating station.

Sec. 29.   Nothing in this Act shall be understood or construed to give the licensing authority the power of censorship over the radio communications or signals transmitted by any radio station, and no regulation or condition shall be promulgated or fixed by the licensing authority which shall interfere with the right of free speech by means of radio communications. No person within the jurisdiction of the United States shall utter any obscene, indecent, or profane language by means of radio communication.

Sec. 30.   The Secretary of the Navy is hereby authorized unless restrained by international agreement, under the terms and conditions and at rates prescribed by him, which rates shall be just and reasonable, and which, upon complaint, shall be subject to review and revision by the Interstate Commerce Commission, to use all radio stations and apparatus, wherever located, owned by the United States and under the control of the Navy Department (a) for the reception and transmission of press messages offered by any newspaper published in the United States, its Territories or possessions, or published by citizens of the United States in foreign countries, or by any press association of the United States, and (b) for the reception and transmission of private commercial messages between ships, between ship and shore, between localities in Alaska and between Alaska and the continental United States: *Provided*, That the rates fixed for the reception and transmission of all such messages, other than press messages between the Pacific coast of the United States, Hawaii, Alaska, the Philippine Islands, and the Orient, and between the United States and the Virgin Islands, shall not be less than the rates charged by privately owned and operated stations for like messages and service: *Provided further*, That the right to use such stations for any of the purposes named in this section shall terminate and cease as between any countries or localities or between any locality and privately operated ships whenever privately owned and operated stations are capable of meeting the normal communication requirements between such countries or localities or between any locality and privately operated ships, and the licensing authority shall have notified the Secretary of the Navy thereof.

Sec. 31.   The expression "radio communication" or "radio communications" wherever used in this Act means any intelligence, message, signal, power, pictures, or communication of any nature transferred by electrical energy from one point to another without the aid of any wire connecting the points from and at which the electrical energy is sent or received and any system by means of which such transfer of energy is effected.

Sec. 32.   Any person, firm, company, or corporation failing or refusing to observe or violating any rule, regulation, restriction, or condition made or imposed by the licensing authority under the authority of this Act or of any international radio convention or treaty ratified or adhered to by the United States, in addition to any other penalties provided by law, upon conviction thereof by a court of competent jurisdiction, shall be punished by a fine of not more than $500 for each and every offense.

Sec. 33.   Any person, firm, company, or corporation who shall violate any provision of this Act, or shall knowingly make any false oath or affirmation in any affidavit required or authorized by this Act, or shall knowingly swear falsely to a material matter in any hearing authorized by this Act, upon conviction thereof in any court of competent jurisdiction shall be punished by a fine of not more than $5,000 or by imprisonment for a term of not more than five years or both for each and every such offense.

Sec. 34.   The trial of any offense under this Act shall be in the district in which it is committed; or if the offense is committed upon the high seas, or out of the jurisdiction of any particular State or district, the trial shall be in the district where the offender may be found or into which he shall be first brought.

Sec. 35.   This Act shall not apply to the Philippine Islands or to the Canal Zone. In international radio matters the Philippine Islands and the Canal Zone shall be represented by the Secretary of State.

Sec. 36.   The licensing authority is authorized to designate any officer or employee of any other department of the Government on duty in any Territory or possession of the United States other than the Philippine Islands and the Canal Zone, to render therein such services in connection with the administration of the radio laws of the United States as such authority may prescribe: *Provided*, That such designation shall be approved by the head of the department in which such person is employed.

Sec. 37.   The unexpended balance of the moneys appropriated in the item for "wireless communication laws," under the caption "Bureau of Navigation" in Title III of the Act entitled "An Act making appropriations for the Departments of State and Justice and for the judiciary, and for the Departments of Commerce and Labor, for the fiscal year ending June 30, 1927, and for other purposes," approved April 29, 1926, and the appropriation for the same purposes for the fiscal year ending June 30, 1928, shall be available both for expenditures incurred in the administration of this Act and for expenditures for the purposes specified in such items. There is hereby authorized to be appropriated for each fiscal year such sums as may be necessary for the administration of this Act and for the purposes specified in such item.

Sec. 38.   If any provision of this Act or the application thereof to any person, firm, company, or corporation, or to any circumstances, is held invalid, the remainder of the Act and the application of such provision to other persons, firms, companies, or corporations, or to other circumstances, shall not be affected thereby.

Sec. 39.   The Act entitled "An Act to regulate radio communication," approved August 13, 1912, the joint resolution to authorize the operation of Government-owned radio stations for the general public, and for other purposes, approved June 5, 1920, as amended, and the joint resolution entitled "Joint resolution limiting the time for which licenses for radio transmission may be granted, and for other purposes," approved December 8, 1926, are hereby repealed.

Such repeal, however, shall not affect any act done or any right accrued or any suit or proceeding had or commenced in any civil cause prior to said repeal, but all liabilities under said laws shall continue and may be enforced in the same manner as if committed; and all penalties, forfeitures, or liabilities incurred prior to taking effect hereof, under any law embraced in, changed, modified, or repealed by this Act, may be prosecuted and punished in the same manner and with the same effect as if this Act had not been passed.

Nothing in this section shall be construed as authorizing any person now using or operating any apparatus for the transmission of radio energy or radio communications or signals to continue such use except under and in accordance with this Act and with a license granted in accordance with the authority hereinbefore conferred.

Sec. 40.   This Act shall take effect and be in force upon its passage and approval, except that for and during a period of sixty days after such approval no holder of a license or an extension thereof issued by the Secretary of Commerce under said Act of August 13, 1912, shall be subject to the penalties provided herein for operating a station without the license herein required.

Sec. 41.   This Act may be referred to and cited as the Radio Act of 1927.

10

FRC Interpretation of the Public Interest

Statement Made by the Commission on

August 23, 1928, Relative to Public Interest,

Convenience, or Necessity

2 FRC Ann. Rep. 166 (1928)

Delayed confirmations and appropriations complicated by death and resignation caused the membership of the Federal Radio Commission to remain incomplete until a year after passage of the Act of 1927. At about the same time, on March 28, 1928, the "Davis Amendment" (Public Law 195, 70th Congress) was signed into law. This amendment directed the FRC to provide "equality of radio broadcasting service, both of transmission and of reception" to each of the five zones established by Section 2 of the Radio Act. The amendment was an administrative nightmare for a new commission plagued with the problems of an overcrowded broadcast spectrum.

Before establishing the quotas required by the Davis Amendment, the Commission acted on its own General Order No. 32, holding expedited hearings during two weeks in July, 1928, in which 164 broadcast licensees were given the opportunity to justify their continued status as station operators under the Radio Act's public interest standard. When the dust had settled there were 62 fewer broadcasters; several others had to settle for power reductions, consolidations, or probationary renewals. Fewer than half of the 164 stations emerged unscathed.

The following statement constitutes the FRC's first comprehensive attempt to put the flesh of administrative interpretation on the bare-boned "public interest" standard with which Congress had endowed it. Although some of the guidelines seem hopelessly archaic today, contemporary technical and programming standards can be traced back to these basic principles of regulatory philosophy.

Related Reading: 106, 131.

Federal Radio Commission, *Washington, D.C.*

The Federal Radio Commission announced on August 23, 1928, the basic principles and its interpretation of the public interest, convenience, or necessity clause of the radio act, which were invoked in reaching decisions in cases recently heard of radio broadcasting stations whose public service was challenged. The commission's statement follows:

Public interest, convenience, or necessity

The only standard (other than the Davis amendment) which Congress furnished to the commission for its guidance in the determination of the complicated questions which arise in connection with the granting of licenses and the renewal or modification of existing licenses is the rather broad one of "public interest, convenience, or necessity." . . .

. . . No attempt is made anywhere in the act to define the term "public interest, convenience, or necessity," nor is any illustration given of its proper application.

The commission is of the opinion that Congress, in enacting the Davis amendment, did not intend to repeal or do away with this standard. While the primary purpose of the Davis amendment is to bring about equality as between the zones, it does not require the commission to grant any application which does not serve public interest, convenience, or necessity simply because the application happens to proceed from a zone or State that is under its quota. The equality is not to be brought about by sacrificing the standard. On the other hand, where a particular zone or State is over its quota, it is true that the commission may on occasions be forced to deny an application the granting of which might, in its opinion, serve public interest, convenience, or necessity. The Davis amendment may, therefore, be viewed as a partial limitation upon the power of the commission in applying the standard.

The cases which the commission has considered as a result of General Order No. 32 are all cases in which it has had before it applications for renewals of station licenses. Under section 2 of the act the commission is given full power and authority to follow the procedure adhered to in these cases, when it has been unable to reach a decision that granting a particular application would serve public interest, convenience, or necessity. In fact, the entire radio act of 1927 makes it clear that no renewal of a license is to be granted, unless the commission shall find that public interest, convenience, or necessity will be served. The fact that all of these stations have been licensed by the commission from time to time in the past, and the further fact that most of them were licensed prior to the enactment of the radio act of 1927 by the Secretary of Commerce, do not, in the opinion of the commission, demonstrate that the continued existence of such stations will serve public interest, convenience, or necessity. The issuance of a previous license by the commission is not in any event to be regarded as a finding further than for the duration of the limited period covered by the license (usually 90 days). There have been a variety of considerations to which the commission was entitled to give weight. For example, when the commission first entered upon its duties it found in existence a large number of stations, much larger than could satisfactorily operate simultaneously and permit good radio reception. Nevertheless, in order to avoid injustice and in order to give the commission an opportunity to determine which stations were best serving the public, it was perfectly consistent for the commission to relicense all of these stations for limited periods. It was in the public interest that a fair test should be conducted to determine which stations were rendering the best service. Furthermore, even if the relicensing of a station in the past would be some indication that it met the test, there is no reason why the United States Government, the commission, or the radio-listening public should be bound by a mistake which has been made in the past. There were no hearings preliminary to granting these licenses in the past, and it can hardly be said that the issue has been adjudicated in any of the cases.

The commission has been urged to give a precise definition of the phrase "public interest, convenience, or necessity," and in the course of the hearings has been frequently criticized for not having done so. It has also been urged that the statute itself is unconstitutional because of the alleged uncertainty and indefiniteness of the phrase. So far as the generality of the phrase is concerned, it is no less certain or definite than other phrases which have found their way into Federal statutes and which have been upheld by the Supreme Court of the United States. An example is "unfair methods of competition." To be able to arrive at a precise definition of such a phrase which will foresee all eventualities is manifestly impossible. The phrase will have to be defined by the United States Supreme Court, and this will probably be done by a gradual process of decisions on particular combinations of fact.

It must be remembered that the standard provided by the act applies not only to broadcasting stations but to each type of radio station which must be licensed, including point-to-point communication, experimental, amateur, ship, airplane, and other kinds of stations. Any definition must be broad enough to include all of these and yet must be elastic enough to permit of definite application to each.

It is, however, possible to state a few general principles which have demonstrated themselves in the course of the experience of the commission and which are applicable to the broadcasting band.

In the first place, the commission has no hesitation in stating that it is in the public interest, convenience, and necessity that a substantial band of frequencies be set aside for the exclusive use of broadcasting stations and the radio listening public, and under the present circumstances believes that the band of 550 to 1,500 kilocycles meets that test.

In the second place, the commission is convinced that public interest, convenience, or necessity will be served by such action on the part of the commission as will bring about the best possible broadcasting reception conditions throughout the United States. By good conditions the commission means freedom from interference of various types as well as good quality in the operation of the broadcasting station. So far as possible, the various types of interference, such as heterodyning, cross talk, and blanketing must be avoided. The commission is convinced that the interest of the broadcast listener is of superior importance to that of the broadcaster and that it is better that there should be a few less broadcasters than that the listening public should suffer from undue interference. It is unfortunate that in the past the most vociferous public expression has been made by broadcasters or by persons speaking in their behalf and the real voice of the listening public has not sufficiently been heard.

The commission is furthermore convinced that within the band of frequencies devoted to broadcasting, public interest, convenience, or necessity will be best served by a fair distribution of different types of service. Without attempting to determine how many channels should be devoted to the various types of service, the commission feels that a certain number should be devoted to stations so equipped and financed as to permit the giving of a high order of service over as large a territory as possible. This is the only manner in which the distant listener in the rural and sparsely settled portions of the country will be reached. A certain number of other channels should be given over to stations which desire to reach a more limited region and as to which there will be large intermediate areas in which there will be objectionable interference. Finally, there should be a provision for stations which are distinctly local in character and which aim to serve only the smaller towns in the United States without any attempt to reach listeners beyond the immediate vicinity of such towns.

The commission also believes that public interest, convenience, or necessity will be best served by avoiding too much duplication of programs and types of programs. Where one community is underserved and another community is receiving duplication of the same order of programs, the second community should be restricted in order to benefit the first. Where one type of service is being rendered by several stations in the same region, consideration should be given to a station which renders a type of service which is not such a duplication.

In view of the paucity of channels, the commission is of the opinion that the limited facilities for broadcasting should not be shared with stations which give the sort of service which is readily available to the public in another form. For example, the public in large cities can easily purchase and use phonograph records of the ordinary commercial type. A station which devotes the main portion of its hours of operation to broadcasting such phonograph records is not giving the public anything which it can not readily have without such a station. If, in addition to this, the station is located in a city where there are large resources in program material, the continued operation of the station means that some other station is being kept out of existence which might put to use such original program material. The commission realizes that the situation is not the same in some of the smaller towns and farming communities, where such program resources are not available. Without placing the stamp of approval on the use of phonograph records under such circumstances, the commission will not go so far at present as to state that the practice is at all times and under all conditions a violation of the test provided by the statute. It may be also that the development of special phonograph records will take such a form that the result can be made available by broadcasting only and not available to the public commercially, and if such proves to be the case the commission will take the fact into consideration. The commission can not close its eyes to the fact that the real purpose of the use of phonograph records in most communities is to provide a cheaper method of advertising for advertisers who are thereby saved the expense of providing an original program.

While it is true that broadcasting stations in this country are for the most part supported or partially supported by advertisers, broadcasting stations are not given these great privileges by the United States Government for the primary benefit of advertisers. Such benefit as is derived by advertisers must be incidental and entirely secondary to the interest of the public.

The same question arises in another connection. Where the station is used for the broadcasting of a considerable amount of what is called "direct advertising," including the quoting of merchandise prices, the advertising is usually offensive to the listening public. Advertising should be only incidental to some real service rendered to the public, and not the main object of a program. The commission realizes that in some communities, particularly in the State of Iowa, there seems to exist a strong sentiment in favor of such advertising on the part of the listening public. At least the broadcasters in that community have succeeded in making an impressive demonstration before the commission on each occasion when the matter has come up for discussion. The commission is not fully convinced that it has heard both sides of the matter, but is willing to concede that in some localities the quoting of direct merchandise prices may serve as a sort of local market, and in that community a service may thus be rendered. That such is not the case generally, however, the commission knows from thousands and thousands of letters which it has had from all over the country complaining of such practices.

Another question which must be taken seriously is the location of the transmitter of the station. This is properly a question of interference. Generally speaking, it is not in the public interest, convenience, or necessity for a station of substantial power (500 watts or more) to be located in the midst of a thickly inhabited community. The question of the proper location of a station with respect to its power is a complicated one and can not here be discussed in detail. Obviously it is desirable that a station serving a particular community or region should cover that community or region with a signal strong enough to constitute adequate service.

It is also desirable that the signal be not so strong as to blanket reception from other stations operating on other frequencies. There is a certain amount of blanketing in the vicinity of every transmitter, even one of 5, 10, or 50 watts. The frequencies used by stations in the same geographical region can be widely enough separated, however, so that the blanketing will not be serious from a transmitter of less than 500 watts, even when located in a thickly inhabited community. With stations of that amount of power, or greater, the problem becomes a serious one. In order to serve the whole of a large metropolitan area a 500-watt station has barely sufficient power even when it is located in the center of the area. If its transmitter is located away from the thickly inhabited portions and out in the country it will not give satisfactory service. Such an area can only be adequately served, without blanketing, by stations of greater power located in sparsely settled portions of the near-by country.

Theoretically, therefore, it may be said that it will not serve public interest, convenience, or necessity to permit the location of a low-powered station in a large city. It can not hope to serve the entire city, and yet it renders the frequency useless for the listeners of the city outside of the small area immediately surrounding the station. On the other hand, such a station might give very good service to a small town or city.

The commission is furthermore convinced that in applying the test of public interest, convenience, or necessity, it may consider the character of the licensee or applicant, his financial responsibility, and his past record, in order to determine whether he is more or less likely to fulfill the trust imposed by the license than others who are seeking the same privilege from the same community, State, or zone.

A word of warning must be given to those broadcasting (of which there have been all too many) who consume much of the valuable time allotted to them under their licenses in matters of a distinctly private nature, which are not only uninteresting but also distasteful to the listening public. Such is the case where two rival broadcasters in the same community spend their time in abusing each other over the air.

A station which does not operate on a regular schedule made known to the public through announcements in the press or otherwise is not rendering a service which meets the test of the law. If the radio listener does not know whether or not a particular station is broadcasting, or what its program will be, but must rely on the whim of the broadcaster and on chance in tuning his dial at the proper time, the service is not such as to justify the commission in licensing such a broadcaster as against one who will give a regular service of which the public is properly advised. A fortiori, where a licensee does not use his transmitter at all and broadcasts his programs, if at all, over some other transmitter separately licensed, he is not rendering any service. It is also improper that the zone and State in which his station is located should be charged with a license under such conditions in connection with the quota of that zone and that State under the Davis amendment.

A broadcaster who is not sufficiently concerned with the public's interest in good radio reception to provide his transmitter with an adequate control or check on its frequency is not entitled to a license. The commission in allowing a latitude of 500 cycles has been very lenient and will necessarily have to reduce this margin in the future. Instability in frequency means that the radio-listening public is subjected to increased interference by heterodyne (and, in some cases, cross-talk) on adjacent channels as well as on the assigned channels.

In conclusion, the commission desires to point out that the test — "public interest, convenience, or necessity" — becomes a matter of a comparative and not an absolute standard when applied to broadcasting stations. Since the number of channels is limited and the number of persons desiring to broadcast is far greater than can be accommodated, the commission must determine from among the applicants before it which of them will, if licensed, best serve the public. In a measure, perhaps, all of them give more or less service. Those who give the least, however, must be sacrificed for those who give the most. The emphasis must be first and foremost on the interest, the convenience, and the necessity of the listening public, and not on the interest, convenience, or necessity of the individual broadcaster or the advertiser.

11

The Great Lakes Statement

In the Matter of the Application of Great

Lakes Broadcasting Co.

FRC Docket No. 4900

3 FRC Ann. Rep. 32 (1929)

The FRC reconstructed its interpretation of the public interest in this early comparative hearing proceeding. The reformulation was unaffected by a court remand [*Great Lakes Broadcasting Company et al.* v. *Federal Radio Commission,* 37 F.2d 993 (D.C. Cir. 1930); *cert. dismissed* 281 U.S. 706].

The 1927 Radio Act's "public interest, convenience, or necessity" phrase was derived from public utility law. The *Great Lakes* statement gives detailed treatment to the contention that although broadcasting was a type of utility, radio stations were not to be thought of as common carriers. This principle was given legislative affirmation in 1934 when Section 3(h) was included in the Communications Act.

The statement is noteworthy for its emphasis on the requirement that radio stations carry diverse and balanced programming to serve the "tastes, needs, and desires" of the general public. This has been an underlying premise of subsequent FCC programming pronouncements, including the currently applied 1960 statement (see Document 26, pp. 262–278). Although the force of this principle has been moderated with respect to the vastly expanded AM and FM radio services, its vigor remains unabated for television broadcasting.

The *Great Lakes* statement also contains the germ of what was promulgated as the "Fairness Doctrine" 20 years later (see Document 22, pp. 217–231). It is clear that by 1929 the FRC had come to view advertising as the economic backbone of broadcasting and was prepared to accept it as an inevitability, within bounds. The last sentence of the statement alludes to listeners' councils, which were the forerunners of the citizens groups of today.

Related Reading: 106, 118, 131, 187.

. . . Broadcasting stations are licensed to serve the public and not for the purpose of furthering the private or selfish interests of individuals or groups of individuals. The standard of public interest, convenience, or necessity means nothing if it does not mean this. The only exception that can be made to this rule has to do with advertising; the exception, however, is only apparent because advertising furnishes the economic support for the service and thus makes it possible. As will be pointed out below, the amount and character of advertising must be rigidly confined within the limits consistent with the public service expected of the station.

The service to be rendered by a station may be viewed from two angles, (1) as an instrument for the communication of intelligence of various kinds to the general public by persons wishing to transmit such intelligence, or (2) as an instrument for the purveying of intangible commodities consisting of entertainment, instruction, education, and information to a listening public. As an instrument for the communication of intelligence, a broadcasting station has frequently been compared to other forms of communication, such as wire telegraphy or telephony, or point-to-point wireless telephony or telegraphy, with the obvious distinction that the messages from a broadcasting station are addressed to and received by the general public, whereas toll messages in point-to-point service are addressed to single persons and attended by safeguards to preserve their confidential nature. If the analogy were pursued with the usual legal incidents, a broadcasting station would have to accept and transmit for all persons on an equal basis without discrimination in charge, and according to rates fixed by a governmental body; this obligation would extend to anything and everything any member of the public might desire to communicate to the listening public, whether it consist of music, propaganda, reading, advertising, or what-not. The public would be deprived of the advantage of the self-imposed censorship exercised by the program directors of broadcasting stations who, for the sake of the popularity and standing of their stations, will select entertainment and educational features according to the needs and desires of their invisible audiences. In the present state of the art there is no way of increasing the number of stations without great injury to the listening public, and yet thousands of stations might be necessary to accommodate all the individuals who insist on airing their views through the microphone. If there are many such persons, as there undoubtedly are, the results would be, first, to crowd most or all of the better programs off the air, and second, to create an almost insoluble problem, i.e., how to choose from among an excess of applicants who shall be given time to address the public and who shall exercise the power to make such a choice.

To pursue the analogy of telephone and telegraph public utilities is, therefore, to emphasize the right of the sender of messages to the detriment of the listening public. The commission believes that such an analogy is a mistaken one when applied to broadcasting stations; the emphasis should be on the receiving of service and the standard of public interest, convenience or necessity should be construed accordingly. This point of view does not take broadcasting stations out of the category of public utilities or relieve them of corresponding obligations; it simply assimilates them to a different group of public utilities, i.e., those engaged in purveying commodities to the general public, such, for example, as heat, water, light, and power companies, whose duties are to consumers, just as the duties of broadcasting stations are to listeners. The commodity may be intangible but so is electric light; the broadcast program has become a vital part of daily life. Just as heat, water, light, and power companies use franchises obtained from city or State to bring their commodities through pipes, conduits, or wires over public highways to the home, so a broadcasting station uses a franchise from the Federal Government to bring its commodity over a channel through the ether to the home. The Government does not try to tell a public utility such as an electric-light company that it must obtain its materials such as coal or wire, from all comers on equal terms; it is not interested so long as the service rendered in the form of light is good. Similarly, the commission believes that the Government is interested mainly in seeing to it that the program service of broadcasting stations is good, i.e., in accordance with the standard of public interest, convenience, or necessity.

It may be said that the law has already written an exception into the foregoing viewpoint in that, by section 18 of the radio act of 1927, a broadcasting station is required to afford equal opportunities for use of the station to all candidates for a public office if it permits any of the candidates to use the station. It will be noticed, however, that in the same section it is provided that "no obligation is hereby imposed upon any licensee to allow the use of its station by any such candidate." This is not only not inconsistent with, but on the contrary it supports, the commission's viewpoint. Again the emphasis is on the listening public, not on the sender of the message. It would not be fair, indeed it would not be good service to the public to allow a one-sided presentation of the political issues of a campaign. In so far as a program consists of discussion of public questions, public interest requires ample play for the free and fair competition of opposing views, and the commission believes that the principle applies not only to addresses by political candidates but to all discussions of issues of importance to the public. The great majority of broadcasting stations are, the commission is glad to say, already tacitly recognizing a broader duty than the law imposes upon them. . . .

An indispensable condition to good service by any station is, of course, modern efficient apparatus, equipped with all devices necessary to insure fidelity in the transmission of voice and music and to avoid frequency instability or other causes of interference. . . .

There are a few negative guides to the evaluation of broadcasting stations. First of these in importance are the injunctions of the statute itself, such, for example, as the requirement for nondiscrimination between political candidates and the prohibition against the utterance of "any obscene, indecent, or profane language" (sec. 29). In the same connection may be mentioned rules and regulations of the commission, including the requirements as to the announcing of call letters and as to the accurate description of mechanical reproductions (such as phonograph records) in announcements. . . .

For more positive guides the commission again finds itself persuaded of the applicability of doctrines analogous to those governing the group of public utilities to which reference has already been made. If the viewpoint is found that the service to the listening public is what must be kept in contemplation in construing the legal standard with reference to broadcasting stations, the service must first of all be continuous during hours when the public usually listens, and must be on a schedule upon which the public may rely. . . .

Furthermore, the service rendered by broadcasting stations must be without discrimination as between its listeners. Obviously, in a strictly physical sense, a station can not discriminate so as to furnish its programs to one listener and not to another; in this respect it is a public utility by virtue of the laws of nature. Even were it technically possible, as it may easily be as the art progresses, so to design both transmitters and receiving sets that the signals emitted by a particular transmitter can be received only by a particular kind of receiving set not available to the general public, the commission would not allow channels in the broadcast band to be used in such fashion. By the same token, it is proceeding very cautiously in permitting television in the broadcast band because, during the hours of such transmission, the great majority of the public audience in the service area of the station, not being equipped to receive television signals, are deprived of the use of the channel.

There is, however, a deeper significance to the principle of nondiscrimination which the commission believes may well furnish the basic formula for the evaluation of broadcasting stations. The entire listening public within the service area of a station, or of a group of stations in one community, is entitled to service from that station or stations. If, therefore, all the programs transmitted are intended for, and interesting or valuable to, only a small portion of that public, the rest of the listeners are being discriminated against. This does not mean that every individual is entitled to his exact preference in program items. It does mean, in the opinion of the commission, that the tastes, needs, and desires of all substantial groups among the listening public should be met, in some fair proportion, by a well-rounded program, in which entertainment, consisting of music of both classical and lighter grades, religion, education and instruction, important public events, discussions of public questions, weather, market reports, and news, and matters of interest to all members of the family find a place. With so few channels in the spectrum and so few hours in the day, there are obvious limitations on the emphasis which can appropriately be placed on any portion of the program. There are parts of the day and of the evening when one type of service is more appropriate than another. There are differences between communities as to the need for one type as against another. The commission does not propose to erect a rigid schedule specifying the hours or minutes that may be devoted to one kind of program or another. What it wishes to emphasize is the general character which it believes must be conformed to by a station in order to best serve the public. . . .

In such a scheme there is no room for the operation of broadcasting stations exclusively by or in the private interests of individuals or groups so far as the nature of the programs is concerned. There is not room in the broadcast band for every school of thought, religious, political, social, and economic, each to have its separate broadcasting station, its mouthpiece in the ether. If franchises are extended to some it gives them an unfair advantage over others, and results in a corresponding cutting down of general public-service stations. It favors the interests and desires of a portion of the listening public at the expense of the rest. Propaganda stations (a term which is here used for the sake of convenience and not in a derogatory sense) are not consistent with the most beneficial sort of discussion of public questions. As a general rule, postulated on the laws of nature as well as on the standard of public interest, convenience, or necessity, particular doctrines, creeds, and beliefs must find their way into the market of ideas by the existing public-service stations, and if they are of sufficient importance to the listening public the microphone will undoubtedly be available. If it is not, a well-founded complaint will receive the careful consideration of the commission in its future action with reference to the station complained of.

The contention may be made that propaganda stations are as well able as other stations to accompany their messages with entertainment and other program features of interest to the public. Even if this were true, the fact remains that the station is used for what is essentially a private purpose for a substantial portion of the time and in addition, is constantly subject to the very human temptation not to be fair to opposing schools of thought and their representatives. By and large, furthermore, propaganda stations do not have the financial resources nor do they have the standing and popularity with the public necessary to obtain the best results in programs of general interest. The contention may also be made that to follow out the commission's viewpoint is to make unjustifiable concessions to what is popular at the expense of what is important and serious. This bears on a consideration which the commission realizes must always be kept carefully in mind and in so far as it has power under the law it will do so in its reviews of the records of particular stations. A defect, if there is any, however, would not be remedied by a one-sided presentation of a controversial subject, no matter how serious. The commission has great confidence in the sound judgment of the listening public, however, as to what types of programs are in its own best interest.

If the question were now raised for the first time, after the commission has given careful study to it, the commission would not license any propaganda station, at least, to an exclusive position on a cleared channel. Unfortunately, under the law in force prior to the radio act of 1927 (see particularly Hoover *v.* Intercity Radio Co., 286 Fed. 1003), the Secretary of Commerce had no power to distinguish between kinds of applicants and it was not possible to foresee the present situation and its problems. Consequently there are and have been for a long time in existence a number of stations operated by religious or similar organizations. Certain enterprising organizations, quick to see the possibilities of radio and anxious to present their creeds to the public, availed themselves of license privileges from the earlier days of broadcasting, and now have good records and a certain degree of popularity among listeners. The commission feels that the situation must be dealt with on a common-sense basis. It does not seem just to deprive such stations of all right to operation and the question must be solved on a comparative basis. While the commission is of the opinion that a broadcasting station engaged in general public service has, ordinarily, a claim to preference over a propaganda station, it will apply this principle as to existing stations by giving preferential facilities to the former and assigning less desirable positions to the latter to the extent that engineering principles permit. In rare cases it is possible to combine a general public-service station and a high-class religious station in a division of time which will approximate a well-rounded program. In other cases religious stations must accept part time on inferior channels or on daylight assignments where they are still able to transmit during the hours when religious services are usually expected by the listening public.

It may be urged that the same reasoning applies to advertising. In a sense this is true. The commission must, however, recognize that, without advertising, broadcasting would not exist, and must confine itself to limiting this advertising in amount and in character so as to preserve the largest possible amount of service for the public. The advertising must, of course, be presented as such and not under the guise of other forms on the same principle that the newspaper must not present advertising as news. It will be recognized and accepted for what it is on such a basis, whereas propaganda is difficult to recognize. If a rule against advertising were enforced, the public would be deprived of millions of dollars worth of programs which are being given out entirely by concerns simply for the resultant good will which is believed to accrue to the broadcaster or the advertiser by the announcement of his name and business in connection with programs. Advertising must be accepted for the present as the sole means of support for broadcasting, and regulation must be relied upon to prevent the abuse and overuse of the privilege.

It may be urged that if what has heretofore been said is law, the listening public is left at the mercy of the broadcaster. Even if this were so, the commission doubts that any improvement would be effected by placing the public at the mercy of each individual in turn who desired to communicate his hobby, his theory, or his grievance over the microphone, or at the mercy of every advertiser without regard to the standing either of himself or his product. That it is not so, however, is demonstrable from two considerations. In the first place, the listener has a complete power of censorship by turning his dial away from a program which he does not like; this results in a keen appreciation by the broadcaster of the necessity of pleasing a large portion of his listeners if he is to hold his audience, and of not displeasing, annoying, or offending the sensibilities of any substantial portion of the public. His failure or success is immediately reflected on the telephone and in the mail, and he knows that the same reaction to his programs will reach the licensing authority. In the second place, the licensing authority will have occasion, both in connection with renewals of his license and in connection with applications of others for his privileges, to review his past performances and to determine whether he has met with the standard. A safeguard which some of the leading stations employ, and which appeals to the commission as a wise precaution, is the association with the station of an advisory board made up of men and women whose character, standing, and occupations will insure a well-rounded program best calculated to serve the greatest portion of the population in the region to be served.

12
Early Self-Regulation

NAB Code of Ethics and Standards of Commercial Practice*

March 25, 1929

The National Association of Broadcasters was organized in 1923 to combat the demands of the American Society of Composers, Authors, and Publishers that radio station operators pay royalties to copyright holders for the use of music on the air. The NAB evolved into a comprehensive trade association. Today it provides a wide range of services to its membership. With headquarters in Washington, D.C., the NAB acts as an effective lobbyist before various agencies of government including the FCC and Congress.

Two years after passage of the Radio Act of 1927 the NAB issued its "Code of Ethics" and "Standards of Commercial Practice," the first industry-wide instruments of self-regulation in broadcasting. The NAB has reformulated its Radio Code many times since 1929. A Television Code was first developed in 1951. (See Document 49, pp. 576–593, for a contemporary edition of the NAB TV Code.) Self-regulation is practiced at the station and network levels also, although the NAB codes have gained wider acceptance than any others. The present-day codes are subscribed to by the networks, approximately two-fifths of commercial radio stations, and almost two-thirds of TV stations.

It should be noted that section I(B) of the "Standards of Commercial Practice" was not intended to prohibit *institutional* advertising during prime time, though the provision reflects the cautious approach to broadcast commercialism widely shared at

*Reprinted with the permission of the Code Authority, National Association of Broadcasters.

the time. Three or four years passed before the national networks, NBC and CBS, permitted advertisers to mention actual
prices over the air.

Related Reading: 216, 241.

NAB CODE OF ETHICS

First.   Recognizing that the Radio audience includes persons of all ages and
all types of political, social and religious belief, every broadcaster will endeavor
to prevent the broadcasting of any matter which would commonly be regarded
as offensive.

Second.   When the facilities of a broadcaster are used by others than the
owner, the broadcaster shall ascertain the financial responsibility and character
of such client, that no dishonest, fraudulent or dangerous person, firm or organization may gain access to the Radio audience.

Third.   Matter which is barred from the mails as fraudulent, deceptive or
obscene shall not be broadcast.

Fourth.   Every broadcaster shall exercise great caution in accepting any
advertising matter regarding products or services which may be injurious to
health.

Fifth.   No broadcaster shall permit the broadcasting of advertising statements or claims which he knows or believes to be false, deceptive or grossly
exaggerated.

Sixth.   Every broadcaster shall strictly follow the provisions of the Radio
Act of 1927 regarding the clear identification of sponsored or paid-for material.

Seventh.   Care shall be taken to prevent the broadcasting of statements
derogatory to other stations, to individuals, or to competing products or services, except where the law specifically provides that the station has no right
of censorship.

Eighth.   Where charges of violation of any article of the Code of Ethics of
The National Association of Broadcasters are filed in writing with the Managing
Director, the Board of Directors shall investigate such charges and notify the
station of its findings.

NAB STANDARDS OF COMMERCIAL PRACTICE

I.   *Program Content and Presentation*

   (A)   There is a decided difference between what may be broadcast before
          and after 6:00 p.m. Time before 6:00 p.m. is included in the

business day and, therefore, may be devoted in part, at least, to broadcasting programs of a business nature; while time after 6:00 p.m. is for recreation and relaxation, and commercial programs should be of the good-will type.

(B) Commercial announcements, as the term is generally understood, should not be broadcast between 7:00 and 11:00 p.m.

(C) A client's business and his product should be mentioned sufficiently to insure him an adequate return on his investment — but never to the extent that it loses listeners to the station.

(D) The use of records should be governed by the following:

1. The order of the Commission with reference to identifying "Phonograph Records" and other means of mechanical reproduction should be completely carried out.

2. Phonograph records (those for sale to the public) should not be broadcast between 6:00 and 11:00 p.m. except in the case of pre-release records used in programs sponsored either by the manufacturer or the local distributor.

3. When mechanical reproductions prepared for radio use only are not for public sale, and are of such quality to recommend their being broadcast, no limitation should be placed on their use, except as individual station policy may determine.

II. *Salesmen and Representatives*

(A) Salesmen on commission or salary should have:

1. Definite responsibility to the station for which they solicit;
2. Some means of identification.

Furthermore, contracts should state specifically that they will not be considered as acceptable until signed by an officer of the station; that no agreements, verbal or understood, can be considered as part of the contract. The salesman's conference with the client should always be confirmed by an officer of the station.

(B) The standard commission allowed by all advertising media to recognized agencies should be allowed by broadcasting stations. If selling representatives are maintained by stations in cities where they otherwise have no representation, the station itself should make its own arrangements as to payment for such representation.

(C) Blanket time should not be sold to clients to be resold by them as they see fit.

III. *Agencies*

(A) Agencies have three functions in broadcasting:

1. Credit responsibility.
2. Account service and contact.
3. Program supervision in the interest of the client.

(B) Commission should be allowed only to agencies of recognized standing.

IV. *Sales Data.* — The best sales data is result data.

V. *Rate Cards*

(A) There should be no deviation whatsoever from rates quoted on a rate card or cards.

(B) Wherever practicable, the standard rate card form recommended by this Association should be used.

VI. *Clients*

(A) Client standards of credit should be maintained similar to those established in other fields of advertising.

(B) In deciding what accounts or classes of business are acceptable for broadcast advertising, member stations should be governed by the Code of Ethics adopted by this Association.

13

The Brinkley Case

KFKB Broadcasting Association, Inc., v. Federal
Radio Commission*
47 F.2d 670 (D.C. Cir.)
February 2, 193˜

> Government censorship of broadcast programming was expressly
> prohibited by Section 29 of the Radio Act and its re-enactment
> as Section 326 of the Communications Act. These provisions
> establish radio as a medium in which free speech enjoys the pro-
> tection of the First Amendment to the Constitution. Yet the
> FRC and FCC were charged with the task of regulating broad-
> casting in the "public interest, convenience, or necessity." Since
> providing a program service to the general public is at the heart
> of any reasonable interpretation of the "public interest" in broad-
> casting, both commissions have found themselves poised on the
> horns of a dilemma: to impose prior restraints on programming
> is contrary to the legal and philosophical underpinnings of free-
> dom of speech, but to exercise absolutely no influence over what
> is broadcast seems inimical to the concept of the public interest.
>   Dr. John R. Brinkley was hardly the only malpractitioner,
> medical or other, who gained access to the airwaves during radio's
> formative era, but he was certainly the most celebrated! His sta-
> tion, KFKB, was among the most popular in the nation for many
> years, and Brinkley himself twice came close to being elected
> governor of Kansas as a political independent. Brinkley had pur-
> chased his medical degrees from diploma mills but was neverthe-
> less reputed to be a skilled surgeon. His medical specialty was a

*Reprinted with the permission of West Publishing Company.

costly "goat gland" operation, the implantation of animal gonads in the scrota of men seeking sexual rejuvenation and salvation from enlarged prostates. Brinkley's questionable surgical practice and sales of his equally dubious prescription remedies earned him millions of dollars over the years—and the wrath of the American Medical Association. In 1930 a three-to-two majority of the Federal Radio Commission voted not to renew KFKB's license.

This Court of Appeals decision stands as the first judicial affirmation of the FRC's right to consider a station's past programming when deciding whether or not license renewal will serve the public interest. After the decision Brinkley continued to broadcast to his American audience from radio stations in Mexico for another decade, though his Kansas medical license was revoked in 1935.

Related Reading: 35, 40, 131, 187, 202, 243.

Robb, Associate Justice.

Appeal from a decision of the Federal Radio Commission denying appellant's application for the renewal of its station license.

The station is located at Milford, Kan., is operating on a frequency of 1,050 kilocycles with 5,000 watts power and is known by the call letters KFKB. The station was first licensed by the Secretary of Commerce on September 20, 1923, in the name of the Brinkley-Jones Hospital Association, and intermittently operated until June 3, 1925. On October 23, 1926, it was relicensed to Dr. J. R. Brinkley with the same call letters and continued to be so licensed until November 26, 1929, when an assignment was made to appellant corporation.

On March 20, 1930, appellant filed its application for renewal of license (Radio Act of 1927, c. 169, 44 Stat. 1162, U. S. C. Supp. 3, tit. 47, § 81, et seq. [47 USCA § 81 et seq.]). The commission, failing to find that public interest, convenience, or necessity would be served thereby, accorded appellant opportunity to be heard. Hearings were had on May 21, 22, and 23, 1930, at which appellant appeared by counsel and introduced evidence on the question whether the granting of the application would be in the public interest, convenience, or necessity. Evidence also was introduced in behalf of the commission. Upon consideration of the evidence and arguments, the commission found that public interest, convenience, or necessity would not be served by granting the application and, therefore, ordered that it be denied, effective June 13, 1930. A stay order was allowed by this court, and appellant has since been operating thereunder.

The evidence tends to show that Dr. J. R. Brinkley established Station KFKB, the Brinkley Hospital, and the Brinkley Pharmaceutical Association, and that these institutions are operated in a common interest. While the record shows that only 3 of the 1,000 shares of the capital stock of appellant are in Dr. Brinkley's name and that his wife owns 381 shares, it is quite apparent that the doctor actually dictates and controls the policy of the station. The Brinkley Hospital, located at Milford, is advertised over Station KFKB. For this advertising the hospital pays the station from $5,000 to $7,000 per month.

The Brinkley Pharmaceutical Association, formed by Dr. Brinkey, is composed of druggists who dispense to the public medical preparations prepared according to formulas of Dr. Brinkley and known to the public only by numerical designations. Members of the association pay a fee upon each sale of certain of those preparations. The amounts thus received are paid the station, presumably for advertising the preparations. It appears that the income of the station for the period February, March, and April, 1930, was as follows :

Brinkley Pharmaceutical Association	$27,856.40
Brinkley Hospital	6,500.00
All other sources	3,544.93
Total	$37,901.33

Dr. Brinkley personally broadcasts during three one-half hour periods daily over the station, the broadcast being referred to as the "medical question box," and is devoted to diagnosing and prescribing treatment of cases from symptoms given in letters addressed either to Dr. Brinkley or to the station. Patients are not known to the doctor except by means of their letters, each letter containing a code signature, which is used in making answer through the broadcasting station. The doctor usually advises that the writer of the letter is suffering from a certain ailment, and recommends the procurement from one of the members of the Brinkley Pharmaceutical Association, of one or more of Dr. Brinkley's prescriptions, designated by numbers. In Dr. Brinkley's broadcast for April 1, 1930, presumably representative of all, he prescribed for forty-four different patients and in all, save ten, he advised the procurement of from one to four of his own prescriptions. We reproduce two as typical:

Here's one from Tillie. She says she had an operation, had some trouble 10 years ago. I think the operation was unnecessary, and it isn't very good sense to have an ovary removed with the expectation of motherhood resulting therefrom. My advice to you is to use Women's Tonic No. 50, 67, and 61. This combination will do for you what you desire if any combination will, after three months' persistent use.

Sunflower State, from Dresden Kans. Probably he has gall stones. No, I don't mean that, I mean kidney stones. My advice to you is to put him on Prescription No. 80 and 50 for men, also 64. I think that he will be a whole lot better. Also drink a lot of water.

In its "Facts and Grounds for Decision," the commission held "that the practice of a physician prescribing treatment for a patient whom he has never seen, and bases his diagnosis upon what symptoms may be recited by the patient in a letter addressed to him, is inimical to the public health and safety, and for that reason is not in the public interest"; that "the testimony in this case shows conclusively that the operation of Station KFKB is conducted only in the personal interest of Dr. John R. Brinkley. While it is to be expected that a licensee of a radio broadcasting station will receive some remuneration for serving the public with radio programs, at the same time the interest of the listening public is paramount, and may not be subordinated to the interests of the station licensee."

This being an application for the renewal of a license, the burden is upon the applicant to establish that such renewal would be in the public interest, convenience, or necessity (Technical Radio Lab. v. Fed. Radio Comm., 59 App. D.C. 125, 36 F.(2d) 111, 114, 66 A.L.R. 1355; Campbell v. Galeno Chem. Co., 281 U.S. 599, 609, 50 S.Ct. 412, 74 L. Ed. 1063), and the court will sustain the findings of fact of the commission unless "manifestly against the evidence." Ansley v. Fed. Radio Comm., 60 App. D.C. 19, 46 F.(2d) 600.

We have held that the business of broadcasting, being a species of interstate commerce, is subject to the reasonable regulation of Congress. Technical Radio Lab. v. Fed. Radio Comm., 59 App. D.C. 125, 36 F.(2d) 111, 66 A.L.R. 1355; City of New York v. Fed. Radio Comm., 59 App. D.C. 129, 36 F.(2d) 115; Chicago Federation of Labor v. Fed. Radio Comm., 59 App. D.C. 333, 41 F.(2d) 422. It is apparent, we think, that the business is impressed with a public interest and that, because the number of available broadcasting frequencies is limited, the commission is necessarily called upon to consider the character and quality of the service to be rendered. In considering an application for a renewal of the license, an important consideration is the past conduct of the applicant, for "by their fruits ye shall know them." Matt. VII:20. Especially is this true in a case like the present, where the evidence clearly justifies the conclusion that the future conduct of the station will not differ from the past.

In its Second Annual Report (1928), p. 169, the commission cautioned broadcasters "who consume much of the valuable time allotted to them under their licenses in matters of a distinctly private nature which are not only uninteresting, but also distasteful to the listening public." When Congress provided that the question whether a license should be issued or renewed should be dependent upon a finding of public interest, convenience, or necessity, it very evidently had in mind that broadcasting should not be a mere adjunct of a particular business but should be of a public character. Obviously, there is no room in the broadcast band for every business or school of thought.

In the present case, while the evidence shows that much of appellant's programs is entertaining and unobjectionable in character, the finding of the commission that the station "is conducted only in the personal interest of Dr.

John R. Brinkley" is not "manifestly against the evidence." We are further of
the view that there is substantial evidence in support of the finding of the
Commission that the "medical question box" as conducted by Dr. Brinkley "is
inimical to the public health and safety, and for that reason is not in the public
interest."

Appellant contends that the attitude of the commission amounts to a
censorship of the station contrary to the provisions of section 29 of the Radio
Act of 1927 (47 USCA s 109). This contention is without merit. There has been
no attempt on the part of the commission to subject any part of appellant's
broadcasting matter to scrutiny prior to its release. In considering the question
whether the public interest, convenience, or necessity will be served by a renewal
of appellant's license, the commission has merely exercised its undoubted right
to take note of appellant's past conduct, which is not censorship.

As already indicated, Congress has imposed upon the commission the
administrative function of determining whether or not a station license should
be renewed, and the commission in the present case has in the exercise of
judgment and discretion ruled against the applicant. We are asked upon the
record and evidence before the commission to substitute our judgment and
discretion for that of the commission. While section 16 of the Radio Act of
1927 (44 Stat. 1162, 1169, U. S. C., Supp. 3, tit. 47, s 96) authorized an appeal
to this court, we do not think it was the intent of Congress that we should
disturb the action of the commission in a case like the present. Support is found
for this view in the Act of July 1, 1930 (46 Stat. 844 [47 USCA s 96]),
amending section 16 of the 1927 Act. The amendment specifically provides
"that the review by the court shall be limited to questions of law and that
findings of fact by the commission, if supported by substantial evidence, shall be
conclusive unless it shall clearly appear that the findings of the commission are
arbitrary or capricious." As to the interpretation that should be placed upon
such provision, see Ma-King v. Blair, 271 U.S. 479, 483, 46 S. Ct. 544, 70 L.Ed.
1046.

We are therefore constrained, upon a careful review of the record. to
affirm the decision.

Affirmed.

14

The Shuler Case

Trinity Methodist Church, South v. Federal Radio Commission*
62 F.2d 850 (D.C. Cir.)
November 28, 1932

Compared to "Doc" Brinkley whose rural charms held sway throughout much of the country, "battling Bob" Shuler was more a local phenomenon. Following the *Brinkley* case by almost 2 years, this appellate decision built on the court's earlier opinion in upholding the FRC's denial of license renewal to Shuler's radio station, KGEF, because of the minister's defamatory and otherwise objectionable utterances.

While the *Brinkley* decision is confined to statutory interpretation, the *Shuler* case grapples with constitutional issues arising from the appellant's reliance on First and Fifth Amendment claims. The Supreme Court declined to review the decision [288 U.S. 599 (1933)].

Despite these unequivocal judicial affirmations of the statutory and constitutional authority of the licensing agency to withhold franchises from broadcasters whose past programming served predominantly private interests rather than the public interest, the FCC has been timid in its exercise of programming powers through the licensing process. Instead, the Commission has relied on broad, marginally enforced policy statements (see Documents 21 and 26, pp. 132–216 and 262–278, respectively) and "regulation by raised eyebrow" through which a commissioner's speech (see Document 28, pp. 281–291) or a proposed (but not enacted) rule motivates program decisions in the broadcasting industry.

*Reprinted with the permission of West Publishing Company.

These methods of encouraging programming in the public interest are subtler than license denial, but their effectiveness is difficult to measure.

In those rare instances in which the FCC declined to renew licenses on programming grounds, other issues have been involved, particularly licensee misrepresentation to the Commission. Judicial affirmations in these cases have tended to rely on the latter ground rather than program content. See *Robinson* v. *FCC*, 334 F.2d 534 (D.C. Cir. 1964) affirming *Palmetto Broadcasting Company (WDKD)*, 33 FCC 250 (1962); *Brandywine–Main Line Radio, Inc.* v. *FCC*, 473 F.2d 16 (D.C. Cir. 1972) affirming 24 FCC 2d 18 (1970).

Related Reading: 35, 131, 187, 243.

Groner, Associate Justice.

Appellant, Trinity Methodist Church, South, was the lessee and operator of a radio-broadcasting station at Los Angeles, Cal., known by the call letters KGEF. The station had been in operation for several years. The Commission, in its findings, shows that, though in the name of the church, the station was in fact owned by the Reverend Doctor Shuler and its operation dominated by him. Dr. Shuler is the minister in charge of Trinity Church. The station was operated for a total of 23¼ hours each week.

In September, 1930, appellant filed an application for renewal of station license. Numerous citizens of Los Angeles protested, and the Commission, being unable to determine that public interest, convenience, and necessity would be served, set the application down for hearing before an examiner. In January, 1931, the matter was heard, and the testimony of ninety witnesses taken. The examiner recommended renewal of the license. Exceptions were filed by one of the objectors, and oral argument requested. This was had before the Commission, sitting in banc, and, upon consideration of the evidence, the examiner's report, the exceptions, etc., the Commission denied the application for renewal upon the ground that the public interest, convenience, and/or necessity would not be served by the granting of the application. Some of the things urging it to this conclusion were that the station had been used to attack a religious organization, meaning the Roman Catholic Church; that the broadcasts by Dr. Shuler were sensational rather than instructive; and that in two instances Shuler had been convicted of attempting in his radio talks to obstruct the orderly administration of public justice.

This court denied a motion for a stay order, and this appeal was taken. The basis of the appeal is that the Commission's decision is unconstitutional, in that it violates the guaranty of free speech, and also that it deprives appellant of his property without due process of law. It is further insisted that the decision violates the Radio Act because not supported by substantial evidence, and therefore is arbitrary and capricious.

We have been at great pains to examine carefully the record of a thousand pages, and have reached the conclusion that none of these assignments is well taken.

We need not stop to review the cases construing the depth and breadth of the first amendment. The subject in its more general outlook has been the source of much writing since Milton's *Areopagitica*, the emancipation of the English press by the withdrawal of the licensing act in the reign of William the Third, and the *Letters* of Junius. It is enough now to say that the universal trend of decisions has recognized the guaranty of the amendment to prevent previous restraints upon publications, as well as immunity of censorship, leaving to correction by subsequent punishment those utterances or publications contrary to the public welfare. In this aspect it is generally regarded that freedom of speech and press cannot be infringed by legislative, executive, or judicial action, and that the constitutional guaranty should be given liberal and comprehensive construction. It may therefore be set down as a fundamental principle that under these constitutional guaranties the citizen has in the first instance the right to utter or publish his sentiments, though, of course, upon condition that he is responsible for any abuse of that right. Near v. Minnesota ex rel. Olson, 283 U.S. 697, 51 S. Ct. 625, 75 L.Ed. 1357. "Every freeman has an undoubted right to lay what sentiments he pleases before the public; to forbid this is to destroy the freedom of the press; but if he publishes what is improper, mischievous, or illegal, he must take the consequences of his own temerity." 4th Bl. Com. 151, 152. But this does not mean that the government, through agencies established by Congress, may not refuse a renewal of license to one who has abused it to broadcast defamatory and untrue matter. In that case there is not a denial of the freedom of speech, but merely the application of the regulatory power of Congress in a field within the scope of its legislative authority. See KFKB Broadcasting Ass'n v. Federal Radio Commission, 60 App. D.C. 79, 47 F.(2d) 670.

Section 1 of the Radio Act of 1927 (44 Stat. 1162, title 47, USCA, § 81) specifically declares the purpose of the act to be to regulate all forms of interstate and foreign radio transmissions and communications within the United States, its territories and possessions; to maintain the control of the United States over all the channels of interstate and foreign radio transmissions; and to provide for the use of such channels for limited periods of time, under licenses granted by federal authority. The federal authority set up by the act to carry out its terms is the Federal Radio Commission, and the Commission is given power, and required, upon examination of an application for a station license, or for a renewal or modification, to determine whether "public interest, convenience, or necessity" will be served by the granting thereof, and any applicant for a renewal of license whose application is refused may of right appeal from such decision to this court.

We have already held that radio communication, in the sense contemplated by the act, constituted interstate commerce, KFKB Broadcasting Ass'n v. Federal Radio Commission, supra; General Elec. Co. v. Federal Radio Commission, 58 App. D.C. 386, 31 F.(2d) 630, and in this respect we are supported by many decisions of the Supreme Court, Pensacola Telegraph Co. v. Western Union Tel. Co., 96 U.S. 1, 9, 24 L.Ed. 708; International Text-Book Co. v. Pigg, 217 U.S. 91, 106, 107, 30 S. Ct. 481, 54 L.Ed. 678, 27 L.R.A. (N.S.) 493, 18 Ann. Cas. 1103; Western Union Teleg. Co. v. Pendelton, 122 U.S. 347, 356, 7 S. Ct. 1126, 30 L. Ed. 1187. And we do not understand it is contended that where, as in the case before us, there is no physical substance between the transmitting and the receiving apparatus, the broadcasting of programs across state lines is not interstate commerce, and, if this be true, it is equally true that the power of Congress to regulate interstate commerce, complete in itself, may be exercised to its utmost extent, and acknowledges no limitation, other than such as prescribed in the Constitution (Gibbons v. Ogden, 9 Wheat. 1, 6 L. Ed. 23), and these powers, as was said by the Supreme Court in Pensacola Tel. Co. v. Western Union Tel. Co., supra, "keep pace with the progress of the country, and adapt themselves to the new developments of time and circumstances."

In recent years the power under the commerce clause has been extended to legislation against interstate commerce in stolen automobiles, Brooks v. United States, 267 U.S. 432, 45 S. Ct. 345, 69 L. Ed. 699, 37 A.L.R. 1407; to transportation of adulterated foods, Hipolite Egg Co. v. United States, 220 U.S. 45, 31 S. Ct. 364, 55 L. Ed. 364; in the suppression of interstate commerce for immoral purposes, Hoke v. United States, 227 U.S. 308, 33 S. Ct. 281, 57 L. Ed. 523, 43 L.R.A. (N.S.) 906, Ann. Cas. 1913E, 905; and in a variety of other subjects never contemplated by the framers of the Constitution. It is too late now to contend that Congress may not regulate, and, in some instances, deny, the facilities of interstate commerce to a business or occupation which it deems inimical to the public welfare or contrary to the public interest. Lottery Cases, 188 U.S. 321, 352, 23 S. Ct. 321, 47 L. Ed. 492. Everyone interested in radio legislation approved the principle of limiting the number of broadcasting stations, or, perhaps, it would be more nearly correct to say, recognized the inevitable necessity. In these circumstances Congress intervened and asserted its paramount authority, and, if it be admitted, as we think it must be, that, in the present condition of the science with its limited facilities, the regulatory provisions of the Radio Act are a reasonable exercise by Congress of its powers, the exercise of these powers is no more restricted by the First Amendment than are the police powers of the States under the Fourteenth Amendment. See In re Kemmler, 136 U.S. 436, 448, 449, 10 S. Ct. 930, 34 L. Ed. 519; Hamilton v.

Kentucky, etc., Co., 251 U.S. 146, at page 156, 40 S. Ct. 106, 64 L. Ed. 194. In either case the answer depends upon whether the statute is a reasonable exercise of governmental control for the public good.

In the case under consideration, the evidence abundantly sustains the conclusion of the Commission that the continuance of the broadcasting programs of appellant is not in the public interest. In a proceeding for contempt against Dr. Shuler, on appeal to the Supreme Court of California, that court said (In re Shuler, 210 Cal. 377, 292 P. 481, 492) that the broadcast utterances of Dr. Shuler disclosed throughout the determination on his part to impose on the trial courts his own will and views with respect to certain causes then pending or on trial, and amounted to contempt of court. Appellant, not satisfied with attacking the judges of the courts in cases then pending before them, attacked the bar association for its activities in recommending judges, charging it with ulterior and sinister purposes. With no more justification, he charged particular judges with sundry immoral acts. He made defamatory statements against the board of health. He charged that the labor temple in Los Angeles was a bootlegging and gambling joint. In none of these matters, when called on to explain or justify his statements, was he able to do more than declare that the statements expressed his own sentiments. On one occasion he announced over the radio that he had certain damaging information against a prominent unnamed man which, unless a contribution (presumably to the church) of a hundred dollars was forthcoming, he would disclose. As a result, he received contributions from several persons. He freely spoke of "pimps" and prostitutes. He alluded slightingly to the Jews as a race, and made frequent and bitter attacks on the Roman Catholic religion and its relations to government. However inspired Dr. Shuler may have been by what he regarded as patriotic zeal, however sincere in denouncing conditions he did not approve, it is manifest, we think, that it is not narrowing the ordinary conception of "public interest" in declaring his broadcasts — without facts to sustain or to justify them — not within that term, and, since that is the test the Commission is required to apply, we think it was its duty in considering the application for renewal to take notice of appellant's conduct in his previous use of the permit, and, in the circumstances, the refusal, we think, was neither arbitrary nor capricious.

If it be considered that one in possession of a permit to broadcast in interstate commerce may, without let or hindrance from any source, use these facilities, reaching out, as they do, from one corner of the country to the other, to obstruct the administration of justice, offend the religious susceptibilities of thousands, inspire political distrust and civic discord, or offend youth and innocence by the free use of words suggestive of sexual immorality, and be answerable for slander only at the instance of the one offended, then this great science, instead of a boon, will become a scourge, and the nation a theater for the display of individual passions and the collision of personal interests. This is neither censorship nor previous restraint, nor is it a whittling away of the rights guaranteed by the First Amendment, or an impairment of their free exercise. Appellant may continue to indulge his strictures upon the characters of men in public office. He may just as freely as ever criticize religious practices of which he does not approve. He may even indulge private malice or personal slander — subject, of course, to be required to answer for the abuse thereof — but he may not, as we think, demand, of right, the continued use of an instrumentality of commerce for such purposes, or any other, except in subordination to all reasonable rules and regulations Congress, acting through the Commission, may prescribe.

Nor are we any more impressed with the argument that the refusal to renew a license is a taking of property within the Fifth Amendment. There is a marked difference between the destruction of physical property, as in Pennsylvania Coal Co. v. Mahon, 260 U.S. 393, 43 S. Ct. 158, 67 L. Ed. 322, 28 A.L.R. 1321, and the denial of a permit to use the limited channels of the air. As was pointed out in American Bond & Mtg. Co. v. United States (C.C.A.) 52 F.(2nd) 318, 320, the former is vested, the latter permissive, and, as was said by the Supreme Court in Chicago, B. & Q. R. Co. v. Illinois, 200 U.S. 561, 593, 26 S. Ct. 341, 350, 50 L.Ed. 596, 4 Ann. Cas. 1175: "If the injury complained of is only incidental to the legitimate exercise of governmental powers for the public good, then there is no taking of property for the public use, and a right to compensation, on account of such injury, does not attach under the Constitution." When Congress imposes restrictions in a field falling within the scope of its legislative authority and a taking of property without compensation is alleged, the test is whether the restrictive measures are reasonably adapted to secure the purposes and objects of regulation. If this test is satisfied, then "the enforcement of uncompensated obedience" to such regulation "is not an unconstitutional taking of property without compensation or without due process of law." Atlantic Coast Line R. Co. v. Goldsboro, 232 U.S. 548, 558, 34 S. Ct. 364, 368, 58 L. Ed. 721.

A case which illustrates this principle is Greenleaf-Johnson Lumber Co. v. Garrison, 237 U.S. 251, 35 S. Ct. 551, 59 L. Ed. 939. In that case the state of Virginia had established lines of navigability in the harbor of Norfolk. The lumber company applied for and obtained permission from the state to build a wharf from its upland into the river to the line of navigability. Some twenty years later the government, in the exercise of its control of the navigable waters and in the interest of commerce and navigation, adopted the lines of navigability formerly established by the state of Virginia, but a few years prior to the commencement of the suit the Secretary of War, by authority conferred on him by the Congress, re-established the lines, as a result of which the riparian proprietor's wharf extended some two hundred feet within the new lines of navigability. The Secretary of War asserted the right to require the demolition of the wharf as an obstruction to navigation. The owner insisted that, having received a grant of privilege from the state of Virginia prior to the exercise by the government of its power over the river, and subsequently acquiesced in by its adoption of the state lines, the property right thus acquired became as stable as any other property, and the privilege so granted irrevocable, and that it could be taken for public use only upon the payment of just compensation. The contention was rejected on the principle that the control of Congress over the navigable streams of the country is conclusive, and its judgment and determination the exercise of a legislative power in respect of a subject wholly within its control. To the same effect is Gibson v. United States, 166 U.S. 269, 17 S. Ct. 578, 41 L. Ed. 996, in which a work of public improvement in the Ohio river diminished greatly the value of the riparian owner's property by destroying his access to navigable water; and Union Bridge Co. v. United States, 204 U.S. 364, 27 S. Ct. 367, 51 L. Ed. 523, where the owner of a bridge was required to remodel the same as an obstruction to navigation, though erected under authority of the state when it was not an obstruction to navigation; and Louisville Bridge Co. v. United States, 242 U.S. 409, 37 S. Ct. 158, 61 L. Ed. 395, in which the same rule was applied in the case of a bridge erected expressly pursuant to an act of Congress. So also in United States v. Chandler-Dunbar Water Power Co., 229 U.S. 53; 33 S. Ct. 667, 57 L. Ed. 1063, the right of the government to destroy the water power of a riparian owner was upheld; and in Lewis Blue Point Oyster Cultivation Co. v. Briggs, 229 U.S. 82, 33 St. Ct. 679, 57 L. Ed. 1083, the right of compensation for the destruction of privately owned oyster beds was denied. All of these cases indubitably show adherence to the principle that one who applies for and obtains a grant or permit from a state, or the United States, to make use of a medium of interstate commerce, under the control and subject to the dominant power of the government, takes such grant or right subject to the exercise of the power of government, in the public interest, to withdraw it without compensation.

Appellant was duly notified by the Commission of the hearing which it ordered to be held to determine if the public interest, convenience, or necessity would be served by granting a renewal of its license. Due notice of this hearing was given and opportunity extended to furnish proof to establish the right under the provisions of the act for a renewal of the grant. There was, therefore, no lack of due process, and, considered from every point of view, the action of the Commission in refusing to renew was in all respects right, and should be, and is, affirmed.

Affirmed.

Van Orsdel, Associate Justice, concurs in the result.

15

The Biltmore Agreement*

December, 1933

News has been an ingredient of broadcasting from its beginning. Newspapers were willing to cooperate with radio stations by publishing program schedules (thereby increasing circulation) and sharing news with the young medium through the 1920's. But the Depression brought an end to this cozy relationship. As newspaper publishers watched their advertising revenues decline, radio stations and networks found commercial sponsors for news broadcasts. Although many stations were owned by newspaper interests, most members of the American Newspaper Publishers Association were unwilling to see radio prosper at their expense.

In 1933 the publishers used several tactics to bring the broadcasters to the bargaining table. They threatened to support anti-broadcasting legislation in Congress; they refused to print program schedules unless broadcasters paid for them; they convinced the three major press associations to withhold news from the radio industry. The last tactic motivated CBS to establish its own news gathering organization, but newspapers retaliated by refusing to publish items about CBS, its programs, and its sponsors. Fearful of losing clients to the rival network, CBS joined NBC in seeking to negotiate a settlement with their print "enemies." The parties to the dispute met for 2 days in New York City's Hotel Biltmore, from which the document below derives its name. The agreement

*This version is taken with permission from pp. 285–86 of *Bulletin No. 6266* of the American Newspaper Publishers Association dated May 3, 1934.

required CBS to abolish its news collecting agency and NBC vowed not to start one of its own. The NAB, representing independent station interests, did not adopt the agreement and named no member to the committee that established the Press–Radio Bureau, which commenced operations on March 1, 1934.

Although the networks were satisfied with this turn of events, many local radio stations that competed with local newspapers for advertising revenues were not. This fostered the creation of several all-radio news services, the most successful of which was the Transradio Press Service. INS and UP started to sell their services to radio stations in 1935 in order to meet the new competition, marking the end of the "Press–Radio War." As the clouds of another war gathered over Europe in the late 1930's, the networks built the framework of their present formidable news organizations. The Press–Radio Bureau ceased to exist in 1940 as even the Associated Press saw the handwriting on the wall and started selling news to broadcasters on an unrestricted basis in 1941. Transradio expired in 1951.

Radio gained its greatest journalistic impetus during World War II. Its ability to be "on the spot" surpassed the best efforts of competing newspapers which could only put out "extra" editions hours after the public heard eyewitness accounts of events broadcast directly from the scene. The popularity of all-news radio formats, the addition of audio feeds by AP and UPI, and the dominance of news among the remaining services provided by radio networks make it inconceivable that modern radio stations would end a newscast with the words, "For further details read your local newspaper," as they did in the 1930's when they temporarily surrendered their journalistic birthright.

Related Reading: 46, 58, 60, 62, 69, 98, 140, 190, 241.

. . . a committee consisting of one representative of The American Newspaper Publishers Association, one representative each from The United Press, The Associated Press and The International News Service, one representative from The National Association of Broadcasters, and one representative each from The National Broadcasting Company and The Columbia Broadcasting System, totalling seven members, with one vote each, should constitute a committee to set up with proper editorial control and supervision a Bureau designed to furnish to the radio broadcasters brief daily news bulletins for broadcasting purposes. The Chairman of the above Committee will be the representative of the American Newspaper Publishers Association and a member of the Publishers' National

Radio Committee. All actions of this committee will be in conjunction with the Publishers' National Radio Committee.

The newspaper and press association members of this committee are authorized and empowered to select such editor or editors, and establish such a Bureau as may be necessary to carry out the purposes of this program, to wit:

To receive from each of the three principal press associations copies of their respective day and night press reports, from which shall be selected bulletins of not more than thirty words each, sufficient to fill two broadcast periods daily of not more than five minutes each.

It is proposed that a broadcast, to be based upon bulletins taken from the morning newspaper report, will be put on the air by the broadcasters not earlier than 9:30, local station time, and the broadcast based upon the day newspaper report will not be put on the air by the broadcasters prior to 9 P.M., local station time.

It is agreed that these news broadcasts will not be sold for commercial purposes.

All expense incident to the functioning of this Bureau will be borne by the broadcasters. Any station may have access to these broadcast reports upon the basis of this program, upon its request and agreement to pay its proportionate share of the expense involved.

Occasional news bulletins of transcendent importance, as a matter of public service, will be furnished to broadcasters, as the occasion may arise at times other than the stated periods above. These bulletins will be written and broadcast in such a manner as to stimulate public interest in the reading of newspapers.

The broadcasters agree to arrange the broadcasts by their commentators in such a manner that these periods will be devoted to a generalization and background of general news situations and eliminate the present practice of the recital of spot news.

A part of this program is to secure the broadcasting of news by newspaper-owned stations and independently owned stations on a basis comparable to the foregoing schedule. The Press Associations will inform their clients or members concerning the broadcasting of news from press association reports as set forth in the foregoing schedule.

The Publishers' National Radio Committee will recommend to all newspaper publishers the above program for their approval, and will urge upon the members of The Associated Press and the management of The International News Service and The United Press the adoption of this program.

By this program it is believed that public interest will be served by making available to any radio station in the United States for broadcasting purposes brief daily reports of authentic news collected by the Press Associations, as well as making available to the public through the radio stations news of transcendent importance with the least possible delay.

16

President Roosevelt's Message to Congress

S. Doc. 144, 73d Congress, 2d Session
February 26, 1934

Bills to unify jurisdiction over all forms of interstate and foreign communication by wire and radio had been debated in Congress as early as 1929. There was particular concern over the less than diligent job of regulating the telephone industry being performed by the Interstate Commerce Commission whose main interest at the time was the railroads.

Soon after assuming office in 1933, President Franklin D. Roosevelt directed an interdepartmental committee to study the need for centralized federal regulation of telecommunications. He submitted the following legislative recommendation after receiving the committee's report, soon after which Senator Dill and Congressman Rayburn introduced bills that eventually emerged with the President's signature on June 19, 1934, as Public Law 416 of the 73d Congress—the Communications Act of 1934. (The Act, as amended through 1976, appears in this volume as Document 47, pp. 511–573.)

The only major controversy that arose during congressional consideration of the legislation occurred on the floor of the Senate when the Wagner–Hatfield amendment was debated. The amendment would have directed the Federal Communications Commission to license 25% of broadcasting facilities to educational and other nonprofit organizations. The broadcasting industry vigorously opposed this proposal, and Section 307(c) (see p. 528) was passed instead as a compromise measure. On January 22, 1935, the FCC recommended against adoption of the proposal contained in Section 307(c) based on its understanding that educational and other similar groups would be given ample access to commercial broadcast facilities. This proved not to be the case.

Congress had lived with the Radio Act of 1927 for 7 years, during which broadcasting, especially the networks, had grown by leaps and bounds. Considering the charges of monopoly and over-commercialization that were made at the time, it may seem strange that Congress saw fit to make no significant modifications in its regulatory philosophy and statutory provisions affecting broadcasting in 1934. It should not appear at all unusual, however, that the prospering radio industry strongly supported passage of the Communications Act, minus the Wagner–Hatfield amendment. The status quo in broadcasting was preserved when the newly created FCC took office on July 11, 1934.

To the Congress:

I have long felt that for the sake of clarity and effectiveness the relationship of the Federal Government to certain services known as utilities should be divided into three fields: Transportation, power, and communications. The problems of transportation are vested in the Interstate Commerce Commission, and the problems of power, its development, transmission, and distribution, in the Federal Power Commission.

In the field of communications, however, there is today no single Government agency charged with broad authority.

The Congress has vested certain authority over certain forms of communications in the Interstate Commerce Commission, and there is in addition the agency known as the Federal Radio Commission.

I recommend that the Congress create a new agency to be known as the Federal Communications Commission, such agency to be vested with the authority now lying in the Federal Radio Commission and with such authority over communications as now lies with the Interstate Commerce Commission — the services affected to be all of those which rely on wires, cables, or radio as a medium of transmission.

It is my thought that a new commission such as I suggest might well be organized this year by transferring the present authority for the control of communications of the Radio Commission and the Interstate Commerce Commission. The new body should, in addition, be given full power to investigate and study the business of existing companies and make recommendations to the Congress for additional legislation at the next session.

Franklin D. Roosevelt

The White House
February 26, 1934

17

"War of the Worlds"

FCC mimeos 30294, 30295, 30405, and 30432

October 31–November 7, 1938

By 1938 radio was firmly entrenched as the average American family's aural conduit to the world of entertainment and news. The audience had become accustomed to hearing President Roosevelt's "fireside chats," up-to-the-minute news bulletins about such events as the trial and execution of Bruno Hauptmann, and first-person descriptions of the explosion of the airship *Hindenburg* and the German occupation of Austria. For nearly three weeks in September, 1938, America riveted its collective ear to the radio loudspeaker to listen to commentators such as CBS' H. V. Kaltenborn describe and analyze the unfolding of the Munich crisis. England's Prime Minister Neville Chamberlain momentarily dissipated the threat of war by allowing Adolph Hitler to take over Czechoslovakia's Sudetenland.

A month later, on October 30, 1938, CBS broadcast the most memorable radio program of all time, "War of the Worlds" performed on the "Mercury Theatre on the Air," presided over by the prodigious 23-year-old stage actor, Orson Welles. Howard Koch's adaptation of H. G. Wells' nineteenth century novel freely deployed certain radio conventions to lend an air of authenticity to the science-fiction tale. The "drama" included what appeared to be remote pickups of hotel dance bands interrupted by bogus "bulletins" about meteor-like objects landing in New Jersey and other specifically identified locales. A fictitious on-the-spot reporter was obliterated on the air by what turned out to be Martian invaders. Actors playing scientists, military commanders, and government officials warned the listening audience of the gravity of the situation as the worsening holocaust was graphically described. Kenny Delmar, later to be featured as "Senator Clag-

horn" on "The Fred Allen Show," did a convincing vocal imper-
sonation of President Roosevelt. It was conservatively estimated
that six million people heard the broadcast. Many of them
panicked, though fortunately no one was killed.

For Orson Welles the show produced instant fame. For the
FCC the program created a touchy problem concerning program
regulation that had to be handled with sensitivity and restraint, as
the following releases indicate. "War of the Worlds" was a grip-
ping demonstration of radio's credibility which pointed out the
need for the broadcasting industry to distinguish clearly between
fact and fancy in the ensuing world crisis.

On October 30, 1974, a local radio station in Providence,
Rhode Island, broadcast its own adaptation of "War of the
Worlds." Complaints from gullible listeners caused the FCC to
sanction the station for failing "to broadcast sufficiently explicit
announcements at the proper times during the program to prevent public alarm or panic." [*Capital Cities Communications, Inc.,*
54 FCC 2d 1035, 1038 (1975).] In 1977 the Swiss Broadcasting
Company had to apologize to listeners for airing an all-too-
convincing satire that conveyed the impression that neutron
bombs had killed half a million people in a fictitious East-West
confrontation in Germany. Yet, American radio broadcasting
stations are credited with calming a distraught public during such
real emergencies as the regional electric power failures of 1965
and 1977. Radio's believability remains an asset to be relied upon
with discretion by broadcasters and the audience alike, lest it become a liability.

Related Reading: 37, 58, 67, 70, 125, 216.

FOR IMMEDIATE RELEASE   Mimeo 30294
                                                 October 31, 1938

FEDERAL COMMUNICATIONS COMMISSION
WASHINGTON, D.C.

Chairman Frank R. McNinch of the Federal Communications Commission
said today: "I have this morning requested the Columbia Broadcasting Company
by telegraph to forward to the Commission at once a copy of the script and also
an electrical transcription of the 'War of the Worlds' which was broadcast last
night and which the press indicates caused widespread excitement, terror and
fright. I shall request prompt consideration of this matter by the Commission.

"I withhold final judgment until later, but any broadcast that creates such general panic and fear as this one is reported to have done is, to say the least, regrettable.

"The widespread public reaction to this broadcast, as indicated by the press, is another demonstration of the power and force of radio and points out again the serious public responsibility of those who are licensed to operate stations."

FOR IMMEDIATE RELEASE   Mimeo 30295
                                                                October 31, 1938

FEDERAL COMMUNICATIONS COMMISSION
WASHINGTON, D.C.

STATEMENT OF COMMISSIONER T.A.M. CRAVEN CONCERNING THE RADIO DRAMATIZATION OF H.G. WELLS' "WAR OF THE WORLDS" AS BROADCAST BY COLUMBIA BROADCASTING SYSTEM ON THE NIGHT OF OCTOBER 30, 1938

In response to numerous requests for a statement concerning the broadcasting by the Columbia Broadcasting System of the radio dramatization of H. G. Wells' book entitled *War of the Worlds*, I am in agreement with the position taken by Chairman McNinch in this matter.

However, I feel that in any action which may be taken by the Commission, utmost caution should be utilized to avoid the danger of the Commission censoring what shall or what shall not be said over the radio.

Furthermore, it is my opinion that the Commission should proceed carefully in order that it will not discourage the presentation by radio of the dramatic arts. It is essential that we encourage radio to make use of the dramatic arts and the artists of this country. The public does not want a "spineless" radio.

It is also my opinion that, in any case, isolated instances of poor program service do not of necessity justify the revocation of a station's license, particularly when such station has an otherwise excellent record of good public service. I do not include in this category, however, criminal action by broadcasting station licensees.

FOR IMMEDIATE RELEASE   Mimeo 30405
                                                                November 5, 1938

FEDERAL COMMUNICATIONS COMMISSION
WASHINGTON, D.C.

Frank R. McNinch, Chairman of the Federal Communications Commission, announced today that he invited the Presidents of National Broadcasting Company, the Columbia Broadcasting System, and the Mutual Broadcasting System to a conference with him next week for an informal discussion of subjects pertaining to broadcast programs and especially the frequent and, at times misleading, use of the newspaper term "Flash" in radio programs of various types.

"I have heard the opinion often expressed," said Chairman McNinch, "within the industry as well as outside, that the practice of using 'Flash' as well as 'Bulletin' is overworked and results in misleading the public. It is hoped and believed that a discussion of this subject may lead to a clearer differentiation between bona fide news matter of first-rank importance and that which is of only ordinary importance or which finds place in dramatics or advertising.

"After having discussed this matter with the three national networks," continued Chairman McNinch, "I shall have further conferences with others in the industry along the same general lines."

FOR IMMEDIATE RELEASE   Mimeo 30432
                                                      November 7, 1938

FEDERAL COMMUNICATIONS COMMISSION
WASHINGTON, D. C.

An informal conference was held today between Chairman Frank R. McNinch of the Federal Communications Commission and Lenox R. Lohr, President of the National Broadcasting Company, William S. Paley, President of the Columbia Broadcasting System, and Alfred J. McCosker, Chairman of the Board of the Mutual Broadcasting System.

Chairman McNinch emphasized that the discussion was necessarily an informal one; first, because the invitations to the meeting were issued by himself and not by the Commission, and, second, because neither he nor the Commission as a whole is attempting to exert any censorship of program content, that being definitely denied the Commission under the law.

In the invitation to the heads of the three networks, Mr. McNinch said that he wanted the informal discussion to center around "the use of the terms 'flash' and 'bulletin' in news broadcasts, dramatic programs and in advertising messages." Chairman McNinch felt that there might be developing an indiscriminate use of these words which could result in misleading or confusing the public.

The three network heads were in agreement that the word "flash" is now rarely used by any network and Lenox R. Lohr, President of the National Broadcasting Company, and William S. Paley, President of the Columbia Broadcasting System, agreed that it should be restricted to items of unusual importance or interest.

Mr. Alfred J. McCosker, Chairman of the Board of the Mutual Broadcasting System, also agreed, for his Station WOR, that "flash" should be restricted to items of unusual importance or interest and that he would submit this matter along with other matters covered by this news release to the members of the Mutual Broadcasting System for their consideration. This, he explained, was necessary because of the autonomous character of the Mutual network, and he had no authority to speak for the members of that network.

The three network heads saw no reason to alter the present practice in broadcasting news labeled as "bulletins."

The network heads agreed that the words "flash" and "bulletin" should be used with great discretion in the dramatization of fictional events, with a view never to using them where they might cause general alarm. It was believed that this could be accomplished without greatly weakening the value of the dramatic technique as such.

Chairman McNinch at the conclusion of the meeting expressed himself to the conferees as well pleased with what the records showed about actual network practices and the assurances to guard against any abuses. He said that he would hold similar informal discussions with other elements of the industry.

"I greatly appreciate," said Chairman McNinch, "the spirit of cooperation shown by the heads of the three networks, and they requested that I express for them their appreciation of the informality and helpfulness of the conference."

18

The Sanders Brothers Case

Federal Communications Commission v.

Sanders Brothers Radio Station

309 U.S. 470

March 25, 1940

How much competition should there be in broadcasting? Aside from prohibiting monopolistic practices, the Communications Act of 1934 is silent on the question, thus leaving its resolution to the FCC. In exercising its discretion to allocate frequencies and issue licenses, the Commission is free to determine the nature and extent of competition that will best serve the "public interest, convenience, and necessity."

This is no easy task. In a broadcasting system almost exclusively supported by advertising, is the public interest best served by licensing as many stations as the electromagnetic spectrum can contain, or by limiting stations to a number determined through economic analysis of available advertising revenues and estimates of capital costs and operating expenses? Is the public interest better served by a large number of competing stations operating on a flimsy financial footing, or by a smaller number of secure, economically protected stations?

Economic considerations frequently arise when a new station seeks to enter an existing station's service area. Broadcasting, after all, is a business. Business enterprises attempt to keep expenses low and revenues high in order to achieve the goal of maximum profitability. Competition enlarges the public's choice of program sources, but it tends to reduce profitability and can even bring about the demise of a station. Allegations of "economic injury," when properly made before the FCC, can forestall the advent of additional competition for program material as well as for audience and advertiser support.

Through the 1930's the FCC regularly took economic injury protests into consideration when acting on applications for new station licenses. A change of policy by the Commission late in the decade gave rise to the 1940 *Sanders Brothers* decision by the Supreme Court which upheld the FCC. Its position thus vindicated, the Commission adopted a highly procompetitive stance whereby it consistently refused to adjudicate economic injury protests until the *Carroll* case was decided in 1958. (See Document 24, pp. 246–250.)

Related Reading: 116, 119.

Mr. Justice Roberts delivered the opinion of the Court.

We took this case to resolve important issues of substance and procedure arising under the Communications Act of 1934, as amended.[1]

January 20, 1936, the Telegraph Herald, a newspaper published in Dubuque, Iowa, filed with the petitioner an application for a construction permit to erect a broadcasting station in that city. May 14, 1936, the respondent, who had for some years held a broadcasting license for, and had operated, Station WKBB at East Dubuque, Illinois, directly across the Mississippi River from Dubuque, Iowa, applied for a permit to move its transmitter and studios to the last named city and install its station there. August 18, 1936, respondent asked leave to intervene in the Telegraph Herald proceeding, alleging in its petition, *inter alia*, that there was an insufficiency of advertising revenue to support an additional station in Dubuque and insufficient talent to furnish programs for an additional station; that adequate service was being rendered to the community by Station WKBB and there was no need for any additional radio outlet in Dubuque and that the granting of the Telegraph Herald application would not serve the public interest, convenience, and necessity. Intervention was permitted and both applications were set for consolidated hearing.

The respondent and the Telegraph Herald offered evidence in support of their respective applications. The respondent's proof showed that its station had operated at a loss; that the area proposed to be served by the Telegraph Herald

---

[1]Act of June 19, 1934, c. 652, 48 Stat. 1064; Act of June 5, 1936, c. 511, 49 Stat. 1475; Act of May 20, 1937, c. 229, 50 Stat. 189, 47 U.S.C. 151, *et seq.*

was substantially the same as that served by the respondent and that, of the advertisers relied on to support the Telegraph Herald station, more than half had used the respondent's station for advertising.

An examiner reported that the application of the Telegraph Herald should be denied and that of the respondent granted. On exceptions of the Telegraph Herald, and after oral argument, the broadcasting division of petitioner made an order granting both applications, reciting that "public interest, convenience, and necessity would be served" by such action. The division promulgated a statement of the facts and of the grounds of decision, reciting that both applicants were legally, technically, and financially qualified to undertake the proposed construction and operation; that there was need in Dubuque and the surrounding territory for the services of both stations, and that no question of electrical interference between the two stations was involved. A rehearing was denied and respondent appealed to the Court of Appeals for the District of Columbia. That court entertained the appeal and held that one of the issues which the Commission should have tried was that of alleged economic injury to the respondent's station by the establishment of an additional station and that the Commission had erred in failing to make findings on that issue. It decided that, in the absence of such findings, the Commission's action in granting the Telegraph Herald permit must be set aside as arbitrary and capricious.[2]

The petitioner's contentions are that under the Communications Act economic injury to a competitor is not a ground for refusing a broadcasting license and that, since this is so, the respondent was not a person aggrieved, or whose interests were adversely affected, by the Commission's action, within the meaning of § 402(b) of the Act which authorizes appeals from the Commission's orders.

The respondent asserts that the petitioner in argument below contented itself with the contention that the respondent had failed to produce evidence requiring a finding of probable economic injury to it. It is consequently insisted that the petitioner is not in a position here to defend its failure to make such findings on the ground that it is not required by the Act to consider any such issue. By its petition for rehearing in the court below, the Commission made clear its position as now advanced. The decision of the court below, and the challenge made in petition for rehearing and here by the Commission, raise a fundamental question as to the function and power of the Commission and we think that, on the record, it is open here.

First.   We hold that resulting economic injury to a rival station is not, in and of itself, and apart from considerations of public convenience, interest, or necessity, an element the petitioner must weigh, and as to which it must make findings, in passing on an application for a broadcasting license.

Section 307(a) of the Communications Act directs that "the Commission,

[2]*Sanders Brothers Radio Station* v. *Federal Communications Commission,* 70 App. D.C. 297; 106 F.2d 321.

if public convenience, interest, or necessity will be served thereby, subject to the limitations of this Act, shall grant to any applicant therefor a station license provided for by this Act." This mandate is given meaning and contour by the other provisions of the statute and the subject matter with which it deals.[3] The Act contains no express command that in passing upon an application the Commission must consider the effect of competition with an existing station. Whether the Commission should consider the subject must depend upon the purpose of the Act and the specific provisions intended to effectuate that purpose.

The genesis of the Communications Act and the necessity for the adoption of some such regulatory measure is a matter of history. The number of available radio frequencies is limited. The attempt by a broadcaster to use a given frequency in disregard of its prior use by others, thus creating confusion and interference, deprives the public of the full benefit of radio audition. Unless Congress had exercised its power over interstate commerce to bring about allocation of available frequencies and to regulate the employment of transmission equipment the result would have been an impairment of the effective use of these facilities by anyone. The fundamental purpose of Congress in respect of broadcasting was the allocation and regulation of the use of radio frequencies by prohibiting such use except under license.

In contradistinction to communication by telephone and telegraph, which the Communications Act recognizes as a common carrier activity and regulates accordingly in analogy to the regulation of rail and other carriers by the Interstate Commerce Commission,[4] the Act recognizes that broadcasters are not common carriers and are not to be dealt with as such.[5] Thus the Act recognizes that the field of broadcasting is one of free competition. The sections dealing with broadcasting demonstrate that Congress has not, in its regulatory scheme, abandoned the principle of free competition, as it has done in the case of the railroads,[6] in respect of which regulation involves the suppression of wasteful practices due to competition, the regulation of rates and charges, and other measures which are unnecessary if free competition is to be permitted.

An important element of public interest and convenience affecting the issue of a license is the ability of the licensee to render the best practicable service to the community reached by his broadcasts. That such ability may be assured the Act contemplates inquiry by the Commission, *inter alia*, into an applicant's financial qualifications to operate the proposed station.[7]

But the Act does not essay to regulate the business of the licensee. The Commission is given no supervisory control of the programs, of business

---

[3] *Radio Commission* v. *Nelson Bros. Co.*, 289 U.S. 266, 285.
[4] See Title II §§ 201-221, 47 U.S.C. §§ 201-221.
[5] See § 3(h), 47 U.S.C. § 153(h).
[6] Compare *Texas & Pacific Ry.* v. *Gulf, C. & S.F. Ry. Co.*, 270 U.S. 266, 277; *Chicago Junction Case*, 264 U.S. 258.
[7] See § 308(b), 47 U.S.C. § 308(b).

management or of policy. In short, the broadcasting field is open to anyone, provided there be an available frequency over which he can broadcast without interference to others, if he shows his competency, the adequacy of his equipment, and financial ability to make good use of the assigned channel.

The policy of the Act is clear that no person is to have anything in the nature of a property right as a result of the granting of a license. Licenses are limited to a maximum of three years' duration, may be revoked, and need not be renewed. Thus the channels presently occupied remain free for a new assignment to another licensee in the interest of the listening public.

Plainly it is not the purpose of the Act to protect a licensee against competition but to protect the public. Congress intended to leave competition in the business of broadcasting where it found it, to permit a licensee who was not interfering electrically with other broadcasters to survive or succumb according to his ability to make his programs attractive to the public.

This is not to say that the question of competition between a proposed station and one operating under an existing license is to be entirely disregarded by the Commission, and, indeed, the Commission's practice shows that it does not disregard that question. It may have a vital and important bearing upon the ability of the applicant adequately to serve his public; it may indicate that both stations − the existing and the proposed − will go under, with the result that a portion of the listening public will be left without adequate service; it may indicate that, by a division of the field, both stations will be compelled to render inadequate service. These matters, however, are distinct from the consideration that, if a license be granted, competition between the licensee and any other existing station may cause economic loss to the latter. If such economic loss were a valid reason for refusing a license this would mean that the Commission's function is to grant a monopoly in the field of broadcasting, a result which the Act itself expressly negatives,[8] which Congress would not have contemplated without granting the Commission powers of control over the rates, programs, and other activities of the business of broadcasting.

We conclude that economic injury to an existing station is not a separate and independent element to be taken into consideration by the Commission in determining whether it shall grant or withhold a license.

Second.   It does not follow that, because the licensee of a station cannot resist the grant of a license to another, on the ground that the resulting competition may work economic injury to him, he has no standing to appeal from an order of the Commission granting the application.

Section 402(b) of the Act provides for an appeal to the Court of Appeals of the District of Columbia (1) by an applicant for a license or permit, or (2) "by any other person aggrieved or whose interests are adversely affected by any decision of the Commission granting or refusing any such application."

The petitioner insists that as economic injury to the respondent was not a

---

[8]See § 311, 47 U.S.C. § 311, relating to unfair competition and monopoly.

proper issue before the Commission it is impossible that § 402(b) was intended to give the respondent standing to appeal, since absence of right implies absence of remedy. This view would deprive subsection (2) of any substantial effect.

Congress had some purpose in enacting § 402(b) (2). It may have been of the opinion that one likely to be financially injured by the issue of a license would be the only person having a sufficient interest to bring to the attention of the appellate court errors of law in the action of the Commission in granting the license. It is within the power of Congress to confer such standing to prosecute an appeal.[9]

We hold, therefore, that the respondent had the requisite standing to appeal and to raise, in the court below, any relevant question of law in respect of the order of the Commission.

Third.   Examination of the findings and grounds of decision set forth by the Commission discloses that the findings were sufficient to comply with the requirements of the Act in respect of the public interest, convenience, or necessity involved in the issue of the permit. In any event, if the findings were not as detailed upon this subject as might be desirable, the attack upon them is not that the public interest is not sufficiently protected but only that the financial interests of the respondent have not been considered. We find no reason for abrogating the Commission's order for lack of adequate findings.

Fourth.   The respondent here renews a contention made in the Court of Appeals to the effect that the Commission used as evidence certain data and reports in its files without permitting the respondent, as intervenor before the Commission, the opportunity of inspecting them. The Commission disavows the use of such material as evidence in the cause and the Court of Appeals has found the disavowal veracious and sufficient. We are not disposed to disturb its conclusion.

The judgment of the Court of Appeals is *Reversed*.

Mr. Justice McReynolds took no part in the decision of this case.

[9]Compare *Interstate Commerce Commission* v. *Oregon-Washington R. Co.*, 288 U.S. 14, 23-25.

19
The Mayflower Doctrine

In the Matter of The Mayflower Broadcasting
Corporation and The Yankee Network, Inc.
(WAAB)
8 FCC 333, 338
January 16, 1941

Many broadcasters took to the air in the 1920's in order to voice their own views. Such licensees regarded their stations as personal soapboxes just as newspaper publishers did in an earlier era. This trend faded as broadcasting developed into an advertiser-supported business operation more interested in avoiding controversy and making money than in spreading ideas. The number of radio stations broadcasting the editorial views of management was small in the 1930's, but stations WAAB and WNAC in Boston, both licensed to John Shepard III's Yankee Network, were among them for a time.

In 1939 WAAB's license renewal application became consolidated in a hearing with the mutually exclusive application of the Mayflower Broadcasting Corporation for a permit to construct a station using WAAB's frequency. One of Mayflower's owners was Lawrence Flynn, a former Yankee Network employee who had complained to the FCC about his ex-employer's editorializing.

In 1940 the FCC proposed to dismiss Mayflower's application because the new applicant had made misrepresentations to the FCC and was not financially qualified to be a licensee. The

Commission also moved to renew WAAB's license without mentioning the editorials that had stopped more than a year before. But Mayflower successfully pressed the Commission to reconsider the case in light of WAAB's past editorializing. The FCC's final decision, reprinted below, changed nothing for Mayflower, but it did contain wording that licensees interpreted as an absolute ban on editorializing.

Why was this administrative fiat never subjected to a court test? Certainly WAAB, which had won its battle for license renewal, was unlikely to appeal. Even if it had, its legal standing to protest the FCC prohibition against editorials was nebulous since it had voluntarily discontinued the practice. This reflected the attitude of the industry at large; even the 1939 NAB Code discouraged editorializing and the sale of time for "presentation of controversial views." The broadcasters, in any case, had more significant matters on their minds as the chain broadcasting proceeding was grinding through its final stages before the Commission.

The subsequent entry of America into World War II precluded broadcaster concern about the ban of a practice in which few engaged. The desire to dissent on the air was remote as the industry lent itself to the harmonious spirit of the war effort through 1945. It wasn't until the issuance of the "Blue Book" a year later (see Document 21, pp. 132-216) that the broadcasting industry became agitated about editorializing. The "Mayflower Doctrine" effectively discouraged broadcast editorials until the FCC issued its "Fairness Doctrine" in 1949. (See Document 22, pp. 217-231.)

Related Reading: 230.

DECISION AND ORDER

These proceedings were instituted upon the filing by The Mayflower Broadcasting Corporation of an application for a construction permit to authorize a new radiobroadcast station at Boston, Mass., to operate on the frequency 1410 kilocycles with power of 500 watts night and 1 kilowatt day, unlimited time. These are the facilities now assigned to Station WAAB, Boston, Mass. The Commission designated this application for hearing along with the applications of The Yankee Network, Inc. (licensee of Station WAAB) for renewal of licenses for this station's main and auxiliary transmitters. The hearing was held in Boston, Mass., during November 1939. On May 31, 1940, the Commission issued proposed findings of fact and conclusions proposing to deny the application of The Mayflower Broadcasting Corporation and to grant the applications of The Yankee Network, Inc., for renewal of licenses. Exceptions to the proposed findings and conclusions were filed by Mayflower Broadcasting Corporation and at its request oral argument was held on July 25, 1940, with The Yankee Network, Inc., participating. Due to the absence of a quorum of the Commission at that time, the case was reargued before the full Commission by counsel for both parties on September 26, 1940.

In its proposed findings the Commission concluded that The Mayflower Broadcasting Corporation was not shown to be financially qualified to construct and operate the proposed station and, moreover, that misrepresentations of fact were made to the Commission in the application. After careful consideration of the applicant's exceptions and of the oral arguments presented, the Commission is unable to change these conclusions. The proposed findings and conclusions as to the application of The Mayflower Broadcasting Corporation will therefore, be adopted and made final.

More difficult and less easily resolvable questions are, however, presented by the applications for renewal of The Yankee Network, Inc. The record shows without contradiction that beginning early in 1937 and continuing through September 1938, it was the policy of Station WAAB to broadcast so-called editorials from time to time urging the election of various candidates for political office or supporting one side or another of various questions in public controversy. In these editorials, which were delivered by the editor-in-chief of the station's news service, no pretense was made at objective, impartial reporting. It is clear — indeed the station seems to have taken pride in the fact — that the purpose of these editorials was to win public support for some person or view favored by those in control of the station.

No attempt will be made here to analyze in detail the large number of broadcasts devoted to editorials. The material in the record has been carefully considered and compels the conclusion that this licensee during the period in question, has revealed a serious misconception of its duties and functions under the law. Under the American system of broadcasting it is clear that responsibility for the conduct of a broadcast station must rest initially with the broadcaster. It is equally clear that with the limitations in frequencies inherent in the nature of radio, the public interest can never be served by a dedication of any broadcast facility to the support of his own partisan ends. Radio can serve as an instrument of democracy only when devoted to the communication of information and the exchange of ideas fairly and objectively presented. A truly free radio cannot be used to advocate the causes of the licensee. It cannot be used to support the candidacies of his friends. It cannot be devoted to the support of principles he happens to regard most favorably. In brief, the broadcaster cannot be an advocate.

Freedom of speech on the radio must be broad enough to provide full and equal opportunity for the presentation to the public of all sides of public issues. Indeed, as one licensed to operate in a public domain the licensee has assumed the obligation of presenting all sides of important public questions, fairly, objectively and without bias. The public interest — not the private — is paramount. These requirements are inherent in the conception of public interest set up by the Communications Act as the criterion of regulation. And while the day to day decisions applying these requirements are the licensee's responsibility, the ultimate duty to review generally the course of conduct of the station over a period of time and to take appropriate action thereon is vested in the Commission.

Upon such a review here, there can be no question that The Yankee Network, Inc., in 1937 and 1938 continued to operate in contravention of these principles. The record does show, however, that, in response to a request of the Commission for details as to the conduct of the station since September 1938, two affidavits were filed with the Commission by John Shepard 3d, president of The Yankee Network, Inc. Apparently conceding the departures from the requirements of public interest by the earlier conduct of the station, these affidavits state, and they are uncontradicted, that no editorials have been broadcast over Station WAAB since September 1938 and that it is not intended to depart from this uninterrupted policy. The station has no editorial policies. In the affidavits there is further a description of the station's procedure for handling news items and the statement is made that since September 1938 "no attempt has ever been or will ever be made to color or editorialize the news received" through usual sources. In response to a question from the bench inquiring whether the Commission should rely on these affidavits in determining whether to renew the licenses, counsel for The Yankee Network, Inc., stated at the second argument, "There are absolutely no reservations whatsoever, or mental reservations of any sort, character, or kind with reference to those affidavits. They mean exactly what they say in the fullest possible amplification that the Commission wants to give to them."

Relying upon these comprehensive and unequivocal representations as to the future conduct of the station and in view of the loss of service to the public involved in the deletion of this station, it has been concluded to grant the applications for renewal. Should any future occasion arise to examine into the conduct of this licensee, however, the Commission will consider the facts developed in this record in its review of the activities as a whole. . . .

20

The Network Case

National Broadcasting Co., Inc., et al. v. United

States et al.

319 U.S. 190

May 10, 1943

A network provides programs and advertising revenues to its affiliated stations. Without networks, broadcasting in a vast country like the United States would not be a national communications medium. Network operations began as early as 1923 in America. The National Broadcasting Company originated in 1926, followed by the Columbia Broadcasting System in 1927 and the Mutual Broadcasting System in 1934. Throughout the "golden age" of radio in the 1930's and 1940's networks were as potent a force in the broadcasting industry as they are in television today.

In the late 1930's the FCC became concerned about the power of radio networks, especially NBC and CBS, whose affiliation contracts hampered the ability of station licensees to program as they saw fit and threatened the very structure of the competitive broadcasting system envisaged by Congress. The Commission was particularly anxious to end NBC's simultaneous operation of two networks, the Red and the Blue, a situation that had arisen as a result of the American Telephone and Telegraph Company's departure from active broadcasting in 1926 (see p. 19). The Red and Blue networks tended to counterprogram against one another, giving NBC a decided competitive advantage over CBS and MBS.

One important outcome of the FCC's chain broadcasting investigation and subsequent rulemaking was the corporate separation of the two networks in 1941, followed by the sale of the

Blue Network in 1943 to Edward J. Noble, licensee of WMCA in New York City (which he sold) and chairman of the board of the Life Savers Corporation. In 1945 Noble's network was renamed the American Broadcasting Company. More than 20 years later, with the power of network radio on the wane, ABC was granted a waiver of the very rule that brought about its creation, when it commenced operating four specialized radio networks. [See 11 FCC 2d 163 (1967).]

This key Supreme Court decision on which the Justices were divided (the vote was five to two) upheld the Commission's authority to issue regulations pertaining to business arrangements between networks and their affiliates. Aside from its treatment of the central issue of the regulation of competition, Justice Frankfurter's opinion is noteworthy for its examination of the legislative history of radio law and its clarification of the relationship between "public interest, convenience, and necessity" and freedom of speech in broadcasting. Justice Murphy's dissent suggests inconsistency between the Court's 1940 *Sanders Brothers* decision (Document 18, pp. 89-94) and this one.

What are perhaps the most misinterpreted words in the judicial history of broadcast regulation appear in this case. The majority opinion states, "But the Act does not restrict the Commission merely to supervision of the [radio] traffic. It puts upon the Commission the burden of determining the composition of that traffic" (p. 117). Many readers of this part of the decision have taken this to mean that the Court was approving FCC dictation of program content. In context, however, these two sentences simply say that the Commission has the authority to *select* licensees as well as to "supervise" them. "Traffic" in the Court's analogy refers to licensees, not to programs.

No decision of the Court has had as much influence on public policy in broadcasting as the "Network" case. By upholding the constitutionality of the Communications Act and stating that the Act confers broad, though elastically enumerated ("not niggardly but expansive") powers, the High Court provided a precedent that has been used ever since to ratify jurisdictional expansions by the FCC.

Networking in television proved to be as natural a part of broadcasting as it had been during radio's era of supremacy. But the limited number of desirable VHF channel assignments and the vastly greater expense of producing programs for TV made the networks a more dominant force than they ever had been prior to the ascendancy of television. Attempts to establish a viable fourth commercial TV network have thus far failed for lack of enough VHF affiliates.

Since 1959 the FCC has applied more and more rules to TV networks in order to moderate their anti-competitive influence. For example, it is illegal for a TV station to option its time to a network; each network show must be individually "cleared" with every affiliate that chooses to carry it. Nevertheless, the economics of television station operation creates a practical reliance on the networks for most programming, and ABC, CBS, and NBC have responded to the stations' need by making available an increasing supply of network programs from dawn to after midnight.

By the late 1960's the dominance of the TV networks as program suppliers had reduced the supply of non-network first-run syndicated shows to a trickle. In 1970 the FCC attempted to encourage "the development of independent program sources" to benefit unaffiliated, affiliated, and UHF stations (23 FCC 2d 382, 395) by issuing rules reducing network programming during prime time, prohibiting domestic syndication by networks, and preventing networks from acquiring an interest in programs produced by others for non-network exhibition. These rules were upheld in *Mt. Mansfield Television, Inc. v. Federal Communications Commission*, 442 F.2d 470 (2d Cir. 1971). The original "prime time access rule" (PTAR I) was modified in 1974 (44 FCC 2d 1081), but court action delayed implementation of PTAR II [*National Association of Independent Television Producers and Distributors et al. v. FCC*, 502 F.2d 249 (2d Cir. 1974)], whereupon the Commission developed PTAR III [50 FCC 2d 829 (1975), affirmed by 516 F.2d 526 (2d Cir. 1975)] which became effective with the 1975–1976 TV season. PTAR III is similar to PTAR I with the addition of exemptions for such network programs as documentaries, children's shows, and live sports coverage that unpredictably runs over into prime time.

PTAR helped to revive the syndication field, but the typical TV viewer noticed little change on the home screen during the first years of PTAR's operation. It does not matter to the public if a game show reaches the local station through a network or through an independent distributor. Therefore, while the diversity of program sources was increased by PTAR, the diversity of programming remained virtually unchanged. TV stations that had formerly opposed PTAR came to favor its retention, for their profits improved under the rule. Even the national networks were ultimate beneficiaries of the rule, for they are licensees of major market television stations.

A renewed testament to the power of the TV networks emerged in 1977 when the FCC responded to a petition for rule making submitted by the Westinghouse Broadcasting Company by instituting a comprehensive inquiry into network TV programming practices and policies (62 FCC 2d 548), the first such investigation in two decades. Undoubtedly, the FCC and other government agencies (notably the Justice Department) will continue to chip away at the television networks, like some latter-day Don Quixote tilting at windmills.

Meanwhile the need to regulate radio networks closely has diminished with the vast increase in the number of AM and FM stations and with the reduced reliance on networks for radio programs in the wake of TV's dominance as a mass medium since the early 1950's. In 1977 the FCC repealed all of the radio chain regulations upheld by the Court in 1943 except the "territorial exclusivity" rule. The Commission accompanied this action with a policy statement cautioning against the restrictive station-network practices formerly prohibited by rule. The FCC said, ". . . [radio] licensees have an affirmative, non-delegable duty to choose independently all programming for broadcast, in light of the tastes and ascertained needs and problems of the community." [63 FCC 2d 674, 690 (1977).]

Related Reading: 7, 57, 75, 96, 113, 129, 165, 186.

Mr. Justice Frankfurter delivered the opinion of the Court.

In view of our dependence upon regulated private enterprise in discharging the far-reaching rôle which radio plays in our society, a somewhat detailed exposition of the history of the present controversy and the issues which it raises is appropriate.

These suits were brought on October 30, 1941, to enjoin the enforcement of the Chain Broadcasting Regulations promulgated by the Federal Communications Commission on May 2, 1941, and amended on October 11, 1941. We held last Term in *Columbia System* v. *United States*, 316 U.S. 407, and *National Broadcasting Co.* v. *United States*, 316 U.S. 447, that the suits could be maintained under § 402(a) of the Communications Act of 1934, 48 Stat. 1093, 47 U.S.C. § 402(a) (incorporating by reference the Urgent Deficiencies Act of October 22, 1913, 38 Stat. 219, 28 U.S.C. § 47), and that the decrees of the District Court dismissing the suits for want of jurisdiction should therefore be reversed. On remand the District Court granted the Government's motions for summary judgment and dismissed the suits on the merits. 47 F. Supp. 940. The cases are now here on appeal. 28 U.S.C. § 47. Since they raise substantially the same issues and were argued together, we shall deal with both cases in a single opinion.

On March 18, 1938, the Commission undertook a comprehensive investigation to determine whether special regulations applicable to radio stations engaged in chain broadcasting[1] were required in the "public interest, convenience, or necessity." The Commission's order directed that inquiry be made, *inter alia*, in the following specific matters: the number of stations licensed to or affiliated with networks, and the amount of station time used or controlled by networks; the contractual rights and obligations of stations under their agreements with networks; the scope of network agreements containing exclusive affiliation provisions and restricting the network from affiliating with other stations in the same area; the rights and obligations of stations with respect to network advertisers; the nature of the program service rendered by stations licensed to networks; the policies of networks with respect to character of programs, diversification, and accommodation to the particular requirements of the areas served by the affiliated stations; the extent to which affiliated stations exercise control over programs, advertising contracts, and related matters; the nature and extent of network program duplication by stations serving the same area; the extent to which particular networks have exclusive coverage in some areas; the competitive practices of stations engaged in chain broadcasting; the effect of chain broadcasting upon stations not licensed to or affiliated with networks; practices or agreements in restraint of trade, or in furtherance of monopoly, in connection with chain broadcasting; and the scope of concentration of control over stations, locally, regionally, or nationally, through contracts, common ownership, or other means.

On April 6, 1938, a committee of three Commissioners was designated to hold hearings and make recommendations to the full Commission. This committee held public hearings for 73 days over a period of six months, from November 14, 1938, to May 19, 1939. Order No. 37, announcing the investigation and specifying the particular matters which would be explored at the hearings, was published in the Federal Register, 3 Fed. Reg. 637, and copies were sent to every station licensee and network organization. Notices of the hearings were also sent to these parties. Station licensees, national and regional networks, and transcription and recording companies were invited to appear and give evidence. Other persons who sought to appear were afforded an opportunity

---

[1]Chain broadcasting is defined in § 3 (p) of the Communications Act of 1934 as the "simultaneous broadcasting of an identical program by two or more connected stations." In actual practice, programs are transmitted by wire, usually leased telephone lines, from their point of origin to each station in the network for simultaneous broadcast over the air.

to testify. 96 witnesses were heard by the committee, 45 of whom were called by the national networks. The evidence covers 27 volumes, including over 8,000 pages of transcript and more than 700 exhibits. The testimony of the witnesses called by the national networks fills more than 6,000 pages, the equivalent of 46 hearing days.

The committee submitted a report to the Commission on June 12, 1940, stating its findings and recommendations. Thereafter, briefs on behalf of the networks and other interested parties were filed before the full Commission, and on November 28, 1940, the Commission issued proposed regulations which the parties were requested to consider in the oral arguments held on December 2 and 3, 1940. These proposed regulations dealt with the same matters as those covered by the regulations eventually adopted by the Commission. On January 2, 1941, each of the national networks filed a supplementary brief discussing at length the questions raised by the committee report and the proposed regulations.

On May 2, 1941, the Commission issued its Report on Chain Broadcasting, setting forth its findings and conclusions upon the matters explored in the investigation, together with an order adopting the Regulations here assailed. Two of the seven members of the Commission dissented from this action. The effective date of the Regulations was deferred for 90 days with respect to existing contracts and arrangements of network-operated stations, and subsequently the effective date was thrice again postponed. On August 14, 1941, the Mutual Broadcasting Company petitioned the Commission to amend two of the Regulations. In considering this petition the Commission invited interested parties to submit their views. Briefs were filed on behalf of all of the national networks, and oral argument was had before the Commission on September 12, 1941. And on October 11, 1941, the Commission (again with two members dissenting) issued a Supplemental Report. together with an order amending three Regulations. Simultaneously, the effective date of the Regulations was postponed until November 15, 1941, and provision was made for further postponements from time to time if necessary to permit the orderly adjustment of existing arrangements. Since October 30, 1941, when the present suits were filed, the enforcement of the Regulations has been stayed either voluntarily by the Commission or by order of court.

Such is the history of the Chain Broadcasting Regulations. We turn now to the Regulations themselves, illumined by the practices in the radio industry disclosed by the Commission's investigation. The Regulations, which the Commission characterized in its Report as "the expression of the general policy we will follow in exercising our licensing power," are addressed in terms to station licensees and applicants for station licenses. They provide, in general, that no licenses shall be granted to stations or applicants having specified relationships with networks. Each Regulation is directed at a particular practice found by the Commission to be detrimental to the "public interest," and we shall consider them *seriatim*. In doing so, however, we do not overlook the admonition of the Commission that the Regulations as well as the network practices at which they are aimed are interrelated:

In considering above the network practices which necessitate the regulations we are adopting, we have taken each practice singly, and have shown that even in isolation each warrants the regulation addressed to it. But the various practices we have considered do not operate in isolation; they form a compact bundle or pattern, and the effect of their joint impact upon licensees necessitates the regulations even more urgently than the effect of each taken singly. (Report, p. 75.)

The Commission found that at the end of 1938 there were 660 commercial stations in the United States, and that 341 of these were affiliated with national networks. 135 stations were affiliated exclusively with the National Broadcasting Company, Inc., known in the industry as NBC, which operated two national networks, the "Red" and the "Blue." NBC was also the licensee of 10 stations, including 7 which operated on so-called clear channels with the maximum power available, 50 kilowatts; in addition, NBC operated 5 other stations, 4 of which had power of 50 kilowatts, under management contracts with their licensees. 102 stations were affiliated exclusively with the Columbia Broadcasting System, Inc., which was also the licensee of 8 stations, 7 of which were clear-channel stations operating with power of 50 kilowatts. 74 stations were under exclusive affiliation with the Mutual Broadcasting System, Inc. In addition, 25 stations were affiliated with both NBC and Mutual, and 5 with both CBS and Mutual. These figures, the Commission noted, did not accurately reflect the relative prominence of the three companies, since the stations affiliated with Mutual were, generally speaking, less desirable in frequency, power, and coverage. It pointed out that the stations affiliated with the national networks utilized more than 97% of the total night-time broadcasting power of all the stations in the country. NBC and CBS together controlled more than 85% of the total night-time wattage, and the broadcast business of the three national network companies amounted to almost half of the total business of all stations in the United States.

The Commission recognized that network broadcasting had played and was continuing to play an important part in the development of radio.

The growth and development of chain broadcasting [it stated], found its impetus in the desire to give widespread coverage to programs which otherwise would not be heard beyond the reception area of a single station. Chain broadcasting makes possible a wider reception for expensive entertainment and cultural programs and also for programs of national or regional significance which would otherwise have coverage only in the locality of origin. Furthermore, the access to greatly enlarged audiences made possible by chain broadcasting has been a strong incentive to advertisers to finance the production of expensive programs. . . . But the fact that the chain broadcasting method brings benefits and advantages to both the listening public and to broadcast station licensees does not mean that the prevailing practices and policies of the networks and their outlets are sound in all respects, or that they should not be altered. The Commission's duty under the Communications Act of 1934 is not only to see that the public receives the advantages and benefits of chain broadcasting, but also, so far as its powers enable it, to see that practices which adversely affect the ability of licensees to operate in the public interest are eliminated. (Report, p. 4.)

The Commission found that eight network abuses were amenable to correction within the powers granted it by Congress:

Regulation 3.101 – Exclusive affiliation of station.   The Commission found that the network affiliation agreements of NBC and CBS customarily contained a provision which prevented the station from broadcasting the programs of any other network. The effect of this provision was to hinder the growth of new networks, to deprive the listening public in many areas of service to which they were entitled, and to prevent station licensees from exercising their statutory duty of determining which programs would best serve the needs of their community. The Commission observed that in areas where all the stations were under exclusive contract to either NBC or CBS, the public was deprived of the opportunity to hear programs presented by Mutual. To take a case cited in the Report: In the fall of 1939 Mutual obtained the exclusive right to broadcast the World Series baseball games. It offered this program of outstanding national interest to stations throughout the country, including NBC and CBS affiliates in communities having no other stations. CBS and NBC immediately invoked the "exclusive affiliation" clauses of their agreements with these stations, and as a result thousands of persons in many sections of the country were unable to hear the broadcasts of the games.

Restraints having this effect [the Commission observed], are to be condemned as contrary to the public interest irrespective of whether it be assumed that Mutual programs are of equal, superior, or inferior quality. The important consideration is that station licensees are denied freedom to choose the programs which they believe best suited to their needs; in this manner the duty of a station licensee to operate in the public interest is defeated. . . . Our conclusion is that the disadvantages resulting from these exclusive arrangements far outweigh any advantages. A licensee station does not operate in the public interest when it enters into exclusive arrangements which prevent it from giving the public the best service of which it is capable, and which, by closing the door of opportunity in the network field, adversely affects the program structure of the entire industry. (Report, pp. 52, 57.)

Accordingly, the Commission adopted Regulation 3.101, providing as follows:

No license shall be granted to a standard broadcast station having any contract, arrangement, or understanding, express or implied, with a network organization under which the station is prevented or hindered from, or penalized for, broadcasting the programs of any other network organization.

Regulation 3.102 – Territorial exclusivity.   The Commission found another type of "exclusivity" provision in network affiliation agreements whereby the network bound itself not to sell programs to any other station in the same area. The effect of this provision, designed to protect the affiliate from the competition of other stations serving the same territory, was to deprive the listening public of many programs that might otherwise be available. If an affiliated station rejected a network program, the "territorial exclusivity" clause of its affiliation agreement prevented the network from offering the program to other stations in the area. For example, Mutual presented a popular program, known as "The American Forum of the Air," in which prominent persons discussed topics of general interest. None of the Mutual stations in the Buffalo area decided to carry the program, and a Buffalo station not affiliated with Mutual attempted to obtain the program for its listeners. These efforts failed, however, on account of the "territorial exclusivity" provision in Mutual's agreements with its outlets. The result was that this program was not available to the people of Buffalo.

The Commission concluded that

It is not in the public interest for the listening audience in an area to be deprived of network programs not carried by one station where other stations in that area are ready and willing to broadcast the programs. It is as much against the public interest for a network affiliate to enter into a contractual arrangement which prevents another station from carrying a network program as it would be for it to drown out that program by electrical interference. (Report, p. 59.)

Recognizing that the "territorial exclusivity" clause was unobjectionable in so far as it sought to prevent duplication of programs in the same area, the Commission limited itself to the situations in which the clause impaired the ability of the licensee to broadcast available programs. Regulation 3.102, promulgated to remedy this particular evil, provides as follows:

No license shall be granted to a standard broadcast station having any contract, arrangement, or understanding, express or implied, with a network organization which prevents or hinders another station serving substantially the same area from broadcasting the network's programs not taken by the former station, or which prevents or hinders another station serving a substantially different area from broadcasting any program of the network organization. This regulation shall not be construed to prohibit any contract, arrangement, or understanding between a station and a network organization pursuant to which the station is granted the first call in its primary service area upon the programs of the network organization.

Regulation 3.103 – Term of affiliation.   The standard NBC and CBS affiliation contracts bound the station for a period of five years, with the network having the exclusive right to terminate the contracts upon one year's notice. The Commission, relying upon § 307(d) of the Communications Act of 1934, under which no license to operate a broadcast station can be granted for a longer term than three years, found the five-year affiliation term to be contrary to the policy of the Act:

Regardless of any changes that may occur in the economic, political, or social life of the Nation or of the community in which the station is located, CBS and NBC affiliates are bound by contract to continue broadcasting the network programs of only one network for 5 years. The licensee is so bound even though the policy and caliber of programs of the network may deteriorate greatly. The future necessities of the station and of the community are not considered. The station licensee is unable to follow his conception of the public interest until the end of the 5-year contract. (Report, p. 61.)

The Commission concluded that under contracts binding the affiliates for five years, "stations become parties to arrangements which deprive the public of the improved service it might otherwise derive from competition in the network field; and that a station is not operating in the public interest when it so limits its freedom of action." (Report, p. 62.) Accordingly, the Commission adopted Regulation 3.103:

No license shall be granted to a standard broadcast station having any contract, arrangement, or understanding, express or implied, with a network organization which provides, by original term, provisions for renewal, or otherwise for the affiliation of the station with the network organization for a period longer than two years:[2] *Provided,* That a contract, arrangement, or understanding for a period up to two years, may be entered into within 120 days prior to the commencement of such period.

Regulation 3.104 – Option time.   The Commission found that network affiliation contracts usually contained so-called network optional time clauses. Under these provisions the network could upon 28 days' notice call upon its affiliates to carry a commercial program during any of the hours specified in the agreement as "network optional time." For CBS affiliates "network optional time" meant the entire broadcast day. For 29 outlets of NBC on the Pacific Coast, it also covered the entire broadcast day; for substantially all of the other NBC affiliates, it included 8½ hours on weekdays and 8 hours on Sundays. Mutual's contracts with about half of its affiliates contained such a

---

[2] Station licenses issued by the Commission normally last two years. Section 3.34 of the Commission's Rules and Regulations governing Standard and High-Frequency Broadcast Stations, as amended October 14, 1941.

provision, giving the network optional time for 3 or 4 hours on weekdays and 6 hours on Sundays.

In the Commission's judgment these optional time provisions, in addition to imposing serious obstacles in the path of new networks, hindered stations in developing a local program service. The exercise by the networks of their options over the station's time tended to prevent regular scheduling of local programs at desirable hours. The Commission found that

shifting a local commercial program may seriously interfere with the efforts of a [local] sponsor to build up a regular listening audience at a definite hour, and the long-term advertising contract becomes a highly dubious project. This hampers the efforts of the station to develop local commercial programs and affects adversely its ability to give the public good program service. . . . A station licensee must retain sufficient freedom of action to supply the program and advertising needs of the local community. Local program service is a vital part of community life. A station should be ready, able, and willing to serve the needs of the local community by broadcasting such outstanding local events as community concerts, civic meetings, local sports events, and other programs of local consumer and social interest. We conclude that national network time options have restricted the freedom of station licensees and hampered their efforts to broadcast local commercial programs, the programs of other national networks, and national spot transcriptions. We believe that these considerations far outweigh any supposed advantages from "stability" of network operations under time options. We find that the optioning of time by licensee stations has operated against the public interest. (Report, pp. 63, 65.)

The Commission undertook to preserve the advantages of option time, as a device for "stabilizing" the industry, without unduly impairing the ability of local stations to develop local program service. Regulation 3.104 called for the modification of the option-time provision in three respects: the minimum notice period for exercise of the option could not be less than 56 days; the number of hours which could be optioned was limited; and specific restrictions were placed upon exercise of the option to the disadvantage of other networks. The text of the Regulation follows:

No license shall be granted to a standard broadcast station which options for network programs any time subject to call on less than 56 days' notice, or more time than a total of three hours within each of four segments of the broadcast day, as herein described. The broadcast day is divided into 4 segments, as follows: 8:00 a.m. to 1:00 p.m.; 1:00 p.m. to 6:00 p.m.; 6:00 p.m. to 11:00 p.m.; 11:00 p.m. to 8:00 a.m. Such options may not be exclusive as against other network organizations and may not prevent or hinder the station from optioning or selling any or all of the time covered by the option, or other time, to other network organizations.

Regulation 3.105 – Right to reject programs.   The Commission found that most network affiliation contracts contained a clause defining the right of the station to reject network commercial programs. The NBC contracts provided simply that the station "may reject a network program the broadcasting of which would not be in the public interest, convenience, and necessity." NBC required a licensee who rejected a program to "be able to support his contention that what he has done has been more in the public interest than had he carried on the network program." Similarly, the CBS contracts provided that if the station had "reasonable objection to any sponsored program or the product advertised thereon as not being in the public interest, the station may, on 3 weeks' prior notice thereof to Columbia, refuse to broadcast such program, unless during such notice period such reasonable objection of the station shall be satisfied."

While seeming in the abstract to be fair, these provisions, according to the Commission's finding, did not sufficiently protect the "public interest." As a practical matter, the licensee could not determine in advance whether the broadcasting of any particular network program would or would not be in the public interest.

It is obvious that from such skeletal information [as the networks submitted to the stations prior to the broadcasts] the station cannot determine in advance whether the program is in the public interest, nor can it ascertain whether or not parts of the program are in one way or another offensive. In practice, if not in theory, stations affiliated with networks have delegated to the networks a large part of their programming functions. In many instances, moreover, the network further delegates the actual production of programs to advertising agencies. These agencies are far more than mere brokers or intermediaries between the network and the advertiser. To an ever-increasing extent, these agencies actually exercise the function of program production. Thus it is frequently neither the station nor the network, but rather the advertising agency, which determines what broadcast programs shall contain. Under such circumstances, it is especially important that individual stations, if they are to operate in the public interest, should have the practical opportunity as well as the contractual right to reject network programs. . . .

It is the station, not the network, which is licensed to serve the public interest. The licensee has the duty of determining what programs shall be broadcast over his station's facilities, and cannot lawfully delegate this duty or transfer the control of his station directly to the network or indirectly to an advertising agency. He cannot lawfully bind himself to accept programs in every case where he cannot sustain the burden of proof that he has a better program. The licensee is obliged to reserve to himself the final decision as to what programs will best serve the public interest. We conclude that a licensee is not fulfilling his obligations to operate in the public interest, and is not operating in accordance with the express requirements of the Communications Act, if he agrees to accept programs on any basis other than his own reasonable decision that the programs are satisfactory. (Report, pp. 39, 66.)

The Commission undertook in Regulation 3.105 to formulate the obligations of licensees with respect to supervision over programs:

No license shall be granted to a standard broadcast station having any contract, arrangement, or understanding, express or implied, with a network organization which (a), with respect to programs offered pursuant to an affiliation contract, prevents or hinders the station from rejecting or refusing network programs which the station reasonably believes to be unsatisfactory or unsuitable; or which (b), with respect to network programs so offered or already contracted for, prevents the station from rejecting or refusing any program which, in its opinion, is contrary to the public interest, or from substituting a program of outstanding local or national importance.

Regulation 3.106 – Network ownership of stations.   The Commission found that NBC, in addition to its network operations, was the licensee of 10 stations, 2 each in New York, Chicago, Washington, and San Francisco, 1 in Denver, and 1 in Cleveland. CBS was the licensee of 8 stations, 1 in each of these cities: New York, Chicago, Washington, Boston, Minneapolis, St. Louis, Charlotte, and Los Angeles. These 18 stations owned by NBC and CBS, the Commission observed, were among the most powerful and desirable in the country, and were permanently inaccessible to competing networks.

Competition among networks for these facilities is nonexistent, as they are completely removed from the network-station market. It gives the network complete control over its policies. This "bottling-up" of the best facilities has undoubtedly had a discouraging effect upon the creation and growth of new networks. Furthermore, common ownership of network and station places the network in a position where its interest as the owner of certain stations may conflict with its interest as a network organization serving affiliated stations. In dealings with advertisers, the network represents its own stations in a proprietary capacity and the affiliated stations in something akin to an agency capacity. The danger is present that the network organization will give preference to its own stations at the expense of its affiliates. (Report, p. 67.)

The Commission stated that if the question had arisen as an original matter, it might well have concluded that the public interest required severance of the business of station ownership from that of network operation. But since substantial business interests have been formed on the basis of the Commission's continued tolerance of the situation, it was found inadvisable to take such a drastic step. The Commission concluded, however, that "the licensing of two stations in the same area to a single network organization is basically unsound and contrary to the public interest," and that it was also against the "public interest" for network organizations to own stations in areas where the available facilities were so few or of such unequal coverage that competition would thereby be substantially restricted. Recognizing that these considerations called for flexibility in their application to particular situations, the Commission provided that "networks will be given full opportunity, on proper application for new facilities or renewal of existing licenses, to call to our attention any reasons why the principle should be modified or held inapplicable." (Report, p. 68.) Regulation 3.106 reads as follows:

No license shall be granted to a network organization, or to any person directly or indirectly controlled by or under common control with a network organization, for more than one standard broadcast station where one of the stations covers substantially the service area of the other station, or for any standard broadcast station in any locality where the existing standard broadcast stations are so few or of such unequal desirability (in terms of coverage, power, frequency, or other related matters) that competition would be substantially restrained by such licensing.

Regulation 3.107 – Dual network operation.   This regulation provides that: "No license shall be issued to a standard broadcast station affiliated with a network organization which maintains more than one network: *Provided*, That this regulation shall not be applicable if such networks are not operated simultaneously, or if there is no substantial overlap in the territory served by the group of stations comprising each such network." In its Supplemental Report of October 11, 1941, the Commission announced the indefinite suspension of this regulation. There is no occasion here to consider the validity of Regulation 3.107, since there is no immediate threat of its enforcement by the Commission.

Regulation 3.108 – Control by networks of station rates.   The Commission found that NBC's affiliation contracts contained a provision empowering the network to reduce the station's network rate, and thereby to reduce the compensation received by the station, if the station set a lower rate for non-network national advertising than the rate established by the contract for the network programs. Under this provision the station could not sell time to a national advertiser for less than it would cost the advertiser if he bought the time from NBC. In the words of NBC's vice-president, "This means simply that a national advertiser should pay the same price for the station whether he buys it through one source or another source. It means that we do not believe that our stations should go into competition with ourselves." (Report, p. 73.)

The Commission concluded that "it is against the public interest for a station licensee to enter into a contract with a network which has the effect of decreasing its ability to compete for national business. We believe that the public interest will best be served and listeners supplied with the best programs if stations bargain freely with national advertisers." (Report, p. 75.) Accordingly, the Commission adopted Regulation 3.108, which provides as follows:

No license shall be granted to a standard broadcast station having any contract, arrangement, or understanding, express or implied, with a network organization under which the station is prevented or hindered from, or penalized for, fixing or altering its rates for the sale of broadcast time for other than the network's programs.

The appellants attack the validity of these Regulations along many fronts. They contend that the Commission went beyond the regulatory powers conferred upon it by the Communications Act of 1934; that even if the Commission were authorized by the Act to deal with the matters comprehended by the Regulations, its action is nevertheless invalid because the Commission misconceived the scope of the Act, particularly § 313 which deals with the application of the anti-trust laws to the radio industry; that the Regulations are arbitrary and capricious; that if the Communications Act of 1934 were construed to authorize the promulgation of the Regulations, it would be an unconstitutional delegation of legislative power; and that, in any event, the Regulations abridge the appellants' right of free speech in violation of the First Amendment. We are thus called upon to determine whether Congress has authorized the Commission to exercise the power asserted by the Chain Broadcasting Regulations, and if it has, whether the Constitution forbids the exercise of such authority.

Federal regulation of radio[3] begins with the Wireless Ship Act of June 24, 1910, 36 Stat. 629, which forbade any steamer carrying or licensed to carry fifty or more persons to leave any American port unless equipped with efficient apparatus for radio communication, in charge of a skilled operator. The enforcement of this legislation was entrusted to the Secretary of Commerce and Labor, who was in charge of the administration of the marine navigation laws. But it was not until 1912, when the United States ratified the first international radio treaty, 37 Stat. 1565, that the need for general regulation of radio communication became urgent. In order to fulfill our obligations under the treaty, Congress enacted the Radio Act of August 13, 1912, 37 Stat. 302. This statute forbade the operation of radio apparatus without a license from the Secretary of Commerce and Labor; it also allocated certain frequencies for the use of the Government, and imposed restrictions upon the character of wave emissions, the transmission of distress signals, and the like.

The enforcement of the Radio Act of 1912 presented no serious problems prior to the World War. Questions of interference arose only rarely because there

---

[3]The history of federal regulation of radio communication is summarized in Herring and Gross, Telecommunications (1936) 239-86; Administrative Procedure in Government Agencies, Monograph of the Attorney General's Committee on Administrative Procedure, Sen. Doc. No. 186, 76th Cong., 3d Sess., Part 3, dealing with the Federal Communications Commission, pp. 82-84; 1 Socolow, Law of Radio Broadcasting (1939) 38-61; Donovan, Origin and Development of Radio Law (1930).

were more than enough frequencies for all the stations then in existence. The war accelerated the development of the art, however, and in 1921 the first standard broadcast stations were established. They grew rapidly in number, and by 1923 there were several hundred such stations throughout the country. The Act of 1912 had not set aside any particular frequencies for the use of private broadcast stations; consequently, the Secretary of Commerce selected two frequencies, 750 and 833 kilocycles, and licensed all stations to operate upon one or the other of these channels. The number of stations increased so rapidly, however, and the situation became so chaotic, that the Secretary, upon the recommendation of the National Radio Conferences which met in Washington in 1923 and 1924, established a policy of assigning specified frequencies to particular stations. The entire radio spectrum was divided into numerous bands, each allocated to a particular kind of service. The frequencies ranging from 550 to 1500 kilocycles (96 channels in all, since the channels were separated from each other by 10 kilocycles) were assigned to the standard broadcast stations. But the problems created by the enormously rapid development of radio were far from solved. The increase in the number of channels was not enough to take care of the constantly growing number of stations. Since there were more stations than available frequencies, the Secretary of Commerce attempted to find room for everybody by limiting the power and hours of operation of stations in order that several stations might use the same channel. The number of stations multiplied so rapidly, however, that by November, 1925, there were almost 600 stations in the country, and there were 175 applications for new stations. Every channel in the standard broadcast band was, by that time, already occupied by at least one station, and many by several. The new stations could be accommodated only by extending the standard broadcast band, at the expense of the other types of services, or by imposing still greater limitations upon time and power. The National Radio Conference which met in November, 1925, opposed both of these methods and called upon Congress to remedy the situation through legislation.

The Secretary of Commerce was powerless to deal with the situation. It had been held that he could not deny a license to an otherwise legally qualified applicant on the ground that the proposed station would interfere with existing private or Government stations. *Hoover* v. *Intercity Radio Co.*, 52 App. D.C. 339, 286 F. 1003. And on April 16, 1926, an Illinois district court held that the Secretary had no power to impose restrictions as to frequency, power, and hours of operation, and that a station's use of a frequency not assigned to it was not a violation of the Radio Act of 1912. *United States* v. *Zenith Radio Corp.*, 12 F. 2d 614. This was followed on July 8, 1926, by an opinion of Acting Attorney General Donovan that the Secretary of Commerce had no power, under the Radio Act of 1912, to regulate the power, frequency or hours of operation of stations. 35 Ops. Atty. Gen. 126. The next day the Secretary of Commerce issued a statement abandoning all his efforts to regulate radio and urging that the stations undertake self-regulation.

But the plea of the Secretary went unheeded. From July, 1926, to February 23, 1927, when Congress enacted the Radio Act of 1927, 44 Stat. 1162, almost 200 new stations went on the air. These new stations used any frequencies they desired, regardless of the interference thereby caused to others. Existing stations changed to other frequencies and increased their power and hours of operation at will. The result was confusion and chaos. With everybody on the air, nobody could he heard. The situation became so intolerable that the President in his message of December 7, 1926, appealed to Congress to enact a comprehensive radio law:

Due to the decisions of the courts, the authority of the department [of Commerce] under the law of 1912 has broken down; many more stations have been operating than can be accommodated within the limited number of wave lengths available; further stations are in course of construction; many stations have departed from the scheme of allocations set down by the department, and the whole service of this most important public function has drifted into such chaos as seems likely, if not remedied, to destroy its great value. I most urgently recommend that this legislation should be speedily enacted. (H. Doc. 483, 69th Cong., 2d Sess., p. 10.)

The plight into which radio fell prior to 1927 was attributable to certain basic facts about radio as a means of communication — its facilities are limited; they are not available to all who may wish to use them; the radio spectrum simply is not large enough to accommodate everybody. There is a fixed natural limitation upon the number of stations that can operate without interfering with one another.[4] Regulation of radio was therefore as vital to its development as traffic control was to the development of the automobile. In enacting the Radio Act of 1927, the first comprehensive scheme of control over radio communication, Congress acted upon the knowledge that if the potentialities of radio were not to be wasted, regulation was essential.

The Radio Act of 1927 created the Federal Radio Commission, composed of five members, and endowed the Commission with wide licensing and regulatory powers. We do not pause here to enumerate the scope of the Radio Act of 1927 and of the authority entrusted to the Radio Commission, for the basic provisions of that Act are incorporated in the Communications Act of 1934, 48 Stat. 1064, 47 U.S.C. § 151 *et seq.*, the legislation immediately before us. As we noted in *Federal Communications Comm'n* v. *Pottsville Broadcasting Co.*, 309 U.S. 134, 137,

In its essentials the Communications Act of 1934 [so far as its provisions relating to radio are concerned] derives from the Federal Radio Act of 1927. . . . By this Act Congress, in order to protect the national interest involved in the new and

---

[4] See Morecroft, Principles of Radio Communication (3d ed. 1933) 355-402; Terman, Radio Engineering (2d ed. 1937) 593-645.

far-reaching science of broadcasting, formulated a unified and comprehensive regulatory system for the industry. The common factors in the administration of the various statutes by which Congress had supervised the different modes of communication led to the creation, in the Act of 1934, of the Communications Commission. But the objectives of the legislation have remained substantially unaltered since 1927.

Section 1 of the Communications Act states its "purpose of regulating interstate and foreign commerce in communication by wire and radio so as to make available, so far as possible, to all the people of the United States a rapid, efficient, Nation-wide, and world-wide wire and radio communication service with adequate facilities at reasonable charges." Section 301 particularizes this general purpose with respect to radio:

It is the purpose of this Act, among other things, to maintain the control of the United States over all the channels of interstate and foreign radio transmission; and to provide for the use of such channels, but not the ownership thereof, by persons for limited periods of time, under licenses granted by Federal authority, and no such license shall be construed to create any right, beyond the terms, conditions, and periods of the license.

To that end a Commission composed of seven members was created, with broad licensing and regulatory powers.

Section 303 provides:

Except as otherwise provided in this Act, the Commission from time to time, as public convenience, interest, or necessity requires, shall—

(a)   Classify radio stations;

(b)   Prescribe the nature of the service to be rendered by each class of licensed stations and each station within any class; . . .

(f)   Make such regulations not inconsistent with law as it may deem necessary to prevent interference between stations and to carry out the provisions of this Act . . . ;

(g)   Study new uses for radio, provide for experimental uses of frequencies, and generally encourage the larger and more effective use of radio in the public interest; . . .

(i)   Have authority to make special regulations applicable to radio stations engaged in chain broadcasting; . . .

(r)   Make such rules and regulations and prescribe such restrictions and conditions, not inconsistent with law, as may be necessary to carry out the provisions of this Act. . . .

The criterion governing the exercise of the Commission's licensing power is the "public interest, convenience, or necessity." § § 307(a)(d), 309(a), 310, 312. In addition, § 307(b) directs the Commission that

In considering applications for licenses, and modifications and renewals thereof, when and insofar as there is demand for the same, the Commission shall make such distribution of licenses, frequencies, hours of operation, and of power among the several States and communities as to provide a fair, efficient, and equitable distribution of radio service to each of the same.

The Act itself establishes that the Commission's powers are not limited to the engineering and technical aspects of regulation of radio communication. Yet we are asked to regard the Commission as a kind of traffic officer, policing the wave lengths to prevent stations from interfering with each other. But the Act does not restrict the Commission merely to supervision of the traffic. It puts upon the Commission the burden of determining the composition of that traffic. The facilities of radio are not large enough to accommodate all who wish to use them. Methods must be devised for choosing from among the many who apply. And since Congress itself could not do this, it committed the task to the Commission.

The Commission was, however, not left at large in performing this duty. The touchstone provided by Congress was the "public interest, convenience, or necessity," a criterion which "is as concrete as the complicated factors for judgment in such a field of delegated authority permit." *Federal Communications Comm'n* v. *Pottsville Broadcasting Co.*, 309 U.S. 134, 138. "This criterion is not to be interpreted as setting up a standard so indefinite as to confer an unlimited power. Compare *New York Central Securities Co.* v. *United States*, 287 U.S. 12, 24. The requirement is to be interpreted by its context, by the nature of radio transmission and reception, by the scope, character and quality of services . . ." *Federal Radio Comm'n* v. *Nelson Bros. Co.*, 289 U.S. 266, 285.

The "public interest" to be served under the Communications Act is thus the interest of the listening public in "the larger and more effective use of radio." § 303(g). The facilities of radio are limited and therefore precious; they cannot be left to wasteful use without detriment to the public interest. "An important element of public interest and convenience affecting the issue of a license is the ability of the licensee to render the best practicable service to the community reached by his broadcasts." *Federal Communications Comm'n* v. *Sanders Radio Station*, 309 U.S. 470, 475. The Commission's licensing function cannot be discharged, therefore, merely by finding that there are no technological objections to the granting of a license. If the criterion of "public interest" were limited to such matters, how could the Commission choose between two applicants for the same facilities, each of whom is financially and technically qualified to operate a station? Since the very inception of federal regulation of radio, comparative considerations as to the services to be rendered have governed the application of the standard of "public interest, convenience, or necessity." See *Federal Communications Comm'n* v. *Pottsville Broadcasting Co.*, 309 U.S. 134, 138 n. 2.

The avowed aim of the Communications Act of 1934 was to secure the maximum benefits of radio to all the people of the United States. To that end Congress endowed the Communications Commission with comprehensive powers to promote and realize the vast potentialities of radio. Section 303(g) provides that the Commission shall "generally encourage the larger and more effective use of radio in the public interest"; subsection (i) gives the Commission specific "authority to make special regulations applicable to radio stations engaged in chain broadcasting"; and subsection (r) empowers it to adopt "such rules and regulations and prescribe such restrictions and conditions, not inconsistent with law, as may be necessary to carry out the provisions of this Act."

These provisions, individually and in the aggregate, preclude the notion that the Commission is empowered to deal only with technical and engineering impediments to the "larger and more effective use of radio in the public interest." We cannot find in the Act any such restriction of the Commission's authority. Suppose, for example, that a community can, because of physical limitations, be assigned only two stations. That community might be deprived of effective service in any one of several ways. More powerful stations in nearby cities might blanket out the signals of the local stations so that they could not be heard at all. The stations might interfere with each other so that neither could be clearly heard. One station might dominate the other with the power of its signal. But the community could be deprived of good radio service in ways less crude. One man, financially and technically qualified, might apply for and obtain the licenses of both stations and present a single service over the two stations, thus wasting a frequency otherwise available to the area. The language of the Act does not withdraw such a situation from the licensing and regulatory powers of the Commission, and there is no evidence that Congress did not mean its broad language to carry the authority it expresses.

In essence, the Chain Broadcasting Regulations represent a particularization of the Commission's conception of the "public interest" sought to be safeguarded by Congress in enacting the Communications Act of 1934. The basic consideration of policy underlying the Regulations is succinctly stated in its Report:

With the number of radio channels limited by natural factors, the public interest demands that those who are entrusted with the available channels shall make the fullest and most effective use of them. If a licensee enters into a contract with a network organization which limits his ability to make the best use of the radio facility assigned him, he is not serving the public interest. . . . The net effect [of the practices disclosed by the investigation] has been that broadcasting service has been maintained at a level below that possible under a system of free competition. Having so found, we would be remiss in our statutory duty of encouraging "the larger and more effective use of radio in the public interest" if we were to grant licenses to persons who persist in these practices. (Report, pp. 81, 82.)

We would be asserting our personal views regarding the effective utilization of radio were we to deny that the Commission was entitled to find that the large public aims of the Communications Act of 1934 comprehend the considerations which moved the Commission in promulgating the Chain Broadcasting Regulations. True enough, the Act does not explicitly say that the Commission shall have power to deal with network practices found inimical to the public interest. But Congress was acting in a field of regulation which was both new and dynamic. "Congress moved under the spur of a widespread fear that in the absence of governmental control the public interest might be subordinated to monopolistic domination in the broadcasting field." *Federal Communications Comm'n v. Pottsville Broadcasting Co.*, 309 U.S. 134, 137. In the context of the developing problems to which it was directed, the Act gave the Commission not niggardly but expansive powers. It was given a comprehensive mandate to "encourage the larger and more effective use of radio in the public interest," if need be, by making "special regulations applicable to radio stations engaged in chain broadcasting." § 303(g)(i).

Generalities unrelated to the living problems of radio communication of course cannot justify exercises of power by the Commission. Equally so, generalities empty of all concrete considerations of the actual bearing of regulations promulgated by the Commission to the subject-matter entrusted to it, cannot strike down exercises of power by the Commission. While Congress did not give the Commission unfettered discretion to regulate all phases of the radio industry, it did not frustrate the purposes for which the Communications Act of 1934 was brought into being by attempting an itemized catalogue of the specific manifestations of the general problems for the solution of which it was establishing a regulatory agency. That would have stereotyped the powers of the Commission to specific details in regulating a field of enterprise the dominant characteristic of which was the rapid pace of its unfolding. And so Congress did what experience had taught it in similar attempts at regulation, even in fields where the subject-matter of regulation was far less fluid and dynamic than radio. The essence of that experience was to define broad areas for regulation and to establish standards for judgment adequately related in their application to the problems to be solved.

For the cramping construction of the Act pressed upon us, support cannot be found in its legislative history. The principal argument is that § 303(i), empowering the Commission "to make special regulations applicable to radio stations engaged in chain broadcasting," intended to restrict the scope of the Commission's powers to the technical and engineering aspects of chain broadcasting. This provision comes from § 4(h) of the Radio Act of 1927. It was introduced into the legislation as a Senate committee amendment to the House bill. (H. R. 9971, 69th Cong., 1st Sess.) This amendment originally read as follows:

(C) The commission, from time to time, as public convenience, interest, or necessity requires, shall— . . .

(j) When stations are connected by wire for chain broadcasting, determine the power each station shall use and the wave lengths to be used during the time stations are so connected and so operated, and make all other regulations necessary in the interest of equitable radio service to the listeners in the communities or areas affected by chain broadcasting.

The report of the Senate Committee on Interstate Commerce, which submitted this amendment, stated that under the bill the Commission was given "complete authority . . . to control chain broadcasting." Sen. Rep. No. 772, 69th Cong., 1st Sess., p. 3. The bill as thus amended was passed by the Senate, and then sent to conference. The bill that emerged from the conference committee, and which became the Radio Act of 1927, phrased the amendment in the general terms now contained in § 303(i) of the 1934 Act: the Commission was authorized "to make special regulations applicable to radio stations engaged in chain broadcasting." The conference reports do not give any explanation of this particular change in phrasing, but they do state that the jurisdiction conferred upon the Commission by the conference bill was substantially identical with that conferred by the bill passed by the Senate. See Sen. Doc. No. 200, 69th Cong., 2d Sess., p.17; H. Rep. 1886, 69th Cong., 2d Sess., p. 17. We agree with the District Court that in view of this legislative history, § 303(i) cannot be construed as no broader than the first clause of the Senate amendment, which limited the Commission's authority to the technical and engineering phases of chain broadcasting. There is no basis for assuming that the conference intended to preserve the first clause, which was of limited scope, by agreeing upon a provision which was broader and more comprehensive than those it supplanted.[5]

A totally different source of attack upon the Regulations is found in §

---

[5]In the course of the Senate debates on the conference report upon the bill that became the Radio Act of 1927, Senator Dill, who was in charge of the bill, said: "While the commission would have the power under the general terms of the bill, the bill specifically sets out as one of the special powers of the commission the right to make specific regulations for governing chain broadcasting. As to creating a monopoly of radio in this country, let me say that this bill absolutely protects the public, so far as it can protect them, by giving the commission full power to refuse a license to anyone who it believes will not serve the public interest, convenience, or necessity. It specifically provides that any corporation guilty of monopoly shall not only not receive a license but that its license may be revoked; and if after a corporation has received its license for a period of three years it is then discovered and found to be guilty of monopoly, its license will be revoked. . . . In addition to that, the bill contains a provision that no license may be transferred from one owner to another without the written consent of the commission, and the commission, of course, having the power to protect against a monopoly, must give such protection. I wish to state further that the only way by which monopolies in the radio business can secure control of radio here, even for a limited period of time, will be by the commission becoming servile to them. Power must be lodged somewhere, and I myself am unwilling to assume in advance that the commission proposed to be created will be servile to the desires and demands of great corporations of this country." 68 Cong. Rec. 2881.

311 of the Act, which authorizes the Commission to withhold licenses from persons convicted of having violated the anti-trust laws. Two contentions are made — first, that this provision puts considerations relating to competition outside the Commission's concern before an applicant has been convicted of monopoly or other restraints of trade, and second, that, in any event, the Commission misconceived the scope of its powers under § 311 in issuing the Regulations. Both of these contentions are unfounded. Section 311 derives from § 13 of the Radio Act of 1927, which expressly commanded, rather than merely authorized, the Commission to refuse a license to any person judicially found guilty of having violated the anti-trust laws. The change in the 1934 Act was made, in the words of Senator Dill, the manager of the legislation in the Senate, because "it seemed fair to the committee to do that." 78 Cong. Rec. 8825. The Commission was thus permitted to exercise its judgment as to whether violation of the anti-trust laws disqualified an applicant from operating a station in the "public interest." We agree with the District Court that "The necessary implication from this [amendment in 1934] was that the Commission might infer from the fact that the applicant had in the past tried to monopolize radio, or had engaged in unfair methods of competition, that the disposition so manifested would continue and that if it did it would make him an unfit licensee." 47 F. Supp. 940, 944.

That the Commission may refuse to grant a license to persons adjudged guilty in a court of law of conduct in violation of the anti-trust laws certainly does not render irrelevant consideration by the Commission of the effect of such conduct upon the "public interest, convenience, or necessity." A licensee charged with practices in contravention of this standard cannot continue to hold his license merely because his conduct is also in violation of the anti-trust laws and he has not yet been proceeded against and convicted. By clarifying in § 311 the scope of the Commission's authority in dealing with persons convicted of violating the anti-trust laws, Congress can hardly be deemed to have limited the concept of "public interest" so as to exclude all considerations relating to monopoly and unreasonable restraints upon commerce. Nothing in the provisions or history of the Act lends support to the inference that the Commission was denied the power to refuse a license to a station not operating in the "public interest," merely because its misconduct happened to be an unconvicted violation of the anti-trust laws.

Alternatively, it is urged that the Regulations constitute an *ultra vires* attempt by the Commission to enforce the anti-trust laws, and that the enforcement of the anti-trust laws is the province not of the Commission but of the Attorney General and the courts. This contention misconceives the basis of the Commission's action. The Commission's Report indicates plainly enough that the Commission was not attempting to administer the anti-trust laws:

The prohibitions of the Sherman Act apply to broadcasting. This Commission, although not charged with the duty of enforcing that law, should administer its regulatory powers with respect to broadcasting in the light of the purposes which the Sherman Act was designed to achieve. . . . While many of the network practices raise serious questions under the antitrust laws, our jurisdiction does not depend on a showing that they do in fact constitute a violation of the antitrust laws. It is not our function to apply the antitrust laws as such. It is our duty, however, to refuse licenses or renewals to any person who engages or proposes to engage in practices which will prevent either himself or other licensees or both from making the fullest use of radio facilities. This is the standard of public interest, convenience or necessity which we must apply to all applications for licenses and renewals. . . . We do not predicate our jurisdiction to issue the regulations on the ground that the network practices violate the antitrust laws. We are issuing these regulations because we have found that the network practices prevent the maximum utilization of radio facilities in the public interest. (Report, pp. 46, 83, 83 n. 3.)

We conclude, therefore, that the Communications Act of 1934 authorized the Commission to promulgate regulations designed to correct the abuses disclosed by its investigation of chain broadcasting. There remains for consideration the claim that the Commission's exercise of such authority was unlawful.

The Regulations are assailed as "arbitrary and capricious." If this contention means that the Regulations are unwise, that they are not likely to succeed in accomplishing what the Commission intended, we can say only that the appellants have selected the wrong forum for such a plea. What was said in *Board of Trade* v. *United States*, 314 U.S. 534, 548, is relevant here: "We certainly have neither technical competence nor legal authority to pronounce upon the wisdom of the course taken by the Commission." Our duty is at an end when we find that the action of the Commission was based upon findings supported by evidence, and was made pursuant to authority granted by Congress. It is not for us to say that the "public interest" will be furthered or retarded by the Chain Broadcasting Regulations. The responsibility belongs to the Congress for the grant of valid legislative authority and to the Commission for its exercise.

It would be sheer dogmatism to say that the Commission made out no case for its allowable discretion in formulating these Regulations. Its long investigation disclosed the existences of practices which it regarded as contrary to the "public interest." The Commission knew that the wisdom of any action it took would have to be tested by experience:

We are under no illusion that the regulations we are adopting will solve all questions of public interest with respect to the network system of program distribution. . . . The problems in the network field are interdependent, and the steps now taken may perhaps operate as a partial solution of problems not directly dealt with at this time. Such problems may be examined again at some future time after the regulations here adopted have been given a fair trial. (Report, p. 88.)

The problems with which the Commission attempted to deal could not be solved at once and for all time by rigid rules-of-thumb. The Commission therefore did not bind itself inflexibly to the licensing policies expressed in the Regulations. In each case that comes before it the Commission must still exercise an ultimate judgment whether the grant of a license would serve the "public interest, convenience, or necessity." If time and changing circumstances reveal that the "public interest" is not served by application of the Regulations, it must be assumed that the Commission will act in accordance with its statutory obligations.

Since there is no basis for any claim that the Commission failed to observe procedural safeguards required by law, we reach the contention that the Regulations should be denied enforcement on constitutional grounds. Here, as in *New York Central Securities Corp.* v. *United States*, 287 U.S. 12, 24-25, the claim is made that the standard of "public interest" governing the exercise of the powers delegated to the Commission by Congress is so vague and indefinite that, if it be construed as comprehensively as the words alone permit, the delegation of legislative authority is unconstitutional. But, as we held in that case, "It is a mistaken assumption that this is a mere general reference to public welfare without any standard to guide determinations. The purpose of the Act, the requirements it imposes, and the context of the provision in question show the contrary." *Ibid.* See *Federal Radio Comm'n* v. *Nelson Bros. Co.*, 289 U.S. 266, 285; *Federal Communications Comm'n* v. *Pottsville Broadcasting Co.*, 309 U.S. 134, 137–38. Compare *Panama Refining Co.* v. *Ryan*, 293 U.S. 388, 428; *Intermountain Rate Cases*, 234 U.S. 476, 486-89; *United States* v. *Lowden*, 308 U.S. 225.

We come, finally, to an appeal to the First Amendment. The Regulations, even if valid in all other respects, must fall because they abridge, say the appellants, their right of free speech. If that be so, it would follow that every person whose application for a license to operate a station is denied by the Commission is thereby denied his constitutional right of free speech. Freedom of utterance is abridged to many who wish to use the limited facilities of radio. Unlike other modes of expression, radio inherently is not available to all. That is its unique characteristic, and that is why, unlike other modes of expression, it is subject to governmental regulation. Because it cannot be used by all, some who wish to use it must be denied. But Congress did not authorize the Commission to choose among applicants upon the basis of their political, economic or social views, or upon any other capricious basis. If it did, or if the Commission by these Regulations proposed a choice among applicants upon some such basis, the issue before us would be wholly different. The question here is simply whether the Commission, by announcing that it will refuse licenses to persons who engage in specified network practices (a basis for choice which we hold is comprehended within the statutory criterion of "public interest"), is thereby denying such persons the constitutional right of free speech. The right of free speech does not include, however, the right to use the facilities of radio without a license. The licensing system established by Congress in the Communications Act of 1934 was a proper exercise of its power over commerce. The standard it provided for the licensing of stations was the "public interest, convenience, or necessity." Denial of a station license on that ground, if valid under the Act, is not a denial of free speech.

A procedural point calls for just a word. The District Court, by granting the Government's motion for summary judgment, disposed of the case upon the pleadings and upon the record made before the Commission. The court below correctly held that its inquiry was limited to review of the evidence before the Commission. Trial *de novo* of the matters heard by the Commission and dealt with in its Report would have been improper. See *Tagg Bros.* v. *United States*, 280 U.S. 420; *Acker* v. *United States*, 298 U.S. 426.

Affirmed.

Mr. Justice Black and Mr. Justice Rutledge took no part in the consideration or decision of these cases.

Mr. Justice Murphy, dissenting:

I do not question the objectives of the proposed regulations, and it is not my desire by narrow statutory interpretation to weaken the authority of government agencies to deal efficiently with matters committed to their jurisdiction by the Congress. Statutes of this kind should be construed so that the agency concerned may be able to cope effectively with problems which the Congress intended to correct, or may otherwise perform the functions given to it. But we exceed our competence when we gratuitously bestow upon an agency power which the Congress has not granted. Since that is what the Court in substance does today, I dissent.

In the present case we are dealing with a subject of extreme importance in the life of the nation. Although radio broadcasting, like the press, is generally conducted on a commercial basis, it is not an ordinary business activity, like the selling of securities or the marketing of electrical power. In the dissemination of information and opinion, radio has assumed a position of commanding importance, rivalling the press and the pulpit. Owing to its physical characteristics radio, unlike the other methods of conveying information, must be regulated and rationed by the government. Otherwise there would be chaos, and radio's usefulness would be largely destroyed. But because of its vast potentialities as a medium of communication, discussion and propaganda, the character and extent of control that should be exercised over it by the government is a matter of deep and vital concern. Events in Europe show that radio may readily be a weapon of authority and misrepresentation, instead of a means of entertainment and enlightenment. It may even be an instrument of oppression. In pointing out these possibilities I do not mean to intimate in the slightest that they are imminent or probable in this country, but they do suggest that the construction of the instant statute should be approached with more than ordinary restraint and caution, to avoid an interpretation that is not clearly justified by the conditions that brought about its enactment, or that would give the Commission greater powers than the Congress intended to confer.

The Communications Act of 1934 does not in terms give the Commission power to regulate the contractual relations between the stations and the networks. *Columbia System* v. *United States*, 316 U.S. 407, 416. It is only as an incident of the power to grant or withhold licenses to individual stations under § § 307, 308, 309 and 310 that this authority is claimed,[1] except as it may have been provided by subdivisions (g), (i) and (r) of § 303, and by § § 311 and 313. But nowhere in these sections, taken singly or collectively, is there to be found by reasonable construction or necessary inference, authority to regulate the broadcasting industry as such, or to control the complex operations of the national networks.

In providing for regulation of the radio, the Congress was under the necessity of vesting a considerable amount of discretionary authority in the Commission. The task of choosing between various claimants for the privilege of using the air waves is essentially an administrative one. Nevertheless, in specifying with some degree of particularity the kind of information to be included in an application for a license, the Congress has indicated what general conditions and considerations are to govern the granting and withholding of station licenses. Thus an applicant is required by § 308(b) to submit information bearing upon his citizenship, character, and technical, financial and other qualifications to operate the proposed station, as well as data relating to the ownership and location of the proposed station, the power and frequencies desired, operating periods, intended use, and such other information as the Commission may require. Licenses, frequencies, hours of operation and power are to be fairly distributed among the several States and communities to provide efficient service to each. § 307(b). Explicit provision is made for dealing with applicants and licensees who are found guilty, or who are under the control of persons found guilty of violating the federal anti-trust laws. § § 311 and 313. Subject to the limitations defined in the Act, the Commission is required to grant a station license to any applicant "if public convenience, interest, or

---

[1] The regulations as first proposed were not connected with denial of applications for initial or renewal station licenses but provided instead that: "No licensee of a standard broadcast station shall enter into any contractual arrangement, express or implied, with a network organization," which contained any of the disapproved provisions. After a short time, however, the regulations were cast in their present form, making station licensing depend upon conformity with the regulations.

necessity will be served thereby." § 307(a). Nothing is said, in any of these sections, about network contracts, affiliations, or business arrangements.

The power to control network contracts and affiliations by means of the Commission's licensing powers cannot be derived from implication out of the standard of "public convenience, interest or necessity." We have held that: "the Act does not essay to regulate the business of the licensee. The Commission is given no supervisory control of the programs, of business management or of policy. In short, the broadcasting field is open to anyone, provided there be an available frequency over which he can broadcast without interference to others, if he shows his competency, the adequacy of his equipment, and financial ability to make good use of the assigned channel." *Federal Communications Comm'n* v. *Sanders Radio Station*, 309 U.S. 470, 475. The criterion of "public convenience, interest or necessity" is not an indefinite standard, but one to be "interpreted by its context, by the nature of radio transmission and reception, by the scope, character and quality of services, . . ." *Federal Radio Comm'n* v. *Nelson Bros. Co.*, 289 U.S. 266, 285. Nothing in the context of which the standard is a part refers to network contracts. It is evident from the record that the Commission is making its determination of whether the public interest would be served by renewal of an existing license or licenses, not upon an examination of written applications presented to it, as required by § § 308 and 309, but upon an investigation of the broadcasting industry as a whole, and general findings made in pursuance thereof which relate to the business methods of the network companies rather than the characteristics of the individual stations and the peculiar needs of the areas served by them. If it had been the intention of the Congress to invest the Commission with the responsibility, through its licensing authority, of exercising far-reaching control – as exemplified by the proposed regulations – over the business operations of chain broadcasting and radio networks as they were then or are now organized and established, it is not likely that the Congress would have left it to mere inference or implication from the test of "public convenience, interest or necessity," or that Congress would have neglected to include it among the considerations expressly made relevant to license applications by § 308(b). The subject is one of such scope and importance as to warrant explicit mention. To construe the licensing sections (§ § 307, 308, 309, 310) as granting authority to require fundamental and revolutionary changes in the business methods of the broadcasting networks – methods which have been in existence for several years and which have not been adjudged unlawful – would inflate and distort their true meaning and extend them beyond the limited purposes which they were intended to serve.

It is quite possible, of course, that maximum utilization of the radio as an instrument of culture, entertainment, and the diffusion of ideas is inhibited by existing network arrangements. Some of the conditions imposed by the broadcasting chains are possibly not conducive to a freer use of radio facilities, however essential they may be to the maintenance of sustaining programs and the operation of the chain broadcasting business as it is now conducted. But I am unable to agree that it is within the present authority of the Commission to prescribe the remedy for such conditions. It is evident that a correction of these conditions in the manner proposed by the regulations will involve drastic changes in the business of radio broadcasting which the Congress has not clearly and definitely empowered the Commission to undertake.

If this were a case in which a station license had been withheld from an individual applicant or licensee because of special relations or commitments that would seriously compromise or limit his ability to provide adequate service to the listening public, I should be less inclined to make any objection. As an incident of its authority to determine the eligibility of an individual applicant in an isolated case, the Commission might possibly consider such factors. In the present case, however, the Commission has reversed the order of things. Its real objective is to regulate the business practices of the major networks, thus bringing within the range of its regulatory power the chain broadcasting industry as a whole. By means of these regulations and the enforcement program, the Commission would not only extend its authority over business activities which represent interests and investments of a very substantial character, which have not been put under its jurisdiction by the Act, but would greatly enlarge its control over an institution that has now become a rival of the press and pulpit as a purveyor of news and entertainment and a medium of public discussion. To assume a function and responsibility of such wide reach and importance in the life of the nation, as a mere incident of its duty to pass on individual applications for permission to operate a radio station and use a specific wave length, is an assumption of authority to which I am not willing to lend my assent.

Again I do not question the need of regulation in this field, or the authority of the Congress to enact legislation that would vest in the Commission such power as it requires to deal with the problem, which it has defined and analyzed in its report with admirable lucidity. It is possible that the remedy indicated by the proposed regulations is the appropriate one, whatever its effect may be on the sustaining programs, advertising contracts, and other characteristics of chain broadcasting as it is now conducted in this country. I do not believe, however, that the Commission was justified in claiming the responsibility and authority it has assumed to exercise without a clear mandate from Congress.

An examination of the history of this legislation convinces me that the Congress did not intend by anything in § 303, or any other provision of the Act, to confer on the Commission the authority it has assumed to exercise by the issuance of these regulations. Section 303 is concerned primarily with technical matters, and the subjects of regulation authorized by most of its subdivisions are exceedingly specific — so specific in fact that it is reasonable to infer that, if Congress had intended to cover the subject of network contracts and affiliations, it would not have left it to dubious implications from general clauses, lifted out of context, in subdivisions (g), (i) and (r). I am unable to agree that in authorizing the Commission in § 303(g) to study new uses for radio, provide for experimental use of frequencies, and "generally encourage the larger and more effective use of radio in the public interest," it was the intention or the purpose of the Congress to confer on the Commission the regulatory powers now being asserted. Manifestly that subdivision dealt with experimental and development work — technical and scientific matters, and the construction of its concluding clause should be accordingly limited to those considerations. Nothing in its legislative history suggests that it had any broader purpose.

It was clearly not the intention of the Congress by the enactment of § 303(i), authorizing the Commission "to make special regulations applicable to radio stations engaged in chain broadcasting," to invest the Commission with the authority now claimed over network contracts. This section is a verbatim reënactment of § 4(h) of the Radio Act of 1927, and had its origin in a Senate amendment to the bill which became that Act. In its original form it provided that the Commission, from time to time, as public convenience, interest, or necessity required, should:

When stations are connected by wire for chain broadcasting, [the Commission should] determine the power each station shall use and the wave lengths to be used during the time stations are so connected and so operated, and make all other regulations necessary in the interest of equitable radio service to the listeners in the communities or areas affected by chain broadcasting.

It was evidently the purpose of this provision to remedy a situation that was described as follows by Senator Dill (who was in charge of the bill in the Senate) in questioning a witness at the hearings of the Senate Committee on Interstate Commerce:

... During the past few months there has grown up a system of chain broadcasting, extending over the United States a great deal of the time. I say a great deal of the time — many nights a month — and the stations that are connected are of such widely varying meter lengths that the ordinary radio set that reaches out any distance is unable to get anything but that one program, and so, in effect, that one program monopolizes the air. I realize it is somewhat of a technical engineering problem, but it has seemed to many people, at least many who have written to me, that when stations are carrying on chain programs that they might be limited to the use of wave lengths adjoining or near enough to one another that they would not cover the entire dial. I do not know whether legislation ought to restrict that or whether it had better be done by regulations of the department. I want to get your opinion as to the advisability in some way protecting people who want to hear some other program than the one being broadcasted by chain broadcast. (Report on Hearings Before Senate

Committee on Interstate Commerce on S. 1 and S. 1754, 69th Cong., 1st Sess. (1926) p. 123.)

In other words, when the same program was simultaneously broadcast by chain stations, the weaker independent stations were drowned out because of the high power of the chain stations. With the receiving sets then commonly in use, listeners were unable to get any program except the chain program. It was essentially an interference problem. In addition to determining power and wave length for chain stations, it would have been the duty of the Commission, under the amendment, to make other regulations necessary for "equitable radio service to the listeners in the communities or areas affected by chain broadcasting." The last clause should not be interpreted out of context and without relation to the problem at which the amendment was aimed. It is reasonably construed as simply authorizing the Commission to remedy other technical problems of interference involved in chain broadcasting in addition to power and wave length by requiring special types of equipment, controlling locations, etc. The statement in the Senate Committee Report that this provision gave the Commission "complete authority . . . to control chain broadcasting" (S. Rep. No. 772, 69th Cong., 1st Sess., p. 3) must be taken as meaning that the provision gave complete authority with respect to the specific problem which the Senate intended to meet, a problem of technical interference.

While the form of the amendment was simplified in the Conference Committee so as to authorize the Commission "to make special regulations applicable to radio stations engaged in chain broadcasting," both Houses were assured in the report of the Conference Committee that "the jurisdiction conferred in this paragraph is substantially the same as the jurisdiction conferred upon the Commission by . . . the Senate amendment." (Sen. Doc. No. 200, 69th Cong., 2d Sess., p. 17; H. Rep. No. 1886, 69th Cong., 2d Sess., p. 17). This is further borne out by a statement of Senator Dill in discussing the conference report on the Senate floor:

What is happening to-day is that the National Broadcasting Co., which is a part of the great Radio Trust, to say the least, if not a monopoly, is hooking up stations in every community on their various wave lengths with high powered stations and sending one program out, and they are forcing the little stations off the board so that the people cannot hear anything except the one program.

There is no power to-day in the hands of the Department of Commerce to stop that practice. The radio commission will have the power to regulate and prevent it and give the independents a chance. (68 Cong. Rec. 3031.)

Section 303(r) is certainly no basis for inferring that the Commission is empowered to issue the challenged regulations. This subdivision is not an independent grant of power, but only an authorization to: "Make such rules and regulations and prescribe such restrictions and conditions, not inconsistent with law, as may be necessary to carry out the provisions of this Act." There is no provision in the Act for the control of network contractual arrangements by the Commission, and consequently § 303(r) is of no consequence here.

To the extent that existing network practices may have run counter to the anti-trust laws, the Congress has expressly provided the means of dealing with the problem. The enforcement of those laws has been committed to the courts and other law enforcement agencies. In addition to the usual penalties prescribed by statute for their violation, however, the Commission has been expressly authorized by § 311 to refuse a station license to any person "finally adjudged guilty by a Federal court" of attempting unlawfully to monopolize radio communication. Anyone under the control of such a person may also be refused a license. And whenever a court has ordered the revocation of an existing license, as expressly provided in § 313, a new license may not be granted by the Commission to the guilty party or to any person under his control. In my opinion these provisions (§ § 311 and 313) clearly do not and were not intended to confer independent authority on the Commission to supervise network contracts or to enforce competition between radio networks by withholding licenses from stations, and do not justify the Commission in refusing a license to an applicant otherwise qualified, because of business arrangements that may constitute an unlawful restraint of trade, when the applicant has not been finally adjudged guilty of violating the anti-trust laws, and is not controlled by one so adjudged.

The conditions disclosed by the Commission's investigation, if they require correction, should be met, not by the invention of authority where none is available or by diverting existing powers out of their true channels and using them for purposes to which they were not addressed, but by invoking the aid of the Congress or the service of agencies that have been entrusted with the enforcement of the anti-trust laws. In other fields of regulation the Congress has made clear its intentions. It has not left to mere inference and guess-work the existence of authority to order broad changes and reforms in the national economy or the structure of business arrangements in the Public Utility Holding Company Act, 49 Stat. 803, the Securities Act of 1933, 48 Stat. 74, the Federal Power Act, 49 Stat. 838, and other measures of similar character. Indeed the Communications Act itself contains cogent internal evidence that Congress did not intend to grant power over network contractual arrangements to the Commission. In § 215(c) of Title II, dealing with common carriers by wire and radio, Congress provided:

The Commission shall examine all contracts of common carriers subject to this Act which prevent the other party thereto from dealing with another common carrier subject to this Act, and shall report its findings to Congress, together with its recommendations as to whether additional legislation on this subject is desirable.

Congress had no difficulty here in expressing the possible desirability of regulating a type of contract roughly similar to the ones with which we are now concerned, and in reserving to itself the ultimate decision upon the matters of policy involved. Insofar as the Congress deemed it necessary in this legislation to safeguard radio broadcasting against arrangements that are offensive to the anti-trust laws or monopolistic in nature, it made specific provision in § § 311 and 313. If the existing network contracts are deemed objectionable because of monopolistic or other features, and no remedy is presently available under these provisions, the proper course is to seek amendatory legislation from the Congress, not to fabricate authority by ingenious reasoning based upon provisions that have no true relation to the specific problem.

Mr. Justice Roberts agrees with these views.

21
The Blue Book

Public Service Responsibility of Broadcast Licensees

March 7, 1946

By 1945 it became clear that the "chain regulations" had done little to change the basic nature of broadcasting in America. Neither the decimation of the system predicted by the industry nor the improvements hoped for by the Commission came to pass. Affiliated stations continued to rely on networks for programming, for it was economically disadvantageous to do otherwise. The FCC questioned whether regulation of competition alone was sufficient to achieve the objectives of the Communications Act. The end of the war would mark the start of a major rise in the number of authorized AM radio stations. FM radio and television broadcasting were soon to emerge from their cocoons as well. Might the Commission have to do something about programming directly?

The FCC began to examine what licensees proposed to broadcast when they filed applications and what they actually programmed. There were many discrepancies between "promise" and "performance." In April, 1945, the Commission started to grant temporary renewals to broadcasters whose applications raised programming questions. In February of 1946 the Hearst station in Baltimore, WBAL, was designated for hearing by the FCC for allegedly failing to operate as it said it would when it was granted a power increase 5 years before. Three weeks later the most thoroughly substantiated and reasoned expression of Commission programming policy was issued.

The "Blue Book" became the common name of the document because of the color of its cover and because of the tendency of the policy statement's opponents to associate it with the "blue pencil" of censorship and/or "blue-blooded" authoritarianism (since official documents of the British government were also called "blue-books"). The three people who were primarily responsible for its contents were FCC Commissioner Clifford Durr, Commission staff member Edward Brecher, and Charles Siepmann, former executive of the British Broadcasting Corporation and American academician who served as a consultant on the project in 1945. Others who collaborated on preparation of the "Blue Book" were consultant Eleanor Bontecue (who wrote the early drafts treating legal aspects of the FCC's authority with respect to programming) and FCC employees Dallas Smythe and Harriet Simons.

Charles Denny, who assumed the chairmanship of the Commission less than 2 weeks prior to issuance of the "Blue Book," vowed that the policy statement would not be "bleached." Denny became an executive for the National Broadcasting Company in 1947, by which time the broadcasting industry's well-orchestrated cries of protest had all but buried the "Blue Book." The FCC proceeded with the WBAL hearings, which became a comparative contest when a competing application for the license was made by a group which included Washington newsman Drew Pearson. The "Blue Book" was interred a few years later when the Commission voted four to two to renew WBAL's license [15 FCC 1149 (1951)].

Neither vigorously enforced nor officially repudiated by the FCC, the very potency of the "Blue Book" rendered it ineffectual. Its theme of balanced programming as a necessary component of broadcast service in the public interest coupled with its emphasis on a reasonable ratio of unsponsored ("sustaining") programs posed too serious a threat to the profitability of commercial radio for either the industry, Congress, or the FCC to want to match regulatory promise with performance.

Related Reading: 29, 151, 152, 187, 204, 241.

PART I.   THE COMMISSION'S CONCERN WITH PROGRAM SERVICE

On April 10, 1945, the Federal Communications Commission announced "a policy of a more detailed review of broadcast station performance when passing upon applications for license renewals."[1]

---

[1] FCC Mimeograph No. 81575, April 10, 1945.

The need for such a policy had earlier been set forth by Chairman Paul A. Porter in an address to the National Association of Broadcasters March 12, 1945. The Chairman stated:

... Briefly the facts are these: an applicant seeks a construction permit for a new station and in his application makes the usual representations as to the type of service he proposes. These representations include specific pledges that time will be made available for civic, educational, agricultural and other public service programs. The station is constructed and begins operations. Subsequently the licensee asks for a three-year renewal and the record clearly shows that he has not fulfilled the promises made to the Commission when he received the original grant. The Commission in the past has, for a variety of reasons, including limitations of staff, automatically renewed these licenses even in cases where there is a vast disparity between promises and performance.

We have under consideration at the present time, however, a procedure whereby promises will be compared with performance. I think the industry is entitled to know of our concern in this matter and should be informed that there is pending before the Commission staff proposals which are designed to strengthen renewal procedures and give the Commission a more definite picture of the station's overall operation when licenses come up for renewal.

A procedure involving more detailed review of renewal applications was instituted experimentally in April 1945; and this report is based in part upon experience since then with renewal applications.

The need for detailed review on renewal can best be illustrated by a series of specific instances. The cases which follow are *not* presented for any substantive light they may throw on policy with respect to program service. Part III of this report will deal with substantive program service matters. The following cases are set forth to show various occasions for detailed review on renewal rather than the principles in terms of which such review should proceed.

A. Comparison of promise and performance: Station KIEV

The KIEV case (8 F.C.C. 207) illustrates primarily the need for sound procedures to compare promises with performance when acting on renewal of licenses.

Under date of January 27, 1932, the Cannon System, Ltd., applied for a construction permit for a new standard broadcast station at Glendale, California. Because the quota[2] for the zone in which California was located had been filled, the Cannon System, Ltd., further requested that the facilities assigned to Station

---

[2] Under Section 9 of the Radio Act of 1927, as amended March 28, 1928, each zone and each state in the United States was assigned a quota, and new applications could not be granted, with certain exceptions, in a zone or state whose quota was already filled. Since the Fifth Zone quota was filled, KIEV was of the opinion that its application would be

KGIX, Las Vegas, Nevada, be withdrawn, in order to make possible a grant of its application.

In prosecuting its application (Docket No. 1595), Cannon System, Ltd., represented that it proposed to operate the station as a civic project; that the central location of its proposed studios would be convenient for the program talent to be broadcast; that the applicant proposed to cooperate with the Glendale Chamber of Commerce and all the local civic, educational, fraternal and religious institutions in donating to them, without charge, periods of time for broadcasting programs of special interest to Glendale listeners; that one-third of the broadcasting time would be devoted to educational and semi-educational matters; that agricultural features would be presented and that programs would include local, state and national news items; that special features would be presented for the large Spanish population in the Glendale area; that 20 percent of all its broadcast hours would be devoted to sustaining programs of an agricultural nature; etc. It further represented that the lack of a broadcast station in Glendale discriminated against "the use of Glendale's excellent talent."

On the basis of such representations, the renewal application of Station KGIX was designated for hearing jointly with the application of the Cannon System, Ltd., for a new station. Following this hearing, the Federal Radio Commission found that "although the Glendale area now receives service from a number of stations situated elsewhere, there appears to be a need in that city for the purely local service, largely civic and educational in character, proposed to be rendered therein by applicant, Cannon System, Ltd."

With respect to Station KGIX, the Commission found that cutting its hours from unlimited to limited would permit the station "to render any substantial service theretofore rendered or proposed to be rendered." Accordingly, the application of the Cannon System, Ltd., was granted, and the authorized time of Station KGIX was cut in half in its renewed license.

On May 22, 1939, Station KIEV filed an application for renewal of its license and the Commission was unable to determine from an examination of the application that a renewal would be in the public interest. Accordingly, the application was designated for hearing[3] and was heard beginning December 7, 1939.

---

granted only at the expense of some other station, and hence requested the withdrawal of the facilities assigned to KGIX. A subsequent change in California quota facilities rendered this question moot. (*In re Cannon System, Ltd.*, F.R.C. Docket 1595, decided Sept. 23, 1932.)

[3] The issues in the hearing included the following:

"1. To determine the nature and character of the program service rendered by the applicant;

"2. To determine whether the station's program service has been and is now in conformity with the representations made to the Commission in support of the original application for construction permit or license, and all subsequent applications by the licensee. . . ."

Commission inspectors had made recordings of the programs broadcast by the applicant on December 15, 21, and 27, 1938. On the basis of these recordings, the Commission found:

. . . On the first of these days the programs consisted of 143 popular records and 9 semi-classical records. There were 264 commercial announcements and 3 minutes of announcements concerning lost and found pets. On December 21, 1938, the programs were made up of 156 popular and 10 semi-classical records and were accompanied by 258 commercial announcements. Ten minutes were devoted to the lost and found pet column. On December 27, 1938, 165 popular, 12 semi-classical records, 10 minutes of the lost and found pet column and 199 commercial announcements made up the day's schedule. During these 3 days, which represented a total of 36 hours of broadcast time, only 23 minutes were devoted to programs other than records and commercial announcements. [4] The alleged policy of the station had been to limit commercial announcements to 160 announcements for each 10-hour day but it appears that the manager, employed on a commission basis, permitted a greater number to be broadcast. Even if the station's definition of a "commercial," which excludes time signals and introductions in the name of the sponsor, is accepted, the number of commercial programs on the dates recorded would be far in excess of those originally proposed.

Further examples of the divergence between promise and performance are found in the following record facts. For a period of over a year no regular news was broadcast over the station. Little effort was made to promote any programs other than those characterized by purely commercial continuity. The musical portions were composed almost entirely of popular records. Each 5-minute program contains at least one commercial announcement and some recorded music. While the licensee made its station available free of charge to civic, charitable, fraternal, and educational organizations, it expended no substantial effort actively to assist and aid such organizations in the preparation and production of programs. As a result, programs of this character became in most instances mere announcements for such organizations. (8 F.C.C. 207, 208-209.)

The Commission's decision, dated September 25, 1940, set forth at some length its views with respect to "the disparity between the proposed service and the programs actually broadcast." It stated:

In the Commission's view the licensee of Station KIEV did not make a reasonable effort to make its programs conform to its representations. The

---

[4]In originally urging that its own application be granted and that the renewal application of Station KGIX be denied, Cannon Systems, Ltd., had called attention to the fact that the KGIX programs were 75 percent transcribed or recorded, and had characterized this as "reprehensible and inexcusable." It appears, however, that the Cannon System programs on the three days monitored were more than 98 percent recorded.

disparity between the proposed service and the programs actually broadcast indicates such a disregard of the representations made as to cast doubt on their sincerity in the first instance, and, therefore, on the qualifications of the licensee. Furthermore, false statements of talent expenditures were made in successive renewal applications. The Commission, in the allocation of frequencies to the various communities, must rely upon the testimony of applicants and upon the representations made in original and renewal applications, to determine whether the public interest will be served by a grant of such applications. Faced here by such a disregard for representations so made, particularly upon the question of service to the public, the Commission is satisfied that a denial of the renewal application might well be justified. It should be noted that the emphasis is here placed upon the question of the truth of representations made to the Commission as a basis for the grant and renewal of a broadcast license. No adverse criticism is directed at the use of a proper proportion of high quality records or electrical transcriptions.

Upon all the facts, however, it has been concluded not to deny the pending application. The record shows that attempts to improve programs have been made. An additional member has been placed on the staff with the duty of arranging programs of a civic, educational and charitable nature. The percentage of time devoted to recorded music and to commercialization has been much reduced, and the remainder of the program schedule dedicated to diversified nonrecorded program material. News programs have been added and a 5-year contract entered into with the United Press. Religious programs are being prepared by the Ministerial Association. Local civic and fraternal organizations are being more actively assisted in the preparation of programs. To a substantial extent the public has come to utilize the transmitting facilities and the broadcast service.

There is, therefore, ground for urging that we may expect the present trend of improvement in program service to be carried forward. With some reluctance the Commission concludes that this application may be granted. The facts developed in this proceeding will, however, be given cumulative weight in dealing with any future questions involving the conduct of this station. (8 F.C.C. 207, 209-210.)

Despite the additional representations made in connection with its 1940 renewal, the KIEV logs for the week beginning April 23, 1944, show that more than 88 percent of its program time was still being devoted to mechanically reproduced music. Less than 3.7 percent of its program time — or 30 minutes a day — was devoted to the "talent" which the applicant assured the Commission was available in the community. This consisted of one singer who sang for 15 minutes 6 times a week, one pianist for 15 minutes on Saturday, one 15-minute school program, and a devotional program daily except Sunday from 6:30 to 6:45 a.m., when audiences, of course, are small. U.P. news was broadcast. The station's programs were still being interspersed with spot announcements on an average of one every 5.5 minutes. A total of 1042 spot announcements were broadcast during the week, of which 1034 were commercial and 8 were broadcast as a public service. A search of the week's logs fails to disclose any "duets, quartets, excerpts from operas, cuttings from great poems," or other special features originally promised when the Cannon System, Ltd., was seeking a license at the expense of Station KGIX. Nor does it reveal an adherence to the representations made in connection with its renewal granted in January 1940.

B.   Competing applications: Station WSNY

In the *Cannon System* case (KIEV), there was an element of competition between applicants, since the Cannon System proposed that the license of an existing station not be renewed. In the *Western Gateway* case (9 F.C.C. 92), the issue of two competing applications for a single available assignment was squarely raised.[1]

On December 8, 1939, the Van Curler Broadcasting Corporation filed an application for a new station to operate in Schenectady, New York, on a frequency of 1210 kilocycles, with power of 250 watts. A month later the Western Gateway Broadcasting Corporation filed a competing application for a new station in the same city, utilizing the same power on the same frequency. The two mutually exclusive applications were jointly heard.

Since both applicants specified similar or identical equipment and both appeared initially to be qualified financially and legally, the hearings were primarily concerned with the program representations of the two applicants. The Van Curler Broadcasting Corporation, for example, represented that it would regularly broadcast programs of the American Legion, the Schenectady Municipal Housing Authority, the Schenectady Council of Churches, etc.; that school programs for the city school system would be broadcast from 1:30 to 2 p.m. daily; that a local town-meeting program, patterned after the "American Town Meeting of the Air," would be broadcast Tuesday evenings from 8 to 9 p.m.; that a special line and studios would be installed at Union College for the broadcasting of its educational programs; etc.[2]

---

[1] This need to decide between competing applicants is a commonplace in the standard broadcast band. It may be somewhat less frequent in the new FM band because of the possibility of a larger number of stations in most communities; but competing applications for FM along the Eastern seaboard and in other metropolitan areas are already on file with the Commission. Television will also in all probability give rise to competing applications for identical facilities.

[2] "The Schenectady Municipal Housing Authority would broadcast a weekly one-quarter hour program, publicizing its activities. The Council of Churches of Schenectady would cooperate with the applicant in presenting religious programs. The proposed religious programs consist of: A one-quarter hour morning devotional program, presented 5 days a week by local ministers; a one-quarter hour Jewish program on Saturday afternoons; morning church services, presented from local churches for 1 hour on Sundays; and Vesper

The other applicant, Western Gateway, also made detailed program representations — for example, that it would broadcast book reviews; a music appreciation series; a local "Radio Workshop" patterned after the CBS program of the same title; round table religious discussions embracing all religious faiths; programs of various local civic organizations, etc. The percentage of time to be devoted to each type of program was explicitly set forth.[3]

On the basis in part of these program service representations, the Commission on February 24, 1942, granted the application of Western Gateway

---

services for one-half hour on Sunday afternoons. Definite arrangements have been made with the city superintendent of schools for the broadcasting of school programs from 1:30 to 2 p.m. daily. Arrangements have been made with the State Forum Counselor, assigned by the United States Office of Education, to the New York Council of School Superintendents to broadcast programs in connection with this group's work in promoting adult civic education. The broadcasts to be presented would consist of: A local town meeting program (patterned after the well-known program, 'American Town Meeting of the Air'), which would be carried on Tuesday evenings from 8 to 9 p.m.; and three one-quarter hour programs each week. The Federation of Women's Clubs of Schenectady, representing some 38 clubs, would broadcast a one-half hour program each week during the seasons of the year when the clubs are most active. Definite arrangements have already been made for the presentation of some 43 programs by affiliates of the Federation. A one-quarter hour book review would be presented each week in cooperation with the city public library; and the applicant has also agreed to broadcast special announcements concerning the library. The City of Scotia would broadcast a weekly program devoted to matters of local interest to the listeners living in that community. The applicant has agreed to contribute to these groups the use of the facilities of the projected station, as well as professional production assistance, and to reserve specific periods of time on an immovable-sustaining basis for their regular programs." (9 F.C.C. 92, 100-101.)

[3] "The proposed station would be operated on the average of about 17 hours daily. According to the applicant's proposed program plans, time would be devoted as follows: Entertainment (51.41 percent), includes various types of music (presented by local and professional talent, records and transcriptions), drama, quiz programs, and programs designed especially for the women (such as shopping and household hints, fashion comments, and advice on the care of children); educational (16.53 percent), includes safety programs, book reviews, a music appreciation series, a program entitled "Radio Workshop" (a local version of CBS program of the same title), patriotic broadcasts, dramatized historical events, local round table discussions, and others; religious (6 percent), includes a morning program of religious hymns (presented by talent furnished by local churches and schools), a daily devotional program conducted by local clergymen, round table discussions embracing all religious faiths, and Sunday services from local churches; agricultural (1.27 percent), includes market and other reports, Farm Bureau topics, Grange notices, and others; news (16.95 percent), includes during each day, 5-minute newscasts every hour, a 10-minute sports review, a one-quarter hour news commentary presented by James T. Healey, two five-minute local newscasts, and two one-quarter hour news digests; civic (7.84 percent), includes programs concerning the activities of various local organizations and institutions, discussions of governmental and civic problems, and programs designed to promote interest in the community, state and nation. Programs presented by means of mechanical reproduction would be broadcast for about 20 percent of the time. Material for newscasts would be obtained from a well-known news service and local newspapers," etc. (9 F.C.C. 92, 96.)

and denied the application of Van Curler. With respect to the successful applicant, the Commission concluded:

Western Gateway Broadcasting Corporation is qualified in every respect to construct and operate the station proposed; it proposes to render a balanced program service comparable to that normally provided by local broadcast stations; and its proposed station would provide a satisfactory technical service throughout the City of Schenectady and the rural areas contiguous thereto. (9 F.C.C. 92, 101.)

With respect to the unsuccessful applicant, Van Curler Broadcasting Corporation, the Commission found that, "while this applicant has made a showing of the public-service programs, newscasts, transcribed features, musical clock programs, and time and other reports, it expects to broadcast, it has not adduced evidence as to its other program plans." Moreover, the Commission raised the question of credibility with respect to the representations made by the unsuccessful applicant. It noted that one of the directors had first testified that $5,000 which he had invested in the company was his own, and subsequently testified instead that it had been borrowed from a brother-in-law. Said the Commission:

In the performance of our duties we must, among other things, determine whether the operation of proposed stations, or the continued operation of existing stations, would serve public interest, and in so doing we are, of necessity, required to rely to a large extent upon statements made by station licensees, or those connected therewith. Caution must, therefore, be exercised to grant station licenses only to those persons whose statements are trustworthy. (9 F.C.C. 92, 102.)

Examinations of the logs of Station WSNY, the Western Gateway station, for the week beginning January 18, 1945, and a consideration of the statement concerning the public service rendered by Station WSNY filed by the licensee under date of May 24, 1945, in connection with its license renewal, warrant the conclusion that while a very genuine effort is being made by the licensee to serve the Schnectady area,[4] nevertheless, the station's present operations clearly fall short of the extreme representations made when Western Gateway was competitively seeking approval of a new station as against Van Curler. For example, Station WSNY represented that approximately 20 percent of its time would be devoted to programs presented by means of mechanical reproduction. An examination of the WSNY logs for the week beginning January 18, 1945,

---

[4]With respect to its statements filed May 24, 1945, Station WSNY declares: "WE BELIEVE THAT NO OTHER STATION IN AMERICA CAN MATCH THE RECORD OF COMMUNITY INTEREST AND PUBLIC SERVICE BROADCASTING INDICATED IN THESE VARIOUS STATEMENTS."

shows in contrast, that 78 percent of the program time of the station is devoted to mechanically reproduced programs. At least some of the types of programs specifically set forth in the original representations do not appear on the program schedules less than 3 years after the station went on the air.

C. Applications for increased facilities: Station WTOL

The relation between the Commission's renewal procedures and its actions in connection with applications for increased facilities for existing broadcast stations is illustrated in the case of Station WTOL, Toledo. (7 F.C.C. 194.)

Station WTOL was originally licensed to operate daytime only; but in 1938 it applied for authority to broadcast unlimited time. In the hearing on its application, the station relied heavily on the need for added evening hours in order to serve local organizations in Toledo, and to make use of the live talent in Toledo after 6 p.m. The applicant represented, for example, that after 6 p.m., 84 percent of its time would be devoted to live-talent broadcasts; that the Toledo Council of Churches, the American Legion, the YMCA and "other worthwhile organizations" desired time over the station *at night*, and that the only other station in Toledo was unable to clear sufficient time for such programs because it was affiliated with a national network.[1]

The president of the licensee corporation testified as follows on direct examination:

Q. What is the purpose of this application for night-time hours?

A. It is to give the people of Toledo an opportunity to have a station which can broadcast a great many events which can not at the present time be

---

[1] "The applicant's proposed weekly program schedule was admitted in evidence, and shows, among other things, that approximately 35.5 percent of the station's time will be devoted to news, drama, education, religious, civic, and sports broadcasts, and the remaining 64.5 percent will be devoted to musical entertainment, approximately one-half of which will be commercial broadcasts. The program service proposed appears somewhat similar in character to its existing service, except that a greater percentage of the total time will be devoted to the use of live talent broadcasts. Approximately 62 percent of the station's time will be devoted to broadcasts using live talent and after 6 p.m. live talent will be used approximately 84 percent of the time. . . .

"The policy of the station has been, and will continue to be, to give free time to the Toledo Council of Churches for religious broadcasts. This organization desires time at night over Station WTOL. The station has also cooperated with the municipal and county governments and the various agencies of both the State and Federal Governments in giving free time to the Toledo Post of the American Legion, the Y.M.C.A., Boy Scouts of America, and other worthwhile organizations. These organizations desire time over the station at night and will cooperate in furnishing program material for broadcasts. Station WSPD is at the present time affiliated with the National Broadcasting Company and has been unable to give sufficient time to these organizations at night." (7 F.C.C. 194, 196-7.)

broadcast, because the only other station there is a regional station with a chain hook-up. For instance, we had during the summer civic opera which, by special permission of the Federal Communications Commission was broadcast. We have had a great many other musical occasions which could not be broadcast, although request was made by the managers of musical organizations for broadcasts. We have many important and interesting speakers who come to Toledo for dinner meetings, and other occasions, where there is a demand made for broadcasting, and these and other educational features can be carried if we have full time operation. (F.C.C. Docket 5320, Tr. 81-82.)

In granting the WTOL application for unlimited time, the Commission concluded:

Station WTOL is rendering a satisfactory local program service to the Toledo, Ohio, audience during daytime hours and a similar program service is proposed for the evening hours which is not now available from any radio broadcast station serving this area. The other existing station (WSPD) in Toledo is of a regional classification and does not adequately meet the local needs of the Toledo area during the evening hours. There is a need in the Toledo, Ohio, area for the service proposed by the applicant. (7 F.C.C. 194, 198.)

The WTOL application was granted on April 17, 1939, and eight months later Station WTOL, like the only other station in Toledo, became affiliated with a national network. By 1944 the "local" programs upon which WTOL had relied were conspicuous by their absence. During the week beginning November 13, 1944, for example, approximately 15 percent of the station's time was devoted to "live" broadcasts rather than the 62 percent originally represented. After 6 p.m., instead of devoting 84 percent of the time to local live broadcasts, as represented, Station WTOL devoted only 13.7 percent of its time to such programs. Nearly half of the "live" programs, moreover, were wire news involving no live talent other than the voice of a news announcer.[2]

In contrast to its allegations that time after 6 p.m. was sought for local public service, the station broadcast only 20 minutes of local live sustaining programs after 6 p.m. during the entire week – 10 minutes of bowling scores and 10 minutes of sports news.

Throughout the week, 91.8 percent of the broadcast time was commercial. No evening time whatever during the week was given to the Toledo American Legion, YMCA, Boy Scouts, or any other local organizations which, according to the representations, desired time over the station at night.

Nor was the time after 6 p.m. filled with commercial programs of such outstanding merit as to leave no room for local service. From 6:15 to 6:30 p.m. on Tuesday, for example, a 15-minute program of transcribed music was interrupted by seven spot announcements – at 6:18, 6:19, 6:22, 6:24½, 6:25½,

---

[2] For discussion of "wire programs" as distinguished from "local live" programs, see "Uniform Definitions and Program Logs."

6:26½, and 6:29 p.m. From 10:10 to 10:30 the same evening, a transcribed musical program entitled "Music Hall" was interrupted by 10 spot announcements in 20 minutes — at 10:15, 10:16, 10:20, 10:21, 10:22, 10:23, 10:25, 10:26, 10:27, and 10:29½ p.m.

D.   Transfer of Control: Station WBAL

In recent years, the purchase of an existing standard broadcast station has become a more common means of entering broadcasting than the erection of a new station.[1] The case of Station WBAL, Baltimore, illustrates the extent to which the service rendered by a station may be affected by a transfer or assignment of license to a purchaser, and the need for integrating Commission transfer and renewal procedures.

Station WBAL was originally licensed to the Consolidated Gas, Electric Light and Power Company of Baltimore, by the Department of Commerce. It began operations November 2, 1925.[2]

When the Federal Radio Commission was established in 1927, Station WBAL was one of many stations which sought to procure a "cleared channel," 25 of which were then being proposed. In support of its claim to a cleared channel, the station submitted "A Description of WBAL, Baltimore," prepared for the information of the Federal Radio Commission, August 1927. The "Description" stated: "Although WBAL is owned by a private corporation, its operation closely approximates that of a public enterprise." The Station's program policy was described as follows:

WBAL has endeavored to be a distinctive personality among broadcasting stations. To attain this end its programs have maintained high musical and artistic standards. The Station's "No Jazz" policy is indicative.

The Station Director is also head of the Baltimore Municipal Department

---

[1] During the four years 1941 through 1944, inclusive, 98 new standard broadcast stations were licensed, while 110 were assigned or transferred in toto, excluding merely formal transfers or assignments involving no actual change of control.

[2] The station began broadcasting with the following statement by the president of the then licensee corporation:

"It is my privilege on this, our opening night, to dedicate this new radio station to Baltimore and Maryland, and to the service of their people in such ways as may be found most useful to them. This station is to be known as 'Baltimore,' and it will be so designated and referred to in the future announcing and operation. The company which has financed its construction and will operate it now dedicates it to the public service of this city and Commonwealth. It will be satisfied to participate along with all others in this great community in such progress and advantage as its operation may bring forth. After tonight the name of this company may not be heard in the announcements of this station, nor is it proposed to commercialize its operation."

of Music. The direct connections which the Director and various members of the musical staff have with the private and public musical activities of the City make possible a selection of the best artistic personnel, and provides a means of coordination which is seldom found possible. The Station has maintained its own features to a unique degree, until quite recently, over ninety percent of its programs being rendered by its own studio organizations.

In addition to the regular features of the Studio, the programs of the Station have included as a regular feature during the winter months, semi-weekly organ recitals from the Peabody Conservatory of Music, at which institution is located the largest single pipe organ south of New York. The Station has also broadcast each season, a number of the most important musical services from various churches throughout the city. During the summer these features were supplanted by outdoor programs from a permanent pick-up point in one of the public parks of the city, featuring two programs each week, one by the Baltimore Municipal Band, the other by the Baltimore City Park Orchestra. Programs of the Baltimore Symphony Orchestra and other orchestral and choral programs of city-wide interest have also been included in the station's broadcasting each season.

The station also employed regular musical organizations:

The following staff organizations which, in line with the policy of not referring to the Gas and Electric Company, are designated simply by the call letters of the Station, have been retained as regular features to insure a uniformly high standard of program. Some appear daily, others semi-weekly, or weekly.

WBAL Concert Orchestra	WBAL String Quartet
WBAL Opera Company	WBAL Dance Orchestra
WBAL Salon Orchestra	WBAL Male Quartet
WBAL Ensemble	WBAL Mixed Quartet
WBAL Dinner Orchestra	WBAL Trio

From the personnel of the various organizations is also drawn talent for special presentations, such as continuity programs, musical scenarios and programs for special events.

The competition among the several hundred stations then on the air for the 25 proposed clear channels was very strenuous, and the Commission made it clear that "superior programs" would be one test, or perhaps the principal test, of eligibility.[3]

On November 20, 1934, application was made for transfer of control of the WBAL Broadcasting Company from the Consolidated Gas, Electric Light and

[3]Thus on December 5, 1927, Commissioner O. H. Caldwell wrote to the Mayor of Baltimore:

"The members of the Commission have asked me to acknowledge yours of December 1st., and to assure you that *the Commission desires to facilitate in every way the presentation of good programs* to the people of Baltimore through the local stations.

Power Company to American Radio News Corporation, an absentee holding company. An amended application was filed December 1, 1934, and the transfer was approved, without a hearing, on January 8, 1935. At that time, no representations concerning program service were required of transferees, so that the purchasers were able to enter broadcasting without the representations which would have been required had they applied for a new station. Currently, transferees are required to state whether the transfer will affect the service, and if so, in what respects.

An examination of the program logs of Station WBAL for the week beginning Sunday, April 23, 1944, shows that its present mode of operation is in marked contrast to its operation described above under the previous licensee.

Thus, during the week beginning Sunday, April 23, 1944, only 12.5 percent of the program time between 8 a.m. and 11 p.m. was sustaining, and no sustaining programs whatever were broadcast on those days between 2 p.m. and 11 p.m. — a total of 45 hours.[4]

Between 8 a.m. and 11 p.m. of the week beginning April 23, 1944, Station WBAL broadcast 507 spot announcements, of which 6 were sustaining public service announcements. An example — not unique — of the piling up of spot announcements is found in the 45-minute period from 8:15 a.m. to 9:00 a.m. on Monday, April 24, 1944, during which 16 spot announcements were broadcast or one every 2.8 minutes.

Less than 2.5 percent of the station's time between 8 a.m. and 11 p.m. during the week was devoted to sustaining programs of local live origin. The only live sustaining programs carried during the entire week, 8 a.m. to 11 p.m., were as follows:

News at various times	95 minutes
"Gif-Ted Children," by remote control, Saturday, 9:45–10:00 a.m.	15 minutes
"The Family Hour," Saturday, 10:15–10:30 a.m.	15 minutes
"Musical Maneuvers," Saturday, 2:00–2:30 p.m.	30 minutes
Total live sustaining for the week	155 minutes

"If there are any channels now in use by other stations to which any Baltimore station feels better entitled, *by reason of superior programs*, the Baltimore station has but to make application, and after a hearing has been held, at which both sides will be given an opportunity to present full testimony, the members of the Commission will endeavor to assign the channel in the best public interest." (Emphasis supplied.)

[4] As used in this paragraph a "commercial" program is any program which is either paid for by a sponsor, or interrupted more than once per 15 minutes by commercial spot announcements. A 15-minute program preceded, followed, and interrupted once by commercial spot announcements is nevertheless classified as sustaining. For the Commission's proposed future definitions of "commercial" and "sustaining" programs, see "Uniform Definitions and Program Logs." For a discussion of the importance of and need for sustaining programs, see below, pp. 156-181.

Station WBAL devoted 9 hours and 50 minutes to religious programs during the week – only 30 minutes of which was on a sustaining basis. The remaining 9 hours and 20 minutes were paid for by the religious organizations involved.

Station WBAL carried one forum or round table discussion-type program, either local or of network origin, during the week. The University of Chicago Round Table was made available to WBAL by NBC; but WBAL carried instead two transcribed commercial music programs and two 5-minute commercial talk programs.

The extent to which Baltimore has long been a world-renowned music center is noted above. During the entire week in question, the only local live music broadcast by Station WBAL between 8 a.m. and 11 p.m. was as follows:

A 10-minute "Music Award" commercial program.
"Musical Maneuvers," Saturday, 2:00–2:30 p.m.
"Songs of Romance," commercial, at various times, totalling 50 minutes for the week.

The National Broadcasting Company designates certain of its outstanding sustaining programs as "Public Service Programs": These programs were until 1945 marked with an American shield on its program schedules. During the week beginning April 23, 1944, NBC designated 19 programs as "Public Service Programs." Of these, Station WBAL carried five[5] and failed to carry 14. The 14 NBC "Public Service Programs" not carried and the programs carried by WBAL in lieu thereof are shown below:

Time	NBC Public Service Program	WBAL Program
SUNDAY		
9:15–9:30 a.m.	"Commando Mary"– War Work for Women.	"Good Tidings Hour." Reverend Peters, commercial program.
10–10:30 a.m.	"National Radio Pulpit" –Reverend John Milton Phillips of the Grand Avenue Baptist Church in Omaha, Guest Speaker; Radio Choristers. Direction George Shackley. (From WOW, Omaha, and New York.)	10–10:05, News; 10:05 –10:30, "Sunday Morning Round-up," transcribed music with four spot announcements for Anderson Motors, Fava Fruit Co., Four Besske Brothers, and Cactus Pills.

[5] "Here's to Youth," "Doctors at War," "American Story," "Army Hour," and "Catholic Hour," all half-hour programs.

Time	NBC Public Service Program	WBAL Program
SUNDAY		
1:15–1:30 p.m.	"Labor for Victory"—Congress of Industrial Organizations; guest speakers.	"Willis Jones," commercial program sponsored by the Willis Jones committee.
1:30–2:00 p.m.	"University of Chicago Round Table Discussion" —guest speakers.	1:30–1:45, transcribed commercial music; 1:45–1:50, commercial talk, "Listen, Motorist"; 1:50–1:55, transcribed commercial music; 1:55–2:00, "Stay Out of Court," commercial talk.
4:30–4:55 p.m.	"Land of the Free"—"Indians of the North." Drama: Inter-American University of the Air; guest speaker (from Canada).	"Women of the Week," local commercial, drama, sponsored by the Schleisner Company.
11:30–12:00 mid.	"The Pacific Story—Hirohito: Eclipse of the Son of Heaven." Dramatization. (From Hollywood.)	"The Open Bible," commercial program sponsored by the Hamilton Baptist Church.
MONDAY		
12:30–1:00 p.m.	"U.S. Navy Band" (from Washington).	12:30–12:45, "Masters of Rhythm," transcribed music with six spot announcements; 12:45–1, "Treasury Salute," transcribed music.
TUESDAY		
12:30–1:00 p.m.	"U.S. Coast Guard on Parade" (from WTIC, Hartford).	12:30–12:45, "Masters of Rhythm," transcribed music with six spot announcements; 12:45–1, "Treasury Salute," transcribed music.
11:30–12:00 mid.	"Words at War"—dramatized stories.	11:30–11:45, "Open Bible," commercial transcribed program sponsored by Hamilton Baptist

Time	NBC Public Service Program	WBAL Program
TUESDAY 11:30–12:00 mid.		Church; 11:45–12, "Treasury Salute," transcribed music.
WEDNESDAY 12:30–1:00 p.m.	"U.S. Air Force Band" –Capt. George S. Howard, Conductor (from Washington).	12:30–12:45, "Masters of Rhythm," transcribed music with six spot announcements; 12:45–1, "Treasury Salute," transcribed music.
FRIDAY 12:30–1:00 p.m.	"U.S. Marine Band" (from Washington).	12:30–12:45, "Masters of Rhythm," transcribed music with six spot announcements; 12:45–1, "Treasury Salute," transcribed music.
SATURDAY 1:30–1:45 p.m.	"The Baxters Invest in Health," drama; National Congress of Parent and Teachers Associations.	1:30–1:35, "Latest News"; spot announcement for Arrid deodorant; 1:35–1:45, "Behind the News."
1:45–2:00 p.m.	"War Telescope"–John MacVane from London via shortwave.	"Front-Page Drama," electrical transcription, commercial program sponsored by Sunday *American.*
6:00–6:30 p.m.	"I Sustain the Wings" –Army Air Force Band, Capt. Glenn Miller conducting.	6–6:05, "Esso News," sponsored by Standard Oil Co.; 6:05–6:15, "National Sports," sponsored by National Beer Co.; transcribed spot announcement for "Whiz Candy"; 6:15–6:30, "Paul Robertson Talk," political speech.

E.   Representations made in court: Station KHMO

The *KHMO* case (4 F.C.C. 505; 70 App. D.C. 80) is of interest because it involves an element of judicial review, and a comparison of representations made in court with present performance.

The Courier Post Publishing Company of Hannibal, Missouri, now the licensee of Station KHMO, originally applied for a new station at Hannibal in 1936, as did a competing applicant. The Commission, after a hearing, was unable to find that a need existed for a local station in Hannibal and accordingly both applications were denied.

On appeal to the U.S. Court of Appeals for the District of Columbia (70 App. D.C. 80, 104 F. (2d) 213), the Court found that the Commission was in error, and that a need did exist for a local broadcast station to serve the particular local interests of the Hannibal community. Speaking through Judge Vinson, the Court noted (pp. 82-83) that service was available from other stations, but that "none of these stations provide for the local needs of Hannibal." The Court cited a Commission definition of a local station as one which would serve "to present programs of local interest to the residents of that community; to utilize and develop local entertainment talent which the record indicates is available; to serve local, religious, educational, civic, patriotic, and other organizations; to broadcast local news; and to generally provide a means of local public expression and a local broadcast service to listeners in that area."[1]

The Court cited in detail the programs which the applicant proposed to broadcast[2] and relied in particular on the applicant's representations that it "planned to use local talent — an abundance of which was shown to be available — and in this manner serve public interest of that area. Thus, it appears that the petition for a construction permit is supported by overwhelming evidence

[1] *Okmulgee Broadcasting Corporation*, 4 FCC 302.

[2] Thus the Court noted that the applicant "proposed to give portions of its time, without charge, to the various local civic, educational, athletic, farming, fraternal, religious, and charitable organizations. Its proposed program consists of: Entertainment 42%, educational 20%, news 9%, religious 9%, agriculture 10%, fraternal 5%, and civic activities 5%. The tentative program contemplated, particularly, the use of the facilities of the station to aid education in supplementing classroom work, and in broadcasting from a secondary studio located at Hannibal La Grange College subjects of scholastic interest and athletic events; the use by the Hannibal Chamber of Commerce to further business relations; the use by the County Agriculture Agent to bring before farmers and farm clubs the subject matter that is offered through the United States Department of Agriculture and Missouri College of Agriculture on farm problems; the use by the County Health Department to give information concerning maternity and child health, public health problems, particularly prevention of disease, food and milk control, and general sanitation; the use of the station by business in advertising; the promotion of literary and philanthropic activities; the promotion of better civic spirit; the furtherance of physical culture, and social activities of the Y.M.C.A. and Boy Scouts; and the broadcasting of daily religious services of the several Hannibal churches." (70 App. D.C. 80, 82-3.)

showing *the local need for a local station to serve in the manner set out."*
(Emphasis supplied.)

Pursuant to this decision of the Court of Appeals, the Commission granted
a license. It appears, however, that the program service rendered is markedly
different from the representations upon which the Court relied. For example,
only 14.2 percent of the station's time for the week beginning April 22, 1945,
was devoted to the "local talent"[3] said to be so abundant in the area. More than
85.8 percent of its time, in contrast, was devoted to network programs and
transcriptions. Instead of giving its time "without charge" to local religious
organizations, as represented, Station KHMO sold 4¾ hours of time during the
week to such organizations on a commercial basis, and provided no time for
local religious programs without charge.

PART II.   COMMISSION JURISDICTION WITH
RESPECT TO PROGRAM SERVICE

The contention has at times been made that Section 326 of the Communications
Act, which prohibits censorship or interference with free speech by the
Commission, precludes any concern on the part of the Commission with the
program service of licensees. This contention overlooks the legislative history of
the Radio Act of 1927, the consistent administrative practice of the Federal
Radio Commission, the re-enactment of identical provisions in the Communications Act of 1934 with full knowledge by the Congress that the language
covered a Commission concern with program service, the relevant court
decisions, and this Commission's concern with program service since 1934.

The Communications Act, like the Radio Act of 1927, directs the
Commission to grant licenses and renewals of licenses only if public interest,
convenience and necessity will be served thereby. The first duty of the Federal
Radio Commission, created by the Act of 1927, was to give concrete meaning to
the phrase "public interest" by formulating standards to be applied in granting
licenses for the use of practically all the then available radio frequencies. From
the beginning it assumed that program service was a prime factor to be taken
into consideration. The renewal forms prepared by it in 1927 included the
following questions:

(11)   Attach printed program for the last week.
(12)   *Why will the operation of the station be in the public convenience,
        interest and necessity?*
        (a)   Average amount of time weekly devoted to the following
               services (1) entertainment (2) religious (3) commercial (4)
               educational (5) agricultural (6) fraternal.

[3] Including news programs read off the ticker by a local announcer.

(b)   Is direct advertising conducted in the interest of the applicant or others?

Copies of this form were submitted for Congressional consideration.[1]

In its Annual Report to Congress for 1928, the Commission stated (p. 161):

The Commission believes it is entitled to consider the program service rendered by the various applicants, to compare them, and to favor those which render the best service.

The Federal Radio Commission was first created for a term of one year only. In 1928 a bill was introduced to extend this term and extensive hearings were held before the House Committee on Merchant Marine and Fisheries. The Commissioners appeared before the Committee and were questioned at length as to their administration of the Act. At that time Commissioner Caldwell reported that the Commission had taken the position that

. . . each station occupying a desirable channel should be kept on its toes to produce and present the best programs possible and, if any station slips from that high standard, another station which is putting on programs of a better standard should have the right to contest the first station's position and after hearing the full testimony, to replace it. (Hearings on Jurisdiction, p. 188.)

The Commissioner also reported that he had concluded, after 18 months' experience, that station selections should not be made on the basis of priority in use and stated that he had found that a policy —

. . . of hearings, by which there is presented full testimony on the demonstrated capacity of the station to render service, is a much better test of who is entitled to those channels. (Ibid.)

By 1929 the Commission had formulated its standard of the program service which would meet, in fair proportion, "the tastes, needs and desires of all substantial groups among the listening public." A well-rounded program service, it said, should consist of

entertainment, consisting of music of both classical and lighter grades, religion, education, and instruction, important public events, discussion of public questions, weather, market reports, and news and matters of interest to all members of the family. (Great Lakes Broadcasting Co., reported in F.R.C., 3d Annual Report, pp. 33-35.)

By the time Congress had under consideration replacing the Radio Act of 1927 with a new regulatory statute, there no longer existed any doubt that the

---

[1]*Hearings on Jurisdiction of Radio Commission,* House Committee on Merchant Marine and Fisheries, 1928, p. 26.

Commission did possess the power to take over-all program service into account. The broadcasting industry itself recognized the "manifest duty" of the Commission to consider program service. In 1934, at hearings before the House Committee on Interstate Commerce on one of the bills which finally culminated in the Communications Act of 1934, the National Association of Broadcasters submitted a statement which contained the following (*Hearings on H.R. 8301*, 73rd Cong., p. 117):

It is the manifest duty of the licensing authority, in passing upon applications for licenses or the renewal thereof, to determine whether or not the applicant is rendering or can render an adequate public service. *Such service necessarily includes* broadcasting of a considerable proportion of programs devoted to education, religion, labor, agricultural and similar activities concerned with human betterment. In actual practice over a period of 7 years, as the records of the Federal Radio Commission amply prove, this has been *the principal test* which the Commission has applied in dealing with broadcasting applications. (Emphasis supplied.)

In hearings before the same committee on the same bill (*H.R. 8301*, 73rd Cong.) Chairman Sykes of the Federal Radio Commission testified (pp. 350-352):

That act puts upon the individual licensee of a broadcast station the private initiative to see that those programs that he broadcasts are in the public interest. . . . Then that act makes those individual licensees responsible to the licensing authority to see that their operations are in the public interest.

Our licenses to broadcasting stations last for 6 months. *The law says that they must operate in the public interest, convenience, and necessity.* When the time for a renewal of those station licenses comes up, *it is the duty of the Commission in passing on whether or not that station should be relicensed for another licensing period, to say whether or not their past performance during the last license period has been in the public interest.* (Emphasis supplied.)

Under the law, of course, we cannot refuse a renewal until there is a hearing before the Commission. We would have to have a hearing before the Commission, to go thoroughly into the nature of all of the broadcasts of those stations, consider all of those broadcasts, and then say whether or not it was operating in the public interest.

In the full knowledge of this established procedure of the Federal Radio Commission, the Congress thereupon re-enacted the relevant provisions in the Communications Act of 1934.

In the course of the discussion of the 1934 Act, an amendment to the Senate bill was introduced which required the Commission to allocate 25 percent of all broadcasting facilities for the use of educational, religious, agricultural, labor, cooperative and similar non-profit-making organizations.

Senator Dill, who was the sponsor in the Senate of both the 1927 and 1934 Acts, spoke against the amendment, stating that the Commission already had the power to reach the desired ends (78 *Cong. Rec.* 8843):

The difficulty probably is in the failure of the present Commission to take the steps that it ought to take to see to it that a larger use is made of radio facilities for education and religious purposes.

I may say, however, that the owners of large radio stations now operating have suggested to me that it might be well to provide in the license that a certain percentage of the time of a radio station shall be allotted to religious, educational, or non-profit users.

Senator Hatfield, a sponsor of the amendment, had also taken the position that the Commission's power was adequate, saying (78 *Cong. Rec.* 8835):

I have no criticism to make of the personnel of the Radio Commission, except that *their refusal literally to carry out the law of the land warrants the Congress of the United States writing into legislation the desire of Congress that educational institutions be given a specified portion of the radio facilities of our country.* (Emphasis supplied.)

The amendment was defeated and Section 307(c) of the Act was substituted which required the Commission to study the question and to report to Congress its recommendations.

The Commission made such a study and in 1935 issued a report advising against the enactment of legislation. The report stated:

Commercial stations are now responsible under the law, to render a public service, and the tendency of the proposal would be to lessen this responsibility.

The Commission feels that present legislation has the flexibility essential to attain the desired ends without necessitating at this time any changes in the law.

There is no need for a change in the existing law to accomplish the helpful purposes of the proposal.

In order for non-profit organizations to obtain the maximum service possible, cooperation in good faith by the broadcasters is required. *Such cooperation should, therefore, be under the direction and supervision of the Commission.* (Report of the Federal Communications Commission to Congress Pursuant to Sec. 307(c) of the Communications Act of 1934, Jan. 22, 1935.) (Emphasis supplied.)

On the basis of the foregoing legislative history there can be no doubt that Congress intended the Commission to consider overall program service in passing on applications. The Federal Communications Commission from the beginning accepted the doctrine that its public interest determinations, like those of its predecessor, must be based in part at least on grounds of program service. Thus early in 1935 it designated for joint hearing the renewal applications of Stations KGFJ, KFWB, KMPC, KRKD, and KIEV, in part "to determine the nature and character of the program service rendered . . ." *In re McGlasham et al.*, 2 F.C.C. 145, 149. In its decision, the Commission set forth the basis of its authority as follows:

Section 309(a) of the Communications Act of 1934 is an exact restatement of Section 11 of the Radio Act of 1927. This section provides that subject to the limitations of the Act the Commission may grant licenses if the public interest, convenience, and necessity will be served thereby. The United States Court of Appeals for the District of Columbia in the case of *KFKB Broadcasting Association, Inc.* v. *Federal Radio Commission*, 60 App. D.C. 79, held that under Section 11 of the Radio Act of 1927 the Radio Commission was necessarily called upon to consider the character and quality of the service to be rendered and that in considering an application for renewal an important consideration is the past conduct of the applicant. (2 F.C.C. 145, 149.)

The courts have agreed that the Commission may consider program service of a licensee in passing on its renewal application. In the first case in which an applicant appealed from a Commission decision denying the renewal of a station license in part because of its program service, the court simply assumed that program service should be considered in determining the question of public interest and summarized and adopted the Commission's findings concerning program service as a factor in its own decision.[2] In 1931, however, the question was squarely presented to the Court of Appeals when the KFKB Broadcasting Association contended that the action of the Commission in denying a renewal of its license because of the type of program material and advertising which it had broadcast, constituted censorship by the Commission. The Court sustained the Commission, saying:

It is apparent, we think, that the business is impressed with a public interest and that, because the number of available broadcasting frequencies is limited, *the Commission is necessarily called upon to consider the character and quality of the service to be rendered.* In considering an application for a renewal of a license, an important consideration is the past conduct of the applicant, for "by their fruits shall ye know them." Matt. VII:20. Especially is this true in a case like the present, where the evidence clearly justifies the conclusion that the future conduct of the station will not differ from the past. (*KFKB Broadcasting Association* v. *Federal Radio Commission*, 47 F. 2d 670.) (Emphasis supplied.)

In 1932, the Court affirmed this position in *Trinity Methodist Church* v. *Federal Radio Commission*, 62 F. (2d) 850, and went on to say that it is the

---

[2] *Technical Radio Laboratory* v. *Federal Radio Commission*, 59 App. D.C. 125, 36 F. (2d) 111.

"duty" of the Commission "to take notice of the appellant's conduct in his previous use of the permit."

The question of the nature of the Commission's power was presented to the Supreme Court in the *network* case. The contention was then made that the Commission's power was limited to technological matters only. The Court rejected this, saying (*National Broadcasting Company* v. *United States*, 319 U.S. 190, 216-217):

The Commission's licensing function cannot be discharged, therefore, merely by finding that there are no technological objections to the granting of a license. If the criterion of "public interest" were limited to such matters, how could the Commission choose between two applicants for the same facilities, each of whom is financially and technically qualified to operate a station? Since the very inception of federal regulation by radio, comparative considerations as to the service to be rendered have governed the application of the standard of "public interest, convenience, or necessity."

The foregoing discussion should make it clear not only that the Commission has the authority to concern itself with program service, but that it is under an affirmative duty, in its public interest determinations, to give full consideration to program service. Part III of this Report will consider some particular aspects of program service as they bear upon the public interest.

PART III.   SOME ASPECTS OF "PUBLIC INTEREST" IN PROGRAM SERVICE

As has been noted, the Commission must determine, with respect to each application granted or denied or renewed, whether or not the program service proposed is "in the public interest, convenience, and necessity."

The Federal Radio Commission was faced with this problem from the very beginning, and in 1928 it laid down a broad definition which may still be cited in part:

Broadcasting stations are licensed to serve the public and not for the purpose of furthering the private or selfish interests of individuals or groups of individuals. The standard of public interest, convenience, or necessity means nothing if it does not mean this. . . . The emphasis should be on the *receiving* of service and the standard of public interest, convenience, or necessity should be construed accordingly. . . . The *entire* listening public within the service area of a station, or of a group of stations in one community, is entitled to service from that station or stations. . . . In a sense a broadcasting station may be regarded as a sort of mouthpiece on the air for the community it serves, over which its public events of general interest, its political campaigns, its election results, its athletic contests, its orchestras and artists, and discussion of its public issues may be broadcast. *If . . . the station performs its duty in furnishing a well rounded program, the rights of the community* have been achieved. (In re Great Lakes Broadcasting Co., F.R.C. Docket No. 4900; cf. 3rd Annual Report of the F.R.C., pp. 32-36.) (Emphasis supplied.)

Commission policy with respect to public interest determinations is for the most part set by opinions in particular cases. (See, for example, cases indexed under "Program Service" in Volumes 1 through 9 of the Commission's Decisions.) A useful purpose is served, however, by occasional overall reviews of Commission policy. This Part will discuss four major issues currently involved in the application of the "public interest" standard to program service policy; namely, (A) the carrying of sustaining programs, (B) the carrying of local live programs, (C) the carrying of programs devoted to public discussion, and (D) the elimination of commercial advertising excesses.

A.   The carrying of sustaining programs

The commercial program, paid for and in many instances also selected, written, casted, and produced by advertisers and advertising agencies, is the staple fare of American listening. More than half of all broadcast time is devoted to commercial programs; the most popular programs on the air are commercial. The evidence is overwhelming that the popularity of American broadcasting as we know it is based in no small part upon its commercial programs.

Nevertheless, since the early days of broadcasting, broadcasters and the Commission alike have recognized that sustaining programs also play an integral and irreplaceable part in the American system of broadcasting. The sustaining program has five distinctive and outstanding functions.

1.   To secure for the station or network a means by which in the overall structure of its program service, it can achieve a *balanced* interpretation of public needs.
2.   To provide programs which by their very nature may not be sponsored with propriety.
3.   To provide programs for significant minority tastes and interests.
4.   To provide programs devoted to the needs and purposes of nonprofit organizations.
5.   To provide a field for experiment in new types of programs, secure from the restrictions that obtain with reference to programs in which the advertiser's interest in selling goods predominates.

(1)   Balance-wheel function of the sustaining program

The sustaining program is the balance-wheel by means of which the imbalance of a station's or network's program structure, which might otherwise result from commercial decisions concerning program structure, can be redressed.

Dr. Frank N. Stanton, then Director of Research and now vice-president of the Columbia Broadcasting System, explained this function to the House Committee on Interstate and Foreign Commerce (*Hearings on H.R. 4597,* 77th Cong., 2nd Sess., May 7, 1942, page 289):

One use Columbia makes of sustaining programs is to supplement commercial offerings in such ways as to achieve, so far as possible, a full and balanced network service. For example, if the commercial programs should be preponderantly musical, Columbia endeavors to restore program balance with drama or the like in its sustaining service.

The Commission, as well as broadcasters themselves, has always insisted that a "well-balanced program structure" is an essential part of broadcasting in the public interest. At least since 1928, and continuing to the present, stations have been asked, on renewal, to set forth the average amount of time, or percentage of time, devoted to entertainment programs, religious programs, educational programs, agricultural programs, fraternal programs, etc.; and the Commission has from time to time relied upon the data thus set forth in determining whether a station has maintained a well-balanced program structure.[1]

In metropolitan areas where the listener has his choice of several stations, balanced service to listeners can be achieved either by means of a balanced program structure for each station or by means of a number of comparatively specialized stations which, considered together, offer a balanced service to the community. In New York City, a considerable degree of specialization on the part of particular stations has already arisen — one station featuring a

---

[1] The question asked on renewal in recent years is as follows:

"State the average percentage of time per month (combined total should equal 100%) devoted to—

"Commercial Programs	*"Sustaining Programs*
"1. Entertainment	[The categories specified under
2. Educational	this column are the same as
3. Religious	those in the adjacent column.—
4. Agricultural	Ed.]
5. Civic (include in this item fraternal, Chamber of Commerce, charitable, and other civic but non-governmental programs)	
6. Governmental (include in this item all municipal, state, and federal programs, including political or controversial broadcasts by public officials, or candidates for public office, and regardless of whether or not the programs included under this item are entertainment, educational, agricultural, etc., in character)	
7. News	
8. —	
9. Total"	

preponderance of classical music, another a preponderance of dance music, etc. With the larger number of stations which FM will make possible, such specialization may arise in other cities. To make possible this development on a sound community basis, the Commission proposes in its application forms hereafter to afford applicants an opportunity to state whether they propose a balanced program structure or special emphasis on program service of a particular type or types.

Experience has shown that in general advertisers prefer to sponsor programs of news and entertainment. There are exceptions; but they do not alter the fact that if decisions today were left solely or predominantly to advertisers, news and entertainment would occupy substantially all of the time. The concept of a well-rounded structure can obviously not be maintained if the decision is left wholly or preponderantly in the hands of advertisers in search of a market, each concerned with his particular half hour, rather than in the hands of stations and networks responsible under the statute for overall program balance in the public interest.

A device by which some networks and stations are seeking to prevent program imbalance is the "package" program, selected, written, casted and produced by the network or station itself, and sold to the advertiser as a ready-built package, with the time specified by the station or network. In order to get a particular period of time, the advertiser must take the package program which occupies that period. This practice, still far from general, appears to be a step in the direction of returning control of programs to those licensed to operate in the public interest. The commercial "package" program is not a substitute for the sustaining program, however, for reasons set forth in subsections (2) through (5) of this section.

What happens when the balance-wheel function of the sustaining program is neglected can be illustrated by the case of the "soap opera," defined as "a continuing serial in dramatic form, in which an understanding of today's episode is dependent upon previous listening."

In January 1940, the four networks provided listeners with 59½ daytime hours of sponsored programs weekly. Of these, 55 hours were devoted to soap operas. *Only 4½ sponsored daytime hours a week on the four networks were devoted to any other type of program.* Advertisers, in short, were permitted to destroy overall program balance by concentration on one type of program. The number of soap operas subsequently increased, reaching in April 1941 a total of some 50 commercially sponsored network soap operas a day.[2] Since then, there has been some decline, and the introduction of some sustaining programs in daytime hours has begun to modify the picture.

The extent of program imbalance still prevalent is indicated by the fact that in September 1945 the National Broadcasting Company was still devoting 4¾ hours per day, Monday through Friday, to 19 soap operas, and the Columbia

[2]C. E. Hooper, Inc., "Year End Review of 1943 Daytime Radio Listening."

Broadcasting System was similarly devoting 4¼ hours daily, Monday through Friday, to 17 such programs.

The following table presents data concerning soap operas during the period December 1944–April 1945.[2a] Column 1 shows the "rating" of the 19 soap operas broadcast by NBC and the 17 broadcast by CBS — that is, the percentage of telephone homes in 32 large cities where a respondent stated that the radio was tuned to the program in question or the station carrying the program. Column 2 shows the size of the available audience as determined by the same telephone calls — that is, the percentage of telephone homes in which someone was at home and awake to answer the telephone. Column 3, which is the "resultant" of columns 1 and 2, thus shows the recruiting power of the program — that is, the percentage of the available audience actually tuned to each soap opera. It will be noted that the most popular soap opera on the air during the period in question recruited 12.5 percent of the available audience. The average NBC soap opera recruited 8.4 percent of the available audience, and the average CBS soap opera recruited 6.7 percent of the available audience. In contrast, approximately 76.8 percent of the available audience answering the telephone during the soap opera hours reported that they had their radios turned off altogether.

NBC SOAP OPERAS

		Program Rating	Available Audience	Recruiting Efficiency
Mon.–Fri. 10:15 a.m.	Lora Lawton	3.3	75.3	4.4
10:30 a.m.	Road of Life	3.0	75.4	4.0
10:45 a.m.	Joyce Jordan	3.0	73.6	4.1
11:45 a.m.	David Harum	2.9	72.2	4.0
2:00 p.m.	Guiding Light	5.5	68.2	8.1
2:15 p.m.	Today's Children	6.0	67.1	8.9
2:30 p.m.	Woman in White	5.6	66.0	8.5
3:00 p.m.	A Woman of America	4.6	66.1	7.0
3:15 p.m.	Oxydol's Own Ma Perkins	6.1	66.2	9.2
3:30 p.m.	Pepper Young's Family	7.1	65.9	10.7
3:45 p.m.	Right to Happiness	7.0	66.4	10.5
4:00 p.m.	Backstage Wife	6.7	67.6	9.9
4:15 p.m.	Stella Dallas	6.9	67.4	10.2
4:30 p.m.	Lorenzo Jones	6.7	68.7	9.8
4:45 p.m.	Young Widder Brown	7.5	69.6	10.7
5:00 p.m.	When a Girl Marries	8.9	71.1	12.5
5:15 p.m.	Portia Faces Life	7.9	71.6	11.0
5:30 p.m.	Just Plain Bill	6.5	73.4	8.9
5:45 p.m.	Front Page Farrell	5.6	74.7	7.5

[2a] See *Fortune*, March 1946, p. 119, "Soap Opera."

CBS SOAP OPERAS

		Program Rating	Available Audience	Recruiting Efficiency
Mon.–Fri. 10:00 a.m.	Valiant Lady	2.9	76.1	3.8
10:15 a.m.	Light of the World	3.7	75.3	4.9
10:30 a.m.	The Strange Romance of Evelyn Winters	3.4	75.4	4.5
10:45 a.m.	Bachelor's Children	4.3	73.6	5.8
11:00 a.m.	Amanda of Honeymoon Hill	2.8	74.5	3.8
11:15 a.m.	Second Husband	3.3	73.3	4.5
11:30 a.m.	Bright Horizon	4.5	73.1	6.2
12:15 p.m.	Big Sister	6.7	72.1	9.3
12:30 p.m.	The Romance of Helen Trent	7.0	72.1	9.7
12:45 p.m.	Our Gal Sunday	6.8	70.8	9.6
1:00 p.m.	Life Can Be Beautiful	7.2	70.4	10.2
1:15 p.m.	Ma Perkins	7.7	69.7	11.0
1:45 p.m.	Young Dr. Malone	5.1	68.2	7.5
2:00 p.m.	Two On a Clue	4.3	68.2	6.3
2:15 p.m.	Rosemary	4.1	67.1	6.1
2:30 p.m.	Perry Mason	3.8	66.0	5.8
2:45 p.m.	Tena & Tim	3.8	66.1	5.7

Source: "Sectional" Hooperatings, Dec. 1944–April 1945, Winter–Spring.

The "ratings" of the NBC and CBS soap operas must be considered in the light of the dominant position in the spectrum occupied by the stations concerned. Thus in the 32 cities in which the surveys in question were made, the power of the stations affiliated with each network was as follows:

	Total power	Average power per station
32 CBS stations	925,000 w	28,906 w
32 NBC stations	835,000 w	26,093 w
32 ABC stations	222,250 w	6,945 w
32 Mutual stations	200,000 w	6,250 w

Several reasons may be suggested for the popularity of soap operas among advertisers.[3] First, the soap opera is among the cheapest of all network shows to

[3] According to the Cooperative Analysis of Broadcasting (CAB), network commercial time during the day from October 1943 to April 1944 was divided as follows:

Serial drama	57.4%
News and talks	10.7%

produce. The weekly production costs of the ordinary soap opera are reported to be less, for five 15-minute periods, than some advertisers spend on a one-minute transcribed spot announcement. Second, advertisers are not interested merely or primarily in the size of the audience which they achieve. They are interested also, and perhaps primarily, in two other indices of program effectiveness. One is the "sponsor identification index" which is defined as "the percent of listeners to a specific program which knows the name of the program's advertiser, or of any of his products." The other is the "product use index," defined as "the use of a sponsor's brand of product and that of his competitors among listeners to his program compared with non-listeners." An advertiser relying on the sponsor identification index, for example, may prefer a soap opera which appeals to only one million listeners and indelibly impresses the name of his product on two-thirds of them, rather than a non-soap opera program which appeals to two million listeners but impresses the sponsor's name on less than one-third. Similarly, an advertiser may prefer a soap opera which, as in an actual instance, results in the use of his product by 46.5 percent of those who listen (as compared with 25.1 percent of use among non-listeners), even though the program in question appeals to comparatively few listeners.

Mr. Duane Jones, head of an advertising agency reputed to be one of the five largest in New York, clearly was considering the special interests of advertisers rather than the public interest, when he declared:

The best radio program is the one that sells the most goods, not necessarily the one that holds the highest Hooper or Crossley rating. [4]

Whether or not the reasons cited for the popularity of soap operas among advertisers are the decisive ones, it is clear that the result on many stations has been a marked imbalance of program structure during the daytime hours; and it is significant that the first steps recently taken to redress this imbalance have been the addition of sustaining programs. It is by means of the sustaining

Variety	8.7%
Drama	6.8%
Children's Programs	4.7%
Classical and Semi-Classical	4.5%
Audience Participation	2.8%
Popular Music	2.2%
Familiar Music	1.3%
Hymns	0.9%
	100 %

[4]The advertiser view cited may be contrasted with one of the "basic principles" in the interpretation of the phrase "public interest, convenience or necessity" laid down by the Federal Radio Commission in 1928:

"While it is true that broadcasting stations in this country are for the most part supported or partially supported by advertisers, broadcasters are not given these great privileges by the United States Government for the primary benefit of advertisers. *Such benefit as is derived by advertisers must be incidental and entirely secondary to the interest of the public.*" (Emphasis in original.)

program that program imbalance, consequent upon sponsor domination of excessive blocks of time, can be redressed by those responsible for program structure — balance — the licensees, including the networks.

(2)   Programs inappropriate for commercial sponsorship

A second role of the sustaining program is to provide time for broadcasts which by their very nature may not be appropriate for sponsorship. As early as 1930, Mr. Merlin H. Aylesworth, then president of the National Broadcasting Company, recognized this role of the sustaining program in testimony before the Senate Committee on Interstate Commerce, even proposing that college football games were by their nature inappropriate for commercial sponsorship.[5] More recently, in 1941, Mr. Niles Trammell, president of the National Broadcasting Co., has stated:

Another reason for the use of sustaining programs was the voluntary recognition on the part of broadcasters that programs of certain types, such as religious programs, informative programs furnished by various governmental agencies and certain programs involving discussions of political principles and other controversial issues, were not suited to advertising sponsorship. The use of high types of sustaining programs also creates goodwill for the station and induces people to become accustomed to listening to certain stations in preference to others.[6]

The *Code of the National Association of Broadcasters* similarly recognized, until 1945, that the presentation of controversial issues (except forums) should be exclusively in sustaining programs. While the Commission has recently held that an absolute ban on the sale of time for the discussion of public issues may under certain circumstances not serve the public interest,[7] it is nevertheless clear that such broadcasts should be primarily of a sustaining nature.

The Commission has never set forth and does not now propose to set forth the particular types of program which, for one reason or another, must remain free from commercial sponsorship. It does, however, recognize along with the stations and networks themselves that there are such programs.[8] Self-regulation

[5] *"Mr. Aylesworth. . . .* We have refused to permit from our system the sponsoring of football games by commercial institutions. That may be a wrong policy; I do not know; but I have assumed that with all these youngsters in their management boards and with all of the commercialism that is talked about, and so forth, that I just did not quite like to see the Yale-Harvard game announced 'through the courtesy of so and so.' " (*Hearings on S. 6,* 1930, p. 1711.)

[6] Affidavit of Niles Trammel, in *National Broadcasting Co.* v. *United States* in the Supreme Court of the U.S., October Term, 1941, No. 1025, Transcript of Record, p. 228.

[7] *In the Matter of United Broadcasting Co. (WHKC),* decided June 26, 1945.

[8] For example, one station has recently stated its refusal to exploit the problems of returning veterans on commercial programs, preferring programs devoted to veteran problems on a sustaining basis. *Variety,* for March 14, 1945, reports:

consonant with public sentiment, and a responsible concern for the public interest, can best insure a suitable interpretation of the basic principle which the industry itself has always recognized, that some programs are by their nature unsuitable for commercial sponsorship. Public interest requires that sustaining time be kept available for such broadcasts.

(3)   Significant minority tastes and interests

It has long been an established policy of broadcasters themselves and of the Commission that the American system of broadcasting must serve significant minorities among our population, and the less dominant needs and tastes which most listeners have from time to time. Dr. Frank Stanton, in his testimony before the House Committee on Interstate and Foreign Commerce in 1942, previously cited, set forth this function of the sustaining program as follows:

There is another feature of sustaining service which differentiates it from commercial programs. While the CBS sustaining service recognizes the broad popular tastes, it also gives attention to smaller groups. It is known that the New York Philharmonic Symphony Orchestra, the Columbia Work Shop, Invitation to Learning, Columbia Broadcasting Symphony, and many other ambitious classical programs never reach the largest audience, but Columbia, nonetheless, puts them on year after year for minorities which are growing steadily.

Many sustaining programs, originally designed for comparatively small audiences, have proved so popular that they have subsequently acquired commercial sponsorship. "Of Men and Books," for example, was a sustaining feature of a literary nature for more than seven years, from May 26, 1938 to September 8, 1945, before a sponsor was obtained. When such a program becomes sponsored, the way is open for devoting sustaining time to still other types of programs having less than maximum audience appeal.

But even if they may not be able to compete, initially or ever, with Fibber McGee and Molly in size of audience, "sponsor identification index," and "product use index," such programs are essential to a well-balanced program structure. It is no doubt partly due to recognition of this fact that time has always been reserved from sponsorship for the carrying of such programs on a sustaining basis.

"WMCA FEELS VETS WOULD RESENT COM'L EXPLOITATION OF REHABILI-TATION SHOW.

"Plans for the production of a new program helping returning GIs rehabilitate themselves, and to aid their families in the readjustment period, are being planned by WMCA, N.Y. Move further reflects the industry-wide consciousness of the vital issue. . . .

"Show will not be for sale, station feeling vets would resent having solution of their problems made the subject of commercial exploitation. As result it's going on as a public service show."

(4)   Service to non-profit organizations

A well-balanced program structure has always been deemed to include programs devoted to the needs and purposes of non-profit organizations.

Section 307(c) of the Communications Act of 1934 specifically directed the Commission to "study the proposal that Congress by statute allocate fixed percentages of radio broadcasting facilities to particular types or kinds of non-profit activities," and to report to Congress its recommendations. The Commission undertook prolonged hearings on the question, at which witnesses for non-profit organizations, networks and stations were heard at length. Such organizations as the National Committee on Education by Radio, individual educational institutions, representatives of many religious organizations, the American Federation of Labor, the Women's National Radio Committee, the Farmers' Union, and many others testified concerning the importance of broadcasting to their organizations and the services which their organizations could render to the public through broadcasting. Networks and stations, in turn, testified without hesitation to their willingness to assist and to supply time for the non-profit organizations.[9]

The Commission, in its report to Congress pursuant to Section 307(c) of the Communications Act, recommended that specific percentages of facilities *not* be reserved by statute for non-profit organizations, specifically on the ground that existing commercial stations were ready and willing to carry programs of non-profit organizations and that non-profit organizations would benefit thereby. Said the Commission:

It would appear that the interests of the non-profit organizations may be better served by the use of the existing facilities, thus giving them access to costly and efficient equipment and to established audiences, than by the establishment of new stations for their peculiar needs. In order for non-profit organizations to obtain the maximum service possible, cooperation in good faith by the broadcasters is required. *Such cooperation should, therefore, be under the direction and supervision of the Commission. . . . It is our firm intention to assist the non-profit organizations to obtain the fullest* opportunities for expression. (Pp. 6, 9-10; emphasis supplied.)

Cooperation between networks, stations, and non-profit organizations has always been present in greater or less degree, and it may be noted that many

---

[9] Merlin A. Aylesworth, then president of the National Broadcasting Company, testified in particular: "We know if we do not render a public service, the Commission will give the license to others who will render better public service." (*Hearings* pursuant to Sec. 307(c), p. A23.)

William S. Paley, until recently president of the Columbia Broadcasting System, similarly testified: "We hold our license by serving the public interest, convenience, and necessity. And only by adequate cooperation with all public spirited groups can we be deemed to perform the conditions of our contract." (*Ibid.*, p. 11151.)

outstanding programs, both network and local, have resulted from such cooperation. Among the programs honored at the 9th Annual Exhibition of Educational Radio Programs, 1945 (the Ohio State University Awards), for example, were the following:

Group I – Regional web, regional or clear-channel station

RELIGIOUS BROADCASTS: First Award, "Salute to Valor" series, planned and produced by National Council of Catholic Men, WEAF, New York, and NBC. Honorable Mention: "Victorious Living" series, planned and produced by International Council of Religious Education, widely used over regional and clear-channel stations.

CULTURAL PROGRAMS: Honorable Mention: "Words at War" series, planned by Council on Books in Wartime, WEAF, New York, and NBC.

PUBLIC DISCUSSION PROGRAMS: First Award, "University of Chicago Round Table" series, planned and produced by U. of Chicago, WMAQ, Chicago, and NBC.

PERSONAL AND FAMILY LIFE PROGRAMS: Honorable Mention: "The Baxters" series, planned by National Congress of Parents-Teachers, WMAQ, Chicago, and NBC. Special Mention: "Alcoholics Anonymous" series, WWJ, Detroit.

PROGRAMS FURTHERING WAR, PEACE: First Award: "The March of Minnesota" series, planned and produced by Minnesota Resources Committee, WCCO, Minneapolis, and special state network. First Award, "Russian War Relief Presents" series, planned and produced by Russian War Relief, Inc.; produced by members of Radio Directors Guild of New York City; released to many stations.

CHILDREN'S PROGRAM, OUT-OF-SCHOOL: First Award, "Books Bring Adventure" series, planned and produced by Association of Junior Leagues of America.

IN SCHOOL PROGRAMS, PRIMARY CHILDREN: First Award, "Your Story Parade" series, planned and produced by Texas State Department of Education, WBAP, Fort Worth, and Texas Quality web.

Group II – Local station or organization

CULTURAL PROGRAMS: Special Mention: "New World A-Coming" series, planned and produced by station WMCA in cooperation with Citywide Citizens Committee on Harlem; WMCA, New York.

PUBLIC DISCUSSION PROGRAMS: First Award, "Free Speech Forum" series, planned and produced by WMCA and New York Newspaper Guild; WMCA, New York.

NEWS INTERPRETATION: First Award, "History in the Making" series, planned and produced by University of Colorado and Rocky Mountain Radio Council; KVOD, Denver.

CHILDREN'S PROGRAMS, OUT-OF-SCHOOL: First Award, "Story Time" series, planned and produced by Colorado State College of Education and Rocky Mountain Radio Council; KLZ, Denver.

IN SCHOOL PROGRAMS, ELEMENTARY CHILDREN: Honorable Mention: "News Today — History Tomorrow" series, planned and produced by Rochester Public Schools, WHAM, Rochester, N.Y.

IN SCHOOL PROGRAMS, JUNIOR-SENIOR HIGHS: First Award, "Our America" series, planned and produced by Radio Council of Chicago Public Schools; WBEZ, Chicago Public Schools.

The *Peabody* and *Variety* awards similarly feature such programs as the WTIC temperance series prepared in cooperation with Alcoholics Anonymous, "Worcester and the World," broadcast by station WTAG in cooperation with the United Nations Information Office; programs of the American Jewish Committee; "Assignment Home," produced by CBS in cooperation with Army Service Forces, etc.

Such programs as these have done much to enrich American broadcasting. It may well be that they have kept in the radio audience many whose tastes and interests would otherwise cause them to turn to other media. Radio might easily deteriorate into a means of amusing only one cultural stratum of the American public if commercially sponsored entertainment were not leavened by programs having a different cultural appeal. Just as the programs of non-profit organizations benefit from being aired along with the mass-appeal programs of advertisers, so, it may be, the programs of the advertisers reach a larger and more varied audience by reason of the serious sustaining programs produced in cooperation with non-profit organizations. The furnishing of time and assistance to non-profit organizations is thus not merely a responsibility of networks and stations, but also an opportunity.

Special problems are involved in connection with program service designed especially for farmers — market reports, crop reports, weather reports, talks on farming, and other broadcasts specifically intended for rural listeners. The question of programs particularly adapted to the needs of rural listeners has been made an issue in the Commission's forthcoming Clear Channel Hearings (Docket No. 6741) and surveys of rural listeners have been made for the Commission by the Division of Program Surveys, Bureau of Agricultural Economics, Department of Agriculture, and by the Bureau of the Census.[10]

[10]*Attitudes of Rural People Toward Radio Service*, Bureau of Agricultural Economics, U.S. Department of Agriculture, January 1946.

(5)   Program experimentation

Dr. Stanton, in his testimony previously cited, has described still another role of the sustaining program in the American system of broadcasting:

. . . It is through the sustaining or noncommercial program service that Columbia has developed its greatest contributions to network radio broadcasting. On its own time and at its own expense, Columbia has pioneered in such experimental fields as that of original radio drama through the Columbia Workshop Series. Further, it was the first to originate news broadcasts involving on-the-spot reports from correspondents located over all the world. The Columbia School of the Air, now in its thirteenth year, is another example of the use to which Columbia puts its sustaining time by providing a balanced curriculum of broadcasts, 5 days a week throughout the school year, suitable for use in the classrooms. Columbia has also taken the leadership in the matter of new program content in adult education, music and public debate.

Various advertisers and advertising agencies have frankly stated the extent to which their commercial requirements make necessary a special tailoring of commercial programs. The president of the American Tobacco Company, a sponsor of many network commercial programs, has been quoted to this effect:

We have some funny things here about radio, and we have been criticized for it. Taking 100% as the total radio value, we give 90% to commercials, to what's said about the product, and we give 10% to the show.

We are commercial and we cannot afford to be anything else. I don't have the right to spend the stockholder's money just to entertain the public. In particular, sponsors are naturally loath to sponsor any program which may offend even a minority of listeners. . . . The last thing I could afford to do is to offend the public.

Similarly Procter & Gamble, probably the largest sponsor in American broadcasting, has been described as having "a policy never to offend a single listener."

In 1935, to take an extreme example, Alexander Woollcott's "Town Crier" broadcasts were discontinued when the sponsor complained Mr. Woollcott had criticized Hitler and Mussolini, and might thus offend some listeners.

In the field of creative and dramatic writing for radio, the sponsor's understandable desire to please, to avoid offense to anyone, and to integrate the tone and content of his program with his sales appeal, may exert an especially restrictive influence on artistic self-expression, and on the development of the radio art. Not a few distinguished writers are known to be unwilling to accept sponsorship because of restraints and stereotypes imposed which reflect the commercial as against the artistic preoccupations of the sponsor. *Variety* comments on this situation in its issue of June 20, 1945:

Radio script writers are turning in increasing numbers to the legit field. . . . What is particularly significant, however, is the motive behind the wholesale transfer of allegiance of the scripters from radio to Broadway. For some time the feeling has been mounting among many of the serious writers for radio that they've been retarded by a lack of freedom of expression . . . and that as long as radio remains more or less of a "duplicating machine" without encouraging creative expression and without establishing an identity of its own, it's inevitable that the guy who has something to say will seek other outlets.

Norman Rosten, himself a writer of commercial programs and winner of a grant from the American Academy of Arts and Letters for his radio writing, has stated the point of view of some radio writers in part as follows:

The sponsor and the advertising agency have taken over radio quietly in this matter of writing. Except for sustaining shows (often worthy, such as "Assignment Home") or special public service programs magnanimously aired after 11:30 p.m., the broadcasting company sells Time. It owns the air. It will sell you a piece. Period.

By "non-commercial radio" I do not mean simply any sustaining series. I mean a non-format show, an experimental show, one which does not have limitations of content or form. Something like the old Columbia Workshop. I mean a half hour each week on each network for a program of original radio plays. With or without love in a cottage. In poetry or prose. Any way we please. No commercial and no strings. All we want is a piece of wavelength and your good auspices. Not a seasonal replacement, but an all-year-round proposition. The present hit-or-miss, one-shot system is a phony. Nor does a new "Thirteen by Corwin" mean the millennium. Mr. Corwin's triumph has not saved his fellow-writers. How about a "Thirteen by Thirteen?" or "Twenty-six by Twenty-six?" The writers are here and some good ones. How about setting the Saga of Lux or the creaking door aside one half hour per week per network? It might well usher in a renaissance in radio drama. How about it NBC, CBS, American and Mutual? Put up or, as the saying quaintly goes, shut up. Prove it, or forever hold your pronouncements about radio coming of age. We are nearing the middle of the 20th century. Shall the singing commercial and the Lone Ranger inherit the earth?

There is no reason to believe that the present boundaries of program service are the ultimate boundaries. If broadcasting is to explore new fields, to devise new types of programs for the American listener, it is clear that the sustaining program must continue as a means by which experimentation and innovation may have the fullest scope, undeterred by the need for immediate financial success or the imposition on writers of restraints deriving from the natural, but limiting, preoccupations of the advertiser.

It is especially important that some sustaining programs be reserved from commercial restraints in view of the degree of concentration of control currently existing among advertisers and advertising agencies. In 1944, for example:

20% of CBS business came from 4 advertisers.

38% of CBS business was handled by 4 advertising agencies.

25% of ABC (Blue Network) business came from 4 advertisers.

37% of ABC (Blue Network) business was handled by 4 advertising agencies.

23% of MBS business came from 4 advertisers.

31% of MBS business was handled by 4 advertising agencies.[11]

One advertiser, Procter & Gamble, is reputed to have spent $22,000,000 on radio advertising in 1944. It purchased approximately 2,000 hours a week of station time — equivalent to the entire weekly time, from sign-on to sign-off, of more than 18 broadcast stations. Procter & Gamble, of course, produces many of its own shows through its own advertising agencies and has control over all its shows. This control is exercised, naturally enough, for the purpose of selling soap. It may incidentally have profound effects on the manners, mores, and opinions of the millions who listen. That is an inevitable feature of the American system of broadcasting; but it is not inevitable that only programs so produced and so controlled shall reach the ear of American listeners. The sustaining program is the necessary makeweight.

(6)   Statistics of sustaining programs

But while networks and stations alike have traditionally recognized the importance of the sustaining program as an integral part of the American system of broadcasting, there is evidence to suggest that such programs are disappearing from the program service of some stations, especially during the best listening hours.

No accurate statistical series has yet been established to determine the proportion of time devoted to sustaining programs, or the trends from year to year. In the most recent annual reports of stations and networks to the Commission, however, station licensees have analyzed their program structure for the month of January 1945. Since no definition of "sustaining" has heretofore been promulgated, these figures must be approached with caution. Some stations, for example, classify a 15-minute "participating" program as sustaining, even though it is interrupted by three, four, or five spot announcements. Some "bonus" stations which carry network programs without direct remuneration from the network classify all their network commercial programs as "sustaining." The returns to the Commission are in some cases carelessly prepared; some stations, for example, report more than 5 hours of programs daily between 6 and 11 p.m. Some of the returns are wholly unusable. Nevertheless, the returns of 703 stations for the month of January 1945 appeared sufficiently complete to warrant tabulation.

[11] *Broadcasting Yearbook*, 1945, pp. 30, 32. Comparable data for NBC not available.

These 703 stations were on the air an average of 16 hours and 5 minutes daily. Of this time, they reported 8 hours and 40 minutes, or 53.9 percent, as commercial, and the remaining 7 hours and 25 minutes, or 46.1 percent, as sustaining.

These overall figures suggest that the sustaining program remains a major part of broadcasting today. On closer analysis, however, certain questions arise.

First, it should be noted that in general, the larger stations carried a considerably smaller percentage of sustaining programs than the smaller stations, as shown on the following table:

AVERAGE HOURS PER DAY AND PERCENTAGE OF TIME ON
THE AIR DEVOTED TO COMMERCIAL AND SUSTAINING
PROGRAMS BY CLASS OF STATION
FOR MONTH OF JANUARY, 1945

	Commercial		*Sustaining*	
	Hours per day	% of time on air	Hours per day	% of time on air
50 kw stations (41)	12:50	67.3	6:14	32.7
500 w—50 kw stations (214)	10:41	61.3	6:45	38.7
250 w or less stations (376)	7:37	47.6	8:23	52.4
Part time stations (72)	5:46	53.3	5:30	46.7
All stations (703)	8:40	53.9	7:25	46.1

Source: Annual Financial Reports, 1944.

Second, the proportion of time devoted to sustaining programs during the best listening hours from 6 to 11 p.m. was lower than during other hours:

AVERAGE HOURS AND PERCENTAGE OF TIME ON THE AIR,
6 TO 11 P.M., DEVOTED TO COMMERCIAL AND
SUSTAINING PROGRAMS BY CLASS OF STATION
FOR MONTH OF JANUARY, 1945

	Commercial		*Sustaining*	
	Hours per day	% of time on air	Hours per day	% of time on air
6 P.M. to 11 P.M. only				
50 kw stations (41)	4:16	84.7	:46	15.3
500 w—50 kw stations (214)	3:38	72.9	1:21	27.1
250 w or less stations (376)	2:38	53.9	2:16	46.1
Part time stations (72)	:46	60.5	:31	39.5
All stations (703)	2:51	62.4	1:43	37.6

Source: Annual Financial Reports, 1944.

The above statistics are, of course, averages, and hence do not illustrate the paucity of sustaining programs on particular stations. The four following charts* show in black the commercial programs, and in white the sustaining programs, of Stations WLW, WBAL, WCAU, and WSIX for a random week. Especially noteworthy is the tendency to crowd sustaining programs into the Saturday afternoon and Sunday morning segments, and to crowd them out of the best listening hours from 6 to 11 p.m.

The following eight charts† similarly illustrate the paucity of sustaining programs during the best listening hours on the stations designated as "basic affiliates" by the four major networks. . . . It will be noted that on Sunday, April 23, 1944, the following stations carried no sustaining programs whatever between the hours of 6 and 11 p.m.:

WHO	WIRE	WCED	WXYZ
WSYR	WTMJ	KOIL	WING
WSPD	WDEL	KMBC	WMAL
WAVE	WHT	WCKY	WEMP

Similarly on Monday, April 24, 1944, the following stations carried no sustaining programs whatever between the hours of 6 and 11 p.m.:

WAGE	WSAI	WFBL	WSPD
WAKR	WNBH	WTOP	WBAL
WXYZ	WEMP	WTAG	WAVE
WING	WTOL	WBBM	WIRE
WENR–WLS	WABC	WADC	WTMJ
WISH	WJR	WMT	WOW
		WHAS	WMAQ

(7)   Statistics of network sustaining programs

More striking even than the dearth on some stations and during some hours of sustaining programs generally, is the dearth of *network* sustaining programs.

The five-fold function of sustaining programs, earlier outlined, has particular significance as it applies to network sustaining programs. These are unique in character. They command resources of talent, of writers, actors, producers, beyond the capacity of all or at least most local stations to offer. They cover many issues and subjects, treatment of which can best be given in the great metropolitan centers where network headquarters are situated. Even more important, the network sustaining program is the primary channel through which a nation-wide audience can be reached for treatment of the subjects

*The four charts are omitted. [Ed.]
†The eight charts are omitted. [Ed.]

earlier referred to as the peculiar province of sustaining programs. It is the very essence of network service that it should reach a nation-wide audience. Any factor intervening to prevent this militates against the principle of network operations.

The failure of American broadcasters to provide nation-wide distribution for even outstanding network sustaining programs can be illustrated by a few examples.

The Columbia Broadcasting System describes "Invitation to Learning" in these terms:

Distinguished scholars, authors, and critics meet informally on this series to discuss the outstanding classics of literature. The summer and fall schedules include a series of 31 great books to bring the total number discussed on the program to 285.

On Sunday, April 2, 1944, the most recent date for which data are available, 39 CBS stations carried this program, while 97 rejected it.

"Transatlantic Call: People to People" is described by CBS as follows:

On alternate Sundays the British Broadcasting Corporation and the Columbia Broadcasting System shake hands across the ocean. In this half-hour program, British and American audiences are presented with a picture of the national characteristics and attitudes of the two countries. The audiences of the two nations learn the reasons for the apparent differences between them, at the same time realizing the basic similarity of their attitudes and behavior.

This program was carried on Sunday, April 2, 1944, by 50 CBS stations and rejected by 86.

"Columbia's Country Journal" is described by CBS as follows:

The farmer's role in war time, his "food for victory" campaign, and his daily problems form the weekly theme of Charles ("Chuck") Worcester's "radio farm magazine." Originating in Washington for national farm news, it frequently switches to various farm regions of the country highlighting local problems. Occasional reports from abroad and native folk music are regular features.

On April 8, 1944, this program was carried by 53 and rejected by 83 CBS affiliates.

"Words at War" is described by NBC as follows:

WORDS AT WAR, a weekly series of dramatizations of current books relating to the war, is presented by NBC in cooperation with the Council on Books in Wartime. This series served as the summer replacement for "Fibber McGee and Molly," and four times in eight months was cited by the Writers' War Board for its programs. Among the outstanding books dramatized on "Words at

War" were "Der Fuehrer," by Konrad Heiden; "The Veteran Comes Back," by Dr. William Waller; "Assignment U.S.A.," by Seldon Menefee; "War Crimes and Punishment," by George Creel; . . .

This program was carried on Tuesday, May 2, 1944, the last date for which data are available, by 52 NBC stations and rejected by 61. It was broadcast over the network at 11:30 p.m., E.W.T., when listeners are comparatively few, and has since been discontinued altogether.

"The NBC Inter-American University of the Air" is described by NBC as:

presenting an integrated schedule of programs of high educational and cultural value . . . Its 1943 schedule included Lands of the Free, Music of the New World, For This We Fight, The Editors Speak, and Music at War — each a series of stimulating programs that proved the worth of radio as an educational medium. Programs of the NBC University of the Air are now "assigned listening" in more than 100 colleges and universities throughout the United States. School teachers taking the "in-service" training courses of the Board of Education of the City of New York receive credits and promotion based upon their study of Lands of the Free and Music of the New World.

The only two programs of the Inter-American University of the Air noted during the week beginning Sunday, April 30, 1944, were "Lands of the Free," broadcast from 4:30 to 4:55 p.m. on Sunday, April 30, and "Music of the New World," broadcast from 11:30 to midnight on Thursday, May 4. *"Lands of the Free" was carried by 24 NBC stations and refused by 114; "Music of the New World" was carried by 66 and refused by 60.*[12]

The NBC labor program was described by the network as follows:

Labor for Victory brought authoritative speakers to discuss labor's role in the war effort, in programs produced by the American Federation of Labor alternating with the Congress of Industrial Organizations.

This program was carried on Sunday, April 30, 1944 by 35 NBC stations and rejected by 104.

"The Reviewing Stand" is an MBS program described by the network as follows:

Roundtable discussion of current problems under auspices of Northwestern University.

It was made available by MBS on Sunday, April 23, 1944 to its full network of 216 stations. Of these, only 40 MBS affiliates carried it.

---

[12] One station broadcast only the second half of "Music of the New World." For the first half it substituted a participating program of spot announcements interspersed with transcribed music.

"Halls of Montezuma," a Marine Corps series from the U.S. Marine Corps base at San Diego, featured the "Sea Soldiers' Chorus" and the "Marine Symphony Orchestra." *It was carried by 50 of the 215 MBS affiliates to which it was made available on Wednesday, April 26, 1944.*

"Mutual's Radio Chapel," a sustaining religious program, was made available to all MBS affiliates. *On Sunday, April 23, 1944, thirteen MBS stations carried it.*

No comparable figures were available from the Blue Network (now the American Broadcasting Company). The extent to which network sustaining programs have been neglected is well illustrated by this failure of the Blue Network even to determine whether or not its sustaining programs were being carried. It is difficult to see how a network can maintain a well-balanced program structure or can determine which of its network sustaining programs to continue and which to replace, if it has not even determined the extent to which such programs are being carried by its affiliates.

The eight charts . . . show the rarity of network sustaining programs from 6 to 11 p.m. on the "basic affiliate" stations of the four major networks. Network sustaining programs are shown by a white "S" superimposed on a black square. It will be noted that the following "basic affiliates" carried no network sustaining programs whatever from 6 to 11 p.m. on Sunday, April 23, 1944:

WXYZ	WTOL	WPRO	WLW
WING	WMT	WJR	WAVE
WHDH	WGAR	WBBM	WCSH
WMAL	WCED	WKRC	WHAM
WISH	KOIL	WIBC	WIRE
WTCN	KMBC	WHO	WTMJ
WCOL	WKBW	WSYR	WDEL
WEMP	WCKY	WSPD	WTIC

Similarly, the following "basic affiliates" carried no network sustaining programs whatever on Monday, April 24, 1944 from 6 to 11 p.m.:

WELI	WISH	WCED	WCKY	WBZA
WAGE	WFIL	WDRC	KMOX	WTIC
WWVA	WEBR	WCAU	WGAR	WDEL
WAKR	WOWO	WPRO	WMT	WRC
WJW	WSAI	WFBL	WHAS	WWJ
WXYZ	WNBH	WTOP	WFBM	WLW
WING	WEMP	WTAG	KDKA	WAVE
WENR–WLS	WTOL	WJAS	KYW	WIRE
KCMO	WABC	KRNT	WSPD	WTMJ
WHDH	WEEI	WBBM	WBAL	KSTP
WMAL	WJR	KMBC	WHAM	WOW
		WADC	WBZ	WMAQ

The paucity of network sustaining programs . . . results from two factors: first, the failure of the networks to supply sustaining programs in quantity during the best listening hours and second, the failure of some stations to carry even those network sustaining programs which are offered.

The mere fact that a station does not carry an outstanding network sustaining program does not mean, of course, that it has sacrificed public interest for private gain. In any particular case, the decision to cancel a network sustaining program may be a wise one, reached on the basis of the availability of a local program of still greater public interest. To determine whether this is the case, it is necessary to compare the network sustaining program rejected with the program scheduled in its stead, and to view the network sustaining program as part of a particular station's schedule.

An example of this technique may be supplied with respect to Station WCAU. This is a 50,000-watt station, occupying an entire clear channel by itself. Station WCAU is affiliated with the Columbia Broadcasting System and is owned by the group which also controls CBS. Hence WCAU might be expected to make available to its listeners at least the outstanding CBS sustaining programs. Indeed, one of the grounds relied on by the Federal Radio Commission when awarding a clear channel to Station WCAU as against competing applicants for such assignments was that WCAU would carry the programs of the Columbia Broadcasting System. (F.R.C. Docket No. 880, decided November 17, 1931.)

Of the 3,165 minutes of network sustaining programs made available to Station WCAU by CBS during the week beginning February 8, 1945, Station WCAU broadcast 1,285 minutes, or 40.6%. From 6 p.m. to 11 p.m. throughout the week, however, Station WCAU broadcast only 55 minutes of network sustaining programs, or 20.8% of the network sustaining programs available to it during this time. On Mondays, Wednesdays, and Thursdays, WCAU broadcast no network sustaining programs whatever from 9:45 a.m. to 11 p.m. The full schedule of network sustaining programs carried by Station WCAU was as follows:

	8 a.m.– 1 p.m.	1 p.m.– 6 p.m.	6 p.m.– 11 p.m.	11 p.m.– 1:02 a.m.	Total
Sunday	180	30	none	95	305
Monday	45	none	none	65	110
Tuesday	45	none	30	65	140
Wednesday	45	none	none	65	110
Thursday	45	none	none	100	145
Friday	45	none	15	65	125
Saturday	45	200	10	95	350
Total	450	230	55	550	1,285

More than 63% of all network sustaining programs carried by WCAU between the hours of 8 a.m. and 11 p.m. were on Saturday and Sunday.

Network sustaining programs from 8 a.m. to 11 p.m., by days, were broadcast as follows:

Sunday	210 minutes
Monday	45 minutes
Tuesday	75 minutes
Wednesday	45 minutes
Thursday	45 minutes
Friday	60 minutes
Saturday	255 minutes
Total	735 minutes

Among the CBS sustaining programs not carried by WCAU, and the WCAU programs substituted therefor, were the following:

SOME NETWORK SUSTAINING PROGRAMS AVAILABLE TO
BUT REFUSED BY STATION WCAU

Name of CBS Sustaining Program	Description[13]	WCAU Program Substituted
FEATURE STORY 4:30–4:45 p.m. Monday through Friday	"Members of CBS' world-wide staff of news correspondents bring to the microphone the many human interest stories that lie under the surface of the latest military and political events and usually miss being told."	"Rhona Lloyd," local talk sponsored by Aristocrat.
TRANS-ATLANTIC CALL: PEOPLE TO PEOPLE 12:30–1 p.m. Sunday	"On alternate Sundays, the British Broadcasting Corporation and the Columbia Broadcasting System shake hands across the ocean. In this half hour program, British and American audiences are presented with a picture of the national characteristics and attitudes of the two countries. The audiences of the two nations learn	"Ranger Joe," transcribed music sponsored by Ranger Joe, Inc.; "Perry Coll," music sponsored by Western Savings Fund.

[13] Quoted from "CBS Program Book – Winter, 1945."

Name of CBS Sustaining Program	*Description*	*WCAU Program Substituted*
	the reasons for the apparent differences between them, at the same time realizing the basic similarity in their attitudes and behavior."	
CALLING PAN-AMERICA 6:15—6:45 p.m. Thursday	"CBS draws the Americas closer together with this weekly program shortwaved from Latin-American capitals. The series 'calls' a different nation to the microphone each Saturday, and presents a vivid radio picture of its life, culture and music."	"Ask Washington," commercial talk sponsored by Hollingshead, 15 minutes; transcribed commercial spot announcement for movie, "National Velvet," sponsored by Metro-Goldwyn-Mayer; phonograph records, "Songs of the Stars" sponsored by Breitenbach, 15 minutes.
SERVICE TIME 5:00—5:30 p.m. Monday through Friday	"Presented in cooperation with the fighting forces, this program devotes itself to the branches of the armed service, spotlighting the activities of a different branch each day. Various service bands and glee clubs are featured, and high ranking officials make personal appearances. There are also interviews with personnel returned from combat zones." Monday — Waves on Parade. Tuesday — It's Maritime. Wednesday — Wacs on Parade. Thursday — Marines in the Making. Friday — First in The Air.	*"Monday* — Phonograph records interspersed with spot announcements for Household Finance Company (5:03:30—5:04:30); Panther Panco Bilt Rite (5:07:30—5:08:30); National Biscuit Premium Crackers (5:11:40—5:12:40); Cuticura-Potter Chemical Company (5:16:00—5:17:00); Glenwood Range (5:19:50—5:20:50); Civil Service (Sustaining) (5:24:15—5:24:35); and weather report (5:29:00—5:29:35). *Tuesday through Friday* — similar phonograph records interspersed with similar spot announcements.

Name of CBS Sustaining Program	Description	WCAU Program Substituted
SALT LAKE TABER-NACLE CHOIR AND ORGAN 12 noon–12:30 p.m. Sunday	"This is the oldest con-secutively presented public-service series in radio, having celebrated its 785th network broadcast on July 30, 1944. The Tabernacle Choir is con-ducted by J. Spencer Cornwall and Richard P. Condie, assistant. Organ-ists are Alexander Schreiner, Dr. Frank Asper and Wade M. Stephens."	"Children's Hour," sponsored by Horn & Hardart, 11:30–12:20; news comment by Carroll Alcott, sponsored by Horn & Hardart, 12:20–12:30.
SALLY MOORE AND THE COLUMBIA CONCERT ORCHESTRA 6:30–6:45 p.m. Monday and Friday	"The young American contralto, CBS' most recent discovery, presents distinctive song recitals of semi-classical music accompanied by the Col-umbia Concert Orchestra."	Phonograph records sponsored by Groves Lax-ative Bromo Quinine.
ENCORE APPEAR-ANCE 6:30–6:45 p.m. Wednesday	"The program offers further opportunity to the new singers who have given outstanding per-formance on CBS' 'New Voices in Song.' They are accompanied by the Col-umbia Concert Orchestra."	Phonograph records sponsored by Groves Lax-ative Bromo Quinine.
WILDERNESS ROAD 5:45–6:00 p.m. Monday through Friday	"A dramatic serial of a pioneering American fam-ily that went through the hazardous Cumberland Gap in 1783 with Daniel Boone as their guide. The story recreates that ad-venture-filled period in American history when every frontier presented a challenge to the New World settlers."	*Monday* – Music by Eliot Lawrence inter-spersed with commercial spot announcements for Rinso (5:48:20–5:49:20); Bell Telephone (5:51:15–5:52:15); and Household Finance Company (5:55:40–5:56:40). *Tuesday through Friday* – similar music interspersed with spot announcements.

Name of CBS *Sustaining Program*	*Description*	WCAU Program *Substituted*
INVITATION TO LEARNING 11:30–12 noon Sunday	"Distinguished scholars, authors, and critics meet informally on this series to discuss the outstanding classics of literature. The winter schedule includes a new series of 30 great books to bring the total number discussed on the program to 254."	"Children's Hour," local commercial program sponsored by Horn & Hardart.
THE PEOPLE'S PLATFORM 6:15–6:45 p.m. Saturday	"The vital issues of today and the postwar world are analyzed weekly on this program, one of radio's most interesting forums. Four eminent guests and Lyman Bryson, CBS Director of Education, who acts as moderator gather informally for these sessions."	"Listen to Lawrence," local commercial music program sponsored by Sun Ship Company.

A special case of failure to carry a network sustaining program is to be noted on Sunday from 2:55 to 3:00 p.m. Beginning at 3 p.m., Station WCAU carries the New York Philharmonic program sponsored by U.S. Rubber. This program is preceded over CBS by a 5-minute introductory talk by Olin Downes, the well-known music critic, on a sustaining basis. WCAU carried the symphony for which it is paid, but rejected the sustaining introduction to the symphony in favor of a five-minute commercial program, "Norman Jay Postscript," sponsored by the Yellow Cab Company.

For a similar analysis of network sustaining programs not carried by Station WBAL, an NBC affiliate, see pp. 146–148.

It has been urged that the network sustaining program is doomed by reason of the fact that a network affiliate can carry local programs only during network sustaining periods, and that station owners quite properly reject network sustaining programs in order to leave some time available for local programs of great public interest. Station owners, on this view, should be praised for eliminating network sustaining programs from their schedules, since in this way they make possible local service to their own communities.

Prior to the enactment of Regulation 3.104, when many stations had all or substantially all of their time under option to the networks, this viewpoint had some cogency. Chain broadcasting Regulation 3.104, however, allows each station freedom to reject network *commercial* programs for two hours out of each five. Thus the individual station licensee's choice is not between broadcasting local live programs during network sustaining hours and not broadcasting them at all. On the contrary, a licensee is free to present during each segment of the broadcast day a well-balanced schedule of network and local, commercial and sustaining programs alike (except to the extent that the network fails to deliver a reasonable proportion of network sustaining programs). The choice is not between network sustaining programs and local programs; rather it is between a balanced program structure and one which lacks such balance.

In recent months, the Commission before renewing the license of a broadcast station has compared the percentage of commercial programs actually broadcast during a sample week with the percentage which the station stated that it would broadcast in its original application. Where a serious discrepancy was noted, and where the proportion of sustaining programs appeared to be so low as to raise a question concerning the station's operation in the public interest, the station's comments were requested. The replies received indicate several widespread misconceptions concerning the basis of Commission policy respecting commercial and sustaining programs.

First, many station licensees stated that they saw no differences between a commercial and a sustaining program, and a few even stated their belief that a station could operate in the public interest with no sustaining programs. (The need for sustaining programs as a balance-wheel to make possible a well-balanced program structure, as a means of broadcasting programs inappropriate for commercial sponsorship, as a service for significant minority tastes and interests, as a service to non-profit organizations, and as a vehicle for program experimentation has been set forth on pp. 156–169.)

Second, a number of stations pointed out that many of their commercial programs were clearly in the public interest. The Commission is in full accord with this view. The fact that some advertisers are broadcasting programs which serve an important public interest, however, does not relieve a station of its responsibility in the public interest. Broadcast licensees properly consider their status to be very different from the status of a common carrier, merely providing physical facilities for the carrying of matter paid for and produced by others. Broadcasters rightly insist that their function in the community and the nation is of a higher order. The maintenance of this independent status and significance, however, is inconsistent with the abnegation of independent responsibility, whether to a network or to advertisers. The conceded merit of many or most programs broadcast during periods which a broadcaster has sold to others does not relieve him of the responsibility for broadcasting his own programs during periods which he has reserved from sponsorship for public service.

Third, a few licensees have alleged that they are unable to estimate the amount of time which they will devote to sustaining programs hereafter because they cannot predict how much demand for time there will be from commercial advertisers. Such licensees have obviously abdicated to advertisers the control over their stations. The requirement of a well-balanced program structure, firmly founded in the public interest provisions of the Communications Act, is a responsibility of the station licensee. To permit advertisers to dictate either the proportion of time which the station shall devote to sustaining programs or any other major policy decision is inconsistent with the basic principles of licensee responsibility on which American broadcasting has always rested.

In their replies, many licensees have pointed out that a comparison of promise and performance with respect to sustaining programs and other categories is difficult or impossible without uniform definitions of what constitutes a commercial program, a sustaining program, etc. To meet this difficulty, the Commission is promulgating herewith uniform definitions of various program categories. (See "Uniform Definitions and Program Logs.")

B.   The carrying of local live programs

All or substantially all programs currently broadcast are of four kinds: (1) network programs, including programs furnished to a station by telephone circuit from another station; (2) recorded (including transcribed) programs; (3) wire programs (chiefly wire news, syndicated to many stations by telegraph or teletype and read off the wire by a local announcer); and (4) local live programs, including remote broadcasts. For definitions of these four main classes, see "Uniform Definitions and Program Logs."

Network programs.   The merit of network programs is universally recognized; indeed, the Commission's Chain Broadcasting Regulations 3.101 and 3.102 were designed in considerable part to insure a freer flow of network programs to the listener. In January 1945, approximately 47.9% of all the time of standard broadcast stations was devoted to network programs.

Transcriptions.   The transcribed or recorded program has not had similar recognition. As early as 1922, the Department of Commerce by regulation prohibited the playing of phonograph records by stations having the better (Class B) channel assignments except in emergencies or to fill in between program periods; and later in the year it amended the regulation to prohibit even such use of records by Class B stations. Through the years the phonograph record, and to a lesser extent the transcription, have been considered inferior program sources.

No good reason appears, however, for not recognizing today the significant role which the transcription and the record, like the network, can play in radio programming. Five particular advantages may be cited:

(a)   Transcriptions are a means of disposing of radio's most ironic anomaly — the dissipation during a single broadcast, in most cases for all time, of all the skill and labor of writer, director, producer, and cast. Transcriptions make possible the compilation of a permanent archive of the best in radio, comparable in other types of programs to the recorded symphony or chamber music. Good programs with timeless interest can thus be repeated not once but many times.

(b)   Transcriptions make possible the placing of programs at convenient hours. For example, a network broadcast may either be inconvenient in time for listeners in a given time zone or may conflict with a station's commitment to its locality. By transcribing the program at the station as it comes in on the network line, the program can be made available at another and still convenient hour.[1]

(c)   Transcriptions make possible the sharing of programs among stations not directly connected by wire lines. Several New York stations, for example, are currently making their outstanding programs available via transcription to stations throughout the country. Similarly, non-radio organizations can produce and distribute programs via transcription, as in the case of the award-winning children's transcription series of the Junior League.

(d)   Transcriptions offer to the writer, director, and producer of programs the same technical advantages that the moving picture industry achieves through cutting-room techniques. Imperfections can be smoothed out; material recorded at different times and places can be blended into a single program, etc. While the basic advantages of this more plastic technique may not yet be fully utilized, recent developments in the transcription field, including those pioneered by the armed forces and the introduction of wire recorders, suggest a significant role for such programs in the future.

(e)   Portable recorders make it possible to present to the listener the event as it occurs rather than a subsequent re-creation of it. The recording of actual press conferences, for example, and the actual battlefront recordings by the Marine Corps and Army Signal Corps point the way to an expansion of recording techniques as a means of radio reporting.

In January, 1945, approximately 32.3% of all the time of standard broadcast stations was devoted to transcriptions and recordings.

Wire Programs.   The wire service, by which spot news and sometimes also other program texts are telegraphically distributed to stations, has in recent years assumed a role of increasing importance.[2] By means of wire service for news and other texts of a timely nature, plus transcriptions for programs of less urgent timeliness, the unaffiliated station can very nearly achieve the breadth of

---

[1] Conversely, however, some stations appear to use the transcription technique for shifting an outstanding network public service program from a good hour to an off hour when listeners are few and commercial programs not available.

[2] For a proposed definition of "wire" programs, see "Uniform Definitions and Program Logs."

service attained through network affiliation No statistics are currently available concerning the proportion of time devoted to wire service programs.

Local Live Programs.   There remains for discussion the local live program, for which also, no precise statistics are available. It is known, however, that in January, 1945, approximately 19.7% of all the time of standard broadcast stations was devoted to local live *and* wire service programs; and that during the best listening hours from 6 to 11 p.m., approximately 15.7% of all the time was devoted to these two classes of programs combined.

In granting and renewing licenses, the Commission has given repeated and explicit recognition to the need for adequate reflection in programs of local interests, activities and talent. Assurances by the applicant that "local talent will be available"; that there will be "a reasonable portion of time for programs which include religious, educational, and civic matters"; that "time will be devoted to local news at frequent intervals, to market reports, agricultural topics and to various civic and political activities that occur in the city" have contributed to favorable decision on many applications. As the Commission noted in its *Supplemental Report on Chain Broadcasting* (1941):

It has been the consistent intention of the Commission to assure that an adequate amount of time *during the good listening hours* shall be made available to meet the needs of the community in terms of public expression and of local interest. If these regulations do not accomplish this objective, the subject will be given further consideration. (Emphasis supplied.)

The networks themselves have recognized the importance of local live programs. Under date of October 9, 1944, the National Broadcasting Company, when requesting the Commission to amend Chain Broadcasting Regulation 3.104, stated:

Over the years our affiliated stations have been producing highly important local programs in these three open hours of the morning segment. From 8 a.m. to 10 a.m. N.Y.T., most of the stations have developed variety or "morning clock" programs which have met popular acceptance. These periods are not only profitable to the individual station but are sought for use by civic, patriotic and religious groups for special appeals because of their local listening audience appeal. Likewise, from 12 noon to 1 p.m. they have developed highly important farm news programs or other local interest shows. *To interfere with local program schedules of many years' standing would deprive our stations of their full opportunity to render a desirable local public service.* (Emphasis supplied.)

The Commission's reply, released December 20, 1944, as Mimeograph No. 79574, stated in part:

One purpose of Regulation 3.104 was to leave 14 of the 35 evening hours in each week free of network option, *in order to foster the development of local programs.*[3] . . . The Commission . . . concurs fully in your statement that interference with local programs which have met with public acceptance and which are sought for use by local civic, patriotic and religious groups, local church services, and other highly important local program schedules of years' standing is to be avoided. (Emphasis supplied.)

The courts have also supported the position taken by the Commission that the interests of the whole listening public require that provision be made for local program service. Where the record showed that of the two stations already functioning in an area, one carried 50 percent network programs and the other 85 percent, the court stated: "In view of this situation it is not difficult to see why the Commission decided that public interest would be served by the construction of a local non-network station."[4]

But the soundness of a local program policy does not rest solely on the consistent Commission policy of encouraging a reasonable proportion of local programs as part of a well-balanced program service. Three examples will serve to suggest that local programming may also be good business policy and may contribute to the popularity of the station. These examples were noted by Professor C. H. Sandage of the Harvard School of Business Administration, during a survey of radio advertising possibilities for retailers financed by the Columbia Broadcasting System.

(a)   One 250-watt station located in the Middle West had struggled along for 4 years and lost money each year until a reorganization was forced in 1942.

The former management had attempted to compete directly with outside stations whose signals were strong in the local community. Good entertainment was provided, but no attempt was made to establish the station as a local institution interested in the life of the community. Neither local listeners nor local businessmen supported the station.

The new management reversed this policy completely. All attempts at copying outside stations were eliminated. Management not only studied the activities peculiar to that community but also took a personal interest in them. Station facilities were made available on a free basis to civic institutions such as the Chamber of Commerce, women's clubs, parent-teacher association, public

---

[3] The failure of Regulation 3.104 to achieve this purpose is illustrated by the eight charts. . . . showing many stations which carried no non-network programs whatever during the evening hours on the two days analyzed.

[4] *Great Western Broadcasting Association* v. *F.C.C.* 94 F. 2d 244, 248. In the KHMO case, the court ordered the Commission to issue a license to an applicant for a local station in an area where three stations were already operating, none of which gave genuine local service. The court expressed approval of the Commission's findings in similar cases, that "under the direct provisions of the statute the *rights of the citizens to enjoy local broadcasting privileges were being denied.*" (*Courier Post Broadcasting Co.* v. *F.C.C.*, 104 F. 2d 213, 218) (Emphasis supplied.)

schools, and Community Chest. School sports contests were broadcast, and other programs of distinctly local interest were developed. In a relatively short time an audience of more than 50 percent of all local radio listeners had been attracted to the station ... At the time the new management came in, gross monthly income was $2,400 and at the end of 12 months this amount has been increased to $6,000. *The new manager attributed all improvement to the policy of making the station a real local institution and a true voice of the community.*[5]

(b)   Amateur shows have been used effectively in developing local talent.

An Illinois retailer has used this type of show for a number of years and has built an audience which in 1942 surpassed in size the audience for any other radio program broadcast at the same time ... It was competing with John Charles Thomas, New York Philharmonic, and the Army Hour. Only the John Charles Thomas program approached the rating for the local program. As in all programs which make use of local talent of fair quality, a considerable audience was attracted because of an interest in local people.[6]

(c)   A feed mill in Missouri developed a quartet called the "Happy Millers" which sang hillbilly and western music.

Public acceptance has been phenomenal, partly *because of the interest of rural people in the type of entertainment afforded but also because the entertainers are all local people and well known in the community.*[7]

These few examples can no doubt be supplemented from their own experience by many alert station managers throughout the country.

While parallels between broadcast stations and newspapers must be approached with caution, their common elements with respect to local interest may be significant. The local newspaper achieves world-wide news coverage through the great press associations, taps the country's foremost writers and cartoonists through the feature syndicates, and from the picture services procures photographs from everywhere in abundant quantity. But the local newspaper editor, faced with such abundant incoming material, does not therefore discharge his local reporters and photographers, nor does he seek to reproduce locally the New York *Times* or *Daily News.* He appreciates the keen interest in local material and makes the most of that material — especially on the front page. The hours from 6 to 11 p.m. are the "front page" of the broadcast station. The statistics of local programming during these hours, or generally, are not impressive.

---

[5] Sandage, *Radio Advertising for Retailers*, p. 210. (Emphasis supplied.)
[6] *Ibid.,* pp. 166–167.
[7] *Ibid.,* p. 161. (Emphasis supplied.)

Extent of local live program service

No reliable statistics are currently available concerning the time devoted to local live programs, partly because there has heretofore been no accepted definition of "local live," partly because "wire" programs of news syndicated to many stations have been included in the local live classification, and partly because programs of phonograph records have been classified as "local live" by some stations if a live announcer intersperses advertising comments among the records. The paucity of local live, and especially local live sustaining programs, is indicated, however, by the following table which shows the time reported by 703 stations as having been devoted to local live programs in January, 1945. The table can perhaps be best interpreted as showing the time devoted to non-network, non-transcribed programs:

AVERAGE HOURS PER DAY AND PERCENTAGE OF TIME ON
THE AIR DEVOTED TO LOCAL LIVE PROGRAMS BY CLASS OF
STATION FOR MONTH OF JANUARY, 1945

	Commercial		Sustaining	
	Hours per day	% of time on air	Hours per day	% of time on air
50 kw stations (41)	3:02	15.9	1:52	9.8
500 w — 50 kw stations (214)	2:23	13.6	1:11	6.8
250 w or less stations (376)	1:43	10.7	1:00	6.3
Part time stations (72)	2:11	20.3	1:09	10.7
All stations (703)	2:02	12.7	1:07	7.0

Source: Annual Financial Reports, 1944.

From 6 to 11 p.m., moreover, non-network, non-transcribed programs are considerably rarer, amounting on the average to only 42 minutes in five hours for all stations. *Sustaining* programs of this type average only 13 minutes in five hours.

AVERAGE HOURS AND PERCENTAGE OF TIME ON THE AIR,
6–11 P.M., DEVOTED TO LOCAL LIVE PROGRAMS BY CLASS
OF STATION FOR MONTH OF JANUARY, 1945

	Commercial		Sustaining	
	Hours per day	% of time on air	Hours per day	% of time on air
6 p.m. to 11 p.m. only				
50 kw stations (41)	:36	12.0	:12	3.9
500 w — 50 kw stations (214)	:34	11.4	:14	4.7
250 w or less stations (376)	:29	9.8	:15	4.9
Part time stations (72)	:11	15.0	:07	8.7
All stations (703)	:29	10.6	:13	4.9

Source: Annual Financial Reports, 1944.

On particular stations, of course, the picture is even more extreme. The eight charts . . . for example, show in white the time devoted to non-network programs by the "basic affiliates" of the four major networks. It will be noted that on Sunday, April 23, 1944, the following stations carried no non-network programs whatever — and hence no local live programs — during the best listening hours from 6 to 11 p.m.:

WORC	WAGE	WMT	WCAU	KDB	WGY
WFCI	KQV	WDRC	WJAS	WBZ	WTAM
WNBC	WADC	WFBM	WTOP	WBZA	WMAQ
WCBM	WCAO	KFAB	WHBF	WJAR	WOW
WTRY	WEEI	WHAS	KWK	WRC	

In the face of this progressive blackout of non-network programs during the best listening hours on many stations, it has been proposed that some stations be licensed exclusively for non-network broadcasting, and that the Commission regulations prohibit the carrying of network programs by stations so licensed. This proposal appears impracticable. In communities where the number of stations does not exceed the number of networks, the result would be to deprive listeners of regular network service from one or more of the networks. In communities where the number of stations exceeds the number of networks, moreover, the regulation would be of little practical value since in such communities one or more of the stations will remain without a network affiliation in any event. The solution to network monopolization of a station's time, accordingly, must be found in terms of a balance of network and non-network programs, rather than in a distinction between network and non-network stations.

The most immediately profitable way to run a station, may be to procure a network affiliation, plug into the network line in the morning, and broadcast network programs throughout the day — interrupting the network output only to insert commercial spot announcements, and to substitute spot announcements and phonograph records for outstanding network sustaining programs. The record on renewal since April, 1945, of standard broadcast stations shows that some stations are approaching perilously close to this extreme. Indeed, it is difficult to see how some stations can do otherwise with the minimal staffs currently employed in programming.

For every three writers employed by 834 broadcast stations in October, 1944, there were four salesmen employed. For every dollar paid to the average writer, the average salesman was paid $2.39. And in terms of total compensation paid to writers and salesmen, the stations paid $3.30 for salesmen for every $1.00 paid for writers. The comparable relationship for 415 local stations is even more unbalanced.[8]

[8] In the week of October 15, 1944, 834 stations employed 863 writers at an average compensation of $40.14, totalling $34,641; and 1195 salesmen at an average compensation of $95.92, totalling $114,624. The 415 local stations employed 259 writers full time at an average salary of $31.87 but employed 409 salesmen at an average of $68.85.

The average local station employed less than $\frac{1}{3}$ of a full time musician and less than $\frac{1}{6}$ of a full time actor.[9]

Such figures suggest, particularly at the local station level, that few stations are staffed adequately to meet their responsibilities in serving the community. A positive responsibility rests upon local stations to make articulate the voice of the community. Unless time is earmarked for such a purpose, unless talent is positively sought and given at least some degree of expert assistance, radio stations have abdicated their local responsibilities and have become mere common carriers of program material piped in from outside the community.

C.   Discussion of public issues

American broadcasters have always recognized that broadcasting is not merely a means of entertainment, but also an unequaled medium for the dissemination of news, information, and opinion, and for the discussion of public issues. Radio's role in broadcasting the election returns of November 1920 is one of which broadcasters are justly proud; and during the quarter of a century which has since elapsed, broadcasting has continued to include news, information, opinion and public discussion in its regular budget of program material.

Especially in recent years, such information programs as news and news commentaries have achieved a popularity exceeding the popularity of any other single type of program. The war, of course, tremendously increased listener interest in such programs; but if broadcasters face the crucial problems of the post-war era with skill, fairness, and courage, there is no reason why broadcasting cannot play as important a role in our democracy hereafter as it has achieved during the war years.

The use of broadcasting as an instrument for the dissemination of news, ideas, and opinions raises a multitude of problems of a complex and sometimes delicate nature, which do not arise in connection with purely entertainment programs. A few such problems may be briefly noted, without any attempt to present an exhaustive list:

(1)   Shall time for the presentation of one point of view on a public issue be sold, or shall all such presentations of points of view be on sustaining time only?

(2)   If presentations of points of view are to be limited only to sustaining time, what measures can be taken to insure that adequate sustaining time during good listening hours is made available for such presentations, and that such time is equitably distributed?

(3)   If time is also on occasion to be sold for presentation of a point of

[9] Many or most stations are financially able to employ far larger program staffs than at present. . . .

view, what precautions are necessary to insure that the most time shall not gravitate to the side prepared to spend the most money?

(4) Are forums, town meetings, and round-table type broadcasts, in which two or more points of view are aired together, intrinsically superior to the separate presentation of points of view at various times?

(5) Should such programs be sponsored?

(6) What measures will insure that such programs be indeed fair and well-balanced among opposing points of view?

(7) Should locally originated discussion programs, in which residents of a community can themselves discuss issues of local, national, or international importance be encouraged, and if so, how?

(8) How can an unbiased presentation of the news be achieved?

(9) Should news be sponsored, and if so, to what extent should the advertiser influence or control the presentation of the news?

(10) How and by whom should commentators be selected?

(11) Should commentators be forbidden, permitted, or encouraged to express their own personal opinions?

(12) Is a denial of free speech involved when a commentator is discharged or his program discontinued because something which he has said has offended (a) the advertiser, (b) the station, (c) a minority of his listeners, or (d) a majority of his listeners?

(13) What provisions, over and above Section 315 of the Communications Act of 1934,[10] are necessary or desirable in connection with the operation of broadcast stations during a political campaign?

(14) Does a station operate in the public interest which charges a higher rate for political broadcasts than for commercial programs?

(15) The Federal Communications Commission is forbidden by law to censor broadcasts. Should station licensees have the absolute right of censorship, or should their review of broadcasts be limited to protection against libel, dissemination of criminal matter, etc.?

(16) Should broadcasters be relieved of responsibility for libel with respect to broadcasts over which they exercise no control?

(17) Should the "right to reply" to broadcasts be afforded; and if so, to whom should the right be afforded, and under what circumstances?

(18) When a station refuses time on the air requested for the discussion of public issues, should it be required to state in writing its reasons for refusal?

---

[10] "Sec. 315: If any licensee shall permit any person who is a legally qualified candidate for any public office to use a broadcasting station, he shall afford equal opportunities to all other such candidates for that office in the use of such broadcasting station, and the Commission shall make rules and regulations to carry this provision into effect: *Provided*, That such licensee shall have no power of censorship over the material broadcast under the provisions of this section. No obligation is hereby imposed upon any licensee to allow the use of its station by any such candidate."

Should it be required to maintain a record of all such requests for time, and of the disposal made of them?

(19)   What measures can be taken to open broadcasting to types of informational programs which contravene the interests of large advertisers — for example, news of the reports and decisions of the Federal Trade Commission concerning unfair advertising; reports of the American Medical Association concerning the effects of cigarette-smoking; temperance broadcasts; etc?

These are only a few of the many questions which are raised in complaints to the Commission from day to day. The future of American broadcasting as an instrument of democracy depends in no small part upon the establishment of sound solutions to such problems, and on the fair and impartial application of general solutions to particular cases.

Under the Communications Act, primary responsibility for solving these and similar issues rests upon the licensees of broadcast stations themselves. Probably no other type of problem in the entire broadcasting industry is as important, or requires of the broadcaster a greater sense of objectivity, responsibility, and fair play.

While primary responsibility in such matters rests with the individual broadcaster, the Commission is required by the statute to review periodically the station's operation, in order to determine whether the station has in fact been operated in the public interest. Certainly, the establishment of sound station policy with respect to news, information, and the discussion of public issues is a major factor in operation in the public interest.

The Commission has never laid down, and does not now propose to lay down, any categorical answers to such questions as those raised above. Rather than enunciating general policies, the Commission reaches decisions on such matters in the crucible of particular cases.[11]

One matter of primary concern, however, can be met by an over-all statement of policy, and must be met as part of the general problem of overall program balance. This is the question of the *quantity* of time which should be made available for the discussion of public issues.

The problems involved in making time available for the discussion of public issues are admittedly complex. Any vigorous presentation of a point of view will of necessity annoy or offend at least some listeners. There may be a temptation, accordingly, for broadcasters to avoid as much as possible any discussion over their stations, and to limit their broadcasts to entertainment programs which offend no one.

To operate in this manner, obviously, is to thwart the effectiveness of broadcasting in a democracy.

[11] See, for example, the *Mayflower* case, 8 F.C.C. 333, and *United Broadcasting Company (WHKC)* case, decided June 26, 1945.

A test case may illustrate the problem here raised. At the request of the Senate Committee on Interstate Commerce, the Commission undertook a study of all network and local programs broadcast from January 1, 1941 through May 31, 1941, relative to the foreign policy issue then before the country, that of isolationism versus intervention in the world conflict. The period reviewed was one of great crisis. The issue at stake would affect the history and even the survival of our country and its institutions. Five major questions of foreign policy were involved — lend-lease, the convoying of ships to Britain, the acquisition of foreign bases, the acquisition of foreign ships, and the maintenance of the British blockade. From this study the following facts emerged.

The four major networks submitted 532 programs. Upon analysis only 203 scripts were deemed relevant; 14 scripts were unobtainable.

Assuming all 14 of these scripts to have been relevant, this means that 217 scripts during a 5-month period dealt with the 5 major issues of foreign policy listed above. Put another way, each network broadcast a program devoted to one or more of these issues every third day.

But while the networks made these programs available, not all affiliated stations carried them. Of 120 CBS affiliates, 59.3% carried the average lend-lease program. Of 165 MBS affiliates, 45.5% carried it. Of the approximately 200 NBC stations on both Red and Blue networks of NBC, 69 stations carried the average NBC program on lend-lease.

Even more significant are the figures relating to non-network programs. Of 742 stations reporting, only 288 claimed to have originated even one program on any subject relevant to this study. The remaining 454 denied having broadcast a single non-network program on foreign policy during the entire 5-month period. While subject to possible sampling error, the study indicates that station time devoted to discussion programs distributed by the four networks exceeded station time devoted to discussion programs originated by the stations in the ratio of 30 to 1.

The carrying of any particular public discussion, of course, is a problem for the individual broadcaster. But the public interest clearly requires that an adequate amount of time be made available for the discussion of public issues; and the Commission, in determining whether a station has served the public interest, will take into consideration the amount of time which has been or will be devoted to the discussion of public issues.

D. Advertising excesses

(1) Value of advertising

Advertising represents the only source of revenue for most American broadcasting stations, and is therefore an indispensable part of our system of broadcasting. In return for spending some 397 million dollars per year[1] on American broadcasting, the advertiser can expect that his name and wares will be effectively made known to the public.

Advertising in general, moreover, and radio advertising in particular, plays an essential role in the distribution of goods and services within our economy. During the postwar era if manufacturers are to dispose of the tremendous output of which our postwar industry will be capable, they must keep their products before the public.

Finally, informative advertising which gives reliable factual data concerning available goods and services is itself of direct benefit to the listener in his role as consumer. Consumer knowledge of the new and improved products which contribute to a higher standard of living is one of the steps toward achieving that higher standard of living.

However, the fact that advertisers have a legitimate interest and place in the American system of broadcasting does not mean that broadcasting should be run solely in the interest of the advertisers rather than that of the listeners. Throughout the history of broadcasting, a limitation on the amount and character of advertising has been one element of "public interest." A brief review will illustrate this point.

(2)   Historic background

Commercial broadcasting began in 1920 or 1921, and by 1922 the dangers of excessive advertising had already been noted. Thus at the First Annual Radio Conference in 1922, Secretary of Commerce Herbert Hoover declared:

It is inconceivable that we should allow so great a possibility for service, for news, for entertainment, for education and for vital commercial purposes to be drowned in advertising chatter. . . .

The Conference itself took heed of Secretary Hoover's warning and recommended:

. . . that direct advertising in radio broadcasting service be absolutely prohibited and that indirect advertising be limited to the announcements of the call letters of the station and of the name of the concern responsible for the matter broadcasted, subject to such regulations as the Secretary of Commerce may impose.

In 1927, following the passage of the Radio Act, advertising abuses were among the first topics to engage the attention of the newly established Federal

---

[1] See p. . . . [This footnote refers to a table, omitted here, comparing annual expenditures for broadcast advertising and listeners' costs for receiver acquisition, operation, and maintenance. — Ed.]

Radio Commission. Thus, in its first formal statement of the "broad underlying principles which . . . must control its decisions on controversies arising between stations in their competition for favorable assignments," one of the "broad underlying principles" set forth was that "the amount and character of advertising must be rigidly confined within the limits consistent with the public service expected of the station." To quote further:

... The Commission must . . . recognize that without advertising, broadcasting would not exist, and *must confine itself to limiting this advertisement in amount and in character* so as to preserve the largest possible amount of service to the public. Advertising must be accepted for the present as the sole means of support of broadcasting, and *regulation must be relied upon to prevent the abuse and over use of the privilege.*[2] (Emphasis supplied.)

This general principle was applied in particular cases, especially in connection with actions on renewal of station licenses. Thus in announcing, on August 23, 1928, its decision not to renew the license of Station WCRW, the Commission stated:

It is clear that a large part of the program is distinctly commercial in character, consisting of advertisers' announcements and of direct advertising, including the quoting of prices. An attempt was made to show a very limited amount of educational and community civic service, but the amount of time thus employed is negligible and evidence of its value to the community is not convincing. Manifestly this station is one which exists chiefly for the purpose of deriving an income from the sale of advertising of a character which must be objectionable to the listening public and without making much, if any, endeavor to render any real service to the public.

The station's license was not renewed.

It was urged in some quarters, then as now, that the Commission need not concern itself with program service because whenever the public found a broadcast irksome, listeners would shift to other stations and the situation would thus automatically correct itself. The Federal Radio Commission, in announcing on August 29, 1928 its decision to place Stations WRAK, WABF, WBRE, and WMBS "on probation" by renewing their license for 30 days only, rather than for the customary 90 days, gave short shrift to this argument. It stated:

Listeners are given no protection unless it is given to them by this Commission, for they are powerless to prevent the ether waves carrying the unwelcome messages from entering the walls of their homes. Their only alternative, which is not to tune in on the station, is not satisfactory, particularly when in a city such as Erie only the local stations can be received during a large

[2] *In re Great Lakes Broadcasting Co.*, F.R.C. Docket No. 4900.

part of the year. When a station is misused for such a private purpose the entire listening public is deprived of the use of a station for a service in the public interest.

Despite the Federal Radio Commission's concern with excessive advertising, there is reason to believe that substantial Congressional sentiment considered the Commission too lax in the exercise of its functions with respect to advertising. Thus on January 12, 1932, the Senate passed Senate Resolution 129, introduced by Senator Couzens, then chairman of the Senate Committee on Interstate Commerce, which provided in part as follows:

Whereas there is growing dissatisfaction with the present use of radio facilities for purposes of commercial advertising: Be it

Resolved, That the Federal Radio Commission is hereby authorized and instructed to make a survey and to report to the Senate on the following questions:

1. What information there is available on the feasibility of Government ownership and operation of broadcasting facilities.
2. To what extent the facilities of a representative group of broadcasting stations are used for commercial advertising purposes.
3. To what extent the use of radio facilities for purposes of commercial advertising varies as between stations having power of one hundred watts, five hundred watts, one thousand watts, five thousand watts, and all in excess of five thousand watts.
4. What plans might be adopted to reduce, to limit, to control, and perhaps, to eliminate the use of radio facilities for commercial advertising purposes.
5. What rules or regulations have been adopted by other countries to control or to eliminate the use of radio facilities for commercial advertising purposes.
6. Whether it would be practicable and satisfactory to permit only the announcement of sponsorship of programs by persons or corporations.[3]

(3)   Evolution of industry standards

(a)   *Commercials in sponsored programs.*   Broadcasters and advertisers themselves have always recognized the basic doctrine that advertising must be limited and abuses avoided. Thus, Mr. Herbert Wilson Smith, of the National Carbon Company, sponsors of the Ever-Ready Hour, testified before the House Merchant Marine and Fisheries Committee concerning radio legislation on January 7, 1926:

---

[3]The Commission's study made pursuant to this Resolution was published as Senate Document 137, 72nd Cong. 1st sess.

. . . When these musical and semi-dramatic programs are given, we precede the program by some such announcement as this one, for example, on December 15, 1925.

"Tuesday evening means the Ever-Ready Hour, for it is on this day and at this time each week that the National Carbon Company, makers of Ever-Ready flashlights and radio batteries, engages the facilities of these 14 radio stations to present its artists in original radio creations. Tonight the sponsors of the hour have included in the program, etc."

Now, that is the extent of the advertising, direct or indirect, of any character which we do in connection with our program. . . . The statement of the name of your company or the sponsorship of the program must be delicately handled so that the listener will not feel that he is having advertising pushed over on him; then throughout the rest of the entertainment, there is given a very high-class program, a musical program, entirely for the pleasure of the listeners. (*Hearings on H.R. 5589*, 69th Cong., 1st sess., pp. 81-82.)

On March 25, 1929 the National Association of Broadcasters, composed at that time of 147 broadcast stations throughout the country, adopted "Standards of Commercial Practice" which specifically provided:

Commercial announcements, as the term is generally understood, shall not be broadcast between 7 and 11 p.m.

In 1930 Mr. William S. Hedges of Station WMAQ, then president of the National Association of Broadcasters and now vice-president of the National Broadcasting Company, testified before the Senate Committee on Interstate Commerce concerning the quantitative limits on advertising which he then enforced.[4]

The Chairman (Senator Couzens).   What portion of a 30-minute program would you say should be devoted to advertising?

Mr. Hedges.   It all depends on the way you do it. Our rule, however, in our station is that no more than one minute out of the 30 minutes is devoted to advertising sponsorship. In other words, the radio listener gets 29 minutes of corking good entertainment, and all he has to do is to learn the name of the organization that has brought to him this fine program.

The Chairman.   Do all of the advertisers on your station confine themselves to 1 minute of advertising out of thirty minutes?

Mr. Hedges.   Some of them do not use as much as that.

The Chairman.   And some use more?

Mr. Hedges.   Very few. (pp. 1752-3)

Mr. William S. Paley, until recently president of the Columbia Broadcasting System, testified in the same hearings that only 22 percent of the time of

[4] Senate Committee on Interstate Commerce, *Hearings on S. 6*, 71st. Cong., 2d sess.

CBS, or 23 hours per week out of 109½ hours of operation, was devoted to commercial programs; the remaining 78 percent of the time was sustaining (pp. 1796-9). He cited the "CBS Credo" on advertising:

No overloading of a program with advertising matter, either through announcements that are too long or by too frequent mention of a trade name or product. (p. 1801)

Mr. Paley testified further:

Senator Dill. How much of the hour do you allow for advertising in a program of an hour, or how much in a program of half an hour?
Mr. Paley. Well, that varies, Senator Dill. I do not know how many seconds or how many minutes during an hour we actually give for the advertising time, but a few weeks ago our research department told me that of all the time used on the air during a particular week, that the actual time taken for advertising mention was seven-tenths of 1 percent of all our time. (p. 1802)

Since 1930, there has been a progressive relaxation of industry standards, so that the NAB standards at present permit as much as one and three-quarter minutes of advertising in a five-minute period, and do not even require this limit on participating programs, "musical clocks," etc. The *NAB Code* provisions in effect from 1937 to 1945 were as follows:

Member stations shall hold the length of commercial copy, including that devoted to contests and offers, to the following number of minutes and seconds:

Daytime

Five-minute programs	2:00
Five-minute news programs*	1:45
Ten-minute programs	2:30
Fifteen-minute programs	3:15
Twenty-five minute programs	4:15
Thirty-minute programs	4:30
Sixty-minute programs	9:00

Nighttime

Five-minute programs	1:45
Five-minute news programs*	1:30
Ten-minute programs	2:00
Fifteen-minute programs	2:30
Twenty-five minute programs	2:45
Thirty-minute programs	3:00
Sixty-minute programs	6:00

*Further restriction by individual stations is recommended.

Exceptions:
The above limitations do not apply to participation programs, announce-

ment programs, "musical clocks," shoppers' guide and local programs falling within these general classifications.

Because of the varying economic and social conditions throughout the United States, members of the NAB shall have the right to present to the NAB for special ruling local situations which in the opinion of the member may justify exceptions to the above prescribed limitations.

In August 1945 these standards were further amended to eliminate the day-night differential, and to apply the former nighttime maxima to all hours.

(b)   *Spot Announcements.*   In addition to the commercials within sponsored programs, there are, of course, commercial spot announcements within or between programs. No standard appears to be generally accepted for limiting spot announcements — though one network has recently announced with respect to its owned stations that commercial spot announcements must be limited to 1 minute or 125 words, that not more than three may be broadcast in any quarter-hour, that "station-break" spot announcements must be limited to 12 seconds or 25 words, and that these must not be more frequent than one each quarter-hour. The result is to permit 12 minutes and 48 seconds of spot announcements per hour. The NAB standards place no limitations whatever on spot announcements.

(4)   Present practices: time devoted to commercials

In addition to the general relaxation of advertising standards in recent years, there is abundant evidence that even the present NAB standards are being flouted by some stations and networks.

As a rough index to contemporary advertising practices, the Commission recorded the programs of the six Washington, D.C., stations for Friday, July 6, 1945, and analyzed the recordings and station logs for that day. The Washington stations comprise:

WRC — a 5,000-watt regional station, owned by the National Broadcasting Company.

WTOP — a 50,000-watt clear-channel station, owned and operated by the Columbia Broadcasting System.

WMAL — a 5,000-watt regional station, owned by the Washington *Evening Star*, affiliated with the American Broadcasting Company (Blue Network).

WOL — a 1,000-watt regional station licensed to the Cowles Broadcasting Company and affiliated with the Mutual Broadcasting System.

WINX — a 250-watt local station licensed to the Washington *Post*.

WWDC — a 250-watt local station licensed to the Capital Broadcasting Company.

It seems reasonable to suppose that these six stations, operating in a major metropolitan area and the capital of the country, including two stations owned by major networks and two others affiliated with major networks would represent practices superior to the practices of stations generally.

Frequent examples of commercial advertising in excess of NAB standards were noted on all four networks and all six stations. The results of the study suggest that on networks and stations alike, the NAB standards are as honored in the breach as in the observance.

(5)   Other advertising problems

The proportion of overall time devoted to advertising commercials, discussed above, is only one of a series of problems raised by present network and station policies. No thorough study has been made of these other advertising problems, and accordingly, the following paragraphs should be considered as suggestive only, and designed to stimulate further research in this field. More light is needed both on the nature of existing practices and on their effect. A partial list of advertising problems other than the proportion of time devoted to advertising includes:

(a)   *Length of individual commercials.*   One commercial recorded by the Commission ran for just five minutes, without program interruption of any kind.

That many advertisers are content with spot announcements of reasonable length is indicated by the following table showing the scheduled length of 70 commercial spot announcements broadcast over Station WCAU on Monday, February 12, 1945, between 8 a.m. and 11 p.m.:

No. of 15-second commercial spot announcements	2
No. of 20-second ” ” ”	2
No. of 25-second ” ” ”	36
No. of 30-second ” ” ”	2
No. of 45-second ” ” ”	1
No. of 60-second ” ” ”	26
No. of 95-second ” ” ”	1
	70

On the other hand, some advertisers are frankly of the opinion that the longer the commercial plug, the more effective the program. Mr. Duane Jones, president of an advertising agency said to be one of the five largest in New York, placing more than 2,000 commercials a week for 26 clients, has given forceful expression to this view:

In dealing with advertising on the air, we in the Duane Jones Co. have found that, when we increase the length and number of commercials on the air to test our programs, invariably their Crossley ratings go up. . . . When making these tests, we load the programs to the limit under NAB rulings with commercials that precede, interrupt, and follow these broadcasts. And we know from the results that any arbitrary curtailment of commercials would seriously impair the audience value of these shows.

This view does not appear to be universally held; and evidence is available that lengthy commercials result in listeners tuning out a program. Thus *Variety* for May 2, 1945, reported:

TOO MANY PLUGS COOL "ROMANCE"

Colgate's "Theatre of Romance" is going way overboard on commercial spiels each week, CBS execs pointed out to Sherman, Marquette agency chiefs on Friday (27) — and it must stop immediately for the good of the program and the web's rating, they added.

A chart-check over a two-month period shows that the commercials on "Romance" run anywhere from three minutes and 15 seconds to four and one-half minutes. CBS' ruling on the commercial's time-limit for 30-minute sponsored shows, proved over the years, is three minutes. Over that, according to researchers at the network, listeners become restless, continuity is uneven and the stanza suffers in rating....

Charts show that the drama picks up rating shortly after going on the air, and that every time a commercial is spieled, the rating sags. On "Romance," too, for a full two minutes before it goes off each week during which the surveys were taken, ratings drop as much as three points. And on many shows, besides the Colgate blurbs, the announcer pitches in with a government-agency plug as well.

Sherman, Marquette will have to hold the commercials within the three-minute limit, or less, from here on in, CBS has informed them.[5]

A study of the six Washington stations for Friday, July 6, 1945, from 8 a.m. to 11 p.m. suggests that commercials one minute or more in length are quite common. More than 150 such announcements were noted on the six Washington stations during that period.

(b) *Number of commercials.* The extreme case of an excessive *number* of spots noted to date is Station KMAC, which broadcast 2215 commercial announcements in 133 hours on the air during the week beginning January 21, 1945. This was an average of 16.7 spots per hour. Spot

---

[5] Television may bring still longer commercials. *Variety* for March 14, 1945, reports:

"A new venture in video experimentation, as far as a Chicago station is concerned, will be tried Tuesday (20) when a 3½-minute commercial is aired over WBKB, Balaban & Katz station here. Designed to fill in the air time between studio programs, the package is completely canned and is composed of slide film, synchronized to a recorded musical background and narration with the video part entirely cartooned.

"Set up as a Red Heart dog food commercial, it was produced by David W. Doyle, associate radio director of the Henri, Hurst & McDonald, Inc., agency; written by Betty Babcock and narrated by Ray Suber. Following tests here it may later be used on WNBT (NBC) and WABD (DuMont), New York."

announcements in excess of 1,000 per week have been noted on a number of stations.

(c)   *Piling up of commercials.*   The listener who has heard one program and wants to hear another has come to expect a commercial plug to intervene. Conversely, the listener who has heard one or more commercial announcements may reasonably expect a program to intervene. Listed below is a series of commercial spot announcements broadcast by Station WTOL in Toledo, on November 14, 1944, during the dinner hour, without program interruption:

6:39:30 p.m.	Transcribed spot announcement.		
6:40:00	Live spot announcement.		
6:41:00	Transcribed spot announcement.		
6:42:00	,,	,,	,,
6:43:00	,,	,,	,,
6:44:00	,,	,,	,,

This programless period occurred each weekday dinner hour during the week of November 13, 1945, except on Thursday, when Station WTOL interrupted its spots to broadcast one minute of transcribed music.

Such series are not unique. The "hitch-hiker" and "cowcatcher" on network programs, now rarer but not yet exterminated, have at times meant that a listener desiring to hear two consecutive network programs must survive five intervening commercial plugs — the closing plug of the first program, a "hitch-hiker" plug for another product of the same sponsor, a local plug in the station break between programs, a "cowcatcher" for a minor product of the sponsor of the second network program, and finally the opening commercial of the second program.

Professor C. H. Sandage, in his survey of radio advertising by retailers, has pointed out that excessive spot announcements may even destroy advertiser confidence in broadcasting:

There is real danger that excessive use of spots will drive not only listeners away from a station but also a number of advertisers whom some refer to as the more respectable. A Midwest jeweler who operated a first-class, noninstallment credit store reported that he had cancelled his use of radio because he felt that radio management in his city had allowed the air to become too crowded with spot announcements. He also believed that many announcements were purchased by firms selling cheap and shoddy merchandise. Another advertiser reported: "Radio announcements are O.K. for loan sharks but not for me." Similar comments were sufficiently frequent to indicate that this factor had kept a number of retailers from using the facilities of radio.[6]

[6] Sandage, *Radio Advertising for Retailers*, p. 186.

(d)   *Time between commercials.*   Listener satisfaction may depend in part upon the length of the intervals between commercials. The National Association of Broadcasters may have been recognizing this feature of the commercial when in 1929 it banned commercial announcements between 7 and 11 p.m., thus affording four hours of listening uninterrupted by commercial advertising — as distinguished from announcement of the name of the advertiser and of his product.

Some stations and some advertisers are becoming aware of the value of uninterrupted listening. Thus the WOL program on July 9, 1945 from 7:30 to 7:58 p.m. made a point of announcing that the four movements of a symphony would be played "without interruption."

(e)   *The middle commercial.*   The Radio Council of Greater Cleveland, composed of representatives of 112 organizations having a total membership of 155,000, conducted a questionnaire survey in 1945 with respect to the "middle commercial" and related problems. The study, while perhaps subject to considerable sampling error, nevertheless indicates roughly the extent of listener dissatisfaction. More than 95 percent of those responding stated that they preferred commercials only at the beginning and end.

Canadian regulations prohibit the middle commercial on newscasts altogether. Canadian Regulation 13(2), adopted November 17, 1941, provides in part:

The only announcement of sponsorship for news . . . shall be two in number, one at the beginning and one at the end, and shall be as follows:

"Through the courtesy of (name and business of sponsor) Station ___ presents (presented) the news of the day furnished by (name of news service)."

The Association of Radio News Analysts, a group whose own livelihood depends upon commercial newscasts, has been among those who believe the middle commercial to be an unhealthy growth. Article IV of the *ARNA Code* of Ethics states:

The association deplores the interruption of a news analysis by commercial announcements.

Many members of the ARNA, which includes outstanding news analysts and commentators throughout the country, refuse to appear on a program which is interrupted by a middle commercial. Raymond Swing, in a telegram to the St. Louis *Post-Dispatch* published February 5, 1945, described his own experience with the middle commercial:

I made my own rebellion against them on May 10, 1940, when writing my broadcast reporting German violation of French, Belgian, Dutch and Luxembourg neutrality in launching the Western offensive. It seemed hideous to have this account interrupted by a sales talk, and I balked.

To the credit of Mutual officials, for whom I was then broadcasting, and the advertising agency handling the program, they supported my stand. Since then my contracts for broadcasts on the Blue network have specified that my program not be interrupted by middle commercials.

Listeners are entitled to hear the news without jarring interruptions, and I feel confident it is sound advertising policy to recognize the right.

Despite the successful revolt of Mr. Swing and some others, it should be noted that as late as Friday, July 6, 1945, recording of broadcasts on the six Washington stations showed some news and analysis programs being interrupted by commercials on all four networks and all six stations.

The St. Louis *Post-Dispatch* has carried on for some months a concerted campaign against the middle commercial in newscasts, and has been followed by newspapers throughout the country. Leaders in the campaign have been other newspapers which, like the *Post-Dispatch*, are themselves the licensees of standard broadcast stations.

Judge Justin Miller, then of the United States Circuit Court of Appeals and now president of the National Association of Broadcasters, commented on the middle commercial and the *Post-Dispatch* campaign in a letter to the editor published April 20, 1945:

I have just read in *Broadcasting* a reprint of your editorial of April 10, "In the Interest of Radio." Let me add my voice to that of others who have commended you for the position which you have taken.

There is no more reason why a newscast should be interrupted for a plug-ugly than that such ads should be inserted in the middle of news stories or editorials in a newspaper; especially when the interruption — deliberately or unconsciously, whichever it may be — is in nauseating contrast to the subject under discussion by the commentator.

It is particularly encouraging that this insistence upon higher professional standards should come from a newspaper — a representative of the profession which has most intelligently through the years defended the guarantees of the first amendment. Only by intelligent anticipation of public reaction and by equally intelligent self-discipline can we prevent legislative intemperance.

While many stations and some sponsors deleted the middle commercial on newscasts following the *Post-Dispatch* campaign, others adopted measures which fall short of elimination. One network, for example, divides 15 minutes of news and comment into a 10-minute program for one sponsor and a 5-minute program for another — with a station-break announcement between. The result is to move the middle commercial from the precise mid-point to the two-thirds point of the quarter-hour — and to subject the listener to two or even three interrupting impacts. Another network claims to have eliminated the middle commercial, but actually it requires that commercials be limited to the first two and the last three minutes of the 15-minute period — as a result of which the news is interrupted twice instead of once. It is clear that such devices, while they eliminate the commercial at the exact middle, fail to meet the chief listener complaint — which is that the news is *interrupted.* Some sponsors, in contrast, have made a sound asset of actual elimination of the middle commercial; their opening announcement ends with some such phrase as: "We bring you now the news — *uninterrupted.*" It may well be that such emphasis upon the essentials of good programming, made explicit to listeners by appropriate announcement over the air, will do much to eliminate inferior procedures indulged in by other networks, stations, or sponsors.

(f) *The patriotic appeal.*   Patriotism, especially in time of war, is an emotion near the forefront of the minds of most listeners. To misuse the listener's deepest patriotic feelings for the sale of commercial products over the air is a violation of a public trust. It is well established that the American flag shall not be used in visual advertising;[7] and the aural symbols of our national life should be similarly immune from commercialization. An example of the patriotic appeal to buy headache remedies is the following announcement over Station WBT, Charlotte, on September 4, 1944:

As every one of you well knows, the United States is face to face with a great challenge. People everywhere are seriously concerned about the Nation's all-out effort. Regardless of how or where you serve, your first duty is to keep well. Get adequate rest. Follow a reasonable diet. Exercise properly. Avoid unnecessary exposures or excesses. When a simple headache develops, or the pain of neuralgia strikes, try a BC Headache Powder. The quick-acting, prescription-type ingredients in the BC formula usually work fast and relieve in a hurry. Remember this. Get one of the 25-cent packages of BC today. You'll like the way BC eases tantalizing headaches and soothes nerves ruffled or upset by pain. USE ONLY ACCORDING TO DIRECTIONS, and consult a physician when pains persist or recur frequently.

Another announcement over the same station said in part:

All of us have a big job on our hands if we want to keep America the land of the free and the home of the brave. The all-out effort means hard work, and lots of it. Production must move forward — fast! . . . Get one of the 10 or 25-cent packages of BC today. . . .

(g) *The physiological commercial.*   Appeals to listeners to "take an internal bath," inquiring of the listener whether he has the common ailment known as "American stomach," discussions of body odors, sluggish bile, etc., are a distinguishing characteristic of American broadcasting.

Various networks and stations impose various restrictions on such physiological advertising. Mr. Lewis Gannett, well-known book critic, sums up listener reaction thus in the New York *Herald Tribune* for February 28, 1945:

The aspect of home-front life which most disgusted me on return was the radio. BBC programs may be dull and army radio programs may be shallow, but

---

[7]Public Law 623, approved June 22, 1942, provides: "The flag should never be used for advertising purposes in any manner whatsoever."

if the soldier in Europe has had a chance to hear the radio at all, he has heard it straight, without the neurotic advertising twaddle which punctuates virtually every American program. . . . The first evening that I sat by a radio at home, I heard one long parade of headaches, coughs, aching muscles, stained teeth, "unpleasant full feeling," and gastric hyperacidity. . . . Our radio evenings are a sick parade of sicknesses and if they haven't yet made us a sick nation, I wonder why.

According to data compiled by the Publisher's Information Bureau, more money is spent for network advertising of drugs and toilet goods than for any other products; 27.9% of all network gross billings is for such products. Drug and cosmetic advertising is said to have trebled between 1939 and 1944. The increasing identification of radio as a purveyor of patent medicines and proprietary remedies raises serious problems which warrant careful consideration by the broadcasting industry.

Professor Sandage's survey, cited above, asked various advertisers who did not use radio advertising the reason for their refraining. His study states:

A common reason for nonuse in a few communities was the character of advertising carried by local stations. Leading merchants commented that radio messages carried on these stations were too much like the patent medicine advertisements of pre-Federal Trade Commission days. These merchants did not wish to be associated on the air with such advertisers.[8]

(h) *Propaganda in commercials.*   The commercial announcement is sometimes used to propagandize for a point of view or one side of a debated issue rather than to sell goods and services. An example is the following announcement over Station KWBU, Corpus Christi, Texas, on August 1, 1944:

When you see a C[entral] P[ower and] L[ight Company] lineman hanging on a pole with one foot in heaven so to speak and hear him holler "headache," you better start running. He is not telling you how he feels but giving warning that he dropped a wrench or hammer and everyone had better look out below. The C[entral] P[ower and] L[ight Company] lineman has a tough job of keeping the electricity flowing to your home. They work night and day to keep headaches from you — to keep your lamps lit and your radio running despite lightning, floods, and storms. Only carefully trained and experienced men could do this job, but there are some in this country who think that the Government should own and operate the light and power industry. Then a lineman might hold his job for political reasons rather than for his ability to render good service to you. Business management under public regulation has brought you good reliable electric service at low prewar prices. That is the American way — let's keep it.

A second example is the following, broadcast over 12 Michigan stations in 1944:

[8] Sandage, *Radio Advertising for Retailers*, p. 73.

American Medicine, the private practice of which represents the cumulative knowledge of decades, the heritage of centuries, the sacrifices and discoveries of countless individuals, has made the United States the healthiest country in the world. Spinal meningitis, diphtheria, smallpox, typhoid fever and other fatal diseases, scourges of yesteryear, are today either preventable or curable, a credit to the tireless efforts of the American medical profession. Thirty-seven states now have voluntary prepayment medical or hospital plans developed by the medical profession and the hospitals. *No theoretical plan, government controlled and operated, and paid for by you, should replace the tried and proved system of the private practice of medicine now in use.*[9]

On January 10, 1944, four days after the U.S. Department of Justice filed suit against the DuPont Company in connection with an alleged cartel agreement, DuPont used its commercial advertising period on the well-known "Cavalcade of America" program over NBC to explain one side of a controversial issue. To quote:

I want to talk to you tonight about an agreement current in the news and of wide public interest. This is the agreement which the DuPont Company has had for years with a British chemical company, Imperial Chemical Industries, Ltd. It provides for a mutual opportunity to acquire patent licenses and technical and scientific information relating to important chemical developments. It has been a matter of public record and known to our government for ten years.

Literally hundreds of transfers of technical and scientific information have occurred for the advancement of chemical science and the benefit of the American people in peace and war. Agreements of a similar character, but limited to specific chemical fields have been made from time to time with continental European companies for the use of scientific data obtained from abroad. Many valuable products have resulted for the use of the American public and necessary to our armed forces. In this war, DuPont chemists have materially improved and have further developed the scientific data flowing from these contractual arrangements.

The scientific and technical information gained has contributed substantially to American progress and to the success of American arms. Many important products have resulted from these agreements to which reference may be made without disclosing military secrets. Developments were made incident to synthetic ammonia manufactured from nitrogen extracted from the air. Without this we could not have smokeless powder and TNT in anything like the quantities needed. The development of Methyl Methacrylate plastic used for the transparent enclosures to be found on every combat airplane stems from these agreements. A new process vital to quantity production of aircraft engines and a

[9] *Journal of the American Medical Association*, Vol. 127, No. 5, p. 283 (February 3, 1945). (Emphasis supplied.)

new plastic polythene, which has gone into the production of new electrical items urgently needed by the Army and Navy. Also high in this last are rayon, dyes, celophane, zelan, — water repellent for military apparel, as well as many other chemical products. All have been improved and perfected here but they came originally from abroad.

These agreements have been of the greatest benefit in giving to the American public products and processes which in the past have materially raised the standard of living, products and processes which are a part of the promise for the future of "Better Things for Better Living Through Chemistry."

(i)   *Intermixture of program and advertising.*   A listener is entitled to know when the program ends and the advertisement begins. The *New York Times* comment on this and related topics is here in point:

The virtual subordination of radio's standards to the philosophy of advertising inevitably has led the networks into an unhealthy and untenable position. It has permitted Gabriel Heatter to shift without emphasis from a discussion of the war to the merits of hair tonic. It has forced the nation's best entertainers to act as candy butchers and debase their integrity as artists. It has permitted screeching voices to yell at our children to eat this or that if they want to be as efficient as some fictional character. ... The broadcaster often has argued that it is not his function to "reform" the public taste, but, be that as it may, it certainly is the broadcaster's responsibility not to lower it.

The Association of Radio News Analysts has particularly inveighed against the practice of having the announcements read by the same voice as the news analysis. Article IV of the ARNA Code of Ethics provides:

The association believes the reading of commercial announcements by radio news analysts is against the best interests of broadcasting.

According to the president of the ARNA, John W. Vandercook:

ARNA has . . . consistently arrayed itself in opposition to the reading of such commercial announcements by news analysts. It is our belief that the major networks and all of the more reputable American advertising agencies are in substantial agreement with us and support our stand.

We, however, recognize and applaud the necessity for perpetual vigilance and unremitting efforts to extirpate the all-too-common breaches of these principles. (St. Louis *Post-Dispatch*, Feb. 5, 1945.)

The above is not to be taken as an exhaustive list of advertising excesses. Since it is not the intention of the Commission to concern itself with advertising excesses other than an excessive ratio of advertising time to program time, no exhaustive study has been undertaken. There is need, however, for a thorough review by the industry itself of current advertising practices, with a view towards the establishment and enforcement of sound standards by the industry itself.

PART IV.   ECONOMIC ASPECTS

The problem of program service is intimately related to economic factors. A prosperous broadcasting industry is obviously in a position to render a better program service to the public than an industry which must pinch and scrape to make ends meet. Since the revenues of American broadcasting come primarily from advertisers, the terms and conditions of program service must not be such as to block the flow of advertising revenues into broadcasting. Finally, the public benefits when the economic foundations of broadcasting are sufficiently firm to insure a flow of new capital into the industry, especially at present when the development of FM and television is imminent.

A review of the economic aspects of broadcasting during recent years indicates that there are no economic considerations to prevent the rendering of a considerably broader program service than the public is currently afforded.*

PART V.   SUMMARY AND CONCLUSIONS –
PROPOSALS FOR FUTURE COMMISSION POLICY

A.   Role of the public

Primary responsibility for the American system of broadcasting rests with the licensee of broadcast stations, including the network organizations. It is to the stations and networks rather than to federal regulation that listeners must primarily turn for improved standards of program service. The Commission, as the licensing agency established by Congress, has a responsibility to consider overall program service in its public interest determinations, but affirmative improvement of program service must be the result primarily of other forces.

One such force is self-regulation by the industry itself, through its trade associations.

Licensees acting individually can also do much to raise program service standards, and some progress has indeed been made. Here and there across the country, some stations have evidenced an increased awareness of the importance of sustaining programs, live programs, and discussion programs. Other stations have eliminated from their own program service the middle commercial, the transcribed commercial, the piling up of commercials, etc. This trend toward self-improvement, if continued, may further buttress the industry against the rising tide of informed and responsible criticism.

Forces outside the broadcasting industry similarly have a role to play in

---

*Sixteen tables of economic data supporting this view are omitted. [Ed.]

improved program service. There is need, for example, for professional radio critics, who will play in this field the role which literary and dramatic critics have long assumed in the older forms of artistic expression. It is, indeed, a curious instance of the time lag in our adjustment to changed circumstances that while plays and concerts performed to comparatively small audiences in the "legitimate" theater or concert hall are regularly reviewed in the press, radio's best productions performed before an audience of millions receive only occasional and limited critical consideration. *Publicity* for radio programs is useful, but limited in the function it performs. Responsible criticism can do much more than mere promotion; it can raise the standards of public appreciation and stimulate the free and unfettered development of radio as a new medium of artistic expression. The independent radio critic, assuming the same role long occupied by the dramatic critic and the literary critic, can bring to bear an objective judgment on questions of good taste and of artistic merit which lie outside the purview of this Commission. The reviews and critiques published weekly in *Variety* afford an illustration of the role that independent criticism can play; newspapers and periodicals might well consider the institution of similar independent critiques for the general public.

Radio listener councils can also do much to improve the quality of program service. Such councils, notably in Cleveland, Ohio, and Madison, Wisconsin, have already shown the possibilities of independent listener organization. First, they can provide a much needed channel through which listeners can convey to broadcasters the wishes of the vast but not generally articulate radio audience. Second, listener councils can engage in much needed research concerning public tastes and attitudes. Third, listener councils can check on the failure of network affiliates to carry outstanding network sustaining programs, and on the local programs substituted for outstanding network sustaining programs. Fourth, they can serve to publicize and to promote outstanding programs — especially sustaining programs which at present suffer a serious handicap for lack of the vast promotional enterprise which goes to publicize many commercial programs. Other useful functions would also no doubt result from an increase in the number and an extension of the range of activities of listener councils, cooperating with the broadcasting industry but speaking solely for the interest of listeners themselves.

Colleges and universities, some of them already active in the field, have a like distinctive role to play. Together with the public schools, they have it in their power to raise a new generation of listeners with higher standards and expectations of what radio can offer.

In radio workshops, knowledge may be acquired of the techniques of radio production. There are already many examples of students graduating from such work who have found their way into the industry, carrying with them standards and conceptions of radio's role, as well as talents, by which radio service cannot fail to be enriched.

Even more important, however, is the role of colleges and universities in the field of radio research. There is room for a vast expansion of studies of the commercial, artistic and social aspects of radio. The cultural aspects of radio's influence provide in themselves a vast and fascinating field of research.

It is hoped that the facts emerging from this report and the recommendations which follow will be of interest to the groups mentioned. With them rather than with the Commission rests much of the hope for improved broadcasting quality.

B.   Role of the Commission

While much of the responsibility for improved program service lies with the broadcasting industry and with the public, the Commission has a statutory responsibility for the public interest, of which it cannot divest itself. The Commission's experience with the detailed review of broadcast renewal applications since April 1945, together with the facts set forth in this report, indicate some current trends in broadcasting which, with reference to licensing procedure, require its particular attention.

In issuing and in renewing the licenses of broadcast stations the Commission proposes to give particular consideration to four program service factors relevant to the public interest. These are: (1) the carrying of sustaining programs, including network sustaining programs, with particular reference to the retention by licensees of a proper discretion and responsibility for maintaining a well-balanced program structure; (2) the carrying of local live programs; (3) the carrying of programs devoted to the discussion of public issues, and (4) the elimination of advertising excesses.

(1)   *Sustaining programs.*   The carrying of sustaining programs has always been deemed one aspect of broadcast operation in the public interest. Sustaining programs, as noted above (pp. 156–169), perform a five-fold function in (a) maintaining an overall program balance, (b) providing time for programs inappropriate for sponsorship, (c) providing time for programs serving particular minority tastes and interests, (d) providing time for non-profit organizations — religious, civic, agricultural, labor, educational, etc., and (e) providing time for experiment and for unfettered artistic self-expression.

Accordingly, the Commission concludes that one standard of operation in the public interest is a reasonable proportion of time devoted to sustaining programs.

Moreover, if sustaining programs are to perform their traditional functions in the American system of broadcasting, they must be broadcast at hours when the public is awake and listening. The time devoted to sustaining programs, accordingly, should be reasonably distributed among the various segments of the broadcast day.

For the reasons set forth on pages 171–181, the Commission, in considering overall program balance, will also take note of network sustaining programs available to but not carried by a station, and of the programs which the station substitutes therefor.

(2)   *Local live programs.*   The Commission has always placed a marked emphasis, and in some cases perhaps an undue emphasis, on the carrying of local live programs as a standard of public interest. The development of network, transcription, and wire news services is such that no sound public interest appears to be served by continuing to stress local live programs exclusively at the expense of these other categories. Nevertheless, reasonable provision for local self-expression still remains an essential function of a station's operation (pp. 181-188), and will continue to be so regarded by the Commission. In particular, public interest requires that such programs should not be crowded out of the best listening hours.

(3)   *Programs devoted to the discussion of public issues.*   The crucial need for discussion programs, at the local, national, and international levels alike is universally realized, as set forth on pp. 188-191. Accordingly, the carrying of such programs in reasonable sufficiency, and during good listening hours, is a factor to be considered in any finding of public interest.

(4)   *Advertising excesses.*   The   evidence   set   forth   above (pp. 191-206), warrants the conclusion that some stations during some or many portions of the broadcast day have engaged in advertising excesses which are incompatible with their public responsibilities, and which threaten the good name of broadcasting itself.

As the broadcasting industry itself has insisted, the public interest clearly requires that the amount of time devoted to advertising matter shall bear a reasonable relationship to the amount of time devoted to programs. Accordingly, in its application forms the Commission will request the applicant to state how much time he proposes to devote to advertising matter in any one hour.

This by itself will not, of course, result in the elimination of some of the particular excesses described on pp. 198-206. This is a matter in which self-regulation by the industry may properly be sought and indeed expected. The Commission has no desire to concern itself with the particular length, content, or irritating qualities of particular commercial plugs.

C.   Procedural proposals

In carrying out the above objectives, the Commission proposes to continue substantially unchanged its present basic licensing procedures – namely, the requiring of a written application setting forth the proposed program service of the station, the consideration of that application on its merits, and subsequently the comparison of promise and performance when an application is received for a renewal of the station license. The ends sought can best be achieved, so far as presently appears, by appropriate modification of the particular forms and procedures currently in use and by a generally more careful consideration of renewal applications.

The particular procedural changes proposed are set forth below. They will not be introduced immediately or simultaneously, but rather from time to time as circumstances warrant. Meanwhile, the Commission invites comment from licensees and from the public.

(1) Uniform definitions and program logs

The Commission has always recognized certain basic categories of programs — e.g., commercial and sustaining, network, transcribed, recorded, local, live, etc. Such classifications must, under Regulation 3.404, be shown upon the face of the program log required to be kept by each standard broadcast station; and the Commission, like its predecessor, has always required data concerning such program classifications in its application forms.

Examination of logs shows, however, that there is no uniformity or agreement concerning what constitutes a "commercial" program, a "sustaining" program, a "network" program, etc. Accordingly, the Commission will adopt uniform definitions of basic program terms and classes, which are to be used in all presentations to the Commission. The proposed definitions are set forth below.

A *commercial program* (C) is any program the time for which is paid for by a sponsor *or* any program which is interrupted by a spot announcement (as defined below), at intervals of less than 15 minutes. A network program shall be classified as "commercial" if it is commercially sponsored on the network, even though the particular station is not paid for carrying it — unless all commercial announcements have been deleted from the program by the station.

(It will be noted that any program which is *interrupted* by a commercial announcement is classified as a commercial program, even though the purchaser of the interrupting announcement has not also purchased the time preceding and following. The result is to classify so-called "participating" programs as commercial. Without such a rule, a 15-minute program may contain 5 or even more minutes of advertising and still be classified as "sustaining." Under the proposed definition, a program may be classified as "sustaining" although preceded and followed by spot announcements, but if a spot announcement *interrupts* a program, the program must be classified as "commercial.")

A *sustaining* program (S) is any program which is *neither* paid for by a sponsor *nor* interrupted by a spot announcement (as defined below).

A *network* program (N) is any program furnished to the station by a network or another station. Transcribed delayed broadcasts of network programs are classified as "network," not "recorded." Programs are classified as network whether furnished by a nationwide, regional, or special network or by another station.

A *recorded* program (R) is any program which uses phonograph records, electrical transcriptions, or other means of mechanical reproduction in whole or in part — except where the recording is wholly incidental to the program and is limited to background sounds, sound effects, identifying themes, musical "bridges," etc. A program part transcribed or recorded and part live is classified as "recorded" unless the recordings are wholly incidental, as above. A transcribed delayed broadcast of a network program, however, is not classified as "recorded" but as "network."

A *wire* program (W) is any program the text of which is distributed to a number of stations by telegraph, teletype, or similar means, and read in whole or in part by a local announcer. Programs distributed by the wire news services are "wire" programs. A news program which is part wire and in part of local non-syndicated origin is classified as "wire" if more than half of the program is usually devoted to the reading verbatim of the syndicated wire text, but is classified as "live" if more than half is usually devoted to local news or comment.

(The above is a new program category. Programs in this category resemble network and transcribed programs in the respect that they are syndicated to scores or hundreds of stations. They resemble local live programs only in the respect that the words are vocalized by a local voice; the text is not local but syndicated. Such programs have an important role in broadcasting, especially in the dissemination of news. With respect to stations not affiliated with a network, the wire program for timely matter, plus the transcription for less urgent broadcasts affords a close approach to the services of a regular network. The only difficulty is that with respect to program classifications heretofore, the wire program has been merged with the local live program, which it resembles only superficially, preventing a statistical analysis of either. By establishing definitions for "wire commercial" and "wire sustaining," the Commission expects to make possible statistical studies with respect to such programs, and also to make more significant the statistical studies with respect to the "local live commercial" and "local live sustaining" categories.)

A *local live* program (L) is any local program which uses live talent exclusively, whether originating in the station's studios or by remote control. Programs furnished to a station by a network or another station, however, are not classified as "live" but as "network." A program which uses recordings in whole or in part, except in a wholly incidental manner, should not be classified as "live" but as "recorded." Wire programs, as defined above, should likewise not be classified as "live."

A *sustaining public service announcement* (PSA) is an announcement which is not paid for by a sponsor and which is devoted to a non-profit cause — e.g., war bonds, Red Cross, public health, civic announcements, etc. Promotional, "courtesy," participating announcements, etc. should not be classified as "sustaining public service announcements" but as "spot announcements." War Bond, Red Cross, civic and similar announcements for which the station receives remuneration should not be classified as "sustaining public service announcements" but as "spot announcements."

A *spot announcement* (SA) is any announcement which is neither a sustaining public service announcement (as above defined) nor a station identification announcement (call letters and location). An announcement should be classified as a "spot announcement," whether or not the station receives remuncration, unless it is devoted to a nonprofit cause. Sponsored time signals, sponsored weather announcements, etc. are spot announcements. Unsponsored time signals, weather announcements, etc., are program matter and not classified as announcements. Station identification announcements should *not* be classified as either sustaining public service or spot announcements, if limited to call letters, location, and identification of the licensee and network.

The Commission further proposes to amend Regulation 3.404 to provide in part that the program log shall contain:

An entry classifying each program as "network commercial" (NC); "network sustaining" (NS); "recorded commercial" (RC); "recorded sustaining" (RS); "wire commercial" (WC); "wire sustaining" (WS); "local live commercial" (LC); or "local live sustaining" (LS); and classifying each announcement as "spot announcement" (SA) or "sustaining public service announcement" (PSA).

The adoption of uniform definitions will make possible a faiter comparison of program representations and performance, and better statistical analyses.

(2)   Segments of the broadcast day

The Commission has always recognized, as has the industry, that different segments of the broadcast day have different characteristics and that different types of programming are therefore permissible. For example, the *NAB Code*, until recently, and many stations permit a greater proportion of advertising during the day than at night. The Commission's Chain Broadcasting Regulations recognize four segments: 8 a.m.–1 p.m., 1 p.m.–6 p.m., 6 p.m.–11 p.m., and all other hours. Most stations make distinctions of hours in their rate cards.

In general, sustaining and live programs have tended to be crowded out of the best listening hours from 6 to 11 p.m., and also in a degree out of the period from 8 a.m. to 6 p.m. At least some stations have improved the ratios shown in reports to the Commission, but not the service rendered the public, by crowding sustaining programs into the hours after 11 p.m. and before dawn when listeners are few and sponsors fewer still. Clearly the responsibility for public service cannot be met by broadcasting public service programs only during such hours. A well-balanced program structure requires balance during the best listening hours.

Statistical convenience requires that categories be kept to a minimum. In general, the segments of the broadcast day established in the Chain Broadcasting Regulations appear satisfactory, except that no good purpose appears to be served in connection with program analysis by calculating separately the segments from 8 a.m. to 1 p.m. and from 1 p.m. to 6 p.m. Accordingly, for present purposes it is proposed to merge these segments, so that the broadcast day will be composed of three segments only: 8 a.m.–6 p.m., 6 p.m.–11 p.m., and all other hours.

The categories set forth above, plus the segments herein defined, make possible a standard program log analysis as in the form shown below.

	8 a.m. 6 p.m.	6 p.m. 11 p.m.	All other hours	Total
Network commercial (NC)				
Network sustaining (NS)				
Recorded commercial (RC)				
Recorded sustaining (RS)				
Wire commercial (WC)				
Wire sustaining (WS)				
Live commercial (LC)				
Live sustaining (LS)				
Total[1]				
No. of Spot Announcements (SA)				
No. of Sustaining Public Service Announcements (PSA)				

[1] Totals should equal full operating time during each segment.

The above schedule will be uniformly utilized in Commission application forms and annual report forms in lieu of the various types of schedules now prevailing. In using it, stations may calculate the length of programs to the nearest five minutes.

(3)   Annual reports and statistics

For some years, the Commission has called for a statement of the number of hours devoted to various classes of programs each year, in connection with the Annual Financial Reports of broadcast stations and networks. Requiring such figures for an entire year may constitute a considerable accounting burden on the stations, and may therefore impair the quality of the reports. Accordingly, the Commission proposes hereafter to require these data in the Annual Financial Reports only for one week.

To make the proposed week as representative as possible of the year as a whole, the Commission will utilize a procedure heretofore sometimes used by stations in presentations to the Commission. At the end of each year, it will select at random a Monday in January or February, a Tuesday in March, a Wednesday in April, a Thursday in May or June, a Friday in July or August, a Saturday in September or October, and a Sunday in November or December, and will ask for detailed program analyses for these seven days. The particular days chosen will vary from year to year, and will be drawn so as to avoid holidays and other atypical occasions.

The information requested will be in terms of the definitions and time periods set forth above. Statistical summaries and trends will be published annually.

The Commission will also call upon the networks for quarterly statements of the stations carrying and failing to carry network sustaining programs during a sample week in each quarter.

(4)   Revision of application forms

Since the establishment of the Federal Radio Commission, applicants for new stations have been required to set forth their program plans, and applications have been granted in part on the basis of representations concerning program plans. Applications for renewal of license, assignment of license, transfer of control of licensee corporation, and modification of license have similarly included, in various forms, representations concerning program service rendered or to be rendered. The program service questions now asked on the Commission's application forms are not uniform, and not closely integrated with current Commission policy respecting program service. It is proposed, accordingly, to revise the program service questions on all Commission forms to bring them into line with the policies set forth in this report.

Specifically, applicants for new stations will be required to fill out, as part of Form 301 or Form 319, a showing of their proposed program structure, utilizing the uniform schedule set forth on page 214. Applicants for renewal of license, consent to transfer of assignment, and modification of license will be required to fill out the same uniform schedule, both for a sample week under their previous licenses, and as an indication of their proposed operation if the application in question is granted.

The Commission, of course, recognizes that there is need for flexibility in broadcast operation. An application to the Commission should not be a straitjacket preventing a licensee from rendering an even better service than originally proposed. To provide the necessary flexibility, the information supplied in the uniform schedule will be treated as a responsible estimate rather than a binding pledge. However, attention should be called to the fact that the need for trustworthiness is at least as important with respect to representations concerning program service as with respect to statements concerning financial matters.

Stations will also be asked whether they propose to render a well-balanced program service, or to specialize in programs of a particular type or addressed to a particular audience. If their proposal is for a specialized rather than a balanced program service, a showing will be requested concerning the relative need for such service in the community as compared with the need for an additional station affording a balanced program service. On renewal, stations which have proposed a specialized service will be expected to show the extent to which they have in fact fulfilled their proposals during the period of their license.

Stations affiliated with a network will further be required to list network sustaining programs not carried during a representative week, and the programs carried in place of such programs.

If the Commission is able to determine from an examination of the application that a grant will serve the public interest, it will grant forthwith, as heretofore. If the Commission is unable to make such a determination on the basis of the application it will, as heretofore, designate the application for hearing.

(5)   Action on renewals

With the above changes in Commission forms and procedures, the Commission will have available in connection with renewal applications, specific data relevant to the finding of public interest required by the statute.

First, it will have available all the data concerning engineering, legal, accounting and other matters, as heretofore.

Second, it will have available a responsible estimate of the overall program structure appropriate for the station in question, as estimated by the licensee himself when making his previous application.

Third, it will have available affirmative representations of the licensee concerning the time to be devoted to sustaining programs, live programs, discussion programs, and advertising matter.

Fourth, it will have available from the annual reports to the Commission data concerning the actual program structure of the station during a sample week in each year under the existing license.

Fifth, it will have available a statement of the overall program structure of the station during a week immediately preceding the filing of the application being considered, and information concerning the carrying of network sustaining programs.

Sixth, it will have available the station's representations concerning program service under the license applied for.

If the Commission is able to determine on the basis of the data thus available that a grant will serve the public interest, it will continue as heretofore, to grant forthwith; otherwise, as heretofore, it will designate the renewal application for hearing.

22

The Fairness Doctrine

In the Matter of Editorializing by Broadcast
Licensees
13 FCC 1246
June 1, 1949

Dissatisfaction with the "Mayflower Doctrine" (Document 19, pp. 95-98) mounted with the end of the war and issuance of the "Blue Book." Several FCC decisions of the time emphasized the need for broadcasters to deal with public controversies in an evenhanded manner [*United Broadcasting Co. (WHKC)*, 10 FCC 515 (1945); *Sam Morris*, 11 FCC 197 (1946); *Robert Harold Scott*, 11 FCC 372 (1946)], but licensee editorials still were apparently banned. In 1947 the Commission was persuaded to take another look at *Mayflower*, and hearings were scheduled for 1948.

While these hearings were under way the "Richards" case surfaced. An organization of professional newspeople charged George A. Richards, licensee of maximum-power radio stations in Los Angeles, Detroit, and Cleveland, with slanting the news. This case would drag on through 1951. Doubtless Richards' attempts to manipulate public opinion through biased news coverage influenced the commissioners who were pondering what to do about *Mayflower*.

The "Fairness Doctrine" in effect reversed the "Mayflower Doctrine's" prohibition against licensee advocacy. More importantly, the policy statement recapitulated two decades of FRC and FCC case law and *dicta* as it set down basic ground rules for the treatment of controversial issues of public importance on the air. The constitutionality of the "Fairness Doctrine" itself was

217

confirmed two decades later by the Supreme Court's *Red Lion* decision (Document 39, pp. 381–402).

The "additional views" of Commissioner Webster and the "separate views" of Commissioner Jones are omitted below, though Commissioner Hennock's brief and prophetic dissent is included. Since two commissioners did not participate at all in the decision, it appears that the "Fairness Doctrine" attracted no more than a bare majority of the full FCC; in fact, if Jones' "separate views" are taken to be a dissent (a not unreasonable interpretation), then this policy statement had the support of only a plurality of the Commission. In 1949 it was inconceivable that the doctrine would achieve its present importance.

While relatively few broadcasters took advantage of the chance to editorialize in the 1950's, a marked increase occurred in the 1960's. The "Fairness Doctrine" was made applicable to news programs exempted from the "equal opportunity" requirement of Section 315 (see p. 538) by a 1959 act of Congress. The FCC issued a "Fairness Primer" in 1964 (29 Fed. Reg. 10415) which summarized 15 years of FCC rulings in a question-and-answer format. Beginning in 1967 the "Fairness Doctrine" was made to apply to a limited class of broadcast advertising (see Document 37, pp. 360-364). This ended in 1974 when the FCC issued its "Fairness Report" (48 FCC 2d 1) which reaffirmed the basic tenets of the "Fairness Doctrine" without significant modification.

Related Reading: 55, 68, 74, 97, 124, 181, 193, 196, 200, 203, 229, 230.

REPORT OF THE COMMISSION

1.   This report is issued by the Commission in connection with its hearings on the above entitled matter held at Washington, D.C., on March 1, 2, 3, 4, and 5, and April 19, 20, and 21, 1948. The hearing had been ordered on the Commission's own motion on September 5, 1947, because of our belief that further clarification of the Commission's position with respect to the obligations of broadcast licensees in the field of broadcasts of news, commentary and opinion was advisable. It was believed that in view of the apparent confusion concerning certain of the Commission's previous statements on these vital matters by broadcast licensees and members of the general public, as well as the professed disagreement on the part of some of these persons with earlier Commission pronouncements, a reexamination and restatement of its views by the Commission would be desirable. And in order to provide an opportunity to

interested persons and organizations to acquaint the Commission with their views, prior to any Commission determination, as to the proper resolution of the difficult and complex problems involved in the presentation of radio news and comment in a democracy, it was designated for public hearing before the Commission *en banc* on the following issues:

1. To determine whether the expression of editorial opinions by broadcast station licensees on matters of public interest and controversy is consistent with their obligations to operate their stations in the public interest.

2. To determine the relationship between any such editorial expression and the affirmative obligation of the licensees to insure that a fair and equal presentation of all sides of controversial issues is made over their facilities.

2. At the hearings testimony was received from some 49 witnesses representing the broadcasting industry and various interested organizations and members of the public. In addition, written statements of their position on the matter were placed into the record by 21 persons and organizations who were unable to appear and testify in person. The various witnesses and statements brought forth for the Commission's consideration, arguments on every side of both of the questions involved in the hearing. Because of the importance of the issues considered in the hearing, and because of the possible confusion which may have existed in the past concerning the policies applicable to the matters which were the subject of the hearing, we have deemed it advisable to set forth in detail and at some length our conclusions as to the basic considerations relevant to the expression of editorial opinion by broadcast licensees and the relationship of any such expression to the general obligations of broadcast licensees with respect to the presentation of programs involving controversial issues.

3. In approaching the issues upon which this proceeding has been held, we believe that the paramount and controlling consideration is the relationship between the American system of broadcasting carried on through a large number of private licensees upon whom devolves the responsibility for the selection and presentation of program material, and the congressional mandate that this licensee responsibility is to be exercised in the interests of, and as a trustee for the public at large which retains ultimate control over the channels of radio and television communications. One important aspect of this relationship, we believe, results from the fact that the needs and interests of the general public with respect to programs devoted to news commentary and opinion can only be satisfied by making available to them for their consideration and acceptance or rejection, of varying and conflicting views held by responsible elements of the community. And it is in the light of these basic concepts that the problems of insuring fairness in the presentation of news and opinion and the place in such a

picture of any expression of the views of the station licensee as such must be considered.

4.   It is apparent that our system of broadcasting, under which private persons and organizations are licensed to provide broadcasting service to the various communities and regions, imposes responsibility in the selection and presentation of radio program material upon such licensees. Congress has recognized that the requests for radio time may far exceed the amount of time reasonably available for distribution by broadcasters. It provided, therefore, in Section 3(h) of the Communications Act that a person engaged in radio broadcasting shall not be deemed a common carrier. It is the licensee, therefore, who must determine what percentage of the limited broadcast day should appropriately be devoted to news and discussion or consideration of public issues, rather than to the other legitimate services of radio broadcasting, and who must select or be responsible for the selection of the particular news items to be reported or the particular local, State, national or international issues or questions of public interest to be considered, as well as the person or persons to comment or analyze the news or to discuss or debate the issues chosen as topics for radio consideration: "The life of each community involves a multitude of interests some dominant and all pervasive such as interest in public affairs, education and similar matters and some highly specialized and limited to few. The practical day-to-day problem with which every licensee is faced is one of striking a balance between these various interests to reflect them in a program service which is useful to the community, and which will in some way fulfill the needs and interests of the many." *Capital Broadcasting Company*, 4 Pike & Fischer, R.R. 21; *The Northern Corporation (WMEX)*, 4 Pike & Fischer, R.R. 333, 338. And both the Commission and the courts have stressed that this responsibility devolves upon the individual licensees, and can neither be delegated by the licensee to any network or other person or group, or be unduly fettered by contractual arrangements restricting the licensee in his free exercise of his independent judgments. *National Broadcasting Company* v. *United States*, 319 U.S. 190 (upholding the Commission's chain broadcasting regulations, Section 3.101-3.108, 3.231-3.238, 3.631-3.638), *Churchhill Tabernacle* v. *Federal Communications Commission*, 160 F. 2d 244 (See, rules and regulations, Sections 3.109, 3.239, 3.639); *Allen T. Simmons* v. *Federal Communications Commission*, 169 F. 2d 670, *certiorari denied* 335 U.S. 846.

5.   But the inevitability that there must be some choosing between various claimants for access to a licensee's microphone, does not mean that the licensee is free to utilize his facilities as he sees fit or in his own particular interests as contrasted with the interests of the general public. The Communications Act of 1934, as amended, makes clear that licenses are to be issued only where the public interest, convenience or necessity would be served thereby. And we think it is equally clear that one of the basic elements of any such operation is the maintenance of radio and television as a medium of freedom of speech and freedom of expression for the people of the Nation as a

whole. Section 301 of the Communications Act provides that it is the purpose of the act to maintain the control of the United States over all channels of interstate and foreign commerce. Section 326 of the act provides that this control of the United States shall not result in any impairment of the right of free speech by means of such radio communications. It would be inconsistent with these express provisions of the act to assert that, while it is the purpose of the act to maintain the control of the United States over radio channels, but free from any regulation or condition which interferes with the right of free speech, nevertheless persons who are granted limited rights to be licensees of radio stations, upon a finding under Sections 307(a) and 309 of the act that the public interest, convenience, or necessity would be served thereby, may themselves make radio unavailable as a medium of free speech. The legislative history of the Communications Act and its predecessor, the Radio Act of 1927 shows, on the contrary, that Congress intended that radio stations should not be used for the private interest, whims, or caprices of the particular persons who have been granted licenses, but in manner which will serve the community generally and the various groups which make up the community.[1] And the courts have consistently upheld Commission action giving recognition to and fulfilling that intent of Congress. *KFKB Broadcasting Association* v. *Federal Radio Commission*, 47 F. 2d 670; *Trinity Methodist Church, South* v. *Federal Radio Commission*, 62 F. 2d 850, *certiorari denied*, 288 U.S. 599.

6. It is axiomatic that one of the most vital questions of mass communication in a democracy is the development of an informed public opinion through the public dissemination of news and ideas concerning the vital public issues of the day. Basically, it is in recognition of the great contribution which radio can make in the advancement of this purpose that portions of the radio spectrum are allocated to that form of radio communications known as

---

[1] Thus in the Congressional debates leading to the enactment of the Radio Act of 1927 Congressman (later Senator) White stated (67 Cong. Rec. 5479, March 12, 1926):

"We have reached the definite conclusion that the right of all our people to enjoy this means of communication can be preserved only by the repudiation of the idea underlying the 1912 law that anyone who will, may transmit and by the assertion in its stead of the doctrine that the right of the public to service is superior to the right of any individual to use the ether ... the recent radio conference met this issue squarely. It recognized that in the present state of scientific development there must be a limitation upon the number of broadcasting stations and it recommended that licenses should be issued only to those stations whose operation would render a benefit to the public, are necessary in the public interest or would contribute to the development of the art. This principle was approved by every witness before your committee. We have written it into the bill. *If enacted into law, the broadcasting privilege will not be a right of selfishness. It will rest upon an assurance of public interest to be served.*" (Italics added.)

And this view that the interest of the listening public rather than the private interests of particular licensees was reemphasized as recently as June 9, 1948, in a unanimous report of the Senate Committee on Interstate and Foreign Commerce on S. 1333 (80th Cong.) which would have amended the present Communications Act in certain respects. See S. Rept. No. 1567, 80th Cong. 2nd Sess., pp. 14-15.

radiobroadcasting. Unquestionably, then, the standard of public interest, convenience and necessity as applied to radiobroadcasting must be interpreted in the light of this basic purpose. The Commission has consequently recognized the necessity for licensees to devote a reasonable percentage of their broadcast time to the presentation of news and programs devoted to the consideration and discussion of public issues of interest in the community served by the particular station. And we have recognized, with respect to such programs, the paramount right of the public in a free society to be informed and to have presented to it for acceptance or rejection the different attitudes and viewpoints concerning these vital and often controversial issues which are held by the various groups which make up the community.[2] It is this right of the public to be informed, rather than any right on the part of the Government, any broadcast licensee or any individual member of the public to broadcast his own particular views on any matter, which is the foundation stone of the American system of broadcasting.

7.   This affirmative responsibility on the part of broadcast licensees to provide a reasonable amount of time for the presentation over their facilities of programs devoted to the discussion and consideration of public issues has been reaffirmed by the Commission in a long series of decisions. The *United Broadcasting Co. (WHKC)* case, 10 FCC 515, emphasized that this duty includes the making of reasonable provision for the discussion of controversial issues of public importance in the community served, and to make sufficient time available for full discussion thereof. The *Scott* case, 3 Pike & Fischer, Radio Regulation 259, stated our conclusions that this duty extends to all subjects of substantial importance to the community coming within the scope of free discussion under the first amendment without regard to personal views and opinions of the licensees on the matter, or any determination by the licensee as to the possible unpopularity of the views to be expressed on the subject matter to be discussed among particular elements of the station's listening audience. Cf., *National Broadcasting Company* v. *United States*, 319 U.S. 190; *Allen T. Simmons*, 3 Pike & Fischer, R.R. 1029, *affirmed; Simmons* v. *Federal Communications Commission*, 169 F. 2d 670, *certiorari denied*, 335 U.S. 846; *Bay State Beacon*, 3 Pike & Fischer, R.R. 1455, *affirmed; Bay State Beacon* v. *Federal Communications Commission*, U.S. App. D.C., decided December 20, 1948; *Petition of Sam Morris*, 3 Pike & Fischer, R.R. 154; *Thomas N. Beach*, 3 Pike & Fischer R.R. 1784. And the Commission has made clear that in such presentation of news and comment the public interest requires that the licensee must operate on a basis of overall fairness, making his facilities available for the expression of the contrasting views of all responsible elements in the community on the various issues which arise. *Mayflower Broadcasting Co.*, 8 F.C.C. 333;

---

[2] Cf., *Thornhill* v. *Alabama*, 310 U.S. 88, 95, 102; *Associated Press* v. *United States*, 326 U.S. 1, 20.

United Broadcasting Co. (WHKC) 10 F.C.C. 515; Cf. *WBNX Broadcasting Co., Inc.,* 4 Pike & Fischer, R.R. 244 (memorandum opinion). Only where the licensee's discretion in the choice of the particular programs to be broadcast over his facilities is exercised so as to afford a reasonable opportunity for the presentation of all responsible positions on matters of sufficient importance to be afforded radio time can radio be maintained as a medium of freedom of speech for the people as a whole. These concepts, of course, do restrict the licensee's freedom to utilize his station in whatever manner he chooses but they do so in order to make possible the maintenance of radio as a medium of freedom of speech for the general public.

8.   It has been suggested in the course of the hearings that licensees have an affirmative obligation to insure fair presentation of all sides of any controversial issue before any time may be allocated to the discussion or consideration of the matter. On the other hand, arguments have been advanced in support of the proposition that the licensee's sole obligation to the public is to refrain from suppressing or excluding any responsible point of view from access to the radio. We are of the opinion, however, that any rigid requirement that licensees adhere to either of these extreme prescriptions for proper station programing techniques would seriously limit the ability of licensees to serve the public interest. Forums and roundtable discussions, while often excellent techniques of presenting a fair cross section of differing viewpoints on a given issue, are not the only appropriate devices for radio discussion, and in some circumstances may not be particularly appropriate or advantageous. Moreover, in many instances the primary "controversy" will be whether or not the particular problem should be discussed at all; in such circumstances, where the licensee has determined that the subject is of sufficient import to receive broadcast attention, it would obviously not be in the public interest for spokesmen for one of the opposing points of view to be able to exercise a veto power over the entire presentation by refusing to broadcast its position. Fairness in such circumstances might require no more than that the licensee make a reasonable effort to secure responsible representation of the particular position and, if it fails in this effort, to continue to make available its facilities to the spokesmen for such position in the event that, after the original programs are broadcast, they then decide to avail themselves of a right to reply to present their contrary opinion. It should be remembered, moreover, that discussion of public issues will not necessarily be confined to questions which are obviously controversial in nature, and, in many cases, programs initiated with no thought on the part of the licensee of their possibly controversial nature will subsequently arouse controversy and opposition of a substantial nature which will merit presentation of opposing views. In such cases, however, fairness can be preserved without undue difficulty since the facilities of the station can be made available to the spokesmen for the groups wishing to state views in opposition to those expressed in the original presentation when such opposition becomes manifest.

9.   We do not believe, however, that the licensee's obligations to serve the public interest can be met merely through the adoption of a general policy of not refusing to broadcast opposing views where a demand is made of the station for broadcast time. If, as we believe to be the case, the public interest is best served in a democracy through the ability of the people to hear expositions of the various positions taken by responsible groups and individuals on particular topics and to choose between them, it is evident that broadcast licensees have an affirmative duty generally to encourage and implement the broadcast of all sides of controversial public issues over their facilities, over and beyond their obligation to make available on demand opportunities for the expression of opposing views. It is clear that any approximation of fairness in the presentation of any controversy will be difficult if not impossible of achievement unless the licensee plays a conscious and positive role in bringing about balanced presentation of the opposing viewpoints.

10.   It should be recognized that there can be no one all embracing formula which licensees can hope to apply to insure the fair and balanced presentation of all public issues. Different issues will inevitably require different techniques of presentation and production. The licensee will in each instance be called upon to exercise his best judgment and good sense in determining what subjects should be considered, the particular format of the programs to be devoted to each subject, the different shades of opinion to be presented, and the spokesmen for each point of view. In determining whether to honor specific requests for time, the station will inevitably be confronted with such questions as whether the subject is worth considering, whether the viewpoint of the requesting party has already received a sufficient amount of broadcast time, or whether there may not be other available groups or individuals who might be more appropriate spokesmen for the particular point of view than the person making the request. The latter's personal involvement in the controversy may also be a factor which must be considered, for elementary considerations of fairness may dictate that time be allocated to a person or group which has been specifically attacked over the station, where otherwise no such obligation would exist. Undoubtedly, over a period of time some licensees may make honest errors of judgment. But there can be no doubt that any licensee honestly desiring to live up to its obligation to serve the public interest and making a reasonable effort to do so, will be able to achieve a fair and satisfactory resolution of these problems in the light of the specific facts.

11.   It is against this background that we must approach the question of "editorialization" — the use of radio facilities by the licensees thereof for the expression of the opinions and ideas of the licensee on the various controversial and significant issues of interest to the members of the general public afforded radio (or television) service by the particular station. In considering this problem it must be kept in mind that such editorial expression may take many forms ranging from the overt statement of position by the licensee in person or

by his acknowledged spokesmen to the selection and presentation of news editors and commentators sharing the licensee's general opinions or the making available of the licensee's facilities, either free of charge or for a fee to persons or organizations reflecting the licensee's viewpoint either generally or with respect to specific issues. It should also be clearly indicated that the question of the relationship of broadcast editorialization, as defined above, to operation in the public interest, is not identical with the broader problem of assuring "fairness" in the presentation of news, comment or opinion, but is rather one specific facet of this larger problem.

12.   It is clear that the licensee's authority to determine the specific programs to be broadcast over his station gives him an opportunity, not available to other persons, to insure that his personal viewpoint on any particular issue is presented in his station's broadcasts, whether or not these views are expressly identified with the licensee. And, in the absence of governmental restraint, he would, if he so choose, be able to utilize his position as a broadcast licensee to weight the scales in line with his personal views, or even directly or indirectly to propagandize in behalf of his particular philosophy or views on the various public issues to the exclusion of any contrary opinions. Such action can be effective and persuasive whether or not it is accompanied by any editorialization in the narrow sense of overt statement of particular opinions and views identified as those of licensee.

13.   The narrower question of whether any overt editorialization or advocacy by broadcast licensees, identified as such is consonant with the operation of their stations in the public interest, resolves itself, primarily into the issue of whether such identification of comment or opinion broadcast over a radio or television station with the licensee, as such, would inevitably or even probably result in such overemphasis on the side of any particular controversy which the licensee chooses to espouse as to make impossible any reasonably balanced presentation of all sides of such issues or to render ineffective the available safeguards of that overall fairness which is the essential element of operation in the public interest. We do not believe that any such consequence is either inevitable or probable, and we have therefore come to the conclusion that overt licensee editorialization, within reasonable limits and subject to the general requirements of fairness detailed above, is not contrary to the public interest.

14.   The Commission has given careful consideration to contentions of those witnesses at the hearing who stated their belief that any overt editorialization or advocacy by broadcast licensee is *per se* contrary to the public interest. The main arguments advanced by these witnesses were that overt editorialization by broadcast licensees would not be consistent with the attainment of balanced presentations since there was a danger that the institutional good will and the production resources at the disposal of broadcast licensees would inevitably influence public opinion in favor of the positions advocated in the name of the licensee and that, having taken an open stand on

behalf of one position in a given controversy, a license is not likely to give a fair break to the opposition. We believe, however, that these fears are largely misdirected, and that they stem from a confusion of the question of overt advocacy in the name of the licensee, with the broader issue of insuring that the station's broadcasts devoted to the consideration of public issues will provide the listening public with a fair and balanced presentation of differing viewpoints on such issues, without regard to the particular views which may be held or expressed by the licensee. Considered, as we believe they must be, as just one of several types of presentation of public issues, to be afforded their appropriate and nonexclusive place in the station's total schedule of programs devoted to balanced discussion and consideration of public issues, we do not believe that programs in which the licensee's personal opinions are expressed are intrinsically more or less subject to abuse than any other program devoted to public issues. If it be true that station good will and licensee prestige, where it exists, may give added weight to opinion expressed by the licensee, it does not follow that such opinion should be excluded from the air any more than it should in the case of any individual or institution which over a period of time has built up a reservoir of good will or prestige in the community. In any competition for public acceptance of ideas, the skills and resources of the proponents and opponents will always have some measure of effect in producing the results sought. But it would not be suggested that they should be denied expression of their opinions over the air by reason of their particular assets. What is against the public interest is for the licensee "to stack the cards" by a deliberate selection of spokesmen for opposing points of view to favor one viewpoint at the expense of the other, whether or not the views of those spokesmen are identified as the views of the licensee or of others. Assurance of fairness must in the final analysis be achieved, not by the exclusion of particular views because of the source of the views, or the forcefulness with which the view is expressed, but by making the microphone available for the presentation of contrary views without deliberate restrictions designed to impede equally forceful presentation.

15.   Similarly, while licensees will in most instances have at their disposal production resources making possible graphic and persuasive techniques for forceful presentation of ideas, their utilization for the promulgation of the licensee's personal viewpoints will not necessarily or automatically lead to unfairness or lack of balance. While uncontrolled utilization of such resources for the partisan ends of the licensee might conceivably lead to serious abuses, such abuses could as well exist where the station's resources are used for the sole use of his personal spokesmen. The prejudicial or unfair use of broadcast production resources would, in either case, be contrary to the public interest.

16.   The Commission is not persuaded that a station's willingness to stand up and be counted on these particular issues upon which the licensee has a definite position may not be actually helpful in providing and maintaining a climate of fairness and equal opportunity for the expression of contrary views.

Certainly the public has less to fear from the open partisan than from the covert propagandist. On many issues, of sufficient importance to be allocated broadcast time, the station licensee may have no fixed opinion or viewpoint which he wishes to state or advocate. But where the licensee, himself, believes strongly that one side of a controversial issue is correct and should prevail, prohibition of his expression of such position will not of itself insure fair presentation of that issue over his station's facilities, nor would open advocacy necessarily prevent an overall fair presentation of the subject. It is not a sufficient answer to state that a licensee *should* occupy the position of an impartial umpire, where the licensee is *in fact* partial. In the absence of a duty to present all sides of controversial issues, overt editorialization by station licensees could conceivably result in serious abuse. But where, as we believe to be the case under the Communications Act, such a responsibility for a fair and balanced presentation of controversial public issues exists, we cannot see how the open espousal of one point of view by the licensee should necessarily prevent him from affording a fair opportunity for the presentation of contrary positions or make more difficult the enforcement of the statutory standard of fairness upon any licensee.

17.   It must be recognized, however, that the licensee's opportunity to express his own views as part of a general presentation of varying opinions on particular controversial issues, does not justify or empower any licensee to exercise his authority over the selection of program material to distort or suppress the basic factual information upon which any truly fair and free discussion of public issues must necessarily depend. The basis for any fair consideration of public issues, and particularly those of a controversial nature, is the presentation of news and information concerning the basic facts of the controversy in as complete and impartial a manner as possible. A licensee would be abusing his position as public trustee of these important means of mass communication were he to withhold from expression over his facilities relevant news or facts concerning a controversy or to slant or distort the presentation of such news. No discussion of the issues involved in any controversy can be fair or in the public interest where such discussion must take place in a climate of false or misleading information concerning the basic facts of the controversy.

18.   During the course of the hearing, fears have been expressed that any effort on the part of the Commission to enforce a reasonable standard of fairness and impartiality would inevitably require the Commission to take a stand on the merits of the particular issues considered in the programs broadcast by the several licensees, as well as exposing the licensees to the risk of loss of license because of "honest mistakes" which they may make in the exercise of their judgment with respect to the broadcasts of programs of a controversial nature. We believe that these fears are wholly without justification, and are based on either an assumption of abuse of power by the Commission or a lack of proper understanding of the role of the Commission, under the Communications Act, in

considering the program service of broadcast licensees in passing upon applications for renewal of license. While this Commission and its predecessor, the Federal Radio Commission, have, from the beginning of effective radio regulation in 1927, properly considered that a licensee's overall program service is one of the primary indicia of his ability to serve the public interest, actual consideration of such service has always been limited to a determination as to whether the licensee's programming, taken as a whole, demonstrates that the licensee is aware of his listening public and is willing and able to make an honest and reasonable effort to live up to such obligations. The action of the station in carrying or refusing to carry any particular program is of relevance only as the station's actions with respect to such programs fits into its overall pattern of broadcast service, and must be considered in the light of its other program activities. This does not mean, of course, that stations may, with impunity, engage in a partisan editorial campaign on a particular issue or series of issues provided only that the remainder of its program schedule conforms to the statutory norm of fairness; a licensee may not utilize the portion of its broadcast service which conforms to the statutory requirements as a cover or shield for other programing which fails to meet the minimum standards of operation in the public interest. But it is clear that the standard of public interest is not so rigid that an honest mistake or error in judgment on the part of a licensee will be or should be condemned where his overall record demonstrates a reasonable effort to provide a balanced presentation of comment and opinion on such issues. The question is necessarily one of the reasonableness of the station's actions, not whether any absolute standard of fairness has been achieved. It does not require any appraisal of the merits of the particular issue to determine whether reasonable efforts have been made to present both sides of the question. Thus, in appraising the record of a station in presenting programs concerning a controversial bill pending before the Congress of the United States, if the record disclosed that the licensee had permitted only advocates of the bill's enactment to utilize its facilities to the exclusion of its opponents, it is clear that no independent appraisal of the bill's merits by the Commission would be required to reach a determination that the licensee has misconstrued its duties and obligations as a person licensed to serve the public interest. The Commission has observed, in considering this general problem that "the duty to operate in the public interest is no esoteric mystery, but is essentially a duty to operate a radio station with good judgment and good faith guided by a reasonable regard for the interests of the community to be served." *Northern Corporation (WMEX)*, 4 Pike & Fischer, R.R. 333, 339. Of course, some cases will be clearer than others, and the Commission in the exercise of its functions may be called upon to weigh conflicting evidence to determine whether the licensee has or has not made reasonable efforts to present a fair and well-rounded presentation of particular public issues. But the standard of reasonableness and the reasonable approximation of a statutory norm is not an arbitrary standard incapable of administrative or judicial determination, but, on the contrary, one of the basic standards of conduct in numerous fields of Anglo-American law. Like all other flexible standards of conduct, it is subject to abuse and arbitrary interpretation and application by the duly authorized reviewing authorities. But the possibility that a legitimate standard of legal conduct might be abused or arbitrarily applied by capricious governmental authority is not and cannot be a reason for abandoning the standard itself. And broadcast licensees are protected against any conceivable abuse of power by the Commission in the exercising of its licensing authority by the procedural safeguards of the Communications Act and the Administrative Procedure Act, and by the right of appeal to the courts from final action claimed to be arbitrary or capricious.

19.   There remains for consideration the allegation made by a few of the witnesses in the hearing that any action by the Commission in this field enforcing a basic standard of fairness upon broadcast licensees necessarily constitutes an "abridgment of the right of free speech" in violation of the first amendment of the United States Constitution. We can see no sound basis for any such conclusion. The freedom of speech protected against governmental abridgment by the first amendment does not extend any privilege to government licensees of means of public communications to exclude the expression of opinions and ideas with which they are in disagreement. We believe, on the contrary, that a requirement that broadcast licensees utilize their franchises in a manner in which the listening public may be assured of hearing varying opinions on the paramount issues facing the American people is within both the spirit and letter of the first amendment. As the Supreme Court of the United States has pointed out in the *Associated Press* monopoly case:

It would be strange indeed, however, if the grave concern for freedom of the press which prompted adoption of the first amendment should be read as a command that the Government was without power to protect that freedom. . . . *That amendment rests on the assumption that the widest possible dissemination of information from diverse and antagonistic sources is essential to the welfare of the public, that a free press is a condition of free society. Surely a command that the Government itself shall not impede the free flow of ideas does not afford nongovernmental combinations a refuge if they impose restraints upon that constitutionally guaranteed freedom.* Freedom to publish means freedom for all and not for some. Freedom to publish is guaranteed by the Constitution but freedom to combine to keep others from publishing is not. (*Associated Press* v. *United States*, 326 U.S. 1 at p. 20.)

20.   We fully recognize that freedom of the radio is included among the freedoms protected against governmental abridgment by the first amendment. *United States* v. *Paramount Pictures, Inc., et al.*, 334 U.S. 131, 166. But this does not mean that the freedom of the people as a whole to enjoy the maximum possible utilization of this medium of mass communication may be subordinated

to the freedom of any single person to exploit the medium for his own private interest. Indeed, it seems indisputable that full effect can only be given to the concept of freedom of speech on the radio by giving precedence to the right of the American public to be informed on all sides of public questions over any such individual exploitation for private purposes. Any regulation of radio, especially a system of limited licensees, is in a real sense an abridgment of the inherent freedom of persons to express themselves by means of radio communications. It is however, a necessary and constitutional abridgment in order to prevent chaotic interference from destroying the great potential of this medium for public enlightenment and entertainment. *National Broadcasting Company* v. *United States*, 319 U.S. 190, . . .; cf. *Federal Radio Commission* v. *Nelson Brothers Bond & Mortgage Co.*, 289 U.S. 266; *Fisher's Blend Station, Inc.* v. *State Tax Commission*, 277 U.S. 650. Nothing in the Communications Act or its history supports any conclusion that the people of the Nation, acting through Congress, have intended to surrender or diminish their paramount rights in the air waves, including access to radio broadcasting facilities to a limited number of private licensees to be used as such licensees see fit, without regard to the paramount interests of the people. The most significant meaning of freedom of the radio is the right of the American people to listen to this great medium of communications free from any governmental dictation as to what they can or cannot hear and free alike from similar restraints by private licensees.

21.   To recapitulate, the Commission believes that under the American system of broadcasting the individual licensees of radio stations have the responsibility for determining the specific program material to be broadcast over their stations. This choice, however, must be exercised in a manner consistent with the basic policy of the Congress that radio be maintained as a medium of free speech for the general public as a whole rather than as an outlet for the purely personal or private interests of the licensee. This requires that licensees devote a reasonable percentage of their broadcasting time to the discussion of public issues of interest in the community served by their stations and that such programs be designed so that the public has a reasonable opportunity to hear different opposing positions on the public issues of interest and importance in the community. The particular format best suited for the presentation of such programs in a manner consistent with the public interest must be determined by the licensee in the light of the facts of each individual situation. Such presentation may include the identified expression of the licensee's personal viewpoint as part of the more general presentation of views or comments on the various issues, but the opportunity of licensees to present such views as they may have on matters of controversy may not be utilized to achieve a partisan or one-sided presentation of issues. Licensee editorialization is but one aspect of freedom of expression by means of radio. Only insofar as it is exercised in conformity with the paramount right of the public to hear a reasonably balanced

presentation of all responsible viewpoints on particular issues can such editorialization be considered to be consistent with the licensee's duty to operate in the public interest. For the licensee is a trustee impressed with the duty of preserving for the public generally radio as a medium of free expression and fair presentation.

DISSENTING VIEWS OF COMMISSIONER HENNOCK

I agree with the majority that it is imperative that a high standard of impartiality in the presentation of issues of public controversy be maintained by broadcast licensees. I do not believe that the Commission's decision, however, will bring about the desired end. The standard of fairness as delineated in the report is virtually impossible of enforcement by the Commission with our present lack of policing methods and with the sanctions given us by law. We should not underestimate the difficulties inherent in the discovery of unfair presentation in any particular situation, or the problem presented by the fact that the sole sanction the Commission possesses is total deprivation of broadcast privileges in a renewal or revocation proceeding which may occur long after the violation.

In the absence of some method of policing and enforcing the requirement that the public trust granted a licensee be exercised in an impartial manner, it seems foolhardy to permit editorialization by licensees themselves. I believe that we should have such a prohibition, unless we can substitute for it some more effective method of insuring fairness. There would be no inherent evil in the presentation of a licensee's viewpoint if fairness could be guaranteed. In the present circumstances, prohibiting it is our only instrument for insuring the proper use of radio in the public interest.

23
The TV Freeze

Television broadcasting began in America on a restricted basis in 1939. The military priorities of World War II impeded TV's growth, and the resumption of peacetime civilian activity was accompanied by slow expansion of the fledgling medium. By 1948, with perhaps a million television receivers in American homes, many new TV stations were planning to go on the air. But only 12 channels (numbered 2–13) in the very high frequency (VHF) portion of the radio spectrum had been allocated to TV broadcasting by the FCC. This was an insufficient supply in light of the burgeoning demand for a limited number of channel assignments in the most populous sections of the country. Additionally, the FCC's postwar assignment table was creating technical interference problems among TV stations already on the air.

The FCC instituted a "freeze" on the issuance of new TV station licenses effective September 30, 1948, in order to give itself time to consider these problems. The freeze, which lasted until July 1, 1952, limited the number of operating TV stations to 108. During the freeze TV set ownership increased almost twenty-fold, coast-to-coast network interconnection lines were built by AT&T, and programming underwent a transition from roller derbies and "simulcasts" of radio shows to "I Love Lucy" and "Today." TV established itself as a profitable mass medium between 1948 and 1952. In fact, the 108 pre-freeze TV stations remain the most lucrative in the industry.

Early in the freeze the FCC established its allocation and assignment goals:

> *Priority No. 1.* To provide at least one television service to all parts of the United States.
> *Priority No. 2.* To provide each community with at least one television broadcasting station.
> *Priority No. 3.* To provide a choice of at least two television services to all parts of the United States.

Priority No. 4. To provide each community with at least two television broadcast stations.

Priority No. 5. Any channels which remain unassigned under the foregoing priorities will be assigned to the various communities depending on the size of the population of such community, the geographical location of such community, and the number of television services available to such community from television stations located in other communities.[1]

To achieve these objectives, the FCC allocated 70 additional channels (numbered 14–83) for TV broadcasting in the ultra high frequency (UHF) spectrum. The *Sixth Report and Order* ended the freeze by assigning 2,053 channels to 1,291 communities. The thaw was a signal for hundreds of additional stations to come on the air.

A paramount issue that arose during the long freeze was a request to establish a separate class of educational noncommercial TV stations. The failure to do so in AM radio had almost completely excluded educators from the first broadcast service. When the FCC initially allocated spectrum space for FM radio broadcasting in 1940, it established the precedent of reserving a portion of the FM band exclusively for educational noncommercial uses. The present-day FM reservation contains the 20 channels from 88 to 92 mHz, or one-fifth of the entire band.

Largely because of the urgings of Commissioner Frieda B. Hennock, the FCC proposed to establish an educational TV reservation in its *Third Notice,* issued late in the freeze. This plan was formally adopted by the Commission in the *Sixth Report and Order.* There were 242 channel assignments (one-third of them VHF) reserved for educational telecasting. This number has almost tripled since 1952.

The documents below elaborate the rationale underlying the FCC decision. Much of the potential and some of the problems of "public television" stem from the policies arrived at during the freeze.

Related Reading: 38, 86.

---

[1] *Notice of Further Proposed Rule Making in Docket Nos. 8736 . . .,* 14 Fed. Reg. 4483, 4485 (1949); restated in *Sixth Report and Order,* 41 FCC 148, 167 (1952).

A. THE THIRD NOTICE

Third Notice of Proposed Rule Making (Appendix A)
16 Fed. Reg. 3072, 3079
March 21, 1951

VI. Non-commercial educational television

The existing channel Assignment Table adopted by the Commission in 1945 did not contain any reserved channels for the exclusive use of non-commercial educational television stations, and no changes in this respect were proposed by the Commission in its proposed table of July 11, 1949. However, in the Notice of Further Proposed Rule Making issued on the latter date the Commission pointed out that it had "received informal suggestions concerning the possible provision for non-commercial educational broadcast stations in the 470–890 mc. band." Interested parties were afforded the opportunity to file comments in the proceeding concerning these suggestions.

Prior to the hearing on this issue, a number of the parties supporting the reservation of channels for noncommercial educational purposes joined together to form the Joint Committee on Educational Television. This committee offered testimony in support of a request for reservation of channels in both the VHF and UHF portions of the spectrum.

In general, the need for non-commercial educational television stations was based upon the important contributions which noncommercial educational television stations can make in educating the people both in school—at all levels—and also the adult public. The need for such stations was justified upon the high quality type of programming which would be available on such stations—programming of an entirely different character from that available on most commercial stations.

The need for a reservation was based upon the fact that educational institutions of necessity proceed more slowly in applying for broadcast stations than commercial stations. Hence, if there is no reservation, the available channels are all assigned to commercial interests long before the educational institutions are ready to apply for them.

Some opposition to the reservation was presented at the hearing. In general, none of the witnesses opposed the idea of noncommercial educational stations. On the contrary, there was general agreement that such stations would be desirable. Objection was made to the idea of reservation because as stated by some witnesses, the experience of educational institutions in the use of AM and FM radio does not furnish sufficient assurance that the educational institutions would make use of the television channels. However, there was no objection even by these witnesses to a certain form of reservation provided it was for a reasonably short time.

In the Commission's view, the need for non-commercial educational television stations has been amply demonstrated on this record. The Commission further believes that educational institutions of necessity need a longer period of time to get prepared for television than do the commercial interests. The only way this can be done is by reserving certain channels for the exclusive use of non-commercial educational stations. Obviously, the period of time during which such reservation should exist is very important. The period must be long enough to give educational institutions a reasonable opportunity to do the preparatory work that is necessary to get authorizations for stations. The period must not be so long that frequencies remain unused for excessively long periods of time. The Commission will survey the general situation from time to time in order to insure that these objectives are not lost sight of.

Accordingly, the Commission in its Table of Assignments has indicated the specific assignments which are proposed to be reserved for non-commercial educational stations.[12] Rules concerning eligibility and use of the stations will be substantially the same as those set forth in subpart C of Part III of the Commission's rules and regulations. The reservation of the non-commercial educational stations is not in a single block as in the case of FM since the assignment problems discussed above would sharply curtail the usefulness of a block assignment.

The following method has been employed in making reservations. In all communities having three or more assignments (whether VHF or UHF) one channel has been reserved for a non-commercial educational station. Where a community has fewer than three assignments, no reservation has been made except in those communities which are primarily educational centers, where reservations have been made even where only one or two channels are assigned.[13] As between VHF and UHF, a UHF channel has been reserved where there are fewer than three VHF assignments, except for those communities which are primarily educational centers where a VHF channel has been reserved. Where three or more VHF channels are assigned to a community, a VHF channel has been reserved except in those communities where all VHF assignments have been taken up. In those cases, a UHF channel has been reserved.

It is recognized that in many communities the number of educational institutions exceed the reservation which is made. In such instances the various institutions concerned must enter into cooperative arrangements so as to make sure that the facilities are available to all on an equitable basis.

[12]The procedure set forth in paragraphs 12 and 13 of the notice is applicable to any specific assignment proposed to be reserved or to any request that a channel not proposed for reservation should be reserved.

[13]Forty-six communities were considered to be primarily educational centers in accordance with the testimony presented by the Joint Committee on Educational Television. However, this enumeration is not binding and consideration will be given to any proposal filed pursuant to paragraphs 12 and 13 of the notice providing for additions to or deletions from the enumeration.

B. SIXTH REPORT AND ORDER

17 Fed. Reg. 3905, 3908; 41 FCC 148, 158
April 14, 1952

The educational reservation

33.   Section VI of Appendix A of the Third Notice contained a statement that as a matter of policy certain assignments in the VHF and UHF would be reserved for the exclusive use of non-commercial television stations. Careful consideration has been given to the exceptions taken to this policy proposal in comments filed by several parties[12] pursuant to paragraph 11 of the Third Notice. For the reasons set forth below, the Commission has concluded that the record does support its proposal[13] and it is hereby adopted in the public interest as the decision of the Commission.

34.   The only comments directed against the proposal which fulfill the requirements of paragraph 11 of the Third Notice are those filed by NARTB-TV and Allen B. DuMont Laboratories, Inc. The others do not specify their objections nor do they cite the evidence on which their objections are based. It is difficult to ascertain in some cases whether the objection is in fact based upon the view that there is a failure of the record to support the proposal or upon some other general disagreement with the proposal. Since, however, the comments filed by NARTB-TV and DuMont clearly cover all the objections to the proposal made by any of the other parties, a discussion of their exceptions will cover those of the other parties, and it will not be necessary to determine whether the latter comments must be rejected for failure to comply with the provisions of paragraph 11 of the Third Notice.

35.   In view of the rather comprehensive and detailed exceptions taken to section VI of Appendix A it is necessary to review the nature and extent of the

---

[12] These parties are: NARTB-TV, Allen B. DuMont Laboratories, Inc., Radio Kentucky, Inc., Capitol Broadcasting Co., and the Tribune Co. Some comments were filed which challenged the power of the Commission under the Communications Act to reserve channels for this purpose. Such contentions have been disposed of by the Commission's Memorandum Opinion of July 13, 1951 (FCC 51-709). Other comments objected to the reservation of a channel in a given community. These objections have been considered in another portion of this report. The Joint Committee on Educational Television filed comments in support of the educational reservation, as did many individual educational institutions, and other civic nonprofit organizations.

[13] Communications Measurements Laboratories, Inc., has taken issue with the use of the words "nation wide" in describing the reservation of channels for this purpose. The proposal is self-explanatory in this respect. Although channels have been reserved throughout the nation, the reservation does not set apart any single channel or group of channels on a nation-wide basis.

Commission's proposal in the Third Notice. An extensive hearing was held by
the Commission on the issue: whether television channels should be reserved for
the exclusive use of noncommercial educational stations. A total of 76 witnesses
testified on this issue.[14] Among the subjects upon which the proponents of reservation presented evidence were: the potential of educational television both for
in-school and adult education, and as an alternative to commercial programming;
the history of education's use of other broadcast media and of visual aids to education; the possibility of immediate or future utilization of television channels
by public and private educational organizations and the methods whereby such
utilization could be effectuated; the type of program material which could be
presented over noncommercial television stations; the history of and prospects
for educational organizations' securing broadcast opportunities from commercial
broadcasters; and the number of channels, both UHF and VHF, which would be
required to satisfy the needs of education throughout the country. The witnesses
who opposed the principle of reservation, contending that it was unlikely that
educators would make sufficient use of the reserved channels to warrant withholding them from commercial applicants, and that the best results could be
achieved by cooperation between educational groups and commercial broadcasters, testified principally about the past record of educators in broadcasting,
the cost of a television station, and cooperation between commercial broadcasters and educational institutions.

36.   On the basis of the record thus compiled, the Commission concluded,
as set forth in the Third Notice, that there is a need for noncommercial educational television stations; that because educational institutions require more time
to prepare for television than commercial interests, a reservation of channels is
necessary to insure that such stations come into existence; that such reservations should not be for an excessively long period and should be surveyed from
time to time; and that channels in both the VHF and UHF bands should be reserved in accordance with the method there set forth.

37.   It has been contended that the record in this proceeding fails to support the Commission's proposal in three basic respects; that it has not been shown
that educational organizations will, in fact, require a longer period of time to
prepare to apply for television stations than commercial broadcasters; that it
should have been found that the reservation of channels for this purpose will
result in a waste of valuable frequency space because of nonusage and because of
the limited audience appeal that educational   stations will have; and that no
feasible plan for stable utilization of channels by educational institutions has
been advanced, particularly with respect to the problem of licensee responsibility.

---

[14]Of this number, all but five were called by educational organizations or testified in
their own behalf in support of the position taken by such organizations in favor of an affirmative resolution of the question. Two other witnesses were in favor of the principle of
reservations but differed with witnesses presented on behalf of educational groups with respect to the manner and extent of reservation.

38.   None of the commenting parties have contended that the record has failed to support the findings of the Commission in the Third Notice that, based on the important contributions such stations can make in the education of the in-school and adult public, there is a need for noncommercial educational stations. The objections to the Commission's proposal must, therefore, refer to the desire and the ability, as evidenced in the record, of the educational community to construct and operate such stations.[15] We conclude that the record shows the desire and ability of education to make a substantial contribution to the use of television. There is much evidence in the record concerning the activities of educational organizations in AM and FM broadcasting. It is true and was to be expected that education has not utilized these media to the full extent that commercial broadcasters have, in terms of number of stations and number of hours of operation. However, it has also been shown that many of the educational institutions which are engaged in aural broadcasting are doing an outstanding job in the presentation of high quality programming, and have been getting excellent public response. And most important in this connection, it is agreed that the potential of television for education is much greater and more readily apparent than that of aural broadcasting, and that the interest of the educational community in the field is much greater than it was in aural broadcasting. Further, the justification for an educational station should not, in our view, turn simply on account of audience size. The public interest will clearly be served if these stations are used to contribute significantly to the educational process of the nation. The type of programs which have been broadcast by educational organizations, and those which the record indicates can and would be televised by educators, will provide a valuable complement to commercial programming.

39.   We do not think there is merit in the contention that the record, with respect to the general phase of the hearing, does not support the general principle of a reservation of channels for educational purposes as set out in the Third Notice because it does not contain detailed information with regard to the desire, ability and qualifications of the educational organizations to construct a noncommercial educational station, or the competing commercial interests which desire to bring television service to the public. In preparing a proposed Assignment Table for the entire nation which would provide the framework for the growth of television for many years to come, we could not limit our perspective to immediate demand for educational stations under circumstances where all communities did not have an opportunity to give full consideration to the possibilities of television for educational purposes and to mobilize their resources. Moreover, evidence of specific demand for educational television was

[15] DuMont, in its Comments in Opposition to Comments and Proposals of Other Parties, has submitted the results of a survey which bear upon this question. Insofar as the survey bears upon any specific reservation, DuMont had the opportunity to present it in the portion of the hearing dealing with Appendix C. The Third Notice was not intended to permit the filing of new material on the matters which were already the subject of hearing. DuMont had an opportunity to present this type of evidence in the general phase of the proceeding.

submitted for several communities in the general phase of the hearing, and in addition there was presented an estimate of the number of channels required for this purpose for one section of the country based upon the size of the various communities and their general educational requirements. We do not think it unreasonable to believe that general principles of assignment may be derived from such evidence, and that such principles may validly be applied to comparable communities for the purposes of drawing up a nation-wide assignment plan. See, e.g., The New England Divisions Case, 261 U.S. 184; 197–199 (1923).

40.   Moreover, the Third Notice provided for the contesting of specific reservations in any community. The Assignment Table adopted below has been prepared after consideration of the specific evidence in support of, as well as in objection to, specific proposed reservations and after consideration of the overall needs of all communities for television service.

41.   The great preponderance of evidence presented to the Commission has been to the effect that the actual process of formulating plans and of enacting necessary legislation or of making adequate financing available is one which will generally require more time for educational organizations than for commercial interests. The record does, of course, show that there are some educational institutions which are now ready to apply for television broadcasting licenses, but this in no wise detracts from the unavoidable conclusion that the great mass of educational institutions must move more slowly and overcome hurdles not present for commercial broadcasters, and that to insure an extensive, rather than a sparse and haphazard development of educational television, channels must be reserved by the Commission at this time. There is moreover, abundant testimony in the record that the very fact of reserving channels would speed the development of educational television. It was pointed out that it is much easier for those seeking to construct educational television stations to raise funds and get other necessary support if the channels are definitely available, than if it is problematical whether a channel may be procured at all.

42.   With regard to possible waste of the reserved channels by nonuse, it is contended that evidence offered in the general portion of the hearing, concerning the record of performance of noncommercial educational agencies in aural broadcasting, and their plans and abilities to meet the installation and programming costs of television, can lead only to the conclusion that waste of limited spectrum space through nonusage will result from the reservation of channels for noncommercial educational stations. To whatever extent the position taken in these exceptions is that any immediate nonuse of channel space available for television constitutes a waste of channels, the Commission cannot agree. The basic nature of a reservation in itself implies some nonuse; to attribute waste of spectrum to the Commission's proposal concerning the use of certain channels by noncommercial educational stations without attributing it to those assignments in the table for smaller cities, which may not be used for some time, is misleading. The very purpose of the Assignment Table is to reserve channels for the communities there listed to forestall a haphazard, inefficient or inequitable

distribution of television service in the United States throughout the many years to come. Moreover, as pointed out in another portion of this report, the whole of the Table of Assignments including the reservations of channels for use by noncommercial educational stations is subject to alteration in appropriate rule making proceedings in the future, and any assignment, whether an educational reservation or not, may be modified if it appears in the public interest to do so.

43.   We do not believe that in order to support our decision to reserve channels for noncommercial educational stations it is necessary that we be able to find on the basis of the record before us, in the general phase of the hearing, that the educational community of the United States has demonstrated either collectively or individually that it is financially qualified at this time to operate television stations. One of the reasons for having the reservation is that the Commission recognizes that it is of the utmost importance to this nation that a reasonable opportunity be afforded educational institutions to use television as a noncommercial educational medium, and that at the same time it will generally take the educational community longer to prepare for the operation of its own television stations than it would for some commercial broadcasters. This approach is exactly the same as that underlying the Assignment Table as a whole, since reservations of commercial channels have been made in many smaller communities to insure that they not be foreclosed from ever having television stations.

44.   Although the record in the general phase of the proceedings does not contain any detailed showing on a community-by-community basis that the educational organizations have made detailed investigation of the costs incident to the construction and operation of television stations and of the exact sources from which such funds could be derived in the near future, nevertheless, the record, as a whole, does indicate that educational organizations in most communities where reservation has finally been made will actually seek the necessary funds. Furthermore, interested persons have had an opportunity to present evidence in the city-by city portion of the hearings as to whether such funds will be sought or will become available in specific communities. It will admittedly be a difficult and time consuming process in most instances, but the likelihood of ultimate success, and the importance to the public of the objective sought, warrants the action taken. Several educational institutions, it was indicated on the record as early as the general portion of the hearing, had applied for television stations. The amounts of money spent by other public and private educational groups in aural broadcasting indicates that the acquisition of sufficient funds for television would not be an insurmountable obstacle. It has been shown, for example, that considerable sums have already been spent on visual aids to education. Television is clearly a fertile field for endowment, and it seems probable that sufficient funds can be raised both through this method and through the usual sources of funds for public and private education to enable the construction and operation of many noncommercial educational stations. As concerns the costs of operation there is the possibility of cooperative programming and

financing among several educational organizations in large communities. The record indicates that educational institutions will unite in the construction and operation of noncommercial educational television stations. Such cooperative effort will, of course, help to make such stations economically feasible. The fact that somewhat novel problems may arise with respect to the selection and designation of licensees in this field does not—as some have contended—constitute a valid argument against the concept of educational reservations.

45. Several alternative methods for utilizing television in education have been presented to the Commission, but we do not think that any of them is satisfactory. One proposal is to utilize a microwave relay or wired circuit system of television for in-school educational programs. It appears that the cost of a wired circuit for the schools in larger cities might be prohibitive; but the determinative objection to such a proposal is that it would ignore very significant aspects of educational television. It is clear from the record that an important part of the educator's effort in television will be in the field of adult education in the home, as well as the provision of after school programs for children.

46. The NARTB-TV contended that the solution lay in the voluntary cooperation of educators and commercial broadcasters in the presentation of educational programs on commercial facilities. We conclude, however, that this sort of voluntary cooperation cannot be expected to accomplish all the important objectives of educational television. In order for an educational program to achieve its purpose it is necessary that broadcast time be available for educators on a regular basis. An audience cannot be built up if educators are forced to shift their broadcast period from time to time. Moreover, the presentation of a comprehensive schedule of programs comprising a number of courses and subjects which are designed for various age and interest groups may require large periods of the broadcast day which would be difficult if not impossible to obtain on commercial stations.

47. Another alternative was proposed by Senator Edwin C. Johnson of Colorado. This proposal is elaborated in the Senator's statement:

It is my belief as I have repeatedly said that the Commission could and should impose a condition on all television licenses that a certain amount of time be made available for educational purposes in the public interest as a sustaining feature. In this manner, television can become available for educational work now without saddling schools with the enormous burden and expense of constructing and operating a noncommercial educational station. . . . It is my considered opinion that the Commission can best serve the public interest and at the same time extend extremely profitable assistance to the educational processes of this country by imposing a condition in each television license issued which would require the availability of appropriate time for educational purposes.

48. It must be remembered that the provision for noncommercial educational television stations does not relieve commercial licensees from their duty to

carry programs which fulfill the educational needs and serve the educational interests of the community in which they operate. This obligation applies with equal force to all commercial licensees whether or not a noncommercial educational channel has been reserved in their community, and similarly will obtain in communities where noncommercial educational stations will be in operation.

49.   Aside from the question of the legal basis of a rule which would accomplish Senator Johnson's proposal, the Commission feels it would be impracticable to promulgate a rule requiring that each commercial television licensee devote a specified amount of time to educational programs. A proper determination as to the appropriate amount of time to be set aside is subject to so many different and complex factors, difficult to determine in advance, that the possibility of such a rule is most questionable. Thus, the number of stations in the community, the total hours operated by each station, the number of educational institutions in the community, the size of the community, and countless other factors, each of which will vary from community to community, would make any uniform rule applicable to all TV stations unrealistic. All things considered, it appears to us that the reservation of channels for noncommercial educational stations, together with continued adherence by commercial stations to the mandate of serving the educational needs of the community, is the best method of achieving the aims of educational television.

Who may be licensed to operate noncommercial educational stations

50.   While the Third Notice did not specify who would be eligible to own and operate a noncommercial educational station, the Commission has in the past restricted the ownership and operation of such stations to nonprofit educational organizations.

51.   The United States Conference of Mayors and the Municipal Broadcasting System, City of New York, have in appropriate comments proposed that eligibility be extended to any municipality operating educational institutions. The Municipal Broadcasting Sytem states that a "more expeditious management of educational television in the City of New York from an administration standpoint" would result if it were permitted to operate a television station. It further stated that "if the Municipal Broadcasting System is eligible to operate television facilities, the station can be utilized by all of the educational institutions over which it has jurisdiction, rather than having responsibility for the operation placed in a particular school."

52.   The Commission is of the opinion that in any community where an independent educational agency is constituted, and is eligible under the Commission's rules to apply for a noncommercial educational television station, there are no compelling reasons for extending eligibility to municipal authorities. The continued operation by the Board of Education of the City of New York since 1939 of noncommercial educational Station WNYE indicates that no insur-

mountable administrative barriers exist which would preclude the Board of Education as a potential licensee in the television field. Similarly, there is no evidence to indicate that the Board of Education of the City of New York, now eligible under the present rules, would give less access to other educational institutions were it the licensee of a television station than would the Municipal Broadcasting System were it eligible and granted a license. It should be noted that in any community the municipal authorities, or any other group, can take the initiative in constituting a consolidated television authority which would represent municipal educational institutions, private universities and other organizations concerned with education.

53.   The Commission has, however, established in its rules an exception providing that where a municipality has no independently constituted educational entity which would be eligible under the rules, the municipality in such case will be eligible to apply for a noncommercial educational station. This exception is designed solely to meet those situations where the municipal authorities do not delegate educational authority but reserve to themselves the management of the municipal educational system.

Partial commercial operation by educational stations

54.   In its comments the University of Missouri[16] requests that the Commission authorize ". . . commercial operation on the channels reserved for educational institutions to an amount equal to 50 percent of the broadcast day." It appears from the evidence that funds in the amount of $350,000 are presently available to the University for the construction of a television station, but that no funds are available for the operation of such a station. Accordingly, the University requests that the Commission permit educational institutions to use the reserved assignments to operate stations on a limited commercial non-profit basis. It is urged that if its request is granted the following objectives will be attained:

A.   More educational institutions will be in a position to construct and operate television stations throughout the country to the benefit of the public at large without materially affecting the strictly commercial stations;

B.   Educational television stations will be able, through income received from commercial programs, to better program their stations; and

C.   That the commercial programs televised will break the monotony of continuous educational subjects so as to permit the stations to attract and hold audiences.

55.   A similar proposal, that the Commission extend the reservation to include all educational institutions which are operated on a nonprofit basis, is

---

[16] See the discussion, elsewhere in this report, of the assignments in Columbia, Missouri.

made by the Bob Jones University (WMUU) Greenville, South Carolina. The Bob Jones University argues that ". . . the reservation of the privilege of a commercial income commensurate with the operating expense of the educational station . . ." will result in the encouragement and aid to television broadcasting by educational institutions.

56.   KFRU, Inc., Columbia, Missouri, opposed the request of the University of Missouri. In its reply to the University, KFRU states that it has no objection to the proposed reservation of Channel 8 for noncommercial educational purposes in Columbia, Missouri. However, it opposes the request of the University for partial commercial operation on the grounds that such an operation would give the educational institution unfair competitive advantages over a commercial licensee.

57.   It is our view that the request of the University of Missouri and the Bob Jones University must be denied. In the Third Notice we stated:

In general, the need for noncommercial educational television stations was based upon the important contributions which noncommercial educational television stations can make in educating the people both in school—at all levels— and also the adult public. The need for such stations was justified upon the high quality type of programming which would be available on such stations—programming of an entirely different character from that available on most commercial stations.

A grant of the requests of the University of Missouri and Bob Jones University for partial commercial operation by educational institutions would tend to vitiate the differences between commercial operation and noncommercial educational operation. It is recognized that the type of operation proposed by these Universities may be accomplished by the licensing of educational institutions in the commercial television broadcast service. But in our view achievement of the objective for which special educational reservations have been established—i.e., the establishment of a genuinely educational type of service—would not be furthered by permitting educational institutions to operate in substantially the same manner as commercial applicants though they may choose to call it limited commercial nonprofit operation.

58.   The Joint Committee on Educational Television suggests in its final brief that, in communities where only one VHF channel is assigned, and that channel is reserved for use by a noncommercial educational station, the noncommercial educational station should be allowed to broadcast programs which at present are available only from commercial network services. This exception would apply until such time as a commercial Grade A service is available in the area.

59.   On January 10, 1952, a Reply and Motion to Strike was filed by Peoria Broadcasting Company, Rock Island Broadcasting Company and Champaign News-Gazette, Inc., with respect to the above described proposal of the

Joint Committee. On January 25, 1952, a response to the Joint Motions was filed by the JCET. In view of the fact that the proposal made by the Joint Committee was not previously raised in any of its prior pleadings, the Motion to Strike is granted and the proposal is being given no further consideration.

The use of the VHF for noncommercial educational television

60.   The Commission's Third Notice proposed to reserve one of the assigned channels for noncommercial educational television use in all communities having a total of three or more assignments (whether VHF or UHF). Where a community had fewer than three assignments no reservation was proposed except in those communities which were designated as primarily educational centers, where reservations were made although only one or two channels were assigned. Except for educational centers, a UHF channel was proposed in those communities where there were fewer than three VHF assignments. In 26 of the 46 educational centers, the Commission proposed to reserve a VHF channel for educational use. In 23 of these 26 centers a VHF educational reservation was proposed where only one VHF channel was assigned to the community. Where three or more VHF channels were assigned to a community, a VHF channel was proposed to be reserved except in those communities where all VHF assignments had been previously licensed. In those cases, the reservation of a UHF channel was proposed.

61.   The Joint Committee on Educational Television in its comment has proposed that a VHF reservation for noncommercial educational institutions in place of a UHF reservation be considered in communities with less than three VHF assignments. On the other hand, some parties have argued that no assignments in the VHF be set aside as educational reservations. The Commission's Third Notice stated that the proposed reservations were not final and that consideration would be given to any specific proposal looking toward additions or deletions. After examining the comments and evidence filed pursuant to the Third Notice, the Commission remains of the view that the bases upon which it determined the apportionment of noncommercial educational assignments by communities are generally sound and should be continued. However, in particular cases the Commission concludes that the evidence warrants deviations from the proposals in the Third Notice, for the reasons stated in the city-by-city portion of this Report.

62.   The Joint Committee on Educational Television also proposes that the Commission should specifically state that an educational interest is not to be foreclosed from applying for a VHF channel in the so-called "closed cities" where all VHF assignments have already been made. No properly qualified applicant is ever precluded from applying for any channel in the broadcast field on the expiration of the existing license. Thus, whether educational interests seek a commercial or noncommercial television operation, they are, just as other applicants, eligible to apply for licensed channels upon expiration of the license term of the stations involved.

24

The Carroll Case

Carroll Broadcasting Company v. Federal Communications Commission*
258 F.2d 440 (D.C. Cir.)
July 10, 1958

The FCC interpreted the 1940 Supreme Court *Sanders Brothers* decision (Document 18, pp. 89-94) to mean that economic injury to a broadcaster was no basis for refusing to grant a license to a potential competitor. Under the Commission's policy the number of stations and broadcast services increased dramatically in the 1940's and 1950's, unfettered by regulations restraining competition. The "Network" case (Document 20, pp. 99-131) shows that the FCC did not hesitate to regulate the broadcasting industry in order to preserve or increase competition; its approach during this era could hardly be described as "hands off." The Commission simply assumed that the more competition there was in broadcasting, the better.

The Court of Appeals' opinion in the *Carroll* case rejected the FCC's narrow reading of *Sanders Brothers* and compelled the Commission to consider economic injury protests when increased competition was alleged to threaten the public interest by diminishing or destroying broadcast service. The FCC's request to appeal this decision to the Supreme Court was turned down by the Department of Justice, whereupon the Commission ingeniously devised a variety of procedural impediments to the successful mounting of an economic injury protest. [See, for example, *WLVA, Inc.* v.

*Reprinted with the permission of West Publishing Company.

FCC, 459 F.2d 1286 (D.C. Cir. 1972) for judicial affirmation of strict pleading standards applied by the FCC to protestants.]

Nevertheless, the FCC found the *Carroll* precedent useful when it sought to exercise regulatory jurisdiction over Cable TV in the 1960's (see Document 30, pp. 296–305). While the Commission offers broadcasters little respite from the competition of other licensees, it has followed a different course in protecting broadcasters from non-broadcast competitors.

Related Reading: 116, 119.

Prettyman, Circuit Judge.

This is an appeal from the Federal Communications Commission and concerns a license for a standard broadcasting station. Carroll, our appellant, is an existing licensee. It unsuccessfully protested the grant of a license to West Georgia, our intervenor.

Carrollton and Bremen are towns in Georgia, twelve miles apart, with populations, respectively, of 8,600 and 2,300. Carroll's main studios are in Carrollton. West Georgia would broadcast from Bremen.

Three issues were prescribed by the Commission for the hearing upon the protest. One of these was upon the request of Carroll and was:

To determine whether a grant of the application would result in such an economic injury to the protestant as would impair the protestant's ability to continue serving the public, and if so, the nature and extent thereof, the areas and populations affected thereby, and the availability of other broadcast service to such areas and populations.

But the Commission ordered "That said issue is not adopted by the Commission and that the burden of proceeding with the introduction of evidence and the burden of proof as to this issue shall be on the protestant." The case was remanded to the examiner for hearings on the added issue and a possible revised decision. The hearings were held, a further initial decision rendered by the examiner, exceptions taken, and oral argument had before the Commission.

On this issue the Commission held that "Congress had determined that free competition shall prevail in the broadcasting industry" and that "The Communications Act does not confer upon the Commission the power to consider the effect of legal competition except perhaps" in Section 307(b) cases. Hence, said the Commission, "it is unnecessary for us to make findings or reach conclusions on this issue." Moreover, the Commission said, pursuant to other decisions by it, as a matter of policy "the possible effects of competition will be disregarded in passing upon applications for new broadcast stations."

It was settled by the Sanders Brothers case[1] that economic injury to an existing station is not a ground for denying a new application. But the Court, it seems to us, made clear the point that economic injury to a licensee and the public interest may be different matters. The Court said, for example:[2]

First.   We hold that resulting economic injury to a rival station is not, in and of itself, and apart from considerations of public convenience, interest, or necessity, an element the petitioner must weigh, and as to which it must make findings, in passing on an application for a broadcasting license.

And the Court said:[3]

This is not to say that the question of competition between a proposed station and one operating under an existing license is to be entirely disregarded by the Commission, and, indeed, the Commission's practice shows that it does not disregard that question. It may have a vital and important bearing upon the ability of the applicant adequately to serve his public; it may indicate that both stations − the existing and the proposed − will go under, with the result that a portion of the listening public will be left without adequate service; it may indicate that, by division of the field, both stations will be compelled to render inadequate service. These matters, however, are distinct from the consideration that, if a license be granted, competition between the licensee and any other existing station may cause economic loss to the latter.

Thus, it seems to us, the question whether a station makes $5,000, or $10,000, or $50,000 is a matter in which the public has no interest so long as service is not adversely affected; service may well be improved by competition. But, if the situation in a given area is such that available revenue will not support good service in more than one station, the public interest may well be in the licensing of one rather than two stations. To license two stations where there is revenue for only one may result in no good service at all. So economic injury to an existing station, while not in and of itself a matter of moment, becomes important when on the facts it spells diminution or destruction of service. At that point the element of injury ceases to be a matter of purely private concern.

The basic charter of the Commission is, of course, to act in the public interest. It grants or denies licenses as the public interest, convenience and necessity dictate. Whatever factual elements make up that criterion in any given problem − and the problem may differ from case to case − must be considered. Such is not only the power but the duty of the Commission.

---

[1]*Federal Communications Commission* v. *Sanders Brothers Radio Station*, 309 U.S. 470, 60 S.Ct. 693, 84 L.Ed. 869 (1940).
[2]Id., 309 U.S. at page 473, 60 S.Ct. at page 696.
[3]Id., 309 U.S. at pages 475-476, 60 S.Ct. at pages 697-698.

So in the present case the Commission had the power to determine whether the economic effect of a second license in this area would be to damage or destroy service to an extent inconsistent with the public interest. Whether the problem actually exists depends upon the facts, and we have no findings upon the point.

This opinion is not to be construed or applied as a mandate to the Commission to hear and decide the economic effects of every new license grant. It has no such meaning. We hold that, when an existing licensee offers to prove that the economic effect of another station would be detrimental to the public interest, the Commission should afford an opportunity for the presentation of such proof and, if the evidence is substantial (*i.e.*, if the protestant does not fail entirely to meet his burden), should make a finding or findings.

The Commission says that, if it has authority to consider economic injury as a factor in the public interest, the whole basic concept of a competitive broadcast industry disappears. We think it does not. Certainly the Supreme Court did not think so in the Sanders Brothers case, supra. Private economic injury is by no means always, or even usually, reflected in public detriment. Competitors may severely injure each other to the great benefit of the public. The broadcast industry is a competitive one, but competitive effects may under some sets of circumstances produce detriment to the public interest. When that happens the public interest controls.

The Commission says it lacks the "tools" — meaning specifications of authority from the Congress — with which to make the computations, valuations, schedules, etc., required in public utility regulation. We think no such elaborate equipment is necessary for the task here. As we have just said, we think it is not incumbent upon the Commission to evaluate the probable economic results of every license grant. Of course the public is not concerned whether it gets service from A or from B or from both combined. The public interest is not disturbed if A is destroyed by B, so long as B renders the required service. The public interest is affected when service is affected. We think the problem arises when a protestant offers to prove that the grant of a new license would be detrimental to the public interest. The Commission is equipped to receive and appraise such evidence. If the protestant fails to bear the burden of proving his point (and it is certainly a heavy burden), there may be an end to the matter. If his showing is substantial, or if there is a genuine issue posed, findings should be made. Perhaps Carroll did not cast its proffer of proof exactly in terms of the public interest, or at least not in terms of the whole public interest. It may be argued that it offered to prove only detriment to its own ability for service. We are inclined to give it the benefit of the most favorable interpretation. In any event, whatever proof Carroll had is already in the record. If it does not support a finding of detriment to the public interest, but merely of a detriment to Carroll, the Commission can readily so find.

The case must be remanded for findings on this point.

Carroll also makes a point about the Commission's findings in respect to West Georgia's basic financial qualifications and about a presumption that a father-in-law, a brother-in-law, and an uncle-in-law form part of the control exercised by a family unit. We find no error in these respects.

Remanded for further findings.

25

"Wires and Lights in a Box"

Address by Edward R. Murrow to the Radio
Television News Directors Association,
Chicago, Illinois*
October 15, 1958

Edward R. Murrow (1908–1965) is the guardian angel of broadcast journalism. He began his 25-year CBS career in 1935. Within
a few years his radio reports of unfolding events from England
and the European continent made his voice known throughout
America. Murrow always preferred radio to television as an instrument of journalism, but in 1951, in association with Fred W.
Friendly, he began the "See It Now" public affairs documentary
series on CBS-TV. His reputation and credibility grew still greater
through exposure on the new medium.

On March 9, 1954, in a well-remembered telecast, Murrow
openly attacked Senator Joseph McCarthy, the anti-communist
demagogue who was later censured by the U.S. Senate. Murrow's
closing remarks, delivered to the camera head-on, display an elo-
quence seldom equaled in the annals of journalism:

This is no time for men who oppose Senator McCarthy's
methods to keep silent, or for those who approve. We can deny
our heritage and our history but we cannot escape responsibility
for the result. There is no way for a citizen of a republic to abdi-

*Reprinted with permission of the Estate of Edward R. Murrow.

cate his responsibilities. As a nation we have come into our full inheritance at a tender age. We proclaim ourselves, as indeed we are, the defenders of freedom—wherever it continues to exist in the world. But we cannot defend freedom abroad by deserting it at home. The actions of the junior senator from Wisconsin have caused alarm and dismay amongst our allies abroad and given considerable comfort to our enemies. And whose fault is that? Not really his. He didn't create this situation of fear, he merely exploited it—and rather successfully. Cassius was right: "The fault, dear Brutus, is not in our stars but in ourselves." Good night, and good luck.*

The program was both hailed and attacked. At the time the TV industry itself was a willing victim of a brand of economic McCarthyism, the vicious and unsubstantiated form of character assassination known as "blacklisting." The "See It Now" McCarthy episode was perhaps TV journalism's bravest moment.

"See It Now" was taken off the air in 1958. Prime commercial TV time had become too precious to be squandered on programs that didn't maximize audience size. Sponsors, networks, and stations wanted to avoid presenting the type of material that was the specialty of "See It Now"—controversy.

Murrow attempted to rouse the conscience of the broadcasting industry in the following speech to the RTNDA. A precursor of Newton Minow's "vast wasteland" address (Document 28, pp. 281–291), the speech had little effect. It took the embarrassment of the quiz show scandals to shame the networks into temporarily increasing their public affairs programming.

Following the speech Murrow's superiors grew as disenchanted with him as he had become disillusioned about broadcasting. In 1959 Murrow took a leave from CBS as the new "CBS Reports" series was launched. Murrow's participation in "Harvest of Shame," a hard-hitting "CBS Reports" documentary about migrant farm workers, aired the day after Thanksgiving, 1960, was his final memorable TV broadcast. He left broadcast journalism to join the Kennedy administration as director of the United States Information Agency early in 1961 at one-tenth his salary at CBS. Declining health caused Murrow to resign 3 years later.

Related Reading: 23, 24, 51, 67, 83, 121, 247.

---

*Reprinted with permission of the Estate of Edward R. Murrow.

This just might do nobody any good. At the end of this discourse a few people may accuse this reporter of fouling his own comfortable nest, and your organization may be accused of having given hospitality to heretical and even dangerous thoughts. But the elaborate structure of networks, advertising agencies and sponsors will not be shaken or altered. It is my desire, if not my duty, to try to talk to you journeymen with some candor about what is happening to radio and television.

I have no technical advice or counsel to offer those of you who labor in this vineyard that produces words and pictures. You will forgive me for not telling you that the instruments with which you work are miraculous, that your responsibility is unprecedented or that your aspirations are frequently frustrated. It is not necessary to remind you that the fact that your voice is amplified to the degree where it reaches from one end of the country to the other does not confer upon you greater wisdom or understanding than you possessed when your voice reached only from one end of the bar to the other. All of these things you know.

You should also know at the outset that, in the manner of witnesses before Congressional committees, I appear here voluntarily—by invitation—that I am an employee of the Columbia Broadcasting System, that I am neither an officer nor a director of that corporation and that these remarks are of a "do-it-yourself" nature. If what I have to say is responsible, then I alone am responsible for the saying of it. Seeking neither approbation from my employers, nor new sponsors, nor acclaim from the critics of radio and television, I cannot well be disappointed. Believing that potentially the commercial system of broadcasting as practiced in this country is the best and freest yet devised, I have decided to express my concern about what I believe to be happening to radio and television. These instruments have been good to me beyond my due. There exists in my mind no reasonable grounds for personal complaint. I have no feud, either with my employers, any sponsors, or with the professional critics of radio and television. But I am seized with an abiding fear regarding what these two instruments are doing to our society, our culture and our heritage.

Our history will be what we make it. And if there are any historians about fifty or a hundred years from now, and there should be preserved the kinescopes for one week of all three networks, they will there find recorded in black and white, or color, evidence of decadence, escapism and insulation from the realities of the world in which we live. I invite your attention to the television schedules of all networks between the hours of 8 and 11 p.m., Eastern Time. Here you will find only fleeting and spasmodic reference to the fact that this nation is in mortal danger. There are, it is true, occasional informative programs presented in that intellectual ghetto on Sunday afternoons. But during the daily peak viewing periods, television in the main insulates us from the realities of the world in which we live. If this state of affairs continues, we may alter an advertising slogan to read: LOOK NOW, PAY LATER. For surely we shall pay for using this most powerful instrument of communication to insulate the citizenry from the hard and demanding realities which must be faced if we are to survive. I mean the word *survive* literally. If there were to be a competition in indifference, or perhaps in insulation from reality, then Nero and his fiddle, Chamberlain and his umbrella, could not find a place on an early afternoon sustaining show. If Hollywood were to run out of Indians, the program schedules would be mangled beyond all recognition. Then some courageous soul with a small budget might be able to do a documentary telling what, in fact, we have done—and are still doing—to the Indians in this country. But that would be unpleasant. And we must at all costs shield the sensitive citizens from anything that is unpleasant.

I am entirely persuaded that the American public is more reasonable, restrained and more mature than most of our industry's program planners believe. Their fear of controversy is not warranted by the evidence. I have reason to know, as do many of you, that when the evidence on a controversial subject is fairly and calmly presented, the public recognizes it for what it is—an effort to illuminate rather than to agitate.

Several years ago, when we undertook to do a program on Egypt and Israel, well-meaning, experienced and intelligent friends shook their heads and said, "This you cannot do—you will be handed your head. It is an emotion-packed controversy, and there is no room for reason in it." We did the program. Zionists, anti-Zionists, the friends of the Middle East, Egyptian and Israeli officials said, with a faint note of surprise, "It was a fair count. The information was there. We have no complaints."

Our experience was similar with two half-hour programs dealing with cigarette smoking and lung cancer. Both the medical profession and the tobacco industry cooperated in a rather wary fashion. But in the end of the day they were both reasonably content. The subject of radioactive fall-out and the banning of nuclear tests was, and is, highly controversial. But according to what little evidence there is, viewers were prepared to listen to both sides with reason and restraint. This is not said to claim any special or unusual competence in the presentation of controversial subjects, but rather to indicate that timidity in these areas is not warranted by the evidence.

Recently, network spokesmen have been disposed to complain that the professional critics of television have been "rather beastly." There have been hints that somehow competition for the advertising dollar has caused the critics of print to gang up on television and radio. This reporter has no desire to defend the critics. They have space in which to do that on their own behalf. But it remains a fact that the newspapers and magazines are the only instruments of mass communication which remain free from sustained and regular critical comment. If the network spokesmen are so anguished about what appears in print, let them come forth and engage in a little sustained and regular comment regarding newspapers and magazines. It is an ancient and sad fact that most people in network television, and radio, have an exaggerated regard for what appears in print. And there have been cases where executives have refused to make even private comment on a program for which they were responsible until they had read the reviews in print. This is hardly an exhibition of confidence.

The oldest excuse of the networks for their timidity is their youth. Their spokesmen say, "We are young; we have not developed the traditions nor acquired the experience of the older media." If they but knew it, they are building these traditions, creating those precedents every day. Each time they yield to a voice from Washington or any political pressure, each time they eliminate something that might offend some section of the community, they are creating their own body of precedent and tradition. They are, in fact, not content to be "half safe."

Nowhere is this better illustrated than by the fact that the chairman of the Federal Communications Commission publicly prods broadcasters to engage in their legal right to editorialize. Of course, to undertake an editorial policy, overt and clearly labeled, and obviously unsponsored, requires a station or a network to be responsible. Most stations today probably do not have the manpower to assume this responsibility, but the manpower could be recruited. Editorials would not be profitable; if they had a cutting edge, they might even offend. It is much easier, much less troublesome, to use the money-making machine of television and radio merely as a conduit through which to channel anything that is not libelous, obscene or defamatory. In that way one has the illusion of power without responsibility.

So far as radio—that most satisfying and rewarding instrument—is concerned, the diagnosis of its difficulties is rather easy. And obviously I speak only of news and information. In order to progress, it need only go backward. To the time when singing commercials were not allowed on news reports, when there was no middle commercial in a 15-minute news report, when radio was rather proud, alert and fast. I recently asked a network official, "Why this great rash of five-minute news reports (including three commercials) on weekends?" He replied, "Because that seems to be the only thing we can sell."

In this kind of complex and confusing world, you can't tell very much about the why of the news in broadcasts where only three minutes is available for news. The only man who could do that was Elmer Davis, and his kind aren't about any more. If radio news is to be regarded as a commodity, only acceptable when saleable, then I don't care what you call it—I say it isn't news.

My memory also goes back to the time when the fear of a slight reduction in business did not result in an immediate cutback in bodies in the news and public affairs department, at a time when network profits had just reached an all-time high. We would all agree, I think, that whether on a station or a network, the stapling machine is a poor substitute for a newsroom typewriter.

One of the minor tragedies of television news and information is that the networks will not even defend their vital interests. When my employer, CBS, through a combination of enterprise and good luck, did an interview with Nikita Khrushchev, the President uttered a few ill-chosen, uninformed words on the subject, and the network practically apologized. This produced a rarity. Many newspapers defended the CBS right to produce the program and commended it for initiative. But the other networks remained silent.

Likewise, when John Foster Dulles, by personal decree, banned American journalists from going to Communist China, and subsequently offered contradictory explanations for his fiat, the networks entered only a mild protest. Then they apparently forgot the unpleasantness. Can it be that this national industry is content to serve the public interest only with the trickle of news that comes out of Hong Kong, to leave its viewers in ignorance of the cataclysmic changes that are occurring in a nation of six hundred million people? I have no illusions about the difficulties of reporting from a dictatorship, but our British and French allies have been better served—in their public interest—with some very useful information from their reporters in Communist China.

One of the basic troubles with radio and television news is that both instruments have grown up as an incompatible combination of show business, advertising and news. Each of the three is a rather bizarre and demanding profession. And when you get all three under one roof, the dust never settles. The top management of the networks, with a few notable exceptions, has been trained in advertising, research, sales or show business. But by the nature of the corporate structure, they also make the final and crucial decisions having to do with news and public affairs. Frequently they have neither the time nor the competence to do this. It is not easy for the same small group of men to decide whether to buy a new station for millions of dollars, build a new building, alter the rate card, buy a new Western, sell a soap opera, decide what defensive line to take in connection with the latest Congressional inquiry, how much money to spend on promoting a new program, what additions or deletions should be made in the existing covey or clutch of vice-presidents, and at the same time—frequently on the same long day—to give mature, thoughtful consideration to the manifold problems that confront those who are charged with the responsibility for news and public affairs.

Sometimes there is a clash between the public interest and the corporate interest. A telephone call or a letter from the proper quarter in Washington is treated rather more seriously than a communication from an irate but not politically potent viewer. It is tempting enough to give away a little air time for frequently irresponsible and unwarranted utterances in an effort to temper the wind of criticism.

Upon occasion, economics and editorial judgment are in conflict. And there is no law which says that dollars will be defeated by duty. Not so long ago the President of the United States delivered a television address to the nation. He was discoursing on the possibility or probability of war between this nation and the Soviet Union and Communist China—a reasonably compelling subject. Two networks, CBS and NBC, delayed that broadcast for an hour and fifteen minutes. If this decision was dictated by anything other than financial reasons, the networks didn't deign to explain those reasons. That hour-and-fifteen-minute delay, by the way, is about twice the time required for an ICBM to travel from the Soviet Union to major targets in the United States. It is difficult to believe that this decision was made by men who love, respect and understand news.

So far, I have been dealing largely with the deficit side of the ledger, and the items could be expanded. But I have said, and I believe, that potentially we have in this country a free enterprise system of radio and television which is superior to any other. But to achieve its promise, it must be both free and enterprising. There is no suggestion here that networks or individual stations should operate as philanthropies. But I can find nothing in the Bill of Rights or the Communications Act which says that they must increase their net profits each year, lest the Republic collapse. I do not suggest that news and information should be subsidized by foundations or private subscriptions. I am aware that the networks have expended, and are expending, very considerable sums of money on public affairs programs from which they cannot hope to receive any financial reward. I have had the privilege at CBS of presiding over a considerable number of such programs. I testify, and am able to stand here and say, that I have never had a program turned down by my superiors because of the money it would cost.

But we all know that you cannot reach the potential maximum audience in marginal time with a sustaining program. This is so because so many stations on the network—any network—will decline to carry it. Every licensee who applies for a grant to operate in the public interest, convenience and necessity makes certain promises as to what he will do in terms of program content. Many recipients of licenses have, in blunt language, welshed on those promises. The money-making machine somehow blunts their memories. The only remedy for this is closer inspection and punitive action by the F.C.C. But in the view of many this would come perilously close to supervision of program content by a federal agency.

So it seems that we cannot rely on philanthropic support or foundation subsidies; we cannot follow the "sustaining route"—the networks cannot pay all the freight—and the F.C.C. cannot or will not discipline those who abuse the facilities that belong to the public. What, then, is the answer? Do we merely stay in our comfortable nests, concluding that the obligation of these instruments has been discharged when we work at the job of informing the public for a minimum of time? Or do we believe that the preservation of the Republic is a seven-day-a-week job, demanding more awareness, better skills and more perseverance than we have yet contemplated.

I am frightened by the imbalance, the constant striving to reach the largest possible audience for everything; by the absence of a sustained study of the state of the nation. Heywood Broun once said, "No body politic is healthy until it begins to itch." I would like television to produce some itching pills, rather than this endless outpouring of tranquilizers. It can be done. Maybe it won't be, but it could. Let us not shoot the wrong piano player. Do not be deluded into believing that the titular heads of the networks control what appears on their networks. They all have better taste. All are responsible to stockholders, and in my experience all are honorable men. But they must schedule what they can sell in the public market.

And this brings us to the nub of the question. In one sense it rather revolves around the phrase heard frequently along Madison Avenue: The Corporate Image. I am not precisely sure what this phrase means, but I would imagine that it reflects a desire on the part of the corporations who pay the advertising bills to have the public imagine, or believe, that they are not merely bodies with no souls, panting in pursuit of elusive dollars. They would like us to believe that they can distinguish between the public good and the private or corporate gain. So the question is this: Are the big corporations who pay the freight for radio and television programs wise to use that time exclusively for the sale of goods and services? Is it in their own interest and that of the stockholders so to do? The sponsor of an hour's television program is not buying merely the six minutes devoted to his commercial message. He is determining, within broad limits, the sum total of the impact of the entire hour. If he always, invariably, reaches for the largest possible audience, then this process of insulation, of escape from reality, will continue to be massively financed, and its apologists will continue to make winsome speeches about giving the public what it wants, or "letting the public decide."

I refuse to believe that the presidents and chairmen of the boards of these big corporations want their corporate image to consist exclusively of a solemn voice in an echo chamber, or a pretty girl opening the door of a refrigerator, or a horse that talks. They want something better, and on occasion some of them have demonstrated it. But most of the men whose legal and moral responsibility it is to spend the stockholders' money for advertising are removed from the realities of the mass media by five, six, or a dozen contraceptive layers of vice-presidents, public relations counsel and advertising agencies. Their business is to sell goods, and the competition is pretty tough.

But this nation is now in competition with malignant forces of evil who are using every instrument at their command to empty the minds of their subjects and fill those minds with slogans, determination and faith in the future. If we go on as we are, we are protecting the mind of the American public from any real contact with the menacing world that squeezes in upon us. We are engaged in a great experiment to discover whether a free public opinion can devise and direct methods of managing the affairs of the nation. We may fail. But we are handicapping ourselves needlessly.

Let us have a little competition. Not only in selling soap, cigarettes and automobiles, but in informing a troubled, apprehensive but receptive public. Why should not each of the 20 or 30 big corporations which dominate radio and television decide that they will give up one or two of their regularly scheduled programs each year, turn the time over to the networks and say in effect: "This is a tiny tithe, just a little bit of our profits. On this particular night we aren't going to try to sell cigarettes or automobiles; this is merely a gesture to indicate our belief in the importance of ideas." The networks should, and I think would, pay for the cost of producing the program. The advertiser, the sponsor, would get name credit but would have nothing to do with the content of the program. Would this blemish the corporate image? Would the stockholders object? I think not. For if the premise upon which our pluralistic society rests, which as I understand it is that if the people are given sufficient undiluted information, they will then somehow, even after long, sober second thoughts, reach the right decision— if that premise is wrong, then not only the corporate image but the corporations are done for.

There used to be an old phrase in this country, employed when someone talked too much. It was: "Go hire a hall." Under this proposal the sponsor would have hired the hall; he has bought the time; the local station operator, no matter how indifferent, is going to carry the program—he has to. Then it's up to the networks to fill the hall. I am not here talking about editorializing but about straightaway exposition as direct, unadorned and impartial as fallible human beings can make it. Just once in a while let us exalt the importance of ideas and information. Let us dream to the extent of saying that on a given Sunday night the time normally occupied by Ed Sullivan is given over to a clinical survey of the state of American education, and a week or two later the time normally used by Steve Allen is devoted to a thoroughgoing study of American policy in the Middle East. Would the corporate image of their respective sponsors be damaged? Would the stockholders rise up in their wrath and complain? Would anything happen other than that a few million people would have received a little illumination on subjects that may well determine the future of this country, and therefore the future of the corporations? This method would also provide real competition between the networks as to which could outdo the others in the palatable presentation of information. It would provide an outlet for the young men of skill, and there are some even of dedication, who would like to do something other than devise methods of insulating while selling.

There may be other and simpler methods of utilizing these instruments of radio and television in the interests of a free society. But I know of none that could be so easily accomplished inside the framework of the existing commercial system. I don't know how you would measure the success or failure of a given program. And it would be hard to prove the magnitude of the benefit accruing to the corporation which gave up one night of a variety or quiz show in order that the network might marshal its skills to do a thoroughgoing job on the present status of NATO, or plans for controlling nuclear tests. But I would reckon that the president, and indeed the majority of shareholders of the corporation who sponsored such a venture, would feel just a little bit better about the corporation and the country.

It may be that the present system, with no modifications and no experiments, can survive. Perhaps the money-making machine has some kind of built-in perpetual motion, but I do not think so. To a very considerable extent the media of mass communications in a given country reflect the political, economic and social climate in which they flourish. That is the reason ours differ from the British and French, or the Russian and Chinese. We are currently wealthy, fat, comfortable and complacent. We have currently a built-in allergy to unpleasant or disturbing information. Our mass media reflect this. But unless we get up off our fat surpluses and recognize that television in the main is being used to distract, delude, amuse and insulate us, then television and those who finance it, those who look at it and those who work at it, may see a totally different picture too late.

I do not advocate that we turn television into a 27-inch wailing wall, where longhairs constantly moan about the state of our culture and our defense. But I would just like to see it reflect occasionally the hard, unyielding realities of the world in which we live. I would like to see it done inside the existing framework, and I would like to see the doing of it redound to the credit of those who finance and program it. Measure the results by Nielsen, Trendex or Silex—it doesn't matter. The main thing is to try. The responsibility can be easily placed, in spite of all the mouthings about giving the public what it wants. It rests on big business, and on big television, and it rests at the top. Responsibility is not something that can be assigned or delegated. And it promises its own reward: good business and good television.

Perhaps no one will do anything about it. I have ventured to outline it against a background of criticism that may have been too harsh only because I could think of nothing better. Someone once said—I think it was Max Eastman—that "that publisher serves his advertiser best who best serves his readers." I cannot believe that radio and television, or the corporations that finance the programs, are serving well or truly their viewers or listeners, or themselves.

I began by saying that our history will be what we make it. If we go on as we are, then history will take its revenge, and retribution will not limp in catching up with us.

We are to a large extent an imitative society. If one or two or three corporations would undertake to devote just a small fraction of their advertising appropriation along the lines that I have suggested, the procedure would grow by contagion; the economic burden would be bearable, and there might ensue a most exciting adventure—exposure to ideas and the bringing of reality into the homes of the nation.

To those who say people wouldn't look; they wouldn't be interested; they're too complacent, indifferent and insulated, I can only reply: There is, in one reporter's opinion, considerable evidence against that contention. But even if they are right, what have they got to lose? Because if they are right, and this instrument is good for nothing but to entertain, amuse and insulate, then the tube is flickering now and we will soon see that the whole struggle is lost.

This instrument can teach, it can illuminate; yes, and it can even inspire. But it can do so only to the extent that humans are determined to use it to those ends. Otherwise it is merely wires and lights in a box. There is a great and perhaps decisive battle to be fought against ignorance, intolerance and indifference. This weapon of television could be useful.

Stonewall Jackson, who knew something about the use of weapons, is reported to have said, "When war comes, you must draw the sword and throw away the scabbard." The trouble with television is that it is rusting in the scabbard during a battle for survival.

26

The 1960 Programming Policy Statement

Report and Statement of Policy re: Commission en banc Programming Inquiry
25 Fed. Reg. 7291; 44 FCC 2303
July 29, 1960

Issued 14 years after the "Blue Book" (Document 21, pp. 132–216), the "1960 Programming Policy Statement" was much milder in tone than its predecessor. The FCC was understandably concerned by the payola and rigged quiz show revelations of the late 1950's. The proposed legislation alluded to in this statement was enacted by Congress the same year (Public Law 86-752, approved September 13, 1960), adding to the Communications Act Sections 503(b), 508, and 509, relating to forfeitures, payola-plugola, and deceptive contests, respectively.

The 1946 and 1960 policy statements are remarkably similar in many respects. Both documents place responsibility for programming with the licensee. Both rely on industry self-regulation to achieve compliance with FCC programming objectives to a great extent. The "Blue Book" and the "1960 Programming Policy Statement" both recognize the need for balanced programming, including local live programs, public affairs presentations, and the elimination of advertising excesses. However, the "Blue Book's" well-supported inclusion of sustaining programs as a necessary element of balanced scheduling is expressly rejected in the 1960 statement.

A new element was introduced by the FCC in the 1960 policy statement—licensee ascertainment. This requires the broadcaster to discover the "tastes, needs, and desires" of people in the local service area through surveys of community leaders and the general public; to evaluate the findings of such surveys; and to propose programs responsive to the evaluated "tastes, needs, and desires." The lawfulness of the ascertainment requirement was upheld in the *Suburban* case (Document 31, pp. 306-309).

The program proposal section of FCC application forms was revised to reflect the growing importance of licensee ascertainment in the 1960's. In 1971 the Commission issued its first ascertainment "primer" (27 FCC 2d 650) in which primary emphasis was placed on programming responsive to community "problems" rather than "tastes, needs, and desires." The same emphasis is exhibited in the more recent "Renewal Ascertainment Primer" (Document 44, pp. 477-485).

Broadcast industry opposition to the "1960 Programming Policy Statement" has been no more than token. Licensees seem to prefer procedural programming requirements (surveys and forms) to substantive ones. The 1960 statement is still adhered to by the FCC, at least officially. But it must be said that Commission enforcement of the spirit of the policy has also been token, and probably for the same reason underlying broadcaster acceptance. Constitutional and statutory prohibitions of censorship favor the licensing agency's choice of form over substance and acquiescence to licensee discretion in the regulation of program content. Thus the policy statement is superficially complied with in most respects.

Related Reading: 78, 162, 187, 198, 238.

. . . On November 9, 1959, the proceeding instituted by the Commission's Order of February 26, 1959 was amended and enlarged to include a general inquiry with respect to programming to determine, among other things, whether the general standards heretofore laid down by the Commission for the guidance of broadcast licensees in the selection of programs and other material intended for broadcast are currently adequate; whether the Commission should, by the exercise of its rule-making power, set out more detailed and precise standards for such broadcasters; whether the Commission's present review and consideration in the field of programming and advertising are adequate, under present conditions in the broadcast industry; and whether the Commission's authority under the Communications Act of 1934, as amended, is adequate, or whether legislation should be recommended to Congress.

This inquiry was heard by the Commission *en banc* between December 7, 1959, and February 1, 1960, and consumed 19 days in actual hearings. Over 90 witnesses testified relative to the problems involved, made suggestions and otherwise contributed from their background and experience to the solution of these problems. Several additional statements were submitted. The record in the *en banc* portion of the inquiry consisted of 3,775 pages of transcript plus 1,000 pages of exhibits. The Interim Report of the staff of the Office of Network Study was submitted to the Commission for consideration on June 15, 1960.

The Commission will make every effort to expedite its consideration of the entire docket proceeding and will take such definitive action as the Commission determines to be warranted. However, the Commission feels that a general statement of policy responsive to the issues in the *en banc* inquiry is warranted at this time.

Prior to the *en banc* hearing, the Commission had made its position clear that, in fulfilling its obligation to operate in the public interest, a broadcast station is expected to exercise reasonable care and prudence with respect to its broadcast material in order to assure that no matter is broadcast which will deceive or mislead the public. In view of the extent of the problem existing with respect to a number of licensees involving such practices as deceptive quiz shows and payola which had become apparent, the Commission concluded that certain proposed amendments to our Rules as well as proposed legislation would provide a basis for substantial improvements. Accordingly, on February 5, 1960, we adopted a Notice of Proposed Rule Making to deal with fixed quiz and other non-bona fide contest programs involving intellectual skill. These rules would prohibit the broadcasting of such programming unless accompanied by an announcement which would in all cases describe the nature of the program in a manner to sufficiently apprise the audience that the events in question are not in fact spontaneous or actual measures of knowledge or intellectual skill. Announcements would be made at the beginning and end of each program. Moreover, the proposed rules would require a station if it obtained such a program from networks, to be assured similarly that the network program has an accompanying announcement of this nature. This, we believe, would go a long way toward preventing any recurrence of problems such as those encountered in the recent quiz show programs.

We have also felt that this sort of conduct should be prohibited by statute. Accordingly, we suggested legislation designed to make it a crime for anyone to wilfully and knowingly participate or cause another to participate in or cause to be broadcast a program of intellectual skill or knowledge where the outcome thereof is prearranged or predetermined. Without the above-described amendment, the Commission's regulatory authority is limited to its licensing function. The Commission cannot reach networks directly or advertisers, producers, sponsors, and others who, in one capacity or another, are associated with the presentation of radio and television programs which may deceive the listening or viewing public. It is our view that this proposed legislation will help to assure that every contest of intellectual skill or knowledge that is broadcast will be in fact a bona fide contest. Under this proposal, all those persons responsible in any way for the broadcast of a deceptive program of this type would be penalized. Because of the far reaching effects of radio and television, we believe such sanctions to be desirable.

The Commission proposed on February 5, 1960 that a new section be added to the Commission's rules which would require the licensee of radio broadcast stations to adopt appropriate procedures to prevent the practice of payola amongst his employees. Here again the standard of due diligence would have to be met by the licensee. We have also approved on February 11 the language of proposed legislation which would impose criminal penalties for failure to announce sponsored programs, such as payola and others, involving hidden payments or other considerations. This proposal looks toward amending the United States Code to provide fines up to $5,000 or imprisonment up to one year, or both, for violators. It would prohibit the payment to any person or the receipt of payment by any person for the purpose of having as a part of the broadcast program any material on either a radio or television show unless an announcement is made as a part of the program that such material has been paid for or furnished. The Commission now has no direct jurisdiction over the employees of a broadcast station with respect to this type of activity. The imposition of a criminal penalty appears to us to be an effective manner for dealing with this practice. In addition, the Commission has made related legislative proposals with respect to fines, temporary suspension of licenses, and temporary restraining orders.

In view of our mutual interest with the Federal Trade Commission and in order to avoid duplication of effort, we have arrived at an arrangement whereby any information obtained by the FCC which might be of interest to FTC will be called to that Commission's attention by our staff. Similarly, FTC will advise our Commission of any information or data which it acquires in the course of its investigations which might be pertinent to matters under jurisdiction of the FCC. This is an understanding supplemental to earlier liaison arrangements between FCC and FTC.

Certain legislative proposals recently made by the Commission as related to the instant inquiry have been mentioned. It is appropriate now to consider whether the statutory authority of the Commission with respect to programming and program practices is, in other respects, adequate.

In considering the extent of the Commission's authority in the area of programming it is essential first to examine the limitations imposed upon it by the First Amendment to the Constitution and Section 326 of the Communications Act.

The First Amendment to the United States Constitution reads as follows:

Congress shall make no law respecting an establishment of religion or prohibiting the free exercise thereof; or abridging the freedom of speech, or of the press; or the right of the people peaceably to assemble, and to petition the Government for a redress of grievances.

Section 326 of the Communications Act of 1934, as amended, provides that:

Nothing in this chapter shall be understood or construed to give the Commission the power of censorship over the radio communications or signals transmitted by any radio station, and no regulation or condition shall be promulgated or fixed by the Commission which shall interfere with the right of free speech by means of radio communication.

The communication of ideas by means of radio and television is a form of expression entitled to protection against abridgement by the First Amendment to the Constitution. In *United States* v. *Paramount Pictures*, 334 U.S. 131, 166 (1948) the Supreme Court stated:

We have no doubt that moving pictures, like newspapers and radio are included in the press, whose freedom is guaranteed by the First Amendment.

As recently as 1954 in *Superior Films* v. *Department of Education*, 346 U.S. 587, Justice Douglas in a concurring opinion stated:

Motion pictures are, of course, a different medium of expression than the radio, the stage, the novel or the magazine. But the First Amendment draws no distinction between the various methods of communicating ideas.

Moreover, the free speech protection of the First Amendment is not confined solely to the exposition of ideas nor is it required that the subject matter of the communication be possessed of some value to society. In *Winters* v. *New York*, 333 U.S. 507, 510 (1948) the Supreme Court reversed a conviction based upon a violation of an ordinance of the City of New York which made it punishable to distribute printed matter devoted to the publication of accounts of criminal deeds and pictures of bloodshed, lust or crime. In this connection the Court said:

We do not accede to appellee's suggestion that the constitutional protection for a free press applies only to the exposition of ideas. The line between the informing and the entertaining is too elusive for the protection of that basic right. . . . Though we can see nothing of any possible value to society in these magazines, they are as much entitled to the protection of free speech as the best of literature.

Notwithstanding the foregoing authorities, the right to the use of the airwaves is conditioned upon the issuance of a license under a statutory scheme established by Congress in the Communications Act in the proper exercise of its power over commerce.[1] The question therefore arises as to whether because of

---

[1] *NBC* v. *United States*, 319 U.S. 190 (1943).

the characteristics peculiar to broadcasting which justifies the government in regulating its operation through a licensing system, there exists the basis for a distinction as regards other media of mass communication with respect to application of the free speech provisions of the First Amendment? In other words, does it follow that because one may not engage in broadcasting without first obtaining a license, the terms thereof may be so framed as to unreasonably abridge the free speech protection of the First Amendment?

We recognize that the broadcasting medium presents problems peculiar to itself which are not necessarily subject to the same rules governing other media of communication. As we stated in our Petition in *Grove Press, Inc.* and *Readers Subscription, Inc.* v. *Robert K. Christenberry* (Case No. 25,861) filed in the U.S. Court of Appeals for the Second Circuit,

radio and TV programs enter the home and are readily available not only to the average normal adult but also to children and to the emotionally immature. . . . Thus, for example, while a nudist magazine may be within the protection of the First Amendment . . . the televising of nudes might well raise a serious question of programming contrary to 18 U.S.C. 1464. . . . Similarly, regardless of whether the "four-letter words" and sexual description, set forth in "Lady Chatterley's Lover," (when considered in the context of the whole book) make the book obscene for mailability purposes, the utterance of such words or the depiction of such sexual activity on radio or TV would raise similar public interest and Section 1464 questions.

Nevertheless it is essential to keep in mind that "the basic principles of freedom of speech and the press like the First Amendment's command do not vary."[2]

Although the Commission must determine whether the total program service of broadcasters is reasonably responsive to the interests and needs of the public they serve, it may not condition the grant, denial or revocation of a broadcast license upon its own subjective determination of what is or is not a good program. To do so would "lay a forbidden burden upon the exercise of liberty protected by the Constitution."[3] The Chairman of the Commission during the course of his testimony recently given before the Senate Independent Offices Subcommittee of the Committee on Appropriations expressed the point as follows:

Mr. Ford. When it comes to questions of taste, unless it is downright profanity or obscenity, I do not think that the Commission has any part in it.

I don't see how we could possibly go out and say this program is good and that program is bad. That would be a direct violation of the law.[4]

[2]*Burstyn* v. *Wilson*, 343 U.S. 495, 503 (1952).

[3]*Cantwell* v. *Connecticut*, 310 U.S. 296, 307.

[4] Hearings before the Subcommittee of the Committee on Appropriations, United States Senate, 86th Congress, 2nd Session on H.R. 11776 at page 775.

In a similar vein Mr. Whitney North Seymour, President-elect of the American Bar Association, stated during the course of this proceeding that while the Commission may inquire of licensees what they have done to determine the needs of the community they propose to serve, the Commission may not impose upon them its private notions of what the public ought to hear.[5]

Nevertheless, several witnesses in this proceeding have advanced persuasive arguments urging us to require licensees to present specific types of programs on the theory that such action would enhance freedom of expression rather than tend to abridge it. With respect to this proposition we are constrained to point out that the First Amendment forbids governmental interference asserted in aid of free speech, as well as governmental action repressive of it. The protection against abridgement of freedom of speech and press flatly forbids governmental interference, benign or otherwise. The First Amendment "while regarding freedom in religion, in speech and printing and in assembling and petitioning the government for redress of grievances as fundamental and precious to all, seeks only to forbid that Congress should meddle therein." (*Powe v. United States*, 109 F. 2nd 147)

As recently as 1959 in *Farmers Educational and Cooperative Union of America* v. *WDAY, Inc.* 360 U.S. 525, the Supreme Court succinctly stated:

. . . expressly applying this country's tradition of free expression to the field of radio broadcasting, Congress has from the first emphatically forbidden the Commission to exercise any power of censorship over radio communication.

An examination of the foregoing authorities serves to explain why the day-to-day operation of a broadcast station is primarily the responsibility of the individual station licensee. Indeed, Congress provided in Section 3(h) of the Communications Act that a person engaged in radio broadcasting shall not be deemed a common carrier. Hence, the Commission in administering the Act and the courts in interpreting it have consistently maintained that responsibility for the selection and presentation of broadcast material ultimately devolves upon the individual station licensee, and that the fulfillment of the public interest requires the free exercise of his independent judgment. Accordingly, the Communications Act "does not essay to regulate the business of the licensee. The Commission is given no supervisory control over programs, of business management or of policy . . . The Congress intended to leave competition in the business of broadcasting where it found it . . . ."[6] The regulatory responsibility of the Commission in the broadcast field essentially involves the maintenance of a balance between the preservation of a free competitive broadcast system, on the one hand, and the reasonable restriction of that freedom inherent in the public interest standard provided in the Communications Act, on the other.

[5]Memorandum of Mr. Whitney North Seymour, Special Counsel to the National Association of Broadcasters at page 7.
[6]*FCC* v. *Sanders Brothers*, 309 U.S. 470 (1940).

In addition, there appears a second problem quite unrelated to the question of censorship that would enter into the Commission's assumption of supervision over program content. The Commission's role as a practical matter, let alone a legal matter, cannot be one of program dictation or program supervision. In this connection we think the words of Justice Douglas are particularly appropriate.

The music selected by one bureaucrat may be as offensive to some as it is soothing to others. The news commentator chosen to report on the events of the day may give overtones to the news that pleases the bureaucrat but which rile the . . . audience. The political philosophy which one radio sponsor exudes may be thought by the official who makes up the programs as the best for the welfare of the people. But the man who listens to it . . . may think it marks the destruction of the Republic. . . . Today it is a business enterprise working out a radio program under the auspices of government. Tomorrow it may be a dominant, political or religious group. . . . Once a man is forced to submit to one type of program, he can be forced to submit to another. It may be but a short step from a cultural program to a political program. . . . The strength of our system is in the dignity, resourcefulness and the intelligence of our people. Our confidence is in their ability to make the wisest choice. That system cannot flourish if regimentation takes hold.[7]

Having discussed the limitations upon the Commission in the consideration of programming, there remains for discussion the exceptions to those limitations and the area of affirmative responsibility which the Commission may appropriately exercise under its statutory obligation to find that the public interest, convenience and necessity will be served by the granting of a license to broadcast.

In view of the fact that a broadcaster is required to program his station in the public interest, convenience and necessity, it follows despite the limitations of the First Amendment and Section 326 of the Act, that his freedom to program is not absolute. The Commission does not conceive that it is barred by the Constitution or by statute from exercising any responsibility with respect to programming. It does conceive that the manner or extent of the exercise of such responsibility can introduce constitutional or statutory questions. It readily concedes that it is precluded from examining a program for taste or content, unless the recognized exceptions to censorship apply: for example, obscenity, profanity, indecency, programs inciting to riots, programs designed or inducing toward the commission of crime, lotteries, etc. These exceptions, in part, are written into the United States Code and, in part, are recognized in judicial decision. See Sections 1304, 1343, and 1464 of Title 18 of the United States Code (lotteries; fraud by radio; utterance of obscene, indecent or profane

[7]*Public Utilities Commission* v. *Pollak*, 343 U.S. 451, 468, Dissenting Opinion.

language by radio). It must be added that such traditional or legislative exceptions to a strict application of the freedom of speech requirements of the United States Constitution may very well also convey wider scope in judicial interpretation as applied to licensed radio than they have had or would have as applied to other communications media. The Commission's petition in the *Grove* case, *supra*, urged the court not unnecessarily to refer to broadcasting, in its opinion, as had the District Court. Such reference subsequently was not made though it must be pointed out there is no evidence that the motion made by the FCC was a contributing factor. It must nonetheless be observed that this Commission conscientiously believes that it should make no policy or take any action which would violate the letter or the spirit of the censorship prohibitions of Section 326 of the Communications Act.

As stated by the Supreme Court of the United States in *Joseph Burstyn, Inc.* v. *Wilson, supra*:

. . . Nor does it follow that motion pictures are necessarily subject to the precise rule governing any other particular method of expression. Each method tends to present its own peculiar problem. But the basic principles of freedom of speech and the press, like the First Amendment's command, do not vary. Those principles, as they have frequently been enunciated by this Court, make freedom of expression the rule.

A review of the Communications Act as a whole clearly reveals that the foundation of the Commission's authority rests upon the public interest, convenience and necessity.[8] The Commission may not grant, modify or renew a broadcast station license without finding that the operation of such station is in the public interest. Thus, faithful discharge of its statutory responsibilities is absolutely necessary in connection with the implacable requirement that the Commission approve no such application for license unless it finds that "public interest, convenience, and necessity would be served." While the public interest standard does not provide a blueprint of all of the situations to which it may apply, it does contain a sufficiently precise definition of authority so as to enable the Commission to properly deal with the many and varied occasions which may give rise to its application. A significant element of the public interest is the broadcaster's service to the community. In the case of *NBC* v. *United States*, 319 U.S. 190, the Supreme Court described this aspect of the public interest as follows:

An important element of public interest and convenience affecting the issue of a license is the ability of the licensee to render the best practicable service to the community reached by broadcasts. . . . The Commission's licensing function cannot be discharged, therefore, merely by finding that there are no technological objections to the granting of a license. If the criterion of "public

---

[8] §307(d), 308, 309, *inter alia*.

interest" were limited to such matters, how could the Commission choose between two applicants for the same facilities, each of whom is financially and technically qualified to operate a station? Since the very inception of federal regulation of radio, comparative considerations as to the services to be rendered have governed the application of the standard of "public interest, convenience, or necessity."

Moreover, apart from this broad standard which we will further discuss in a moment, there are certain other statutory indications.

It is generally recognized that programming is of the essence of radio service. Section 307(b) of the Communications Act requires the Commission to "make such distribution of licenses . . . among the several States and communities as to provide a fair, efficient, and equitable distribution of radio service to each of the same." Under this section the Commission has consistently licensed stations with the end objective of either providing new or additional programming service *to* a community, area or state, or of providing a new or additional "outlet" for broadcasting *from* a community, area, or state. Implicit in the former alternative is increased radio reception; implicit in the latter alternative is increased radio transmission and, in this connection, appropriate attention to local live programming is required.

Formerly by reason of administrative policy, and since September 14, 1959, by necessary implication from the amended language of Section 315 of the Communications Act, the Commission has had the responsibility for determining whether licensees "afford reasonable opportunity for the discussion of conflicting views on issues of public importance." This responsibility usually is of the generic kind and thus, in the absence of unusual circumstances, is not exercised with regard to particular situations but rather in terms of operating policies of stations as viewed over a reasonable period of time. This, in the past, has meant a review, usually in terms of filed complaints, in connection with the applications made each three year period for renewal of station licenses. However, that has been a practice largely traceable to workload necessities, and therefore not so limited by law. Indeed the Commission recently has expressed its views to the Congress that it would be desirable to exercise a greater discretion with respect to the length of licensing periods within the maximum three year license period provided by Section 307(d). It has also initiated rulemaking to this end.

The foundation of the American system of broadcasting was laid in the Radio Act of 1927 when Congress placed the basic responsibility for all matter broadcast to the public at the grass roots level in the hands of the station licensee. That obligation was carried forward into the Communications Act of 1934 and remains unaltered and undivided. The licensee, is, in effect, a "trustee" in the sense that his license to operate his station imposes upon him a non-delegable duty to serve the public interest in the community he had chosen to represent as a broadcaster.

Great confidence and trust are placed in the citizens who have qualified as broadcasters. The primary duty and privilege to select the material to be broadcast to his audience and the operation of his component of this powerful medium of communication is left in his hands. As was stated by the Chairman in behalf of this Commission in recent testimony before a Congressional Committee:[9]

Thus far Congress has not imposed by law an affirmative programming requirement on broadcast licenses. Rather, it has heretofore given licensees a broad discretion in the selection of programs. In recognition of this principle, Congress provided in section 3(h) of the Communications Act that a person engaged in radio broadcasting shall not be deemed a common carrier. To this end the Commission in administering the Act and the courts in interpreting it have consistently maintained that responsibility for the selection and presentation of broadcast material ultimately devolves upon the individual station licensee, and that the fulfillment of such responsibility requires the free exercise of his independent judgment.

As indicated by former President Hoover, then Secretary of Commerce, in the Radio Conference of 1922-25:

The dominant element for consideration in the radio field is, and always will be, the great body of the listening public, millions in number, country wide in distribution. There is no proper line of conflict between the broadcaster and the listener, nor would I attempt to array one against the other. Their interests are mutual, for without the one the other could not exist.

There have been few developments in industrial history to equal the speed and efficiency with which genius and capital have joined to meet radio needs. The great majority of station owners today recognize the burden of service and gladly assume it. Whatever other motive may exist for broadcasting, the pleasing of the listener is always the primary purpose . . .

The greatest public interest must be the deciding factor. I presume that few will dissent as to the correctness of this principle, for all will agree that public good must ever balance private desire; but its acceptance leads to important and far-reaching practical effects, as to which there may not be the same unanimity, but from which, nevertheless, there is no logical escape.

The confines of the licensee's duty are set by the general standard "the public interest, convenience or necessity."[10] The initial and principal execution

---

[9] Testimony of Frederick W. Ford, May 16, 1960, before the Subcommittee on Communications of the Committee on Interstate & Foreign Commerce, United States Senate.

[10] *Cf.* Communications Act of 1934, as amended, *inter alia*, Secs. 307, 309.

of that standard, in terms of the area he is licensed to serve, is the obligation of the licensee. The principal ingredient of such obligation consists of a diligent, positive and continuing effort by the licensee to discover and fulfill the tastes, needs and desires of his service area. If he has accomplished this, he has met his public responsibility. It is the duty of the Commission, in the first instance, to select persons as licensees who meet the qualifications laid down in the Act, and on a continuing basis to review the operations of such licensees from time to time to provide reasonable assurance to the public that the broadcast service it receives is such as its direct and justifiable interest requires.

Historically it is interesting to note that in its review of station performance the Federal Radio Commission sought to extract the general principles of broadcast service which should (1) guide the licensee in his determination of the public interest and (2) be employed by the Commission as an "index" or general frame of reference in evaluating the licensee's discharge of his public duty. The Commission attempted no precise definition of the components of the public interest but left the discernment of its limit to the practical operation of broadcast regulation. It required existing stations to report the types of service which had been provided and called on the public to express its views and preferences as to programs and other broadcast services. It sought information from as many sources as were available in its quest of a fair and equitable basis for the selection of those who might wish to become licensees and the supervision of those who already engaged in broadcasting.

The spirit in which the Radio Commission approached its unprecedented task was to seek to chart a course between the need of arriving at a workable concept of the public interest in station operation, on the one hand, and the prohibition laid on it by the First Amendment to the Constitution of the United States and by Congress in Section 29 of the Federal Radio Act against censorship and interference with free speech, on the other. The Standards or guidelines which evolved from that process, in their essentials, were adopted by the Federal Communications Commission and have remained as the basis for evaluation of broadcast service. They have in the main, been incorporated into various codes and manuals of network and station operation.

It is emphasized, that these standards or guidelines should in no sense constitute a rigid mold for station performance, nor should they be considered as a Commission formula for broadcast service in the public interest. Rather, they should be considered as indicia of the types and areas of service which, on the basis of experience, have usually been accepted by the broadcasters as more or less included in the practical definition of community needs and interests.

Broadcasting licensees must assume responsibility for all material which is broadcast through their facilities. This includes all programs and advertising material which they present to the public. With respect to advertising material the licensee has the additional responsibility to take all reasonable measures to eliminate any false, misleading, or deceptive matter and to avoid abuses with respect to the total amount of time devoted to advertising continuity as well as the frequency with which regular programs are interrupted for advertising messages. This duty is personal to the licensee and may not be delegated. He is obligated to bring his positive responsibility affirmatively to bear upon all who have a hand in providing broadcast matter for transmission through his facilities so as to assure the discharge of his duty to provide acceptable program schedule consonant with operating in the public interest in his community. The broadcaster is obligated to make a positive, diligent and continuing effort, in good faith, to determine the tastes, needs and desires of the public in his community and to provide programming to meet those needs and interests. This again, is a duty personal to the licensee and may not be avoided by delegation of the responsibility to others.

Although the individual station licensee continues to bear legal responsibility for all matter broadcast over his facilities, the structure of broadcasting, as developed in practical operation, is such — especially in television — that, in reality, the station licensee has little part in the creation, production, selection, and control of network program offerings. Licensees place "practical reliance" on networks for the selection and supervision of network programs which, of course, are the principal broadcast fare of the vast majority of television stations throughout the country. [11]

In the fulfillment of his obligation the broadcaster should consider the tastes, needs and desires of the public he is licensed to serve in developing his programming and should exercise conscientious efforts not only to ascertain them but also to carry them out as well as he reasonably can. He should reasonably attempt to meet all such needs and interests on an equitable basis. Particular areas of interest and types of appropriate service may, of course, differ from community to community, and from time to time. However, the Commission does expect its broadcast licensees to take the necessary steps to inform themselves of the real needs and interests of the areas they serve and to provide programming which in fact constitutes a diligent effort, in good faith, to provide for those needs and interests.

The major elements usually necessary to meet the public interest, needs and desires of the community in which the station is located as developed by the industry, and recognized by the Commission, have included: (1) Opportunity for Local Self-Expression, (2) The Development and Use of Local Talent, (3) Programs for Children, (4) Religious Programs, (5) Educational Programs, (6) Public Affairs Programs, (7) Editorialization by Licensees, (8) Political Broadcasts, (9) Agricultural Programs, (10) News Programs, (11) Weather and Market Reports, (12) Sports Programs, (13) Service to Minority Groups, (14) Entertainment Programming.

---

[11] The Commission, in recognition of this problem as it affects the licensees, has recently recommended to the Congress enactment of legislation providing for direct regulation of networks in certain respects. [Enactment did not occur.—Ed.]

The elements set out above are neither all-embracing nor constant. We re-emphasize that they do not serve and have never been intended as a rigid mold or fixed formula for station operations. The ascertainment of the needed elements of the broadcast matter to be provided by a particular licensee for the audience he is obligated to serve remains primarily the function of the licensee. His honest and prudent judgments will be accorded great weight by the Commission. Indeed, any other course would tend to substitute the judgment of the Commission for that of the licensee.

The programs provided first by "chains" of stations and then by networks have always been recognized by this Commission as of great value to the station licensee in providing a well-rounded community service. The importance of network programs need not be re-emphasized as they have constituted an integral part of the well-rounded program service provided by the broadcast business in most communities.

Our own observations and the testimony in this inquiry have persuaded us that there is no public interest basis for distinguishing between sustaining and commercially sponsored programs in evaluating station performance. However, this does not relieve the station from responsibility for retaining the flexibility to accommodate public needs.

Sponsorship of public affairs, and other similar programs may very well encourage broadcasters to greater efforts in these vital areas. This is borne out by statements made in this proceeding in which it was pointed out that under modern conditions sponsorship fosters rather than diminishes the availability of important public affairs and "cultural" broadcast programming. There is some convincing evidence, for instance, that at the network level there is a direct relation between commercial sponsorship and "clearance" of public affairs and other "cultural" programs. Agency executives have testified that there is unused advertising support for public affairs type programming. The networks and some stations have scheduled these types of programs during "prime time."

The Communications Act[12] provides that the Commission may grant construction permits and station licenses, or modifications or renewals thereof, "only upon written application" setting forth the information required by the Act and the Commission's Rules and Regulations. If, upon examination of any such application, the Commission shall find the public interest, convenience, and necessity would be served by the granting thereof, it shall grant said application. If it does not so find, it shall so advise the applicant and other known parties in interest of all objections to the application and the applicant shall then be given an opportunity to supply additional information. If the Commission cannot then make the necessary finding, the application is designated for hearing and the applicant bears the burden of providing proof of the public interest.

During our hearings there seemed to be some misunderstanding as to the

[12] Section 308(a).

nature and use of the "statistical" data regarding programming and advertising required by our application forms. We wish to stress that no one may be summarily judged as to the service he has performed on the basis of the information contained in his application. As we said long ago:

It should be emphasized that the statistical data before the Commission constitute an index only of the manner of operation of the stations and are not considered by the Commission as conclusive of the over-all operation of the stations in question.

Licensees will have an opportunity to show the nature of their program service and to introduce other relevant evidence which would demonstrate that in actual operation the program service of the station is, in fact, a well rounded program service and is in conformity with the promises and representations previously made in prior applications to the Commission.[13]

As we have said above, the principal ingredient of the licensee's obligation to operate his station in the public interest is the diligent, positive, and continuing effort by the licensee to discover and fulfill the tastes, needs, and desires of his community or service area, for broadcast service.

To enable the Commission in its licensing functions to make the necessary public interest finding, we intend to revise Part IV of our application forms to require a statement by the applicant, whether for new facilities, renewal or modification, as to: (1) the measures he has taken and the effort he has made to determine the tastes, needs and desires of his community or service area, and (2) the manner in which he proposes to meet those needs and desires.

Thus we do not intend to guide the licensee along the path of programming; on the contrary the licensee must find his own path with the guidance of those whom his signal is to serve. We will thus steer clear of the bans of censorship without disregarding the public's vital interest. What we propose will not be served by pre-planned program format submissions accompanied by complimentary references from local citizens. What we propose is documented program submissions prepared as the result of assiduous planning and consultation covering two main areas: first, a canvass of the listening public who will receive the signal and who constitute a definite public interest figure; second, consultation with leaders in community life – public officials, educators, religious, the entertainment media, agriculture, business, labor – professional and eleemosynary organizations, and others who bespeak the interests which make up the community.

By the care spent in obtaining and reflecting the views thus obtained, which clearly cannot be accepted without attention to the business judgment of the licensee if his station is to be an operating success, will the standard of programming in the public interest be best fulfilled. This would not ordinarily be

[13] Public Notice (98501), Sept. 20, 1946, "Status of Standard Broadcast Applications."

the case if program formats have been decided upon by the licensee before he undertakes his planning and consultation, for the result would show little stimulation on the part of the two local groups above referenced. And it is the composite of their contributive planning, led and sifted by the expert judgment of the licensee, which will assure to the station the appropriate attention to the public interest which will permit the Commission to find that a license may issue. By his narrative development, in his application, of the planning, consulting, shaping, revising, creating, discarding and evaluation of programming thus conceived or discussed, the licensee discharges the public interest facet of his business calling without Government dictation or supervision and permits the Commission to discharge its responsibility to the public without invasion of spheres of freedom properly denied to it. By the practicality and specificity of his narrative the licensee facilitates the application of expert judgment by the Commission. Thus, if a particular kind of educational program could not be feasibly assisted (by funds or service) by educators for more than a few time periods, it would be idle for program composition to place it in weekly focus. Private ingenuity and educational interest should look further, toward imple- mental suggestions of practical yet constructive value. The broadcaster's license is not intended to convert his business into "an instrumentality of the federal government"; [14] neither, on the other hand, may he ignore the public interest which his application for a license should thus define and his operations thereafter reasonably observe.

Numbers of suggestions were made during the *en banc* hearings concerning possible uses by the Commission of codes of broadcast practices adopted by segments of the industry as part of a process of self-regulation. While the Commission has not endorsed any specific code of broadcast practices, we consider the efforts of the industry to maintain high standards of conduct to be highly commendable and urge that the industry persevere in these efforts.

The Commission recognizes that submissions, by applicants, concerning their past and future programming policies and performance provide one important basis for deciding whether — insofar as broadcast services are concerned — we may properly make the public interest finding requisite to the grant of an application for a standard FM or television broadcast station. The particular manner in which applicants are required to depict their proposed or past broadcast policies and services (including the broadcasting of commercial announcements) may therefore, have significant bearing upon the Commission's ability to discharge its statutory duties in the matter. Conscious of the importance of reporting requirements, the Commission on November 24, 1958 initiated proceedings (Docket No. 12673) to consider revisions to the rules prescribing the form and content of reports on broadcast programming.

---

[14] "The defendant is not an instrumentality of the federal government but a privately owned corporation." *McIntire* v. *Wm. Penn Broadcasting Co.*, 151 F. 2d 597, 600.

Aided by numerous helpful suggestions offered by witnesses in the recent *en banc* hearings on broadcast programming, the Commission is at present engaged in a thorough study of this subject. Upon completion of that study we will announce, for comment by all interested parties, such further revisions to the present reporting requirements as we think will best conduce to an awareness, by broadcasters, of their responsibilities to the public and to effective, efficient processing, by the Commission, of applications for broadcast licenses and renewals.

To this end, we will initiate further rule making on the subject at the earliest practicable date.

27

The Great Debates Law

Public Law 677, 86th Congress
August 24, 1960

This temporary suspension of Section 315 permitted broadcast stations to carry the so-called "Great Debates" between John F. Kennedy and Richard M. Nixon in 1960 without offering "equal time" to the many, splinter party presidential aspirants. The Senate Joint Resolution was passed only after the major parties' candidates were selected at the national political conventions. Congress has passed no similar suspension, and 1964, 1968, and 1972 saw no joint broadcast appearances by presidential candidates.

In 1972 Congress made "failure to allow reasonable access to . . . the use of a broadcasting station" by candidates for federal office a ground for license revocation (Section 312(a)(7) of the Communications Act; see pp. 535-536). In 1975 the FCC reinterpreted Section 315(a)(4)'s exemption of "on-the-spot coverage of bona fide news events" (p. 538) to permit licensees to carry candidates' debates and news conferences free of the "equal time" obligation (*Aspen Institute*, 55 FCC 2d 697). Accordingly, when the League of Women Voters arranged debates between Gerald Ford and Jimmy Carter in 1976, broadcast coverage was allowed.

Related Reading: 45, 54, 55, 66, 93, 128, 149, 232, 233, 246.

Resolved by the Senate and House of Representatives of the United States of America in Congress assembled, That that part of section 315(a) of the Communications Act of 1934, as amended, which requires any licensee of a broadcast station who permits any person who is a legally qualified candidate for any public office to use a broadcasting station to afford equal opportunities to all other such candidates for that office in the use of such broadcasting station, is suspended for the period of the 1960 presidential and vice presidential campaigns with respect to nominees for the offices of President and Vice President of the United States. Nothing in the foregoing shall be construed as relieving broadcasters from the obligation imposed upon them under this Act to operate in the public interest.

(2) The Federal Communications Commission shall make a report to the Congress, not later than March 1, 1961, with respect to the effect of the provisions of this joint resolution and any recommendations the Commission may have for amendments to the Communications Act of 1934 as a result of experience under the provisions of this joint resolution.

28

The "Vast Wasteland"

Address by Newton N. Minow to the National Association of Broadcasters, Washington, D.C.* May 9, 1961

Newton N. Minow served only 28 months as FCC Chairman, but no commissioner before or since matched his impact on the general public and broadcasting. A Chicago lawyer and associate of Adlai E. Stevenson, Minow was named to the Commission early in 1961 by President John F. Kennedy. He resigned in the middle of 1963 to take a more lucrative legal position in private industry.

This speech alarmed broadcasters, made newspaper headlines, and evoked favorable public response and comment in the print media. It signaled the start of a new regulatory activism and an end to the corruption that riddled the FCC in the closing years of the Eisenhower administration, when two commissioners (including a chairman) were forced to resign because of their scandalous dealings with some of the broadcasters they were supposed to regulate.

Some aspects of Minow's regulatory program, outlined in this address, attracted wide support and were realized in the following 2 years. Educational television station construction was given a $32 million boost when Congress passed the "ETV Facilities Act of 1962" (Public Law 87-447, approved May 1, 1962). The prospects for UHF television brightened with enactment of the "All Channel Receiver Law" (Public Law 87-529, approved July 10, 1962) which added Sections 303(s) and 330 to the

*Reprinted with permission from Newton N. Minow, *Equal Time: The Private Broadcaster and the Public Interest*, ed. Lawrence Laurent (New York: Atheneum, 1964), pp. 48-64.

Communications Act (see pp. 526 and 543). But protection of Pay TV from infanticide and reduction of broadcast advertising excesses were among the regulatory objectives Minow failed to achieve because of his short stay in office and the shifting regulatory climate following his departure.

It was Minow's outspoken discontent with television programming and his vow to lead the FCC to review broadcast content more closely when acting on license renewals that made broadcasters apprehensive. Anxious not to find out if the Chairman really meant what he said, networks and stations alike attempted to make the "vast wasteland" bloom with more public affairs programs, improved children's offerings, and a de-emphasis on violent action shows. The change proved to be as temporary as Minow's tenure at the FCC. More lasting was the technique of "regulation by raised eyebrow" that Minow used with considerable success in this speech and which his successors have continued to employ in the delicate area of broadcast programming with varied results.

Related Reading: 3, 64, 127, 156, 171, 187, 198, 238.

Governor Collins, Distinguished Guests, Ladies and Gentlemen:

Thank you for this opportunity to meet with you today. This is my first public address since I took over my new job. When the New Frontiersmen rode into town, I locked myself in my office to do my homework and get my feet wet. But apparently I haven't managed to stay out of hot water. I seem to have detected a certain nervous apprehension about what I might say or do when I emerged from that locked office for this, my maiden station break.

First, let me begin by dispelling a rumor. I was not picked for this job because I regard myself as the fastest draw on the New Frontier.

Second, let me start a rumor. Like you, I have carefully read President Kennedy's messages about the regulatory agencies, conflict of interest and the dangers of *ex parte* contacts. And of course, we at the Federal Communications Commission will do our part. Indeed, I may even suggest that we change the name of the FCC to The Seven Untouchables!

It may also come as a surprise to some of you, but I want you to know that you have my admiration and respect. Yours is a most honorable profession. Anyone who is in the broadcasting business has a tough row to hoe. You earn your bread by using public property. When you work in broadcasting, you volunteer for public service, public pressure and public regulation. You must compete with other attractions and other investments, and the only way you can do it is to prove to us every three years that you should have been in business in the first place.

I can think of easier ways to make a living.

But I cannot think of more satisfying ways.

I admire your courage—but that doesn't mean I would make life any easier for you. Your license lets you use the public's airwaves as trustees for 180 million Americans. The public is your beneficiary. If you want to stay on as trustees, you must deliver a decent return to the public—not only to your stockholders. So, as a representative of the public, your health and your product are among my chief concerns.

As to your health: let's talk only of television today. In 1960 gross broadcast revenues of the television industry were over $1,268,000,000; profit before taxes was $243,900,000—an average return on revenue of 19.2 per cent. Compare this with 1959, when gross broadcast revenues were $1,163,900,000, and profit before taxes was $222,300,000, an average return on revenue of 19.1 per cent. So, the percentage increase of total revenues from 1959 to 1960 was 9 per cent, and the percentage increase of profit was 9.7 per cent. This, despite a recession. For your investors, the price has indeed been right.

I have confidence in your health.

But not in your product.

It is with this and much more in mind that I come before you today.

One editorialist in the trade press wrote that "the FCC of the New Frontier is going to be one of the toughest FCC's in the history of broadcast regulation." If he meant that we intend to enforce the law in the public interest, let me make it perfectly clear that he is right—we do.

If he meant that we intend to muzzle or censor broadcasting, he is dead wrong.

It would not surprise me if some of you had expected me to come here today and say in effect, "Clean up your own house or the government will do it for you."

Well, in a limited sense, you would be right—I've just said it.

But I want to say to you earnestly that it is not in that spirit that I come before you today, nor is it in that spirit that I intend to serve the FCC.

I am in Washington to help broadcasting, not to harm it; to strengthen it, not weaken it; to reward it, not punish it; to encourage it, not threaten it; to stimulate it, not censor it.

Above all, I am here to uphold and protect the public interest.

What do we mean by "the public interest"? Some say the public interest is merely what interests the public.

I disagree.

So does your distinguished president, Governor Collins. In a recent speech he said, "Broadcasting, to serve the public interest, must have a soul and a conscience, a burning desire to excel, as well as to sell; the urge to build the character, citizenship and intellectual stature of people, as well as to expand the gross national product. . . . By no means do I imply that broadcasters disregard the public interest. . . . But a much better job can be done, and should be done."

I could not agree more.

And I would add that in today's world, with chaos in Laos and the Congo aflame, with Communist tyranny on our Caribbean doorstep and relentless pressure on our Atlantic alliance, with social and economic problems at home of the gravest nature, yes, and with technological knowledge that makes it possible, as our President has said, not only to destroy our world but to destroy poverty around the world—in a time of peril and opportunity, the old complacent, unbalanced fare of action-adventure and situation comedies is simply not good enough.

Your industry possesses the most powerful voice in America. It has an inescapable duty to make that voice ring with intelligence and with leadership. In a few years this exciting industry has grown from a novelty to an instrument of overwhelming impact on the American people. It should be making ready for the kind of leadership that newspapers and magazines assumed years ago, to make our people aware of their world.

Ours has been called the jet age, the atomic age, the space age. It is also, I submit, the television age. And just as history will decide whether the leaders of today's world employed the atom to destroy the world or rebuild it for mankind's benefit, so will history decide whether today's broadcasters employed their powerful voice to enrich the people or debase them.

If I seem today to address myself chiefly to the problems of television, I don't want any of you radio broadcasters to think we've gone to sleep at your switch—we haven't. We still listen. But in recent years most of the controversies and crosscurrents in broadcast programing have swirled around television. And so my subject today is the television industry and the public interest.

Like everybody, I wear more than one hat. I am the Chairman of the FCC. I am also a television viewer and the husband and father of other television viewers. I have seen a great many television programs that seemed to me eminently worthwhile, and I am not talking about the much-bemoaned good old days of "Playhouse 90" and "Studio One."

I am talking about this past season. Some were wonderfully entertaining, such as "The Fabulous Fifties," the "Fred Astaire Show" and the "Bing Crosby Special"; some were dramatic and moving, such as Conrad's "Victory" and "Twilight Zone"; some were marvelously informative, such as "The Nation's Future," "CBS Reports," and "The Valiant Years." I could list many more—programs that I am sure everyone here felt enriched his own life and that of his family. When television is good, nothing—not the theater, not the magazines or newspapers—nothing is better.

But when television is bad, nothing is worse. I invite you to sit down in front of your television set when your station goes on the air and stay there without a book, magazine, newspaper, profit-and-loss sheet or rating book to distract you—and keep your eyes glued to that set until the station signs off. I can assure you that you will observe a vast wasteland.

You will see a procession of game shows, violence, audience participation shows, formula comedies about totally unbelievable families, blood and thunder, mayhem, violence, sadism, murder, Western badmen, Western good men, private eyes, gangsters, more violence and cartoons. And, endlessly, commercials—many screaming, cajoling and offending. And most of all, boredom. True, you will see a few things you will enjoy. But they will be very, very few. And if you think I exaggerate, try it.

Is there one person in this room who claims that broadcasting can't do better?

Well, a glance at next season's proposed programing can give us little heart. Of seventy-three and a half hours of prime evening time, the networks have tentatively scheduled fifty-nine hours to categories of "action-adventure," situation comedy, variety, quiz and movies.

Is there one network president in this room who claims he can't do better?

Well, is there at least one network president who believes that the other networks can't do better?

Gentlemen, your trust accounting with your beneficiaries is overdue.

Never have so few owed so much to so many.

Why is so much of television so bad? I have heard many answers: demands of your advertisers; competition for ever higher ratings; the need always to attract a mass audience; the high cost of television programs; the insatiable appetite for programing material—these are some of them. Unquestionably these are tough problems not susceptible to easy answers.

But I am not convinced that you have tried hard enough to solve them.

I do not accept the idea that the present over-all programing is aimed accurately at the public taste. The ratings tell us only that some people have their television sets turned on, and of that number, so many are tuned to one channel and so many to another. They don't tell us what the public might watch if they were offered half a dozen additional choices. A rating, at best, is an indication of how many people saw what you gave them. Unfortunately it does not reveal the depth of the penetration, or the intensity of reaction, and it never reveals what the acceptance would have been if what you gave them had been better—if all the forces of art and creativity and daring and imagination had been unleashed. I believe in the people's good sense and good taste, and I am not convinced that the people's taste is as low as some of you assume.

My concern with the rating services is not with their accuracy. Perhaps they are accurate. I really don't know. What, then, is wrong with the ratings? It's not been their accuracy—it's been their use.

Certainly I hope you will agree that ratings should have little influence where children are concerned. The best estimates indicate that during the hours of 5 to 6 P.M., 60 per cent of your audience is composed of children under twelve. And most young children today, believe it or not, spend as much time watching television as they do in the schoolroom. I repeat—let that sink in—most young children today spend as much time watching television as they do in the schoolroom. It used to be said that there were three great influences on a child: home, school and church. Today there is a fourth great influence, and you ladies and gentlemen control it.

If parents, teachers and ministers conducted their responsibilities by following the ratings, children would have a steady diet of ice cream, school holidays and no Sunday School. What about your responsibilities? Is there no room on television to teach, to inform, to uplift, to stretch, to enlarge the capacities of our children? Is there no room for programs deepening their understanding of children in other lands? Is there no room for a children's news show explaining something about the world to them at their level of understanding? Is there no room for reading the great literature of the past, teaching them the great traditions of freedom? There are some fine children's shows, but they are drowned out in the massive doses of cartoons, violence and more violence. Must these be your trademarks? Search your consciences and see if you cannot offer more to your young beneficiaries, whose future you guide so many hours each and every day.

What about adult programing and ratings? You know, newspaper publishers take popularity ratings too. The answers are pretty clear; it is almost always the comics, followed by the advice-to-the-lovelorn columns. But, ladies and gentlemen, the news is still on the front page of all newspapers, the editorials are not replaced by more comics, the newspapers have not become one long collection of advice to the lovelorn. Yet newspapers do not need a license from the government to be in business—they do not use public property. But in television— where your responsibilities as public trustees are so plain—the moment that the ratings indicate that Westerns are popular, there are new imitations of Westerns on the air faster than the old coaxial cable could take us from Hollywood to New York. Broadcasting cannot continue to live by the numbers. Ratings ought to be the slave of the broadcaster, not his master. And you and I both know that the rating services themselves would agree.

Let me make clear that what I am talking about is balance. I believe that the public interest is made up of many interests. There are many people in this great country, and you must serve all of us. You will get no argument from me if you say that, given a choice between a Western and a symphony, more people will watch the Western. I like Westerns and private eyes too—but a steady diet for the whole country is obviously not in the public interest. We all know that people would more often prefer to be entertained than stimulated or informed. But your obligations are not satisfied if you look only to popularity as a test of what to broadcast. You are not only in show business; you are free to communicate ideas as well as relaxation. You must provide a wider range of choices, more diversity, more alternatives. It is not enough to cater to the nation's whims—you must also serve the nation's needs.

And I would add this—that if some of you persist in a relentless search for the highest rating and the lowest common denominator, you may very well lose your audience. Because, to paraphrase a great American who was recently my law partner, the people are wise, wiser than some of the broadcasters—and politicians—think.

As you may have gathered, I would like to see television improved. But how is this to be brought about? By voluntary action by the broadcasters themselves? By direct government intervention? Or how?

Let me address myself now to my role, not as a viewer, but as Chairman of the FCC. I could not if I would chart for you this afternoon in detail all of the actions I contemplate. Instead, I want to make clear some of the fundamental principles which guide me.

First: the people own the air. They own it as much in prime evening time as they do at 6 o'clock Sunday morning. For every hour that the people give you, you owe them something. I intend to see that your debt is paid with service.

Second: I think it would be foolish and wasteful for us to continue any worn-out wrangle over the problems of payola, rigged quiz shows, and other mistakes of the past. There are laws on the books which we will enforce. But there is no chip on my shoulder. We live together in perilous, uncertain times; we face together staggering problems; and we must not waste much time now by rehashing the clichés of past controversy. To quarrel over the past is to lose the future.

Third: I believe in the free enterprise system. I want to see broadcasting improved and I want you to do the job. I am proud to champion your cause. It is not rare for American businessmen to serve a public trust. Yours is a special trust because it is imposed by law.

Fourth: I will do all I can to help educational television. There are still not enough educational stations, and major centers of the country still lack usable educational channels. If there were a limited number of printing presses in this country, you may be sure that a fair proportion of them would be put to educational use. Educational television has an enormous contribution to make to the future, and I intend to give it a hand along the way. If there is not a nationwide educational television system in this country, it will not be the fault of the FCC.

Fifth: I am unalterably opposed to governmental censorship. There will be no suppression of programing which does not meet with bureaucratic tastes. Censorship strikes at the taproot of our free society.

Sixth: I did not come to Washington to idly observe the squandering of the public's airwaves. The squandering of our airwaves is no less important than the lavish waste of any precious natural resource. I intend to take the job of Chairman of the FCC very seriously. I believe in the gravity of my own particular sector of the New Frontier. There will be times perhaps when you will consider that I take myself or my job *too* seriously. Frankly, I don't care if you do. For I am convinced that either one takes this job seriously—or one can be seriously taken.

Now, how will these principles be applied? Clearly, at the heart of the FCC's authority lies its power to license, to renew or fail to renew, or to revoke a license. As you know, when your license comes up for renewal, your performance is compared with your promises. I understand that many people feel that in the past licenses were often renewed *pro forma*. I say to you now: renewal will not be *pro forma* in the future. There is nothing permanent or sacred about a broadcast license.

But simply matching promises and performance is not enough. I intend to do more. I intend to find out whether the people care. I intend to find out whether the community which each broadcaster serves believes he has been serving the public interest. When a renewal is set down for hearing, I intend—wherever possible—to hold a well-advertised public hearing, right in the community you have promised to serve. I want the people who own the air and the homes that television enters to tell you and the FCC what's been going on. I want the people—if they are truly interested in the service you give them—to make notes, document cases, tell us the facts. For those few of you who really believe that the public interest is merely what interests the public—I hope that these hearings will arouse no little interest.

The FCC has a fine reserve of monitors—almost 180 million Americans gathered around 56 million sets. If you want those monitors to be your friends at court—it's up to you.

Some of you may say, "Yes, but I still do not know where the line is between a grant of a renewal and the hearing you just spoke of." My answer is: why should you want to know how close you can come to the edge of the cliff? What the Commission asks of you is to make a conscientious good-faith effort to serve the public interest. Every one of you serves a community in which the people would benefit by educational, religious, instructive or other public service programing. Every one of you serves an area which has local needs—as to local elections, controversial issues, local news, local talent. Make a serious, genuine effort to put on that programing. When you do, you will not be playing brinkmanship with the public interest.

What I've been saying applies to broadcast stations. Now a station break for the networks:

You know your importance in this great industry. Today, more than one-half of all hours of television station programing comes from the networks; in prime time, this rises to more than three-fourths of the available hours.

You know that the FCC has been studying network operations for some time. I intend to press this to a speedy conclusion with useful results. I can tell you right now, however, that I am deeply concerned with concentration of power in the hands of the networks. As a result, too many local stations have foregone any efforts at local programing, with little use of live talent and local service. Too many local stations operate with one hand on the network switch and the other on a projector loaded with old movies. We want the individual stations to be free to meet their legal responsibilities to serve their communities.

I join Governor Collins in his views so well expressed to the advertisers who use the public air. I urge the networks to join him and undertake a very special mission on behalf of this industry: you can tell your advertisers, "This is the high quality we are going to serve—take it or other people will. If you think you can find a better place to move automobiles, cigarettes and soap—go ahead and try."

Tell your sponsors to be less concerned with costs per thousand and more concerned with understanding per millions. And remind your stockholders that an investment in broadcasting is buying a share in public responsibility.

The networks can start this industry on the road to freedom from the dictatorship of numbers.

But there is more to the problem than network influences on stations or advertiser influences on networks. I know the problems networks face in trying to clear some of their best programs—the informational programs that exemplify public service. They are your finest hours, whether sustaining or commercial, whether regularly scheduled or special; these are the signs that broadcasting knows the way to leadership. They make the public's trust in you a wise choice.

They should be seen. As you know, we are readying for use new forms by which broadcast stations will report their programing to the Commission. You probably also know that special attention will be paid in these reports to public service programing. I believe that stations taking network service should also be required to report the extent of the local clearance of network public service programing, and when they fail to clear them, they should explain why. If it is to put on some outstanding local program, this is one reason. But, if it is simply to carry some old movie, that is an entirely different matter. The Commission should consider such clearance reports carefully when making up its mind about the licensee's over-all programing.

We intend to move—and as you know, indeed the FCC was rapidly moving in other new areas before the new administration arrived in Washington. And I want to pay my public respects to my very able predecessor, Fred Ford, and my colleagues on the Commission who have welcomed me to the FCC with warmth and cooperation.

We have approved an experiment with pay TV, and in New York we are testing the potential of UHF broadcasting. Either or both of these may revolutionize television. Only a foolish prophet would venture to guess the direction they will take, and their effect. But we intend that they shall be explored fully— for they are part of broadcasting's new frontier.

The questions surrounding pay TV are largely economic. The questions surrounding UHF are largely technological. We are going to give the infant pay TV a chance to prove whether it can offer a useful service; we are going to protect it from those who would strangle it in its crib.

As for UHF, I'm sure you know about our test in the canyons of New York City. We will take every possible positive step to break through the allocations barrier into UHF. We will put this sleeping giant to use, and in the years ahead we may have twice as many channels operating in cities where now there are only two or three. We may have a half-dozen networks instead of three.

I have told you that I believe in the free enterprise system. I believe that most of television's problems stem from lack of competition. This is the importance of UHF to me: with more channels on the air, we will be able to provide every community with enough stations to offer service to all parts of the public. Programs with a mass-market appeal required by mass-product advertisers certainly will still be available. But other stations will recognize the need to appeal to more limited markets and to special tastes. In this way we can all have a much wider range of programs.

Television should thrive on this competition—and the country should benefit from alternative sources of service to the public. And, Governor Collins, I hope the NAB will benefit from many new members.

Another, and perhaps the most important, frontier: television will rapidly join the parade into space. International television will be with us soon. No one knows how long it will be until a broadcast from a studio in New York will be viewed in India as well as in Indiana, will be seen in the Congo as it is seen in Chicago. But as surely as we are meeting here today, that day will come—and once again our world will shrink.

What will the people of other countries think of us when they see our Western badmen and good men punching each other in the jaw in between the shooting? What will the Latin American or African child learn of America from our great communications industry? We cannot permit television in its present form to be our voice overseas.

There is your challenge to leadership. You must reexamine some fundamentals of your industry. You must open your minds and open your hearts to the limitless horizons of tomorrow.

I can suggest some words that should serve to guide you:

Television and all who participate in it are jointly accountable to the American public for respect for the special needs of children, for community responsibility, for the advancement of education and culture, for the acceptability of the program materials chosen, for decency and decorum in production, and for propriety in advertising. This responsibility cannot be discharged by any given group of programs, but can be discharged only through the highest standards of respect for the American home, applied to every moment of every program presented by television.

Program materials should enlarge the horizons of the viewer, provide him with wholesome entertainment, afford helpful stimulation, and remind him of the responsibilities which the citizen has toward his society.

These words are not mine. They are yours. They are taken literally from your own Television Code. They reflect the leadership and aspirations of your own great industry. I urge you to respect them as I do. And I urge you to respect the intelligent and farsighted leadership of Governor LeRoy Collins and to make this meeting a creative act. I urge you at this meeting and, after you leave, back home, at your stations and your networks, to strive ceaselessly to improve your product and to better serve your viewers, the American people.

I hope that we at the FCC will not allow ourselves to become so bogged down in the mountain of papers, hearings, memoranda, orders and the daily routine that we close our eyes to the wider view of the public interest. And I hope that you broadcasters will not permit yourselves to become so absorbed in the chase for ratings, sales and profits that you lose this wider view. Now more than ever before in broadcasting's history the times demand the best of all of us.

We need imagination in programing, not sterility; creativity, not imitation; experimentation, not conformity; excellence, not mediocrity. Television is filled with creative, imaginative people. You must strive to set them free.

Television in its young life has had many hours of greatness—its "Victory at Sea," its Army-McCarthy hearings, its "Peter Pan," its "Kraft Theater," its "See It Now," its "Project 20," the World Series, its political conventions and campaigns, the Great Debates—and it has had its endless hours of mediocrity and its moments of public disgrace. There are estimates that today the average viewer spends about 200 minutes daily with television, while the average reader spends thirty-eight minutes with magazines and forty minutes with newspapers. Television has grown faster than a teenager, and now it is time to grow up.

What you gentlemen broadcast through the people's air affects the people's taste, their knowledge, their opinions, their understanding of themselves and of their world. And their future.

The power of instantaneous sight and sound is without precedent in mankind's history. This is an awesome power. It has limitless capabilities for good— and for evil. And it carries with it awesome responsibilities—responsibilities which you and I cannot escape.

In his stirring Inaugural Address, our President said, "And so, my fellow Americans: ask not what your country can do for you—ask what you can do for your country."

Ladies and Gentlemen:

Ask not what broadcasting can do for you—ask what you can do for broadcasting.

I urge you to put the people's airwaves to the service of the people and the cause of freedom. You must help prepare a generation for great decisions. You must help a great nation fulfill its future.

Do this, and I pledge you our help.

29

President Kennedy's Statement on Communication Satellite Policy

Senate Report No. 1584, 87th Congress, 2d Session
(pp. 25-27)
July 24, 1961

Russia's successful launch of the first artificial Earth satellite, Sputnik I, on October 4, 1957, was hailed as an event of major significance throughout the world. For America it marked the start of efforts to equal or surpass the Soviet accomplishment. President Kennedy gave high priority to the United States' space effort, pledging even to land a man on the moon—a feat that was first achieved in July, 1969.

The National Aeronautics and Space Administration launched its first experimental communications satellite, Echo I, on August 12, 1960. Others followed, including synchronous satellites, heralding the arrival of global communication free of land lines. The potential of satellites to serve as functional alternatives to cable, telephone, telegraph, and even terrestrial broadcast transmitters presented thorny questions of public policy. Early in his administration President Kennedy provided policy leadership in the statement below, which led to enactment of the Communications Satellite Act a year later (Public Law 87–624, approved August 31, 1962). The Communications Satellite Corporation (Comsat) authorized by this law was incorporated on February 1, 1963, as a private firm, regulated by the FCC, and given a monopoly over American international communications via satellite. Through interaction with the International Telecommunications Satellite Consortium (INTELSAT), Comsat became an effective "carrier's carrier," a common carrier providing services to other common carriers such as AT&T.

The 1962 Comsat Act said little about the use of satellites for domestic communications. When the FCC was faced with the first proposal to operate a domestic system in 1965, it found itself sailing in uncharted waters. It took 7 years before the Commission finally enunciated its policy guidelines [*Domestic Communications-Satellite Facilities*, 35 FCC 2d 844 (1972)], which encouraged competition in domestic satellite operations by permitting open entry in a branch of communication that had previously been dominated by monopolistic policies and practices.

By the late 1970's both international and domestic communication via satellite had become commonplace. Although direct broadcasting by satellite to the home is technologically feasible, the powerful vested broadcasting interests favor the status quo. However, domestic satellites are often used instead of terrestrial relay systems to interconnect cable TV systems, and plans are being implemented to apply this concept to broadcasting stations affiliated with networks.

Related Reading: 43, 56, 65, 72, 87, 122, 147, 220.

Science and technology have progressed to such a degree that communication through the use of space satellites has become possible. Through this country's leadership, this competence should be developed for global benefit at the earliest practicable time.

To accomplish this practical objective, increased resources must be devoted to the task and a coordinated national policy should guide the use of those resources in the public interest. Consequently, on May 25, 1961, I asked the Congress for additional funds to accelerate the use of space satellites for worldwide communications. Also, on June 15, I asked the Vice President to have the Space Council make the necessary studies and policy recommendations for the optimum development and operation of such system. This has been done. The primary guideline for the preparation of such recommendations was that public interest objectives be given the highest priority.

I again invite all nations to participate in a communication satellite system, in the interest of world peace and closer brotherhood among peoples throughout the world.

The present status of the communication satellite programs, both civil and military, is that of research and development. To date, no arrangements between the Government and private industry contain any commitments as to an operational system.

A.   POLICY OF OWNERSHIP AND OPERATION

Private ownership and operation of the U.S. portion of the system is favored, provided that such ownership and operation meet the following policy requirements:

1.   New and expanded international communications services be made available at the earliest practicable date;

2.   Make the system global in coverage so as to provide efficient communication service throughout the whole world as soon as technically feasible, including service where individual portions of the coverage are not profitable;

3.   Provide opportunities for foreign participation through ownership or otherwise, in the communications satellite system;

4.   Nondiscriminatory use of and equitable access to the system by present and future authorized communications carriers;

5.   Effective competition, such as competitive bidding, in the acquisition of equipment used in the system;

6.   Structure of ownership or control which will assure maximum possible competition;

7.   Full compliance with antitrust legislation and with the regulatory controls of the Government;

8.   Development of an economical system, the benefits of which will be reflected in oversea communication rates.

B.   POLICY OF GOVERNMENT RESPONSIBILITY

In addition to its regulatory responsibilities, the U.S. Government will—

1.   Conduct and encourage research and development to advance the state of the art and to give maximum assurance of rapid and continuous scientific and technological progress;

2.   Conduct or maintain supervision of international agreements and negotiations;

3.   Control all launching of U.S. spacecraft;

4.   Make use of the commercial system for general governmental purposes and establish separate communications satellite systems when required to meet unique government needs which cannot, in the national interest, be met by the commercial system;

5.   Assure the effective use of the radio-frequency spectrum;

6.   Assure the ability to discontinue the electronic functioning of satellites when required in the interest of communication efficiency and effectiveness;

7.   Provide technical assistance to newly developing countries in order to help attain an effective global system as soon as practicable;

8.   Examine with other countries the most constructive role for the United Nations, including the ITU, in international space communications.

C.   COORDINATION

I have asked the full cooperation of all agencies of the Government in the vigorous implementation of the policies stated herein. The National Aeronautics and Space Council will provide continuing policy coordination and will also have responsibility for recommending to me any actions needed to achieve full and prompt compliance with the policy With the guidelines provided here, I am anxious that development of this new technology to bring the farthest corner of the globe within reach by voice and visual communication, fairly and equitably available for use, proceed with all possible promptness.

30

The Carter Mountain Case

In re Carter Mountain Transmission Corp.

32 FCC 459

February 14, 1962

Cable television (CATV) systems began operating in the United States during the TV "freeze" in 1949, when they were known as "community antenna television systems." At first they merely served as a small town equivalent of urban apartment house master antenna systems by bringing TV reception by wire to subscribers unable to obtain clear reception on their own because of their distance from the small number of television station transmitters or because of terrain features that blocked TV signals.

In the early 1950's some CATV systems began to "import" TV station signals from distant cities via point-to-point microwave relay facilities. Cable systems grew in number and size. They expanded the services they offered to their subscribers to include not only local and distant broadcast signals but locally originated ("cablecast") programming as well. Cable's growth threatened the economic health of TV broadcasters in the small markets that started to receive local television service from one or two stations following the end of the "freeze" in 1952. By the end of the decade the FCC found it impossible to ignore the growing clamor of complaining TV licensees.

When the Commission first considered CATV's competitive impact on open circuit television, the agency disclaimed jurisdiction over cable, for it was neither an interstate common carrier by wire (therefore not subject to regulation under Title II of the

Communications Act) nor was it engaged in radio communication over the air (thereby falling outside the reach of Title III). The FCC requested legislative authority to exercise modest control over CATV, but in 1960 Congress failed to act favorably on the measure. As CATV continued to grow and broadcasters' protests mounted, the Commission became convinced that it would have to take matters into its own hands.

It was through the *Carter Mountain* case that the FCC finally opened the jurisdictional door. This decision relies on the Court of Appeals' 1958 *Carroll* opinion (Document 24, pp. 246–250) to establish the Commission's power and duty to deny applications for microwave relay facilities serving CATV systems if existing TV stations would be economically injured by increased CATV competition to the degree that over-the-air broadcast service—and thus the public interest—would be impaired. It is interesting to note that broadcast licensees protesting grants to other broadcasters are required to meet stringent pleading standards in order for the FCC to hold an economic injury hearing, whereas licensees protesting CATV competition need not bear so heavy a burden of proof.

This FCC decision was affirmed by the Court of Appeals [321 F.2d 359 (D.C. Cir. 1963)] and the Supreme Court declined to review the case [375 U.S. 951 (1963)]. The *Carter Mountain* case became a "dispositive" precedent a few years later when the Commission adopted its first set of rules for microwave-served CATV systems [38 FCC 683, 687, n. 5 (1965)]. In 1968 the FCC's statutory authority to regulate CATV was upheld by the Supreme Court in the *Southwestern* case (Document 38, pp. 365–380).

Related Reading: 42, 52, 63, 117, 130, 167, 170.

By the Commission: Commissioner Bartley not participating; Commissioner Cross dissenting and issuing a statement.

1.   This is a protest proceeding under 47 U.S.C. 309(c)[1] and 405, arising out of the application of Carter Mountain Transmission Corp. ("Carter"), for a permit to install microwave radio relay pickup television signals to community antenna systems in Riverton, Lander, and Thermopolis, Wyo. Our grant without hearing was protested by Joseph P. and Mildred V. Ernst, d/b as Chief Washakie TV, licensee of station KWRB-TV, channel 10, Riverton, Wyo. ("KWRB-TV"),

---

[1]The protest was filed under the then provisions of sec. 309(c) of the Communications Act of 1934, 48 Stat. 1085, as amended, 47 U.S.C.A. sec. 309(c).

protestants alleging, inter alia, that by providing additional service to existing and operating CATV systems located in Thermopolis, Riverton, and Lander, Wyo., the microwave facilities would enhance their competitive standing to the economic detriment of KWRB-TV; and further, that Carter "is not eligible" to hold common carrier authorizations. By memorandum opinion and order of June 29, 1959 (FCC 59-617; 24 F.R. 5402), the effective date of the grant was postponed and the protest was set for oral argument before the Commission, en banc, with the licensee of KWRB-TV, Carter, and the Chief, Common Carrier Bureau, designated as parties. By memorandum opinion and order of May 20, 1960 (FCC 60-564; 25 F.R. 4606), the matter was designated for hearing. On May 25, 1961 (FCC 61D-74), Hearing Examiner Walther W. Guenther released an initial decision looking toward a denial of the protest, a setting aside of the stay of the effectiveness of the grant, and a reinstatement of the grant of the subject application. KWRB-TV filed exceptions and requested oral argument. The National Association of Broadcasters and Tri-State TV Translator Association sought and were granted leave to file memoranda of law, and the NAB was granted further leave to participate in the oral argument, which was held December 14, 1961.

2.   The initial decision sets forth the background and history of the proceeding, which need not be repeated here. Except as modified herein and in the rulings on the exceptions, the Commission is in general agreement with the examiner's findings, which are hereby adopted. Except as modified herein, and in the rulings on the exceptions, the examiner's conclusions not inconsistent with this decision are hereby adopted. For reasons hereinafter stated, the Commission disagrees with the ultimate result reached by the examiner and, as to that portion of the decision reverses the examiner.

3.   Two basic questions are presented for determination: (a) whether Carter is in fact a bona fide common carrier eligible for a common carrier microwave facility; and (b) whether, a determination having been made that Carter is a common carrier of a microwave facility to a CATV system, the public interest is inherent and the economic impact is of no legal significance. Each will be discussed in order.

4.   KWRB-TV excepts to the examiner's findings and ultimate conclusion that Carter is a bona fide common carrier and to the examiner's failure to find that Carter is the alter ego of Western (a CATV operator). The examiner amply described the situation, adequately discussed the legal proposition, and ultimately concluded correctly. The burden of adducing facts concerning the interlocking ownership between itself and CATV was placed on the applicant, who proved to the examiner's satisfaction that Carter and CATV are separate legal entities, and that the existing degree of common or interlocking ownership would support no contrary inference. KWRB-TV failed to prove anything adverse to this conclusion. In view of the conclusion herein, we do not reach the

question of the legal significance of a greater degree of, or a total identity of, ownership, and we refrain from expressing an opinion thereon. The applicant held itself out for hire, invited the public to use its facilities, and indicated its willingness and ability to carry out this hire. As a matter of fact, station KOOK-TV, with which Carter has no affinity of interest, accepted Carter's offer and the examiner rightfully took official notice thereof. Thus, in accordance with the facts gathered pursuant to issues (3) and (4), issue (5) was properly resolved in applicant's favor.

5. After such findings, the examiner stated "[since] a grant of the subject application will serve the public interest [because it is a bona fide common carrier], . . . it is unnecessary to consider, in particular, the nature of the showing made by protestant under issue (2). . . . whatever impact the operations of the CATV systems may have upon protestant's operation of station KWRB-TV, . . . are matters of no legal significance to the ultimate determination made that a grant of the subject application of Carter, a bona fide communications common carrier, will serve the public interest." KWRB-TV urges that the examiner erred in so concluding. The National Association of Broadcasters, Tri-State TV Translator Association, and the Broadcast Bureau join.

6. When this application was designated for hearing, the Commission recognized that the grant of the microwave facility which is to be used to carry CATV into a community could conceivably destroy the only local television service. The Commission retained the right to make a determination on the facts by specifically including issues (1) and (2), which seek respectively to determine the areas and population now being served by KWRB-TV and the nature and type of said service; and to determine the impact which a grant of the instant application would have upon the operation of KWRB-TV, and the resulting injury, if any, to the public now served. Thus, it is clear that the Commission did not consider the impact of no legal significance, but sought facts on which an ultimate conclusion could be predicated. The examiner made adequate findings with respect to these issues, but gave these facts no weight in his conclusions.

7. Carter urges however, that even were the Commission to find an impact and were it to take cognizance of any adverse effect this impact may have on KWRB-TV, it must recognize that the CATV not the carrier (Carter in this instance) is responsible for the impact, and that the two systems are separate legal entities. This argument, appearing meritorious on its face, is set forth by the examiner (initial decision, p. 28, footnote 8). However, the Commission does not construe its responsibilities this narrowly. We find no justification for ignoring our obligations in the field of television simply because it happens to be common carrier activities that are being regulated at the moment. A grant of common carrier radio facilities requires a finding that the public interest will be served thereby; certainly the well-being of existing television facilities is an aspect of this public interest. Thus it is not only appropriate, it is necessary that

we determine whether the use of the facility applied for would directly or indirectly bring about the elimination of the only television transmission or reception service to the public. In examining the entire instant situation, we may reasonably assume that the carrier (over which we do have jurisdiction) seeks to improve its present service and add additional services so that it may utilize any customer (i.e., CATV) potential. Carter contends that because we have no jurisdiction over the customer, we cannot consider the activities of the customer in regulating the carrier. We do not agree. If making the grant enables this customer potential to destroy a basic Commission policy, then even assuming, arguendo, that the applicant is not the direct cause of the impact, the ability to create such a situation in this particular instance is sufficient to warrant an examination into the entire problem. We will not shut our eyes to the impact upon the public service which is our ultimate concern, when it appears that the grant may serve to deprive a substantially large number of the public of a service merely because the common carrier classification is used. The Commission does not operate in a vacuum. We will not permit a subsequent grant to be issued if it be demonstrated that the same would vitiate a prior grant, without weighing the public-interest considerations involved.

8.   Carter further urges that considering the use which the common carrier subscriber may make of its facility places the Commission in the position of censoring public communications. Here again we do not agree with this position. As guardian of the public interest, we are entrusted with a wide range of discretionary authority and under that authority we may not only appraise the facts and draw inferences from them, but also bring to bear upon the problem an expert judgment from our analysis of the total situation as to just where the public interest lies.[2] We are not in this instance attempting to do anything more than make a valued judgment in this direction. There is no attempt to examine, limit, or interfere with the actual material to be transmitted. We are merely considering the question of whether the use of the facility is in the public interest, a conclusion which must be reached prior to the issuance of the grant. In seeking this ultimate answer, we must look at the situation in its entirety, and we do not agree that we are acting in any fashion which would constitute "censorship."

9.   It would be helpful at this time to set down some of the pertinent facts. KWRB-TV's grade A and B contours include a total of 36,918 persons (1950 U.S. census), in an area of 13,845 square miles, encompassing approximately 10,548 homes.[3] However, only 6 of the towns included in the aforementioned area have a population in excess of 1,000 persons; namely,

---

[2]In *Television Corporation of Michigan, Inc.* v. *FCC* (294 F. 2d 730 (1961)), the Court of Appeals for the District of Columbia Circuit stated, at p. 733, that "[N]either the statutory sections nor the 'priorities' express rigid and inflexible standards: the Commission has a broad measure of discretion in dealing with the many and complicated problems of allocation and distribution of service."

[3]U.S. census national average of approximately 3.5 persons per "household" or "home."

Lander, Riverton, Thermopolis, Worland, Basin, and Greybull. We are primarily concerned here with the first four towns, having populations of 4,182, 6,845, 3,955, and 5,806 persons, respectively, totaling 20,788 persons, or 5,940 homes. The towns of Lander and Riverton had a relatively small number of subscribers to CATV operations, although from 1958 through 1960 they slowly increased the number of homes placed on the cable. The towns of Thermopolis and Worland had a large number of CATV subscribers, and these numbers had been decreasing during the years 1958 through 1960 with resultant increased sale of spots for KWRB-TV.

10.   KWRB-TV's overall programing serves the public interest. It has permission from each of the three networks with which it is affiliated to carry their entire schedules by deleting the "commercials" and substituting "public service," and it carries public service spots on behalf of the local town and community. It has a good local operating record and programs for the community it serves. If KWRB-TV were no longer to operate, no local programs of this type would be available to persons residing within the grade B contour, and they depend on this station for the airing of this local material.

11.   The largest revenue returns are received from the towns of Lander and Riverton. Despite the fact that Worland has approximately 1,600 more persons than does Lander, the revenue from Lander is approximately 6 times that of Worland. This is attributed to the fact that CATV did not make any substantial inroad in Lander, while approximately 75 percent of the homes in Worland are on the cable. A similar type of comparison may be made between the towns of Riverton and Thermopolis.

12.   Since its inception, station KWRB-TV has been operating in the "red"; that is, its operating expenses have exceeded its income. However, in each succeeding year of operation the gap between the two has become smaller, and as contended by protestant, should eventually be closed and then changed to "black." KWRB-TV points to a number of contributing factors, some of which are: the closing of the CATV station in Thermopolis (then under another operator) for approximately 6 months during 1960; a decrease in the number of homes carried on the CATV cable in the towns of Thermopolis and Worland where CATV has 44 percent and 75 percent subscriptions; KWRB-TV's being a "family enterprise" with resultant low expense and high productivity; reduction in the amount of syndicated film purchases and the substitution of network programing for which charges are no longer being exacted; but primarily, KWRB-TV's ability to show inroads on the number of cable subscribers together with an increase in its network affiliation status, enabled it to sell its spot advertising more readily, thus increasing its revenue.

13.   Duplication of network programing exists not only between the imported programs entering the towns here involved over the cable system, but also with KWRB-TV signal. Network programs carried on KWRB-TV may also appear on one or more of the cable channels, without the local spot advertising. KWRB-TV states that at the present time, however, its picture is clearer and

better than the one appearing on the CATV cable in the area. Thus, although a good deal of difficulty is encountered in attempting to sell spots in face of the division of audience, it manages to do so on the basis of better performance. However, it is urged that a grant of the instant application would permit the CATV to improve its facilities to match that of KWRB-TV, rendering the sale to local advertisers impossible in view of the fact that they would not be able to guarantee any viewing on its channel. Reason and logic cause us to agree with the conclusion that should the CATV system be permitted to expand its services and furnish better technical facilities, KWRB-TV will be placed in the economically disadvantageous position of finding it more difficult to sell its advertising; it would have nothing to point to which would indicate to a potential advertiser that a popular program was being viewed over KWRB-TV vis-a-vis other potential channels. Its one balancing factor of a better picture will have been removed.

14.   Licenses are granted by the Commission only if the operations proposed are found to be in the public interest, convenience, and necessity. Hence, when the impact of economic injury is such as to adversely affect the public interest, it is not only within our power, but it is our duty to determine the ultimate effect, study the facts, and act in a manner most advantageous to the public.[4] Although most of the network programs carried by KWRB-TV would continue to be available to the present CATV subscribers in the 6 towns of over 1,000 persons, via translators or CATV's, such programs would not be available to persons not residing in the immediate vicinity of the towns in which the CATV systems and VHF translators operate, nor to persons in the towns unable to pay the CATV charges. Therefore, if KWRB-TV is eventually forced off the air as a result of a grant of the instant application, the public stands to lose its only local outlet, an outlet on which a considerable part of the population in northwestern Wyoming relies.

15.   A review of KWRB-TV's revenue for the year 1959 indicates that Lander and Riverton each return $14,191.31 and $17,429.14, respectively, as against a return of $6,457.20 and $2,485.45 from Thermopolis and Worland, respectively, notwithstanding the fact that Worland has a larger population than does Lander. Thus, the four towns made up $40,563.10 of a total revenue of $66,812.03 for the year 1959. If the CATV pattern is permitted to be altered, and the substantial return from Riverton in particular is reduced, KWRB-TV, despite the fact that it would strive harder, would find it more difficult to sell its advertising in face of the split audience, and this situation, together with facts of record, results in our judgment that the demise of this local operation would result.

[4]The courts have held that economic injury to a licensee and public interest may be different matters. However, the former "becomes important when on the facts it spells diminution or destruction of service." *Carroll Broadcasting Company* v. *FCC*, 258 F. 2d 440, 443 (1958).

16. At the time KWRB-TV was granted its license, the Commission concluded that it was in the public interest to make such a grant. The Commission must now find it in the public interest to grant the instant application. Standing alone, it might appear that each does in fact serve the public interest, with KWRB-TV showing, inter alia, that it is the only local television outlet for the community, while Carter would show that an increase in its facilities would permit the rendition of better and more efficient service to the CATV serving the community. However, neither stands alone; the effect of one upon the other must be weighed, and the ultimate conclusion must be made to the best interest of the public. True, a grant of the instant application would permit the rendition of better service by the CATV, but at the expense of destroying the local station and its rural coverage. The CATV would permit the urban areas a choice of coverage, but the local station, especially in this case of a single-station market, serves a wider area. A grant of this application will not contemplate an extension of coverage for the entire area included in KWRB-TV's contours, since it is too costly for CATV to enter the rural areas. Thus, the rural people would be left with nothing at all. This is not a true competitive situation where one or the other of the applicants would render the service. In this instance, if KWRB-TV, the local outlet, should be forced to cease operation, the rural people would be left without any service. We do not agree that we are powerless to prevent the demise of the local television station, and the eventual loss of service to a substantial population; nor do we agree that the Commission's expertise may not be invoked in this instance to predict this ultimate situation. Thus, after weighing the public interest involved in Carter's improved facility against the loss of the local station, it must be concluded, beyond peradventure of a doubt, the need for the local outlet and the service which it would provide to outlying areas outweighs the need for the improved service which Carter would furnish under the terms of the instant application. To the extent that this decision departs from our views in the report and order in docket No. 12443, 26 FCC 403 (released April 14, 1959), those views are modified.

17. In view of the foregoing and in light of the evidence adduced, we fail to find that a grant of the instant application would serve the public interest, convenience, and necessity, and therefore the application is denied, without prejudice however, to Carter's refiling when it is able to show that the CATV operation will avoid the duplication of KWRB-TV programing which now exists and that the CATV system will carry the local KWRB-TV signal. Placing of these latter conditions upon the refiling without prejudice is being done with full recognition of the separate corporate entities of Carter and the CATV. The realities of the situation, however, force a recognition of the fact that the conditions we impose upon Carter are a sine qua non to our finding that its operation will be in the public interest. Neither the Commission nor KWRB-TV can bring them about. Carter may accomplish this by a contract relationship

between itself and the corporation with which it has some interlocking ownership [Western], or by some less formal means.

Accordingly, *It is ordered*, This 14th day of February 1962, that protest of Joseph P. Ernst and Mildred V. Ernst, d/b as Chief Washakie TV (KWRB-TV), *Is granted*; and the aforementioned application of Carter Mountain Transmission Corp. *Is denied* without prejudice to refiling when a showing can be made that the duplication of programing is adequately avoided and a satisfactory arrangement is arrived at by which the cable system will carry the local KWRB-TV service.

Dissenting statement of Commissioner Cross

I dissent. Even though I sympathize with the plight of station KWRB-TV (channel 10, Riverton, Wyo.) in this instance, I nevertheless consider the relief being granted by the majority sets an undesirable precedent that is against the best overall interests of the broadcasting industry in this country.

In docket No. 12443 (released April 14, 1959), the Commission, after lengthy consideration and deliberation, properly, in my view, determined the rationale for deciding cases like this one. In paragraph 75 of the report and order in docket No. 12443, the Commission stated:

... it is neither proper, pertinent, nor necessary for us to consider the specific lawful use which the common carrier subscriber may make of the facilities of the carrier. To take a different view would place the Commission in the anomalous position of acting as censor over public communications, and put us under the burden of policing, not only the use of such facilities but the content of communications transmitted on the facilities. The logical extension of such a philosophy would require us to deny communications facilities of any kind (message telephone, telegraph, etc.) to CATV's and, for example, to deny access to facilities to those acting contrary to our concept of the public welfare. The adjudication of these matters is beyond our province.

Despite this previous statement by the Commission (and the other portions of the report and order in docket No. 12443 on this general subject), the protestant and others have now apparently convinced the majority that the Commission should consider the specific lawful use which the common carrier subscriber may make of the facilities of the carrier. The thrust of their argument in this regard is that the Commission should not, on the one hand, license microwave facilities to a common carrier when part or all of such facilities will be used by a CATV system to the economic detriment of the only television station in the community, which has also been licensed by the Commission with its other hand.

Admittedly, this is a hard case, but there is an old saying that hard cases make bad law and, in my opinion, that is what is being done here by the decision of the majority. Having the Commission examine into the specific lawful use which the common carrier subscriber may make of the facilities of the carrier is, in my opinion, not only contrary to common carrier communications law and practice but could open up a veritable Pandora's box which in the end may well redound to the serious detriment of the broadcasting industry itself.

The Commission was aware of these undesirable possibilities at the time it released its report and order in docket No. 12443. Indeed, these factors were significant in persuading the Commission that the best way to protect the broadcaster in situations like this was not through the common carrier licensees but through legislation that would authorize the Commission to have some degree of regulation over the users; i.e., the CATV systems. Such legislation was, in fact, proposed to the Congress by the Commission and is still before the Congress.[5] Accordingly, it is my view that we should not try to correct one isolated situation in the instant case by departing from our previously well-considered and soundly bottomed actions on the subject; i.e., the report and order in docket No. 12443 and our subsequent request to the Congress for the legislation noted above. I would therefore deny the protest and wait for the enactment of the requested legislation to deal with this matter.

[5] S. 1044 and H.R. 6840 were introduced on Feb. 16, 1961, at the Commission's request.

31

The Suburban Case

Patrick Henry et al., d/b as Suburban Broadcasters

v. Federal Communications Commission*

302 F.2d 191 (D.C. Cir.)

March 29, 1962

It looked as if the FCC, under Newton Minow's chairmanship, was getting serious about broadcast programming when, in mid-1961, it denied the application of Suburban Broadcasters to construct Elizabeth, New Jersey's first FM station because of the applicant's failure to comply with the ascertainment requirement stated in the "1960 Programming Policy Statement" (Document 26, pp. 262–278). There was no competing applicant for the Elizabeth station. Was the Commission's denial legal, or was it (in the words of *Broadcasting* magazine, the industry's leading trade journal) "censorship in the raw"? The stage was set for a court test of the FCC's statutory and constitutional authority to require prospective licensees to base program proposals on an informed awareness of local community needs.

This Court of Appeals decision relies on the Supreme Court's opinion in the 1943 "Network" case (Document 20, pp. 99–131) in affirming the FCC and, in effect, placing the judicial stamp of approval on the community surveys mandated by the 1960 statement of policy. (Warren E. Burger, a member of the three-judge panel deciding this case, was made Chief Justice of the United States 7 years later.) The Supreme Court declined to review the case [371 U.S. 821 (1962)].

Even though the FCC's ascertainment requirements subsequently centered on community *problems* rather than "tastes,

---

*Reprinted with the permission of West Publishing Company.

needs, and desires" (Document 44, pp. 477–485), the appellate
court's tangential remarks about music formats ("questions . . .
that we need not here decide") presage the judicial concern
clearly expressed a dozen years later in the *WEFM* case (Document 43, pp. 453–476).

Related Reading: 5, 78.

Bazelon, Circuit Judge.

Appellants, doing business as Suburban Broadcasters, filed the sole
application for a permit to construct the first commercial F.M. station in
Elizabeth, New Jersey.[1] Although the Federal Communications Commission
found Suburban legally, technically and financially qualified, it designated the
application for hearing on the issues raised by the claim of Metropolitan
Broadcasting Company, the licensee of WNEW in New York, that a grant would
result in objectionable interference. At Metropolitan's request, the Commission
subsequently added another issue for hearing:

To determine whether the program proposals of Suburban Broadcasters
are designed to and would be expected to serve the needs of the proposed service
area.

Upon hearing, the trial examiner found for Suburban on both issues. The
Commission affirmed on the issue of objectionable interference but reversed on
the issue relating to the program proposals and denied the application. Suburban
appeals.

These are the pertinent facts disclosed by the record. None of Suburban's
principals were residents of Elizabeth. They made no inquiry into the
characteristics or programming needs of that community and offered no
evidence thereon. Suburban's program proposals were identical with those
submitted in its application for an F.M. facility in Berwyn, Illinois, and in the
application of two of its principals for an F.M. facility in Alameda, California.[2]

Although the trial examiner resolved the program planning issue in favor
of Suburban, he noted that its approach might be characterized as "cavalier" or
little more than a "quick shrug." He also referred to the "Program Policy
Statement," released by the Commission July 29, 1960, to the effect that the
broadcaster's programming responsibility is measured by the statutory standard
of "public interest, convenience or necessity," and that in meeting such standard

---

[1] The Communications Act of 1934 § 319, 48 Stat. 1089, 47 U.S.C.A. § 319 (1958),
forbids the Commission to license a station unless its construction has previously been
authorized by a permit issued pursuant to §§ 308 and 309, 48 Stat. 1084-1085 (1934), 47
U.S.C.A. §§ 308, 309 (1958).

[2] The application for the Berwyn facility was dismissed; the one for Alameda was granted.

the broadcaster is "obligated to make a positive, diligent and continuing effort, in good faith, to determine the tastes, needs and desires of the public in his community and to provide programming to meet those needs and interests." But the examiner stated that these standards were intended for existing licensees, rather than applicants for new stations, and were therefore inapplicable here.

In reversing the examiner, the Commission (with one Commissioner absent and two dissenting) stated:

We agree [with the examiner] that Elizabeth has a presumptive need for a first local FM transmission service. We have generally presumed that an applicant for such a community would satisfy its programming needs, assuming that the applicant had at least a rudimentary knowledge of such needs. However, we cannot indulge in that presumption where the validity of the underlying assumption is questioned, a specific issue is added, and it is demonstrated that the applicant has taken no steps to familiarize himself with the community or its needs. It is not sufficient that the applicant will bring a first transmission service to the community — it must in fact provide a first local outlet for community self-expression. Communities may differ, and so may their needs; an applicant has the responsibility of ascertaining his community's needs and of programming to meet those needs. As found by the Examiner, Suburban's principals made no inquiry into the characteristics of Elizabeth or its particular programming needs. The instant program proposals were drawn up on the basis of the principals' apparent belief — unsubstantiated by inquiry, insofar as the record shows — that Elizabeth's needs duplicated those of Alameda, California, and Berwyn, Illinois, or, in the words of the Examiner, could "be served in the same manner that such 'needs' are served by FM broadcasters generally."

The Commission found that the "program proposals were not 'designed' to serve the needs of Elizabeth"; and that it could not determine whether the proposals "would be expected" to serve these needs, since no evidence of these needs was offered. "In essence," said the Commission, "we are asked to grant an application prepared by individuals totally without knowledge of the area they seek to serve. We feel the public deserves something more in the way of preparation for the responsibilities sought by applicant than was demonstrated on this record." Accordingly, the Commission held that "it cannot be concluded that a grant . . . would serve the public interest, convenience and necessity."

Appellants contend that the statutory licensing scheme requires a grant where, as here, it is established that the sole applicants for a frequency are legally, financially and technically qualified. This view reflects an arbitrarily narrow understanding of the statutory words "public convenience, interest, or necessity."[3] It leaves no room for Commission consideration of matters relating

[3] Communications Act of 1934 § 307(a), 48 Stat. 1083, 47 U.S.C.A. § 307(a) (1958). The statute directs the Commission to grant a station license to any applicant "if public convenience, interest, or necessity will be served thereby."

to programming. Moreover, appellants urge that consideration of such matters is precluded by the statute's proscription of censorship[4] and the constitutional guarantee of free speech.

We think these broad contentions are beside the narrow point at issue upon this record. It may be that a licensee must have freedom to broadcast light opera even if the community likes rock and roll music, although that question is not uncomplicated. Even more complicated is the question whether he may feed a diet of rock and roll music to a community which hungers for opera. These are questions, however, that we need not here decide. As we see it, the question presented on the instant record is simply whether the Commission may require that an applicant demonstrate an earnest interest in serving a local community by evidencing a familiarity with its particular needs and an effort to meet them.

We think National Broadcasting Co. v. United States, 319 U.S. 190, 63 S.Ct. 997, 87 L.Ed. 1344 (1943), settles the narrow question before us in the affirmative. There, the Commission promulgated regulations which provided, *inter alia*, that no license would be granted to stations whose network contracts would prevent them from developing programs "to serve the needs of the local community." 319 U.S. at 203, 63 S.Ct. at 1003. National Broadcasting Company challenged the regulations on precisely the grounds appellants advance here: that since the regulations were calculated to affect program content, they exceeded statutory and constitutional limitations. In sustaining the regulations, the Supreme Court held that the Commission may impose reasonable restrictions upon the grant of licenses to assure programming designed to meet the needs of the local community. We think it clear that the Commission's action in the instant case reflects no greater interference with a broadcaster's alleged right to choose its programs free from Commission control than the interference involved in National Broadcasting Co.[5]

Affirmed.

---

[4]"Nothing in this Act shall be understood or construed to give the Commission the power of censorship over the radio communications or signals transmitted by any radio station, and no regulation or condition shall be promulgated or fixed by the Commission which shall interfere with the right of free speech by means of radio communication." Communications Act of 1934 § 326, 48 Stat. 1091, 47 U.S.C.A. § 326 (1958).

[5]Appellants also complain that they were surprised by the Commission's insistence that they be familiar with the needs of the community they sought to serve. But that requirement is not new. See Kentucky Broadcasting Corp. v. Federal Communications Comm., 84 U.S. App. D.C. 383, 174 F. 2d 38 (1949); Sanders, 2 F.C.C. 365, 372 (1936); Egeland, 6 F.C.C. 278 (1938); Brownsville Broadcasting Co., 2 F.C.C. 336, 340 (1936) (alternative ground); Martin, 3 F.C.C. 461 (1936) (alternative ground); Goldwasser, 4 F.C.C. 223 (1937) (alternative ground); Kraft, 4 F.C.C. 354 (1937) (alternative ground). And the question whether appellants had demonstrated such familiarity was within the scope of the issues designated for hearing.

32

The Pacifica Case

In re Pacifica Foundation

36 FCC 147

January 22, 1964

This FCC decision resulted in grants to the Pacifica Foundation for an initial license for KPFK, Los Angeles, renewals of the licenses of KPFA-FM and KPFB, Berkeley, and WBAI-FM, New York City, and permission to transfer control of the stations. The authorizations were made by the Commission despite complaints from some people who found the stations' programming offensive. At the time, the *Pacifica* decision was hailed as affirmation by the FCC of free speech principles applied to broadcasting.

Section 1464 of the U.S. Criminal Code (see p. 575) makes the broadcasting of "obscene, indecent, or profane language" a crime, and Section 503(b) of the Communications Act (p. 566) authorizes the FCC to levy forfeitures on licensees who violate the obscenity statute. The years of sexual liberation following the *Pacifica* decision were marked by changing language standards, and the problems posed by candid broadcast programming mounted. In 1970 the FCC fined a noncommercial radio station $100 for broadcasting a recorded interview at 10:00 p.m. in which recording artist Jerry Garcia peppered his remarks with commonly used words denoting excrement and sexual intercourse [(*WUHY-FM, Eastern Educational Radio*, 24 FCC 2d 408 (1970)]. The Commission held the program to be "indecent" (rather than "obscene") and invited a court test, but the licensee chose to pay the fine instead. For judicial review of a later related case involving Pacifica, see Document 46 (pp. 497–510).

Related Reading: 15, 150, 163, 174, 215.

BY THE COMMISSION: COMMISSIONER LEE CONCURRING AND ISSUING A STATEMENT.

1. The Commission has before it for consideration the above-pending applications of the listed broadcast stations licensed to Pacifica Foundation. There are three aspects to our consideration: (*a*) Certain programming issues raised by complaints; (*b*) issues of possible Communist Party affiliation of principals of Pacifica; and (*c*) a question of possible unauthorized transfer of control. We shall consider each in turn.

2. *The programming issues.* — The principal complaints are concerned with five programs: (i) a December 12, 1959, broadcast over KPFA, at 10 p.m., of certain poems by Lawrence Ferlinghetti (read by the poet himself); (ii) "The Zoo Story," a recording of the Edward Albee play broadcast over KPFK at 11 p.m., January 13, 1963; (iii) "Live and Let Live," a program broadcast over KPFK at 10:15 p.m. on January 15, 1963, in which eight homosexuals discussed their attitudes and problems; (iv) a program broadcast over KPFA at 7:15 p.m. on January 28, 1963, in which the poem, "Ballad of the Despairing Husband," was read by the author Robert Creeley; and (v) "The Kid," a program broadcast at 11 p.m. on January 8, 1963, over KPFA, which consisted of readings by Edward Pomerantz from his unfinished novel of the same name. The complaints charge that these programs were offensive or "filthy" in nature, thus raising the type of issue we recently considered in *Palmetto Bctg. Co.*, 33 FCC 483; 34 FCC 101. We shall consider the above five matters in determining whether, on an overall basis, the licensee's programing met the public-interest standard laid down in the Communications Act.[1] *Report and Statement of Policy re: Commission En Banc Programing Inquiry,* 20 Pike & Fischer R.R. 1901.

3. When the Commission receives complaints of the general nature here involved, its usual practice is to refer them to the licensee so as to afford the latter an opportunity to comment. When the Commission reviews, on an overall basis, the station's operation at the time of renewal, it thus has before it a complete file, containing all the sides of any matter which may have arisen during the license period. Specifically, with respect to the programing issue in this case, the Commission, barring the exceptions noted in the *Programing Statement (supra,* at p. 1909), is not concerned with individual programs — nor is it at any time concerned with matters essentially of licensee taste or judgment. Cf. *Palmetto Bctg. Co., supra,* paragraph 22. As shown by the cited case, its very limited concern in this type of case is whether, upon the overall examination, some substantial pattern of operation inconsistent with the public-interest

---

[1]The Commission may also enforce the standard of sec. 1464 of title 18 (dealing with "obscene, indecent, or profane language"). See secs. 312(a), (b); sec. 503(b)(1)(E). In our view, enforcement proceedings under sec. 1464 are not warranted, and therefore, no further consideration need be given this section.

standard clearly and patently emerges. Unlike *Palmetto* where there was such a substantial pattern (id. at par. 23; see par. 7, infra), here we are dealing with a few isolated programs, presented over a 4-year period. It would thus appear that there is no substantial problem, on an overall basis, warranting further inquiry.[2] While this would normally conclude the matter, we have determined to treat the issues raised by Pacifica's response to the complaints, because we think it would serve a useful purpose, both to the industry and the public. We shall therefore turn to a more detailed consideration of the issues raised by the complaints as to these five programs. Because of Pacifica's different response to the complaints as to (i) and (iv), paragraph 2 above, we shall treat these two broadcasts separately. (See pars. 6-7, infra.)

4.   There is, we think, no question but that the broadcasts of the programs, "The Zoo Story," "Live and Let Live," and "The Kid," lay well within the licensee's judgment under the public-interest standard. The situation here stands on an entirely different footing than *Palmetto, supra*, where the licensee had devoted a substantial period of his broadcast day to material which we found to be patently offensive — however much we weighed that standard in the licensee's favor — and as to which programming the licensee himself never asserted that it was not offensive or vulgar, *or that it served the needs of his area or had any redeeming features.* In this case, Pacifica has stated its judgment that the three above-cited programs served the public interests and specifically, the needs and interests of its listening public. Thus, it has pointed out that in its judgment, "The Zoo Story" is a "serious work of drama" by an eminent and "provocative playwright" — that it is "an honest and courageous play" which Americans "who do not live near Broadway ought to have the opportunity to hear and experience. . . ." Similarly, as to "The Kid," Pacifica states, with supporting authority, that Mr. Pomerantz is an author who has obtained notable recognition for his writings and whose readings from his unfinished novel were fully in the public interest as a serious work meriting the attention of its listeners; Pacifica further states that prior to broadcast, the tape was auditioned by one of its employees who edited out two phrases because they did not meet Pacifica's broadcast standards of good taste; and that while "certain minor swear words are used, . . . these fit well within the context of the material being read and conform to the standards of acceptability of reasonably intelligent listeners." Finally, as to the program, "Live and Let Live," Pacifica states that "so long as the program is handled in good taste, there is no reason why subjects like homosexuality should not be discussed on the air"; and that it "conscientiously believes that the American people will be better off as a result of hearing

---

[2]While, for reasons developed in this opinion, it is unnecessary to detail the showings here, we have examined the licensee's overall showings as to its stations' operations and find that those operations did serve the needs and interests of the licensee's areas. *Programing Statement, supra*, at pp. 1913-1916. In this connection, we have also taken into account the showing made in the letter of Apr. 16, 1963.

a constructive discussion of the problem rather than leaving the subject to ignorance and silence."

5.   We recognize that as shown by the complaints here, such provocative programing as here involved may offend some listeners. But this does not mean that those offended have the right, through the Commission's licensing power, to rule such programing off the airwaves. Were this the case, only the wholly inoffensive, the bland, could gain access to the radio microphone or TV camera. No such drastic curtailment can be countenanced under the Constitution, the Communications Act, or the Commission's policy, which has consistently sought to insure "the maintenance of radio and television as a medium of freedom of speech and freedom of expression for the people of the Nation as a whole" (*Editorializing Report,* 13 FCC 1246, 1248). In saying this, we do not mean to indicate that those who have complained about the foregoing programs are in the wrong as to the worth of these programs and should listen to them. This is a matter solely for determination by the individual listeners. Our function, we stress, is not to pass on the merits of the program – to commend or to frown. Rather, as we stated (par. 3), it is the very limited one of assaying, at the time of renewal, whether the licensee's programming, on an overall basis, has been in the public interest and, in the context of this issue, whether he has made programing judgments reasonably related to the public interest. This does not pose a close question in the case: Pacifica's judgments as to the above programs clearly fall within the very great discretion which the act wisely vests in the licensee. In this connection, we also note that Pacifica took into account the nature of the broadcast medium when it scheduled such programing for the late evening hours (after 10 p.m., when the number of children in the listening audience is at a minimum).[3]

6.   As to the Ferlinghetti and Creeley programs, the licensee asserts that in both instances, some passages did not measure up to "Pacifica's own standards of good taste." Thus, it states that it did not carefully screen the Ferlinghetti tape to see if it met its standards, "because it relied upon Mr. Ferlinghetti's national reputation and also upon the fact that the tape came to it from a reputable FM station." It acknowledges that this was a mistake in its procedures and states that "in the future, Pacifica will make its own review of all broadcasts. . . ." With respect to the Creeley passage (i.e., the poem, "Ballad of a Despairing Husband"),[4] Pacifica again states that in its judgment it should not have been broadcast. It "does not excuse the broadcast of the poem in question," but it does explain how the poem "slipped by" KPFA's drama and literature editor

---

[3]Pacifica states that it "is sensitive to its responsibilities to its listening audience and carefully schedules for late night broadcasts those programs which may be misunderstood by children although thoroughly acceptable to an adult audience."

[4]The program containing this passage was a taped recording of Mr. Creeley's readings of selections from his poetry to students at the University of California. KPFA broadcasts many such poetry readings at the university, which are recorded by a university employee for the school's archives (and made available to the station).

who auditioned the tape. It points out that prior to the offending poem, Mr. Creeley, who "has a rather flat, monotonous voice," read 18 other perfectly acceptable poems — and that the station's editor was so lulled thereby that he did not catch the few offensive words on the 19th poem. It also points out that each of the nine poems which followed was again perfectly acceptable, and that before rebroadcasting the poem on its Los Angeles station, it deleted the objectionable verse.

7.   In view of the foregoing, we find no impediment to renewal on this score. We are dealing with two isolated errors in the licensee's application of its own standards — one in 1959 and the other in 1963. The explanations given for these two errors are credible. Therefore, even assuming, arguendo, that the broadcasts were inconsistent with the public-interest standard, it is clear that no unfavorable action upon the renewal applications is called for. The standard of public interest is not so rigid that an honest mistake or error on the part of a licensee results in drastic action against him where his overall record demonstrates a reasonable effort to serve the needs and interests of his community. (See note 2, supra.) Here again, this case contrasts sharply with *Palmetto*, where instead of two isolated instances, years apart, we found that the patently offensive material was broadcast for a substantial period of the station's broadcast day for many years. (See par. 3, supra.)

8.   We find, therefore, that the programing matters raised with respect to the Pacifica renewals pose no bar to a grant of renewal.[5] Our holding, as is true of all such holdings in this sensitive area, is necessarily based on, and limited to, the facts of the particular case. But we have tried to stress here, as in *Palmetto*, an underlying policy — that the licensee's judgment in this freedom-of-speech area is entitled to very great weight and that the Commission, under the public-interest standard, will take action against the licensee at the time of renewal only where the facts of the particular case, established in a hearing record, flagrantly call for such action. We have done so because we are charged under the act with "promoting the larger and more effective use of radio in the public interest" (sec. 303(g)), and obviously, in the discharge of that responsibility, must take every precaution to avoid inhibiting broadcast licensees' efforts at experimenting or diversifying their programing. Such diversity of programing has been the goal of many Commission policies (e.g., multiple ownership, development of UHF, the fairness doctrine). Clearly, the Commission must remain faithful to that goal in discharging its functions in the actual area of programing itself. . . .

[5]One other programing aspect deserves emphasis. Complaint has also been made concerning Pacifica's presentation of "far-left" programing. Pacifica has stated that it follows a policy of presenting programs covering the widest range of the political or controversial issue spectrum — from the members of the Communist Party on the left to members of the John Birch Society on the right. Again, we point out that such a policy (which must, of course, be carried out consistently with the requirements of the fairness doctrine) is within the licensee's area of programing judgment.

Conclusion

14.   In view of the foregoing, *It is ordered*, This 22d day of January 1964, that the above-entitled applications of Pacifica Foundation *Are granted* as serving the public interest, convenience, and necessity.

Concurring statement of Commissioner Robert E. Lee

I concur in the action of the Commission in granting the several applications of Pacifica Foundation. However, I feel constrained to comment on at least one program coming to our attention insofar as it may or may not reflect these stations' program policies.

Having listened carefully and painfully to a 1½-hour tape recording of a program involving self-professed homosexuals, I am convinced that the program was designed to be, and succeeded in being, contributory to nothing but sensationalism. The airing of a program dealing with sexual aberrations is not to my mind, per se, a violation of good taste nor contrary to the public interest. When these subjects are discussed by physicians and sociologists, it is conceivable that the public could benefit. But a panel of eight homosexuals discussing their experiences and past history does not approach the treatment of a delicate subject one could expect by a responsible broadcaster. A microphone in a bordello, during slack hours, could give us similar information on a related subject. Such programs, obviously designed to be lurid and to stir the public curiosity, have little place on the air.

I do not hold myself to be either a moralist or a judge of taste. Least of all do I have a clear understanding of what may constitute obscenity in broadcasting.

33

Broadcasting from the Courtroom

Estes v. Texas

381 U.S. 532

June 7, 1965

As a result of the notoriously publicized trial of Bruno Richard Hauptmann, convicted of kidnapping the son of Charles A. Lindbergh, in 1937 the American Bar Association enacted Canon 35 of its Canons of Judicial Ethics barring radio microphones from covering court proceedings. Canon 35 was amended in 1952 to ban television as well. In 1972 the American Bar Association adopted a new Code of Judicial Conduct. The former Canon 35 has been replaced by Canon 3A(7):

> A judge should prohibit broadcasting, televising, recording, or taking photographs in the courtroom and areas immediately adjacent thereto during sessions of court or recesses between sessions, except that a judge may authorize:
>
> (a) the use of electronic or photographic means for the presentation of evidence, for the perpetuation of a record, or for other purposes of judical administration;
>
> (b) the broadcasting, televising, recording, or photographing of investitive, ceremonial, or nationalization proceedings;
>
> (c) the photographic or electronic recording and reproduction of appropriate court proceedings under the following conditions:
>
> (i) the means of recording will not distract participants or impair the dignity of the proceedings;

(ii) the parties have consented, and the consent to being depicted or recorded has been obtained from each witness appearing in the recording and reproduction;

(iii) the reproduction will not be exhibited until after the proceeding has been concluded and all direct appeals have been exhausted; and

(iv) the reproduction will be exhibited only for instructional purposes in education institutions.

Billie Sol Estes was convicted by a federal court of mail fraud and conspiracy. (He was released from prison in 1971 after serving 6 years of a 15-year sentence.) Estes was also accused of violating Texas state laws and was tried for these acts in a state court that found him guilty. The state conviction was appealed to the United States Supreme Court because of the constitutional question presented by the presence of television apparatus in the Texas courtroom. The conflict between the First, Fifth, Sixth, and Fourteenth Amendments is typically characterized as "Free Press versus Fair Trial," thus posing the broadcast journalist's right of free expression against a criminal defendant's right to due process of law.

This five-to-four Supreme Court decision reversed the state conviction, holding that when First and Fourteenth Amendment rights conflict, the latter takes precedence over the former. The Court decided that such a conflict occurs whenever pretrial disclosures create notorious publicity and courtroom proceedings are disrupted by television equipment and personnel. *Estes* v. *Texas* constitutes an important precedent for the decision in *Sheppard* v. *Maxwell* [384 U.S. 333 (1966)]. Six opinions were written in the *Estes* case; only the opinion of the Court appears below.

Related Reading: 14, 50, 82, 89, 104, 124, 133, 134, 210.

Mr. Justice Clark delivered the opinion of the Court.

The question presented here is whether the petitioner, who stands convicted in the District Court for the Seventh Judicial District of Texas at Tyler for swindling,[1] was deprived of his right under the Fourteenth Amendment to

---

[1] The evidence indicated that petitioner, through false pretenses and fraudulent representations, induced certain farmers to purchase fertilizer tanks and accompanying equipment, which in fact did not exist, and to sign and deliver to him chattel mortages on the fictitious property.

due process by the televising and broadcasting of his trial. Both the trial court and the Texas Court of Criminal Appeals found against the petitioner. We hold to the contrary and reverse his conviction.

I

While petitioner recites his claim in the framework of Canon 35 of the Judicial Canons of the American Bar Association he does not contend that we should enshrine Canon 35 in the Fourteenth Amendment, but only that the time-honored principles of a fair trial were not followed in his case and that he was thus convicted without due process of law. Canon 35, of course, has of itself no binding effect on the courts but merely expresses the view of the Association in opposition to the broadcasting, televising and photographing of court proceedings. Likewise, Judicial Canon 28 of the Integrated State Bar of Texas, 27 Tex. B. J. 102 (1964), which leaves to the trial judge's sound discretion the telecasting and photographing of court proceedings, is of itself not law. In short, the question here is not the validity of either Canon 35 of the American Bar Association or Canon 28 of the State Bar of Texas, but only whether petitioner was tried in a manner which comports with the due process requirement of the Fourteenth Amendment.

Petitioner's case was originally called for trial on September 24, 1962, in Smith County after a change of venue from Reeves County, some 500 miles west. Massive pretrial publicity totaling 11 volumes of press clippings, which are on file with the Clerk, had given it national notoriety. All available seats in the courtroom were taken and some 30 persons stood in the aisles. However, at that time a defense motion to prevent telecasting, broadcasting by radio and news photography and a defense motion for continuance were presented, and after a two-day hearing the former was denied and the latter granted.

These initial hearings were carried live by both radio and television, and news photography was permitted throughout. The videotapes of these hearings clearly illustrate that the picture presented was not one of that judicial serenity and calm to which petitioner was entitled. Cf. *Wood* v. *Georgia*, 370 U.S. 375, 383 (1962); *Turner* v. *Louisiana*, 379 U.S. 466, 472 (1965); *Cox* v. *Louisiana*, 379 U.S. 559, 562 (1965). Indeed, at least 12 cameramen were engaged in the courtroom throughout the hearing taking motion and still pictures and televising the proceedings. Cables and wires were snaked across the courtroom floor, three microphones were on the judge's bench and others were beamed at the jury box and the counsel table. It is conceded that the activities of the television crews and news photographers led to considerable disruption of the hearings. Moreover, veniremen had been summoned and were present in the courtroom during the entire hearing but were later released after petitioner's motion for continuance had been granted. The court also had the names of the witnesses called; some answered but the absence of others led to a continuance of the case until October 22, 1962. It is contended that this two-day pretrial hearing cannot be considered in determining the question before us. We cannot agree. Pretrial can create a major problem for the defendant in a criminal case. Indeed, it may be more harmful than publicity during the trial for it may well set the community opinion as to guilt or innocence. Though the September hearings dealt with motions to prohibit television coverage and to postpone the trial, they are unquestionably relevant to the issue before us. All of this two-day affair was highly publicized and could only have impressed those present, and also the community at large, with the notorious character of the petitioner as well as the proceeding. The trial witnesses present at the hearing, as well as the original jury panel, were undoubtedly made aware of the peculiar public importance of the case by the press and television coverage being provided, and by the fact that they themselves were televised live and their pictures rebroadcast on the evening show.

When the case was called for trial on October 22 the scene had been altered. A booth had been constructed at the back of the courtroom which was painted to blend with the permanent structure of the room. It had an aperture to allow the lens of the cameras an unrestricted view of the courtroom. All television cameras and newsreel photographers were restricted to the area of the booth when shooting film or telecasting.

Because of continual objection, the rules governing live telecasting, as well as radio and still photos, were changed as the exigencies of the situation seemed to require. As a result, live telecasting was prohibited during a great portion of the actual trial. Only the opening[2] and closing arguments of the State, the return of the jury's verdict and its receipt by the trial judge were carried live with sound. Although the order allowed videotapes of the entire proceeding without sound, the cameras operated only intermittently, recording various portions of the trial for broadcast on regularly scheduled newscasts later in the day and evening. At the request of the petitioner, the trial judge prohibited coverage of any kind, still or television, of the defense counsel during their summations to the jury.

Because of the varying restrictions placed on sound and live telecasting the telecasts of the trial were confined largely to film clips shown on the stations' regularly scheduled news programs. The news commentators would use the film of a particular part of the day's trial activities as a backdrop for their reports. Their commentary included excerpts from testimony and the usual reportorial remarks. On one occasion the videotapes of the September hearings were rebroadcast in place of the "late movie."

[2]Due to mechanical difficulty there was no picture during the opening argument.

II

In *Rideau* v. *Louisiana*, 373 U.S. 723 (1963), this Court constructed a rule that the televising of a defendant in the act of confessing to a crime was inherently invalid under the Due Process Clause of the Fourteenth Amendment even without a showing of prejudice or a demonstration of the nexus between the televised confession and the trial. See *id.*, at 729 (dissenting opinion of Clark, J.). Here, although there was nothing so dramatic as a home-viewed confession, there had been a bombardment of the community with the sights and sounds of a two-day hearing during which the original jury panel, the petitioner, the lawyers and the judge were highly publicized. The petitioner was subjected to characterization and minute electronic scrutiny to such an extent that at one point the photographers were found attempting to picture the page of the paper from which he was reading while sitting at the counsel table. The two-day hearing and the order permitting television at the actual trial were widely known throughout the community. This emphasized the notorious character that the trial would take and, therefore, set it apart in the public mind as an extraordinary case or, as Shaw would say, something "not conventionally unconventional." When the new jury was empaneled at the trial four of the jurors selected had seen and heard all or part of the broadcasts of the earlier proceedings.

III

We start with the proposition that it is a "public trial" that the Sixth Amendment guarantees to the "accused." The purpose of the requirement of a public trial was to guarantee that the accused would be fairly dealt with and not unjustly condemned. History had proven that secret tribunals were effective instruments of oppression. As our Brother Black so well said in *In re Oliver*, 333 U.S. 257 (1948):

The traditional Anglo-American distrust for secret trials has been variously ascribed to the notorious use of this practice by the Spanish Inquisition, to the excesses of the English Court of Star Chamber, and to the French monarchy's abuse of the *lettre de cachet*. . . . Whatever other benefits the guarantee to an accused that his trial be conducted in public may confer upon our society, the guarantee has always been recognized as a safeguard against any attempt to employ our courts as instruments of persecution. At 268-270. (Footnotes omitted.)

It is said, however, that the freedoms granted in the First Amendment extend a right to the news media to televise from the courtroom, and that to refuse to honor this privilege is to discriminate between the newspapers and television. This is a misconception of the rights of the press.

The free press has been a mighty catalyst in awakening public interest in governmental affairs, exposing corruption among public officers and employees and generally informing the citizenry of public events and occurrences, including court proceedings. While maximum freedom must be allowed the press in carrying on this important function in a democratic society its exercise must necessarily be subject to the maintenance of absolute fairness in the judicial process. While the state and federal courts have differed over what spectators may be excluded from a criminal trial, 6 Wigmore, Evidence § 1834 (3d ed. 1940), the *amici curiae* brief of the National Association of Broadcasters and the Radio Television News Directors Association, says, as indeed it must, that "neither of these two amendments [First and Sixth] speaks of an unlimited right of access to the courtroom on the part of the broadcasting media. . . ." At 7. Moreover, they recognize that the "primary concern of all must be the proper administration of justice"; that "the life or liberty of any individual in this land should not be put in jeopardy because of actions of any news media"; and that "the due process requirements in both the Fifth and Fourteenth Amendments and the provisions of the Sixth Amendment require a procedure that will assure a fair trial. . . ." At 3-4.

Nor can the courts be said to discriminate where they permit the newspaper reporter access to the courtroom. The television and radio reporter has the same privilege. All are entitled to the same rights as the general public. The news reporter is not permitted to bring his typewriter or printing press. When the advances in these arts permit reporting by printing press or by television without their present hazards to a fair trial we will have another case.

IV

Court proceedings are held for the solemn purpose of endeavoring to ascertain the truth which is the *sine qua non* of a fair trial. Over the centuries Anglo-American courts have devised careful safeguards by rule and otherwise to protect and facilitate the performance of this high function. As a result, at this time those safeguards do not permit the televising and photographing of a criminal trial, save in two States and there only under restrictions. The federal courts prohibit it by specific rule. This is weighty evidence that our concepts of a fair trial do not tolerate such an indulgence. We have always held that the atmosphere essential to the preservation of a fair trial — the most fundamental of all freedoms — must be maintained at all costs. Our approach has been through rules, contempt proceedings and reversal of convictions obtained under unfair conditions. Here the remedy is clear and certain of application and it is our duty to continue to enforce the principles that from time immemorial have proven efficacious and necessary to a fair trial.

V

The State contends that the televising of portions of a criminal trial does not constitute a denial of due process. Its position is that because no prejudice has been shown by the petitioner as resulting from the televising, it is permissible; that claims of "distractions" during the trial due to the physical presence of television are wholly unfounded; and that psychological considerations are for psychologists, not courts, because they are purely hypothetical. It argues further that the public has a right to know what goes on in the courts; that the court has no power to "suppress, edit, or censor events which transpire in proceedings before it," citing *Craig* v. *Harney*, 331 U.S. 367, 374 (1947); and that the televising of criminal trials would be enlightening to the public and would promote greater respect for the courts.

At the outset the notion should be dispelled that telecasting is dangerous because it is new. It is true that our empirical knowledge of its full effect on the public, the jury or the participants in a trial, including the judge, witnesses and lawyers, is limited. However, the nub of the question is not its newness but, as Mr. Justice Douglas says, "the insidious influences which it puts to work in the administration of justice." Douglas, The Public Trial and the Free Press, 33 Rocky Mt. L. Rev. 1 (1960). These influences will be detailed below, but before turning to them the State's argument that the public has a right to know what goes on in the courtroom should be dealt with.

It is true that the public has the right to be informed as to what occurs in its courts, but reporters of all media, including television, are always present if they wish to be and are plainly free to report whatever occurs in open court through their respective media. This was settled in *Bridges* v. *California*, 314 U.S. 252 (1941), and *Pennekamp* v. *Florida*, 328 U.S. 331 (1946), which we reaffirm. These reportorial privileges of the press were stated years ago:

> The law, however, favors publicity in legal proceedings, so far as that object can be attained without injustice to the persons immediately concerned. The public are permitted to attend nearly all judicial inquiries, and there appears to be no sufficient reason why they should not also be allowed to see in print the reports of trials, if they can thus have them presented as fully as they are exhibited in court, or at least all the material portion of the proceedings impartially stated, so that one shall not, by means of them, derive erroneous impressions, which he would not have been likely to receive from hearing the trial itself. 2 Cooley's Constitutional Limitations 931-932 (Carrington ed. 1927).

The State, however, says that the use of television in the instant case was "without injustice to the person immediately concerned," basing its position on the fact that the petitioner has established no isolatable prejudice and that this must be shown in order to invalidate a conviction in these circumstances. The State paints too broadly in this contention, for this Court itself has found instances in which a showing of actual prejudice is not a prerequisite to reversal. This is such a case. It is true that in most cases involving claims of due process deprivations we require a showing of identifiable prejudice to the accused. Nevertheless, at times a procedure employed by the State involves such a probability that prejudice will result that it is deemed inherently lacking in due process. Such a case was *In re Murchison*, 349 U.S. 133 (1955), where Mr. Justice Black for the Court pointed up with his usual clarity and force:

A fair trial in a fair tribunal is a basic requirement of due process. Fairness of course requires an absence of actual bias in the trial of cases. But our system of law has always endeavored to prevent even the *probability* of unfairness. . . . [T]o perform its high function in the best way "justice must satisfy the appearance of justice." *Offutt* v. *United States*, 348 U.S. 11, 14. At 136. (Emphasis supplied.)

And, as Chief Justice Taft said in *Tumey* v. *Ohio*, 273 U.S. 510, almost 30 years before:

the requirement of due process of law in judicial procedure is not satisfied by the argument that men of the highest honor and the greatest self-sacrifice could carry it on without danger or injustice. Every procedure which would offer a *possible* temptation to the average man ... to forget the burden of proof required to convict the defendant, or which might lead him not to hold the balance nice, clear and true between the State and the accused, denies the latter due process of law. At 532. (Emphasis supplied.)

This rule was followed in *Rideau, supra*, and in *Turner* v. *Louisiana*, 379 U.S. 466 (1965). In each of these cases the Court departed from the approach it charted in *Stroble* v. *California*, 343 U.S. 181 (1952), and in *Irvin* v. *Dowd*, 366 U.S. 717 (1961), where we made a careful examination of the facts in order to determine whether prejudice resulted. In *Rideau* and *Turner* the Court did not stop to consider the actual effect of the practice but struck down the conviction on the ground that prejudice was inherent in it. Likewise in *Gideon* v. *Wainwright*, 372 U.S. 335 (1963), and *White* v. *Maryland*, 373 U.S. 59 (1963), we applied the same rule, although in different contexts.

In this case it is even clearer that such a rule must be applied. In *Rideau, Irvin* and *Stroble*, the pretrial publicity occurred outside the courtroom and could not be effectively curtailed. The only recourse other than reversal was by contempt proceedings. In *Turner* the probability of prejudice was present through the use of deputy sheriffs, who were also witnesses in the case, as shepherds for the jury. No prejudice was shown but the circumstances were held to be inherently suspect, and, therefore, such a showing was not held to be a requisite to reversal. Likewise in this case the application of this principle is especially appropriate. Television in its present state and by its very nature, reaches into a variety of areas in which it may cause prejudice to an accused.

Still one cannot put his finger on its specific mischief and prove with particularity wherein he was prejudiced. This was found true in *Murchison, Tumey, Rideau* and *Turner*. Such untoward circumstances as were found in those cases are inherently bad and prejudice to the accused was presumed. Forty-eight of our States and the Federal Rules have deemed the use of television improper in the courtroom. This fact is most telling in buttressing our conclusion that any change in procedure which would permit its use would be inconsistent with our concepts of due process in this field.

VI

As has been said, the chief function of our judicial machinery is to ascertain the truth. The use of television, however, cannot be said to contribute materially to this objective. Rather its use amounts to the injection of an irrelevant factor into court proceedings. In addition experience teaches that there are numerous situations in which it might cause actual unfairness — some so subtle as to defy detection by the accused or control by the judge. We enumerate some in summary:

1.   The potential impact of television on the jurors is perhaps of the greatest significance. They are the nerve center of the fact-finding process. It is true that in States like Texas where they are required to be sequestered in trials of this nature the jurors will probably not see any of the proceedings as televised from the courtroom. But the inquiry cannot end there. From the moment the trial judge announces that a case will be televised it becomes a *cause célèbre*. The whole community, including prospective jurors, becomes interested in all the morbid details surrounding it. The approaching trial immediately assumes an important status in the public press and the accused is highly publicized along with the offense with which he is charged. Every juror carries with him into the jury box these solemn facts and thus increases the chance of prejudice that is present in every criminal case. And we must remember that realistically it is only the notorious trial which will be broadcast, because of the necessity for paid sponsorship. The conscious or unconscious effect that this may have on the juror's judgment cannot be evaluated, but experience indicates that it is not only possible but highly probable that it will have a direct bearing on his vote as to guilt or innocence. Where pretrial publicity of all kinds has created intense public feeling which is aggravated by the telecasting or picturing of the trial the televised jurors cannot help but feel the pressures of knowing that friends and neighbors have their eyes upon them. If the community be hostile to an accused a televised juror, realizing that he must return to neighbors who saw the trial themselves, may well be led "not to hold the balance nice, clear and true between the State and the accused. . . ."

　　Moreover, while it is practically impossible to assess the effect of television on jury attentiveness, those of us who know juries realize the problem of jury "distraction." The State argues this is *de minimis* since the physical disturbances have been eliminated. But we know that distractions are not caused solely by the physical presence of the camera and its telltale red lights. It is the awareness of the fact of telecasting that is felt by the juror throughout the trial. We are all self-conscious and uneasy when being televised. Human nature being what it is, not only will a juror's eyes be fixed on the camera, but also his mind will be preoccupied with the telecasting rather than with the testimony.

　　Furthermore, in many States, the jurors serving in the trial may see the broadcasts of the trial proceedings. Admittedly, the Texas sequestration rule would prevent this occurring there.[3] In other States following no such practice jurors would return home and turn on the TV if only to see how they appeared upon it. They would also be subjected to re-enactment and emphasis of the selected parts of the proceedings which the requirements of the broadcasters determined would be telecast and would be subconsciously influenced the more by that testimony. Moreover, they would be subjected to the broadest commentary and criticism and perhaps the well-meant advice of friends, relatives and inquiring strangers who recognized them on the streets.

　　Finally, new trials plainly would be jeopardized in that potential jurors will often have seen and heard the original trial when it was telecast. Yet viewers may later be called upon to sit in the jury box during the new trial. These very dangers are illustrated in this case where the court, due to the defendant's objections, permitted only the State's opening and closing arguments to be broadcast with sound to the public.

　　2.　The quality of the testimony in criminal trials will often be impaired. The impact upon a witness of the knowledge that he is being viewed by a vast audience is simply incalculable. Some may be demoralized and frightened, some cocky and given to overstatement; memories may falter, as with anyone speaking publicly, and accuracy of statement may be severely undermined. Embarrassment may impede the search for the truth, as may a natural tendency toward overdramatization. Furthermore, inquisitive strangers and "cranks" might approach witnesses on the street with jibes, advice or demands for explanation of testimony. There is little wonder that the defendant cannot "prove" the existence of such factors. Yet we all know from experience that they exist.

　　In addition the invocation of the rule against witnesses is frustrated. In most instances witnesses would be able to go to their homes and view broadcasts of the day's trial proceedings, notwithstanding the fact that they had been admonished not to do so. They could view and hear the testimony of preceding

[3]Only six States, in addition to Texas, require sequestration of the jury prior to its deliberations in a non-capital felony trial. The great majority of jurisdictions leave the matter to the trial judge's discretion, while in at least one State the jury will be kept together in such circumstances only upon a showing of cause by the defendant.

witnesses, and so shape their own testimony as to make its impact crucial. And even in the absence of sound, the influences of such viewing on the attitude of the witness toward testifying, his frame of mind upon taking the stand or his apprehension of withering cross-examination defy objective assessment. Indeed, the mere fact that the trial is to be televised might render witnesses reluctant to appear and thereby impede the trial as well as the discovery of the truth.

While some of the dangers mentioned above are present as well in newspaper coverage of any important trial, the circumstances and extraneous influences intruding upon the solemn decorum of court procedure in the televised trial are far more serious than in cases involving only newspaper coverage.

3.   A major aspect of the problem is the additional responsibilities the presence of television places on the trial judge. His job is to make certain that the accused receives a fair trial. This most difficult task requires his undivided attention. Still when television comes into the courtroom he must also supervise it. In this trial, for example, the judge on several different occasions — aside from the two days of pretrial — was obliged to have a hearing or enter an order made necessary solely because of the presence of television. Thus, where telecasting is restricted as it was here, and as even the State concedes it must be, his task is made much more difficult and exacting. And, as happened here, such rulings may unfortunately militate against the fairness of the trial. In addition, laying physical interruptions aside, there is the ever-present distraction that the mere awareness of television's presence prompts. Judges are human beings also and are subject to the same psychological reactions as laymen. Telecasting is particularly bad where the judge is elected, as is the case in all save a half dozen of our States. The telecasting of a trial becomes a political weapon, which, along with other distractions inherent in broadcasting, diverts his attention from the task at hand — the fair trial of the accused.

But this is not all. There is the initial decision that must be made as to whether the use of television will be permitted. This is perhaps an even more crucial consideration. Our judges are high-minded men and women. But it is difficult to remain oblivious to the pressures that the news media can bring to bear on them both directly and through the shaping of public opinion. Moreover, where one judge in a district or even in a State permits telecasting, the requirement that the others do the same is almost mandatory. Especially is this true where the judge is selected at the ballot box.

4.   Finally, we cannot ignore the impact of courtroom television on the defendant. Its presence is a form of mental — if not physical — harassment, resembling a police line-up or the third degree. The inevitable close-ups of his gestures and expressions during the ordeal of his trial might well transgress his personal sensibilities, his dignity, and his ability to concentrate on the proceedings before him — sometimes the difference between life and death — dispassionately, freely and without the distraction of wide public surveillance. A defendant on trial for a specific crime is entitled to his day in court, not in a

stadium, or a city or nationwide arena. The heightened public clamor resulting from radio and television coverage will inevitably result in prejudice. Trial by television is, therefore, foreign to our system. Furthermore, telecasting may also deprive an accused of effective counsel. The distractions, intrusions into confidential attorney-client relationships and the temptation offered by television to play to the public audience might often have a direct effect not only upon the lawyers, but the judge, the jury and the witnesses. See Pye, The Lessons of Dallas — Threats to Fair Trial and Free Press, National Civil Liberties Clearing House, 16th Annual Conference.

The television camera is a powerful weapon. Intentionally or inadvertently it can destroy an accused and his case in the eyes of the public. While our telecasters are honorable men, they too are human. The necessity for sponsorship weighs heavily in favor of the televising of only notorious cases, such as this one, and invariably focuses the lens upon the unpopular or infamous accused. Such a selection is necessary in order to obtain a sponsor willing to pay a sufficient fee to cover the costs and return a profit. We have already examined the ways in which public sentiment can affect the trial participants. To the extent that television shapes that sentiment, it can strip the accused of a fair trial.

The State would dispose of all these observations with the simple statement that they are for psychologists because they are purely hypothetical. But we cannot afford the luxury of saying that, because these factors are difficult of ascertainment in particular cases, they must be ignored. Nor are they "purely hypothetical." They are no more hypothetical than were the considerations deemed controlling in *Tumey, Murchison, Rideau* and *Turner*. They are real enough to have convinced the Judicial Conference of the United States, this Court and the Congress that television should be barred in federal trials by the Federal Rules of Criminal Procedure; in addition they have persuaded all but two of our States to prohibit television in the courtroom. They are effects that may, and in some combination almost certainly will, exist in any case in which television is injected into the trial process.

VII

The facts in this case demonstrate clearly the necessity for the application of the rule announced in *Rideau*. The sole issue before the court for two days of pretrial hearing was the question now before us. The hearing was televised live and repeated on tape in the same evening, reaching approximately 100,000 viewers. In addition, the courtroom was a mass of wires, television cameras, microphones and photographers. The petitioner, the panel of prospective jurors, who were sworn the second day, the witnesses and the lawyers were all exposed to this untoward situation. The judge decided that the trial proceedings would be telecast. He announced no restrictions at the time. This emphasized the notorious nature of the coming trial, increased the intensity of the publicity on the petitioner and together with the subsequent televising of the trial beginning 30 days later inherently prevented a sober search for the truth. This is underscored by the fact that the selection of the jury took an entire week. As might be expected, a substantial amount of that time was devoted to ascertaining the impact of the pretrial televising on the prospective jurors. As we have noted, four of the jurors selected had seen all or part of those broadcasts. The trial, on the other hand, lasted only three days.

Moreover, the trial judge was himself harassed. After the initial decision to permit telecasting he apparently decided that a booth should be built at the broadcasters' expense to confine its operations; he then decided to limit the parts of the trial that might be televised live; then he decided to film the testimony of the witnesses without sound in an attempt to protect those under the rule; and finally he ordered that defense counsel and their argument not be televised, in the light of their objection. Plagued by his original error — recurring each day of the trial — his day-to-day orders made the trial more confusing to the jury, the participants and to the viewers. Indeed, it resulted in a public presentation of only the State's side of the case.

As Mr. Justice Holmes said in *Patterson* v. *Colorado*, 205 U.S. 454, 462 (1907):

The theory of our system is that the conclusions to be reached in a case will be induced only by evidence and argument in open court, and not by any outside influence, whether of private talk or public print.

It is said that the ever-advancing techniques of public communication and the adjustment of the public to its presence may bring about a change in the effect of telecasting upon the fairness of criminal trials. But we are not dealing here with future developments in the field of electronics. Our judgment cannot be rested on the hypothesis of tomorrow but must take the facts as they are presented today.

The judgment is therefore reversed.

34

Policy Statement on Comparative Broadcast Hearings

1 FCC 2d 393

July 28, 1965

Until 1965 the FCC weighed the relative public interest merits of licensing each of several prospective broadcasters competing for a single authorization without the benefit of clear standards to guide the outcome of the comparative hearing that determined the victorious applicant. Commission decisions in such cases were justly criticized for their inconsistency and arbitrariness. The issuance of this policy statement helped to clarify the major comparative criteria and their relative importance. Two commissioners dissented because they felt that adoption of the statement deprived the FCC and applicants of a desirable degree of flexibility.

Although footnote number 1 disclaims the applicability of the policy statement to comparative *renewal* proceedings, in 1969 the FCC applied the document's criteria in favoring the application of a challenger over a Boston telecaster's renewal bid [(*WHDH, Inc.,* 16 FCC 2d 1 (1969)]. On reconsideration, the Commission pointed out that the incumbent was anything but a typical renewal applicant [17 FCC 2d 856, 872-3 (1969)]. But the fears of those who wondered if their licenses would be renewed if similarly challenged could not be allayed when two court decisions adverse to broadcasters were handed down within the month following FCC reconsideration of the Boston case: the Supreme Court's *Red Lion* opinion (Document 39, pp. 381–402) and the Court of Appeals' reversal of FCC renewal of TV station WLBT (see p. 340). Broadcasters felt that the regulatory walls were tumbling down on them in mid-1969.

Concerned that a rash of license challengers would force the FCC to favor new applicants over incumbent licensees with absentee ownership and holdings in other media, the broadcasting industry urged Congress to pass protective legislation. When the measure (S. 2004, also known as the "Pastore bill") appeared unlikely to gain passage, the FCC issued a "Policy Statement Concerning Comparative Hearings Involving Regular Renewal Applicants" [22 FCC 2d 424 (1970)] that virtually guaranteed renewal to licensees whose programming was unmarred by serious deficiencies. The renewal policy statement was struck down in court [*Citizens Communications Center et al. v. FCC*, 447 F.2d 1201 (D.C. Cir. 1971)], whereupon the Commission resumed dealing with comparative renewals on a case-by-case basis that consistently-favored incumbents without the need for a statement of policy. See, e.g., *Cowles Florida Broadcasting Inc., et al.*, 60 FCC 2d 372 (1976), clarified by 62 FCC 2d 953 (1977), vacated and remanded *sub nom. Central Florida Enterprises, Inc. v. FCC,* 598 F. 2d 37(D.C. Cir. 1979).

Related Reading: 27, 88, 91, 108, 110, 127, 182, 197, 207, 227.

One of the Commission's primary responsibilities is to choose among qualified new applicants for the same broadcast facilities.[1] This commonly requires extended hearings into a number of areas of comparison. The hearing and decision process is inherently complex, and the subject does not lend itself to precise categorization or to the clear making of precedent. The various factors cannot be assigned absolute values, some factors may be present in some cases and not in others, and the differences between applicants with respect to each factor are almost infinitely variable.

Furthermore, membership on the Commission is not static and the views of individual Commissioners on the importance of particular factors may change. For these and other reasons, the Commission is not bound to deal with all cases at all times as it has dealt in the past with some that seem comparable, *Federal Communications Commission v. WOKO, Inc.*, 329 U.S. 223, 228,[2] and changes

---

[1]This statement of policy does not attempt to deal with the somewhat different problems raised where an applicant is contesting with a licensee seeking renewal of license.

[2]"[T]he doctrine of *stare decisis* is not generally applicable to the decisions of administrative tribunals," *Kentucky Broadcasting Corp. v. Federal Communications Commission*, 84 U.S. App. D.C. 383, 385, 174 F. 2d 38, 40.

of viewpoint, if reasonable, are recognized as both inescapable and proper. *Pinellas Broadcasting Co.* v. *Federal Communications Commission*, 97 U.S. App. D.C. 236, 230 F. 2d 204, *cert. den.* 350 U.S. 1007.

All this being so, it is nonetheless important to have a high degree of consistency of decision and of clarity in our basic policies. It is also obviously of great importance to prevent undue delay in the disposition of comparative hearing cases. A general review of the criteria governing the disposition of comparative broadcast hearings will, we believe, be useful to parties appearing before the Commission. It should also be of value to the examiners who initially decide the cases and to the Review Board to which the basic review of examiners' decisions in this area has been delegated. See Section 0.365 of our Rules, 47 CFR 0.365.[3]

This statement is issued to serve the purpose of clarity and consistency of decision, and the further purpose of eliminating from the hearing process time-consuming elements not substantially related to the public interest. We recognize, of course, that a general statement cannot dispose of all problems or decide cases in advance. Thus, for example, a case where a party proposes a specialized service will have to be given somewhat different consideration. Difficult cases will remain difficult. Our purpose is to promote stability of judgment without foreclosing the right of every applicant to a full hearing.

We believe that there are two primary objectives toward which the process of comparison should be directed. They are, first, the best practicable service to the public, and, second, a maximum diffusion of control of the media of mass communications. The value of these objectives is clear. Diversification of control is a public good in a free society, and is additionally desirable where a government licensing system limits access by the public to the use of radio and television facilities.[4] Equally basic is a broadcast service which meets the needs of the public in the area to be served, both in terms of those general interests which all areas have in common and those special interests which areas do not share. An important element of such a service is the flexibility to change as local needs and interests change. Since independence and individuality of approach

---

[3]On June 15, 1964 the rule was amended to give the Review Board authority to review initial decisions of hearing examiners in comparative television cases, a function formerly performed only by the Commission itself.

[4]As the Supreme Court has stated, the First Amendment to the Constitution of the United States "rests on the assumption that the widest possible dissemination of information from diverse and antagonistic sources is essential to the welfare of the public," *Associated Press* v. *United States*, 326 U.S. 1, 20. That radio and television broadcast stations play an important role in providing news and opinion is obvious. That it is important in a free society to prevent a concentration of control of the sources of news and opinion and, particularly, that government should not create such a concentration, is equally apparent, and well established. *United States* v. *Storer Broadcasting Co.*, 351 U.S. 192; *Scripps-Howard Radio, Inc.* v. *Federal Communications Commission*, 89 U.S. App. D.C. 13, 189 F. 2d 677, *cert. den.* 342 U.S. 830.

are elements of rendering good program service, the primary goals of good service and diversification of control are also fully compatible.

Several factors are significant in the two areas of comparison mentioned above, and it is important to make clear the manner in which each will be treated.

1. *Diversification of control of the media of mass communications.* Diversification is a factor of primary significance since, as set forth above, it constitutes a primary objective in the licensing scheme.

As in the past, we will consider both common control and less than controlling interests in other broadcast stations and other media of mass communications. The less the degree of interest in other stations or media, the less will be the significance of the factor. Other interests in the principal community proposed to be served will normally be of most significance, followed by other interests in the remainder of the proposed service area[5] and, finally, generally in the United States. However, control of large interests elsewhere in the same state or region may well be more significant than control of a small medium of expression (such as a weekly newspaper) in the same community. The number of other mass communication outlets of the same type in the community proposed to be served will also affect to some extent the importance of this factor in the general comparative scale.

It is not possible, of course, to spell out in advance the relationships between any significant number of the various factual situations which may be presented in actual hearings. It is possible, however, to set forth the elements which we believe significant. Without indicating any order of priority, we will consider interests in existing media of mass communications to be more significant in the degree that they:

(A)   are larger, i.e., go towards complete ownership and control;

and to the degree that the existing media:

(B)   are in, or close to, the community being applied for;
(C)   are significant in terms of numbers and size, i.e., the area covered, circulation, size of audience, etc.;
(D)   are significant in terms of regional or national coverage; and
(E)   are significant with respect to other media in their respective localities.

2. *Full-time participation in station operation by owners.* We consider this factor to be of substantial importance. It is inherently desirable

[5]Sections 73.35(a), 73.240(a)(1) and 73.636(a)(1) of our rules, 47 CFR 73.35(a), 73.240(a)(1), 73.636(a)(1), prohibit common control of stations in the same service (AM, FM and TV) within prescribed overlap areas. Less than controlling ownership interests and significant managerial positions in stations and other media within and without such areas will be considered when held by persons with any ownership or significant managerial interest in an applicant.

that legal responsibility and day-to-day performance be closely associated. In addition, there is a likelihood of greater sensitivity to an area's changing needs, and of programming designed to serve these needs, to the extent that the station's proprietors actively participate in the day-to-day operation of the station. This factor is thus important in securing the best practicable service.[6] It also frequently complements the objective of diversification, since concentrations of control are necessarily achieved at the expense of integrated ownership.

We are primarily interested in full-time participation. To the extent that the time spent moves away from full time, the credit given will drop sharply, and no credit will be given to the participation of any person who will not devote to the station substantial amounts of time on a daily basis. In assessing proposals, we will also look to the positions which the participating owners will occupy, in order to determine the extent of their policy functions and the likelihood of their playing important roles in management. We will accord particular weight to staff positions held by the owners, such as general manager, station manager, program director, business manager, director of news, sports or public service broadcasting, and sales manager. Thus, although positions of less responsibility will be considered, especially if there will be full-time integration by those holding those positions, they cannot be given the decisional significance attributed to the integration of stockholders exercising policy functions. Merely consultative positions will be given no weight.

Attributes of participating owners, such as their experience and local residence, will also be considered in weighing integration of ownership and management. While, for the reasons given above, integration of ownership and management is important *per se,* its value is increased if the participating owners are local residents and if they have experience in the field. Participation in station affairs on the basis described above by a local resident indicates a likelihood of continuing knowledge of changing local interests and needs.[7] Previous broadcast experience, while not so significant as local residence, also has some value when put to use through integration of ownership and management.

Past participation in civic affairs will be considered as a part of a participating owner's local residence background, as will any other local activities indicating a knowledge of and interest in the welfare of the community. Mere diversity of business interests will not be considered. Generally speaking, residence in the principal community to be served will be of primary importance, closely followed by residence outside the community, but within the proposed service area. Proposed future local residence (which is expected to accompany meaningful participation) will also be accorded less weight than present residence of several years' duration.

---

[6]As with other proposals, it is important that integration proposals be adhered to on a permanent basis. See *Tidewater Teleradio, Inc.*, 24 Pike & Fischer, R.R. 653.
[7]Of course, full-time participation is also necessarily accompanied by residence in the area.

Previous broadcasting experience includes activity which would not qualify as a past broadcast record, i.e., where there was not ownership responsibility for a station's performance. Since emphasis upon this element could discourage qualified newcomers to broadcasting, and since experience generally confers only an initial advantage,[8] it will be deemed of minor significance. It may be examined qualitatively, upon an offer of proof of particularly poor or good previous accomplishment.

The discussion above has assumed full-time, or almost full-time, participation in station operation by those with ownership interests. We recognize that station ownership by those who are local residents and, to a markedly lesser degree, by those who have broadcasting experience, may still be of some value even where there is not the substantial participation to which we will accord weight under this heading. Thus, local residence complements the statutory scheme and Commission allocation policy of licensing a large number of stations throughout the country, in order to provide for attention to local interests, and local ownership also generally accords with the goal of diversifying control of broadcast stations. Therefore, a slight credit will be given for the local residence of those persons with ownership interests who cannot be considered as actively participating in station affairs on a substantially full-time basis but who will devote some time to station affairs, and a very slight credit will similarly be given for experience not accompanied by full-time participation. Both of these factors, it should be emphasized, are of minor significance. No credit will be given either the local residence or experience of any person who will not put his knowledge of the community (or area) or experience to any use in the operation of the station.

3.   *Proposed program service.*   The United States Court of Appeals for the District of Columbia Circuit has stated that, "in a comparative consideration, it is well recognized that comparative service to the listening public is the vital element, and programs are the essence of that service." *Johnston Broadcasting Co.* v. *Federal Communications Commission*, 85 U.S. App. D.C. 40, 48, 175 F. 2d 351, 359. The importance of program service is obvious. The feasibility of making a comparative evaluation is not so obvious. Hearings take considerable time and precisely formulated program plans may have to be changed not only in details but in substance, to take account of new conditions obtaining at the time a successful applicant commences operation. Thus, minor differences among applicants are apt to prove to be of no significance.

The basic elements of an adequate service have been set forth in our July 29, 1960 "Report and Statement of Policy Re: Commission *en banc* Programming Inquiry," 25 F.R. 7291, 20 Pike & Fischer, R.R. 1901, and need

---

[8] Lack of experience, unlike a high concentration of control, is remediable. See *Sunbeam Television Corp.* v. *Federal Communications Commission*, 100 U.S. App. D.C. 82, 243 F. 2d 26.

not be repeated here.[9] And the applicant has the responsibility for a reasonable knowledge of the community and area, based on surveys or background, which will show that the program proposals are designed to meet the needs and interests of the public in that area. See *Henry* v. *Federal Communications Commission*, 112 U.S. App. D.C. 257, 302 F. 2d 191, *cert. den.* 371 U.S. 821. Contacts with local civic and other groups and individuals are also an important means of formulating proposals to meet an area's needs and interests. Failure to make them will be considered a serious deficiency, whether or not the applicant is familiar with the area.

Decisional significance will be accorded only to material and substantial differences between applicants' proposed program plans. See *Johnston Broadcasting Co.* v. *Federal Communications Commission*, 85 U.S. App. D.C. 40, 175 F. 2d 351. Minor differences in the proportions of time allocated to different types of programs will not be considered. Substantial differences will be considered to the extent that they go beyond ordinary differences in judgment and show a superior devotion to public service. For example, an unusual attention to local community matters for which there is a demonstrated need, may still be urged. We will not assume, however, that an unusually high percentage of time to be devoted to local or other particular types of programs is necessarily to be preferred. Staffing plans and other elements of planning will not be compared in the hearing process except where an inability to carry out proposals is indicated.[10]

In light of the considerations set forth above, and our experience with the similarity of the program plans of competing applicants, taken with the desirability of keeping hearing records free of immaterial clutter, no comparative issue will ordinarily be designated on program plans and policies, or on staffing plans or other program planning elements, and evidence on these matters will not be taken under the standard issues. The Commission will designate an issue where examination of the applications and other information before it makes such action appropriate, and applicants who believe they can demonstrate significant differences upon which the reception of evidence will be useful may petition to amend the issues.

No independent factor of likelihood of effectuation of proposals will be utilized. The Commission expects every licensee to carry out its proposals, subject to factors beyond its control, and subject to reasonable judgment that the public's needs and interests require a departure from original plans. If there

---

[9]Specialized proposals necessarily have to be considered on a case-to-case basis. We will examine the need for the specialized service as against the need for a general-service station where the question is presented by competing applicants.

[10]We will similarly not give independent consideration to proposed studios or other equipment. These are also elements of a proposed operation which are necessary to carry out the program plans, and which are expected to be adequate. They will be inquired into only upon a petition to amend the issues which indicates a serious deficiency.

is a substantial indication that any party will not be able to carry out its proposals to a significant degree, the proposals themselves will be considered deficient.[11]

4.   *Past broadcast record.*   This factor includes past ownership interest and significant participation in a broadcast station by one with an ownership interest in the applicant. It is a factor of substantial importance upon the terms set forth below.

A past record within the bounds of average performance will be disregarded, since average future performance is expected. Thus, we are not interested in the fact of past ownership *per se*, and will not give a preference because one applicant has owned stations in the past and another has not.

We are interested in records which, because either unusually good or unusually poor, give some indication of unusual performance in the future. Thus, we shall consider past records to determine whether the record shows (i) unusual attention to the public's needs and interests, such as special sensitivity to an area's changing needs through flexibility of local programs designed to meet those needs, or (ii) either a failure to meet the public's needs and interests or a significant failure to carry out representations made to the Commission (the fact that such representations have been carried out, however, does not lead to an affirmative preference for the applicant, since it is expected, as a matter of course, that a licensee will carry out representations made to the Commission).

If a past record warrants consideration, the particular reasons, if any, which may have accounted for that record will be examined to determine whether they will be present in the proposed operation. For example, an extraordinary record compiled while the owner fully participated in operation of the station will not be accorded full credit where the party does not propose similar participation in the operation of the new station for which he is applying.

5.   *Efficient use of frequency.*[12]   In comparative cases where one of two or more competing applicants proposes an operation which, for one or more engineering reasons, would be more efficient, this fact can and should be considered in determining which of the applicants should be preferred. The nature of an efficient operation may depend upon the nature of the facilities applied for, i.e., whether they are in the television or FM bands where geographical allocations have been made, or in the standard broadcast (AM) band where there are no such fixed allocations. In addition, the possible variations of situations in comparative hearings are numerous. Therefore, it is not feasible here to delineate the outlines of this element, and we merely take

[11] It should be noted here that the absence of an issue on program plans and policies will not preclude cross-examination of the parties with respect to their proposals for participation in station operation, i.e., to test the validity of integration proposals.

[12] This factor as discussed here is not to be confused with the determination to be made of which of two communities has the greater need for a new station. See *Federal Communications Commission* v. *Allentown Broadcasting Corp.* 349 U.S. 358.

this occasion to point out that the element will be considered where the facts warrant.

6. *Character.* The Communications Act makes character a relevant consideration in the issuance of a license. See Section 308(b), 47 U.S.C. 308(b). Significant character deficiencies may warrant disqualification, and an issue will be designated where appropriate. Since substantial demerits may be appropriate in some cases where disqualification is not warranted, petitions to add an issue on conduct relating to character will be entertained. In the absence of a designated issue, character evidence will not be taken. Our intention here is not only to avoid unduly prolonging the hearing process, but also to avoid those situations where an applicant converts the hearing into a search for his opponents' minor blemishes, no matter how remote in the past or how insignificant.

7. *Other Factors.* As we stated at the outset, our interest in the consistency and clarity of decision and in expedition of the hearing process is not intended to preclude the full examination of any relevant and substantial factor. We will thus favorably consider petitions to add issues when, but only when, they demonstrate that significant evidence will be adduced.[13]

We pointed out at the outset that in the normal course there may be changes in the views of individual commissioners as membership on the Commission changes or as commissioners may come to view matters differently with the passage of time. Therefore, it may be well to emphasize that by this attempt to clarify our present policy and our views with respect to the various factors which are considered in comparative hearings, we do not intend to stultify the continuing process of reviewing our judgment on these matters. Where changes in policy are deemed appropriate they will be made, either in individual cases or in further general statements, with an explanation of the reason for the change. In this way, we hope to preserve the advantages of clear policy enunciation without sacrificing necessary flexibility and open-mindedness.

Cases to be decided by either the Review Board or, where the Review Board has not been delegated that function, by the Commission itself, will be decided under the policies here set forth. So too, future designations for hearing will be made in accordance with this statement. Where cases are now in hearing, the hearing examiner will be expected to follow this statement to the extent practicable. Issues already designated will not be changed, but evidence should be adduced only in accordance with this statement. Thus, evidence on issues which we have said will no longer be designated in the absence of a petition to add an issue, should not be accepted unless the party wishing to adduce the evidence makes an offer of proof to the examiner which demonstrates that the evidence will be of substantial value under the criteria discussed herein. Since we

---

[13]Where a narrow question is raised, for example on one aspect of financial qualification, a narrowly drawn issue will be appropriate. In other circumstances, a broader inquiry may be required. This is a matter for *ad hoc* determination.

are not adopting new criteria which would call for the introduction of new evidence, but rather restricting the scope somewhat of existing factors and explaining their importance more clearly, there will be no element of surprise which might affect the fairness of a hearing. It is, of course, traditional judicial practice to decide cases in accordance with principles in effect at the time of decision. Administrative finality is also important. Therefore, cases which have already been decided, either by the Commission or, where appropriate, by the Review Board, will not be reconsidered. We believe that our purpose to improve the hearing and decisional process in the future does not require upsetting decisions already made, particularly in light of the basically clarifying nature of this document.

35

The United Church of Christ Case

Office of Communication of the United Church of Christ v. Federal Communications Commission*
359 F.2d 994 (D.C. Cir.)
March 25, 1966

Throughout its history the FCC had received comments and complaints from the public. These were dutifully filed away and rarely was anything done about them. Although the Commission required licensees to seek out conflicting views on controversial issues of public importance and ascertain community needs, tastes, and desires (or "problems"), the agency itself seldom actively solicited the public's views on the radio and television services' they were receiving. Like other federal regulatory bodies, the FCC gradually aligned itself with the interests of the broadcasting industry it was established to regulate. It was as if the Commission believed the public was an entity whose interests could best be served by ignoring them.

The *United Church of Christ* case changed this situation by providing a degree of legal clout to ordinary citizens. This 1966 decision establishes the right of representatives of the general public to intervene in broadcast licensing proceedings before the FCC. Prior to this historic decision only other broadcasters alleging economic injury or electrical interference (see, for example, Documents 18, 24, 30, and 31, pp. 89-94, 246-250, 296-305,

*Reprinted with the permission of West Publishing Company.

and 306–309, respectively) were granted standing to intervene. *United Church of Christ* is the Magna Carta (but not a carte blanche) for active public participation in broadcast regulation. Document 42 (pp. 426–452) provides a comprehensive perspective of the range of citizens' rights in broadcasting as of 1974.

Following this decision, the FCC held the required hearing, but it placed the major burden of proof on the public intervenors instead of the renewal applicant. Since little weight or credence was given to the intervenors' testimony, WLBT's license was renewed. The case then returned to the Court of Appeals. In Warren Burger's last opinion before he was appointed Chief Justice of the Supreme Court, the appellate body sternly vacated the renewal and ordered the FCC to consider new applicants for the channel [*Office of Communication of the United Church of Christ* v. *FCC*, 425 F.2d 543 (D.C. Cir. 1969)]. WLBT was operated on an interim basis by a non-profit and racially mixed group of local residents while the FCC's comparative proceeding slowly wended its way through the 1970's.

Related Reading: 27, 92, 94, 114, 146, 166, 201.

Burger, Circuit Judge:

This is an appeal from a decision of the Federal Communications Commission granting to the Intervenor a one-year renewal of its license to operate television station WLBT in Jackson, Mississippi. Appellants filed with the Commission a timely petition to intervene to present evidence and arguments opposing the renewal application. The Commission dismissed Appellants' petition and, without a hearing, took the unusual step of granting a restricted and conditional renewal of the license. Instead of granting the usual three-year renewal, it limited the license to one year from June 1, 1965, and imposed what it characterizes here as "strict conditions" on WLBT's operations in that one-year probationary period.

The questions presented are (a) whether Appellants, or any of them, have standing before the Federal Communications Commission as parties in interest under Section 309(d) of the Federal Communications Act[1] to contest the renewal of a broadcast license; and (b) whether the Commission was required by Section 309(e)[2] to conduct an evidentiary hearing on the claims of the Appellants prior to acting on renewal of the license.

Because the question whether representatives of the listening public have

---

[1] 74 Stat. 890 (1960), 47 U.S.C. § 309(d) (1964).
[2] 78 Stat. 193 (1964), 47 U.S.C. § 309(e) (1964).

standing to intervene in a license renewal proceeding is one of first impression, we have given particularly close attention to the background of these issues and to the Commission's reasons for denying standing to Appellants.

BACKGROUND

The complaints against Intervenor embrace charges of discrimination on racial and religious grounds and of excessive commercials. As the Commission's order indicates, the first complaints go back to 1955 when it was claimed that WLBT had deliberately cut off a network program about race relations problems on which the General Counsel of the NAACP was appearing and had flashed on the viewers' screens a "Sorry, Cable Trouble" sign. In 1957 another complaint was made to the Commission that WLBT had presented a program urging the maintenance of racial segregation and had refused requests for time to present the opposing viewpoint. Since then numerous other complaints have been made.

When WLBT sought a renewal of its license in 1958, the Commission at first deferred action because of complaints of this character but eventually granted the usual three-year renewal because it found that, while there had been failures to comply with the Fairness Doctrine, the failures were isolated instances of improper behavior and did not warrant denial of WLBT's renewal application.

Shortly after the outbreak of prolonged civil disturbances centering in large part around the University of Mississippi in September 1962, the Commission again received complaints that various Mississippi radio and television stations, including WLBT, had presented programs concerning racial integration in which only one viewpoint was aired. In 1963 the Commission investigated and requested the stations to submit detailed factual reports on their programs dealing with racial issues. On March 3, 1964, while the Commission was considering WLBT's responses, WLBT filed the license renewal application presently under review.

To block license renewal, Appellants filed a petition in the Commission urging denial of WLBT's application and asking to intervene in their own behalf and as representatives of "all other television viewers in the State of Mississippi." The petition[3] stated that the Office of Communication of the United Church of Christ is an instrumentality of the United Church of Christ, a national denomination with substantial membership within WLBT's prime service area. It listed Appellants Henry and Smith as individual residents of Mississippi, and asserted that both owned television sets and that one lived within the prime service area of WLBT; both are described as leaders in Mississippi civic and civil

---

[3] By "petition," we refer to both the original petition and the reply to WLBT's opposition to the initial petition.

rights groups. Dr. Henry is president of the Mississippi NAACP; both have been politically active. Each has had a number of controversies with WLBT over allotment of time to present views in opposition to those expressed by WLBT editorials and programs. Appellant United Church of Christ at Tougaloo is a congregation of the United Church of Christ within WLBT's area.

The petition claimed that WLBT failed to serve the general public because it provided a disproportionate amount of commercials and entertainment and did not give a fair and balanced presentation of controversial issues, especially those concerning Negroes, who comprise almost forty-five per cent of the total population within its prime service area;[4] it also claimed discrimination against local activities of the Catholic Church.

Appellants claim standing before the Commission on the grounds that:

(1)   They are individuals and organizations who were denied a reasonable opportunity to answer their critics, a violation of the Fairness Doctrine.

(2)   These individuals and organizations represent the nearly one half of WLBT's potential listening audience who were denied an opportunity to have their side of controversial issues presented, equally a violation of the Fairness Doctrine, and who were more generally ignored and discriminated against in WLBT's programs.

(3)   These individuals and organizations represent the total audience, not merely one part of it, and they assert the right of all listeners, regardless of race or religion, to hear and see balanced programming on significant public questions as required by the Fairness Doctrine[5] and also their broad interest that the station be operated in the public interest in all respects.

The Commission denied the petition to intervene on the ground that standing is predicated upon the invasion of a legally protected interest or an injury which is direct and substantial and that "petitioners . . . can assert no

---

[4] The specific complaints of discrimination were that Negro individuals and institutions are given very much less television exposure than others are given and that programs are generally disrespectful toward Negroes. The allegations were particularized and accompanied by a detailed presentation of the results of Appellants' monitoring of a typical week's programming.

[5] In promulgating the Fairness Doctrine in 1949 the Commission emphasized the "right of the public to be informed, rather than any right on the part of the Government, any broadcast licensee or any individual member of the public to broadcast his own particular views on any matter . . ." The Commission characterized this as "the foundation stone of the American system of broadcasting." *Editorializing by Broadcast Licensees*, 13 F.C.C. 1246, 1249 (1949). This policy received Congressional approval in the 1959 amendment of Section 315 which speaks in terms of "the obligation imposed upon [licensees] under this Act to operate in the public interest and to afford reasonable opportunity for the discussion of conflicting views on issues of public importance." 73 Stat. 557 (1959), 47 U.S.C. § 315(a) (1964).

greater interest or claim of injury than members of the general public." The Commission stated in its denial, however, that as a general practice it "does consider the contentions advanced in circumstances such as these, irrespective of any questions of standing or related matters," and argues that it did so in this proceeding.

Upon considering Petitioners' claims and WLBT's answers to them on this basis, the Commission concluded that

serious issues are presented whether the licensee's operations have fully met the public interest standard. Indeed, it is a close question whether to designate for hearing these applications for renewal of license.

Nevertheless, the Commission conducted no hearing but granted a license renewal, asserting a belief that renewal would be in the public interest since broadcast stations were in a position to make worthwhile contributions to the resolution of pressing racial problems, this contribution was "needed immediately" in the Jackson area, and WLBT, if operated properly,[6] could make such a contribution. Indeed the renewal period was explicitly made a test of WLBT's qualifications in this respect.

We are granting a renewal of license, so that the licensee can demonstrate and carry out its stated willingness to serve fully and fairly the needs and interests of its entire area — so that it can, in short, meet and resolve the questions raised.

The one-year renewal was on conditions which plainly put WLBT on notice that the renewal was in the nature of a probationary grant; the conditions were stated as follows:

(a)   "That the licensee comply strictly with the established requirements of the fairness doctrine."

(b)   ". . . [T]hat the licensee observe strictly its representations to the Commission in this [fairness] area . . ."

(c)   "That, in the light of the substantial questions raised by the United Church petition, the licensee immediately have discussions with community leaders, including those active in the civil rights movement (such as petitioners), as to whether its programming is fully meeting the needs and interests of its area."

(d)   "That the licensee immediately cease discriminatory programming patterns."

(e)   That "the licensee will be required to make a detailed report as to its efforts in the above four respects . . ."

Appellants contend that, against the background of complaints since 1955 and the Commission's conclusion that WLBT was in fact guilty of "discrimi-

---

[6]". . . we cannot stress too strongly that the licensee must operate in complete conformity with its representations and the conditions laid down."

natory programming," the Commission could not properly renew the license even for one year without a hearing to resolve factual issues raised by their petition and vitally important to the public. The Commission argues, however, that it in effect accepted Petitioners' view of the facts, took all necessary steps to insure that the practices complained of would cease, and for this reason granted a short-term renewal as an exercise by the Commission of what it describes as a "'political' decision, 'in the higher sense of that abused term,' which is peculiarly entrusted to the agency."[7] The Commission seems to have based its "political decision" on a blend of what the Appellants alleged, what its own investigation revealed, its hope that WLBT would improve, and its view that the station was needed.

STANDING OF APPELLANTS[8]

The Commission's denial of standing to Appellants was based on the theory that, absent a potential direct, substantial injury or adverse effect from the administrative action under consideration, a petitioner has no standing before the Commission and that the only types of effects sufficient to support standing are economic injury and electrical interference. It asserted its traditional position that members of the listening public do not suffer any injury peculiar to them and that allowing them standing would pose great administrative burdens.[9]

Up to this time, the courts have granted standing to intervene only to those alleging electrical interference, NBC v. FCC (KOA), 76 U.S. App. D.C. 238, 132 F. 2d 545 (1942), aff'd, 319 U.S. 239, 63 S.Ct. 1035, 87 L.Ed. 1374 (1943), or alleging some economic injury, e.g., FCC v. Sanders Bros. Radio Station, 309 U.S. 470, 60 S.Ct. 693, 84 L.Ed. 869 (1940). It is interesting to

[7]Intervenor and the Commission depart from the record to argue that WLBT has fully complied with the conditions and that the Commission's hope that WLBT would make a valuable contribution to the problems of race relations is being fulfilled. Appellants respond that WLBT has not adequately corrected unbalanced programming. We do not consider these claims as to the alleged success of the Commission's effort to permit WLBT to purge itself of misconduct relevant either to the question of standing or to the correctness of the grant of a renewal without a hearing. We confine ourselves to the record as made before the Commission.

[8]All parties seem to consider that the same standards are applicable to determining standing before the Commission and standing to appeal a Commission order to this court. See Philco Corp. v. FCC, 103 U.S. App. D.C. 278, 257 F. 2d 656 (1958), cert. denied, 358 U.S. 946, 79 S.Ct. 350, 3 L.Ed. 2d 352 (1959); Metropolitan Television Co. v. FCC, 95 U.S. App. D.C. 326, 221 F. 2d 879 (1955). We have, therefore, used the cases dealing with standing in the two tribunals interchangeably.

[9]See Northern Pacific Radio Corp., 23 P & F Rad. Reg. 186 (1962); Gordon Broadcasting of San Francisco, Inc., 22 P & F Rad. Reg. 236 (1962).

note, however, that the Commission's traditionally narrow view of standing initially led it to deny standing to the very categories it now asserts are the only ones entitled thereto. In *Sanders* the Commission argued that economic injury was not a basis for standing,[10] and in *KOA* that electrical interference was insufficient. This history indicates that neither administrative nor judicial concepts of standing have been static.

What the Commission apparently fails to see in the present case is that the courts have resolved questions of standing as they arose and have at no time manifested an intent to make economic interest and electrical interference the exclusive grounds for standing. *Sanders*, for instance, granted standing to those economically injured on the theory that such persons might well be the only ones sufficiently interested to contest a Commission action. 309 U.S. 470, 477, 60 S.Ct. 693. In *KOA* we noted the anomalous result that, if standing were restricted to those with an economic interest, educational and non-profit radio stations, a prime source of public-interest broadcasting, would be defaulted. Because such a rule would hardly promote the statutory goal of public-interest broadcasting, we concluded that non-profit stations must be heard without a showing of economic injury and held that all broadcast licensees could have standing by showing injury other than financial (there, electrical interference). Our statement that *Sanders* did not limit standing to those suffering direct economic injury was not disturbed by the Supreme Court when it affirmed *KOA*. 319 U.S. 239, 63 S.Ct. 1035 (1943).

It is important to remember that the cases allowing standing to those falling within either of the two established categories have emphasized that standing is accorded to persons not for the protection of their private interest but only to vindicate the public interest.

"The Communications Act of 1934 did not create new private rights. The purpose of the Act was to protect the public interest in communications. By § 402(b)(2), Congress gave the right of appeal to persons 'aggrieved or whose interests are adversely affected' by Commission action. ... But *these private litigants have standing only as representatives of the public interest.* Federal Communications Commission v. Sanders Radio Station, 309 U.S. 470, 477, 642, 60 S.Ct. 693, 698, 84 L.Ed. 869, 1037." Associated Industries of New York State, Inc. v. Ickes, 134 F. 2d 694, 703 (2d Cir. 1943), vacated as moot, 320 U.S. 707, 64 S.Ct. 74, 88 L.Ed. 414 (1943), quoting Scripps-Howard Radio, Inc. v. FCC, 316 U.S. 4, 14, 62 S.Ct. 875, 86 L.Ed. 1229 (1942).

On the other hand, some Congressional reports have expressed apprehensions, possibly representing the views of both administrative agencies and

---

[10] It argued that, since economic injury was not a ground for refusing a license, it could not be a basis of standing. See generally Chicago Junction Case, 264 U.S. 258, 44 S.Ct. 317, 68 L.Ed. 667 (1924).

broadcasters, that standing should not be accorded lightly so as to make possible intervention into proceedings "by a host of parties who have no legitimate interest but solely with the purpose of delaying license grants which properly should be made."[11] But the recurring theme in the legislative reports is not so much fear of a plethora of parties in interest as apprehension that standing might be abused by persons with no *legitimate* interest in the proceedings but with a desire only to delay the granting of a license for some private selfish reason.[12] The Congressional Committee which voiced the apprehension of a "host of parties" seemingly was willing to allow standing to anyone who could show economic injury or electrical interference. Yet these criteria are no guarantee of the legitimacy of the claim sought to be advanced, for, as another Congressional Committee later lamented, "In many of these cases the protests are based on grounds which have little or no relationship to the public interest."[13]

We see no reason to believe, therefore, that Congress through its committees had any thought that electrical interference and economic injury were to be the exclusive grounds for standing or that it intended to limit participation of the listening public to writing letters to the Complaints Division of the Commission. Instead, the Congressional reports seem to recognize that the issue of standing was to be left to the courts.[14]

The Commission's rigid adherence to a requirement of direct economic injury in the commercial sense operates to give standing to an electronics manufacturer who competes with the owner of a radio-television station only in the sale of appliances,[15] while it denies standing to spokesmen for the listeners, who are most directly concerned with and intimately affected by the performance of a licensee. Since the concept of standing is a practical and functional one designed to insure that only those with a genuine and legitimate interest can participate in a proceeding, we can see no reason to exclude those with such an obvious and acute concern as the listening audience. This much seems essential to insure that the holders of broadcasting licenses be responsive to the needs of the audience, without which the broadcaster could not exist.

There is nothing unusual or novel in granting the consuming public standing to challenge administrative actions. In Associated Industries of New York State, Inc. v. Ickes, 134 F. 2d 694 (2d Cir. 1943), vacated as moot, 320 U.S. 707, 64 S.Ct. 74, 88 L.Ed. 414 (1943), coal consumers were found to have

---

[11] S. Rep. No. 44, 82d Cong., 1st Sess. 8 (1951).

[12] See, *e.g., ibid.*; S. Rep. No. 1231, 84th Cong., 1st Sess. 1-3 (1955); H.R. Rep. No. 1051, 84th Cong., 1st Sess. 2-3 (1955); H.R. Rep. No. 1800, 86th Cong., 2d Sess. 9-10, U.S. Code Cong. & Admin. News 1960, p. 3516 (1960).

[13] H.R. Rep. No. 1051, 84th Cong., 1st Sess. 3 (1955).

[14] Perhaps the mention in these reports of economic and electrical injury arose out of preoccupation with problems surrounding initial licensing procedures, as distinguished from those involved in renewal proceedings. See . . . *infra.*

[15] Philco Corp. v. FCC, 103 U.S. App. D.C. 278, 257 F. 2d 656 (1958); cert. denied, 358 U.S. 946, 79 S.Ct. 350, 3 L.Ed. 2d 35 (1959).

standing to review a minimum price order. In United States v. Public Utilities Commission, 80 U.S. App. D.C. 227, 151 F. 2d 609 (1945), we held that a consumer of electricity was affected by the rates charged and could appeal an order setting them. Similarly in Bebchick v. Public Utilities Commission, 109 U.S. App. D.C. 298, 287 F. 2d 337 (1961), we had no difficulty in concluding that a public transit rider had standing to appeal a rate increase. A direct economic injury, even if small as to each user, is involved in the rate cases, but standing has also been granted to a passenger to contest the legality of Interstate Commerce Commission rules allowing racial segregation in railroad dining cars. Henderson v. United States, 339 U.S. 816, 70 S.Ct. 843, 94 L.Ed. 1302 (1950). Moreover, in Reade v. Ewing, 205 F. 2d 630 (2d Cir. 1953), a consumer of oleomargarine was held to have standing to challenge orders affecting the ingredients thereof.[16]

These "consumer" cases were not decided under the Federal Communications Act, but all of them have in common with the case under review the interpretation of language 'granting standing to persons "affected" or "aggrieved." The Commission fails to suggest how we are to distinguish these cases from those involving standing of broadcast "consumers" to oppose license renewals in the Federal Communications Commission. The total number of potential individual suitors who are consumers of oleomargarine or public transit passengers would seem to be greater than the number of responsible representatives of the listening public who are potential intervenors in a proceeding affecting a single broadcast reception area. Furthermore, assuming we look only to the commercial economic aspects and ignore vital public interest, we cannot believe that the economic stake of the consumers of electricity or public transit riders is more significant than that of listeners who collectively have a huge aggregate investment in receiving equipment. [17]

The argument that a broadcaster is not a public utility is beside the point. True it is not a public utility in the same sense as strictly regulated common carriers or purveyors of power, but neither is it a purely private enterprise like a newspaper or an automobile agency. A broadcaster has much in common with a newspaper publisher, but he is not in the same category in terms of public obligations imposed by law. A broadcaster seeks and is granted the free and exclusive use of a limited and valuable part of the public domain; when he accepts that franchise it is burdened by enforceable public obligations. A

---

[16] In the most recent case on the subject, the Second Circuit, relying on cases under the Federal Communications Act, held that non-profit conservation associations have standing to protect the aesthetic, conservational, and recreational aspects of power development. Scenic Hudson Preservation Conference v. FPC, 354 F. 2d 608 (2d Cir. 1965).

[17] According to Robert Sarnoff of NBC the total investment in television, by American viewers is 40 billion dollars, a figure perhaps twenty times as large as the total investment of broadcasters. FCC, *Television Network Program Procurement*, H.R. Rep. No. 281, 88th Cong., 1st Sess. 57 (1963). Forty billion dollars would seem to afford at least one substantial brick in a foundation for standing.

newspaper can be operated at the whim or caprice of its owners; a broadcast station cannot. After nearly five decades of operation the broadcast industry does not seem to have grasped the simple fact that a broadcast license is a public trust subject to termination for breach of duty.

Nor does the fact that the Commission itself is directed by Congress to protect the public interest constitute adequate reason to preclude the listening public from assisting in that task. *Cf.* UAW v. Scofield, 382 U.S. 205, 86 S.Ct. 335, 15 L.Ed. 2d 304 (1965). The Commission of course represents and indeed is the prime arbiter of the public interest, but its duties and jurisdiction are vast, and it acknowledges that it cannot begin to monitor or oversee the performance of every one of thousands of licensees. Moreover, the Commission has always viewed its regulatory duties as guided if not limited by our national tradition that public response is the most reliable test of ideas and performance in broadcasting as in most areas of life. The Commission view is that we have traditionally depended on this public reaction rather than on some form of governmental supervision or "censorship" mechanisms.

[I]t is the public in individual communities throughout the length and breadth of our country who must bear final responsibility for the quality and adequacy of television service — whether it be originated by local stations or by national networks. Under our system, the interests of the public are dominant. The commercial needs of licensed broadcasters and advertisers must be integrated into those of the public. *Hence, individual citizens and the communities they compose owe a duty to themselves and their peers to take an active interest in the scope and quality of the television service* which stations and networks provide and which, undoubtedly, has a *vast impact on their lives and the lives of their children.* Nor need the public feel that in taking a hand in broadcasting they are unduly interfering in the private business affairs of others. On the contrary, *their interest in television programming is direct* and their responsibilities important. *They are the owners* of the channels of television — indeed, of all broadcasting.
FCC, *Television Network Program Procurement*, H.R. Rep. No. 281, 88th Cong., 1st Sess. 20 (1963). (Emphasis added.)

Taking advantage of this "active interest in the ... quality" of broadcasting rather than depending on governmental initiative is also desirable in that it tends to cast governmental power, at least in the first instance, in the more detached role of arbiter rather than accuser.

The theory that the Commission can always effectively represent the listener interests in a renewal proceeding without the aid and participation of legitimate listener representatives fulfilling the role of private attorneys general is one of those assumptions we collectively try to work with so long as they are reasonably adequate. When it becomes clear, as it does to us now, that it is no longer a valid assumption which stands up under the realities of actual experience, neither we nor the Commission can continue to rely on it. The gradual expansion and evolution of concepts of standing in administrative law attests that experience rather than logic or fixed rules has been accepted as the guide.

The Commission's attitude in this case is ambivalent in the precise sense of that term. While attracted by the potential contribution of widespread public interest and participation in improving the quality of broadcasting, the Commission rejects effective public participation by invoking the oft-expressed fear that a "host of parties" will descend upon it and render its dockets "clogged" and "unworkable." The Commission resolves this ambivalence for itself by contending that in this renewal proceeding the viewpoint of the public was adequately represented since it fully considered the claims presented by Appellants even though denying them standing. It also points to the general procedures for public participation that are already available, such as the filing of complaints with the Commission, [18] the practice of having local hearings, [19] and the ability of people who are not parties in interest to appear at hearings as witnesses. [20] In light of the Commission's procedure in this case and its stated willingness to hear witnesses having complaints, it is difficult to see how a grant of formal standing would pose undue or insoluble problems for the Commission.

We cannot believe that the Congressional mandate of public participation which the Commission says it seeks to fulfill [21] was meant to be limited to writing letters to the Commission, to inspection of records, to the Commission's grace in considering listener claims, or to mere non-participating appearance at hearings. We cannot fail to note that the long history of complaints against WLBT beginning in 1955 had left the Commission virtually unmoved in the subsequent renewal proceedings, and it seems not unlikely that the 1964 renewal application might well have been routinely granted except for the determined and sustained efforts of Appellants at no small expense to themselves. [22] Such beneficial contribution as these Appellants, or some of them, can make must not be left to the grace of the Commission.

Public participation is especially important in a renewal proceeding, since the public will have been exposed for at least three years to the licensee's performance, as cannot be the case when the Commission considers an initial grant, unless the applicant has a prior record as a licensee. In a renewal proceeding, furthermore, public spokesmen, such as Appellants here, may be the only objectors. In a community served by only one outlet, the public interest focus is perhaps sharper and the need for airing complaints often greater than where, for example, several channels exist. Yet if there is only one outlet, there

---

[18] 47 C.F.R. § 1.587 (1965).

[19] 74 Stat. 892 (1960), 47 U.S.C. § 311 (1964).

[20] 47 C.F.R. § 1.225 (1965).

[21] See 30 Fed. Reg. 4543 (1965).

[22] We recognize, of course, the existence of strong tides of public opinion and other forces at work outside the listening area of the Licensee which may not have been without some effect on the Commission.

are no rivals at hand to assert the public interest, and reliance on opposing applicants to challenge the existing licensee for the channel would be fortuitous at best. Even when there are multiple competing stations in a locality, various factors may operate to inhibit the other broadcasters from opposing a renewal application. An imperfect rival may be thought a desirable rival, or there may be a "gentleman's agreement" of deference to a fellow broadcaster in the hope he will reciprocate on a propitious occasion.

Thus we are brought around by analogy to the Supreme Court's reasoning in *Sanders*; unless the listeners — the broadcast consumers — can be heard, there may be no one to bring programming deficiencies or offensive overcommercialization to the attention of the Commission in an effective manner. By process of elimination those "consumers" willing to shoulder the burdensome and costly processes of intervention in a Commission proceeding are likely to be the only ones "having a sufficient interest" to challenge a renewal application. The late Edmond Cahn addressed himself to this problem in its broadest aspects when he said, "Some consumers need bread; others need Shakespeare; others need their rightful place in the national society — what they all need is processors of law who will consider the people's needs more significant than administrative convenience." *Law in the Consumer Perspective*, 112 U.Pa.L.Rev. 1, 13 (1963).

Unless the Commission is to be given staff and resources to perform the enormously complex and prohibitively expensive task of maintaining constant surveillance over every licensee, some mechanism must be developed so that the *legitimate* interests of listeners can be made a part of the record which the Commission evaluates. An initial applicant frequently floods the Commission with testimonials from a host of representative community groups as to the relative merit of their champion, and the Commission places considerable reliance on these vouchers; on a renewal application the "campaign pledges" of applicants must be open to comparison with "performance in office" aided by a limited number of responsible representatives of the listening public when such representatives seek participation.

We recognize the risks alluded to by Judge Madden in his cogent dissent in *Philco*;[23] regulatory agencies, the Federal Communications Commission in particular, would ill serve the public interest if the courts imposed such heavy burdens on them as to overtax their capacities. The competing consideration is that experience demonstrates consumers are generally among the best vindicators of the public interest. In order to safeguard the public interest in broadcasting, therefore, we hold that some "audience participation" must be allowed in license renewal proceedings. We recognize this will create problems for the Commission but it does not necessarily follow that "hosts" of protestors must be granted standing to challenge a renewal application or that the Commission need allow the administrative processes to be obstructed or

---

[23]103 U.S. App. D.C. at 281, 257 F. 2d at 659 (1958), cert. denied, 358 U.S. 946, 79 S.Ct. 350, 3 L.Ed. 2d 352 (1959).

overwhelmed by captious or purely obstructive protests. The Commission can avoid such results by developing appropriate regulations by statutory rule-making. Although it denied Appellants standing, it employed *ad hoc* criteria in determining that these Appellants were responsible spokesmen for representative groups having significant roots in the listening community. These criteria can afford a basis for developing formalized standards to regulate and limit public intervention to spokesmen who can be helpful. A petition for such intervention must "contain specific allegations of fact sufficient to show that the petitioner is a party in interest and that a grant of the application would be prima facie inconsistent" with the public interest. 74 Stat. 891 (1960), 47 U.S.C. 309(d) (1) (1964).

The responsible and representative groups eligible to intervene cannot here be enumerated or categorized specifically; such community organizations as civic associations, professional societies, unions, churches, and educational institutions or associations might well be helpful to the Commission. These groups are found in every community; they usually concern themselves with a wide range of community problems and tend to be representatives of broad as distinguished from narrow interests, public as distinguished from private or commercial interests.

The Commission should be accorded broad discretion in establishing and applying rules for such public participation, including rules for determining which community representatives are to be allowed to participate and how many are reasonably required to give the Commission the assistance it needs in vindicating the public interest.[24] The usefulness of any particular petitioner for intervention must be judged in relation to other petitioners and the nature of the claims it asserts as basis for standing. Moreover it is no novelty in the administrative process to require consolidation of petitions and briefs to avoid multiplicity of parties and duplication of effort.

The fears of regulatory agencies that their processes will be inundated by expansion of standing criteria are rarely borne out. Always a restraining factor is the expense of participation in the administrative process, an economic reality which will operate to limit the number of those who will seek participation; legal and related expenses of administrative proceedings are such that even those with large economic interests find the costs burdensome. Moreover, the listening public seeking intervention in a license renewal proceeding cannot attract

---

[24]Professor Jaffe concedes there are strong reasons to reject public or listener standing but he believes "it does have much to commend it" in certain areas if put in terms of "jurisdiction subject to judicial discretion to be exercised with due regard for the character of the interests and the issues involved in each case." Jaffe, *Standing to Secure Judicial Review: Private Actions*, 75 Harv. L. Rev. 255, 282 (1961). "There are many persons . . . who feel that neither the industry nor the FCC can be trusted to protect the listener interest. If this is so, the public action is appropriate. But a frank recognition that the action is a public action and not a private remedy would allow us to introduce the notion of discretion at both the administrative and judicial levels." *Id.* at 284.

lawyers to represent their cause by the prospect of lucrative contingent fees, as can be done, for example, in rate cases.

We are aware that there may be efforts to exploit the enlargement of intervention, including spurious petitions from private interests not concerned with the quality of broadcast programming, since such private interests may sometimes cloak themselves with a semblance of public interest advocates. But this problem, as we have noted, can be dealt with by the Commission under its inherent powers and by rulemaking.

In line with this analysis, we do not now hold that all of the Appellants have standing to challenge WLBT's renewal. We do not reach that question. As to these Appellants we limit ourselves to holding that the Commission must allow standing to one or more of them as responsible representatives to assert and prove the claims they have urged in their petition.

It is difficult to anticipate the range of claims which may be raised or sought to be raised by future petitioners asserting representation of the public interest. It is neither possible nor desirable for us to try to chart the precise scope or patterns for the future. The need sought to be met is to provide a means for reflection of listener appraisal of a licensee's performance as the performance meets or fails to meet the licensee's statutory obligation to operate the facility in the public interest. The matter now before us is one in which the alleged conduct adverse to the public interest rests primarily on claims of racial discrimination, some elements of religious discrimination, oppressive over-commercialization by advertising announcements, and violation of the Fairness Doctrine. Future cases may involve other areas of conduct and programming adverse to the public interest; at this point we can only emphasize that intervention on behalf of the public is not allowed to press private interests but only to vindicate the broad public interest relating to a licensee's performance of the public trust inherent in every license.

HEARING

We hold further that in the circumstances shown by this record an evidentiary hearing was required in order to resolve the public interest issue. Under Section 309(e) the Commission must set a renewal application for hearing where "a substantial and material question of fact is presented *or* the Commission for any reason is unable to make the finding" that the public interest, convenience, and necessity will be served by the license renewal. (Emphasis supplied.)

The Commission argues in this Court that it accepted all Appellants' allegations of WLBT's misconduct and that for this reason no hearing was necessary.[25] Yet the Commission recognized that WLBT's past behavior, as

---

[25]The Commission also argues that Appellants do not have standing in this Court as persons aggrieved or adversely affected under 66 Stat. 718 (1952), as amended, 47 U.S.C. § 402(b) (1964), because all their allegations were accepted as true. However, denial of the relief they sought rendered them persons aggrieved.

described by Appellants, would preclude the statutory finding of public interest necessary for license renewal;[26] hence its grant of the one-year license on the policy ground that there was an urgent need at the time for a properly run station in Jackson must have been predicated on a belief that the need was so great as to warrant the risk that WLBT might continue its improper conduct.

We agree that a history of programming misconduct of the kind alleged would preclude, as a matter of law, the required finding that renewal of the license would serve the public interest. It is important to bear in mind, moreover, that although in granting an initial license the Commission must of necessity engage in some degree of forecasting future performance, in a renewal proceeding past performance is its best criterion. When past performance is in conflict with the public interest, a very heavy burden rests on the renewal applicant to show how a renewal can be reconciled with the public interest. Like public officials charged with a public trust, a renewal applicant, as we noted in our discussion of standing, must literally "run on his record."

The Commission in effect sought to justify its grant of the one-year license, in the face of accepted facts irreconcilable with a public interest finding, on the ground that as a matter of policy the immediate need warranted the risks involved, and that the "strict conditions" it imposed on the grant would improve *future* operations. However the conditions which the Commission made explicit in the one-year license are implicit in every grant. The Commission's opinion reveals how it labored to justify the result it thought was dictated by the urgency of the situation.[27] The majority considered the question of setting the application for hearing a "close" one; Chairman Henry and Commissioner Cox would have granted a hearing to Appellants as a matter of right.

[26]In the 1959 renewal proceedings the Commission conceded that WLBT's misconduct then shown would preclude a grant except that there were only "isolated instances."

[27]"24. The discussion in B and C, above, establishes that serious issues are presented whether the licensee's operations have fully met the public interest standard. Indeed, it is a close question whether to designate for hearing these applications for renewal of license. In making its judgment, the Commission has taken into account that this particular area is entering a critical period in race relations, and that the broadcast stations, such as here involved, can make a most worthwhile contribution to the resolution of problems arising in this respect. That contribution is needed now — and should not be put off for the future. We believe that the licensee, operating in strict accordance with the representations made and other conditions specified herein, can make that needed contribution, and thus that its renewal would be in the public interest.

25. But we cannot stress too strongly that the licensee must operate in complete conformity with its representations and the conditions laid down. In the last *two* renewal periods, questions have been raised whether the licensee has complied with the requirements of the fairness doctrine; in the last renewal period, substantial public interest questions have been raised by the petition filed by most responsible community leaders. We are granting a renewal of license, so that the licensee can demonstrate and carry out its stated willingness to serve fully and fairly the needs and interests of its entire area — so that it can, in short, meet and resolve the questions raised. Further, in line with the basic policy determination set out in par. 24, the licensee's efforts in this respect must be made now, and continue throughout the license period."

The Commission's "policy" decision is not a reflection of some long standing or accepted proposition but represents an *ad hoc* determination in the context of Jackson's contemporary problem. Granted the basis for a Commission "policy" recognizing the value of properly run broadcast facilities to the resolution of community problems, if indeed this truism rises to the level of a policy, it is a determination valid in the abstract but calling for explanation in its application.

Assuming *arguendo* that the Commission's acceptance of Appellants' allegations would satisfy one ground for dispensing with a hearing, *i.e.*, absence of a question of fact, Section 309(e) also commands that in order to avoid a hearing the Commission must make an affirmative finding that renewal will serve the public interest. Yet the only finding on this crucial factor is a qualified statement that the public interest would be served, provided WLBT thereafter complied strictly with the specified conditions. Not surprisingly, having asserted that it accepted Petitioners' allegations, the Commission thus considered itself unable to make a categorical determination that on WLBT's record of performance it was an appropriate entity to receive the license. It found only that *if* WLBT changed its ways, something which the Commission did not and, of course, could not guarantee, the licensing would be proper. The statutory public interest finding cannot be inferred from a statement of the obvious truth that a properly operated station will serve the public interest.

We view as particularly significant the Commission's summary:

We are granting a renewal of license, so that the licensee can demonstrate and carry out its stated willingness to serve fully and fairly the needs and interests of its entire area — so that it can, in short, meet and resolve the questions raised.

The only "stated willingness to serve fully and fairly" which we can glean from the record is WLBT's protestation that it had always fully performed its public obligations. As we read it the Commission's statement is a strained and strange substitute for a public interest finding.

We recognize that the Commission was confronted with a difficult problem and difficult choices, but it would perhaps not go too far to say it elected to post the Wolf to guard the Sheep in the hope that the Wolf would mend his ways because some protection was needed at once and none but the Wolf was handy. This is not a case, however, where the Wolf had either promised or demonstrated any capacity and willingness to change, for WLBT had stoutly denied Appellants' charges of programming misconduct and violations.[28] In these circumstances a pious hope on the Commission's part for better things from WLBT is not a substitute for evidence and findings. *Cf.* Interstate Broadcasting Co. v. FCC, 116 U.S. App. D.C. 327, 323 F. 2d 797 (1963).

---

[28]The Commission should have discretion to experiment and even to take calculated risks on renewals where a licensee confesses the error of its ways; this is not such a case.

Even if the embodiment of the Commission's hope be conceded *arguendo* to be a finding, there was not sufficient evidence in the record to justify a "policy determination" that the need for a properly run station in Jackson was so pressing as to justify the risk that WLBT might well continue with an inadequate performance. The issues which should have been considered could be resolved only in an evidentiary hearing in which all aspects of its qualifications and performance could be explored.

It is open to question whether the public interest would not be as well, if not better served with one TV outlet acutely conscious that adherence to the Fairness Doctrine is a *sine qua non* of every licensee. Even putting aside the salutary warning effect of a license denial, there are other reasons why one station in Jackson might be better than two for an interim period. For instance, in a letter to the Commission, Appellant Smith alleged that the other television station in Jackson had agreed to sell him time only if WLBT did so.[29] It is arguable that the pressures on the other station might be reduced if WLBT were in other hands — or off the air. The need which the Commission thought urgent might well be satisfied by refusing to renew the license of WLBT and opening the channel to new applicants under the special temporary authorization procedures available to the Commission on the theory that another, and better suited, operator could be found to broadcast on the channel with brief, if any, interruption of service. The Commission's opinion reflects no consideration of these or other alternatives.

We hold that the grant of a renewal of WLBT's license for one year was erroneous. The Commission is directed to conduct hearings on WLBT's renewal application, allowing public intervention pursuant to this holding. Since the Commission has already decided that Appellants are responsible representatives of the listening public of the Jackson area, we see no obstacle to a prompt determination granting standing to Appellants or some of them. Whether WLBT should be able to benefit from a showing of good performance, if such is the case, since June 1965 we do not undertake to decide. The Commission has had no occasion to pass on this issue and we therefore refrain from doing so.[30]

The record is remanded to the Commission for further proceedings consistent with this opinion; jurisdiction is retained in this court.

Reversed and remanded.

---

[29] Letter to Commission from Rev. Robert L. T. Smith, received Jan. 17, 1962, Record, p. 1.

[30] In light of our holding, the special form of license granted here is not unlike a special temporary authorization. Under the Commission's position in Community Broadcasting Co., Inc. v. FCC, 107 U.S. App. D.C. 95, 274 F. 2d 753 (1960), it may be that the Commission will conclude that good performance under this conditional or probationary license should not weigh in favor of WLBT.

36

President Johnson's Message to Congress

H.R. Doc. 68, 90th Congress, 1st Session

February 28, 1967

Earlier pages (see pp. 82–83, 232–245, 281) sketch the progress of noncommercial broadcasting in America to 1962. By 1965 only about 100 educational noncommercial television (ETV) stations were on the air (and about 250 educational FM stations, most of which were low powered and student operated). The main impediment to a larger, more effective noncommercial broadcasting establishment was the lack of money. True, many states and local communities had supported ETV generously, and since 1962 federal dollars were used to help construct ETV stations. But many areas of the country were left unserved by noncommercial broadcasting, and the medium had failed to achieve anything approaching national impact. For one thing, there was no interconnected network to facilitate program sharing among stations. And while dollars for hardware could often be found, funds to support program production on a fully professional scale were scarce, even though the Ford Foundation had pumped more than $100 million into the medium by the mid-1960's.

A sweeping plan to finance and revitalize the service that had been established 15 years earlier by the FCC was proposed by the Carnegie Commission on Educational Television in 1967. The Commission was headed by Dr. James R. Killian and supported by a $500,000 grant from the Carnegie Corporation of New York. Its report recommended the creation of a federally financed "Corporation for Public Television." President Lyndon B. Johnson, himself a former schoolteacher, requested legislation embodying the major aspects of the Carnegie Commission's proposal in the following excerpt from his "Message on Education and Health in America." The question of long-range funding was left for future determination, and both radio and TV were included in President Johnson's recommendations.

Congress responded with the Public Broadcasting Act of 1967 (Public Law 90-129, approved November 7, 1967), which is incorporated into Part IV of Title III of the Communications Act of 1934, as amended (see pp. 543-560). Intermediate-range funding was initiated through a 1975 law authorizing federal funds for public broadcasting over a 5-year period. [See Section 396(k)(3) of the Communications Act, pp. 554-555.]

The Corporation for Public Broadcasting's first decade of operation saw more than a doubling in the number of educational TV and FM radio stations on the air accompanied by the creation of the Public Broadcasting Service (interconnecting TV stations), National Public Radio (linking the larger and professionally managed noncommercial radio stations), and the Children's Television Workshop (producing series such as "Sesame Street" and "Electric Company"). The cultural, children's, and minority interest programming provided by noncommercial television stations constitutes an increasingly effective alternative to the programs offered by commercial stations. In 1977 the "Carnegie Commission on the Future of Public Broadcasting" was activated under the leadership of Dr. William J. McGill. Its recommendations will influence the progress of noncommercial radio and television in the 1980's.

Related Reading: 22, 32, 39, 41, 55, 102, 120, 138, 145, 169, 189, 222, 231, 244.

Building for tomorrow

Public television

In 1951, the Federal Communications Commission set aside the first 242 television channels for noncommercial broadcasting, declaring: "The public interest will be clearly served if these stations contribute significantly to the educational process of the Nation."

The first educational television station went on the air in May 1953. Today, there are 178 noncommercial television stations on the air or under construction. Since 1963 the Federal Government has provided $32 million under the Educational Television Facilities Act to help build towers, transmitters and other facilities. These funds have helped stations with an estimated potential audience of close to 150 million citizens.

Yet we have only begun to grasp the great promise of this medium, which, in the words of one critic, has the power to "arouse our dreams, satisfy our hunger for beauty, take us on journeys, enable us to participate in events, present great drama and music, explore the sea and the sky and the winds and the hills."

Noncommercial television can bring its audience the excitement of excellence in every field. I am convinced that a vital and self-sufficient noncommercial television system will not only instruct, but inspire and uplift our people.

Practically all noncommercial stations have serious shortages of the facilities, equipment, money and staff which they need to present programs of high quality. There are not enough stations. Interconnections between stations are inadequate and seldom permit the timely scheduling of current programs.

Noncommercial television today is reaching only a fraction of its potential audience — and achieving only a fraction of its potential worth.

Clearly, the time has come to build on the experience of the past 14 years, the important studies that have been made, and the beginnings we have made.

I recommend that Congress enact the Public Television Act of 1967 to:

—Increase federal funds for television and radio facility construction to $10.5 million in fiscal 1968, more than three times this year's appropriations.

—Create a Corporation for Public Television authorized to provide support to noncommercial television and radio.

—Provide $9 million in fiscal 1968 as initial funding for the Corporation.

Next year, after careful review, I will make further proposals for the Corporation's long-term financing.

Noncommercial television and radio in America, even though supported by Federal funds, must be absolutely free from any Federal Government interference over programming. As I said in the state of the Union message, "We should insist that the public interest be fully served through the public's airwaves."

The Board of Directors of the Corporation for Public Television should include American leaders in education, communications and the creative arts. I recommend that the Board be comprised of 15 members, appointed by the President and confirmed by the Senate.

The Corporation would provide support to establish production centers and to help local stations improve their proficiency. It would be authorized to accept funds from other sources, public and private.

The strength of public television should lie in its diversity. Every region and community should be challenged to contribute its best.

Other opportunities for the Corporation exist to support vocational training for young people who desire careers in public television, to foster research and development, and to explore new ways to serve the viewing public.

One of the Corporation's first tasks should be to study the practicality and the economic advantages of using communication satellites to establish an educational television and radio network. To assist the Corporation, I am directing the Administrator of the National Aeronautics and Space Administration and the Secretary of Health, Education, and Welfare to conduct experiments on the requirements for such a system, and for instructional television, in cooperation with other interested agencies of the Government and the private sector.

Formulation of long-range policies concerning the future of satellite communications requires the most detailed and comprehensive study by the executive branch and the Congress. I anticipate that the appropriate committees of Congress will hold hearings to consider these complex issues of public policy. The executive branch will carefully study these hearings as we shape our recommendations.

37

The Fairness Doctrine Applied to Cigarette Advertising

Letter from Federal Communications Commission
to Television Station WCBS-TV
8 FCC 2d 381
June 2, 1967

During an era of growing consumer activism the FCC, in 1967, responded to a citizen's complaint by holding that health aspects of cigarette smoking constituted a controversial issue of public importance to which the Fairness Doctrine (Document 22, pp. 217–231) applied. Broadcasters were required to "provide a significant amount of time for the other viewpoint" if they carried cigarette commercials. The Commission pointed out that cigarettes were a "unique" product category and that the doctrine would not apply to commercial messages on behalf of other products.

A dizzying sequence of events followed this ruling. After the FCC elaborated its decision on reconsideration [9 FCC 2d 921 (1967)], the Court of Appeals upheld the ruling on general public interest grounds [405 F.2d 1082 (D.C. Cir. 1968)], and the Supreme Court refused to review the case [396 U.S. 842 (1969)]. The FCC proposed to ban cigarette commercials entirely [16 FCC 2d 284 (1969)] as the NAB "volunteered" to effect a gradual phase-out of the ads through industry self-regulation. Congress settled the matter by banning all cigarette commercials on radio and TV effective January 2, 1971 [Public Law 91–222 (1970)], whereupon the Commission ruled that in the absence of such ads, smoking was no longer a matter to which it would apply the Fairness Doctrine [27 FCC 2d 453 (1970)]. The result of all this was confusion about the scope of the Fairness Doctrine and the loss of more than $200 million annually in tobacco advertising revenue.

The cigarette ruling turned out to be a precedent, despite Commission protestations to the contrary. The FCC's reluctance to apply the Fairness Doctrine to other types of commercial advertising was upset in 1971 by the Court of Appeals which found the health hazards posed by air pollution stemming from the use of such advertised products as super-powered cars and high-test gasolines were sufficiently akin to those in the cigarette ruling to mandate similar Fairness Doctrine treatment [*Friends of the Earth* v. *FCC*, 449 F.2d 1164 (D.C. Cir. 1971)].

The Commission finally extricated itself from its self-made dilemma when it issued its "Fairness Report" in 1974, following 3 years of re-examining selected aspects of the Fairness Doctrine [48 FCC 2d 1 (1974)]. The FCC rescinded the cigarette ruling, holding that ordinary product commercials do not "inform the public on any side of a controversial issue of public importance" or make "a meaningful contribution to public debate" (*id.* at 26). Hence the Fairness Doctrine is no longer applicable to ordinary commercial advertising, unless a controversial issue is explicitly raised in a sponsor's message. See, e.g., *Energy Action Committee Inc., et al.*, 64 FCC 2d 787 (1977).

Related Reading: 141, 196, 205, 225, 245.

FEDERAL COMMUNICATIONS COMMISSION
Washington 25, D.C.
June 2, 1967

Television Station WCBS-TV
51 West 52 Street
New York, New York.

Gentlemen:

This letter constitutes the Commission's ruling upon the complaint of Mr. John F. Banzhaf, III, against Station WCBS-TV, New York, N.Y. Mr. Banzhaf, by letter dated January 5, 1967, filed a fairness doctrine complaint, asserting that WCBS-TV, after having aired numerous commercial advertisements for cigarette manufacturers, has not afforded him or some other responsible spokesman an opportunity "to present contrasting views on the issue of the benefits and advisability of smoking."

Mr. Banzhaf's letter cites as examples three particular commercials over WCBS-TV which present the point of view that smoking is "socially acceptable and desirable, manly, and a necessary part of a rich full life." Mr. Banzhaf, in his letter to you of December 1, 1966, requested free time be made available to "responsible groups" roughly approximate to that spent on the promotion of "the virtues and values of smoking."

Your responsive letter of December 30, 1966, cites programs which WCBS-TV has broadcast dealing with the effect of smoking on health, beginning in September 1962 and continuing to date. It cites six reports on this issue in its evening news programs since May 1966, five major reports by its Science Editor since September 1966 and five one minute messages, which advance the view that smoking is undesirable, broadcast without charge within the last few months for the American Cancer Society. The letter also refers to half hour and hour programs on smoking and health broadcast in 1962 and 1964. You take the position that the above programs have provided contrasting viewpoints on this issue by responsible authorities, and therefore, that it is unnecessary to consider whether the "fairness doctrine" may be applied to commercial announcements solely aimed at selling products. You state your view that it may not.

In Mr. Banzhaf's complaint to the Commission, he asserts that the programs cited by you as showing compliance with the "fairness doctrine" are insufficient to offset the effects of paid advertisements broadcast daily for a total of five to ten minutes each broadcast day. He also states that the very point of his letters is to establish the applicability of the doctrine to cigarette advertisements.

We hold that the fairness doctrine is applicable to such advertisements. We stress that our holding is limited to this product — cigarettes. Governmental and private reports (e.g., the 1964 Report of the Surgeon General's Committee) and Congressional action (e.g., the Federal Cigarette Labeling and Advertising Act of 1965) assert that normal use of this product can be a hazard to the health of millions of persons. The advertisements in question clearly promote the use of a particular cigarette as attractive and enjoyable. Indeed, they understandably have no other purpose. We believe that a station which presents such advertisements has the duty of informing its audience of the other side of this controversial issue of public importance — that however enjoyable, such smoking may be a hazard to the smoker's health.

We reject, however, Mr. Banzhaf's claim that the time to be afforded "roughly approximate" that devoted to the cigarette commercials. The fairness doctrine does not require "equal time" (see Ruling No. II C. 12, 29 F.R. 10416) and, equally important, a requirement of such "rough approximation" would, we think, be inconsistent with the Congressional direction in this field — the 1965 Cigarette Labeling and Advertising Act. The practical result of any roughly one-to-one correlation would probably be either the elimination or substantial curtailment of broadcast cigarette advertising. But in the 1965 Act Congress made clear that it did not favor such a "drastic" step, but rather wished to afford an opportunity to consider "the combined impact of voluntary limitations on advertising under the Cigarette Advertising Code, the extensive smoking education campaigns now underway, and the compulsory warning on the package . . . [on the problem of] adequately alert[ing] the public to the potential hazard from smoking" (Sen. Rept. No. 195, 89th Cong., 1st Sess., p. 5). At the conclusion of a three year period (to end July 1, 1969), and upon the basis of reports from the Federal Trade Commission and the Department of Health, Education, and Welfare (HEW) and other pertinent sources, the Congress would then decide what further remedial action, if any, is appropriate. In the meantime, Congress has promoted extensive smoking education campaigns by appropriating substantial sums for HEW in this area. See P.L. 89-156, Title II, Public Health Service, Chronic Diseases and Health of the Aged.

Our action here, therefore, must be tailored so as to carry out the above Congressional purpose. We believe that it does. It requires a station which carries cigarette commercials to provide a significant amount of time for the other viewpoint, thus implementing the "smoking education campaigns" referred to as a basis for Congressional action in the 1965 Act. See Cigarette Labeling and Advertising Act; remarks of Senator Warren Magnuson, floor manager in the Senate of the bill which became that Act, Cong. Rec. (Daily Edition) Jan. 16, 1967, p. S. 317, 319. But this requirement will not preclude or curtail presentation by stations of cigarette advertising which they choose to carry.

A station might, for example, reasonably determine that the above noted responsibility would be discharged by presenting each week, in addition to appropriate news reports or other programming dealing with the subject, a number of the public service announcements of the American Cancer Society or HEW in this field. We stress, however, that in this, as in other areas under the fairness doctrine, the type of programming and the amount and nature of time to be afforded is a matter for the good faith, reasonable judgment of the licensee, upon the particular facts of his situation. See Cullman Broadcasting Co., F.C.C. 63-849 (Sept. 18, 1963).

In this case, we note that WCBS-TV is aware of its responsibilities in this area, in light of the programming described in the third paragraph. While we have rejected Mr. Banzhaf's claim of "rough approximation of time," the question remains whether in the circumstances a sufficient amount of time is being allocated each week to cover the viewpoint of the health hazard posed by smoking. We note in this respect that, particularly in light of the recent

American Cancer Society announcements, you appear to have a continuing program in this respect. The guidelines in the foregoing discussion are brought to your attention so that in connection with the above continuing program you may make the judgment whether sufficient time is being allocated each week in this area.

By Direction of the Commission
Ben F. Waple
Secretary

38

The Southwestern Case

United States et al. v. Southwestern Cable Co. et al.
392 U.S. 157
June 10, 1968

In 1965 the FCC shifted from a case-by-case approach to CATV regulation to the issuance of rules (see Document 30, pp. 296–305). The first regulations [38 FCC 683 (1965)] placed local TV station carriage and non-duplication requirements on cable systems that used microwave relay to import distant television station signals. A year later the Commission modified its 1965 rules and made them applicable to all CATV systems, whether or not they employed microwave facilities [2 FCC 2d 725 (1966)]. The 1966 rules also prohibited importation of distant TV signals by cable systems into the top 100 television markets without a burdensome hearing. This protected telecasters in the big cities from CATV "encroachment" and hampered the development of cable where the nation's population was concentrated.

    This unanimous Supreme Court decision in *Southwestern* (sometimes referred to as the "San Diego case") declared the FCC's cable rules legally valid under the broad authority over interstate communication vested in the Commission by the Communications Act. (Justice White's concurring opinion has been omitted.) In 1972 the Court narrowly upheld the legality of a rule first adopted by the FCC in 1969 that required cable systems with more than 3,500 subscribers to engage in local program origination; the five-to-four decision pivoted on the "reasonably ancillary" standard, the precedent established in the *Southwestern* case [*United States* v. *Midwest Video Corp.*, 406 U.S. 649, 662 (1972)]. Despite judicial affirmation, the FCC rescinded the cable program origination rule a few years later [49 FCC 2d 1090 (1974)].

In the 4 years between *Southwestern* and *Midwest* a torrent of CATV rules issued from the Commission. The most comprehensive set of cable regulations was promulgated in 1972 (36 FCC 2d 143), but within 5 years these rules had become decimated by waivers, amendments, suspensions, and new regulations. In the meantime, widespread criticism of the FCC's policy of regulating cable in order to protect over-the-air broadcasting mounted. The Commission suffered a major setback in 1977, when the Court of Appeals reversed its 1975 rules restricting CATV systems from providing certain types of subscription services because, *inter alia*, the rules fell short of the "reasonably ancillary" standard of *Southwestern* [*Home Box Office* v. *FCC*, 567 F.2d 9 (D.C. Cir. 1977)]. The Supreme Court declined to review the appellate decision.*

New challenges to the Commission's regulatory philosophy can be expected as the cable penetration rate continues to grow. Despite the hostile regulatory climate, subscription services via CATV ("pay-cable") provide additional income to form a more solid economic base from which cable can expand, while simultaneously fractionalizing TV station audiences. The question of how jurisdiction over cable can best be shared by the "three tiers" (federal, state, and local) of government regulation is unsettled. Experience under the Copyright Act of 1976 (Document 45, pp. 486–496) will test the workability of the FCC's historic approach to cable regulation, as what was once thought of as a mere supplement to conventional broadcasting becomes a mass medium in its own right.

Related Reading: 26, 33, 34, 42, 44, 53, 55, 130, 157, 168, 170, 172, 178, 180, 188, 206, 209, 217, 218, 223, 236, 237.

Mr. Justice Harlan delivered the opinion of the Court.

These cases stem from proceedings conducted by the Federal Communications Commission after requests by Midwest Television[1] for relief under

---

[1] Midwest's petition was premised upon its status as licensee of KFMB-TV, San Diego, California. It is evidently also the licensee of various other broadcasting stations. See Second Report and Order, 2 F.C.C. 2d 725, 739.

* Cable rules requiring "access" channels were struck down as contrary to the "reasonably ancillary" standard by the Supreme Court in FCC v. *Midwest Video Corp.*, 440 U.S. 689 (1979). In 1980 the FCC repealed its rules restricting cable carriage of distant signals and protecting local exclusivity of syndicated programs, stimulating broadcasters to seek judicial, legislative and Copyright Royalty Tribunal relief.

§ § 74.1107[2] and 74.1109[3] of the rules promulgated by the Commission for the regulation of community antenna television (CATV) systems. Midwest averred that respondents' CATV systems transmitted the signals of Los Angeles broadcasting stations into the San Diego area, and thereby had, inconsistently with the public interest, adversely affected Midwest's San Diego station.[4] Midwest sought an appropriate order limiting the carriage of such signals by respondents' systems. After consideration of the petition and of various responsive pleadings, the Commission restricted the expansion of respondents' service in areas in which they had not operated on February 15, 1966, pending hearings to be conducted on the merits of Midwest's complaints.[5] 4 F.C.C. 2d 612. On petitions for review, the Court of Appeals for the Ninth Circuit held that the Commission lacks authority under the Communications Act of 1934, 48

[2]47 CFR § 74.1107(a) provides that "[n]o CATV system operating in a community within the predicted Grade A contour of a television broadcast station in the 100 largest television markets shall extend the signal of a television broadcast station beyond the Grade B contour of that station, except upon a showing approved by the Commission that such extension would be consistent with the public interest, and specifically the establishment and healthy maintenance of television broadcast service in the area. Commission approval of a request to extend a signal in the foregoing circumstances will be granted where the Commission, after consideration of the request and all related materials in a full evidentiary hearing, determines that the requisite showing has been made. The market size shall be determined by the rating of the American Research Bureau, on the basis of the net weekly circulation for the most recent year." San Diego is the Nation's 54th largest television market. *Midwest Television, Inc*, 11 Pike & Fischer Radio Reg. 2d 273, 276.

[3]47 CFR § 74.1109 creates "procedures applicable to petitions for waiver of the rules, additional or different requirements and rulings on complaints or disputes." It provides that petitions for special relief "may be submitted informally, by letter, but shall be accompanied by an affidavit of service on any CATV system, station licensee, permittee, applicant, or other interested person who may be directly affected if the relief requested in the petition should be granted." 47 CFR § 74.1109(b). Provisions are made for comments or opposition to the petition, and for rejoinders by the petitioner. 47 CFR § § 74.1109(d), (e). Finally, the Commission "may specify other procedures, such as oral argument, evidentiary hearing, or further written submissions directed to particular aspects, as it deems appropriate." 47 CFR § 74.1109(f).

[4]Midwest asserted that respondents' importation of Los Angeles signals had fragmented the San Diego audience, that this would reduce the advertising revenues of local stations, and that the ultimate consequence would be to terminate or to curtail the services provided in the San Diego area by local broadcasting stations. Respondents' CATV systems now carry the signals of San Diego stations, but Midwest alleged that the quality of the signals, as they are carried by respondents, is materially degraded, and that this serves only to accentuate the fragmentation of the local audience.

[5]February 15, 1966, is the date on which grandfather rights accrued under 47 CFR § 74.1107(d). The initial decision of the hearing examiner, issued October 3, 1967, concluded that permanent restrictions on the expansion of respondents' services were unwarranted. *Midwest Television, Inc.*, 11 Pike & Fischer Radio Reg. 2d 273. The Commission has declined to terminate its interim restrictions pending consideration by the Commission of the examiner's decision. *Midwest Television, Inc., id.*, at 721.

Stat. 1064, 47 U.S.C. § 151, to issue such an order.[6] 378 F. 2d 118. We granted certiorari to consider this important question of regulatory authority.[7] 389 U.S. 911. For reasons that follow, we reverse.

I.

CATV systems receive the signals of television broadcasting stations, amplify them, transmit them by cable or microwave, and ultimately distribute them by wire to the receivers of their subscribers.[8] CATV systems characteristically do not produce their own programming,[9] and do not recompense producers or broadcasters for use of the programming which they receive and redistribute. [10] Unlike ordinary broadcasting stations, CATV systems commonly charge their subscribers installation and other fees.[11]

The CATV industry has grown rapidly since the establishment of the first commercial system in 1950.[12] In the late 1950's, some 50 new systems were established each year; by 1959, there were 550 "nationally known and

[6]The opinion of the Court of Appeals could be understood to hold either that the Commission may not, under the Communications Act, regulate CATV, or, more narrowly, that it may not issue the prohibitory order involved here. We take the court's opinion, in fact, to have encompassed both positions.

[7]We note that the Court of Appeals for the District of Columbia Circuit has concluded that the Communications Act permits the regulation of CATV systems. See *Buckeye Cablevision, Inc.* v. *F.C.C.*, 128 U.S. App. D.C. 262, 387 F. 2d 220.

[8]CATV systems are defined by the Commission for purposes of its rules as "any facility which . . . receives directly or indirectly over the air and amplifies or otherwise modifies the signals transmitting programs broadcast by one or more television stations and distributes such signals by wire or cable to subscribing members of the public who pay for such service, but such term shall not include (1) any such facility which serves fewer than 50 subscribers, or (2) any such facility which serves only the residents of one or more apartment dwellings under common ownership, control, or management, and commercial establishments located on the premises of such an apartment house." 47 CFR § 74.1101(a).

[9]There is, however, no technical reason why they may not. See Note, The Wire Mire: The FCC and CATV, 79 Harv. L. Rev. 366, 367. Indeed, the examiner was informed in this case that respondent Mission Cable TV "intends to commence program origination in the near future." *Midwest Television, Inc., supra,* at 283.

[10]The question whether a CATV system infringes the copyright of a broadcasting station by its reception and retransmission of the station's signals is presented in *Fortnightly Corp.* v. *United Artists TV, Inc.*, No. 618, now pending before the Court.

[11]The installation costs for CATV systems in 16 Connecticut communities were, for example, found to range from $31 to $147 per home. M. Seiden, An Economic Analysis of Community Antenna Television Systems and the Television Broadcasting Industry 24 (1965).

[12]CATV systems were evidently first established on a noncommercial basis in 1949. H.R. Rep. No. 1635, 89th Cong., 2d Sess., 5.

identified" systems serving a total audience of 1,500,000 to 2,000,000 persons.[13] It has been more recently estimated that "new systems are being founded at the rate of more than one per day, and . . . subscribers . . . signed on at the rate of 15,000 per month."[14] By late 1965, it was reported that there were 1,847 operating CATV systems, that 758 others were franchised but not yet in operation, and that there were 938 applications for additional franchises.[15] The statistical evidence is incomplete, but, as the Commission has observed, "whatever the estimate, CATV growth is clearly explosive in nature." Second Report and Order, 2 F.C.C. 2d 725, 738, n. 15.

CATV systems perform either or both of two functions. First, they may supplement broadcasting by facilitating satisfactory reception of local stations in adjacent areas in which such reception would not otherwise be possible; and second, they may transmit to subscribers the signals of distant stations entirely beyond the range of local antennae. As the number and size of CATV systems have increased, their principal function has more frequently become the importation of distant signals.[16] In 1959, only 50 systems employed microwave relays, and the maximum distance over which signals were transmitted was 300 miles; by 1964, 250 systems used microwave, and the transmission distances sometimes exceeded 665 miles. First Report and Order, 38 F.C.C. 683, 709. There are evidently now plans "to carry the programing of New York City independent stations by cable to . . . upstate New York, to Philadelphia, and even as far as Dayton."[17] And see *Channel 9 Syracuse, Inc.* v. *F.C.C.*, 128 U.S. App. D.C. 187, 385 F. 2d 969; *Hubbard Broadcasting, Inc.* v. *F.C.C.*, 128 U.S. App. D.C. 197, 385 F. 2d 979. Thus, "while the CATV industry originated in sparsely settled areas and areas of adverse terrain . . . it is now spreading to metropolitan centers . . ." First Report and Order, *supra*, at 709. CATV systems, formerly no more than local auxiliaries to broadcasting, promise for the future to provide a national communications system, in which signals from selected broadcasting centers would be transmitted to metropolitan areas throughout the country.[18]

[13]CATV and TV Repeater Services, 26 F.C.C. 403, 408; Note, The Wire Mire: The FCC and CATV, *supra*, at 368.

[14]Note, The Wire Mire: The FCC and CATV, *supra*, at 368.

[15]Second Report and Order, 2 F.C.C. 2d 725, 738. The franchises are granted by state or local regulatory agencies. It was reported in 1965 that two States, Connecticut and Nevada, regulate CATV systems, and that some 86% of the systems are subject at least to some local regulation. Seiden, *supra*, at 44-47. See Conn. Gen. Stat. Rev., Tit. 16, c. 289 (1958); Nev. Stat. 1967, c. 458.

[16]The term "distant signal" has been given a specialized definition by the Commission, as a signal "which is extended or received beyond the Grade B contour of that station." 47 CFR § 74.1101 (i). The Grade B contour is a line along which good reception may be expected 90% of the time at 50% of the locations. See 47 CFR § 73.683(a).

[17]Note, The Wire Mire: The FCC and CATV, *supra*, at 368 (notes omitted).

[18]It has thus been suggested that "a nationwide grid of wired CATV systems, inter-connected by microwave frequencies and financed by subscriber fees, may one day offer a

The Commission has on various occasions attempted to assess the relationship between community antenna television systems and its conceded regulatory functions. In 1959, it completed an extended investigation of several auxiliary broadcasting services, including CATV. CATV and TV Repeater Services, 26 F.C.C. 403. Although it found that CATV is "related to interstate transmission," the Commission reasoned that CATV systems are neither common carriers nor broadcasters, and therefore are within neither of the principal regulatory categories created by the Communications Act. *Id.*, at 427-428. The Commission declared that it had not been given plenary authority over "any and all enterprises which happen to be connected with one of the many aspects of communications." *Id.*, at 429. It refused to premise regulation of CATV upon assertedly adverse consequences for broadcasting, because it could not "determine where the impact takes effect, although we recognize that it may well exist." *Id.*, at 431.

The Commission instead declared that it would forthwith seek appropriate legislation "to clarify the situation." *Id.*, at 438. Such legislation was introduced in the Senate in 1959,[19] favorably reported,[20] and debated on the Senate floor.[21] The bill was, however, ultimately returned to committee.[22]

Despite its inability to obtain amendatory legislation, the Commission has, since 1960, gradually asserted jurisdiction over CATV. It first placed restrictions upon the activities of common carrier microwave facilities that serve CATV systems. See *Carter Mountain Transmission Corp.*, 32 F.C.C. 459, aff'd, 321 F. 2d 359. Finally, the Commission in 1962 conducted a rule-making proceeding in which it re-evaluated the significance of CATV for its regulatory responsibilities. First Report and Order, *supra*. The proceeding was explicitly restricted to those systems that are served by microwave, but the Commission's conclusions plainly were more widely relevant. The Commission found that "the likelihood or probability of [CATV's] adverse impact upon potential and existing service has become too substantial to be dismissed." *Id.*, at 713-714. It reasoned that the importation of distant signals into the service areas of local stations necessarily creates "substantial competition" for local broadcasting. *Id.*, at 707. The Commission acknowledged that it could not "measure precisely the degree of . . . impact," but found that "CATV competition can have a substantial negative effect upon station audience and revenues . . ." *Id.*, at 710-711.

---

viable economic alternative to the advertiser-supported broadcast service." Levin, New Technology and the Old Regulation in Radio Spectrum Management, 56 Am. Econ. Rev. 339, 341 (Proceedings, May 1966).

[19] See S. 2653, 86th Cong., 1st Sess.

[20] S. Rep. No. 923, 86th Cong., 1st Sess.

[21] See 106 Cong. Rec. 10416-10436, 10520-10548.

[22] *Id.*, at 10547. The Commission in 1966 made additional efforts to obtain suitable modifications in the Communications Act. See n. 30, *infra*.

The Commission attempted to "accommodat[e]" the interests of CATV and of local broadcasting by the imposition of two rules. *Id.*, at 713. First, CATV systems were required to transmit to their subscribers the signals of any station into whose service area they have brought competing signals.[23] Second, CATV systems were forbidden to duplicate the programming of such local stations for periods of 15 days before and after a local broadcast. See generally First Report and Order, *supra*, at 719-730. These carriage and nonduplication rules were expected to "insur[e] many stations' ability to maintain themselves as their areas' outlets for highly popular network and other programs . . ." *Id.*, at 715.

The Commission in 1965 issued additional notices of inquiry and proposed rule-making, by which it sought to determine whether all forms of CATV, including those served only by cable, could properly be regulated under the Communications Act. 1 F.C.C. 2d 453. After further hearings, the Commission held that the Act confers adequate regulatory authority over all CATV systems. Second Report and Order, *supra*, at 728-734. It promulgated revised rules, applicable both to cable and to microwave CATV systems, to govern the carriage of local signals and the nonduplication of local programming. Further, the Commission forbade the importation by CATV of distant signals into the 100 largest television markets, except insofar as such service was offered on February 15, 1966, unless the Commission has previously found that it "would be consistent with the public interest," *id.*, at 782; see generally *id.*, at 781-785, "particularly the establishment and healthy maintenance of television broadcast service in the area," 47 CFR § 74.1107(c). Finally, the Commission created "summary, nonhearing procedures" for the disposition of applications for separate or additional relief. 2 F.C.C. 2d, at 764; 47 CFR § 74.1109. Thirteen days after the Commission's adoption of the Second Report, Midwest initiated these proceedings by the submission of its petition for special relief.

II.

We must first emphasize that questions as to the validity of the specific rules promulgated by the Commission for the regulation of CATV are not now before

[23] See generally First Report and Order, *supra*, at 716-719. The Commission held that a CATV system must, within the limits of its channel capacity, carry the signals of stations that place signals over the community served by the system. The stations are to be given priority according to the strength of the signal available in the community, with the strongest signals given first priority. Exceptions are made for situations in which there would be substantial duplication or in which an independent or noncommercial station would be excluded. *Id.*, at 717.

the Court. The issues in these cases are only two: whether the Commission has authority under the Communications Act to regulate CATV systems, and, if it has, whether it has, in addition, authority to issue the prohibitory order here in question.[24]

The Commission's authority to regulate broadcasting and other communications is derived from the Communications Act of 1934, as amended. The Act's provisions are explicitly applicable to "all interstate and foreign communication by wire or radio . . ." 47 U.S.C. § 152(a). The Commission's responsibilities are no more narrow: it is required to endeavor to "make available . . . to all the people of the United States a rapid, efficient, Nation-wide, and world-wide wire and radio communication service . . ." 47 U.S.C. § 151. The Commission was expected to serve as the "single Government agency"[25] with "unified jurisdiction"[26] and "regulatory power over all forms of electrical communication, whether by telephone, telegraph, cable, or radio."[27] It was for this purpose given "broad authority."[28] As this Court emphasized in an earlier case, the Act's terms, purposes, and history all indicate that Congress "formulated a unified and comprehensive regulatory system for the [broadcasting] industry." F.C.C. v. Pottsville Broadcasting Co., 309 U.S. 134, 137.

Respondents do not suggest that CATV systems are not within the term "communication by wire or radio." Indeed, such communications are defined by the Act so as to encompass "the transmission of . . . signals, pictures, and sounds of all kinds," whether by radio or cable, "including all instrumentalities, facilities, apparatus, and services (among other things, the receipt, forwarding, and delivery of communications) incidental to such transmission." 47 U.S.C. § § 153(a), (b). These very general terms amply suffice to reach respondents' activities.

Nor can we doubt that CATV systems are engaged in interstate communication, even where, as here, the intercepted signals emanate from

---

[24] It must also be noted that the CATV systems involved in these cases evidently do not employ microwave. We intimate no views on what differences, if any, there might be in the scope of the Commission's authority over microwave and nonmicrowave systems.

[25] The phrase is taken from the message to Congress from President Roosevelt, dated February 26, 1934, in which he recommended the Commission's creation. See H. R. Rep. No. 1850, 73d Cong., 2d Sess., 1.

[26] S. Rep. No. 781, 73d Cong., 2d Sess., 1.

[27] Ibid. The Committee also indicated that there was a "vital need" for such a commission, with jurisdiction "over all of these methods of communication." Ibid.

[28] The phrase is taken from President Roosevelt's message to Congress. H. R. Rep. No. 1850, supra, at 1. The House Committee added that "the primary purpose of this bill [is] to create such a commission armed with adequate statutory powers to regulate all forms of communication . . ." Id., at 3.

stations located within the same State in which the CATV system operates. [29] We may take notice that television broadcasting consists in very large part of programming devised for, and distributed to, national audiences; respondents thus are ordinarily employed in the simultaneous retransmission of communications that have very often originated in other States. The stream of communication is essentially uninterrupted and properly indivisible. To categorize respondents' activities as intrastate would disregard the character of the television industry, and serve merely to prevent the national regulation that "is not only appropriate but essential to the efficient use of radio facilities." *Federal Radio Comm'n* v. *Nelson Bros. Co.*, 289 U.S. 266, 279.

Nonetheless, respondents urge that the Communications Act, properly understood, does not permit the regulation of CATV systems. First, they emphasize that the Commission in 1959 and again in 1966[30] sought legislation that would have explicitly authorized such regulation, and that its efforts were unsuccessful. In the circumstances here, however, this cannot be dispositive. The Commission's requests for legislation evidently reflected in each instance both its uncertainty as to the proper width of its authority and its understandable preference for more detailed policy guidance than the Communications Act now provides. [31] We have recognized that administrative agencies should, in such situations, be encouraged to seek from Congress clarification of the pertinent statutory provisions. *Wong Yang Sung* v. *McGrath*, 339 U.S. 33, 47.

Nor can we obtain significant assistance from the various expressions of congressional opinion that followed the Commission's requests. In the first

[29]Respondents assert only that this "is subject to considerable question." Brief for Respondent Southwestern Cable Co. 24, n. 25. They rely chiefly upon the language of § 152(b), which provides that nothing in the Act shall give the Commission jurisdiction over "carriers" that are engaged in interstate communication solely through physical connection, or connection by wire or radio, with the facilities of another carrier, if they are not directly or indirectly controlled by such other carrier. The terms and history of this provision, however, indicate that it was "merely a perfecting amendment" intended to "obviate any possible technical argument that the Commission may attempt to assert common-carrier jurisdiction over point-to-point communication by radio between two points within a single State . . ." S. Rep. No. 1090, 83d Cong., 2d Sess., 1. See also H. R. Rep. No. 910, 83d Cong., 1st Sess. The Commission and the respondents are agreed, we think properly, that these CATV systems are not common carriers within the meaning of the Act. See 47 U.S.C. § 153(h); *Frontier Broadcasting Co.* v. *Collier*, 24 F.C.C. 251; *Philadelphia Television Broadcasting Co.* v. *F.C.C.*, 123 U.S. App. D.C. 298, 359 F. 2d 282; CATV and TV Repeater Services, *supra*, at 427-428.

[30]See H. R. 13286, 89th Cong., 2d Sess. The bill was favorably reported by the House Committee on Interstate and Foreign Commerce, H. R. Rep. No. 1635, 89th Cong., 2d Sess., but failed to reach the floor for debate.

[31]See, for the legislation proposed in 1959, CATV and TV Repeater Services, *supra*, at 427-431, 438-439. The Commission in 1966 explicitly stated in its explanation of its proposed amendments to the Act that "we believe it highly desirable that Congress . . . confirm [the Commission's] jurisdiction and . . . establish such basic national policy as it deems appropriate." H. R. Rep. No. 1635, *supra*, at 16.

place, the views of one Congress as to the construction of a statute adopted many years before by another Congress have "very little, if any, significance." *Rainwater* v. *United States*, 356 U.S. 590, 593; *United States* v. *Price*, 361 U.S. 304, 313; *Haynes* v. *United States*, 390 U.S. 85, 87, n. 4. Further, it is far from clear that Congress believed, as it considered these requests for legislation, that the Commission did not already possess regulatory authority over CATV. In 1959, the proposed legislation was preceded by the Commission's declarations that it "did not intend to regulate CATV," and that it preferred to recommend the adoption of legislation that would impose specified requirements upon CATV systems.[32]   Congress may well have been more troubled by the Commission's unwillingness to regulate than by any fears that it was unable to regulate.[33]   In 1966, the Commission informed Congress that it desired legislation in order to "confirm [its] jurisdiction and to establish such basic national policy as [Congress] deems appropriate." H. R. Rep. No. 1635, 89th Cong., 2d Sess., 16. In response, the House Committee on Interstate and Foreign Commerce said merely that it did not "either agree or disagree" with the jurisdictional conclusions of the Second Report, and that "the question of whether or not . . . the Commission has authority under present law to regulate CATV systems is for the courts to decide . . ." *Id.*, at 9. In these circumstances, we cannot derive from the Commission's requests for legislation anything of significant bearing on the construction question now before us.

Second, respondents urge that § 152(a)[34] does not independently confer regulatory authority upon the Commission, but instead merely prescribes the forms of communication to which the Act's other provisions may separately be made applicable. Respondents emphasize that the Commission does not contend either that CATV systems are common carriers, and thus within Title II of the Act, or that they are broadcasters, and thus within Title III. They conclude that CATV, with certain of the characteristics both of broadcasting and of common carriers, but with all of the characteristics of neither, eludes altogether the Act's grasp.

[32] See S. Rep. No. 923, 86th Cong., 1st Sess., 5-6.

[33] Thus, the Senate Committee on Interstate and Foreign Commerce observed in its 1959 Report that although the Commission's staff had recommended that authority be asserted over CATV, the Commission had "long hesitated," and had only recently made clear "that it did not intend to regulate CATV systems in any way whatsoever." S. Rep. No. 923, *supra*, at 5. Nonetheless, it must be acknowledged that the debate on the Senate floor centered on the broad question whether the Commission should have authority to regulate CATV. See, *e.g.*, 106 Cong. Rec. 10426.

[34] 47 U.S.C. § 152(a) provides that "[t]he provisions of this chapter shall apply to all interstate and foreign communication by wire or radio and all interstate and foreign transmission of energy by radio, which originates and/or is received within the United States, and to all persons engaged within the United States in such communication or such transmission of energy by radio, and to the licensing and regulating of all radio stations as hereinafter provided; but it shall not apply to persons engaged in wire or radio communication or transmission in the Canal Zone, or to wire or radio communication or transmission wholly within the Canal Zone."

We cannot construe the Act so restrictively. Nothing in the language of §
152(a), in the surrounding language, or in the Act's history or purposes limits
the Commission's authority to those activities and forms of communication that
are specifically described by the Act's other provisions. The section itself states
merely that the "provisions of [the Act] shall apply to all interstate and foreign
communication by wire or radio . . ." Similarly, the legislative history indicates
that the Commission was given "regulatory power over all forms of electrical
communication . . ." S. Rep. No. 781, 73d Cong., 2d Sess., 1. Certainly Congress
could not in 1934 have foreseen the development of community antenna
television systems, but it seems to us that it was precisely because Congress
wished "to maintain, through appropriate administrative control, a grip on the
dynamic aspects of radio transmission," *F.C.C.* v. *Pottsville Broadcasting Co.,
supra*, at 138, that it conferred upon the Commission a "unified jurisdiction"[35]
and "broad authority."[36] Thus, "[u]nderlying the whole [Communications
Act] is recognition of the rapidly fluctuating factors characteristic of the
evolution of broadcasting and of the corresponding requirement that the
administrative process possess sufficient flexibility to adjust itself to these
factors." *F.C.C.* v. *Pottsville Broadcasting Co., supra*, at 138. Congress in 1934
acted in a field that was demonstrably "both new and dynamic," and it
therefore gave the Commission "a comprehensive mandate," with "not niggardly
but expansive powers." *National Broadcasting Co.* v. *United States*, 319 U.S.
190, 219. We have found no reason to believe that § 152 does not, as its terms
suggest, confer regulatory authority over "all interstate . . communication by
wire or radio."[37]

Moreover, the Commission has reasonably concluded that regulatory
authority over CATV is imperative if it is to perform with appropriate
effectiveness certain of its other responsibilities. Congress has imposed upon the
Commission the "obligation of providing a widely dispersed radio and television
service,"[38] with a "fair, efficient, and equitable distribution" of service among

[35] S. Rep. No. 781, *supra*, at 1.
[36] H. R. Rep. No. 1850, *supra*, at 1.
[37] Respondents argue, and the Court of Appeals evidently concluded, that the opinion of the
Court in *Regents* v. *Carroll*, 338 U.S. 586, supports the inference that the Commission's
authority is limited to licensees, carriers, and others specifically reached by the Act's
other provisions. We find this unpersuasive. The Court in *Carroll* considered the very
general contention that the Commission had been given authority "to determine the
validity of contracts between licensees and others." *Id.*, at 602. It was concerned, not
with the limits of the Commission's authority over a form of communication by wire or
radio, but with efforts to enforce a contract that had been repudiated upon the demand
of the Commission. The Court's discussion of the Commission's authority under § 303(r),
see *id.*, at 600, must be read in that context, and as thus read it cannot be controlling
here.
[38] S. Rep. No. 923, *supra*, at 7. The Committee added that "Congress and the people" have
no particular interest in the success of any given broadcaster, but if the failure of a station
"leaves a community with inferior service," this becomes "a matter of real and immediate
public concern." *Ibid.*

the "several States and communities." 47 U.S.C. § 307(b). The Commission has, for this and other purposes, been granted authority to allocate broadcasting zones or areas, and to provide regulations "as it may deem necessary" to prevent interference among the various stations. 47 U.S.C. §§ 303(f), (h). The Commission has concluded, and Congress has agreed, that these obligations require for their satisfaction the creation of a system of local broadcasting stations, such that "all communities of appreciable size [will] have at least one television station as an outlet for local self-expression."[39] In turn, the Commission has held that an appropriate svstem of local broadcasting may be created only if two subsidiary goals are realized. First, significantly wider use must be made of the available ultra-high frequency channels.[40] Second, communities must be encouraged "to launch sound and adequate programs to utilize the television channels now reserved for educational purposes."[41] These subsidiary goals have received the endorsement of Congress.[42]

The Commission has reasonably found that the achievement of each of these purposes is "placed in jeopardy by the unregulated explosive growth of CATV." H. R. Rep. No. 1635, 89th Cong., 2d Sess., 7. Although CATV may in some circumstances make possible "the realization of some of the [Com-

---

[39] H. R. Rep. No. 1559, 87th Cong., 2d Sess., 3; Sixth Report and Order, 17 Fed. Reg. 3905. And see Staff of the Senate Comm. on Interstate and Foreign Commerce, 85th Cong., 2d Sess., The Television Inquiry: The Problem of Television Service for Smaller Communities 3-4 (Comm. Print 1959). The Senate Committee has elsewhere stated that "[t]here should be no weakening of the Commission's announced goal of local service." S. Rep. No. 923, *supra*, at 7.

[40] The Commission has allocated 82 channels for television broadcasting, of which 70 are in the UHF portion of the radio spectrum. This permits a total of 681 VHF stations and 1,544 UHF stations. H. R. Rep. No. 1559, *supra*, at 2. In December 1964, 454 VHF stations were on the air, 25 permittees were not operating, and 11 applications were awaiting Commission action, leaving 63 unreserved VHF allocations available. Seiden, *supra*, 162, n. 11, at 10. At the same time, 90 UHF stations were operating, 66 were assigned but not operating, 52 applications were pending before the Commission, and 1,108 allocations were still available. *Ibid.* The Commission has concluded that, in these circumstances, "an adequate national television system can be achieved" only if more of the available UHF channels are utilized. H. R. Rep. No. 1559, *supra*, at 4.

[41] S. Rep. No. 67, 87th Cong., 1st Sess., 8-9. The Committee indicated that it was "of utmost importance to the Nation that a reasonable opportunity be afforded educational institutions to use television as a noncommercial educational medium." *Id.*, at 3. Similarly, the House Committee on Interstate and Foreign Commerce has concluded that educational television will "provide a much needed source of cultural and informational programing for all audiences . . ." H. R. Rep. No. 1559, *supra*, at 3. It is thus an essential element of "an adequate national television system." *Id.*, at 4. See also H. R. Rep. No. 572, 90th Cong., 1st Sess.; S. Rep. No. 222, 90th Cong., 1st Sess.

[42] Legislation was adopted in 1962 to amend the Communications Act in order to require that all television receivers thereafter shipped in interstate commerce for sale or resale to the public be capable of receiving both UHF and VHF frequencies. 76 Stat. 150. The legislation was plainly intended to assist the growth of UHF broadcasting. See H. R. Rep. No. 1559, *supra*. Moreover, legislation has been adopted to provide construction grants and other assistance to educational television systems. 76 Stat. 68, 81 Stat. 365.

mission's] most important goals," First Report and Order, *supra*, at 699, its importation of distant signals into the service areas of local stations may also "destroy or seriously degrade the service offered by a television broadcaster," *id.*, at 700, and thus ultimately deprive the public of the various benefits of a system of local broadcasting stations.[43] In particular, the Commission feared that CATV might, by dividing the available audiences and revenues, significantly magnify the characteristically serious financial difficulties of UHF and educational television broadcasters.[44] The Commission acknowledged that it could not predict with certainty the consequences of unregulated CATV, but reasoned that its statutory responsibilities demand that it "plan in advance of foreseeable events, instead of waiting to react to them." *Id.*, at 701. We are aware that these consequences have been variously estimated,[45] but must conclude that there is

---

[43]See generally Second Report and Order, *supra*, at 736-745. It is pertinent that the Senate Committee on Interstate and Foreign Commerce feared even in 1959 that the unrestricted growth of CATV would eliminate local broadcasting, and that, in turn, this would have four undesirable consequences: (1) the local community "would be left without the local service which is necessary if the public is to receive the maximum benefits from the television medium"; (2) the "suburban and rural areas surrounding the central community may be deprived not only of local service but of any service at all"; (3) even "the resident of the central community may be deprived of all service if he cannot afford the connection charge and monthly service fees of the CATV system"; (4) "[u]nrestrained CATV, booster, or translator operation might eventually result in large regions, or even entire States, being deprived of all local television service — or being left, at best, with nothing more than a highly limited satellite service." S. Rep No. 923, *supra*, at 7-8. The Committee concluded that CATV competition "does have an effect on the orderly development of television." *Id.*, at 8.

[44]The Commission has found that "we are in a critical period with respect to UHF development. Most of the new UHF stations will face considerable financial obstacles." First Report and Order, *supra*, at 712. It concluded that "one general factor giving cause for serious concern," *ibid.*, was that there is "likely" to be a "severe" impact between new local stations, particularly UHF stations, and CATV systems. *Id.*, at 713. Further, the Commission believed that there was danger that CATV systems would "siphon off sufficient local financial support" for educational television, with the result that such stations would fail or not be established at all. It feared that "the loss would be keenly felt by the public." Second Report and Order, *supra*, at 761. The Commission concluded that the hazards to educational television were "sufficiently strong to warrant some special protection . . ." *Id.*, at 762. Similarly, a recent study has found that CATV systems may have a substantial impact upon station revenues, that many stations, particularly in small markets, cannot readily afford such competition, and that in consequence a "substantial percentage of potential new station entrants, particularly UHF, are likely to be discouraged . . ." Fisher & Ferrall, Community Antenna Television Systems and Local Television Station Audience, 80 Q. J. Econ. 227, 250.

[45]Compare the following. Seiden, *supra*, at 69-90; Note, The Federal Communications Commission and Regulation of CATV, 43 N.Y.U. L. Rev. 117, 133-139; Note, The Wire Mire: The FCC and CATV, *supra* at 376-383; Fisher & Ferrall, *supra*. We note, in addition, that the dispute here is in part whether local, advertiser-supported stations are an appropriate foundation for a national system of television broadcasting. See generally Coase, The Economics of Broadcasting and Government Policy, 56 Am. Econ. Rev. 440 (May 1966); Greenberg, Wire Television and the FCC's Second Report and Order on CATV Systems, 10 J. Law & Econ. 181.

substantial evidence that the Commission cannot "discharge its overall responsibilities without authority over this important aspect of television service." Staff of Senate Comm. on Interstate and Foreign Commerce, 85th Cong., 2d Sess., The Television Inquiry: The Problem of Television Service for Smaller Communities 19 (Comm. Print 1959).

The Commission has been charged with broad responsibilities for the orderly development of an appropriate system of local television broadcasting. The significance of its efforts can scarcely be exaggerated, for broadcasting is demonstrably a principal source of information and entertainment for a great part of the Nation's population. The Commission has reasonably found that the successful performance of these duties demands prompt and efficacious regulation of community antenna television systems. We have elsewhere held that we may not, "in the absence of compelling evidence that such was Congress' intention . . . prohibit administrative action imperative for the achievement of an agency's ultimate purposes." *Permian Basin Area Rate Cases*, 390 U.S. 747, 780. Compare *National Broadcasting Co.* v. *United States, supra*, at 219-220; *American Trucking Assns.* v. *United States*, 344 U.S. 298, 311. There is no such evidence here, and we therefore hold that the Commission's authority over "all interstate . . . communication by wire or radio" permits the regulation of CATV systems.

There is no need here to determine in detail the limits of the Commission's authority to regulate CATV. It is enough to emphasize that the authority which we recognize today under § 152(a) is restricted to that reasonably ancillary to the effective performance of the Commission's various responsibilities for the regulation of television broadcasting. The Commission may, for these purposes, issue "such rules and regulations and prescribe such restrictions and conditions, not inconsistent with law," as "public convenience, interest, or necessity requires." 47 U.S.C. § 303(r). We express no views as to the Commission's authority, if any, to regulate CATV under any other circumstances or for any other purposes.

III.

We must next determine whether the Commission has authority under the Communications Act to issue the particular prohibitory order in question in these proceedings. In its Second Report and Order, *supra*, the Commission concluded that it should provide summary procedures for the disposition both of requests for special relief and of "complaints or disputes." *Id.*, at 764. It feared that if evidentiary hearings were in every situation mandatory they would prove "time consuming and burdensome" to the CATV systems and broadcasting stations involved. *Ibid.* The Commission considered that appropriate notice and opportunities for comment or objection must be given, and it declared that "additional procedures, such as oral argument, evidentiary hearing, or further written submissions" would be permitted "if they appear necessary or appropriate . . ." *Ibid.* See 47 CFR § 74.1109(f). It was under the authority of these provisions that Midwest sought, and the Commission granted, temporary relief.

The Commission, after examination of various responsive pleadings but without prior hearings, ordered that respondents generally restrict their carriage of Los Angeles signals to areas served by them on February 15, 1966, pending hearings to determine whether the carriage of such signals into San Diego contravenes the public interest. The order does not prohibit the addition of new subscribers within areas served by respondents on February 15, 1966; it does not prevent service to other subscribers who began receiving service or who submitted an "accepted subscription request" between February 15, 1966, and the date of the Commission's order; and it does not preclude the carriage of San Diego and Tijuana, Mexico, signals to subscribers in new areas of service. 4 F.C.C. 2d 612, 624-625. The order is thus designed simply to preserve the situation as it existed at the moment of its issuance.

Respondents urge that the Commission may issue prohibitory orders only under the authority of § 312(b), by which the Commission is empowered to issue cease-and-desist orders. We shall assume that, consistent with the requirements of § 312(c), cease-and-desist orders are proper only after hearing or waiver of the right to hearing. Nonetheless, the requirement does not invalidate the order issued in this case, for we have concluded that the provisions of §§ 312(b), (c) are inapplicable here. Section 312(b) provides that a cease-and-desist order may issue only if the respondent "has violated or failed to observe" a provision of the Communications Act or a rule or regulation promulgated by the Commission under the Act's authority. Respondents here were not found to have violated or to have failed to observe any such restriction; the question before the Commission was instead only whether an existing situation should be preserved pending a determination "whether respondents' present or planned CATV operations are consistent with the public interest and what, if any, action should be taken by the Commission." 4 F.C.C. 2d, at 626. The Commission's order was thus not, in form or function, a cease-and-desist order that must issue under §§ 312(b), (c).[46]

The Commission has acknowledged that, in this area of rapid and significant change, there may be situations in which its generalized regulations are inadequate, and special or additional forms of relief are imperative. It has

---

[46]Respondents urge that the legislative history of § 312(b) indicates that the Commission may issue prohibitory orders only under, and in conformity with, that section. We find this unpersuasive. Nothing in that history suggests that the Commission was deprived of its authority, granted elsewhere in the Act, to issue orders "necessary in the execution of its functions." 47 U.S.C. § 154(i). See also 47 U.S.C. § 303(r).

found that the present case may prove to be such a situation, and that the public interest demands "interim relief ... limiting further expansion," pending hearings to determine appropriate Commission action. Such orders do not exceed the Commission's authority. This Court has recognized that "the administrative process [must] possess sufficient flexibility to adjust itself" to the "dynamic aspects of radio transmission," *F.C.C.* v. *Pottsville Broadcasting Co., supra*, at 138, and that it was precisely for that reason that Congress declined to "stereotyp[e] the powers of the Commission to specific details ..." *National Broadcasting Co.* v. *United States, supra*, at 219. And compare *American Trucking Assns.* v. *United States*, 344 U.S. 298, 311; *R. A. Holman & Co.* v. *S.E.C.*, 112 U.S. App. D.C. 43, 47-48, 299 F. 2d 127, 131-132. Thus, the Commission has been explicitly authorized to issue "such orders, not inconsistent with this [Act], as may be necessary in the execution of its functions." 47 U.S.C. § 154(i). See also 47 U.S.C. § 303(r). In these circumstances, we hold that the Commission's order limiting further expansion of respondents' service pending appropriate hearings did not exceed or abuse its authority under the Communications Act. And there is no claim that its procedure in this respect is in any way constitutionally infirm.

The judgments of the Court of Appeals are reversed, and the cases are remanded for further proceedings consistent with this opinion.

It is so ordered.

Mr. Justice Douglas and Mr. Justice Marshall took no part in the consideration or decision of these cases.

39

The Red Lion Case

Red Lion Broadcasting Co., Inc., et al. v. Federal
Communications Commission et al.
395 U.S. 367
June 9, 1969

In this landmark decision the Supreme Court unanimously upheld the constitutional and statutory soundness of the FCC's
Fairness Doctrine (Document 22, pp. 217–231) and related right-
of-reply rules issued by the Commission in 1967. Justice White's
opinion is premised on the technological scarcity of frequencies
that places broadcasting in a different posture with respect to the
First Amendment than other modes of communication. Thus,
although government *abridgment* of free expression is prohibited
by the Constitution, *enhancement* of that freedom, reasonably
related to the public interest in broadcasting, is permissible—even
if the freedom of licensees is lessened thereby.

The *Red Lion* decision raised as many questions as it settled.
The biggest riddle had to do with the notion that the First
Amendment, a pre-mass media "relic" of the eighteenth century,
required substantial judicial re-interpretation if it was to serve
the informational needs of the public in the media-dominated
twentieth century. Those urging a limited right of access to broadcasting for editorial advertising were disappointed by a 1973
Supreme Court decision that established limits on how far *Red
Lion*'s broad holding could be stretched (see Document 41, pp.
407–425). Then, a year later, the nine Justices dashed the hopes
of media access advocates by declaring unconstitutional a 1913
Florida right-of-reply law that required newspapers to provide
free and equal space for replies to published attacks on political

candidates [*Miami Herald* v. *Tornillo*, 418 U.S. 241 (1974)]. The Court held that the First Amendment prohibits government intrusion into the editorial prerogatives of control and judgment.

While the language of *Red Lion* appears to carve the Fairness Doctrine out of constitutional stone, subsequent developments have weakened prospects for the metamorphosis of "fairness" into legally enforceable "access" to broadcasting and the print media. The foundation of the Fairness Doctrine itself has suffered some erosion, for the view persists that there is little practical difference between the technological scarcity that permits approximately 10,000 broadcasting stations and the economic scarcity that limits daily newspapers to fewer than 2,000. Why, then, should different First Amendment standards apply to the treatment of public controversy in different mass media? Is it conceivable that the public interest standard of the Communications Act supersedes the Constitution? Can the river run higher than its source?

Related Reading: 12, 13, 16, 21, 84, 105, 109, 153, 196.

Mr. Justice White delivered the opinion of the Court.

The Federal Communications Commission has for many years imposed on radio and television broadcasters the requirement that discussion of public issues be presented on broadcast stations, and that each side of those issues must be given fair coverage. This is known as the fairness doctrine, which originated very early in the history of broadcasting and has maintained its present outlines for some time. It is an obligation whose content has been defined in a long series of FCC rulings in particular cases, and which is distinct from the statutory requirement of § 315 of the Communications Act[1] that equal time be allotted

---

[1]Communications Act of 1934, Tit. III, 48 Stat. 1081, as amended, 47 U.S.C. § 301 *et seq.* Section 315 now reads:

"315. Candidates for public office; facilities; rules.

"(a) If any licensee shall permit any person who is a legally qualified candidate for any public office to use a broadcasting station, he shall afford equal opportunities to all other such candidates for that office in the use of such broadcasting station: *Provided,* That such licensee shall have no power of censorship over the material broadcast under the provisions of this section. No obligation is imposed upon any licensee to allow the use of its station by any such candidate. Appearance by a legally qualified candidate on any –

"(1) bona fide newscast,

"(2) bona fide news interview,

"(3) bona fide news documentary (if the appearance of the candidate is incidental to the presentation of the subject or subjects covered by the news documentary), or

"(4) on-the-spot coverage of bona fide news events (including but not limited to political conventions and activities incidental thereto), shall not be deemed to be use of a

all qualified candidates for public office. Two aspects of the fairness doctrine, relating to personal attacks in the context of controversial public issues and to political editorializing, were codified more precisely in the form of FCC regulations in 1967. The two cases before us now, which were decided separately below, challenge the constitutional and statutory bases of the doctrine and component rules. *Red Lion* involves the application of the fairness doctrine to a particular broadcast, and *RTNDA** arises as an action to review the FCC's 1967 promulgation of the personal attack and political editorializing regulations, which were laid down after the *Red Lion* litigation had begun.

I.

A.

The Red Lion Broadcasting Company is licensed to operate a Pennsylvania radio station, WGCB. On November 27, 1964, WGCB carried a 15-minute broadcast by the Reverend Billy James Hargis as part of a "Christian Crusade" series. A book by Fred J. Cook entitled "Goldwater – Extremist on the Right" was discussed by Hargis, who said that Cook had been fired by a newspaper for making false charges against city officials; that Cook had then worked for a Communist-affiliated publication, that he had defended Alger Hiss and attacked J. Edgar Hoover and the Central Intelligence Agency; and that he had now written a "book to smear and destroy Barry Goldwater."[2] When Cook heard of

---

broadcasting station within the meaning of this subsection. Nothing in the foregoing sentence shall be construed as relieving broadcasters, in connection with the presentation of newscasts, news interviews, news documentaries, and on-the-spot coverage of news events, from the obligation imposed upon them under this chapter to operate in the public interest and to afford reasonable opportunity for the discussion of conflicting views on issues of public importance..

"(b) The charges made for the use of any broadcasting station for any of the purposes set forth in this section shall not exceed the charges made for comparable use of such station for other purposes.

"(c) The Commission shall prescribe appropriate rules and regulations to carry out the provisions of this section."

*RTNDA denotes Radio Television News Directors Association. [Ed.]

[2] According to the record, Hargis asserted that his broadcast included the following statement:

"Now, this paperback book by Fred J. Cook is entitled, 'GOLDWATER–EXTREMIST ON THE RIGHT.' Who is Cook? Cook was fired from the New York World Telegram after he made a false charge publicly on television against an un-named official of the New York City government. New York publishers and NEWSWEEK Magazine for December 7, 1959. showed that Fred Cook and his pal, Eugene Gleason, had made up the whole story and this confession was made to New York District Attorney, Frank Hogan. After losing his job,

the broadcast he concluded that he had been personally attacked and demanded free reply time, which the station refused. After an exchange of letters among Cook, Red Lion, and the FCC, the FCC declared that the Hargis broadcast constituted a personal attack on Cook; that Red Lion had failed to meet its obligation under the fairness doctrine as expressed in *Times-Mirror Broadcasting Co.*, 24 P & F Radio Reg. 404 (1962), to send a tape, transcript, or summary of the broadcast to Cook and offer him reply time; and that the station must provide reply time whether or not Cook would pay for it. On review in the Court of Appeals for the District of Columbia Circuit,[3] the FCC's position was upheld as constitutional and otherwise proper. 127 U.S. App. D.C. 129, 381 F. 2d 908 (1967).

B.

Not long after the *Red Lion* litigation was begun, the FCC issued a Notice of Proposed Rule Making, 31 Fed. Reg. 5710, with an eye to making the personal attack aspect of the fairness doctrine more precise and more readily enforceable,

---

Cook went to work for the left-wing publication, THE NATION, one of the most scurrilous publications of the left which has championed many communist causes over many years. Its editor, Carry McWilliams, has been affiliated with many communist enterprises, scores of which have been cited as subversive by the Attorney General of the U.S. or by other government agencies. . . . Now, among other things Fred Cook wrote for THE NATION, was an article absolving Alger Hiss of any wrong doing . . . there was a 208 page attack on the FBI and J. Edgar Hoover; another attack by Mr. Cook was on the Central Intelligence Agency . . . now this is the man who wrote the book to smear and destroy Barry Goldwater called 'Barry Goldwater — Extremist of the Right!' "

[3]The Court of Appeals initially dismissed the petition for want of a reviewable order, later reversing itself en banc upon argument by the Government that the FCC rule used here, which permits it to issue "a declaratory ruling terminating a controversy or removing uncertainty," 47 CFR § 1.2, was in fact justified by the Administrative Procedure Act. That Act permits an adjudicating agency, "in its sound discretion, with like effect as in the case of other orders, to issue a declaratory order to terminate a controversy or remove uncertainty." § 5, 60 Stat. 239, 5 U.S.C. § 1004(d). In this case, the FCC could have determined the question of Red Lion's liability to a cease-and-desist order or license revocation, 47 U.S.C. § 312, for failure to comply with the license's condition that the station be operated "in the public interest," or for failure to obey a requirement of operation in the public interest implicit in the ability of the FCC to revoke licenses for conditions justifying the denial of an initial license, 47 U.S.C. § 312(a)(2), and the statutory requirement that the public interest be served in granting and renewing licenses, 47 U.S.C. §§ 307(a), (d). Since the FCC could have adjudicated these questions it could, under the Administrative Procedure Act, have issued a declaratory order in the course of its adjudication which would have been subject to judicial review. Although the FCC did not comply with all of the formalities for an adjudicative proceeding in this case, the petitioner itself adopted as its own the Government's position that this was a reviewable order, waiving any objection it might have had to the procedure of the adjudication.

and to specifying its rules relating to political editorials. After considering written comments supporting and opposing the rules, the FCC adopted them substantially as proposed, 32 Fed. Reg. 10303. Twice amended, 32 Fed. Reg. 11531, 33 Fed. Reg. 5362, the rules were held unconstitutional in the *RTNDA* litigation by the Court of Appeals for the Seventh Circuit, on review of the rule-making proceeding, as abridging the freedoms of speech and press. 400 F. 2d 1002 (1968).

As they now stand amended, the regulations read as follows:

"Personal attacks; political editorials.

"(a) When, during the presentation of views on a controversial issue of public importance, an attack is made upon the honesty, character, integrity or like personal qualities of an identified person or group, the licensee shall, within a reasonable time and in no event later than 1 week after the attack, transmit to the person or group attacked (1) notification of the date, time and identification of the broadcast; (2) a script or tape (or an accurate summary if a script or tape is not available) of the attack; and (3) an offer of a reasonable opportunity to respond over the licensee's facilities.

"(b) The provisions of paragraph (a) of this section shall not be applicable (1) to attacks on foreign groups or foreign public figures; (2) to personal attacks which are made by legally qualified candidates, their authorized spokesmen, or those associated with them in the campaign, on other such candidates, their authorized spokesmen, or persons associated with the candidates in the campaign; and (3) to bona fide newscasts, bona fide news interviews, and on-the-spot coverage of a bona fide news event (including commentary or analysis contained in the foregoing programs, but the provisions of paragraph (a) of this section shall be applicable to editorials of the licensee).

"NOTE: The fairness doctrine is applicable to situations coming within [(3)], above, and, in a specific factual situation, may be applicable in the general area of political broadcasts [(2)], above. See, section 315(a) of the Act, 47 U.S.C. 315(a); Public Notice: *Applicability of the Fairness Doctrine in the Handling of Controversial Issues of Public Importance.* 29 F.R. 10415. The categories listed in [(3)] are the same as those specified in section 315(a) of the Act.

"(c) Where a licensee, in an editorial, (i) endorses or (ii) opposes a legally qualified candidate or candidates, the licensee shall, within 24 hours after the editorial, transmit to respectively (i) the other qualified candidate or candidates for the same office or (ii) the candidate opposed in the editorial (1) notification of the date and the time of the editorial; (2) a script or tape of the editorial; and (3) an offer of a reasonable opportunity for a candidate or a spokesman of the candidate to respond over the licensee's facilities: *Provided, however,* That where such editorials are broadcast within 72 hours prior to the day of the election, the licensee shall comply with the provisions of this paragraph sufficiently far in advance of the broadcast to enable the candidate or candidates to have a reasonable opportunity to prepare a response and to present it in a timely fashion." 47 CFR § § 73.123, 73.300, 73.598, 73.679 (all identical).

C.

Believing that the specific application of the fairness doctrine in *Red Lion*, and the promulgation of the regulations in *RTNDA*, are both authorized by Congress and enhance rather than abridge the freedoms of speech and press protected by the First Amendment, we hold them valid and constitutional, reversing the judgment below in *RTNDA* and affirming the judgment below in *Red Lion.*

II.

The history of the emergence of the fairness doctrine and of the related legislation shows that the Commission's action in the *Red Lion* case did not exceed its authority, and that in adopting the new regulations the Commission was implementing congressional policy rather than embarking on a frolic of its own.

A.

Before 1927, the allocation of frequencies was left entirely to the private sector, and the result was chaos.[4] It quickly became apparent that broadcast

---

[4] Because of this chaos, a series of National Radio Conferences was held between 1922 and 1925, at which it was resolved that regulation of the radio spectrum by the Federal Government was essential and that regulatory power should be utilized to ensure that allocation of this limited resource would be made only to those who would serve the public interest. The 1923 Conference expressed the opinion that the Radio Communications Act of 1912, 37 Stat. 302, conferred upon the Secretary of Commerce the power to regulate frequencies and hours of operation, but when Secretary Hoover sought to implement this claimed power by penalizing the Zenith Radio Corporation for operating on an unauthorized frequency, the 1912 Act was held not to permit enforcement. *United States* v. *Zenith Radio Corporation*, 12 F. 2d 614 (D.C.N.D. Ill. 1926). Cf. *Hoover* v. *Intercity Radio Co.*, 52 App. D.C. 339, 286 F. 1003 (1923) (Secretary had no power to deny licenses, but was empowered to assign frequencies). An opinion issued by the Attorney General at Hoover's request confirmed the impotence of the Secretary under the 1912 Act. 35 Op. Atty. Gen. 126 (1926). Hoover thereafter appealed to the radio industry to regulate itself, but his appeal went largely unheeded. See generally L. Schmeckebier, The Federal Radio Commission 1-14 (1932).

frequencies constituted a scarce resource whose use could be regulated and rationalized only by the Government. Without government control, the medium would be of little use because of the cacophony of competing voices, none of which could be clearly and predictably heard.[5] Consequently, the Federal Radio Commission was established to allocate frequencies among competing applicants in a manner responsive to the public "convenience, interest, or necessity."[6]

Very shortly thereafter the Commission expressed its view that the "public interest requires ample play for the free and fair competition of opposing views, and the commission believes that the principle applies ... to all discussions of issues of importance to the public." *Great Lakes Broadcasting Co.*, 3 F.R.C. Ann. Rep. 32, 33 (1929), rev'd on other grounds, 59 App. D.C. 197, 37 F. 2d 993, cert. dismissed, 281 U.S. 706 (1930). This doctrine was applied through denial of license renewals or construction permits, both by the FRC, *Trinity Methodist Church, South v. FRC*, 61 App. D.C. 311, 62 F. 2d 850 (1932), cert. denied, 288 U.S. 599 (1933), and its successor FCC, *Young People's Association for the Propagation of the Gospel*, 6 F.C.C. 178 (1938). After an extended period during which the licensee was obliged not only to cover and to cover fairly the views of others, but also to refrain from expressing his own personal views, *Mayflower Broadcasting Corp.*, 8 F.C.C. 333 (1940), the latter limitation on the licensee was abandoned and the doctrine developed into its present form.

There is a twofold duty laid down by the FCC's decisions and described by the 1949 Report on Editorializing by Broadcast Licensees, 13 F.C.C. 1246 (1949). The broadcaster must give adequate coverage to public issues, *United Broadcasting Co.*, 10 F.C.C. 515 (1945), and coverage must be fair in that it accurately reflects the opposing views. *New Broadcasting Co.*, 6 P & F Radio Reg. 258 (1950). This must be done at the broadcaster's own expense if sponsorship is unavailable. *Cullman Broadcasting Co.*, 25 P & F Radio Reg. 895 (1963). Moreover, the duty must be met by programming obtained at the licensee's own initiative if available from no other source. *John J. Dempsey*, 6

---

[5] Congressman White, a sponsor of the bill enacted as the Radio Act of 1927, commented upon the need for new legislation:

"We have reached the definite conclusion that the right of all our people to enjoy this means of communication can be preserved only by the repudiation of the idea underlying the 1912 law that anyone who will may transmit and by the assertion in its stead of the doctrine that the right of the public to service is superior to the right of any individual. ... The recent radio conference met this issue squarely. It recognized that in the present state of scientific development there must be a limitation upon the number of broadcasting stations and it recommended that licenses should be issued only to those stations whose operation would render a benefit to the public, are necessary in the public interest, or would contribute to the development of the art. This principle was approved by every witness before your committee. We have written it into the bill. If enacted into law, the broadcasting privilege will not be a right of selfishness. It will rest upon an assurance of public interest to be served." 67 Cong. Rec. 5479.

[6] Radio Act of 1927, § 4, 44 Stat. 1163. See generally Davis, The Radio Act of 1927, 13 Va. L. Rev. 611 (1927).

P & F Radio Reg. 615 (1950); see *Metropolitan Broadcasting Corp.*, 19 P & F Radio Reg. 602 (1960); *The Evening News Assn.*, 6 P & F Radio Reg. 283 (1950). The Federal Radio Commission had imposed these two basic duties on broadcasters since the outset, *Great Lakes Broadcasting Co.*, 3 F.R.C. Ann. Rep. 32 (1929), rev'd on other grounds, 59 App. D.C. 197, 37 F. 2d 993, cert. dismissed, 281 U.S. 706 (1930); *Chicago Federation of Labor* v. *FRC*, 3 F.R.C. Ann. Rep. 36 (1929), aff'd, 59 App. D.C. 333, 41 F. 2d 422 (1930); *KFKB Broadcasting Assn.* v. *FRC*, 60 App. D.C. 79, 47 F. 2d 670 (1931), and in particular respects the personal attack rules and regulations at issue here have spelled them out in greater detail.

When a personal attack has been made on a figure involved in a public issue, both the doctrine of cases such as *Red Lion* and *Times-Mirror Broadcasting Co.*, 24 P & F Radio Reg. 404 (1962), and also the 1967 regulations at issue in *RTNDA* require that the individual attacked himself be offered an opportunity to respond. Likewise, where one candidate is endorsed in a political editorial, the other candidates must themselves be offered reply time to use personally or through a spokesman. These obligations differ from the general fairness requirement that issues be presented, and presented with coverage of competing views, in that the broadcaster does not have the option of presenting the attacked party's side himself or choosing a third party to represent that side. But insofar as there is an obligation of the broadcaster to see that both sides are presented, and insofar as that is an affirmative obligation, the personal attack doctrine and regulations do not differ from the preceding fairness doctrine. The simple fact that the attacked men or unendorsed candidates may respond themselves or through agents is not a critical distinction, and indeed, it is not unreasonable for the FCC to conclude that the objective of adequate presentation of all sides may best be served by allowing those most closely affected to make the response, rather than leaving the response in the hands of the station which has attacked their candidacies, endorsed their opponents, or carried a personal attack upon them.

B.

The statutory authority of the FCC to promulgate these regulations derives from the mandate to the "Commission from time to time, as public convenience, interest, or necessity requires" to promulgate "such rules and regulations and prescribe such restrictions and conditions . . . as may be necessary to carry out the provisions of this chapter . . ." 47 U.S.C. § 303 and § 303 (r).[7] The

---

[7] As early as 1930, Senator Dill expressed the view that the Federal Radio Commission had the power to make regulations requiring a licensee to afford an opportunity for presentation of the other side on "public questions." Hearings before the Senate Committee on Interstate Commerce on S. 6, 71st Cong., 2d Sess., 1616 (1930):

Commission is specifically directed to consider the demands of the public interest in the course of granting licenses, 47 U.S.C. § § 307(a), 309(a); renewing them, 47 U.S.C. § 307; and modifying them. *Ibid.* Moreover, the FCC has included among the conditions of the Red Lion license itself the requirement that operation of the station be carried out in the public interest, 47 U.S.C. § 309(h). This mandate to the FCC to assure that broadcasters operate in the public interest is a broad one, a power "not niggardly but expansive," *National Broadcasting Co.* v. *United States*, 319 U.S. 190, 219 (1943), whose validity we have long upheld. *FCC* v. *Pottsville Broadcasting Co.*, 309 U.S. 134, 138 (1940); *FCC* v. *RCA Communications, Inc.*, 346 U.S. 86, 90 (1953); *FRC* v. *Nelson Bros. Bond & Mortgage Co.*, 289 U.S. 266, 285 (1933). It is broad enough to encompass these regulations.

The fairness doctrine finds specific recognition in statutory form, is in part modeled on explicit statutory provisions relating to political candidates, and is approvingly reflected in legislative history.

In 1959 the Congress amended the statutory requirement of § 315 that equal time be accorded each political candidate to except certain appearances on news programs, but added that this constituted no exception *"from the obligation imposed upon them under this Act to operate in the public interest and to afford reasonable opportunity for the discussion of conflicting views on issues of public importance."* Act of September 14, 1959, § 1, 73 Stat. 557, amending 47 U.S.C. § 315(a) (emphasis added). This language makes it very plain that Congress, in 1959, announced that the phrase "public interest," which had been in the Act since 1927, imposed a duty on broadcasters to discuss both sides of controversial public issues. In other words, the amendment vindicated the FCC's general view that the fairness doctrine inhered in the public interest standard. Subsequent legislation declaring the intent of an earlier statute is entitled to great weight in statutory construction.[8] And here this principle is

---

"Senator Dill. Then you are suggesting that the provision of the statute that now requires a station to give equal opportunity to candidates for office shall be applied to all public questions?

"Commissioner Robinson. Of course, I think in the legal concept the law requires it now. I do not see that there is any need to legislate about it. It will evolve one of these days. Somebody will go into court and say, 'I am entitled to this opportunity,' and he will get it.

"Senator Dill. Has the Commission considered the question of making regulations requiring the stations to do that?

"Commissioner Robinson. Oh, no.

"Senator Dill. It would be within the power of the commission, I think, to make regulations on that subject."

[8] *Federal Housing Administration* v. *Darlington, Inc.*, 358 U.S. 84, 90 (1958); *Glidden Co.* v. *Zdanok*, 370 U.S. 530, 541 (1962) (opinion of Mr. Justice Harlan, joined by Mr. Justice Brennan and Mr. Justice Stewart). This principle is a venerable one. *Alexander* v. *Alexandria*, 5 Cranch 1 (1809); *United States* v. *Freeman*, 3 How. 556 (1845); *Stockdale* v. *The Insurance Companies*, 20 Wall. 323 (1874).

given special force by the equally venerable principle that the construction of a
statute by those charged with its execution should be followed unless there are
compelling indications that it is wrong,[9] especially when Congress has refused to
alter the administrative construction.[10] Here, the Congress has not just kept its
silence by refusing to overturn the administrative construction,[11] but has
ratified it with positive legislation. Thirty years of consistent administrative
construction left undisturbed by Congress until 1959, when that construction
was expressly accepted, reinforce the natural conclusion that the public interest
language of the Act authorized the Commission to require licensees to use their
stations for discussion of public issues, and that the FCC is free to implement
this requirement by reasonable rules and regulations which fall short of
abridgment of the freedom of speech and press, and of the censorship proscribed
by § 326 of the Act.[12]

---

[9]*Zemel* v. *Rusk*, 381 U.S. 1, 11-12 (1965); *Udall* v. *Tallman*, 380 U.S. 1, 16-18 (1965);
Commissioner v. *Sternberger's Estate*, 348 U.S. 187, 199 (1955); *Hastings & D.R. Co.* v.
Whitney, 132 U.S. 357, 366 (1889); *United States* v. *Burlington & Missouri River R. Co.*,
98 U.S. 334, 341 (1879); *United States* v. *Alexander*, 12 Wall. 177, 179-181 (1871);
Surgett v. *Lapice*, 8 How. 48, 68 (1850).

[10]*Zemel* v. *Rusk*, 381 U.S. 1, 11-12 (1965); *United States* v. *Bergh*, 352 U.S. 40, 46-47
(1956); *Alstate Construction Co.* v. *Durkin*, 345 U.S. 13, 16-17 (1953); *Costanzo* v.
Tillinghast, 287 U.S. 341, 345 (1932).

[11]An attempt to limit sharply the FCC's power to interfere with programming practices
failed to emerge from Committee in 1943. S. 814, 78th Cong., 1st Sess. (1943). See
Hearings on S. 814 before the Senate Committee on Interstate Commerce, 78th Cong., 1st
Sess. (1943). Also, attempts specifically to enact the doctrine failed in the Radio Act of
1927, 67 Cong. Rec. 12505 (1926) (agreeing to amendment proposed by Senator Dill
eliminating coverage of "question affecting the public"), and a similar proposal in the
Communications Act of 1934 was accepted by the Senate, 78 Cong. Rec. 8854 (1934);
see S. Rep. No. 781, 73d Cong., 2d Sess., 8 (1934), but was not included in the bill
reported by the House Committee, see H. R. Rep. No. 1850, 73d Cong., 2d Sess. (1934).
The attempt which came nearest success was a bill, H. R. 7716, 72d Cong., 1st Sess.
(1932), passed by Congress but pocket-vetoed by the President in 1933, which would
have extended "equal opportunities" whenever a public question was to be voted on at an
election or by a government agency. H. R. Rep. No. 2106, 72d Cong., 2d Sess., 6 (1933).
In any event, unsuccessful attempts at legislation are not the best of guides to legislative
intent. *Fogarty* v. *United States*, 340 U.S. 8, 13-14 (1950); *United States* v. *United Mine
Workers*, 330 U.S. 258, 281-282 (1947). A review of some of the legislative history over
the years, drawing a somewhat different conclusion, is found in Staff Study of the House
Committee on Interstate and Foreign Commerce, Legislative History of the Fairness
Doctrine, 90th Cong., 2d Sess. (Comm. Print. 1968). This inconclusive history was, of
course, superseded by the specific statutory language added in 1959.

[12]" § 326. Censorship.

"Nothing in this chapter shall be understood or construed to give the Commission
the power of censorship over the radio communications or signals transmitted by any
radio station, and no regulation or condition shall be promulgated or fixed by the
Commission which shall interfere with the right of free speech by means of radio
communication."

The objectives of § 315 themselves could readily be circumvented but for the complementary fairness doctrine ratified by § 315. The section applies only to campaign appearances by candidates, and not by family, friends, campaign managers, or other supporters. Without the fairness doctrine, then, a licensee could ban all campaign appearances by candidates themselves from the air[13] and proceed to deliver over his station entirely to the supporters of one slate of candidates, to the exclusion of all others. In this way the broadcaster could have a far greater impact on the favored candidacy than he could by simply allowing a spot appearance by the candidate himself. It is the fairness doctrine as an aspect of the obligation to operate in the public interest, rather than § 315, which prohibits the broadcaster from taking such a step.

The legislative history reinforces this view of the effect of the 1959 amendment. Even before the language relevant here was added, the Senate report on amending § 315 noted that "broadcast frequencies are limited and, therefore, they have been necessarily considered a public trust. Every licensee who is fortunate in obtaining a license is mandated to operate in the public interest and has assumed the obligation of presenting important public questions fairly and without bias." S. Rep. No. 562, 86th Cong., 1st Sess., 8-9 (1959). See also, specifically adverting to Federal Communications Commission doctrine, *id.*, at 13.

Rather than leave this approval solely in the legislative history, Senator Proxmire suggested an amendment to make it part of the Act. 105 Cong. Rec. 14457. This amendment, which Senator Pastore, a manager of the bill and a ranking member of the Senate Committee, considered "rather surplusage," 105 Cong. Rec. 14462, constituted a positive statement of doctrine[14] and was altered to the present merely approving language in the conference committee. In explaining the language to the Senate after the committee changes, Senator Pastore said: "We insisted that ·that provision remain in the bill, to be a continuing reminder and admonition to the Federal Communications Commission and to the broadcasters alike, that we were not abandoning the philosophy that gave birth to section 315, in giving the people the right to have a full and complete disclosure of conflicting views on news of interest to the people of the country." 105 Cong. Rec. 17830. Senator Scott, another Senate manager, added that: "It is intended to encompass all legitimate areas of public importance which are controversial," not just politics. 105 Cong. Rec. 17831.

---

[13]*John P. Crommelin*, 19 P & F Radio Reg. 1392 (1960).

[14]The Proxmire amendment read: "[B]ut nothing in this sentence shall be construed as changing the basic intent of Congress with respect to the provisions of this act, which recognizes that television and radio frequencies are in the public domain, that the license to operate in such frequencies requires operation in the public interest, and that in newscasts, news interviews, news documentaries, on-the-spot coverage of news events, and panel discussions, all sides of public controversies shall be given as equal an opportunity to be heard as is practically possible." 105 Cong. Rec. 14457.

It is true that the personal attack aspect of the fairness doctrine was not actually adjudicated until after 1959, so that Congress then did not have those rules specifically before it. However, the obligation to offer time to reply to a personal attack was presaged by the FCC's 1949 Report on Editorializing, which the FCC views as the principal summary of its *ratio decidendi* in cases in this area:

"In determining whether to honor specific requests for time, the station will inevitably be confronted with such questions as . . . whether there may not be other available groups or individuals who might be more appropriate spokesmen for the particular point of view than the person making the request. The latter's personal involvement in the controversy may also be a factor which must be considered, for elementary considerations of fairness may dictate that time be allocated to a person or group which has been specifically attacked over the station, where otherwise no such obligation would exist." 13 F.C.C., at 1251-1252.

When the Congress ratified the FCC's implication of a fairness doctrine in 1959 it did not, of course, approve every past decision or pronouncement by the Commission on this subject, or give it a completely free hand for the future. The statutory authority does not go so far. But we cannot say that when a station publishes personal attacks or endorses political candidates, it is a misconstruction of the public interest standard to require the station to offer time for a response rather than to leave the response entirely within the control of the station which has attacked either the candidacies or the men who wish to reply in their own defense. When a broadcaster grants time to a political candidate, Congress itself requires that equal time be offered to his opponents. It would exceed our competence to hold that the Commission is unauthorized by the statute to employ a similar device where personal attacks or political editorials are broadcast by a radio or television station.

In light of the fact that the "public interest" in broadcasting clearly encompasses the presentation of vigorous debate of controversial issues of importance and concern to the public; the fact that the FCC has rested upon that language from its very inception a doctrine that these issues must be discussed, and fairly; and the fact that Congress has acknowledged that the analogous provisions of § 315 are not preclusive in this area, and knowingly preserved the FCC's complementary efforts, we think the fairness doctrine and its component personal attack and political editorializing regulations are a legitimate exercise of congressionally delegated authority. The Communications Act is not notable for the precision of its substantive standards and in this respect the explicit provisions of § 315, and the doctrine and rules at issue here which are closely modeled upon that section, are far more explicit than the generalized "public interest" standard in which the Commission ordinarily finds its sole guidance, and which we have held a broad but adequate standard before. *FCC* v. *RCA Communications, Inc.*, 346 U.S. 86, 90 (1953); *National*

Broadcasting Co. v. *United States*, 319 U.S. 190, 216-217 (1943); *FCC* v. *Pottsville Broadcasting Co.*, 309 U.S. 134, 138 (1940); *FRC* v. *Nelson Bros. Bond & Mortgage Co.*, 289 U.S. 266, 285 (1933). We cannot say that the FCC's declaratory ruling in *Red Lion*, or the regulations at issue in *RTNDA*, are beyond the scope of the congressionally conferred power to assure that stations are operated by those whose possession of a license serves "the public interest."

III.

The broadcasters challenge the fairness doctrine and its specific manifestations in the personal attack and political editorial rules on conventional First Amendment grounds, alleging that the rules abridge their freedom of speech and press. Their contention is that the First Amendment protects their desire to use their allotted frequencies continuously to broadcast whatever they choose, and to exclude whomever they choose from ever using that frequency. No man may be prevented from saying or publishing what he thinks, or from refusing in his speech or other utterances to give equal weight to the views of his opponents. This right, they say, applies equally to broadcasters.

A.

Although broadcasting is clearly a medium affected by a First Amendment interest, *United States* v. *Paramount Pictures, Inc.*, 334 U.S. 131, 166 (1948), differences in the characteristics of new media justify differences in the First Amendment standards applied to them.[15] *Joseph Burstyn, Inc.* v. *Wilson*, 343 U.S. 495, 503 (1952). For example, the ability of new technology to produce

---

[15] The general problems raised by a technology which supplants atomized, relatively informal communication with mass media as a prime source of national cohesion and news were discussed at considerable length by Zechariah Chafee in Government and Mass Communications (1947). Debate on the particular implications of this view for the broadcasting industry has continued unabated. A compendium of views appears in Freedom and Responsibility in Broadcasting (J. Coons ed.) (1961). See also Kalven, Broadcasting, Public Policy and the First Amendment, 10 J. Law & Econ. 15 (1967); M. Ernst, The First Freedom, 125-180 (1946); T. Robinson, Radio Networks and the Federal Government, especially at 75-87 (1943). The considerations which the newest technology brings to bear on the particular problem of this litigation are concisely explored by Louis Jaffe in The Fairness Doctrine, Equal Time, Reply to Personal Attacks, and the Local Service Obligation; Implications of Technological Change, Printed for Special Subcommittee on Investigations of the House Committee on Interstate and Foreign Commerce (1968).

sounds more raucous than those of the human voice justifies restrictions on the sound level, and on the hours and places of use, of sound trucks so long as the restrictions are reasonable and applied without discrimination. *Kovacs* v. *Cooper*, 336 U.S. 77 (1949).

Just as the Government may limit the use of sound-amplifying equipment potentially so noisy that it drowns out civilized private speech, so may the Government limit the use of broadcast equipment. The right of free speech of a broadcaster, the user of a sound truck, or any other individual does not embrace a right to snuff out the free speech of others. *Associated Press* v. *United States*, 326 U.S. 1, 20 (1945).

When two people converse face to face, both should not speak at once if either is to be clearly understood. But the range of the human voice is so limited that there could be meaningful communications if half the people in the United States were talking and the other half listening. Just as clearly, half the people might publish and the other half read. But the reach of radio signals is incomparably greater than the range of the human voice and the problem of interference is a massive reality. The lack of know-how and equipment may keep many from the air, but only a tiny fraction of those with resources and intelligence can hope to communicate by radio at the same time if intelligible communication is to be had, even if the entire radio spectrum is utilized in the present state of commercially acceptable technology.

It was this fact, and the chaos which ensued from permitting anyone to use any frequency at whatever power level he wished, which made necessary the enactment of the Radio Act of 1927 and the Communications Act of 1934,[16] as the Court has noted at length before. *National Broadcasting Co.* v. *United States*, 319 U.S. 190, 210-214 (1943). It was this reality which at the very least necessitated first the division of the radio spectrum into portions reserved respectively for public broadcasting and for other important radio uses such as amateur operation, aircraft, police, defense, and navigation; and then the subdivision of each portion, and assignment of specific frequencies to individual users or groups of users. Beyond this, however, because the frequencies reserved for public broadcasting were limited in number, it was essential for the Government to tell some applicants that they could not broadcast at all because there was room for only a few.

Where there are substantially more individuals who want to broadcast than there are frequencies to allocate, it is idle to posit an unabridgeable First Amendment right to broadcast comparable to the right of every individual to speak, write, or publish. If 100 persons want broadcast licenses but there are only 10 frequencies to allocate, all of them may have the same "right" to a

[16]The range of controls which have in fact been imposed over the last 40 years, without giving rise to successful constitutional challenge in this Court, is discussed in W. Emery, Broadcasting and Government: Responsibilities and Regulations (1961); Note, Regulation of Program Content by the FCC, 77 Harv. L. Rev. 701 (1964).

license; but if there is to be any effective communication by radio, only a few can be licensed and the rest must be barred from the airwaves. It would be strange if the First Amendment, aimed at protecting and furthering communications, prevented the Government from making radio communication possible by requiring licenses to broadcast and by limiting the number of licenses so as not to overcrowd the spectrum.

This has been the consistent view of the Court. Congress unquestionably has the power to grant and deny licenses and to eliminate existing stations. *FRC v. Nelson Bros. Bond & Mortgage Co.*, 289 U.S. 266 (1933). No one has a First Amendment right to a license or to monopolize a radio frequency; to deny a station license because "the public interest" requires it "is not a denial of free speech." *National Broadcasting Co.* v. *United States*, 319 U.S. 190, 227 (1943).

By the same token, as far as the First Amendment is concerned those who are licensed stand no better than those to whom licenses are refused. A license permits broadcasting, but the licensee has no constitutional right to be the one who holds the license or to monopolize a radio frequency to the exclusion of his fellow citizens. There is nothing in the First Amendment which prevents the Government from requiring a licensee to share his frequency with others and to conduct himself as a proxy or fiduciary with obligations to present those views and voices which are representative of his community and which would otherwise, by necessity, be barred from the airwaves.

This is not to say that the First Amendment is irrelevant to public broadcasting. On the contrary, it has a major role to play as the Congress itself recognized in § 326, which forbids FCC interference with "the right of free speech by means of radio communication." Because of the scarcity of radio frequencies, the Government is permitted to put restraints on licensees in favor of others whose views should be expressed on this unique medium. But the people as a whole retain their interest in free speech by radio and their collective right to have the medium function consistently with the ends and purposes of the First Amendment. It is the right of the viewers and listeners, not the right of the broadcasters, which is paramount. See *FCC* v. *Sanders Bros. Radio Station*, 309 U.S. 470, 475 (1940); *FCC* v. *Allentown Broadcasting Corp.*, 349 U.S. 358, 361-362 (1955); 2 Z. Chafee, Government and Mass Communications 546 (1947). It is the purpose of the First Amendment to preserve an uninhibited marketplace of ideas in which truth will ultimately prevail, rather than to countenance monopolization of that market, whether it be by the Government itself or a private licensee. *Associated Press* v. *United States*, 326 U.S. 1, 20 (1945); *New York Times Co.* v. *Sullivan*, 376 U.S. 254, 270 (1964); *Abrams* v. *United States*, 250 U.S. 616, 630 (1919) (Holmes, J., dissenting). "[S]peech concerning public affairs is more than self-expression; it is the essence of self-government." *Garrison* v. *Louisiana*, 379 U.S. 64, 74-75 (1964). See Brennan, The Supreme Court and the Meiklejohn Interpretation of the First Amendment, 79 Harv. L. Rev. 1 (1965). It is the right of the public to receive suitable access to social, political, esthetic, moral, and other ideas and experiences which is crucial here. That right may not constitutionally be abridged either by Congress or by the FCC.

B.

Rather than confer frequency monopolies on a relatively small number of licensees, in a Nation of 200,000,000, the Government could surely have decreed that each frequency should be shared among all or some of those who wish to use it, each being assigned a portion of the broadcast day or the broadcast week. The ruling and regulations at issue here do not go quite so far. They assert that under specified circumstances, a licensee must offer to make available a reasonable amount of broadcast time to those who have a view different from that which has already been expressed on his station. The expression of a political endorsement, or of a personal attack while dealing with a controversial public issue, simply triggers this time sharing. As we have said, the First Amendment confers no right on licensees to prevent others from broadcasting on "their" frequencies and no right to an unconditional monopoly of a scarce resource which the Government has denied others the right to use.

In terms of constitutional principle, and as enforced sharing of a scarce resource, the personal attack and political editorial rules are indistinguishable from the equal-time provision of § 315, a specific enactment of Congress requiring stations to set aside reply time under specified circumstances and to which the fairness doctrine and these constituent regulations are important complements. That provision, which has been part of the law since 1927, Radio Act of 1927, § 18, 44 Stat. 1170, has been held valid by this Court as an obligation of the licensee relieving him of any power in any way to prevent or censor the broadcast, and thus insulating him from liability for defamation. The constitutionality of the statute under the First Amendment was unquestioned.[17] *Farmer Educ. & Coop. Union* v. *WDAY*, 360 U.S. 525 (1959).

Nor can we say that it is inconsistent with the First Amendment goal of producing an informed public capable of conducting its own affairs to require a broadcaster to permit answers to personal attacks occurring in the course of discussing controversial issues, or to require that the political opponents of those

---

[17]This has not prevented vigorous argument from developing on the constitutionality of the ancillary FCC doctrines. Compare Barrow, The Equal Opportunities and Fairness Doctrines in Broadcasting: Pillars in the Forum of Democracy, 37 U. Cin. L. Rev. 447 (1968), with Robinson, The FCC and the First Amendment: Observations on 40 Years of Radio and Television Regulation, 52 Minn. L. Rev. 67 (1967), and Sullivan, Editorials and Controversy: The Broadcaster's Dilemma, 32 Geo. Wash. L. Rev. 719 (1964).

endorsed by the station be given a chance to communicate with the public. [18]
Otherwise, station owners and a few networks would have unfettered power to
make time available only to the highest bidders, to communicate only their own
views on public issues, people and candidates, and to permit on the air only
those with whom they agreed. There is no sanctuary in the First Amendment for
unlimited private censorship operating in a medium not open to all. "Freedom
of the press from governmental interference under the First Amendment does
not sanction repression of that freedom by private interests." *Associated Press* v.
United States, 326 U.S. 1, 20 (1945).

C.

It is strenuously argued, however, that if political editorials or personal attacks
will trigger an obligation in broadcasters to afford the opportunity for
expression to speakers who need not pay for time and whose views are
unpalatable to the licensees, then broadcasters will be irresistibly forced to
self-censorship and their coverage of controversial public issues will be
eliminated or at least rendered wholly ineffective. Such a result would indeed be
a serious matter, for should licensees actually eliminate their coverage of
controversial issues, the purposes of the doctrine would be stifled.

At this point, however, as the Federal Communications Commission has
indicated, that possibility is at best speculative. The communications industry,
and in particular the networks, have taken pains to present controversial issues in
the past, and even now they do not assert that they intend to abandon their
efforts in this regard. [19] It would be better if the FCC's encouragement were
never necessary to induce the broadcasters to meet their responsibility. And if
experience with the administration of these doctrines indicates that they have
the net effect of reducing rather than enhancing the volume and quality of

---

[18]The expression of views opposing those which broadcasters permit to be aired in the first
place need not be confined solely to the broadcasters themselves as proxies. "Nor is it
enough that he should hear the arguments of adversaries from his own teachers, presented
as they state them, and accompanied by what they offer as refutations. That is not the
way to do justice to the arguments, or bring them into real contact with his own mind. He
must be able to hear them from persons who actually believe them; who defend them in
earnest, and do their very utmost for them." J. Mill, On Liberty 32 (R. McCallum ed.
1947).

[19]The President of the Columbia Broadcasting System has recently declared that despite the
Government, "we are determined to continue covering controversial issues as a public
service, and exercising our own independent news judgment and enterprise. I, for one,
refuse to allow that judgment and enterprise to be affected by official intimidation." F.
Stanton, Keynote Address, Sigma Delta Chi National Convention, Atlanta, Georgia,
November 21, 1968. Problems of news coverage from the broadcaster's viewpoint are
surveyed in W. Wood, Electronic Journalism (1967).

coverage, there will be time enough to reconsider the constitutional implications. The fairness doctrine in the past has had no such overall effect.

That this will occur now seems unlikely, however, since if present licensees should suddenly prove timorous, the Commission is not powerless to insist that they give adequate and fair attention to public issues. It does not violate the First Amendment to treat licensees given the privilege of using scarce radio frequencies as proxies for the entire community, obligated to give suitable time and attention to matters of great public concern. To condition the granting or renewal of licenses on a willingness to present representative community views on controversial issues is consistent with the ends and purposes of those constitutional provisions forbidding the abridgment of freedom of speech and freedom of the press. Congress need not stand idly by and permit those with licenses to ignore the problems which beset the people or to exclude from the airways anything but their own views of fundamental questions. The statute, long administrative practice, and cases are to this effect.

Licenses to broadcast do not confer ownership of designated frequencies, but only the temporary privilege of using them. 47 U.S.C. § 301. Unless renewed, they expire within three years. 47 U.S.C. § 307(d). The statute mandates the issuance of licenses if the "public convenience, interest, or necessity will be served thereby." 47 U.S.C. § 307(a). In applying this standard the Commission for 40 years has been choosing licensees based in part on their program proposals. In *FRC* v. *Nelson Bros. Bond & Mortgage Co.*, 289 U.S. 266, 279 (1933), the Court noted that in "view of the limited number of available broadcasting frequencies, the Congress has authorized allocation and licenses." In determining how best to allocate frequencies, the Federal Radio Commission considered the needs of competing communities and the programs offered by competing stations to meet those needs; moreover, if needs or programs shifted, the Commission could alter its allocations to reflect those shifts. *Id.*, at 285. In the same vein, in *FCC* v. *Pottsville Broadcasting Co.*, 309 U.S. 134, 137-138 (1940), the Court noted that the statutory standard was a supple instrument to effect congressional desires "to maintain . . . a grip on the dynamic aspects of radio transmission" and to allay fears that "in the absence of governmental control the public interest might be subordinated to monopolistic domination in the broadcasting field." Three years later the Court considered the validity of the Commission's chain broadcasting regulations, which among other things forbade stations from devoting too much time to network programs in order that there be suitable opportunity for local programs serving local needs. The Court upheld the regulations, unequivocally recognizing that the Commission was more than a traffic policeman concerned with the technical aspects of broadcasting and that it neither exceeded its powers under the statute nor transgressed the First Amendment in interesting itself in general program format and the kinds of programs broadcast by licensees. *National Broadcasting Co.* v. *United States*, 319 U.S. 190 (1943).

D.

The litigants embellish their First Amendment arguments with the contention that the regulations are so vague that their duties are impossible to discern. Of this point it is enough to say that, judging the validity of the regulations on their face as they are presented here, we cannot conclude that the FCC has been left a free hand to vindicate its own idiosyncratic conception of the public interest or of the requirements of free speech. Past adjudications by the FCC give added precision to the regulations; there was nothing vague about the FCC's specific ruling in *Red Lion* that Fred Cook should be provided an opportunity to reply. The regulations at issue in *RTNDA* could be employed in precisely the same way as the fairness doctrine was in *Red Lion*. Moreover, the FCC itself has recognized that the applicability of its regulations to situations beyond the scope of past cases may be questionable, 32 Fed. Reg. 10303, 10304 and n. 6, and will not impose sanctions in such cases without warning. We need not approve every aspect of the fairness doctrine to decide these cases, and we will not now pass upon the constitutionality of these regulations by envisioning the most extreme applications conceivable, *United States* v. *Sullivan*, 332 U.S. 689, 694 (1948), but will deal with those problems if and when they arise.

We need not and do not now ratify every past and future decision by the FCC with regard to programming. There is no question here of the Commission's refusal to permit the broadcaster to carry a particular program or to publish his own views; of a discriminatory refusal to require the licensee to broadcast certain views which have been denied access to the airwaves; of government censorship of a particular program contrary to § 326; or of the official government view dominating public broadcasting. Such questions would raise more serious First Amendment issues. But we do hold that the Congress and the Commission do not violate the First Amendment when they require a radio or television station to give reply time to answer personal attacks and political editorials.

E.

It is argued that even if at one time the lack of available frequencies for all who wished to use them justified the Government's choice of those who would best serve the public interest by acting as proxy for those who would present differing views, or by giving the latter access directly to broadcast facilities, this condition no longer prevails so that continuing control is not justified. To this there are several answers.

Scarcity is not entirely a thing of the past. Advances in technology, such as microwave transmission, have led to more efficient utilization of the frequency spectrum, but uses for that spectrum have also grown apace.[20] Portions of the spectrum must be reserved for vital uses unconnected with human communication, such as radio-navigational aids used by aircraft and vessels. Conflicts have even emerged between such vital functions as defense preparedness and experimentation in methods of averting midair collisions through radio warning devices.[21] "Land mobile services" such as police, ambulance, fire department, public utility, and other communications systems have been occupying an increasingly crowded portion of the frequency spectrum[22] and there are, apart from licensed amateur radio operators' equipment, 5,000,000 transmitters operated on the "citizens' band" which is also increasingly congested.[23] Among the various uses for radio frequency space, including marine, aviation, amateur, military, and common carrier users, there are easily enough claimants to permit use of the whole with an even smaller allocation to broadcast radio and television uses than now exists.

Comparative hearings between competing applicants for broadcast spectrum space are by no means a thing of the past. The radio spectrum has become so congested that at times it has been necessary to suspend new applications.[24] The very high frequency television spectrum is, in the country's major markets, almost entirely occupied, although space reserved for ultra high frequency television transmission, which is a relatively recent development as a commercially viable alternative, has not yet been completely filled.[25]

[20]Current discussions of the frequency allocation problem appear in Telecommunication Science Panel, Commerce Technical Advisory Board, U.S. Dept. of Commerce, Electromagnetic Spectrum Utilization — The Silent Crisis (1966); Joint Technical Advisory Committee, Institute of Electrical and Electronics Engineers and Electronic Industries Assn., Report on Radio Spectrum Utilization (1964); Note, The Crisis in Electromagnetic Frequency Spectrum Allocation, 53 Iowa L. Rev. 437 (1967). A recently released study is the Final Report of the President's Task Force on Communications Policy (1968).

[21]*Bendix Aviation Corp.* v. *FCC*, 106 U.S. App. D.C. 304, 272 F.2d 533 (1959), cert. denied, 361 U.S. 965 (1960).

[22]1968 FCC Annual Report 65-69.

[23]New limitations on these users, who can also lay claim to First Amendment protection, were sustained against First Amendment attack with the comment, "Here is truly a situation where if everybody could say anything, many could say nothing." *Lafayette Radio Electronics Corp.* v. *United States*, 345 F. 2d 278, 281 (1965). Accord, *California Citizens Band Assn.* v. *United States*, 375 F. 2d 43 (C.A. 9th Cir.), cert. denied, 389 U.S. 844 (1967).

[24]*Kessler* v. *FCC*, 117 U.S. App. D.C. 130, 326 F. 2d 673 (1963).

[25]In a table prepared by the FCC on the basis of statistics current as of August 31, 1968, VHF and UHF channels allocated to and those available in the top 100 market areas for television are set forth:

COMMERCIAL

Market Areas	Channels Allocated		Channels On the Air, Authorized, or Applied for		Available Channels	
	VHF	UHF	VHF	UHF	VHF	UHF
Top 10	40	45	40	44	0	1
Top 50	157	163	157	136	0	27
Top 100	264	297	264	213	0	84

The rapidity with which technological advances succeed one another to create more efficient use of spectrum space on the one hand, and to create new uses for that space by ever growing numbers of people on the other, makes it unwise to speculate on the future allocation of that space. It is enough to say that the resource is one of considerable and growing importance whose scarcity impelled its regulation by an agency authorized by Congress. Nothing in this record, or in our own researches, convinces us that the resource is no longer one for which there are more immediate and potential uses than can be accommodated, and for which wise planning is essential.[26] This does not mean, of course, that every possible wavelength must be occupied at every hour by some vital use in order to sustain the congressional judgment. The substantial capital investment required for many uses, in addition to the potentiality for confusion and interference inherent in any scheme for continuous kaleidoscopic reallocation of all available space may make this unfeasible. The allocation need not be made at such a breakneck pace that the objectives of the allocation are themselves imperiled.[27]

	NONCOMMERCIAL					
			Channels On the Air, Authorized, or			
	Channels Reserved		*Applied for*		*Available Channels*	
Market Areas	VHF	UHF	VHF	UHF	VHF	UHF
Top 10	7	17	7	16	0	1
Top 50	21	79	20	47	1	32
Top 100	35	138	34	69	1	69

1968 FCC Annual Report 132–135.

[26]RTNDA argues that these regulations should be held invalid for failure of the FCC to make specific findings in the rule-making proceeding relating to these factual questions. Presumably the fairness doctrine and the personal attack decisions themselves, such as *Red Lion*, should fall for the same reason. But this argument ignores the fact that these regulations are no more than the detailed specification of certain consequences of long-standing rules, the need for which was recognized by the Congress on the factual predicate of scarcity made plain in 1927, recognized by this Court in the 1943 *National Broadcasting Co.* case, and reaffirmed by the Congress as recently as 1959. "If the number of radio and television stations were not limited by available frequencies, the committee would have no hesitation in removing completely the present provision regarding equal time and urge the right of each broadcaster to follow his own conscience . . . However, broadcast frequencies are limited and, therefore, they have been necessarily considered a public trust." S. Rep. No. 562, 86th Cong., 1st Sess., 8-9 (1959). In light of this history; the opportunity which the broadcasters have had to address the FCC and show that somehow the situation had radically changed, undercutting the validity of the congressional judgment; and their failure to adduce any convincing evidence of that in the record here, we cannot consider the absence of more detailed findings below to be determinative.

[27]The "airwaves [need not] be filled at the earliest possible moment in all circumstances without due regard for these important factors." *Community Broadcasting Co.* v. *FCC*, 107 U.S. App. D.C. 95, 105, 274 F. 2d 753, 763 (1960). Accord, enforcing the fairness doctrine, *Office of Communication of the United Church of Christ* v. *FCC*, 123 U.S. App. D.C. 328, 343, 359 F. 2d 994, 1009 (1966).

Even where there are gaps in spectrum utilization, the fact remains that existing broadcasters have often attained their present position because of their initial government selection in competition with others before new technological advances opened new opportunities for further uses. Long experience in broadcasting, confirmed habits of listeners and viewers, network affiliation, and other advantages in program procurement give existing broadcasters a substantial advantage over new entrants, even where new entry is technologically possible. These advantages are the fruit of a preferred position conferred by the Government. Some present possibility for new entry by competing stations is not enough, in itself, to render unconstitutional the Government's effort to assure that a broadcaster's programming ranges widely enough to serve the public interest.

In view of the scarcity of broadcast frequencies, the Government's role in allocating those frequencies, and the legitimate claims of those unable without governmental assistance to gain access to those frequencies for expression of their views, we hold the regulations and ruling at issue here are both authorized by statute and constitutional.[28] The judgment of the Court of Appeals in *Red Lion* is affirmed and that in *RTNDA* reversed and the causes remanded for proceedings consistent with this opinion.

It is so ordered.

Not having heard oral argument in these cases, Mr. Justice Douglas took no part in the Court's decision.*

[28]We need not deal with the argument that even if there is no longer a technological scarcity of frequencies limiting the number of broadcasters, there nevertheless is an economic scarcity in the sense that the Commission could or does limit entry to the broadcasting market on economic grounds and license no more stations than the market will support. Hence, it is said, the fairness doctrine or its equivalent is essential to satisfy the claims of those excluded and of the public generally. A related argument, which we also put aside, is that quite apart from scarcity of frequencies, technological or economic, Congress does not abridge freedom of speech or press by legislation directly or indirectly multiplying the voices and views presented to the public through time sharing, fairness doctrines, or other devices which limit or dissipate the power of those who sit astride the channels of communication with the general public. Cf. *Citizen Publishing Co.* v. *United States,* 394 U.S. 131 (1969)

*Justice Douglas declared in a concurring opinion 4 years later, "The Fairness Doctrine has no place in our First Amendment regime. It puts the head of the camel inside the tent and enables administration after administration to toy with TV or radio in order to serve its sordid or its benevolent ends." [*Columbia Broadcasting System, Inc.* v. *Democratic National Committee,* 412 U.S. 94, 154 (1973).] [Ed.]

40

President Nixon's Message to Congress

H.R. Doc. 222, 91st Congress, 2d Session
February 9, 1970

Federal involvement in electronic communication has increased as the importance and complexity of this field have grown. Congress has been the dominant articulator of public policy in telecommunications, both directly and through the agencies it has created, especially the FCC.

Presidential prerogatives in this sphere have been limited by the traditional scope of executive authority implicit in the Constitution's enumeration and separation of powers. Presidents Coolidge and Roosevelt confined their roles to exhorting Congress to enact legislation that was clearly needed and largely uncontroversial (see Documents 7 and 16, pp. 28-29 and 82-83); by rallying around Congress, these chief executives served as catalysts in a legislative process already under way. Presidents Kennedy and Johnson exercised a greater degree of leadership (see Documents 29 and 36, pp. 292-295 and 356-359) by developing policy initiatives around which Congress rallied.

The centralized, executive branch Office of Telecommunications Policy (OTP) came about through congressional acquiescence; since Congress did not veto President Nixon's reorganization plan, it became effective 60 days after its submission. OTP's creation added a powerful executive voice to the impressive congressional chorus that determines public policy in broadcasting and related media.

Dr. Clay T. Whitehead, President Nixon's former telecommunications aide, served as the first Director of OTP from 1970 to 1974. During these 4 years there was no major aspect of government relations with broadcasting about which OTP was silent. The wide range of issues on which Whitehead acted as administration spokesman included radio "de-regulation," longer license terms, reduction of "ideological plugola" in TV news, abolition of the Fairness Doctrine, federal funding for public broadcasting, network reruns, and the addition of more VHF channels in the top 100 markets. Whitehead chaired the Cabinet Committee on Cable Communications, whose 1974 report took a libertarian view of CATV that advocated a lessening of FCC control.

Dr. Whitehead left OTP shortly after President Nixon's resignation. Nixon's immediate successors did not deploy OTP so aggressively, and the Carter administration abolished the office and transferred most of its functions to the Commerce Department in 1977. The unit was named the National Telecommunications and Information Administration in 1978.

Related Reading: 1, 73, 95, 173, 175, 176, 212, 213.

The White House, February 9, 1970.

To the Congress of the United States:

We live in a time when the technology of telecommunications is undergoing rapid change which will dramatically affect the whole of our society. It has long been recognized that the executive branch of the Federal government should be better equipped to deal with the issues which arise from telecommunications growth. As the largest single user of the nation's telecommunications facilities, the Federal government must also manage its internal communications operations in the most effective manner possible.

Accordingly, I am today transmitting to the Congress Reorganization Plan No. 1 of 1970, prepared in accordance with chapter 9 of title 5 of the United States Code.

That plan would establish a new Office of Telecommunications Policy in the Executive Office of the President. The new unit would be headed by a Director and a Deputy Director who would be appointed by the President with the advice and consent of the Senate. The existing office held by the Director of Telecommunications Management in the Office of Emergency Preparedness would be abolished.

In addition to the functions which are transferred to it by the reorganization plan, the new Office would perform certain other duties which I intend to assign to it by Executive order as soon as the reorganization plan takes effect. That order would delegate to the new Office essentially those functions which are now assigned to the Director of Telecommunications Management. The Office of Telecommunications Policy would be assisted in its research and analysis responsibilities by the agencies and departments of the Executive Branch including another new office, located in the Department of Commerce.

The new Office of Telecommunications Policy would play three essential roles:

1. It would serve as the President's principal adviser on telecommunications policy, helping to formulate government policies concerning a wide range of domestic and international telecommunications issues and helping to develop plans and programs which take full advantage of the nation's technological capabilities. The speed of economic and technological advance in our time means that new questions concerning communications are constantly arising, questions on which the government must be well informed and well advised. The new Office will enable the President and all government officials to share more fully in the experience, the insights, and the forecasts of government and non-government experts.

2. The Office of Telecommunications Policy would help formulate policies and coordinate operations for the Federal government's own vast communications systems. It would, for example, set guidelines for the various departments and agencies concerning their communications equipment and services. It would regularly review the ability of government communications systems to meet the security needs of the nation and to perform effectively in time of emergency. The Office would direct the assignment of those portions of the radio spectrum which are reserved for government use, carry out responsibilities conferred on the President by the Communications Satellite Act, advise State and local governments, and provide policy direction for the National Communications System.

3. Finally, the new Office would enable the executive branch to speak with a clearer voice and to act as a more effective partner in discussions of communications policy with both the Congress and the Federal Communications Commission. This action would take away none of the prerogatives or functions assigned to the Federal Communications Commission by the Congress. It is my hope, however, that the new Office and the Federal Communications Commission would cooperate in achieving certain reforms in telecommunications policy, especially in their procedures for allocating portions of the radio spectrum for government and civilian use. Our current procedures must be more flexible if they are to deal adequately with problems such as the worsening spectrum shortage.

Each reorganization included in the plan which accompanies this message is necessary to accomplish one or more of the purposes set forth in section 901(a) of title 5 of the United States Code. In particular, the plan is responsive to section 901(a)(1), "to promote the better execution of the laws, the more effective management of the executive branch and of its agencies and functions, and the expeditious administration of the public business;" and section 901(a)(3), "to increase the efficiency of the operations of the government to the fullest extent practicable."

The reorganizations provided for in this plan make necessary the appointment and compensation of new officers, as specified in sections 3(a) and 3(b) of the plan. The rates of compensation fixed for these officers are comparable to those fixed for other officers in the executive branch who have similar responsibilities.

This plan should result in the more efficient operation of the government. It is not practical, however, to itemize or aggregate the exact expenditure reductions which will result from this action.

The public interest requires that government policies concerning telecommunications be formulated with as much sophistication and vision as possible. This reorganization plan — and the executive order which would follow it — are necessary instruments if the government is to respond adequately to the challenges and opportunities presented by the rapid pace of change in communications. I urge that the Congress allow this plan to become effective so that these necessary reforms can be accomplished.

Richard Nixon.

41

CBS v. DNC

Columbia Broadcasting System, Inc. v.

Democratic National Committee

412 U.S. 94

May 29, 1973

In the wake of the *Red Lion* decision (Document 39, pp. 381–402) many groups sought access to broadcast facilities to express their opinions. Some were willing to pay for the privilege, but when station policy precluded the sale of time for editorial advertising they tried to turn privilege into legal right.

In *CBS* v. *DNC* the Supreme Court upset an appellate court's reversal of the FCC's refusal to mandate a limited right of access for paid messages advocating viewpoints on controversial public issues. This seven-to-two decision vindicated the Commission's view that the Fairness Doctrine was sufficient to protect the public interest by providing for the broadcast access of *issues* (rather than *persons*) selected by responsible licensees serving as gatekeepers. The six separate opinions issued by nine Justices indicate the complexity of the procedural and substantive matters at stake. Parts I and II of the opinion below were supported by six Justices, but Part IV attracted only the barest majority of the Court. All concurring and dissenting opinions have been omitted.

The FCC concluded the Fairness Doctrine inquiry referred to in this decision (pp. 424–425) with the adoption of the "Fairness Report" on June 27, 1974—two days after the High Court decided the *Miami Herald* case (see pp. 381–382). The "Fairness Report" reaffirmed the Commission's commitment to the Fairness Doctrine and specifically rejected the notion of government dictated access, whether paid or free [48 FCC 2d 1, 28–31 (1974)].

Two years later the FCC set a precedent when it required a broadcasting station to provide coverage of the previously untreated local issue of strip mining [*Patsy Mink and O. D. Hagedorn* v. *Station WHAR*, 59 FCC 2d 987 (1976)]. This somewhat belated enforcement of the "affirmative responsibility" aspect of the Fairness Doctrine (see paragraph 7 of the doctrine on p. 222), if not an aberration, may signal a quasi-access manifestation of the doctrine that causes it to flourish—or collapse under its own weight.

Related Reading: 12, 13, 16, 84, 105, 153, 196.

Mr. Chief Justice Burger delivered the opinion of the Court. . . .

We granted the writs of certiorari in these cases to consider whether a broadcast licensee's general policy of not selling advertising time to individuals or groups wishing to speak out on issues they consider important violates the Federal Communications Act of 1934, 48 Stat. 1064, as amended, 47 U.S.C. § 151 *et seq.*, or the First Amendment.

In two orders announced the same day, the Federal Communications Commission ruled that a broadcaster who meets his public obligation to provide full and fair coverage of public issues is not required to accept editorial advertisements. *Democratic National Committee*, 25 F.C.C. 2d 216; *Business Executives' Move for Vietnam Peace*, 25 F.C.C. 2d 242. A divided Court of Appeals reversed the Commission, holding that a broadcaster's fixed policy of refusing editorial advertisements violates the First Amendment; the court remanded the cases to the Commission to develop procedures and guidelines for administering a First Amendment right of access. *Business Executives' Move for Vietnam Peace* v. *FCC*, 146 U.S. App. D.C. 181, 450 F.2d 642 (1971).

The complainants in these actions are the Democratic National Committee (DNC) and the Business Executives' Move for Vietnam Peace (BEM), a national organization of businessmen opposed to United States involvement in the Vietnam conflict. In January 1970, BEM filed a complaint with the Commission charging that radio station WTOP in Washington, D.C., had refused to sell it time to broadcast a series of one-minute spot announcements expressing BEM views on Vietnam. WTOP, in common with many, but not all, broadcasters, followed a policy of refusing to sell time for spot announcements to individuals and groups who wished to expound their views on controversial issues. WTOP took the position that since it presented full and fair coverage of important public questions, including the Vietnam conflict, it was justified in refusing to accept editorial advertisements. WTOP also submitted evidence showing that the station had aired the views of critics of our Vietnam policy on numerous occasions. BEM challenged the fairness of WTOP's coverage of criticism of that policy, but it presented no evidence in support of that claim.

Four months later, in May 1970, DNC filed with the Commission a request for a declaratory ruling:

"That under the First Amendment to the Constitution and the Communications Act, a broadcaster may not, as a general policy, refuse to sell time to responsible entities, such as the DNC, for the solicitation of funds and for comment on public issues."

DNC claimed that it intended to purchase time from radio and television stations and from the national networks in order to present the views of the Democratic Party and to solicit funds. Unlike BEM, DNC did not object to the policies of any particular broadcaster but claimed that its prior "experiences in this area make it clear that it will encounter considerable difficulty—if not total frustration of its efforts—in carrying out its plans in the event the Commission should decline to issue a ruling as requested." DNC cited *Red Lion Broadcasting Co.* v. *FCC*, 395 U.S. 367 (1969), as establishing a limited constitutional right of access to the airwaves.

In two separate opinions, the Commission rejected respondents' claims that "responsible" individuals and groups have a right to purchase advertising time to comment on public issues without regard to whether the broadcaster has complied with the Fairness Doctrine. The Commission viewed the issue as one of major significance in administering the regulatory scheme relating to the electronic media, one going "to the heart of the system of broadcasting which has developed in this country. . . ." 25 F.C.C. 2d, at 221. After reviewing the legislative history of the Communications Act, the provisions of the Act itself, the Commission's decisions under the Act, and the difficult problems inherent in administering a right of access, the Commission rejected the demands of BEM and DNC.

The Commission also rejected BEM's claim that WTOP had violated the Fairness Doctrine by failing to air views such as those held by members of BEM; the Commission pointed out that BEM had made only a "general allegation" of unfairness in WTOP's coverage of the Vietnam conflict and that the station had adequately rebutted the charge by affidavit. The Commission did, however, uphold DNC's position that the statute recognized a right of political parties to purchase broadcast time for the purpose of soliciting funds. The Commission noted that Congress has accorded special consideration for access by political parties, see 47 U.S.C. § 315 (a), and that solicitation of funds by political parties is both feasible and appropriate in the short space of time generally allotted to spot advertisements.[1]

A majority of the Court of Appeals reversed the Commission, holding that

---

[1] The Commission's rulings against BEM's Fairness Doctrine complaint and in favor of DNC's claim that political parties should be permitted to purchase air time for solicitation of funds were not appealed to the Court of Appeals and are not before us here.

"a flat ban on paid public issue announcements is in violation of the First Amendment, at least when other sorts of paid announcements are accepted." 146 U.S. App. D.C., at 185, 450 F.2d, at 646. Recognizing that the broadcast frequencies are a scarce resource inherently unavailable to all, the court nevertheless concluded that the First Amendment mandated an "abridgeable" right to present editorial advertisements. The court reasoned that a broadcaster's policy of airing commercial advertisements but not editorial advertisements constitutes unconstitutional discrimination. The court did not, however, order that either BEM's or DNC's proposed announcements must be accepted by the broadcasters; rather, it remanded the cases to the Commission to develop "reasonable procedures and regulations determining which and how many 'editorial advertisements' will be put on the air." *Ibid.*

Judge McGowan dissented; in his view, the First Amendment did not compel the Commission to undertake the task assigned to it by the majority:

"It is presently the obligation of a licensee to advance the public's right to know by devoting a substantial amount of time to the presentation of controversial views on issues of public importance, striking a balance which is always subject to redress by reference to the fairness doctrine. Failure to do so puts continuation of the license at risk—a sanction of tremendous potency, and one which the Commission is under increasing pressure to employ.

"This is the system which Congress has, wisely or not, provided as the alternative to public ownership and operation of radio and television communications facilities. This approach has never been thought to be other than within the permissible limits of constitutional choice." 146 U.S. App. D.C., at 205, 450 F.2d, at 666.

Judge McGowan concluded that the court's decision to overrule the Commission and to remand for development and implementation of a constitutional right of access put the Commission in a "constitutional straitjacket" on a highly complex and far-reaching issue.

I

Mr. Justice White's opinion for the Court in *Red Lion Broadcasting Co. v. FCC,* 395 U.S. 367 (1969), makes clear that the broadcast media pose unique and special problems not present in the traditional free speech case. Unlike other media, broadcasting is subject to an inherent physical limitation. Broadcast frequencies are a scarce resource; they must be portioned out among applicants. All who possess the financial resources and the desire to communicate by television or radio cannot be satisfactorily accommodated. The Court spoke to this reality when, in *Red Lion,* we said "it is idle to posit an unabridgeable First Amendment right to broadcast comparable to the right of every individual to speak, write, or publish." *Id.,* at 388.

Because the broadcast media utilize a valuable and limited public resource, there is also present an unusual order of First Amendment values. *Red Lion* discussed at length the application of the First Amendment to the broadcast media. In analyzing the broadcasters' claim that the Fairness Doctrine and two of its component rules violated their freedom of expression, we held that "[n]o one has a First Amendment right to a license or to monopolize a radio frequency; to deny a station license because 'the public interest' requires it 'is not a denial of free speech.'" *Id.,* at 389. Although the broadcaster is not without protection under the First Amendment, *United States* v. *Paramount Pictures, Inc.,* 334 U.S. 131, 166 (1948), "[i]t is the right of the viewers and listeners, not the right of the broadcasters, which is paramount. . . . It is the right of the public to receive suitable access to social, political, esthetic, moral, and other ideas and experiences which is crucial here. That right may not constitutionally be abridged either by Congress or by the FCC." *Red Lion, supra,* at 390.

Balancing the various First Amendment interests involved in the broadcast media and determining what best serves the public's right to be informed is a task of a great delicacy and difficulty. The process must necessarily be undertaken within the framework of the regulatory scheme that has evolved over the course of the past half century. For, during that time, Congress and its chosen regulatory agency have established a delicately balanced system of regulation intended to serve the interests of all concerned. The problems of regulation are rendered more difficult because the broadcast industry is dynamic in terms of technological change; solutions adequate a decade ago are not necessarily so now, and those acceptable today may well be outmoded 10 years hence.

Thus, in evaluating the First Amendment claims of respondents, we must afford great weight to the decisions of Congress and the experience of the Commission. Professor Chafee aptly observed:

"Once we get away from the bare words of the [First] Amendment, we must construe it as part of a Constitution which creates a government for the purpose of performing several very important tasks. The [First] Amendment should be interpreted so as not to cripple the regular work of the government. A part of this work is the regulation of interstate and foreign commerce, and this has come in our modern age to include the job of parceling out the air among broadcasters, which Congress has entrusted to the FCC. Therefore, every free-speech problem in the radio has to be considered with reference to the satisfactory performance of this job as well as to the value of open discussion. Although free speech should weigh heavily in the scale in the event of conflict, still the Commission should be given ample scope to do its job." 2 Z. Chafee, Government and Mass Communications 640–641 (1947).

The judgment of the Legislative Branch cannot be ignored or undervalued simply because one segment of the broadcast constituency casts its claims under the umbrella of the First Amendment. That is not to say we "defer" to the judgment of the Congress and the Commission on a constitutional question, or that we would hesitate to invoke the Constitution should we determine that the Commission has not fulfilled its task with appropriate sensitivity to the interests in free expression. The point is, rather, that when we face a complex problem with many hard questions and few easy answers we do well to pay careful attention to how the other branches of Government have addressed the same problem. Thus, before confronting the specific legal issues in these cases, we turn to an examination of the legislative and administrative development of our broadcast system over the last half century.

II

This Court has on numerous occasions recounted the origins of our modern system of broadcast regulation. See, *e.g., Red Lion, supra,* at 375-386; *National Broadcasting Co.* v. *United States,*   319 U.S. 190, 210-217 (1943); *FCC* v. *Sanders Brothers Radio Station,* 309 U.S. 470, 474 (1940); *FCC* v. *Pottsville Broadcasting Co.,* 309 U.S. 134, 137-138 (1940). We have noted that prior to the passage of the Radio Act of 1927, 44 Stat. 1162, broadcasting was marked by chaos. The unregulated and burgeoning private use of the new media in the 1920's had resulted in an intolerable situation demanding congressional action:

"It quickly became apparent that broadcast frequencies constituted a scarce resource whose use could be regulated and rationalized only by the Government. Without government control, the medium would be of little use because of the cacaphony of competing voices, none of which could be clearly and predictably heard." *Red Lion, supra,* at 376.

But, once it was accepted that broadcasting was subject to regulation, Congress was confronted with a major dilemma: how to strike a proper balance between private and public control. Cf. *Farmers Union* v. *WDAY,* 360 U.S. 525, 528 (1959).

One of the earliest and most frequently quoted statements of this dilemma is that of Herbert Hoover, when he was Secretary of Commerce. While his Department was making exploratory attempts to deal with the infant broadcasting industry in the early 1920's, he testified before a House Committee:

"We can not allow any single person or group to place themselves in [a] position where they can censor the material which shall be broadcasted to the public, nor do I believe that the Government should ever be placed in the position of censoring this material." Hearings on H.R. 7357 before the House Committee on the Merchant Marine and Fisheries, 68th Cong., 1st Sess., 8 (1924).

That statement foreshadowed the "tightrope" aspects of Government regulation of the broadcast media, a problem the Congress, the Commission, and the courts have struggled with ever since. Congress appears to have concluded, however, that of these two choices—private or official censorship—Government censorship would be the most pervasive, the most self-serving, the most difficult to restrain and hence the one most to be avoided.

The legislative history of the Radio Act of 1927, the model for our present statutory scheme, see *FCC* v. *Pottsville Broadcasting Co., supra,* at 137, reveals that in the area of discussion of public issues Congress chose to leave broad journalistic discretion with the licensee. Congress specifically dealt with—and firmly rejected—the argument that the broadcast facilities should be open on a non-selective basis to all persons wishing to talk about public issues. Some members of Congress—those whose views were ultimately rejected—strenuously objected to the unregulated power of broadcasters to reject applications for service. See, *e.g.,* H.R. Rep. No. 404, 69th Cong., 1st Sess., 18 (minority report). They regarded the exercise of such power to be "private censorship," which should be controlled by treating broadcasters as public utilities.[2] The provision that came closest to imposing an unlimited right of access to broadcast time was part of the bill reported to the Senate by the Committee on Interstate Commerce. The bill that emerged from the Committee contained the following provision:

"[I]f any licensee shall permit a broadcasting station to be used . . . by a candidate or candidates for any public office, *or for the discussion of any question affecting the public,* he shall make no discrimination as to the use of such broadcasting station, *and with respect to said matters the licensee shall be deemed a common carrier in interstate commerce:* Provided, that such licensee shall have no power to censor the material broadcast." 67 Cong. Rec. 12503 (1926) (emphasis added).

When the bill came to the Senate floor, the principal architect of the Radio Act of 1927, Senator Dill, offered an amendment to the provision to eliminate the common carrier obligation and to restrict the right of access to candidates for public office. Senator Dill explained the need for the amendment:

---

[2] Congressman Davis, for example, stated on the floor of the House the view that Congress found unacceptable:
"I do not think any member of the committee will deny that it is absolutely inevitable that we are going to have to regulate the radio public utilities just as we regulate other public utilities. We are going to have to regulate the rates and the service, and to force them to give equal service and equal treatment to all." 67 Cong. Rec. 5483 (1926). See also *id.,* at 5484.

"When we recall that broadcasting today is purely voluntary, and the listener-in pays nothing for it, that the broadcaster gives it for the purpose of building up his reputation, it seemed unwise to put the broadcaster under the hampering control of being a common carrier and compelled to accept anything and everything that was offered him so long as the price was paid." 67 Cong. Rec. 12502.

The Senators were also sensitive to the problems involved in legislating "equal opportunities" with respect to the discussion of public issues. Senator Dill stated:

"['Public questions'] is such a general term that there is probably no question of any interest whatsoever that could be discussed but that the other side of it could demand time; and thus a radio station would be placed in the position that the Senator from Iowa mentions about candidates, namely, that they would have to give all their time to that kind of discussion, or no public question could be discussed." *Id.*. at 12504.

The Senate adopted Senator Dill's amendment. The provision finally enacted, § 18 of the Radio Act of 1927, 44 Stat. 1170, was later re-enacted as § 315 (a) of the Communications Act of 1934,[3] but only after Congress rejected another proposal that would have imposed a limited obligation on broadcasters to turn over their microphones to persons wishing to speak out on certain public issues.[4]

---

[3] Section 315(a) now reads:
"If any licensee shall permit any person who is a legally qualified candidate for any public office to use a broadcasting station, he shall afford equal opportunities to all other such candidates for that office in the use of such broadcasting station: *Provided,* That such licensee shall have no power of censorship over the material broadcast under the provisions of this section. No obligation is imposed under this subsection upon any licensee to allow the use of its station by any such candidate. Appearance by a legally qualified candidate on any—
"(1) bona fide newscast,
"(2) bona fide news interview,
"(3) bona fide news documentary (if the appearance of the candidate is incidental to the presentation of the subject or subjects covered by the news documentary), or
"(4) on-the-spot coverage of bona fide news events (including but not limited to political conventions and activities incidental thereto),
"shall not be deemed to be use of a broadcasting station within the meaning of this subsection. Nothing in the foregoing sentence shall be construed as relieving broadcasters, in connection with the presentation of newscasts, news interviews, news documentaries, and on-the-spot coverage of news events, from the obligation imposed upon them under this chapter to operate in the public interest and to afford reasonable opportunity for the discussion of conflicting views on issues of public importance." 47 U.S.C. § 315(a).
[4] The Senate passed a provision stating that:

"[I]f any licensee shall permit any person to use a broadcasting station in support of or in opposition to any candidate for public office, *or in the presentation of views on a public question to be voted upon at an election, he shall afford equal opportunity to an equal number of other persons to use such station* in support of an opposing candidate for such public office, or to reply to a person who has used such broadcasting station in support of

Instead, Congress after prolonged consideration adopted § 3 (h), which specifically provides that "a person engaged in radio broadcasting shall not, insofar as such person is so engaged, be deemed a common carrier."[5]

Other provisions of the 1934 Act also evince a legislative desire to preserve values of private journalism under a regulatory scheme which would insure fulfillment of certain public obligations. Although the Commission was given the authority to issue renewable three-year licenses to broadcasters[6] and to promulgate rules and regulations governing the use of those licenses,[7] both consistent

---

or in opposition to a candidate, *or for the presentation of opposite views on such public questions.*"

See Hearings on S. 2910 before the Senate Committee on Interstate Commerce, 73d Cong., 2d Sess., 19 (1934) (emphasis added). The provision for discussion of public issues was deleted by the House-Senate Conference. See H.R. Conf. Rep. No. 1918 on S. 3285, 73d Cong., 2d Sess., 49.

Also noteworthy are two bills offered in 1934 that would have restricted the control of broadcasters over the discussion of certain issues. Congressman McFadden proposed a bill that would have forbidden broadcasters to discriminate against programs sponsored by religious, charitable, or educational associations. H.R. 7986, 73d Cong., 2d Sess. The bill was not reported out of committee. And, during the debates on the 1934 Act, Senators Wagner and Hatfield offered an amendment that would have ordered the Commission to "reserve and allocate only to educational, religious, agricultural, labor, cooperative, and similar nonprofit making associations one-fourth of all the radio broadcasting facilities within its jurisdiction." 78 Cong. Rec. 8828. Senator Dill explained why the Committee had rejected the proposed amendment, indicating that the practical difficulties and the dangers of censorship were crucial:

"MR. DILL. . . . If we should provide that 25 percent of time shall be allocated to non-profit organizations, someone would have to determine—Congress or somebody else—how much of the 25 percent should go to education, how much of it to religion, and how much of it to agriculture, how much of it to labor, how much of it to fraternal organizations, and so forth. When we enter this field we must determine how much to give to the Catholics probably and how much to the Protestants and how much to the Jews." 78 Cong. Rec. 8843.

Senator Dill went on to say that the problem of determining the proper allocation of time for discussion of these subjects should be worked out by the Commission. *Id.*, at 8844. The Senate rejected the amendment. *Id.*, at 8846.

[5] Section 3 (h) provides as follows:

"'Common carrier' or 'carrier' means any person engaged as a common carrier for hire, in interstate or foreign communication by wire or radio or in interstate or foreign radio transmission of energy, except where reference is made to common carriers not subject to this chapter; but a person engaged in radio broadcasting shall not, insofar as such person is so engaged, be deemed a common carrier." 48 Stat. 1066, as amended, 47 U.S.C. § 153 (h).

[6] 48 Stat. 1083, as amended, 47 U.S.C. § 307.

[7] Section 303, 48 Stat. 1082, as amended, 47 U.S.C. § 303, provides in relevant part:

"Except as otherwise provided in this chapter, the Commission from time to time, as public convenience, interest, or necessity requires, shall—

•   •   •   •   •   •

"(b) Prescribe the nature of the service to be rendered by each class of licensed stations and each station within any class;

•   •   •   •   •

"(r) Make such rules and regulations and prescribe such restrictions and conditions, not inconsistent with law, as may be necessary to carry out the provisions of this chapter . . . ."

with the "public convenience, interest, or necessity," § 326 of the Act specifically provides that:

"Nothing in this chapter shall be understood or construed to give the Commission the power of censorship over the radio communications or signals transmitted by any radio station, and no regulation or condition shall be promulgated or fixed by the Commission which shall interfere with the right of free speech by means of radio communication." 47 U.S.C. § 326.

From these provisions it seems clear that Congress intended to permit private broadcasting to develop with the widest journalistic freedom consistent with its public obligations. Only when the interests of the public are found to outweigh the private journalistic interests of the broadcasters will government power be asserted within the framework of the Act. License renewal proceedings, in which the listening public can be heard, are a principal means of such regulation. See *Office of Communication of United Church of Christ* v. *FCC*, 123 U.S. App. D.C. 328, 359 F.2d 994 (1966), and 138 U.S. App. D.C. 112, 425 F.2d 543 (1969).

Subsequent developments in broadcast regulation illustrate how this regulatory scheme has evolved. Of particular importance, in light of Congress' flat refusal to impose a "common carrier" right of access for all persons wishing to speak out on public issues, is the Commission's "Fairness Doctrine," which evolved gradually over the years spanning federal regulation of the broadcast media.[8] Formulated under the Commission's power to issue regulations consistent with the "public interest," the doctrine imposes two affirmative responsibilities on the broadcaster: coverage of issues of public importance must be adequate and must fairly reflect differing viewpoints. See *Red Lion,* 395 U.S., at 377. In fulfilling the Fairness Doctrine obligations, the broadcaster must provide free time for the presentation of opposing views if a paid sponsor is unavailable, *Cullman Broadcasting Co.,* 25 P & F Radio Reg. 895 (1963), and must initiate programming on public issues if no one else seeks to do so. See *John J. Dempsey,* 6 P & F Radio Reg. 615 (1950); *Red Lion, supra,* at 378.

Since it is physically impossible to provide time for all viewpoints, however, the right to exercise editorial judgment was granted to the broadcaster. The broadcaster, therefore, is allowed significant journalistic discretion in deciding how best to fulfill the Fairness Doctrine obligations,[9] although that discretion

---

[8] In 1959, Congress amended § 315 of the Act to give statutory approval to the Fairness Doctrine. Act of Sept. 14, 1959, § 1, 73 Stat. 557, 47 U.S.C. § 315 (a).

For a summary of the development and nature of the Fairness Doctrine, see *Red Lion Broadcasting Co.* v. *FCC,* 395 U.S. 367, 375–386 (1969).

[9] See *Madalyn Murray,* 5 P & F Radio Reg. 2d 263 (1965). Factors that the broadcaster must take into account in exercising his discretion include the following:

"In determining whether to honor specific requests for time, the station will inevitably be confronted with such questions as whether the subject is worth considering, whether the

is bounded by rules designed to assure that the public interest in fairness is furthered. In its decision in the instant cases, the Commission described the boundaries as follows:

"The most basic consideration in this respect is that the licensee cannot rule off the air coverage of important issues or views because of his private ends or beliefs. As a public trustee, he must present representative community views and voices on controversial issues which are of importance to his listeners. . . . This means also that some of the voices must be partisan. A licensee policy of excluding partisan voices and always itself presenting views in a bland, inoffensive manner would run counter to the 'profound national commitment that debate on public issues should be uninhibited, robust, and wide-open.' *New York Times Co. v. Sullivan,* 376 U.S. 254, 270 (1964); see also *Red Lion Broadcasting Co., Inc. v. F.C.C.,* 395 U.S. 367, 392 (n. 18) (1969). . . ." 25 F.C.C. 2d, at 222–223.

Thus, under the Fairness Doctrine broadcasters are responsible for providing the listening and viewing public with access to a balanced presentation of information on issues of public importance.[10] The basic principle underlying that responsibility is "the right of the public to be informed, rather than any right on the part of the Government, any broadcast licensee or any individual member of the public to broadcast his own particular views on any matter. . . ." Report on Editorializing by Broadcast Licensees, 13 F.C.C. 1246, 1249 (1949). Consistent with that philosophy, the Commission on several occasions has ruled that no private individual or group has a right to command the use of broadcast facilities.[11] See, *e.g., Dowie A. Crittenden,* 18 F.C.C. 2d 499 (1969); *Margaret Z.*

---

viewpoint of the requesting party has already received a sufficient amount of broadcast time, or whether there may not be other available groups or individuals who might be more appropriate spokesmen for the particular point of view than the person [or group] making the request." Report on Editorializing by Broadcast Licensees, 13 F.C.C. 1246, 1251–1252 (1949).

[10] The Commission has also adopted various component regulations under the Fairness Doctrine, the most notable of which are the "personal attack" and "political editorializing" rules which we upheld in *Red Lion.* The "personal attack" rule provides that "[w]hen, during the presentation of views on a controversial issue of public importance, an attack is made upon the honesty, character, integrity or like personal qualities of an identified person," the licensee must notify the person attacked and give him an opportunity to respond. *E.g.,* 47 CFR § 73.123. Similarly, the "political editorializing" rule provides that, when a licensee endorses a political candidate in an editorial, he must give other candidates or their spokesmen an opportunity to respond. *E.g., id.,* § 73.123.

The Commission, of course, has taken other steps beyond the Fairness Doctrine to expand the diversity of expression on radio and television. The chain broadcasting and multiple ownership rules are established examples. *E.g., id.,* §§ 73.131, 73.240. More recently, the Commission promulgated rules limiting television network syndication practices and reserving 25% of prime time for non-network programs. *Id.,* §§ 73.658 (j), (k).

[11] The Court of Appeals, respondents, and the dissent in this case have relied on dictum in *United Broadcasting Co.,* 10 F.C.C. 515 (1945), as illustrating Commission approval of a private right to purchase air time for the discussion of controversial issues. In that case the complaint alleged not only that the station had a policy of refusing to sell time for the

Scherbina, 21 F.C.C. 2d 141 (1969); *Boalt Hall Student Assn.,* 20 F.C.C. 2d 612 (1969); *Madalyn Murray,* 40 F.C.C. 647 (1965); *Democratic State Central Committee of California,* 19 F.C.C. 2d 833 (1968); *U.S. Broadcasting Corp.,* 2 F.C.C. 208 (1935). Congress has not yet seen fit to alter that policy, although since 1934 it has amended the Act on several occasions[12] and considered various proposals that would have vested private individuals with a right of access.[13]

. . .

[Part III of Chief Justice Burger's opinion drew the support of only two other Justices. Because it does not constitute part of the Court's opinion, it is omitted here. —Ed.]

IV

There remains for consideration the question whether the "public interest" standard of the Communications Act requires broadcasters to accept editorial advertisements or, whether, assuming governmental action, broadcasters are required to do so by reason of the First Amendment. In resolving those issues, we are guided by the "venerable principle that the construction of a statute

---

discussion of public issues, but also that the station had applied its policy in a discriminatory manner, a factor not shown in the cases presently before us. Furthermore, the decision was handed down four years before the Commission had fully developed and articulated the Fairness Doctrine. See Report on Editorializing by Broadcast Licensees, 13 F.C.C. 1246 (1949). Thus, even if the decision is read without reference to the allegation of discrimination, it stands as merely an isolated statement, made during the period in which the Commission was still working out the problems associated with the discussion of public issues; the dictum has not been followed since and has been modified by the Fairness Doctrine.

[12] In 1959, as noted earlier, Congress amended § 315 (a) of the Act to give statutory approval to the Commission's Fairness Doctrine. Act of Sept. 14, 1959, § 1, 73 Stat. 557, 47 U.S.C. § 315 (a). Very recently, Congress amended § 312 (a) of the 1934 Act to authorize the Commission to revoke a station license "for willful or repeated failure to allow reasonable access to or to permit purchase of reasonable amounts of time for the use of a broadcasting station by a legally qualified candidate for Federal elective office on behalf of his candidacy." Campaign Communications Reform Act of 1972, Pub. L. 92–225, 86 Stat. 4. This amendment essentially codified the Commission's prior interpretation of § 315 (a) as requiring broadcasters to make time available to political candidates. *Farmers Union* v. *WDAY,* 360 U.S. 525, 534 (1959). See FCC Memorandum on Second Sentence of Section 315 (a), in Political Broadcasts—Equal Time, Hearings before Subcommittee of the House Committee on Interstate and Foreign Commerce, 88th Cong., 1st Sess., on H.J. Res. 247, pp. 84–90.

[13] See, *e.g.,* H.R. 3595, 80th Cong., 1st Sess. (1947). A more recent proposal was offered by Senator Fulbright. His bill would have amended § 315 of the Act to provide:

"(d) Licensees shall provide a reasonable amount of public service time to authorized representatives of the Senate of the United States, and the House of Representatives of the United States, to present the views of the Senate and the House of Representatives on issues of public importance. The public service time required to be provided under this subsection shall be made available to each such authorized representative at least, but not limited to, four times during each calender year." S.J. Res. 209, 91st Cong., 2d Sess. (1970).

by those charged with its execution should be followed unless there are compelling indications that it is wrong. . . ." *Red Lion,* 395 U.S., at 381. Whether there are "compelling indications" of error in these cases must be answered by a careful evaluation of the Commission's reasoning in light of the policies embodied by Congress in the "public interest" standard of the Act. Many of those policies, as the legislative history makes clear, were drawn from the First Amendment itself; the "public interest" standard necessarily invites reference to First Amendment principles. Thus, the question before us is whether the various interests in free expression of the public, the broadcaster, and the individuals require broadcasters to sell commercial time to persons wishing to discuss controversial issues. In resolving that issue it must constantly be kept in mind that the interest of the public is our foremost concern. With broadcasting, where the available means of communication are limited in both space and time, the admonition of Professor Alexander Meiklejohn that "[w]hat is essential is not that everyone shall speak, but that everything worth saying shall be said" is peculiarly appropriate. Political Freedom 26 (1948).

At the outset we reiterate what was made clear earlier that nothing in the language of the Communications Act or its legislative history compels a conclusion different from that reached by the Commission. As we have seen, Congress has time and again rejected various legislative attempts that would have mandated a variety of forms of individual access. That is not to say that Congress' rejection of such proposals must be taken to mean that Congress is opposed to private rights of access under all circumstances. Rather, the point is that Congress has chosen to leave such questions with the Commission, to which it has given the flexibility to experiment with new ideas as changing conditions require. In this case, the Commission has decided that on balance the undesirable effects of the right of access urged by respondents would outweigh the asserted benefits. The Court of Appeals failed to give due weight to the Commission's judgment on these matters.

The Commission was justified in concluding that the public interest in providing access to the marketplace of "ideas and experiences" would scarcely be served by a system so heavily weighted in favor of the financially affluent, or those with access to wealth. Cf. *Red Lion, supra,* at 392. Even under a first-come-first-served system, proposed by the dissenting Commissioner in these cases,[16] the views of the affluent could well prevail over those of others, since they would have it within their power to purchase time more frequently. Moreover, there is the substantial danger, as the Court of Appeals acknowledged, 146 U.S. App. D.C., at 203, 450 F.2d, at 664, that the time allotted for editorial advertising could be monopolized by those of one political persuasion.

These problems would not necessarily be solved by applying the Fairness Doctrine, including the *Cullman* doctrine, to editorial advertising. If broad-

---

[16] See 25 F.C.C. 2d 216, 230, 234–235 (Johnson, dissenting).

casters were required to provide time, free when necessary, for the discussion of the various shades of opinion on the issue discussed in the advertisement, the affluent could still determine in large part the issues to be discussed. Thus, the very premise of the Court of Appeals' holding—that a right of access is necessary to allow individuals and groups the opportunity for self-initiated speech—would have little meaning to those who could not afford to purchase time in the first instance.[17]

If the Fairness Doctrine were applied to editorial advertising, there is also the substantial danger that the effective operation of that doctrine would be jeopardized. To minimize financial hardship and to comply fully with its public responsibilities a broadcaster might well be forced to make regular programming time available to those holding a view different from that expressed in an editorial advertisement; indeed, BEM has suggested as much in its brief. The result would be a further erosion of the journalistic discretion of broadcasters in the coverage of public issues, and a transfer of control over the treatment of public issues from the licensees who are accountable for broadcast performance to private individuals who are not. The public interest would no longer be "paramount" but, rather, subordinate to private whim especially since, under the Court of Appeals' decision, a broadcaster would be largely precluded from rejecting editorial advertisements that dealt with matters trivial or insignificant or already fairly covered by the broadcaster. 146 U.S. App. D.C., at 196 n. 36, 197, 450 F.2d, at 657 n. 36, 658. If the Fairness Doctrine and the *Cullman* doctrine were suspended to alleviate these problems, as respondents suggest might be appropriate, the question arises whether we would have abandoned more than we have gained. Under such a regime the congressional objective of balanced coverage of public issues would be seriously threatened.

Nor can we accept the Court of Appeals' view that every potential speaker is "the best judge" of what the listening public ought to hear or indeed the best judge of the merits of his or her views. All journalistic tradition and experience is to the contrary. For better or worse, editing is what editors are for; and editing is selection and choice of material. That editors—newspaper or broadcast—can and do abuse this power is beyond doubt, but that is no reason to deny the discretion Congress provided. Calculated risks of abuse are taken in order to preserve higher values. The presence of these risks is nothing new; the authors of the Bill of Rights accepted the reality that these risks were evils for which there was no acceptable remedy other than a spirit of moderation and a sense of responsibility—and civility—on the part of those who exercise the guaranteed freedoms of expression.

It was reasonable for Congress to conclude that the public interest in being

---

[17]To overcome this inconsistency it has been suggested that a "submarket rate system" be established for those unable to afford the normal cost for air time. See Note, 85 Harv. L. Rev. 689, 695–696 (1972). That proposal has been criticized, we think justifiably, as raising "incredible administrative problems." Jaffe, The Editorial Responsibility of the Broadcaster: Reflections on Fairness and Access, 85 Harv. L. Rev. 768, 789 (1972).

informed requires periodic accountability on the part of those who are entrusted with the use of broadcast frequencies, scarce as they are. In the delicate balancing historically followed in the regulation of broadcasting Congress and the Commission could appropriately conclude that the allocation of journalistic priorities should be concentrated in the licensee rather than diffused among many. This policy gives the public some assurance that the broadcaster will be answerable if he fails to meet its legitimate needs. No such accountability attaches to the private individual, whose only qualifications for using the broadcast facility may be abundant funds and a point of view. To agree that debate on public issues should be "robust, and wide-open" does not mean that we should exchange "public trustee" broadcasting, with all its limitations, for a system of self-appointed editorial commentators.

The Court of Appeals discounted those difficulties by stressing that it was merely mandating a "modest reform," requiring only that broadcasters be required to accept some editorial advertising. 146 U.S. App. D.C., at 202, 450 F.2d, at 663. The court suggested that broadcasters could place an "outside limit on the total amount of editorial advertising they will sell" and that the Commission and the broadcasters could develop "'reasonable regulations' designed to prevent domination by a few groups or a few viewpoints." Id., at 202, 203, 450 F.2d, at 663, 664. If the Commission decided to apply the Fairness Doctrine to editorial advertisements and as a result broadcasters suffered financial harm, the court thought the "Commission could make necessary adjustments." Id., at 203, 450 F.2d, at 664. Thus, without providing any specific answers to the substantial objections raised by the Commission and the broadcasters, other than to express repeatedly its "confidence" in the Commission's ability to overcome any difficulties, the court remanded the cases to the Commission for the development of regulations to implement a constitutional right of access.

By minimizing the difficult problems involved in implementing such a right of access, the Court of Appeals failed to come to grips with another problem of critical importance to broadcast regulation and the First Amendment—the risk of an enlargement of Government control over the content of broadcast discussion of public issues. See, e.g., Fowler v. Rhode Island, 345 U.S. 67 (1953); Niemotko v. Maryland, 340 U.S. 268 (1951). This risk is inherent in the Court of Appeals' remand requiring regulations and procedures to sort out requests to be heard—a process involving the very editing that licensees now perform as to regular programming. Although the use of a public resource by the broadcast media permits a limited degree of Government surveillance, as is not true with respect to private media, see National Broadcasting Co. v. United States, 319 U.S., at 216-219, the Government's power over licensees, as we have noted, is by no means absolute and is carefully circumscribed by the Act itself.[18]

Under a constitutionally commanded and Government supervised right-of-

[18] See n. 8, supra.

access system urged by respondents and mandated by the Court of Appeals, the Commission would be required to oversee far more of the day-to-day operations of broadcasters' conduct, deciding such questions as whether a particular individual or group has had sufficient opportunity to present its viewpoint and whether a particular viewpoint has already been sufficiently aired. Regimenting broadcasters is too radical a therapy for the ailment respondents complain of.

Under the Fairness Doctrine the Commission's responsibility is to judge whether a licensee's overall performance indicates a sustained good-faith effort to meet the public interest in being fully and fairly informed.[19] The Commission's responsibilities under a right-of-access system would tend to draw it into a continuing case-by-case determination of who should be heard and when. Indeed, the likelihood of Government involvement is so great that it has been suggested that the accepted constitutional principles against control of speech content would need to be relaxed with respect to editorial advertisements.[20] To sacrifice First Amendment protections for so speculative a gain is not warranted, and it was well within the Commission's discretion to construe the Act so as to avoid such a result.[21]

The Commission is also entitled to take into account the reality that in a very real sense listeners and viewers constitute a "captive audience." Cf. *Public Utilities Comm'n* v. *Pollak,* 343 U.S., at 463; *Kovacs* v. *Cooper,* 336 U.S. 77 (1949). The "captive" nature of the broadcast audience was recognized as early as 1924, when Commerce Secretary Hoover remarked at the Fourth [*sic*] National Radio Conference that "the radio listener does not have the same option that the reader of publications has—to ignore advertising in which he is not interested—and he may resent its invasion of his set."[22] As the broadcast media became more pervasive in our society, the problem has become more acute. In a recent decision upholding the Commission's power to promulgate rules regarding cigarette advertising, Judge Bazelon, writing for a unanimous Court of Appeals, noted some of the effects of the ubiquitous commercial:

"Written messages are not communicated unless they are read, and reading requires an affirmative act. Broadcast messages, in contrast, are 'in the air.' In an age of omnipresent radio, there scarcely breathes a citizen who does not know some part of a leading cigarette jingle by heart. Similarly, an ordinary habitual television watcher can *avoid* these commercials only by frequently leaving the room, changing the channel, or by doing some other such affirmative act. It is

[19] See Report on Editorializing by Broadcast Licensees, 13 F.C.C., at 1251–1252.
[20] See Note, 85 Harv. L. Rev. 689, 697 (1973).
[21] DNC has urged in this Court that we at least recognize a right of our national parties to purchase air time for the purpose of discussing public issues. We see no principled means under the First Amendment of favoring access by organized political parties over other groups and individuals.
[22] Reprinted in Hearings before the Senate Committee on Interstate Commerce on Radio Control, 69th Cong., 1st Sess., 54 (1926).

difficult to calculate the subliminal impact of this pervasive propaganda, which may be heard even if not listened to, but it may reasonably be thought greater than the impact of the written word." *Banzhaf* v. *FCC,* 132 U.S. App. D.C. 14, 32–33, 405 F.2d 1082, 1100–1101 (1968), cert. denied, 396 U.S. 842 (1969).

It is no answer to say that because we tolerate pervasive commercial advertisements we can also live with its political counterparts.

The rationale for the Court of Appeals' decision imposing a constitutional right of access on the broadcast media was that the licensee impermissibly discriminates by accepting commercial advertisements while refusing editorial advertisements. The court relied on decisions holding that state-supported school newspapers and public transit companies were prohibited by the First Amendment from excluding controversial editorial advertisements in favor of commercial advertisements.[23] The court also attempted to analogize this case to some of our decisions holding that States may not constitutionally ban certain protected speech while at the same time permitting other speech in public areas. *Cox* v. *Louisiana,* 379 U.S. 536 (1965); *Fowler* v. *Rhode Island,* 345 U.S. 67 (1953); *Niemotko* v. *Maryland,* 340 U.S. 268 (1951). This theme of "invidious discrimination" against protected speech is echoed in the briefs of BEM and DNC to this Court. Respondents also rely on our recent decisions in *Grayned* v. *City of Rockford,* 408 U.S. 104 (1972), and *Police Dept. of Chicago* v. *Mosley,* 408 U.S. 92 (1972), where we held unconstitutional city ordinances that permitted "peaceful picketing of any school involved in a labor dispute," *id.,* at 93, but prohibited demonstrations for any other purposes on the streets and sidewalks within 150 feet of the school.

Those decisions provide little guidance, however, in resolving the question whether the First Amendment requires the Commission to mandate a private right of access to the broadcast media. In none of those cases did the forum sought for expression have an affirmative and independent statutory obligation to provide full and fair coverage of public issues, such as Congress has imposed on all broadcast licensees. In short, there is no "discrimination" against controversial speech present in this case. The question here is not whether there is to be discussion of controversial issues of public importance on the broadcast media, but rather who shall determine what issues are to be discussed by whom, and when.

The opinion of the Court of Appeals asserted that the Fairness Doctrine, insofar as it allows broadcasters to exercise certain journalistic judgments over the discussion of public issues, is inadequate to meet the public's interest in

---

[23] *Lee* v. *Board of Regents of State Colleges,* 306 F. Supp. 1097 (WD Wis. 1969), aff'd, 441 F.2d 1257 (CA7 1971); *Zucker* v. *Panitz,* 299 F. Supp. 102 (SDNY 1969); *Kissinger* v. *New York City Transit Authority,* 274 F. Supp. 438 (SDNY 1967); *Hillside Community Church, Inc.* v. *City of Tacoma,* 76 Wash. 2d 63, 455 P.2d 350 (1969); *Wirta* v. *Alameda-Contra Costa Transit District,* 68 Cal. 2d 51, 434 P.2d 982 (1967).

being informed. The present system, the court held, "conforms . . . to a paternalistic structure in which licensees and bureaucrats decide what issues are 'important,' and how 'fully' to cover them, and the format, time and style of the coverage." 146 U.S. App. D.C., at 195, 450 F.2d, at 656. The forced sale of advertising time for editorial spot announcements would, according to the Court of Appeals majority, remedy this deficiency. That conclusion was premised on the notion that advertising time, as opposed to programming time, involves a "special and separate mode of expression" because advertising content, unlike programming content, is generally prepared and edited by the advertiser. Thus, that court concluded, a broadcaster's policy against using advertising time for editorial messages "may well ignore opportunities to enliven and enrich the public's overall information." *Id.*, at 197, 450 F.2d, at 658. The Court of Appeals' holding would serve to transfer a large share of responsibility for balanced broadcasting from an identifiable, regulated entity—the licensee—to unregulated speakers who could afford the cost.

We reject the suggestion that the Fairness Doctrine permits broadcasters to preside over a "paternalistic" regime. See *Red Lion,* 395 U.S., at 390. That doctrine admittedly has not always brought to the public perfect or, indeed, even consistently high-quality treatment of all public events and issues; but the remedy does not lie in diluting licensee responsibility. The Commission stressed that, while the licensee has discretion in fulfilling its obligations under the Fairness Doctrine, it is required to "present representative community views and voices on controversial issues which are of importance to [its] listeners," and it is prohibited from "excluding partisan voices and always itself presenting views in a bland, inoffensive manner. . . ." 25 F.C.C. 2d, at 222. A broadcaster neglects that obligation only at the risk of losing his license.

Conceivably at some future date Congress or the Commission—or the broadcasters—may devise some kind of limited right of access that is both practicable and desirable. Indeed, the Commission noted in these proceedings that the advent of cable television will afford increased opportunities for the discussion of public issues. In its proposed rules on cable television the Commission has provided that cable systems in major television markets

"shall maintain at least one specially designated, noncommercial public access channel available on a first-come, nondiscriminatory basis. The system shall maintain and have available for public use at least the minimal equipment and facilities necessary for the production of programming for such a channel." 37 Fed. Reg. 3289, § 76.251(a)(4).

For the present, the Commission is conducting a wide-ranging study into the effectiveness of the Fairness Doctrine to see what needs to be done to improve the coverage and presentation of public issues on the broadcast media. Notice of Inquiry in Docket 19260, 30 F.C.C. 2d 26, 36 Fed. Reg. 11825. Among other things, the study will attempt to determine whether "there is any feasible method of providing access for discussion of public issues outside the requirements of the fairness doctrine." 30 F.C.C. 2d, at 33. The Commission made it clear, however, that it does not intend to discard the Fairness Doctrine or to require broadcasters to accept all private demands for air time.[24] The Commission's inquiry on this score was announced prior to the decision of the Court of Appeals in this case and hearings are under way.

The problems perceived by the Court of Appeals majority are by no means new; as we have seen, the history of the Communications Act and the activities of the Commission over a period of 40 years reflect a continuing search for means to achieve reasonable regulation compatible with the First Amendment rights of the public and the licensees. The Commission's pending hearings are but one step in this continuing process. At the very least, courts should not freeze this necessarily dynamic process into a constitutional holding. See *American Commercial Lines, Inc.* v. *Louisville & N.R. Co.,* 392 U.S. 571, 590-593 (1968).

The judgment of the Court of Appeals is

Reversed.

---

[24] Subsequent to the announcement of the Court of Appeals' decision, the Commission expanded the scope of the inquiry to comply with the Court of Appeals' mandate. Further Notice of Inquiry in Docket 19260, 33 F.C.C. 2d 554, 37 Fed. Reg. 3383. After we granted certiorari and stayed the mandate of the Court of Appeals, the Commission withdrew that notice of an expanded inquiry and continued its study as originally planned. Order and Further Notice of Inquiry in Docket 19260, 33 F.C.C. 2d 790, 37 Fed. Reg. 4980.

42

Broadcast Procedure Manual

The Public and Broadcasting—A Procedure
Manual (revised edition)

49 FCC 2d 1

September 5, 1974

Active public participation in broadcast regulation became commonplace following the *United Church of Christ* court decisions
of the 1960's. (See Document 35, pp. 339–355.) Numerous petitions to deny license renewals and transfers of ownership have
been lodged by citizens groups, and national organizations such
as Action for Children's Television have achieved results by
petitioning the FCC to issue rules [*Action for Children's Television*, 50 FCC 2d 1 (1974)].

The most effective way in which one can influence broadcasting is to become a broadcaster. But citizens groups already
committed to other pursuits cannot consider this as a realistic
alternative to filing complaints and petitions; such groups are
like earnest students who want to see education improved, but
are either unable or unwilling to become teachers.

Although some petitions to deny have met with success before the FCC [see *Alabama Educational Television Commission*,
50 FCC 2d 461 (1975)], most citizens groups have been unable
to present sufficiently specific proof of their claims to convince
the Commission that a hearing is required [see *Stone* v. *FCC*, 466
F.2d 316 (D.C. Cir. 1972)]. However, when the petitioner's
claims are supported by factual evidence, the licensee, threatened

by a hearing that might end with non-renewal, has often come to terms with citizens groups by granting concessions in programming and employment practices if complaints and petitions to deny are withdrawn [see *KCMC, Inc. (KTAL-TV),* 19 FCC 2d 109, 120–122 (1969); a much earlier example of this sort of arrangement is *United Broadcasting Co. (WHKC),* 10 FCC 515 (1945)]. More recently, the FCC has made these points clear: (1) a licensee does not have to enter into agreements with citizens groups and may not delegate his "obligation to determine how to serve the public interest" to anyone, even voluntarily; (2) the Commission must consider the issues raised in a petition to deny, even if the petition is later withdrawn pursuant to an agreement between petitioner and licensee; (3) ". . . clauses in agreements barring petitions to deny would be improper . . ." [*Agreements between Broadcast Licensees and the Public,* 57 FCC 2d 42 (1975).]

The "Broadcast Procedure Manual," below, is a useful primer for members of the general public seeking to influence broadcasting through contact with broadcasters and the FCC. Readers desiring to obtain the publications mentioned in paragraphs 11, 15, and 69 should request them by writing to:

Public Information Officer
Federal Communications Commission
1919 M Street, N.W.
Washington, D.C.   20554

Individuals or groups seeking advice from the FCC about Commission policies and procedures may direct their requests to the Consumer Assistance Office at the above address. The National Citizens Committee for Broadcasting (NCCB) is a non-governmental source of help for members of the public wishing to act on their interests in broadcasting. NCCB publishes a monthly magazine called *access* which is directed to the concerns of broadcast consumers. NCCB's address is 1028 Connecticut Avenue, N.W., Washington, D.C. 20036.

Related Reading: 17, 92, 94, 112, 114, 135, 146, 166, 194, 201.

INTRODUCTION

1. Establishing and maintaining quality broadcasting services in a community is the responsibility of broadcast station licensees and the Federal Communica-

tions Commission.[1] It is also, however, a matter in which members of the community have a vital concern and in which they can and should play a prominent role.

2. Licensees of radio and television stations are required to make a diligent, positive, and continuing effort to discover and fulfill the problems, needs, and interests of the communities they serve. The Commission encourages a continuing dialog between stations and community members as a means of ascertaining the community's problems, needs, and interests and of devising ways to meet and fulfill them. Members of the community can help a station to provide better broadcast service and more responsive programing by making their needs, interests, and problems known to the station and by commenting, whether favorably or unfavorably, on the programing and practices of the station. Complaints concerning a station's operation should be communicated promptly to the station, and every effort should be made, by both the complainant and the licensee, to resolve any differences through discussion at the local level.

3. The Commission is responsible for seeing that stations do in fact meet their obligations to the community. It considers complaints by members of the community against a station and before issuing or renewing a broadcast station license, must find that its action will serve the public interest, convenience, and necessity. However, to effectively invoke the Commission's processes, the citizen must not only concern himself with the quality of broadcasting but must know when, how, and to whom, to express his concern. On the one hand, the Commission is in large measure dependent on community members to bring up matters which warrant its attention. On the other, if resolute efforts are not first made to clear up problems at the local level, the Commission's processes become clogged by the sheer bulk of the matters brought before it.

4. If direct contact with a station does not produce satisfactory results, there are a number of formal and informal ways for members of the community to convey their grievances to the Commission and to participate in proceedings in

---

[1] The Federal Communications Commission is an independent Government agency responsible for regulating interstate and foreign communication by radio and wire. One of its responsibilities is to determine who is to operate the limited number of broadcast stations, to regulate the manner in which they are operated, and to generally supervise their operation, to the end that such operation may serve the interests of the public. This booklet deals only with this one aspect of the Commission's responsibilities.

The FCC is composed of seven members, who are appointed by the President subject to confirmation by the Senate. Normally, one Commissioner is appointed or reappointed each year, for a term of 7 years. One of the Commissioners is designated by the President to serve as Chairman, or chief executive officer, of the Commission.

The Commissioners, functioning as a unit, supervise all activities of the Commission. They are assisted by a staff of approximately 1,500 persons. Note that the term "Commission" refers both to the seven Commissioners as a unit and to the entire agency, including the staff. For a general description of the Commission and its organization, see 47 CFR 0.1–0.5. For a full description of the Commission's functions and of authority delegated by the Commission to its staff, see 47 CFR Part 0. [The Commission's rules are printed in Volume 47 of the Code of Federal Regulations (CFR). See paras. 60 and 61 below.]

which the performance of a station is judged and legitimate grievances are redressed. The purpose of this manual is to outline the procedures available to the concerned citizen and to provide information and practical advice concerning their use. It is not a substitute for the rules of practice and procedure (47 CFR Part 1).[2] We are hopeful, however, that it will help community members to participate effectively and in a manner which is helpful to the Commission.

PROCEEDINGS INVOLVING PARTICULAR APPLICANTS AND LICENSEES

Initiating a proceeding

5. *Complaints generally.* A complaint against a broadcast station[3] can be filed with the Commission by any person at any time. You can go about it any way you wish; there are no particular procedural requirements, except as noted below. You should, however, bear the following facts in mind:

(a) During fiscal year 1973, the Commission received 84,525 complaints, comments, and inquiries concerning broadcast stations. Of this total, 61,322 were complaints.

(b) Almost all of these communications are initially considered and dealt with by approximately five Commission employees who are specially assigned this function. Additional personnel are assigned to a matter only if, on the initial examination, the complaint appears to raise novel or difficult legal questions or appears to warrant extensive inquiry, investigation, or formal proceedings.

In light of this situation, there are a number of practical steps you can take which will be helpful to the Commission and will increase your effectiveness in making a complaint. These are set out below:

(1) Limit your complaint to matters on which the Commission can act. With minor exceptions (the provision of "equal time" for candidates for public office, for example), we cannot direct that a particular program be put on or taken off the air. Nor are we arbiters of taste. Our concern, moreover, is with matters which affect the community generally (the public interest) rather than with the personal preferences or grievances of individuals. Another publication, "The

---

[2] The manual reflects procedures and policies in effect on August 1, 1974. Persons using this manual are cautioned that these procedures and policies are subject to change and that any changes made after August 1, 1974 are not reflected in this manual.

[3] Complaints relating to some of the operations of networks and other organizations associated with broadcasting can also be filed.

FCC and Broadcasting," contains more detailed information (in areas in which numerous complaints are received) regarding what the Commission can and cannot do. Copies will be furnished by the Complaints and Compliance Division of the Commission's Broadcast Bureau upon request.

(2) Submit your complaint first to the station involved. The station may well recognize the merit of your complaint and take corrective action, or may explain the matter to your satisfaction. If you are not satisfied with the station's response, it will aid and expedite action on your complaint to the Commission to enclose a copy of your complaint to the station and all subsequent correspondence between you and the station. (Though this way of proceeding is generally far preferable to complaining initially to the Commission, this is not always the case. If, for example, the complainant has reason for not disclosing his identity to the station, he may complain directly to the Commission, requesting that his identity not be disclosed.)

(3) Submit your complaint promptly after the event to which it relates.

(4) Include at least the following information in your letter of complaint:

   a. The full name and address of the complainant.

   b. The call letters and location of the station.

   c. The name of any program to which the complaint relates and the date and time of its broadcast.

   d. A statement of what the station has done or failed to do which causes you to file a complaint. Be as specific as possible: Furnish names, dates, places and other details.

   e. A statement setting forth what you want the station and/or the Commission to do.

   f. A copy of any previous correspondence between you and the station concerning the subject of the complaint.

(5) Try to appreciate that the person reviewing your complaint must make rapid judgments regarding the gravity of the matters related and the action to be taken. There are a number of simple things you can do to make his job easier and to aid your own cause: State the facts fully and at the beginning. Subject to fully stating the facts, be as brief as possible. If the facts are self-explanatory, avoid argument; let the facts speak for themselves. Avoid repetition or exaggeration. If you think a specific law or regulation has been violated, tell us what it is. If possible, use a typewriter, but if you do write by hand, take special pains to write legibly.

6. A complaint received by the Commission is dealt with as follows:

(1) If the complaint does not allege a substantial violation of statute or of Commission rule or policy, if inadequate information is submitted, or if the factual statement is not sufficiently specific, a letter (which is often a form letter) explaining these matters is directed to the complainant.

(2) If the complaint does allege specific facts sufficient to indicate a sub-

stantial violation, it is investigated, either by correspondence with the station (which may produce a satisfactory explanation or remedial action) or, in rare instances, by field inquiry. (Since the Commission's investigatory staff is small, the number of complaints which can be investigated by field inquiry is limited.) If further information from the complainant is needed, he is asked to furnish it. If the staff concludes that there has been a violation, it may recommend to the Commission that sanctions be imposed on the station; it may direct remedial action (such as equal opportunities for a candidate for public office); or, where extenuating circumstances are present (as where the violation follows from an honest mistake or misjudgment or where the station otherwise has a good record), it may note the violation but not recommend a sanction. Possible Commission actions range from the imposition of monetary forfeitures not exceeding $10,000 and short-term renewal of license to revocation of license or denial of an application for renewal of license. The imposition of sanctions involves formal proceedings (which may include a hearing) and, in connection with such proceedings, the complainant may be asked to submit a sworn statement or to appear and give testimony at a hearing before an administrative law judge. In some circumstances, the complainant is entitled, and may choose, to participate as a party to the proceeding. A hearing is ordered in a renewal or revocation proceeding only if substantial questions have been raised concerning the licensee's qualifications.

7. Four types of complaint require compliance with specific procedures and submission of specific information. These complaints involve compliance with the requirement of equal time for political candidates, the fairness doctrine, the personal attack rule, and the rule governing political editorials. Generally, these matters should be taken up with the station before a complaint is filed with the Commission. However, where time is an important factor, you may find it advisable to complain simultaneously to the station and the Commission. In such circumstances, complaints are often submitted and answered by telegraph and, where the matter is most urgent, by telephone.

8. *Political broadcasting.* Section 315 of the Communications Act, 47 U.S.C. 315,[4] provides that if any Commission licensee shall permit any person "who is a legally qualified candidate for any public office" to use a broadcast station, he shall afford to all other candidates for that office equal opportunities to use the station's facilities. Appearances by candidates on the following types of programs are exempt from the equal opportunities requirement:

1. Bona fide newscast;
2. Bona fide news interview;
3. Bona fide news documentary (if the appearance of the candidate is inci-

---

[4]The Communications Act is printed in title 47 of the United States Code (U.S.C.). See paragraph 59 below.

dental to the presentation of the subject or subjects covered by the news documentary); or

4.   On-the-spot coverage of bona fide news events (including but not limited to political conventions and activities incidental thereto).

However, where candidates appear on programs exempt from the equal opportunities requirement, broadcasters must nevertheless meet the obligation imposed upon them under the Communications Act (to operate in the public interest) and the fairness doctrine (to afford reasonable opportunity for the discussion of conflicting views on controversial issues of public importance). See paragraph 12 below. The equal opportunities and fairness doctrine requirements are applied to networks as well as to stations.

9. A request for equal opportunities must be made directly to the station or network and must be submitted within 1 week after the first broadcast giving rise to your right of equal opportunities. This is most important, as your right is lost by failure to make a timely request. To make it as clear as possible, we offer the folowing example:

A, B, and C are legally qualified candidates for the same public office. A makes an appearance on April 5 on a program not exempted by the statute. On April 12, B asks for an equal opportunity to appear on the station and does, in fact, appear on April 15. On April 16, C asks for an equal opportunity to appear. However, he is not entitled to do so, as he has failed to make his request within 1 week after A's appearance.

There is an exception to this requirement where the person requesting equal opportunities was not a candidate at the time of the first broadcast giving rise to the right of equal opportunities. See 47 CFR 73.120(e).

10. If you are a candidate or his designated agent and think that the candidate has been denied equal opportunities you may complain to the Commission. A copy of this complaint should be sent to the station. Your letter of complaint should state (1) the name of the station or network involved; (2) the name of the candidate for the same office and the date of his appearance on the station's facilities; (3) whether the candidate who appeared was a legally qualified candidate for the office at the time of his appearance (this is determined by reference to the law of the State in which the election is being held); (4) whether the candidate seeking equal time is a legally qualified candidate for the same office; and (5) whether you or your candidate made a request for equal opportunities to the licensee within 1 week of the day on which the first broadcast giving rise to the right to equal opportunities occurred.

11. A political broadcasting primer ("Use of Broadcast Facilities by Candidates for Public Office"), containing a summary of rulings interpreting the equal opportunities requirement, has been published in the *Federal Register* and in

the FCC Reports[5] (35 F.R. 13048, 24 F.C.C. 2d 832) and is available from the Commission upon request, as is a question and answer pamphlet ("Use of Broadcast and Cablecast Facilities by Candidates for Public Office") (37 F.R. 5796, 34 F.C.C. 2d 510). See also 47 U.S.C. 315 and 47 CFR 73.120.

12. *Fairness doctrine.* Under the fairness doctrine, if there is a presentation of a point of view on a controversial issue of public importance over a station (or network), it is the duty of the station (or network), in its overall programing, to afford a reasonable opportunity for the presentation of contrasting views as to that issue. This duty applies to all station programing and not merely to editorials stating the station's position. The station may make offers of time to spokesmen for contrasting views or may present its own programing on the issue. It must present suitable contrasting views without charge if it is unable to secure payment from, or a sponsor for, the spokesman for such views. The broadcaster has considerable discretion as to the format of programs, the different shades of opinion to be presented, the spokesman for each point of view, and the time allowed. He is not required to provide equal time or equal opportunities; this requirement applies only to broadcasts by candidates for public office. The doctrine is based on the right of the public to be informed and not on the proposition that any particular person or group is entitled to be heard.

13. If you believe that a broadcaster (station or network) is not meeting its obligation to the public under the fairness doctrine, you should complain first to the broadcaster. If you believe that a point of view is not being presented and wish to act as spokesman for that point of view, you should first notify the broadcaster. Barring unusual circumstances, complaints should not be made to the Commission without affording the broadcaster an opportunity to rectify the situation, comply with your request, or explain its position.

14. If you do file a fairness doctrine complaint with the Commission, a copy should be sent to the station. The complaint should contain specific information concerning the following matters: (1) The name of the station or network involved; (2) the controversial issue of public importance on which a view was presented; (3) the date and time of its broadcast; (4) the basis for your claim that the issue is controversial and of public importance; (5) an accurate summary of the view or views broadcast; (6) the basis for your claim that the station or network has not broadcast contrasting views on the issue or issues in its overall programing; and (7) whether the station or network has afforded, or has expressed the intention to afford, a reasonable opportunity for the presentation of contrasting viewpoints on that issue. The requirement that you state the basis for your claim that the station or network has not broadcast contrasting views on the issue or issues in its overall programing does not mean that you must constantly monitor the station. As the Commission stated in its *Fairness Report:*

While the Complainant must state the basis for this claim that the station has

[5] See paragraph 62 below.

not presented contrasting views, that claim might be based on an assertion that the complainant is a regular listener or viewer; that is, a person who consistently or as a matter of routine listens to the news, public affairs and other non-entertainment carried by the station involved. This does not require that the complainant listen to or view the station 24 hours a day, seven days a week ... Complainants should specify the nature and should indicate the period of time during which they have been regular members of the station's audience. *Fairness Report,* 39 Fed. Reg. 26372, 26379 (1974).

Further, a basis for your claim that the station has failed to present contrasting views might be provided by correspondence between you and the station or network involved. Thus if the station's or network's response to your correspondence states that no other programing has been presented on the subject and none is planned, such response would also provide a basis for your claim.

15. Following the Commission's broad-ranging inquiry into the efficacy of the fairness doctrine and related public interest policies, the Commission issued its *Fairness Report,* 39 Fed. Reg. 26372 (1974). Copies of this and an earlier fairness primer containing a summary of rulings interpreting the fairness doctrine ["Applicability of the Fairness Doctrine in the Handling of Controversial Issues of Public Importance," 29 Fed. Reg. 10416, 40 FCC 598 (1964)] are available from the Commission upon request.

16. *Personal attacks.* The personal attack rule requires that when, during the presentation of views on a controversial issue of public importance, an attack is made upon the honesty, character, integrity, or like personal qualities of an identified person or group, the broadcaster must, within 1 week after the attack, transmit to the person or group attacked (1) notification of the date, time and identification of the broadcast; (2) a script or tape (or an accurate summary if a script or tape is not available) of the attack; and (3) an offer of a reasonable opportunity to respond over the station's facilities free of charge. See 47 CFR 73.123(a). The personal attack rule does not apply to attacks made in the course of a bona fide newscast, a bona fide news interview, or on-the-spot coverage of a bona fide news event (including commentary or analysis by newsmen offered as part of such programs). Though the specific requirements of notice and an offer of an opportunity to respond do not apply to such programs, the other requirements of the fairness doctrine do apply. For other circumstances in which the personal attack rule does not apply, see 47 CFR 73.123(b). See also, the fairness primer, described above in paragraph 15.

17. If you believe that you or your group has been personally attacked during presentation of a controversial issue, and if you are not offered an opportunity to respond, you should complain first to the station or network involved. If you are not satisfied with the response, you may then complain to the Commission.

18. If you file a complaint with the Commission, a copy should be sent to the station. The complaint should contain specific information concerning the following matters: (1) The name of the station or network involved; (2) the

words or statements broadcast; (3) the date and time the broadcast was made; (4) the basis for your view that the words broadcast constitute an attack upon the honesty, character, integrity, or like personal qualities of you or your group; (5) the basis for your view that the personal attack was broadcast during the presentation of views on a controversial issue of public importance; (6) the basis for your view that the matter discussed was a controversial issue of public importance, either nationally or in the station's local area, at the time of the broadcast; and (7) whether the station within 1 week of the alleged attack: (i) Notified you or your group of the broadcast; (ii) transmitted a script, tape, or accurate summary of the broadcast if a script or tape was not available; and (iii) offered a reasonable opportunity to respond over the station's facilities.

19. *Political editorials.* When a broadcast station, in an editorial, endorses a legally qualified candidate for public office, it is required to transmit to other qualified candidates for the same office (1) notice as to the date and time of the editorial, (2) a script or tape of the editorial, and (3) an offer of a reasonable opportunity for the other candidates or their spokesmen to respond to the editorial over the licensee's facilities free of charge. Where a broadcast station, in an editorial, opposes a legally qualified candidate for public office, it is required to send the notice and offer to the candidate opposed. The notice and offer must be sent within 24 hours after the editorial is broadcast. If the editorial is to be broadcast within 72 hours of election day, the station must transmit the notice and offer "sufficiently far in advance of the broadcast to enable the candidate or candidates to have a reasonable opportunity to prepare a response and to present it in timely fashion." See 47 CFR 73.123(c). See also, the fairness primer, described above in paragraph 15.

20. If you are a candidate or his authorized spokesman and believe that the station, in an editorial, has opposed the candidate or supported his opponent and has not complied fully with these requirements, you should complain to the station or network involved. If, in response to your complaint, the station does not offer what you consider to be a reasonable opportunity to respond to the editorial, you may complain to the Commission. Send a copy of your complaint to the station.

Participation in application proceedings

21. *General.* Public expression regarding the operation of broadcast stations is not limited to letters of complaint. You can also support or object to applications filed with the Commission, such as an application for a new license, a change in existing facilities (for example, an increase in tower height or transmitter power or a change in studio location), or the renewal or transfer of a current license. You may proceed either formally, by filing a "petition to deny," or informally, by filing an "informal objection." (See below.) You may raise any

public interest question relating to the application or the applicant. Allegations have been made in the past, for example, that the station's programing does not serve the needs and interests of the community or that the station has engaged in discriminatory employment practices. The question raised need not relate directly to the authority sought by the applicant. Your purpose in participating could properly be to effect a change in the station's policies or practices, by negotiation or by Commission direction, rather than to have the application denied. It is desirable and important that you discuss your grievances with the station, as they occur, and try to work out a mutually acceptable solution, either prior to or in lieu of filing an objection to the grant of an application. The Commission does not look with favor on objections to a grant where grievances have been "stored up" during the license term, without being brought to the station's attention, and are disclosed for the first time in objections to an application.

22. With certain minor exceptions, all broadcast applicants are required to give notice to the community that they have filed an application with the Commission. See 47 CFR 1.580. In the case of most existing licensee-applicants the notice is broadcast over their facilities. Public notice of the filing of the application is also given by the Commission. Applicants and licensees are required to maintain locally for public inspection copies of applications and other documents as specified in the Commission's rules. See 47 CFR 1.526. The notice given locally by the station will state the address at which these documents can be inspected. Additional papers relating to the station, including most of those kept locally, are available for inspection at the Commission's office in the District of Columbia.[6] Except in the case of certain minor applications (see 47 U.S.C. 309), the Commission must give notice of the acceptance of the application for filing at least 30 days before acting on it. See paragraphs 33 and 34 below.

23. *Informal objection.* If you have information which you believe should be considered by the Commission in determining whether the grant of an application would serve the public interest, convenience and necessity, you may file an "informal objection." See 47 CFR 1.587. Such objections may be filed in writing with the Secretary of the Commission, Washington, D.C. 20554, at any time prior to action on the application, and must be signed by the person making them. There are no other requirements.

24. The informal objection procedure is designed for use by persons who cannot qualify as "parties in interest" (see paragraph 30 below) or who (though

[6]Most Commission records are routinely available for inspection under the Public Information Act (5 U.S.C. 552) and Commission rules implementing that Act (47 CFR 0.441–0.467). See, in particular, §§ 0.453 and 0.455. A person wishing to inspect such records has only to go to the office where they are kept and ask to see them. Requests for inspection of records not routinely available for inspection may be submitted, and are considered, under procedures set out in § 0.461 of the rules (47 CFR 0.461). Copies of records may be obtained for a fee from a private firm which contracts with the Commission to perform this service (see 47 CFR 0.465).

they qualify as parties in interest) do not choose to assert the rights or to assume the burdens of parties to the proceeding. In addition, pleadings, or communications, submitted by persons who desire to participate as parties to the proceeding but which fail to meet the requirements for "petitions to deny" (see paragraph 29 below) are treated as informal objections.

25. Informal objections are dealt with much in the same manner as complaints and should include at least the minimum information required for an effective complaint (see paragraph 5 above). They are associated with the application to which they relate, however, and are reviewed by elements of the staff responsible for taking or recommending action on that application.

26. If in the judgment of the Commission's staff the objection does not raise a substantial public interest question, it will not be referred to the Commission (that is, the Commissioners) for consideration. In such cases, the staff will give notice of Commission or staff action on the application to persons who have filed an objection, advising them that their objection has been rejected by the staff as a basis for denying the application. An application for review of staff action by the Commission may be filed. Such an application must be filed prior to seeking judicial review. See 47 U.S.C. 155(d)(7); 47 CFR 1.115.

27. If in the judgment of the staff the objection raises a substantial public interest question, it is made the subject of field inquiry or is forwarded to the applicant for comment. If the applicant is asked to comment, he is required to serve a copy of his comments on the person who filed the objection, and that person is entitled to file a reply. If there is still a substantial question, it is referred to the Commission and is dealt with on its merits in conjunction with action on the application. If the Commission concludes that a substantial and material question of fact has been presented or if it is for any reason unable to find that a grant of the application would serve the public interest, it will order a hearing. Otherwise, it will grant the application. If a hearing is ordered, a person who has filed an informal objection will not ordinarily be named as a party to the proceeding, but may seek to participate as a witness or, within 30 days after publication of the hearing issues in the *Federal Register,* petition for intervention as a party. See paragraph 39 below.

28. If the objection is considered and disposed of in a Commission opinion granting the application, you may within 30 days petition for reconsideration or seek judicial review. If you appeal or petition for reconsideration, you should be prepared to show that you are aggrieved or adversely affected by the Commission action [47 U.S.C. 402(b)(6) and 405]. If you have not participated in proceedings resulting in a grant of the application (as by filing an informal objection), or if the Commission has not been afforded an opportunity to pass on the questions you intend to raise in court, you must file a petition for reconsideration before seeking judicial review.

29. *Petition to deny.* A petition to deny, which is a formal objection to grant of an application, is subject to the following statutory requirements [47 U.S.C. 309(d)] :

1.   The petition must contain specific allegations of fact sufficient to show that the petitioner is a party in interest and which, if true, would demonstrate that a grant of the application would be inconsistent with the public interest, convenience and necessity.

2.   "Such allegations of fact shall, except for those of which official notice may be taken, be supported by affidavit of a person or persons with personal knowledge thereof."

3.   The petitioner must serve a copy of the petition upon the applicant.

4.   The petition must be filed with the Commission within the time prescribed by the rules.

The requirements are discussed below at paragraphs 30-34. A petition opposing grant of an application which does not meet these requirements is treated as an informal objection. If you intend to appeal a grant of the application or wish to participate in any hearing held to determine whether the application should be granted or denied, or if you wish to assure Commission (rather than staff) action on your objections to the application, it is advisable to file a petition to deny rather than an informal objection. If you file a petition to deny, subsequent communication with Commissioners and certain other Commission personnel is limited by the rules governing ex parte communications, 47 CFR 1.1201-1.1251.[7]

30. There is no hard and fast rule for determining whether a member of the listening public or a community group qualifies as a party in interest. Generally, under court precedents, members of the listening public who show that they would be aggrieved or adversely affected by a Commission action granting an application of a station in their area have standing to raise public interest questions. It is important to bear in mind this last point—that arguments for denial of the application must be directed to the public interest rather than to your own personal interest. For example, you may show that you are hurt by the activities or failing of the station to which you object, as by showing that you live or work in the area served by the station and, if the charges relate to racial discrimination, that you are a member of a racial minority being discriminated against; but the substance of your arguments must be related to the interests of the community as a whole. Since the purpose of your participation is to argue for the interests of your community as a whole, it is relevant to show your ties to the community and knowledge of its problems and needs. To make a stronger

[7]It is important that you not communicate privately concerning the merits or outcome of any aspect of the case with persons who may participate in deciding it. Written communications must be served on parties to the proceeding. Oral communication must be preceded by notice to the parties affording them an opportunity to be present. Persons who may participate in the decision are (1) the Commissioners and their personal office staffs, (2) the Chief of the Office of Opinions and Review and his staff, (3) the Review Board and its staff, (4) the Chief Administrative Law Judge, the administrative law judges, and the staff of the Office of Administrative Law Judges, (5) the General Counsel and his staff, and (6) the Chief Engineer and his staff.

showing,[8] it is also helpful to demonstrate that you are well qualified to represent the interests of the community and to aid the Commission in reaching a decision that best serves the interests of the community. You may, for example, have a background which specifically qualifies you on matters relating to your charges against the station. You may have a background in broadcasting or previous experience in Commission proceedings which would contribute to your effectiveness as a representative of the community. You may have access to information concerning the station's operations which is not generally available, as would be indicated by previous correspondence (or discussion) with the station concerning the charges set out in your petition. You may be the only member of the community who is prepared to assume the personal and financial burden which participation in Commission proceedings involves. It will help to show that others join with you in your petition or that you are serving as an authorized spokesman for a representative community group or groups. If other members of the public have separately petitioned to deny the application, you should endeavor to show that the contribution you can make would be superior to or different from that made by others. You should consider the possibility of joining with other members of the public for the purpose of participating in the hearing. If a large number of persons or groups seek to participate on behalf of the public, it is possible that some would be required to consolidate their efforts.

31. In determining whether the grant of an application is consistent or inconsistent with the public interest, the Commission is guided by the Communications Act, other laws pertinent to the facts of the case and the matters at issue, its own rules and regulations and policy statements, and past decisions of both the Commission and the courts. Although the facts set out in the petition to deny and the precise public interest question presented may be novel, it would be rare indeed if none of these guides could be brought to bear upon the question. It is possible, of course, to simply set out allegations of fact in a petition to deny and assert that they show that "a grant of the application would be prima facie inconsistent with the public interest" [47 U.S.C. 309(d)]. Obviously, however, it is far more effective for you, and helpful to the Commission, if the facts alleged are related specifically to the policy and precedent guidelines utilized by the Commission in making its determination. An experienced attorney will be familiar with these materials and will know how to use them in effectively presenting your position.

32. Note that the statute requires specific allegations of fact. Hearsay, rumor, opinion, or broad generalizations, do not meet this requirement. Note also that

---

[8]We do not wish to imply that a showing with respect to all of these matters, or as to any particular matter, is necessarily required to sustain your claim, or that other information may not also be appropriate. To the extent that the suggested information is set forth, however, it will enhance your showing. Do not, however, be discouraged by the number of factors listed. Our intent is to give you a general idea as to the type of information which can be submitted in support of a claim—not to indicate that the required showing is necessarily difficult to make.

the allegations must "be supported by affidavit of a person or persons with personal knowledge" of the facts. The petitioner need not, himself, have personal knowledge of the facts if he submits affidavits signed by others who do. An affidavit is a written statement, the truth of which is sworn to or affirmed before an officer who has authority to administer an oath, such as a notary public. Service of the petition is accomplished by delivering or mailing a copy to the applicant, on or before the day on which the document is filed. See 47 CFR 1.47. If the applicant is represented by an attorney, it is the attorney who should be served. A certificate of service, signed by the person who delivered or mailed the petition and reciting the fact and method of service, must be attached to the petition.

33. With minor exceptions [see 47 U.S.C. 309 (c) and (f)], no broadcast application may be granted earlier than 30 days following the Commission's issuance of a public notice stating that the application, or any substantial amendment thereof, has been "accepted for filing" [47 U.S.C. 309(b)]. Except in the case of standard broadcast (AM radio) applications and renewal applications, the petition to deny must be filed within this 30-day period. In the case of standard broadcast (other than renewal) applications, the Commission issues a second public notice stating that the application is "available and ready for processing" and specifying a "cutoff" date, on which processing of the application will commence. Petitions to deny must be filed before the cutoff date. See 47 CFR 1.580(i).

34. Applications for renewal of licenses of broadcast stations (except experimental and developmental stations) must be filed not later than the first day of the fourth full calendar month prior to the expiration date of the license (47 CFR 1.539).[9] A petition to deny a renewal application must be filed by the end

---

[9] Licenses for standard broadcast (AM), FM and television broadcast stations ordinarily expire at 3-year intervals from the following dates:

(1) For stations located in Iowa and Missouri, February 1, 1977.

(2) For stations located in Minnesota, North Dakota, South Dakota, Montana, and Colorado, April 1, 1977.

(3) For stations located in Kansas, Oklahoma, and Nebraska, June 1, 1977.

(4) For stations located in Texas, August 1, 1974.

(5) For stations located in Wyoming, Nevada, Arizona, Utah, New Mexico, and Idaho, October 1, 1974.

(6) For stations located in California, December 1, 1974.

(7) For stations located in Washington, Oregon, Alaska, Guam, and Hawaii, February 1, 1975.

(8) For stations located in Connecticut, Maine, Massachusetts, New Hampshire, Rhode Island, and Vermont, April 1, 1975.

(9) For stations located in New Jersey and New York, June 1, 1975.

(10) For stations located in Delaware and Pennsylvania, August 1, 1975.

(11) For stations located in Maryland, District of Columbia, Virginia, and West Virginia, October 1, 1975.

(12) For stations located in North Carolina and South Carolina, December 1, 1975.

(13) For stations located in Florida, Puerto Rico, and Virgin Islands, February 1, 1976.

(14) For stations located in Alabama and Georgia, April 1, 1976.

(15) For stations located in Arkansas, Louisiana, and Mississippi, June 1, 1976.

of the first day of the last full calendar month of the expiring license term (47 CFR 1.580(i) and 1.516(e)). Thus, for example, the license of a television station located in Pennsylvania would ordinarily expire on August 1, 1975; the renewal application would be filed on or before April 1, 1975 and a petition to deny would have to be filed on or before July 1, 1975. There are two exceptions to the foregoing. First, the Commission may previously have issued a short-term license to the station in question; the license would in that case expire on a date specified by the Commission in its order making the short-term grant rather than on the date specified in footnote 9. Second, if the renewal application is filed late, the deadline for filing a petition to deny is the 90th day after the Commission has given public notice that the late filed application has been accepted for filing.

35. The applicant may file an opposition to your petition to deny within 30 days after the petition is filed. You may file a reply to the opposition within 20 days after the opposition is due or within 20 days after the opposition is filed, whichever is longer. Note that the papers must reach the Commission within these periods. Reasonable requests for extensions of time will be granted if both parties consent or upon a showing of good cause. Note that requirements applicable to the petition to deny (service, supporting affidavits, etc.) also apply to the opposition and the reply. The purpose of a reply pleading is to respond to points made in the opposition pleading; it is not intended to give a petitioner an opportunity to present new matters. Also, pursuant to § 1.45(c) of the Commission rules (47 CFR 1.45(c)), additional pleadings may not be filed unless specifically requested and authorized by the Commission.

36. Questions raised in a petition to deny are dealt with on their merits in conjunction with action on the application in an opinion issued by the Commission (that is, by the Commissioners and not by the staff under delegated authority). The Commission will either deny your petition and grant the application, deny your petition and set the application for hearing on issues other than those you have raised, or grant your petition and set the application for hearing on some or all of the issues you have raised. If the application is granted, you may petition for reconsideration (see 47 U.S.C. 405; 47 CFR 1.106) or appeal to the U.S. Court of Appeals for the District of Columbia Circuit (see 47 U.S.C. 402(b)(6)). If a hearing is ordered and you are not named as a party, you may petition for reconsideration or (if you have previously made clear your wish to participate as a party) you may appeal; you may also file a petition to intervene (see 47 U.S.C. 309(e); 47 CFR 1.223) or seek participation as a witness. See paragraph 39 below.

37. If you file a petition to deny but do not intend to participate as a party

---

(16) For stations located in Tennessee, Kentucky, and Indiana, August 1, 1976.
(17) For stations located in Ohio and Michigan, October 1, 1976.
(18) For stations located in Illinois and Wisconsin, December 1, 1976.
For the expiration date of licenses of other classes of broadcast stations (for example, television booster and translator stations), see 47 CFR 74.15.

to a hearing on the application, you should so advise the Commission in your petition. Otherwise, it will be assumed that you are asserting the right to participate and offering to prove the allegations set out in your petition; and if a hearing is ordered and you have established your right to participate, you will be named as a party and may be assigned the burden of proceeding with the introduction of evidence and the burden of proof on the issues raised in your petition. You will be expected to appear at the hearing, present evidence, and proceed in other respects as a party. You are not required to retain an attorney. However, it is most advisable that you do so, as it is unlikely that you will be able to participate effectively without the assistance of counsel. If you do intend to retain counsel, it is advisable to do so at an early date, so as to have his assistance in preparing the petition to deny.

Participation in a hearing proceeding

38. The rules governing hearing proceedings are set out in Subpart B of Part 1 of Title 47 of the Code of Federal Regulations. If you do not retain an attorney, it is important that you familiarize yourself thoroughly with those rules. It is also important that you become familiar with Subpart A, the general rules of practice and procedure, many of which apply in hearing proceedings. Though the following outline of the procedural stages of a hearing proceeding may be helpful, effective participation will require a more detailed knowledge of the rules.

39. When the Commission determines that a hearing should be held, it issues an order (called a designation order) specifying the issues upon which evidence will be received and naming known parties in interest as parties to the proceeding. Shortly thereafter, the Chief Administrative Law Judge issues an order naming a presiding officer, setting a time and place for an initial prehearing conference, and specifying the place of the hearing and the date for its commencement. If you are named as a party, and wish to participate, you should, within 20 days after the designation order is mailed, file a notice of appearance stating that you will appear at the hearing. See 47 CFR 1.221. This notice and (except as otherwise expressly provided) all papers subsequently filed must be served on all other parties to the proceeding. See 47 CFR 1.47 and 1.211; see also, the rules governing ex parte presentations, 47 CFR 1.1201-1.1251. The notice of appearance should list the address at which you wish other parties to serve papers on you. If you are not named as a party, you may petition to intervene. See 47 CFR 1.223. To intervene as of right, you must show that you are a party in interest (see paragraph 30 above) and must file the petition within 30 days after the designation order is published in the *Federal Register*. It is not necessary for you to

have participated in earlier stages of the proceeding. If the petition is filed late or if it fails to show that petitioner is a party in interest, his intervention as a party lies within the discretion of the presiding officer. You may appeal to the Review Board, as a matter of right, from an order denying your petition to intervene. See 47 CFR 1.301(a)(1). (For a description of the Review Board and its functions, see 47 CFR 0.361 and 0.365.) If the petition is denied, the person objecting may nevertheless request Commission counsel to call him as a witness. He may request other parties to the proceeding to call him as a witness. And, if these measures fail, he may appear at the hearing and ask that the presiding officer allow him to testify. If he shows that his testimony will be relevant, material, and competent, he will be allowed to testify. See 47 CFR 1.225(b). A person who has been permitted to participate as a party may move before the Chief Administrative Law Judge to hold the hearing in the community where the station is located, rather than in the District of Columbia. Action on that request lies within the discretion of the Chief Administrative Law Judge. Subject to budgetary limitations, hearings are held in the local community when it appears that there will be a sizable number of witnesses who live in that community.

40. If you are permitted to participate as a party, a number of new rights accrue to you. If you are dissatisfied with the issues listed by the Commission, you may petition for the addition or deletion of an issue or for the modification of those which are listed. See 47 CFR 1.229. Such petitions are acted on by the Review Board. You may utilize procedures for the discovery of facts relevant to the proceeding. See 47 CFR 1.311-1.325. You may file pleadings and oppose or support any motion or petition filed by any other party to the proceeding. You may ask the presiding officer to issue subpenas requiring the attendance of witnesses or the production of documents at the hearing. See 47 CFR 1.331-1.340. You may examine witnesses, object to the introduction of evidence, and cross-examine the witnesses of other parties. You are expected to be present at the hearing (either personally or by attorney) and to participate in the proceedings. If you subpena witnesses, you are responsible for payment of witness fees.

41. About 4 weeks after the proceeding is designated for hearing, the presiding officer holds an initial prehearing conference. See 47 CFR 1.248. Additional conferences may be held. At such conferences, the presiding officer works with counsel for the parties to devise a schedule for the completion of procedures (such as discovery and summary decision procedures) to be followed by counsel and to settle as many matters as possible before the evidentiary hearing. Counsel may, for example, enter into stipulations regarding undisputed facts and reach agreement as to the scope of the issues set for hearing. They may also agree as to the authenticity of exhibits and as to the qualifications of expert witnesses. Such agreement aids counsel in the preparation of his case, allowing him to concentrate on matters which remain in dispute. It also saves the time and expense which would otherwise be involved in establishing the facts agreed upon by testimony at the hearing. By the time you attend the conference, you

should have a clear understanding of what you intend to prove, how (by what witnesses and exhibits) you intend to prove it, and of any collateral procedures you intend to follow, so that you can make full use of the prehearing technique.

42. A Commission hearing is much like a trial in a civil case in a court of law. Instead of a judge, there is a presiding officer, usually one of the Commission's administrative law judges. The administrative law judge is independent of the remainder of the agency and, with minor exceptions, his sole function is to preside over and initially decide Commission hearing proceedings. The Commission's Broadcast Bureau usually participates as a party to the proceeding, on behalf of the public, and is represented at the hearing by an attorney from its Hearing Division. At the hearing proper, witnesses testify under oath, are examined and cross-examined, and a transcript is made of their testimony; exhibits are offered in evidence; the rules of evidence are applied; and various motions are made, argued, and acted on. The transcript of testimony and exhibits, together with all papers and requests filed in the proceeding, constitute the exclusive record for decision.

43. When the testimony of all witnesses has been heard, the presiding officer closes the record (47 CFR 1.258) and certifies the transcript and exhibits as to identity (47 CFR 1.260). Parties are afforded an opportunity to move for correction of the transcript (47 CFR 1.261) and to file proposed findings of fact and conclusions of law, which may be supported by a brief (47 CFR 1.263, 1.264). The presiding officer then prepares and issues an initial decision, which becomes effective 50 days after its issuance unless it is appealed by a party or reviewed by the Commission on its own motion (47 CFR 1.267 and 1.277(d)).

44. If you are dissatisfied with the initial decision you may, within 30 days, file exceptions to the decision, which may be accompanied by a brief. See 47 CFR 1.271–1.279. You may also, within this period, file a statement supporting the initial decision. Reply briefs may be filed within 10 days. In cases involving the revocation or renewal of a broadcast station license, the decision is reviewed by the Commission. In other broadcast cases, unless the Commission specifies otherwise, the decision is reviewed by the Review Board (47 CFR 0.365(a)). After exceptions have been filed, the parties may request an opportunity for oral argument before the Commission or the Review Board, as the case may be (47 CFR 1.277). Such requests are ordinarily granted. Thereafter the Commission (or the Board) issues a final decision (47 CFR 1.282). Within 30 days after release of a final Commission decision, you may petition for reconsideration (47 U.S.C. 405; 47 CFR 1.106) or file a notice of appeal with the U.S. Court of Appeals for the District of Columbia Circuit (47 U.S.C. 402(b)). In the case of a Review Board decision, you may, within 30 days, file either a petition for reconsideration by the Board or an application for review of the decision by the Commission. See 47 U.S.C. 155(d); 47 CFR 1.101, 1.102, 1.104, 1.106, 1.113, 1.115, and 1.117. You must seek Commission review of a Board decision before seeking judicial review.

RULE MAKING

45. A rule is similar to a law. It is a statement of policy to be applied generally in the future. A rule making proceeding is the process, required by law, through which the Commission seeks information and ideas from interested persons, concerning a particular rule or rule amendment, which will aid it in making a sound policy judgment. There are other ways, when a rule is not under consideration, in which the Commission seeks information needed to meet its regulatory responsibilities. It may issue a Notice of Inquiry, in which interested persons are asked to furnish information on a given matter and their views as to whether and how the Commission should deal with it. If needed information cannot be obtained in proceedings on a Notice of Inquiry, the Commission can order an investigatory hearing, in which witnesses and records can be subpenaed. If the information obtained indicates that rules should be adopted, the Commission then initiates a rule making proceeding.

Petition for rule making

46. The principal rules relating to broadcast matters are set out in the rules and regulations of the Commission as Subpart D of Part 1, Part 73 and Part 74. Other provisions relating to broadcasting will be found in Parts 0 and 1. If you think that any of these rules should be changed or that new rules relating to broadcasting should be adopted by the Commission, you are entitled to file a petition for rule making. 5 U.S.C. 553(e); 47 CFR 1.401-1.407. No specific form is required for such a petition, but it should be captioned "Petition for Rule Making" to make it clear that you regard your proposal as more than a casual suggestion. An original and 14 copies of the petition and all other pleadings in rule making matters should be filed.

47. The petition "shall set forth the text or substance of the proposed rule * * * together with views, arguments and data deemed to support the action requested * * *." 47 CFR 1.401(c). This is important, for unless statements supporting or opposing your proposal are filed, you are afforded no further opportunity, prior to Commission action on the petition, to explain or justify your proposal.

48. When a petition for rule making is received, it is given a file number (such as RM-1000) and public notice of its filing is given. The public notice briefly describes the proposal and invites interested persons to file statements supporting or opposing it. Statements must be filed within 30 days after the notice is issued and must be served on the petitioner, who may reply to such a

statement within 15 days after it is filed. The reply must be served on the person who filed the statement to which the reply is directed.

49. If a petition for rule making is repetitive or moot or for other reasons plainly does not warrant consideration by the Commission, it can be dismissed or denied by the Chief of the Broadcast Bureau. See 47 CFR 0.280(bb). In that event, petitioner may file an application for review of the Bureau Chief's action by the Commission. See 47 CFR 1.115. In most cases, however, the petition for rule making is acted on by the Commission. Action is ordinarily deferred pending passage of the time for filing statements and replies. Where the changes proposed obviously have (or lack) merit, however, action may be taken without waiting for the submission of statements or replies. In acting on a petition for rule making, the Commission will issue (1) an order amending the rules, as proposed or modified, or (2) a notice of rule making proposing amendment of the rules, as proposed or modified, or (3) an order denying the petition. In the event of adverse action by the Commission, you may petition for reconsideration (47 CFR 1.106).

Rule making without prior notice and public procedure

50. Rule making proceedings are conducted under section 4 of the Administrative Procedure Act, 5 U.S.C. 553. See also, 47 CFR 1.411–1.427. Section 4 provides that an agency may make rules without prior notice and public procedure in any of the following circumstances:

(a)   Where the subject matter involves a military or foreign affairs function of the United States.

(b)   Where the subject matter relates to agency management or personnel or to public property, loans, grants, benefits, or contracts.

(c)   Where the rules made are interpretative rules, general statements of policy, or rules of agency organization, procedure or practice.

(d)   Where the agency for good cause finds (and incorporates the finding and a brief statement of reasons therefore in the rules issued) that notice and public procedure are impracticable, unnecessary, or contrary to the public interest.

The rules of organization practice and procedure (47 CFR Parts 0 and 1) are rather frequently amended, often without prior notice and public procedure. However, prior public comment is requested if the matters involved are particularly significant or there is doubt or controversy concerning the wisdom, precise effect, or details of the rule. Where notice is omitted pursuant to (d) above, it is in circumstances where the effect of the rule could be undermined by actions taken during the period allowed for comment, where the rule merely repeats the provisions of a statute, where the provisions of the rule are beneficial to all and there is no reason to expect unfavorable public comment, or in other similar circumstances constituting good cause under the statute. The other exceptions to the requirement of prior notice are of lesser importance.

51. If you are dissatisfied with a rule made by the Commission without prior notice, you may file a petition for reconsideration. You may also request that the effect of the rule be stayed pending action on your petition. All orders changing the Commission's rules are published in the *Federal Register,* and the 30-day period for filing the petition for reconsideration runs from the date of publication.

Rule making with prior notice and public procedure

52. Except in circumstances listed in paragraph 50 above, the Commission is required to give prior notice and to afford an opportunity for public comment before making or changing a rule. If you have something to say concerning the proposed rule, you are entitled to file comments. Notice is given by issuance of a notice of proposed rule making, and by publishing that notice in the *Federal Register.* The text of the proposed rule is usually set out in the notice. On occasion, however, the notice will instead indicate the subject involved and the result intended, leaving the precise method for obtaining that result to a later stage of the proceeding following consideration of public comment. Whether or not the text is set out, the notice contains an explanation of the proposed rule and a statement both as to the Commission's reasons for proposing the rule and its authority to adopt it. The notice also lists the dates by which comments and reply comments should be submitted and states whether there are limitations on Commission consideration of nonrecord communications concerning the proceeding.[10] Requests for extension of the time allowed for filing comments and reply comments may be filed.

53. Rule making proceedings are relatively informal. When a notice of proposed rule making is issued, the proceeding is given a docket number (such as Docket No. 15000). Papers relating to the proceeding are placed in a docket file bearing this number. This file is available for inspection in the Commission's Public Reference Room in Washington, D.C. Because comments and reply comments are sometimes filed by hundreds of persons, the Commission does not require that copies be served on others. To find out what others have said in their comments, you may inspect the docket file or arrange with a private firm

---

[10] In rule making proceedings which involve "conflicting private claims to a valuable privilege," fairness precludes nonrecord communication between Commission personnel involved in making a decision and interested persons concerning the merits of the proceeding. Sangamon Valley Television Corp. v. F.C.C., 269 F.2d 221, 224. In such proceedings, limitations on communication with the Commission are stated in the notice of proposed rule making.

(for a fee) to furnish copies of comments filed in the proceeding. See 47 CFR 0.465. Often, those who have filed comments will furnish copies as a courtesy upon request. All papers placed in the docket file are considered by the Commission before taking final action in the proceeding. To assure that your views are placed in the docket file and considered by the Commission, all comments, pleadings, and correspondence relating to the proceeding should (in the caption or otherwise) show the docket number.

54. The rules require that an original and 14 copies of comments be filed, that they be typed, doubled-spaced, timely filed, and so forth. See, e.g., 47 CFR 1.419. As a practical matter, it is important for you to meet these requirements. The 14 copies are needed for distribution to Commissioners and members of the staff involved in making a decision. If you submit only an original, it will be placed in or associated with the docket file and considered by the staff member assigned to write a decision but probably will not be seen by other Commission officials. Handwritten communications are also placed in the docket file and so considered. You should appreciate, however, that you are more likely to get your point of view across to the persons making the decision if your presentation is typewritten. In making a rule, the Commission is interested in getting as much information and the best thinking possible from the public before making a decision and does not reject comments on narrow technical grounds. However, failure to comply with the filing requirements adversely affects your right to have the comments considered and to complain if they do not receive what you consider to be full consideration.

55. The comments should explain who you are and what your interest is. They should recite the facts and authority which support your position. They should not ignore facts and authorities which tend to support a different position, but should deal with them and demonstrate that the public interest requires that the matter be resolved as you proposed. They should be carefully worded and well organized and free of exaggeration or vituperative comment. They should be explicit. If the details of the proposed rule or one of several provisions only are objectionable, this should be made clear. Counterproposals may be submitted. If the rule would be acceptable only with certain safeguards, these should be spelled out, with the reasons why they are needed.

56. In rule making proceedings, the Commission's responsibility is to make a policy judgment and, in making that judgment, to obtain and consider comments filed in the proceeding. It may tap other sources of information. Unless otherwise expressly stated in the notice,[11] staff members working on the proceeding are generally prepared to meet with and discuss the proposed rule with anyone who is sufficiently interested. They may initiate correspondence or organize meetings to further develop pertinent information and ideas. They will utilize information available in the Commission's files and draw upon the knowl-

---

[11] See footnote 10 above.

edge and experience of other Commission personnel or of other Government agencies. Generally, the Commission hears oral argument only in rule making proceedings involving policy decisions of the greatest importance. However, you may request the Commission to hear argument in any proceeding, and that request will be considered and ruled upon. When argument is heard, interested persons appear before the Commissioners, orally present their views, and are questioned by the Commissioners. Other devices, such as panel discussions, have, on occasion, been used to further develop the information and ideas presented. An evidentiary hearing is not usual in rule making proceedings. Nevertheless, if you think the circumstances require an evidentiary hearing, you are entitled to ask that one be held.

57. After comments and reply comments and the record of oral argument (if any) have been reviewed, a policy judgment is made and a document announcing and explaining it is issued. There are a number of possibilities. The proposed rules may be adopted, with or without changes. They may be adopted in part and, in that event, further comment may be requested on portions of the proceeding which remain. The Commission may decide that no rules should be adopted or that inadequate information has been obtained and, thus, either terminate the proceeding or issue a further notice of proposed rule making requesting additional comment on particular matters. If final action as to all or any part of the proceeding is taken, the final action taken is subject to reconsideration (47 U.S.C. 405).

Petition for waiver of a rule

58. Except as they implement mandatory statutory provisions, all of the Commission's rules are subject to waiver, 47 CFR 1.3. If there is something the rules prohibit which you wish to do, or if there is something the rules require which you do not wish to do, you may petition for waiver of the rules in question. The petition must contain a showing sufficient to convince the Commission that waiver is justified on public interest grounds (that is, the public interest would be served by not applying the rule in a particular situation) or, in some instances, on grounds of hardship or undue burden.

PUBLIC INSPECTION OF STATION DOCUMENTS

59. *Local public inspection file.* All radio and television stations maintain a local public inspection file which contains materials specified in 47 CFR 1.526. The file, which is available for public inspection at any time during regular busi-

ness hours, is usually maintained at the main studio of the station, but the rules permit it to be located at any other publicly accessible place, such as a public registry for documents or an attorney's office. A prior appointment to examine the file is not required, but may prove of mutual benefit to the station and the inspecting party.

60. The local public inspection files of all radio and television stations include recent renewal applications (FCC-Form 303), ownership reports (FCC-Form 323), various reports regarding broadcasts by candidates for public office, annual employment reports (FCC-Form 395), letters received from members of the public concerning operation of the station (see 47 CFR 73.1202(f)), and a copy of this Manual. In addition, the local public inspection files of commercial television stations also include annual programing reports (FCC-Form 303-A) and annual listings of what the licensee believes to have been some of the significant problems and needs of the area served by the station during the preceding twelve months. All television licensees are required to make the materials in their local public inspection files available for machine reproduction, providing the requesting party pays any reasonable costs incurred in producing machine copies.

61. *Public inspection of television station program logs.* In response to formal requests from various citizen groups, the Commission's rules were amended in March 1974 to require television stations to make their program logs available for public inspection under certain circumstances. The contents of these logs are specified. See 47 CFR 73.112. It should be emphasized that because the logs are intended primarily to serve Commission needs, the information they contain is limited and is essentially statistical in nature. Although, for example, the logs include the title and type (that is, the program category such as news, entertainment, etc.) of the various programs carried by the station, and the times these programs were broadcast, the logging rules do not require descriptions of the actual content of individual programs nor a listing of program participants or issues discussed. Despite their limitations, however, the logs do contain relevant information concerning station programing, including commercial practices.

62. Television station program logs are available upon request for public inspection and reproduction at a location convenient and accessible for the residents of the community to which the station is licensed. All such requests for inspection are subject to the following procedural requirements set forth in 47 CFR 73.674:

(1)   Parties wishing to inspect the logs shall make a prior appointment with the licensee and, at that time, identify themselves by name and address; identify the organization they represent, if any; and state the general purpose of the examination.

(2)   Inspection of the logs shall take place at the station or at such other convenient and accessible location as may be specified by the licensee. The licensee, at its option, may make an exact copy available in lieu of the original program logs.

(3) Machine copies of the logs shall be made available upon request, provided the party making the request shall pay the reasonable costs of machine reproduction.

(4) An inspecting party shall have a reasonable time to examine the program logs. If examination is requested beyond a reasonable time, the licensee may condition such further inspection upon the inspecting party's willingness either to assume the expense of machine duplication of the logs or to reimburse the licensee for any reasonable expense incurred if supervision of continued examination of the original logs is deemed necessary.

(5) No log need be made available for public inspection until 45 days have elapsed from the day covered by the log in question.

63. 47 CFR 73.674 provides that the licensee may refuse to permit public inspection of the program logs where good cause exists. When it included this provision in its 1974 amendments to 47 CFR 73.674, the Commission indicated that lacking experience with the operation of public inspection of program logs, it was in no position to describe all situations in which there would be good cause for refusing to permit access. Two illustrations which it did offer, however, were (1) a request from a financial competitor of the station or of the station's advertisers which was based solely on competitive considerations and (2) a situation in which the request represented an attempt at harassment. Harassment would exist if the primary goal of requesting examination of the logs was the disruption of station operation or the creation of an annoyance. If, for example, an inspecting party or parties situated themselves in the inspection location hour after hour, day after day, refusing to indicate which, if any, logs it wished to have duplicated, and refusing to engage in dialogue with the licensee regarding further inspection, it would not be inappropriate to characterize that inspection as an attempt at harassment.

64. While the probability of misuse and abuse of requests to inspect program logs and the danger of harassment was not sufficient to cause the Commission to refrain from making the logs generally available, the provision regarding refusal of access for good cause was inserted in amended 47 CFR 73.674 as a recognition of legitimate concerns of broadcasters. In the rare case where an unresolved dispute arises between members of the public and a station regarding whether good cause exists for not making the logs available, the dispute can, of course, be brought to the Commission for resolution.

REFERENCE MATERIALS

65. Laws relating to communications have been compiled in Title 47 of the United States Code, which is available in most libraries. The basic law under which the Commission operates is the Communications Act of 1934, as amended,

47 U.S.C. 151–609. A pamphlet containing the Communications Act, the Administrative Procedure Act, and other statutory materials pertaining to communications may be purchased from the Superintendent of Documents, U.S. Government Printing Office, Washington, D.C. 20402. Ask for the "The Communications Act of 1934" which includes all changes in the Act through January 1969.

66. The Commission's rules and regulations have been compiled in Chapter I of Title 47 of the Code of Federal Regulations, which is available in many libraries. Chapter I is divided into four subchapters, which are printed in separate volumes, which may be purchased separately from the Superintendent of Documents. Those wishing to participate in broadcast matters will need two of these volumes:

Subchapter A–General
Subchapter C–Broadcast Radio Services

These volumes are revised annually.

67. The Commission's rules may also be purchased from the Superintendent of Documents in looseleaf form on a subscription basis. The rules are divided into 10 volumes, each containing several related parts. Each volume may be purchased separately. The purchase price includes a subscription to replacement pages reflecting changes in the rules until such time as the volume is revised. Those wishing to participate in broadcast matters will need two of these volumes:

Volume I–containing Parts 0, 1, 13, 17, and 19
Volume III–containing Parts 73, 74, 76, and 78

68. All documents adopted by the Commission which have precedential or historical significance are published in the FCC reports, which are available in some libraries. The reports are usually published weekly in pamphlet form. The pamphlets are available from the Superintendent of Documents on a subscription basis and are subsequently compiled and published in bound volumes.

69. A list of the Commission's printed publications (with prices) will be furnished by the Commission on request.

43

The WEFM Case

Citizens Committee to Save WEFM v.

Federal Communications Commission*

506 F.2d 246 (D.C. Cir.) (en banc)

October 4, 1974

Citizens groups have met with considerable success in their attempts to preserve radio formats threatened with extinction as a
result of a change of station ownership. A series of court decisions
starting in 1970 required the FCC to conduct hearings in such
cases to determine if the threatened format was unique and economically viable. The Court of Appeals reasoned that under the
Communications Act, minority programming preferences must be
taken into account by the FCC when allocating the public airwaves "for the greatest good of the greatest number" [*Citizens
Committee to Preserve the Voice of the Arts in Atlanta* v. *FCC*,
436 F.2d 263, 269 (D.C. Cir. 1970)].

The *WEFM* decision reprinted here is a most significant ruling.
It was decided on rehearing by the District of Columbia Court of
Appeals *en banc*, that is, by all the circuit judges instead of the
usual panel of three. Judge McGowan's opinion for the court
carefully reviews prior format change case law and the facts of
the WEFM controversy before remanding the case to the FCC for
hearing on specified issues. Part III of the opinion is especially
interesting both for what it says and for the manner in which law
and policy are intertwined. (Chief Judge Bazelon, who concurred
in the result of this decision, issued a long exegesis on the First
Amendment matters the majority opinion declined to treat. Al-

*Reprinted with the permission of West Publishing Company.

though it is omitted below, some of its concerns are expressed in the dissents of Judges Robb and MacKinnon that follow the court's opinion.)

In 1976, while the WEFM case was still being heard before the FCC, the Commission issued a policy statement declaring its intention not to consider format changes in the future and to rely instead on unregulated competitive forces to achieve programming diversity in the public interest: ". . . the marketplace is the best way to allocate entertainment formats in radio . . ." [*Development of Policy re: Changes in the Entertainment Formats of Broadcast Stations*, 60 FCC 2d 858, 863 (1976).] Implementation of this policy was delayed pending disposition of petitions for reconsideration [66 FCC 2d 78 (1977)] and appellate proceedings [*WNCN Listeners Guild* v. *FCC*, 610 F. 2d 838 (D.C. Cir. 1979) (*en banc*)] that will ultimately be decided by the Supreme Court. For the time being, at least, the *WEFM* decision remains the law of the land. At the heart of the matter's resolution is the fundamental question of how much deference is to be accorded the FCC in formulating and implementing public policy in broadcasting when the Court of Appeals holds that the law prohibits such policy.

Related Reading: 94, 103, 118, 160, 162, 166, 201, 235.

McGowan, Circuit Judge:

This is a statutory review proceeding involving the Federal Communications Commission. It has been thought appropriate for *en banc* consideration because it presents important questions with respect to the utilization of the publicly-owned airwaves in such manner as to serve the divergent interests and tastes of the largest possible number of their owners. A Citizens Committee was organized to contest the assignment of the license of radio station WEFM (FM), Chicago, Illinois, by Zenith Radio Corporation to GCC Communications of Chicago, Inc. The FCC denied the Committee's petition to deny the application to transfer the license or, alternatively, to conduct a hearing on certain questions. 38 FCC 2d 838; 40 FCC 2d 223 (on reconsideration).

The case was originally heard and decided by a division of the court which affirmed the action of the Commission in authorizing the assignment of the license in issue without a hearing. Judge Fahy dissented from this disposition in an opinion which, after noting that (1) the statute (47 U.S.C. § 309(e)) requires hearings to resolve factual disputes which are substantial and material and (2) the Commission in approving the assignment had relied materially and substantially upon alleged financial losses suffered by the assignor, expressed agreement with the dissenting Commissioner that "the attribution of such financial losses to the assignor's classical musical format was a question which could not be answered without further investigation," especially since the assignor "continued to use the station to advertise its own manufactured products."

We find that the Committee has raised substantial and material questions necessitating a hearing before final disposition of the transfer application, and that the present record is inadequate to support the Commission's purported public interest finding.[1] The orders of the Commission are set aside and the case remanded for further proceedings consistent herewith.

I

Since it was first licensed to Zenith in 1940, WEFM's format has always been one of classical music. For twenty-five years Zenith operated the station on an entirely non-commercial basis, at the same time using the station as a developmental adjunct to, and laboratory for, its FM receiver manufacturing business. As such, WEFM has had a distinguished history, being the first Chicago station to broadcast in high-fidelity (1953), the pioneer in stereophonic broadcasting (1959), the source of experiments leading to the FCC's national standards for multiplex (stereo) operations (1961), and the first station in its area to introduce the dual polarization antenna, which radiates both horizontal and vertical signals (1966).

The increased costs that Zenith incurred with its 1966 expansion of WEFM's studio and technical facilities caused the company for the first time "to seek advertising support" for its operations.[2] Both the degree of Zenith's commitment to commercial operation, and the relevance of commercial benefits realized by it over and above the advertising revenues received, remain the subject of dispute, but, according to the Commission, statements filed with it show that advertising income failed to cover costs in each succeeding year.

In March, 1972, Zenith contracted to sell WEFM to GCC, a corporation organized for the purpose of the purchase, for $1,000,000.[3] Thereafter Zenith

---

[1] 47 U.S.C. § 310(b) provides as follows:
No construction permit or station license, or any rights thereunder, shall be transferred, assigned, or disposed of in any manner, voluntarily or involuntarily, directly or indirectly, or by transfer of control of any corporation holding such permit or license, to any person except upon application to the Commission *and upon finding by the Commission that the public interest, convenience, and necessity will be served thereby.* Any such application shall be disposed of as if the proposed transferee or assignee were making application under section 308 of this title for the permit or license in question; but in acting thereon the Commission may not consider whether the public interest, convenience, and necessity might be served by the transfer, assignment, or disposal of the permit or license to a person other than the proposed transferee or assignee. (Emphasis supplied.)

[2] Statement of Assignor's Purpose in Requesting Assignment of the License of WEFM, J.A. 240.

[3] GCC is a subsidiary of General Cinema Corporation, which controls several stations in other cities.

and GCC applied to the FCC for assignment of the license of WEFM to GCC. In the application GCC proposed to "present a format of contemporary music approximately 70% of the time," twenty-four hours a day. In this manner, it was said, "[t]he applicant will contribute to the overall diversity of program services in the Chicago area."[4]

Notice of the proposed assignment was broadcast over WEFM once daily for four consecutive days and published four times in one of Chicago's four daily newspapers. The notice identified the type of application filed, the parties (assignor and assignee) thereto, the officers and directors of each, and stated that the application was available for inspection at Zenith's offices. No mention of the proposed format change was required, and none was made. 47 C.F.R. § 1.580 (d).

In its petition filed with the FCC, the Committee related that the 7.5 million residents of the metropolitan area served by WEFM received classical music from no AM stations and, in the greater part of the service area, from only one other FM station, WFMT-FM.[5] It alleged that the program formats of these stations varied somewhat, but did not claim that any part of the service area would be left entirely without a classical music station.[6] The Committee asserted that it had received hundreds of letters in opposition to the sale, and that the FCC had received over 1,000 such letters. It detailed the financial relations between General Cinema Corporation and GCC,[7] alleged that General Cinema had lost $1 million from its five other radio operations the prior year, and pointed out that there was "no indication that Zenith's management claiming losses prior to its 1970 [license] renewal instituted measures designed to produce such profit by increasing its advertising time from 2½ minutes per hour to 5 or 6 minutes," presumably standard in the industry, nor took any other step indicating that its claimed losses, which were also doubted by the Committee, occurred despite efforts to operate WEFM on a truly commercial basis. The Committee also pointed out that in its 1970 license renewal application, approved by the FCC in 1971 to run through 1973, Zenith had represented that continuation of WEFM's classical music format was in the public interest and that it would be continued.

---

[4] As explained in GCC's later opposition to the petition to deny, "contemporary" music is rock music. J.A. 91. According to GCC's own account (J.A. 343), however, five of the sixty-one stations serving the Chicago area play rock, progressive rock, or jazz rock music, while another eight concentrate on "pop," or "pop contemporary" music. Ascertainment of Community Interests, Needs and Problems 70–73, J.A. 253–256.

[5] Part of the area is also served by WNIB. GCC has proposed to give the classical music library acquired from WEFM, along with technical assistance and that station's call letters, to WNIB. WNIB would then, so it is said, be able to reach a larger portion of WEFM's service area with classical music.

[6] In its petition for rehearing in this court, the Committee refers to a study introduced as Exhibit 1A but not part of the administrative record, see note 12, infra, said to document "the degree to which WEFM has its own identity and audience loyalty" and makes unique contributions to diversity "significantly different from and in addition to those of WFMT."

[7] Alexander Tanger, who organized GCC, purchased all 500 of its common shares at $1.00 per share. The company then got an unsecured loan of $1,250,000 from General Cinema, of which $1,000,000 was to be used to purchase WEFM. General Cinema purchased GCC's preferred stock for $50,000.

On the basis of these and other allegations of fact, the Committee asserted that it had made out a case to deny the proposed assignment of WEFM's license on public interest grounds, or at least raised "substantial and material question[s] of fact," necessitating a hearing, 47 U.S.C. § 309(d), about the public interest in the proposed format change, Zenith's claimed losses, and GCC's qualifications as a licensee. It also challenged the constitutional adequacy of the public notice that the assignment was pending, and that a format change was contemplated.

Zenith and GCC filed oppositions to the Committee's petition. For its part, Zenith asserted facts intended to show the bona fides of its attempt to operate WEFM on a commercial basis and the amount of its losses, said to be almost $2 million over six years. GCC controverted the Committee's assertion that it had already decided to abandon WEFM's classical music format when it agreed to purchase the station, stating that "[i]t was only after the study of [community] needs [which the FCC requires of each license applicant] was completed and it was determined that the station would program for the young adults of the Chicago area that it was determined that a classical music format would not be consistent with programming directed to this age group." It also asserted that Chicago-area classical music broadcasting would be of overall higher quality when only WFMT and a strengthened WNIB shared that market than it could be with three stations competing for the classical music audience, but no facts were alleged to buttress either the premise that present service is poor or the likelihood that it would be improved by WEFM's format change.

The Committee's reply alleged that WNIB reached at most 15% of the area served by WEFM, further questioned Zenith's claimed losses, although it alleged no specific facts to the contrary,[8] and by a later amendment, challenged the validity of GCC's community leaders survey. The Committee wrote to some fifty of the 116 representative community leaders GCC had personally interviewed in order to ascertain community needs, issues, and problems. The Committee asked each interviewee whether he or she had in fact been personally approached by GCC, had been informed of any plans to change the WEFM format to rock music, and whether they approved of that change. Twenty-four persons responded, and eighteen of these responses were submitted to the FCC. J.A. 141–158. Five said they had been told there would be a format change, but only one recalled being told that the new format would be rock music. Nine said they were not informed that any change was contemplated, and one recalled being told specifically that no change was contemplated. As it happens, all eighteen personally disapproved of the change, some quite vehemently, and one had already protested the matter in letters to Zenith and the FCC.

While the application and petition to deny were pending before the FCC, the

[8] The Committee did allege that "WEFM is not operated by a separate corporation. Petitioners have not been apprised of, nor have they had the opportunity to examine, Zenith's records to determine the method under which Zenith allocates expenses and revenues or includes in Zenith's income revenues attributable to the use of Station WEFM by Zenith for advertising its products."

Committee on November 20, 1972, also filed a complaint requesting that WEFM be dedicated to classical music and cultural programming so long as any licensee willing to operate it for that purpose could be found. Zenith and GCC moved that the complaint be dismissed as a pleading not provided for in the FCC rules of practice.

On December 21, 1972 the FCC issued a Memorandum Opinion denying the Committee all relief and granting the assignment application without a hearing.[9] The FCC acknowledged that it had "received over 1,000 letters from Chicago area listeners protesting the proposed format change." It stated however, that "[t]he Chicago metropolitan area is served by two additional classical music stations," WFMT and WNIB, and that "[t]he issue here simply put is whether the assignee without a hearing can change the musical format of WEFM from classical music to a 'contemporary music' format where there are two other classical music stations serving Chicago and the station has been suffering continuous operating losses."

The Commission's resolution of this issue, however, depended not on the claimed losses, but rather on its view of its own role in cases where the format to be abandoned is not unique. In these circumstances, the FCC opined, competition among broadcasters will produce the optimal distribution of formats. Citizens Committee to Preserve the Voice of the Arts in Atlanta (WGKA-FM) v. FCC, 141 U.S. App. D.C. 109, 436 F.2d 263 (1970) (hereinafter *Citizens Committee of Atlanta*), where this court had held that abandonment of a unique format was "material" in gauging the public interest and that "substantial" factual questions therefore had to be resolved in a public hearing before the assignment application could be approved as being in the public interest, was thus distinguished. In the FCC's view, abandonment of a non-unique format is not a matter affected with the public interest but a business judgment within the licensee's discretion.[10]

To hamper the licensee's discretion in this area with the ominous threat of a hearing in a case like this would only serve to discourage licensees from choosing or experimenting with a format . . . . Accordingly, we find no basis to question the applicants [sic] discretion in the choice of format . . . . 38 FCC 2d at 846.

Finding the Committee's factual allegations concerning the assignee's financial structure and its parent's losses, and community leader opposition to a format change, to have been met adequately by the applicant's responses, the FCC

---

[9] The Opinion issued for four Commissioners; a fifth joined in the result, one did not participate, and one (Johnson) dissented in a separate opinion.

[10] In support of this position, the FCC quoted from and relied on its then recent decision in Twin States Broadcasting, 35 FCC 2d 969 (1972), which we later reversed and remanded for a hearing under the doctrine of Citizens Committee of Atlanta. Citizens Committee to Keep Progressive Rock v. FCC, 156 U.S. App. D.C. 16, 478 F.2d 926 (1973).

held that there were presented no material and substantial questions of fact on which to require a hearing.[11]

Commissioner Johnson in his dissenting opinion argued that *Citizens Committee of Atlanta* could not be confined to instances where a unique format is involved, since the assignee in that case had alleged that another classical music station did indeed serve much of Atlanta and yet this court held that a hearing was required to determine the actual availability of the asserted alternative. The touchstone of the public interest consideration in the prior case, he insisted, was the effect of the proposed change in lessening the diversity of radio service, not necessarily the total elimination of a particular format. He would thus have required a hearing on the degree, if any, to which the assignee's proposed assistance would strengthen WNIB's service, as well as on the causal relationship between Zenith's losses and WEFM's classical music format. In addition, he charged that the majority, by adhering to its doctrine of licensee discretion in format matters, was placing on the public the burden of establishing that the assignee's format change is *not* in the public interest, and abdicating its responsibility to determine whether a proposed format change that would decrease the diversity of formats available to an area "can possibly serve the public interest."

In petitioning the FCC for reconsideration, the Committee principally argued that the Commission had failed to consider the public interest in retaining WEFM as a distinctive cultural facility,[12] disregarded the fact that the limited service area of WNIB made it an inadequate substitute for WEFM, and resolved the dispute over Zenith's losses by relying on confidential financial reports not in the record and not disclosed to the Committee. On March 22, 1973, the FCC denied reconsideration in an opinion that reiterated its view of the agency's role in non-unique format cases, affirmed that two classical music stations would still remain after a change in WEFM's format,[13] and refused to question Zenith's

---

[11] The Commission was also of the view that "no substantial question exists regarding the WEFM operational losses," but was quick to add that the existence *vel non* of such a question was not critical to its decision inasmuch as financial viability was not a material consideration outside of the unique format context. 38 FCC 2d at 845 & n. 12.

The FCC rejected the Committee's attack on the adequacy of the public notice required to be given under its rules. With respect to the Committee's November 20 complaint requesting that station WEFM be dedicated to classical music as long as a qualified licensee could be found to operate it, the FCC relied on Section 310(b) of the Communications Act, 47 U.S.C. § 310(b), which prohibits it from considering whether the public interest might be served by assignment of a license to any person other than the proposed transferee before it, and reiterated its view that "the choice of a particular musical format is primarily a business judgment which a licensee or applicant must make in determining whether he can successfully operate the station and render service to his community of license." 38 FCC 2d at 848. Accordingly, it held that a hearing on the complaint was not warranted.

[12] The Committee offered to present at a hearing a study then in progress of the value of WEFM's programming in order to assist the FCC in weighing the public interest. *See* D. Bogue, The Radio Audience for Classical Music: The Case of WEFM, Chicago (Communication Laboratory, Community and Family Study Center, The University of Chicago, 1973).

[13] The dispute over WNIB's suitability as a substitute reflects a difference in premises as to the relevant service area. The FCC considered service to the city of license of primary

claimed losses since the Committee had alleged "no facts" casting doubt upon them.

Appended to the Commission's opinion on reconsideration was an opinion entitled "Additional Views of Chairman Burch In Which Commissioners Robert E. Lee, H. Rex Lee, Reid, Wiley, and Hooks Join." 40 FCC 2d at 230. Since Commissioners Reid and Wiley did not join in the opinion on reconsideration but only concurred in the result, these "Additional Views," to which six of the seven FCC Commissioners adhere, take on peculiar significance. They differ from the opinion itself in being broader than the facts of the particular case, but at the same time explain the underlying analysis on which the FCC's decision in this case was based. Indeed, they were offered because the Commissioners believed "that an explanation of the many policy considerations underlying our decision here is both appropriate and necessary." According to the six Commissioners, the starting point for discerning the appropriate FCC policy on format choice is in striking the "balance between the preservation of a free competitive broadcast system, on the one hand, and the reasonable restriction of that freedom inherent in the public interest standard provided in the Communications Act, on the other," *quoting* FCC v. Sanders Bros. Radio Station, 309 U.S. 470, 474, 60 S.Ct. 693, 84 L.Ed. 869 (1940). Thus:

The Commission has struck this balance by requiring licensees to conduct formal surveys to ascertain the need for certain types of nonentertainment programming, while allowing licensees wide discretion in the area of entertainment programming. Thus with respect to the provision of news, public affairs, and other informational services to the community, we have required that broadcasters conduct thorough surveys designed to assure familiarity with community problems and then develop programming responsive to those identified needs.[3] *In contrast, we have generally left entertainment programming decisions to the licensee or applicant's judgment and competitive marketplace forces.* As the Commission stated in its Programming Policy Statement, 25 Fed. Reg. 7293 (1960), "[o]ur view has been that the station's [entertainment] program format is a matter best left to the discretion of the licensee or applicants, since as a matter of public acceptance and of economic necessity he will tend to program to meet the preferences of his area and fill whatever void is left by the programming of other stations." (Emphasis added.)

[3]Primer on Ascertainment of Community Problems by Broadcast Applicants, 27 FCC 2d 650 (1971).

In further support of this policy, the Commissioners expressed their view of the unwisdom of "locking" a broadcaster in to a particular format, lest it have "the

---

importance, thereby mooting the relevance of the Committee's contention that WNIB serves at most 20% of WEFM's listener area, which has a radius from Chicago of about 100 miles. *See* Section II. B. 1, *infra.*

effect of lessening the likelihood that ['program formats appealing to minority tastes'] will be attempted in the first place."

II

The Committee presses several grounds for reversal of the FCC in this court. Its principal arguments are that (1) the FCC failed to, and could not on this record, determine whether the assignment and format change would be in the public interest; (2) substantial and material questions of fact necessitate a hearing; and (3) the public notice of the impending assignment required by the FCC is insufficient on due process criteria.[14] Before turning to these arguments *seriatim*, we explicate very briefly the statutory scheme to which they relate, as we have had so many occasions to do at greater length in the recent past, *e.g.,* Stone v. FCC, 151 U.S. App. D.C. 145, 466 F.2d 316, 321-323 (1972).

A. Analytic framework.

Under the Communications Act, 47 U.S.C. § 309(a), the Commission must determine, with respect to each license application, whether the public interest, convenience, and necessity would be served by granting the application, and, if it determines that it would be, must grant the application.[15] Subsection (d) (1) provides that any party in interest may petition the FCC to deny the application, and that such petition "shall contain specific allegations of fact sufficient to show . . . that a grant of the application would be prima facie inconsistent with [the public interest, convenience, and necessity]." 47 U.S.C. § 309 (d) (1). Subsection (d) (2) provides as follows:

[14] The Committee also challenges on First Amendment grounds Zenith's refusal, sanctioned by the FCC's interpretation of its own regulations, to grant the Committee's request that the question of Zenith's format change be discussed on WEFM. Our disposition of the case makes it unnecessary to reach this point, but, as the Committee notes, it is closely related to the notice problem and could likewise be usefully reconsidered by the FCC in this or another case. *See* note 34, *infra*. Neither do we reach the Committee's claim that the FCC failed to make a public interest finding *in haec verba,* as required in Joseph v. FCC, 131 U.S. App. D.C. 207, 404 F.2d 207 (1968), where the FCC acted without issuing the kind of opinion from which it could fairly be inferred that it had "taken a 'hard look' at the salient problems." Greater Boston Television Corp. v. FCC, 143 U.S. App. D.C. 383, 444 F.2d 841, 851 (1970), cert. denied, 403 U.S. 923, 91 S.Ct. 2229, 2233, 29 L. Ed. 2d 701 (1971).

[15] Assignment applications are subject to the same standards and treated in the same manner as initial license applications unless they do not entail a substantial change in ownership or control. 47 U.S.C. § 308, 309 (a); *see id.* § 309(c)(2)(B).

(2) If the Commission finds on the basis of the application, the pleadings filed, or other matters which it may officially notice that there are no substantial and material questions of fact *and* that a grant of the application would be consistent with [the public interest, convenience, and necessity], it shall make the grant, deny the petition, and issue a concise statement of the reasons for denying the petition, which statement shall dispose of all substantial issues raised by the petition. If a substantial and material question of fact is presented *or* if the Commission for any reason is unable to find that grant of the application would be consistent with [the public interest, convenience, and necessity], it shall proceed as provided in subsection (e) of this section. (Emphasis added.)

Subsection (e) governs the procedures for setting the application down for a hearing and notifying interested parties, and, in the case of issues presented by a petition to deny, authorizes the FCC to assign the burden of going forward and the burden of proof.

It is clear from the face of the statute that there are two situations in which a hearing is required before the FCC is either empowered or obliged to grant an application. The first, and the only one with which this court has previously dealt, arises when substantial and material questions of fact are raised by the petition to deny. The second occurs when the Commission is "for any reason" unable, on the basis of the application, pleadings, and officially noticeable matters, to make the requisite finding that the public interest would be served. It would seem that this situation might obtain with respect to a particular application regardless of whether anyone has intervened to oppose the application,[16] or indeed regardless of whether there are disputed fact issues as opposed to a simple need for more information. In any event, where, as here, there is a petitioner in opposition, there is certainly no barrier to its invoking both grounds in urging that a hearing is in order.

In this case, the two asserted grounds for requiring a hearing are intimately related, as an examination of the prior case law reveals. It is common ground among all hands, as it was between the majority and dissenting positions on the FCC, that the need for a hearing in this case turns largely on the reach of our decision in *Citizens Committee of Atlanta, supra,* which is factually like the instant case to a startling degree.

The Atlanta case also involved a proposed sale and abandonment of a classical music format. Public notice of the application produced an outcry against the format change, the FCC received a large number of protestant letters, and a citizens committee arose to intervene before the FCC in opposition. The FCC approved the application without a hearing. It relied upon the applicant's community leader survey to demonstrate informed support for the proposed change

---

[16]The FCC's failure to designate an unopposed application for a hearing *sua sponte* would not, of course, be reviewed, since there would be no party in interest to seek review.

in format, determined from the applicant's surveys that the proposed programming would be in the public interest, and "recited as a fact" that the transfer in ownership was a financial necessity. 436 F.2d at 266.

In the proceedings on reconsideration, the Atlanta committee questioned the significance of the community leader survey and alleged that the applicant had misrepresented the views of interviewees. The applicant responded with affidavits from the community leaders vouching for the accuracy of the applicant's summary of their views. Additionally, the applicant both proposed to air classical music for a portion of each evening in recognition of the expressed interest of the large number of protestants, and asserted that a station licensed to nearby Decatur, Georgia, "adequately served the daytime needs" of Atlantans. The FCC denied reconsideration, stating that "[T]he case here comes down to a choice of program formats—a choice which in the circumstances is one for the judgment of the licensee." It took to be the fact that the Decatur station served "a large portion of the City of Atlanta."

As in this case, in *Atlanta* one Commissioner (Cox) was of the view that a hearing was required. WGKA had had a classical music format for ten years; it was the only classical music station of the twenty licensed to Atlanta; and 16% of the area audience, according to the applicant's own survey, preferred that format. Commissioner Cox characterized the proposed sale and format change as an effort not to cut losses, which he disputed, but to maximize profits, and "did not see how the requisite public interest finding could be made short of the illumination afforded by a hearing."

This court reversed the FCC. We held that a format change involving abandonment of a unique format, protested by a significant sector of the community, is a matter material to the public interest and thus one on which a hearing must be held if there are substantial questions of fact. Accordingly, we remanded for a hearing to determine (1) the true financial situation of the assignor, (2) the actual views of the community leaders interviewed by the assignee, and (3) the degree to which the Decatur station provided Atlantans with classical music during the daytime.

The theory underlying the court's decision in *Citizens Committee of Atlanta* is that the FCC does have *some* responsibility, under its public interest mandate, for programming content. The Commission had forsworn any such role on the theory that, because it is not authorized to be a "national arbiter of taste," it must rely entirely on the licensee's discretion in matters of entertainment format. As we pointed out, however, the alternatives are not so stark. "The Commission is not dictating tastes when it seeks to discover what they presently are, and to consider what assignment of channels is feasible and fair in terms of their gratification." 436 F.2d at 272 n. 7. In discharging its public interest obligation, the court thought it to be within the Congressional contemplation that the FCC would seek to assure that, within technical and economic constraints, as many as possible of the various formats preferred by segments of the public would be provided.

Thus, if 16% of the populace wanted access to classical music on radio, the public interest would, *pro tanto,* be served by its continued availability *provided* that the format is not economically unviable in the particular market. If a proposed format change would introduce a new format for a larger segment of the public that is not presently being served, it could not be denied by giving disproportionate weight to the preference of the audience for classical music, but that was not the situation in Atlanta. We repeat what we said in 1970 (436 F.2d at 269):[17]

The Commission's point of departure seems to be that, if the programming contemplated by intervenor is shown to be favored by a significant number of the residents of Atlanta, then a determination to use that format is a judgment for the broadcaster to make, and not the Commission. Thus, so the argument proceeds, since only some 16% of the residents of Atlanta appear to prefer classical music, there can be no question that the public interest is served if the much larger number remaining are given what they say they like best.

In a democracy like ours this might, of course, make perfect sense if there were only one radio channel available to Atlanta. Its rationality becomes less plain when it is remembered that there are some 20 such channels, all owned by the people as a whole, classics lovers and rock enthusiasts alike. The "public interest, convenience, and necessity" can be served in the one case in a way that it cannot be in the other, since it is surely in the public interest, as that was conceived of by a Congress representative of all the people, for all major aspects of contemporary culture to be accommodated by the commonly-owned public resources whenever that is technically and economically feasible.

The Atlanta case was applied in two decisions of this court rendered immediately after the FCC's decision to deny reconsideration in the instant case. Citizens Committee to Keep Progressive Rock v. FCC, 156 U.S. App. D.C. 16, 478 F.2d 926 (1973), involved a proposed license assignment and format change (from "progressive rock" to "middle of the road" music) on a station that had experimented unsuccessfully with two formats and switched to yet a third during the pendency of the assignment application. We adhered to our holding in *Citizens Committee of Atlanta* that "the public has an interest in diversity of entertainment formats and therefore that format changes can be detrimental to the public interest. Consequently, in compliance with its statutory mandate to approve only those assignment applications which it finds to serve the public interest, convenience, and necessity, . . . the Commission must consider format changes and their effect upon the desired diversity." *Id.* at 928–929.

---

[17] As Judge Tamm has said, "We suspect, not altogether facetiously, that the Commission would be more than willing to limit the precedential effect of *Citizens Committee [of Atlanta]* to cases involving Atlanta classical music stations." Citizens Committee to Keep Progressive Rock v. FCC, 156 U.S. App. D.C. 16, 478 F.2d 926, 930 (1973).

Most format changes, we observed, do not diminish the diversity available, and "are thus left to the give and take of each market environment and the business judgment of the licensee." In that case, however, the format proposed to be abandoned was allegedly unique and its loss would affect diversity, thereby implicating the public interest in the change. Even that would have been of no moment were it shown that the endangered format was not viable economically, but affidavits from some station employees indicated that, while the station had not yet made a profit with the recently adopted format, it was "rapidly achieving financial viability." We clarified the "financial viability" constraint on the doctrine of the Atlanta case as follows (at p. 931):

The question is not whether the licensee is in such dire financial straits that an assignment should be granted, but whether the *format* is so economically unfeasible that an assignment encompassing a *format change* should be granted. (Emphasis in original.)

Once a proposed format change engenders "public grumbling [of] significant proportions," the causal relationship between format and finance must be established, and if that requires the resolution of substantial factual questions, as it did in that case, then a hearing must be held.

The result was different in Lakewood Broadcasting Service, Inc. v. FCC, 156 U.S. App. D.C. 9, 478 F.2d 919 (1973), decided the same day, because the FCC had properly found, in a "painstakingly thorough decision," that no substantial factual questions existed. The assignor's financial losses due to the all-news format were undisputed, as was the availability of a substantial amount of news programming on other area stations. What was really being challenged, we found, was "not the authenticity or accuracy of the [community needs] surveys, composites, or economic reports, but rather the inferences which the Commission may draw therefrom." *Id.* at 924. The question of the inferences and legal conclusions to be drawn from substantially undisputed facts, we held, is preeminently the province of the FCC and does not require the holding of an evidentiary hearing.[18] Nothing in *Citizens Committee of Atlanta* was to be understood to impose upon the Commission a hearing requirement where there are no substantial questions material to the public interest determination.[19]

The teaching of these decisions may be briefly summarized. There is a public interest in a diversity of broadcast entertainment formats. The disappearance of a distinctive format may deprive a significant segment of the public of the benefits of radio, at least at their first-preference level. When faced with a proposed

[18]*Accord,* Hartford Communications Committee v. FCC, 151 U.S. App. D.C. 354, 467 F.2d 408 (1972) ("format" cases distinguished on basis of FCC's inference that a proposed change involving greater emphasis on religious programming in an expanded overall schedule that did not reduce service of other types did not constitute a format change).

[19]For a full explication of the substantiality criterion, *see* Stone v. FCC, 151 U.S. App. D.C. 145, 466 F.2d 316, 321-323 (1972).

license assignment encompassing a format change, the FCC is obliged to determine whether the format to be lost is unique or otherwise serves a specialized audience that would feel its loss. If the endangered format is of this variety, then the FCC must affirmatively consider whether the public interest would be served by approving the proposed assignment, which may, if there are substantial questions of fact or inadequate data in the application or other officially noticeable materials, necessitate conducting a public hearing in order to resolve the factual issues or assist the Commission in discerning the public interest. Finally, it is not sufficient justification for approving the application that the assignor has asserted financial losses in providing the special format; those losses must be attributable to the format itself in order logically to support an assignment that occasions a loss of the format.

B. The public interest issues

In its petition to deny, the Citizens Committee did not attempt to portray WEFM as significantly unique in format. Of the 61 stations serving the Chicago area, WEFM, WFMT, and WNIB, all FM stations, were identified as having a "classical music and related cultural program format," with the qualification that "[s]ome variation, however, exists in the program [sic] of the three stations." J.A. 55. The importance of WNIB as an alternative source of classical music was discounted with the allegation that it reaches "only a small part of the audience devoted to classical music," and the letters of protest received by the FCC were said to reveal that "the great majority of WEFM's audience believe that only one other classical music station (WFMT) is available."

In its original decision, the FCC stated flatly that, unlike the situation in Atlanta, "there are two other classical music stations in Chicago." 38 FCC 2d at 845. On reconsideration the FCC responded to the Committee's contention that WNIB's limited service area made it an inadequate substitute for WEFM. On the basis of an attached contour map showing the service areas of all three stations, it found that WNIB, while it does not reach anything like as great an area as WEFM, does reach "all of the city of Chicago, its city of license."[20] In addition, WFMT was shown to reach all of WEFM's service area, so that the withdrawal of WEFM from service to the classical music audience would not leave that segment of the public without access to classical music. Accordingly, the FCC concluded that "this is not a 'format' change case where there is no appropriate substitute for the service being lost." 40 FCC 2d at 226.

The FCC's assertion that abandonment of WEFM's classical music format

---

[20] Mere inspection of the map indicates that either this statement or the map is not entirely accurate. See 40 FCC 2d at 228.

will not leave its service area bereft of similar programming cannot be sustained on the record before us.[21]

1. The relevant service area

We may assume that WNIB serves all of its city of license, Chicago, and, as the Commission stated, that "secondary agreements between WNIB and GCC provide for the enrichment of the programming fare offered by WNIB and substantial assistance is to be provided in increasing that station's power." Without further elaboration, however, it is impossible to say, and the FCC did not find, that WNIB will ultimately serve substantially the area now served by WEFM.[22]

Insofar as WNIB fails to reach the area served by WEFM, we think it is, *pro tanto,* not an available substitute for WEFM. The FCC's reliance on WNIB as a substitute clearly reflected its view that the public interest in format change cases is defined by metes and bounds of the city of license. In Stone v. FCC, *supra,* we found it unnecessary to decide finally whether a licensee "has a *primary* obligation to serve the needs and interests of its city of license," 466 F.2d at 327 (emphasis added), as opposed to the full service area it reaches, because the FCC had properly determined that the television licensee in that renewal case had adequately served its city of license. But we did think it "clear that a broadcast licensee has an obligation to meet the needs and interests of its entire area of service. . . . Suburban and other outlying areas are not cities of license, although their needs and interests must be met by television stations licensed to central cities."

We now hold that the public interest implicated in a format change is the

---

[21] The FCC's mandate to approve applications consistent with the public interest, and only such applications, is not dependent upon the assiduousness of intervenors such as the Committee. An agency charged with regulation in the public interest cannot abdicate its responsibility, preferring for itself the role of an umpire between the regulated industry and public protestants. Office of Communication, United Church of Christ v. FCC, 138 U.S. App. D.C. 112, 425 F.2d 543 (1969) (Burger, J.); *see* Greene County Planning Bd. v. FPC, 455 F.2d 412 (2d Cir. 1972). Even in the absence of intervention, the FCC is obliged to be certain it is not dealing with a format change affected with the public interest by reason of the uniqueness of the format to be abandoned. Public silence, after adequate public notice, would provide such assurance, just as "public grumbling [of] significant proportions," *Progressive Rock, supra,* raises the question.

[22] The Committee variously puts WNIB's service area at 15% or "at best" 20% of that of WEFM, but it is not clear whether these percentages represent potential audience figures or geographical area, or whether they take account of anticipated improvements. GCC's opposition to petition for reconsideration refers to an attached "engineering affidavit" (not in the Joint Appendix) indicating that WNIB serves all of the city of Chicago and 41% of the total area served by WEFM, and predicting that it could be improved to serve "an area almost comparable in size to that of WEFM." J.A. 191. On the view that the FCC took of the matter, the horizons of which were drawn at the boundaries of the city of Chicago, these differences were not in need of resolution.

interest of the public in the service area, not just the city of license.[23] No other view consists with our explication, here and in *Citizens Committee of Atlanta,* of the requirements of "the public interest, as that was conceived of by a Congress representative of all the people." *Id.* 436 F.2d at 269. National Broadcasting Co. v. United States, 319 U.S. 190, 217, 63 S.Ct. 997, 87 L.Ed. 1344 (1943).[24] In considering the availability *vel non* of an alternative source for a particular format, reliance on an alternative that reaches less than a substantial portion of the area served by the station to be assigned gives disproportionate weight to the interests of one portion of the public, and none at all to those of another. Unless the Commission has considered this effect, and reasonably determined that the overall public interest is, on balance, better served by this arrangement, we cannot say that it has discharged its obligation to assess and act in the public interest.[25]

2. WFMT as an alternative source of classical music.

Insofar as WNIB is not an available alternative to listeners presently served by WEFM, WFMT is the only remaining station on which the FCC could rely in support of its thesis that WEFM's abandonment of classical music does not come within the unique format doctrine of *Citizens Committee of Atlanta.* There is, however, a problem with the FCC's bald characterization of WFMT as a classical music station in this proceeding.

A challenge to a proposed assignment of the license of WFMT came before this court in 1968. Joseph v. FCC, 131 U.S. App. D.C. 207, 404 F.2d 207. The issue posed in that case was the propriety of the Commission's approval of the

[23] Areas that receive a distant station under unusual or occasional circumstances or because of fortuitous physical phenomena are not contemplated by this discussion, which relates directly to the problem of metropolitan areas that encompass a major city to which stations are typically licensed.

[24] We note that GCC's Ascertainment of Community Interests, Needs and Problems, which the FCC accepted as adequate, takes as the relevant "community" an area said to be coextensive with "the essential broadcast coverage area of WEFM and, hence, it is the area which WEFM serves." J.A. 369. This area encompasses six counties in Illinois and four in Indiana. Its Community Leader Survey encompassed "the Chicago Metropolitan Area," with the exception of cities within a 75-mile radius of Chicago that are themselves cities of license for a radio station (such as Milwaukee, Wisconsin; Rockford, Illinois; and Gary, Indiana). Its "Study of Desired Radio Programming and Desired Music in Chicago and the Chicago Metropolitan Area," also said to be approximately coextensive with the area reached by WEFM's signal, is based on the musical preferences of persons in six Illinois and four Indiana counties.

[25] GCC's own preference survey of the "kind of music respondents like to hear" reveals that 18% preferred "rock and roll" and 18% preferred "serious music (classical)." J.A. 354. If WEFM's format is unique, therefore, its abandonment in favor of rock music would not bring service to a larger segment of the public and would leave that part of the classical music audience beyond the reach of WNIB without any service, except as WFMT may be found to fill the void.

assignment, without a hearing and without an express public interest finding, from an independent broadcasting company to a corporate group that controlled several broadcast stations and newspapers. We remanded the case to the FCC for a determination of whether a grant of the assignment application would create an undue concentration of media control in contravention of the FCC's regulations and the diversification policy on which they rested.

In this court WFMT represented itself to be, and the court referred to it as, "an award-winning fine arts station," *id.* at 208, and not as a classical music station. After the hearing on remand, the proposed assignee amended its portion of the assignment application to reflect its intention, if the FCC approved, to donate a 100% interest in WFMT to the Chicago Educational Television Association.[26] The FCC approved the application as amended. In the course of doing so, it recited that "CETA has given assurances that it intends to cause WFMT to maintain the *unique fine arts programming* of the station for the benefit of the people of Chicago." 21 FCC 2d 401, 403 (1970). Nowhere in the FCC's opinion was WFMT described as a classical music station, and it was three times described in other terms.[27]

Against this background[28] we think the Commission has an affirmative obli-

---

[26] The FCC describes the proposed donee as a non-profit corporation operating educational television stations in Chicago. Its membership was said to be "composed of some 38 colleges, universities, schools, libraries, etc., as members and some 53 other educational, religious, research, civic, and cultural organizations as associate members." 21 FCC 2d at 403 (1970).

[27] In addition to the passage quoted in the text, the FCC stated that "[a] grant of the application as amended, will make possible the continuation of a *unique* and valuable *fine arts* program service. . . ." Waiver of its interim policy against acting on applications filed during the pendency of its rule making on the subject of common ownership was predicated on "the overriding importance of promoting *educational* broadcasting in the public interest." (Emphases added.)

[28] In addition, we refer to Zenith's 1970 application for renewal of its current license for WEFM. *See* J.A. 115. Question 8 of the application asks "how and to what extent (if any) applicant's station contributed during the past license period to the over-all diversity of program services available in the area or communities served," Zenith responded as follows:

There are upwards of 25 commercial FM stations in the Chicago area. Only one major station other than WEFM offers classical music to the extent that we do. Adherence to our classical music format provides a choice for lovers of fine music. Changing our basic programming would inevitably lessen the over-all diversity of program services available in this area.

From the WNIB program guide, made a part of the record in this case, Zenith's reference would appear to be to that station, thus indicating that Zenith itself did not consider WFMT a "classical music" station. In any event, WEFM's representation to the FCC that its present format enhances diversity requires explanation if abandonment of that format is predicated upon the notion that diversity will not be lessened. The explanation may well lie in the breadth of the term "classical music," if that rubric is used so broadly as to cover formats that do not substantially overlap. One station might not, for example, play music composed in this century, while another might concentrate on twentieth century works. In popular parlance both would be termed "classical music" stations, yet the loss of either would unquestionably lessen diversity in the area.

gation to establish that WFMT is in fact a reasonable substitute for the service previously offered by WEFM before relying on the affirmative of that proposition to avoid the necessity of weighing the public interest in a change of WEFM's format. WFMT's format may have changed since the FCC received assurances that CETA would maintain it as a "fine arts" station, or the FCC's definition of such a station may involve such substantial overlap with its definition of a "classical music" station that they are rough substitutes. But nothing in the present record gives any indication of whether this is so. It may be noteworthy, moreover, that while WNIB's monthly program guide was made part of the record by the applicants in support of their contention that WNIB offers a service comparable to that of WEFM, neither WFMT's program guide nor a summary thereof was submitted to buttress the same thesis with respect to that station.

The substitutability of WFMT's "fine arts" programming for WEFM's classical music format may perhaps be capable of demonstration without the benefit of a hearing. The FCC retains a discretion commensurate with its expertise to make reasonable categorical determinations. If its exercise of that discretion requires information that can best be developed in a public hearing, *see* Citizens for Allegan County, Inc. v. FPC, 134 U.S. App. D.C. 229, 414 F.2d 1125, 1129 (1969), or if substantial questions concerning format similarity arise with the issue thus framed on remand, however, a hearing may well be necessary to resolve this issue. Since a hearing will be required in any event on the questions discussed in II. C, *infra,* we see no reason why its scope should be limited to exclude the question of WFMT's substitutability for WEFM.

C. Questions of fact requiring a hearing.

The FCC also held that the non-format questions raised by the Committee were not material and substantial, and thus that no hearing was required to resolve them. As to two such questions, we cannot agree.

1. Zenith's alleged losses.

Zenith claims to have incurred an operating loss of almost $2 million in the six years during which WEFM sold advertising time, and to have suffered a net after tax loss of approximately $1 million.[29] The Committee disputed this claim by alleging that Zenith continued to advertise its own products on WEFM, and did not really attempt to sell enough other advertising to make WEFM self-

[29] The difference is explained by the fact that Zenith had offsetting income from its other enterprises and thus was able to deduct its losses in determining taxable income, thereby reducing tax liability by approximately one half the amount of its broadcasting loss.

supporting. Neither the FCC nor Zenith referred to any evidence, nor does the record reveal any, either controverting the Committee's allegations or demonstrating that losses resulted despite the use of an accounting method that would give proper recognition to the institutional advertising and other promotional or developmental values derived by Zenith from WEFM.

The Committee did not itself base its disputation of the losses on Zenith's financial reports because, it says, the FCC considers such reports confidential and would not have given the Committee access to them had a request been made. In these circumstances, it is fundamentally unfair for the FCC to dismiss the Committee's challenge to Zenith's claim of losses because the Committee "neither alleged any facts which would cast doubt on the reliability of the losses claimed by Zenith in the operation of WEFM nor has it seriously questioned those figures." It did seriously question those losses in two respects, and the FCC should have used its authority under Section 309(e) to set the matters down for hearing and to assign the burden of proof respecting such losses and Zenith's claimed efforts to make WEFM self-sustaining after twenty-five years on non-commercial operation to the party with access to the relevant information, viz., Zenith.[30] Until these questions are resolved, there is simply no basis from which the FCC can infer that WEFM's classical music format is financially nonviable. *See Progressive Rock, supra.*

2. GCC's community leader survey

In seeking reconsideration by the Commission, the Committee asserted that GCC had deliberately misled the FCC about its intentions to change WEFM's format. GCC represented that it approached the question of format with an open mind and then, on the basis of its community needs survey, determined to direct its programming to young adults, the group it considered most in need of service. Having made that decision, it first set out to determine how best to reach that audience and discovered that a rock music format would be the best vehicle for doing so. Thus, it did not inform community leaders interviewed at the outset of this process that it would change WEFM's format to rock music because it had not yet then determined whether to change the format at all.

There is a fact introduced by the Committee that casts some doubt on the bona fides of GCC's representation. The Committee, it will be recalled, inquired of and received answers from a number of the community leaders that GCC had surveyed about community needs and problems. Five of the twenty-four who answered the Committee's inquiry stated that they had been told that there *would* be a format change once GCC became the licensee of WEFM, and one recalled being told specifically that the new format would be rock music.

---

[30] *Cf.* Bilingual Bicultural Coalition of Mass Media, Inc. v. FCC, 160 U.S. App. D.C. 390, 393, 492 F.2d 656, 659 (1974).

This situation is covered by what we said in *Citizens Committee of Atlanta* (436 F.2d at 271) where it was urged that discrepancies of exactly this sort

demonstrate actual misrepresentation on [the applicant's] part which disqualifies it from being a licensee. We are not disposed, at least on this record, to attribute such a purpose to [the applicant] . . . . Confusion, conflict, misunderstanding, obscurity—all are inherent in a process in which the statements and opinions of one individual are sought to be determined from what two adversary parties say that he said or thinks. . . .

The truth is most likely to be refined and discovered in the crucible of an evidentiary hearing; and it is precisely a situation like the one revealed by this record which motivated Congress to stress the availability to the Commission of the hearing procedure.

A hearing is equally in order on the question of misrepresentation in this case.[31]

III

This court's role as the sole forum for appeals from FCC licensing decisions impels us to add a further comment on the Commission's approach to the public interest in matters of format, and what it termed the "ominous threat of a hearing." As stated in Section I, *supra,* the six Commissioners who voted to deny reconsideration in this case spoke directly, through Chairman Burch, to the "policy considerations underlying [their] decision."[32] Their analysis contains an apparent error, and failure to identify it will only result in a continuation of this series of similar cases that began with *Citizens Committee of Atlanta* four years ago.

The crux of the Commissioners' reason for believing that entertainment "program format is a matter best left to the discretion of the licensee or applicant" is that "as a matter of public acceptance and economic necessity he will tend to program to meet the preferences of his area and fill whatever void is left by the programming of other stations." But this analysis is not applied uniformly by the FCC, which distinguishes entertainment fare from other services, such as news and public affairs coverage, as to which the FCC "require[s] that

---

[31] The authority granted the FCC in Section 309(d)(2) to dispose of a petition without a hearing was directed at "petitions which were of no real consequence." H.Rep. No. 1800, 86th Cong., 2d Sess. 12 (1960), U.S. Code Cong. & Admin. News, p. 3520. *See* Hudson Valley Broadcasting Corp v. FCC, 116 U.S. App. D.C. 1, 320 F.2d 723, 727 (1963).

[32] 40 FCC 2d 230. There is no doubt that the Commission has adopted the view there expressed. It appears in the Programming Policy Statement, 25 Fed. Reg. 7293 (1960), and is quoted at length in the FCC's brief to this court.

broadcasters conduct thorough surveys designed to assure familiarity with community problems and then develop programming responsive to those needs." In this way, the FCC has attempted to strike a balance between free competition in broadcasting "and the reasonable restriction of that freedom inherent in the public interest standard." FCC v. Sanders Brothers Radio Station, 309 U.S. 470, 474, 60 S.Ct. 693, 84 L.Ed. 869 (1940).

Precisely why the balance should be struck with entertainment programming in one pan and everything else in the other is not clear. The Programming Policy Statement pays a great deal of attention to First Amendment considerations in justifying the FCC's non-interference in entertainment matters, but familiar First Amendment concepts, would, if anything, indicate a lesser—not a greater—governmental role in matters affecting news, public affairs, and religious programming. We need not today, however, wade into such deep waters.

The Supreme Court has, more recently than *Sanders,* made it clear that "[t]he 'public interest' to be served under the Communications Act is . . . the interest of the listening public in 'the larger and more effective use of radio.' § 303(g)."

The Commission's licensing function cannot be discharged, therefore, merely by finding that there are no technological objections to the granting of a license. If the criterion of "public interest" were limited to such matters, how could the Commission choose between two applicants for the same facilities, each of whom is financially and technically qualified to operate a station?

.   .   .   .

The avowed aim of the Communications Act of 1934 was to secure the maximum benefits of radio to all the people of the United States.

National Broadcasting Co. v. United States, 319 U.S. 190, 216-217, 63 S.Ct. 997, 87 L.Ed. 1344 (1943) (emphasis added). Moreover, there is no longer any room for doubt that, if the FCC is to pursue the public interest, it may not be able at the same time to pursue a policy of free competition.[33]

The very fact that Congress has seen fit to enter into the comprehensive regulation of communications embodied in the Federal Communications Act of 1934 contradicts the notion that national policy unqualifiedly favors competition in communications.

FCC v. RCA Communications, Inc., 346 U.S. 86, 93, 73 S.Ct. 998, 97 L.Ed. 1470 (1953).

This court does not sit to make radio policy, but to protect Congress's "avowed aim" of "secur[ing] the maximum benefits of radio to all the people

[33] *See,* in this regard, Judge Wilkey's recent opinion for the court in Hawaiian Telephone Co. v. FCC, 162 U.S. App. D.C. 229, 498 F.2d 771, 776-777 (1974).

of the United States." What is a benefit, and of what magnitude, is a question ordinarily best left to the agency charged with regulating the industry in the public interest. But whether the diverse interests of all the people of the United States are being served by radio to the maximum extent possible is a question we cannot ignore in the context of a controversy like the one before us.

There is, in the familiar sense, no free market in radio entertainment because over-the-air broadcasters do not deal directly with their listeners. They derive their revenue from the sale of advertising time. More time may be sold, and at higher rates, by a station that has a larger *or* a demographically more desirable audience for advertisers. Broadcasters therefore find it to their interest to appeal, through their entertainment format, to the particular audience that will enable them to maximize advertising revenues. If advertisers on the whole prefer to reach an audience of a certain type, *e.g.,* young adults with their larger discretionary incomes, then broadcasters, left entirely to themselves by the FCC, would shape their programming to the tastes of that segment of the public.

This is inherently inconsistent with "secur[ing] the maximum benefits of radio to all the people of the United States," and not a situation that we can square with the statute as construed by the Supreme Court. We think it axiomatic that preservation of a format that would otherwise disappear, although economically and technologically viable and preferred by a significant number of listeners, is generally in the public interest.[34] There may well be situations in which that is not the case for reasons within the discretion of the FCC to consider, but a policy of mechanistic deference to "competition" in entertainment program format will not focus the FCC's attention on the necessity to discern such reasons before allowing diversity, serving the public interest because it serves more of the public, to disappear from the airwaves.[35]

---

[34] It cannot be otherwise when it is remembered that the radio channels are priceless properties in limited supply, owned by all of the people but for the use of which the licensees pay nothing. If the marketplace alone is to determine programming format, then different tastes among the totality of the owners may go ungratified. Congress, having made the essential decision to license at no charge for private operation as distinct from putting the channels up for bids, can hardly be thought to have had so limited a concept of the aims of regulation. In any event, the language of the Act, by its terms and as read by the Supreme Court, is to the contrary.

[35] Our disposition of this case makes it unnecessary presently to measure the adequacy of the FCC's minimum notice requirement, which need not alert the public directly to the fact that a proposed license assignment encompasses a format change, against the constitutional rule that, "within the limits of practicability," due process requires "notice reasonably calculated, under all the circumstances, to apprise interested parties of the pendency of the action and afford them an opportunity to present their objections." Mullane v. Central Hanover Trust Co., 339 U.S. 306, 314, 70 S.Ct. 652, 657, 94 L.Ed. 865 (1950). We have had previous occasion to note that "the question as to the adequacy of the notice does not evoke the principle of judicial deference to administrative expertise," Ridge Radio Corp. v. FCC, 110 U.S. App. D.C. 277, 292 F.2d 770, 773 (1961), but we will give the question full attention only in a case where constitutional considerations cannot be avoided. The FCC's present notice requirement may in any event be so related to its expressed reluctance to consider matters of format, much less raise the "ominous threat of a hearing," that reexamination by the agency in light of this opinion's explication of the public interest standard will make such consideration unnecessary in the future as well.

The orders under review are set aside, and the matter is remanded for further proceedings consistent herewith.

It is so ordered.

Robb, Circuit Judge, (dissenting):

As a member of the original panel in this case I concurred in the views cogently expressed by Chief Judge Bazelon in Part II of his opinion for the panel. I adhere to those views. Since Chief Judge Bazelon's opinion has been vacated I here reproduce Part II, after renumbering the footnotes.

In recent years this Court and the FCC have begun to develop principles governing government control of format changes.[1] This Court has held that the public has an interest in the diversity of entertainment formats.[2] Consequently the Commission has had to consider format changes in its statutory determination that a proposed assignment of a license comports with "the public interest, convenience, and necessity."[3] Factual disputes surrounding the format change are material and if substantial become subject to the statutory requirement that a hearing be held.[4]

In this case appellants contend that substantial factual disputes exist on two issues relating to the proposed format change—the diversity of available formats and Zenith's alleged financial losses.

As to diversity, appellants maintain that a substantial issue of fact exists as to whether the Chicago public demands and needs the continuation of classical music on WEFM as opposed to "yet another contemporary music station."[5] Appellants point to the numerous letters and petitions of protest which greeted the news that WEFM was about to abandon its classical format. They note that Chicago has numerous rock stations already, while the demise of WEFM will leave only one classical music station with the power to reach the entire Chicago area.

Our previous opinions and the Commission's actions indicate that the majority of format changes are left to the give and take of the market environment and the business judgment of the licensee.[6] It is only when the format to be discontinued is apparently unique to the area served that a hearing on the public interest must be held.[7] In such cases the public interest in diversity may outweigh the dangers of government intrusion into the content of programming.

In this case it is undisputed that the entire area served by WEFM is served by

---

[1] *See* Citizens Committee to Preserve the Voice of the Arts in Atlanta v. FCC, 141 U.S. App. D.C. 109, 436 F.2d 263 (1970); Hartford Communications Committee v. FCC, 151 U.S. App. D.C. 354, 467 F.2d 408 (1972); Lakewood Broadcasting Service, Inc. v. FCC, 156 U.S. App. D.C. 9, 478 F.2d 919 (1973); Citizens Committee to Keep Progressive Rock v. FCC, 156 U.S. App. D.C. 16, 478 F.2d 926 (1973).

[2] *Citizens Committee to Keep Progressive Rock,* 478 F.2d at 929.

[3] *Lakewood Broadcasting Service, Inc.,* 478 F.2d at 922.

[4] *Id.*

[5] Appellants' brief, at 38.

[6] *Citizens Committee to Keep Progressive Rock,* 478 F.2d at 929.

[7] *Id.* at 929.

another classical music station, WFMT–FM.[8] Thus we are unable to find a substantial issue of fact requiring a hearing on the diversity point.[9]

Appellants also contend that a substantial issue of fact exists concerning the losses Zenith alleges it sustained during its operation of WEFM. Even assuming that such an issue would require a hearing in the absence of a substantial diversity issue, we do not find that appellants have raised a substantial issue of fact here. The Commission had sufficient evidence to support its finding that WEFM had incurred substantial losses in the period after 1965, when the station was operated on a commercial basis and not as a research and development adjunct to the Zenith corporation.[10]

MacKinnon, Circuit Judge, (dissenting):

The majority opinion indicates that we are beginning to open the door wider for intrusion of the courts and the Government into the content of radio broadcasts. To my mind such governmental interference should be held to a minimum and the power should not be exercised except upon the clearest grounds. I fail to see that such grounds exist when we are forced to draw a distinction based on differences in "classical" music to sustain jurisdiction to interfere. Generally my view of the facts and the law is expressed in Judge Robb's dissent with which I concur.

[8] A third classical music station, WNIB-FM, currently serves a smaller part of the Chicago area. GCC has agreed that if their license application is approved, they will relinquish the call letters WEFM to WNIB and give WNIB the WEFM classical music library as well as technical assistance designed to enable WNIB to increase its power.

[9] The long history of WEFM's service does not diminish the impact of WFMT's similar programming. The length of time that a format has been on the air is usually relevant only when that format is unique. *See Citizens Committee to Keep Progressive Rock,* at 933 note 22:

> Naturally the length of time that a specific format has been on the air is a factor to be considered in the ultimate public interest determination, for it can have a direct bearing on the degree of attachment which the public has to the *unique* format. (Emphasis added).

This approach to the diversity issue cannot be applied in a mechanistic fashion. Whether a format to be discontinued is unique can be a subtle question requiring that more than mere labels be examined. The fact, for example, that two stations are labelled "classical" does not automatically mean that they provide substantially similar programming. One of the stations might never play music composed in this century, while the other devotes considerable amounts of time to such music. In this case, however, it is apparent that WEFM and WFMT have substantially similar programming, both covering a broad range of classical music. *Cf. Citizens Committee to Keep Progressive Rock,* at 932, where this Court noted that "Top 40" stations cannot automatically be assumed to provide substantial amounts of "progressive rock" music.

[10] Zenith was not, for example, able to obtain enough advertising to fill the two and one-half minutes per hour it allotted for ads. Joint Appendix at 73.

Appellants' contention concerning the adequacy of the notice of the application for voluntary transfer is also without merit. The Commission properly found that Zenith complied with the notice requirements of the Commission's rules. The notice given was not constitutionally defective.

Similarly, appellants' contention that the Commission's *ex parte* rules had an unconstitutional impact on the public discussion of the format change is without merit in the setting of this case.

44

Renewal Ascertainment Primer

Primer on Ascertainment of Community
Problems by Broadcast Renewal Applicants
57 FCC 2d 418, 441 (Appendix B)
January 7, 1976
[Amended by 61 FCC 2d 1 (1976)]

The notion of formal licensee ascertainment of community problems, needs, and interests was introduced by the FCC's *1960 Programming Policy Statement* (Document 26, pp. 262–278) and
judicially affirmed in the "Suburban" case (Document 31, pp.
306–309). The Commission's application forms were revised in
the 1960's to reflect the increased emphasis placed on the relationship between ascertainment and programming. Ascertainment
requirements were first spelled out with specificity in the *Primer
on Ascertainment of Community Problems by Broadcast Applicants*, 27 FCC 2d 650, 682 (1971), whose standards continue to
pertain to parties seeking initial commercial broadcast licenses.

The "Renewal Ascertainment Primer" establishes a somewhat
different set of standards for incumbent broadcasters, the most
novel of which is the requirement that licensees engage in *continuous* ascertainment during each term of license. Commercial
broadcasters serving populations of 10,000 or fewer persons outside a metropolitan area are free to conduct their ascertainment
surveys as they see fit, although such licensees "must continue to

maintain their awareness of local problems and needs" [57 FCC 2d 418 at 435 (1976)].

A few months after promulgating the "Renewal Ascertainment Primer" the FCC adopted modified ascertainment requirements for noncommercial stations that had previously been exempt [*Ascertainment of Community Problems by Noncommercial Educational Broadcast Applicants*, 58 FCC 2d 526 (1976)].

Related Reading: 5, 77, 162.

INTRODUCTION

The principal ingredient of a licensee's obligation to operate in the public interest is the diligent, positive and continuing effort by the licensee to discover and fulfill the problems, needs and interests of the public within the station's service area. *Statement of Policy Re: Commission En Banc Programming Inquiry*, 25 Fed. Reg. 7291, 20 RR 1901 (1960). In the fulfillment of this obligation, the licensee must consult with leaders who represent the interests of the community and members of the general public who receive the station's signal. *1960 Programming Policy Statement, supra.* This Primer provides guidelines for the licensee of a commercial broadcast station to follow in conducting these consultations. The types of consultations required can best be summarized in a question and answer format.

A. GENERAL

Question 1. When must the community survey be conducted?

Answer. The licensee's obligation is to ascertain the problems, needs and interests of the public within the station's service area on a *continuing* basis. The licensee, therefore, must make reasonable and good faith efforts to ascertain community problems, needs and interests throughout the station's license term.

Question 2. What area should the community survey encompass?

Answer. The licensee is obligated to provide service to the station's entire service area. As a practical matter, however, it is realized that the service contours of a station cover a substantial geographical area. Thus, the licensee is permitted to place primary emphasis on the station's city of license and secondary emphasis outside that area. In any event, no community located more than 75 miles from the city of license need be included in the licensee's survey. Further, if a licensee chooses not to serve a community within the station's contours, a brief statement should be placed in the station's public inspection file explaining the reason(s) therefor.

Question 3. What is the purpose of the community survey?

Answer. The purpose of the community survey is to discover the problems, needs and interests of the public as distinguished from its programming preferences. However, a licensee may, if it wishes, also seek to discover the public's programming preferences.

Question 4. Who must be consulted during the community survey?

Answer. The licensee must interview leaders who represent the interests of the service area and members of the general public.

Question 5. Must a compositional study of the community be conducted?

Answer. A special compositional study of the community need not be conducted. We have identified typical community institutions and elements normally present in most communities and we expect the licensee to utilize this listing in conducting its community leader survey. (See Question and Answer 7, below.) We recognize that all communities are not the same and that other significant institutions or elements may be indigenous to a particular community. However, if a licensee interviews a representative sample of leaders from among the elements in this listing that apply to its community, its coverage of all significant elements will not be open to question. The licensee may, at its option, interview leaders within elements not found on this list.

Question 6. Must the licensee obtain demographic data relating to its community of license?

Answer. A licensee should have on file information relating to the population characteristics of its city of license. The population data required can be extracted from the U.S. Census Bureau's *County and City Data Book* and *General Population Characteristics* (two separate publications), or similarly reliable reference material. The information needed relates to the total population of the city of license; the numbers and proportions of males and females, of minorities, of youths (age 17 and under), and of the elderly (age 65 or older). Inclusion of data on portions of the station's service area outside the city of license is optional.

B. COMMUNITY LEADER SURVEY

Question 7. What community leaders should be consulted?

Answer. The community leaders consulted should constitute a representative cross-section of those who speak for the interests of the service area. This requirement may be met by interviews within the following institutions and elements commonly found in a community: (1) Agriculture; (2) Business; (3) Charities; (4) Civic, Neighborhood and Fraternal Organizations; (5) Consumer Services;

(6) Culture; (7) Education; (8) Environment; (9) Government (local, county, state & federal); (10) Labor; (11) Military; (12) Minority and ethnic groups; (13) Organizations of and for the Elderly; (14) Organizations of and for Women; (15) Organizations of and for Youth (including children) and Students; (16) Professions; (17) Public Safety, Health and Welfare; (18) Recreation; and (19) Religion. A licensee is permitted to show that one or more of these institutions or elements is not present in its community. At its option it may also utilize the "other" category to interview leaders in elements not found on the Checklist.

Question 8. If a licensee interviews in all of the above categories will the licensee be considered to have contacted all the significant groups in its community?

Answer. The Checklist is thorough enough for most communities and yet not overly detailed. Interviews in all of its elements will establish the requisite coverage of significant community groups. Whether this coverage is also representative will depend on such factors as number of interviews in each element, size and influence of that element in the community, etc. A licensee is permitted to show that one or more of these categories is not present in its community. It may also, at its option, interview leaders in other categories which may not be found on the Checklist.

Question 9. How many community leaders should be consulted?

Answer. A licensee should consult with leaders on a continuous basis. The Commission's concern, in this regard, is not one of numbers but of representativeness. The licensee's reasonable and good faith discretion as to how many community leaders should be interviewed to establish representativeness will be accorded great weight. However, we have established a reasonable number of interviews (see table below) that a licensee may conduct during the license term, if it wishes to remove any question as to the gross quantitative sufficiency of its community leader survey. Fewer interviews may be conducted if, in the exercise of its discretion, a licensee determines that a lesser number results in a leadership survey that is representative of its service area.

Population of City of License	Number of Consultations
Under 25,001	60
25,001–50,000	100
50,001–200,000	140
200,001–500,000	180
Over 500,000	220

Question 10. What leaders in each significant institution or element should be consulted?

Answer. There are many community leaders in each of the enumerated institutions and elements. Due to the physical impossibility of interviews with all community leaders, and the practical impossibility of requiring interviews with leaders based on some ratio to population of their constituencies, each licensee is accorded wide discretion in determining what leaders in each of the institutions or elements should be interviewed from time to time. The leadership of some institutions or elements (e.g., government) may remain relatively stable throughout the license term and, thus, interviews with such leaders on several occasions can be expected. In this respect, each consultation with a community leader constitutes a separate ascertainment interview. The licensee should, of course, make reasonable and good faith efforts to consult with various leaders in each significant institution or element and not limit the consultations to the same leaders throughout the license term.

Question 11. Who can conduct the community leader consultations?

Answer. Principals, management level and other employees of the station may conduct the community leader consultations. (See Question and Answer 12, below.) When such interviews are conducted by non-management level employees, their efforts must be under the direction and supervision of a principal or management level employee. Also, the results of the interview must be reported to a principal or management level employee within a reasonable period of time after the consultation.

Question 12. Since non-management level employees may conduct community leader interviews, is it necessary for principals and management level employees to be involved in the consultations at all?

Answer. Yes. Community leader consultations may be conducted by any employee who the licensee believes is qualified for the assignment. However, a substantial degree of participation, as interviewers, by principals and management level employees is still necessary. Accordingly, 50 percent of all interviews must be conducted by management level employees.

Question 13. Can a professional research firm conduct the community leader survey on behalf of the licensee?

Answer. No. The licensee is expected on its own behalf to consult with a cross-section of community leaders who represent the interests of the service area. Thus, a professional research firm cannot be used for this purpose.

Question 14. Must the community leader interviews take place in a formal meeting called for the specific purpose of inquiring about community problems, needs and interests?

Answer. The interview process allows for a multiplicity of dialogue techniques. Such interviews, for example, may take place during a meeting called for the specific purpose of discussing community problems, needs and interests, or in a business meeting with a community leader by a principal, management level or other employee of the licensee where community problems, needs and interests are also the subject of discussion. Additionally, such an interview may take place during community leader luncheons, joint consultations (see Question and Answer 15, below), on the air broadcasts (see Question and Answer 16, below), and during news interviews. In any event, appropriate documentation must be obtained (see Question 18, below).

Question 15. Are joint consultations between licensees and community leaders permitted?

Answer. Joint consultations between licensees and community leaders are permitted, provided: (i) each community leader who participates is on a roughly equivalent plane of interest or responsibility; (ii) each community leader is given ample opportunity to freely present his or her opinions as to community problems, needs and interests; and (iii) each licensee participating is given ample opportunity to question each leader.

Question 16. Can community leader interviews taking place during an on-the-air broadcast be used as evidence of a licensee's ascertainment process?

Answer. Ordinarily, a licensee should not rely on this method to ascertain community problems. When, however, such an on-the-air interview reveals a community problem, need or interest which results in the consideration of a future program concerning that problem, need or interest, the consultation may be used as evidence of the licensee's ascertainment efforts.

Question 17. Can community leaders be interviewed via telephone?

Answer. Face-to-face interviews should be the staple of the licensee's ascertainment process. The limited use of the telephone to conduct community leader interviews is permitted, particularly in areas outside the community of license, and other situations where reasons of convenience, efficiency or necessity might apply. However, a licensee should not, through over-reliance on ascertainment by telephone, abuse the flexibility that this medium gives the station.

Question 18. What documentation is required to be placed in the station's public inspection file regarding community leader interviews?

Answer. Within a reasonable time after completion of an interview, which we perceive ordinarily to be 30 to 45 days, the licensee must place in its public inspection file information identifying: (a) the name and address of the community leader consulted; (b) the institution or element in the community represented; (c) the date, time and place of the interview; (d) problems, needs or interests discussed during the interview (unless the leader requests that his comments be kept confidential); (e) the name of the licensee representative conducting the interview; and (f) where a non-manager performed the interview, the name of the principal or management level employee who reviewed the completed interview record. No credit will be given for interviews placed in the public file after the date on which the licensee's renewal application is filed with the Commission.

Question 19. What documentation relating to the community leader interviews must be submitted with the station's application for renewal of license?

Answer. Upon the filing of an application for renewal of license, the licensee must certify that the documentation noted in Question and Answer 18, above, has been placed in the station's public inspection file at the appropriate times. Additionally, the licensee must submit as part of its renewal application a checklist indicating the number of community leaders interviewed during the license term in the enumerated categories set forth at Question and Answer 7, above. If one or more of the institutions or elements is not present in the community, a brief explanation must be included with the Checklist.

C. GENERAL PUBLIC SURVEY

Question 20. With what members of the general public should consultations be held?

Answer. A random sample of members of the general public should be consulted. For our purposes, a random sampling may be taken from a general city telephone directory or may be done on a geographical distribution basis by means of "man-in-the-street" interviews or questionnaires collected by the licensee. These techniques are illustrative, not exhaustive. Whatever survey technique is utilized by the licensee, there must be a full description of the methodology used to assure a roughly random sampling of the general public and an indication of the total number of general public interviews conducted by that survey technique.

Question 21. What is the purpose of the general public survey?

Answer. Here, again, the primary purpose of the general public survey is to discover the community problems, needs and interests of the public as distinguished from its programming preferences. (See Questions and Answers 3 and 4 above.)

Question 22. How many members of the general public should be surveyed?

Answer. No set number or formula has been adopted. A sufficient number of members of the general public should be consulted to assure a generally random sample. The number, of course, will vary with the size of the community in question.

Question 23. When should the general public survey be conducted?

Answer. Either throughout the license term or within some specific period during the license term, at the licensee's option. In either event, appropriate documentation must be placed in the station's public file within a reasonable time after its completion, which we perceive ordinarily to be 30 to 45 days, but in no event later than the date on which its renewal application is filed with the Commission.

Question 24. Who should consult with members of the general public?

Answer. Principals, station employees, or a professional research or survey service. If consultations are conducted by employees who are below the management level, the consultation process must be supervised by principals or management level employees.

Question 25. What documentation concerning the general public survey is required?

Answer. Each licensee must place in the station's public inspection file a narrative statement concerning the method used to conduct the general public survey, the number of people consulted, and the ascertainment results of the survey. (See also the reference to demographic data in Question and Answer 6.)

Question 26. What documentation relating to the general public survey must be filed with the station's application for renewal of license?

Answer. Upon the filing of an application for renewal of license, the licensee must certify that the documentation noted in Question and Answer 25, above, has been placed in the station's public inspection file. No other submission is necessary unless specifically requested by the Commission.

D. PROGRAMMING

Question 27. Must all community problems revealed by the licensee's consultations with community leaders and members of the general public be treated by the station?

Answer. In serving the needs of its community, a licensee is not required to program to meet all community problems ascertained. There are a number of problems which may deserve attention by the broadcast media. The evaluation of the relative importance and immediacy of these many and varied problems, and the determination of how the station can devote its limited broadcast time to meeting the problems that merit treatment, is left to the good faith judgment of the licensee. In making this determination, the licensee may consider the programming offered by other stations in the area as well as its station's program format and the composition of its audience. With respect to the latter factor, however, it should be borne in mind that many problems affect and are pertinent to diverse groups within the community. All members of the public are entitled to some service from each station. While a station may focus relatively more attention on community problems affecting the audience to which it orients its program service, it cannot exclude all other members of the community from its ascertainment efforts and its non-entertainment programming. Indeed, many special interests may be adequately dealt with in programming which has a wide range of audience appeal.

Question 28. Must all community problems revealed by the ascertainment consultations be included in the licensee's showing placed in the public inspection file?

Answer. Yes. The purpose of the community leader and general public consultations is to elicit from those interviewed what they believe to be the community's problems, needs and interests. All ascertained community problems should, therefore, be reflected in the community leader contact reports and in the general public narrative retained in the station's public inspection file.

Question 29. In what form may matter be broadcast to treat ascertained community problems, needs and interests?

Answer. Programs, news and public service announcements. This includes station editorials, ordinary and special news inserts, program vignettes, and the like. (But see Question and Answer 33, below, regarding the exclusion from the yearly problems-programs list of announcements and ordinary news inserts of breaking events.)

Question 30. Can a licensee use only news and public service announcements to treat community problems, needs and interests?

Answer. Not necessarily. It is the responsibility of the individual licensee to determine the appropriate amount, kind, and time period of broadcast matter which should be presented in response to the ascertained problems, needs and interests of its community and service area. Where the licensee, however, has chosen a brief and usually superficial manner of presentation, such as news and public service announcements, to the exclusion of all others, a question could be raised as to the reasonableness of the licensee's action. The licensee would then be required to clearly demonstrate that its single type of presentation would be the most effective method for its station to respond to the community's ascertained problems.

Question 31. When should matter broadcast in response to the community's ascertained problems, needs and interests be presented?

Answer. The Commission does not prescribe the time of day at which specific program matter responsive to the community's ascertained problems should be broadcast. Rather, the licensee is expected to schedule the time of presentation based upon its good faith judgment as to when the broadcast reasonably could be expected to be effective.

Question 32. If a licensee utilizes a specialized program format—such as all-news, classical music, religious—must it present broadcast matter to meet community problems, needs and interests?

Answer. Yes. It is the responsibility of the licensee to be attentive and responsive to the problems, needs and interests of the public it is licensed to serve. The licensee's choice of a particular program format does not alter its obligation to meet community problems, needs and interests. The manner in which the licensee presents such responsive programming may, of course, be tailored to the particular format of the station. (See, however, Question and Answer 27, above.)

Question 33. What documentation must be placed in the station's public inspection file regarding the licensee's efforts to program to meet ascertained community problems, needs and interests?

Answer. Each year on the anniversary date of the filing of the station's application for renewal of license, the licensee must place in its public inspection file a list of no more than ten significant problems, needs and interests ascertained during the preceding twelve months. Concerning each problem, need or interest listed the licensee must also indicate typical and illustrative programs broadcast in response to those problems, needs and interests indicating the title of the program or program series, its source, type, a brief description thereof, time broadcast and duration. Such programs do not include announcements (such as PSA's) or news inserts of breaking events (the daily or ordinary news coverage of breaking newsworthy events).

45

CATV and Copyright

Section 111 of the Copyright Act of 1976

Public Law 553, 94th Congress

October 19, 1976

The U.S. Constitution (Document 1, pp. 1-2) bestows on Congress the authority to enact copyright legislation. Broadcasting developed and matured under the provisions of the Copyright Act of 1909, which made the public performance for profit of a copyrighted work without permission of the copyright holder an infringement of legally protected exclusive rights. By 1955 it seemed clear that this law was in need of revision to reflect technological developments and experience in the copyright field since 1909. Congress initiated a comprehensive examination of the subject. Bills were introduced in the early 1960's, hearings were held, and committee reports urging passage of proposed legislation were issued, but no law emerged for more than a decade.

A formidable barrier to passage of new copyright legislation in the late 1960's and most of the 1970's was the difficulty of determining the appropriate copyright liability for CATV systems. For a time the FCC appeared to be waiting for Congress to set copyright policy for cable television before it would establish communication policy, while Congress refrained from resolving the copyright controversy until the Commission clarified CATV's role in communication policy. During this stalemate the judiciary was called on to resolve copyright conflicts. In 1968 the Supreme Court held that, under the Copyright Act of 1909, cable television was immune from copyright infringement action when relaying TV station signals to system subscribers because CATV did not "perform" the material but was merely an extension of the viewer's TV set, like any other receiving antenna [*Fortnightly* v. *United Artists*, 392 U.S. 390 (1968)]. When the cable-copyright question came before the Court again a few years later it was complicated by such developments as cable systems originating their own programming, accepting paid advertising, interconnecting with other CATV systems to form cable "networks," and importing TV signals from areas hundreds of miles away via microwave relays. Nevertheless, the High Court, following the *Fortnightly* precedent and noting the need for congressional revision of the archaic law, ratified CATV's immunity from copyright liability even when carrying distant station signals [*Teleprompter* v. *CBS*, 415 U.S. 394 (1974)]. Cable systems, however, are fully liable for copyrighted materials they originate or "cablecast."

Congress passed and President Ford signed a new copyright law 2 years later. Section 111 of the Copyright Act of 1976 (fully effective January 1, 1978) establishes a legislative resolution of the cable-copyright dispute by making CATV systems liable for payments (under a compulsory copyright licensing scheme) when carrying distant non-network TV station programming. The intricate provisions of Section 111 become easier to comprehend if subsection (f), "Definitions," is read first instead of last. The influence of Section 111 on FCC cable policy remains to be seen. (See p. 366.)

Related Reading: 25, 33, 130, 206, 226, 234, 240.

SEC. 111. LIMITATIONS ON EXCLUSIVE RIGHTS: SECONDARY TRANSMISSIONS

(a) *Certain Secondary Transmissions Exempted.* The secondary transmission of a primary transmission embodying a performance or display of a work is not an infringement of copyright if—

(1) the secondary transmission is not made by a cable system, and consists entirely of the relaying, by the management of a hotel, apartment house, or similar establishment, of signals transmitted by a broadcast station licensed by the Federal Communications Commission, within the local service area of such station, to the private lodgings of guests or residents of such establishment, and no direct charge is made to see or hear the secondary transmission; or

(2) the secondary transmission is made solely for the purpose and under the conditions specified by clause (2) of section 110; or

(3) the secondary transmission is made by any carrier who has no direct or indirect control over the content or selection of the primary transmission or over the particular recipients of the secondary transmission, and whose activities with respect to the secondary transmission consist solely of providing wires, cables, or other communications channels for the use of others: *Provided,* That the provisions of this clause extend only to the activities of said carrier with respect to secondary transmissions and do not exempt from liability the activities of others with respect to their own primary or secondary transmissions; or

(4) the secondary transmission is not made by a cable system but is made by a governmental body, or other nonprofit organization, without any purpose of direct or indirect commercial advantage, and without charge to the recipients of the secondary transmission other than assessments necessary to defray the actual and reasonable costs of maintaining and operating the secondary transmission service.

(b) *Secondary Transmission of Primary Transmission to Controlled Group.* Notwithstanding the provisions of subsections (a) and (c), the secondary transmission to the public of a primary transmission embodying a performance or display of a work is actionable as an act of infringement under section 501, and is fully subject to the remedies provided by sections 502 through 506 and 509, if the primary transmission is not made for reception by the public at large but is controlled and limited to reception by particular members of the public: *Provided,* however, That such secondary transmission is not actionable as an act of infringement if—

(1) the primary transmission is made by a broadcast station licensed by the Federal Communications Commission; and

(2) the carriage of the signals comprising the secondary transmission is required under the rules, regulations, or authorizations of the Federal Communications Commission; and

(3) the signal of the primary transmitter is not altered or changed in any way by the secondary transmitter.

(c) *Secondary Transmissions by Cable Systems.*

(1) Subject to the provisions of clauses (2), (3), and (4) of this subsection, secondary transmissions to the public by a cable system of a primary transmission made by a broadcast station licensed by the Federal Communications Commission or by an appropriate governmental authority of Canada or Mexico and embodying a performance or display of a work shall be subject to compulsory licensing upon compliance with the requirements of subsection (d) where the carriage of the signals comprising the secondary transmission is permissible under the rules, regulations, or authorizations of the Federal Communications Commission.

(2) Notwithstanding the provisions of clause (1) of this subsection, the willful or repeated secondary transmission to the public by a cable system of a

primary transmission made by a broadcast station licensed by the Federal Communications Commission or by an appropriate governmental authority of Canada or Mexico and embodying a performance or display of a work is actionable as an act of infringement under section 501, and is fully subject to the remedies provided by sections 502 through 506 and 509, in the following cases:

(A) where the carriage of the signals comprising the secondary transmission is not permissible under the rules, regulations, or authorizations of the Federal Communications Commission; or

(B) where the cable system has not recorded the notice specified by subsection (d) and deposited the statement of account and royalty fee required by subsection (d).

(3) Notwithstanding the provisions of clause (1) of this subsection and subject to the provisions of subsection (e) of this section, the secondary transmission to the public by a cable system of a primary transmission made by a broadcast station licensed by the Federal Communications Commission or by an appropriate governmental authority of Canada or Mexico and embodying a performance or display of a work is actionable as an act of infringement under section 501, and is fully subject to the remedies provided by sections 502 through 506 and sections 509 and 510, if the content of the particular program in which the performance or display is embodied, or any commercial advertising or station announcements transmitted by the primary transmitter during, or immediately before or after, the transmission of such program, is in any way willfully altered by the cable system through changes, deletions, or additions, except for the alteration, deletion, or substitution of commercial advertisements performed by those engaged in television commercial advertising market research: *Provided,* That the research company has obtained the prior consent of the advertiser who has purchased the original commercial advertisement, the television station broadcasting that commercial advertisement, and the cable system performing the secondary transmission: *And provided further,* That such commercial alteration, deletion, or substitution is not performed for the purpose of deriving income from the sale of that commercial time.

(4) Notwithstanding the provisions of clause (1) of this subsection, the secondary transmission to the public by a cable system of a primary transmission made by a broadcast station licensed by an appropriate governmental authority of Canada or Mexico and embodying a performance or display of a work is actionable as an act of infringement under section 501, and is fully subject to the remedies provided by sections 502 through 506 and section 509, if (A) with respect to Canadian signals, the community of the cable system is located more than 150 miles from the United States-Canadian border and is also located south of the forty-second parallel of latitude, or (B) with respect to Mexican signals, the secondary transmission is made by a cable system which received the primary transmission by means other than direct interception of a free space radio wave emitted by such broadcast television station,

unless prior to April 15, 1976, such cable system was actually carrying, or was specifically authorized to carry, the signal of such foreign station on the system pursuant to the rules, regulations, or authorizations of the Federal Communications Commission.

(d) *Compulsory License for Secondary Transmissions by Cable Systems.*

(1) For any secondary transmission to be subject to compulsory licensing under subsection (c), the cable system shall, at least one month before the date of the commencement of operations of the cable system or within one hundred and eighty days after the enactment of this Act, whichever is later, and thereafter within thirty days after each occasion on which the ownership or control or the signal carriage complement of the cable system changes, record in the Copyright Office a notice including a statement of the identity and address of the person who owns or operates the secondary transmission service or has power to exercise primary control over it, together with the name and location of the primary transmitter or primary transmitters whose signals are regularly carried by the cable system, and thereafter, from time to time, such further information as the Register of Copyrights, after consultation with the Copyright Royalty Tribunal (if and when the Tribunal has been constituted), shall prescribe by regulation to carry out the purpose of this clause.

(2) A cable system whose secondary transmissions have been subject to compulsory licensing under subsection (c) shall, on a semiannual basis, deposit with the Register of Copyrights, in accordance with requirements that the Register shall, after consultation with the Copyright Royalty Tribunal (if and when the Tribunal has been constituted), prescribe by regulation—

(A) a statement of account, covering the six months next preceding, specifying the number of channels on which the cable system made secondary transmissions to its subscribers, the names and locations of all primary transmitters whose transmissions were further transmitted by the cable system, the total number of subscribers, the gross amounts paid to the cable system for the basic service of providing secondary transmissions of primary broadcast transmitters, and such other data as the Register of Copyrights may, after consultation with the Copyright Royalty Tribunal (if and when the Tribunal has been constituted), from time to time prescribe by regulation. Such statement shall also include a special statement of account covering any non-network television programing that was carried by the cable system in whole or in part beyond the local service area of the primary transmitter, under rules, regulations, or authorizations of the Federal Communications Commission permitting the substitution or addition of signals under certain circumstances, together with logs showing the times, dates, stations, and programs involved in such substituted or added carriage; and

(B) except in the case of a cable system whose royalty is specified in subclause (C) or (D), a total royalty fee for the period covered by the statement, computed on the basis of specified percentages of the gross receipts from subscribers to the cable service during said period for the basic service of providing secondary transmissions of primary broadcast transmitters, as follows:

(i) 0.675 of 1 per centum of such gross receipts for the privilege of further transmitting any nonnetwork programing of a primary transmitter in whole or in part beyond the local service area of such primary transmitter, such amount to be applied against the fee, if any, payable pursuant to paragraphs (ii) through (iv);

(ii) 0.675 of 1 per centum of gross receipts for the first distant signal equivalent;

(iii) 0.425 of 1 per centum of such gross receipts for each of the second, third, and fourth distant signal equivalents;

(iv) 0.2 of 1 per centum of such gross receipts for the fifth distant signal equivalent and each additional distant signal equivalent thereafter; and
in computing the amounts payable under paragraph (ii) through (iv), above, any fraction of a distant signal equivalent shall be computed at its fractional value and, in the case of any cable system located partly within and partly without the local service area of a primary transmitter, gross receipts shall be limited to those gross receipts derived from subscribers located without the local service area of such primary transmitter; and

(C) if the actual gross receipts paid by subscribers to a cable system for the period covered by the statement for the basic service of providing secondary transmissions of primary broadcast transmitters total $80,000 or less, gross receipts of the cable system for the purpose of this subclause shall be computed by subtracting from such actual gross receipts the amount by which $80,000 exceeds such actual gross receipts, except that in no case shall a cable system's gross receipts be reduced to less than $3,000. The royalty fee payable under this subclause shall be 0.5 of 1 per centum, regardless of the number of distant signal equivalents, if any; and

(D) if the actual gross receipts paid by subscribers to a cable system for the period covered by the statement, for the basic service of providing secondary transmissions of primary broadcast transmitters, are more than $80,000 but less than $160,000, the royalty fee payable under this subclause shall be (i) 0.5 of 1 per centum of any gross receipts up to $80,000; and (ii) 1 per centum of any gross receipts in excess of $80,000 but less than $160,000, regardless of the number of distant signal equivalents, if any.

(3) The Register of Copyrights shall receive all fees deposited under this section and, after deducting the reasonable costs incurred by the Copyright Office under this section, shall deposit the balance in the Treasury of the United States, in such manner as the Secretary of the Treasury directs. All funds held by the Secretary of the Treasury shall be invested in interest-bearing United States securities for later distribution with interest by the Copyright Royalty Tribunal as provided by this title. The Register shall submit to the

Copyright Royalty Tribunal, on a semiannual basis, a compilation of all statements of account covering the relevant six-month period provided by clause (2) of this subsection.

(4) The royalty fees thus deposited shall, in accordance with the procedures provided by clause (5), be distributed to those among the following copyright owners who claim that their works were the subject of secondary transmissions by cable systems during the relevant semiannual period:

(A) any such owner whose work was included in a secondary transmission made by a cable system of a non-network television program in whole or in part beyond the local service area of the primary transmitter; and

(B) any such owner whose work was included in a secondary transmission identified in a special statement of account deposited under clause (2)(A); and

(C) any such owner whose work was included in non-network programing consisting exclusively of aural signals carried by a cable system in whole or in part beyond the local service area of the primary transmitter of such programs.

(5) The royalty fees thus deposited shall be distributed in accordance with the following procedures:

(A) During the month of July in each year, every person claiming to be entitled to compulsory license fees for secondary transmissions shall file a claim with the Copyright Royalty Tribunal, in accordance with requirements that the Tribunal shall prescribe by regulation. Notwithstanding any provisions of the antitrust laws, for purposes of this clause any claimants may agree among themselves as to the proportionate division of compulsory licensing fees among them, may lump their claims together and file them jointly or as a single claim, or may designate a common agent to receive payment on their behalf.

(B) After the first day of August of each year, the Copyright Royalty Tribunal shall determine whether there exists a controversy concerning the distribution of royalty fees. If the Tribunal determines that no such controversy exists, it shall, after deducting its reasonable administrative costs under this section, distribute such fees to the copyright owners entitled, or to their designated agents. If the Tribunal finds the existence of a controversy, it shall, pursuant to chapter 8 of this title, conduct a proceeding to determine the distribution of royalty fees.

(C) During the pendency of any proceeding under this subsection, the Copyright Royalty Tribunal shall withhold from distribution an amount sufficient to satisfy all claims with respect to which a controversy exists, but shall have discretion to proceed to distribute any amounts that are not in controversy.

(e) *Nonsimultaneous Secondary Transmissions by Cable Systems.*

(1) Notwithstanding those provisions of the second paragraph of subsection (f) relating to nonsimultaneous secondary transmissions by a cable system, any

such transmissions are actionable as an act of infringement under section 501, and are fully subject to the remedies provided by sections 502 through 506 and sections 509 and 510, unless—

(A) the program on the videotape is transmitted no more than one time to the cable system's subscribers; and

(B) the copyrighted program, episode, or motion picture videotape, including the commercials contained within such program, episode, or picture, is transmitted without deletion or editing; and

(C) an owner or officer of the cable system (i) prevents the duplication of the videotape while in the possession of the system, (ii) prevents unauthorized duplication while in the possession of the facility making the videotape for the system if the system owns or controls the facility, or takes reasonable precautions to prevent such duplication if it does not own or control the facility, (iii) takes adequate precautions to prevent duplication while the tape is being transported, and (iv) subject to clause (2), erases or destroys, or causes the erasure or destruction of, the videotape; and

(D) within forty-five days after the end of each calendar quarter, an owner or officer of the cable system executes an affidavit attesting (i) to the steps and precautions taken to prevent duplication of the videotape, and (ii) subject to clause (2), to the erasure or destruction of all videotapes made or used during such quarter; and

(E) such owner or officer places or causes each such affidavit, and affidavits received pursuant to clause (2)(C), to be placed in a file, open to public inspection, at such system's main office in the community where the transmission is made or in the nearest community where such system maintains an office; and

(F) the nonsimultaneous transmission is one that the cable system would be authorized to transmit under the rules, regulations, and authorizations of the Federal Communications Commission in effect at the time of the nonsimultaneous transmission if the transmission had been made simultaneously, except that this subclause shall not apply to inadvertent or accidental transmissions.

(2) If a cable system transfers to any person a videotape of a program nonsimultaneously transmitted by it, such transfer is actionable as an act of infringement under section 501, and is fully subject to the remedies provided by sections 502 through 506 and 509, except that, pursuant to a written, nonprofit contract providing for the equitable sharing of the costs of such videotape and its transfer, a videotape nonsimultaneously transmitted by it, in accordance with clause (1), may be transferred by one cable system in Alaska to another system in Alaska, by one cable system in Hawaii permitted to make such nonsimultaneous transmissions to another such cable system in Hawaii, or by one cable system in Guam, the Northern Mariana Islands, or the Trust Territory of the Pacific Islands, to another cable system in any of those three territories, if—

(A) each such contract is available for public inspection in the offices of the cable systems involved, and a copy of such contract is filed, within thirty days after such contract is entered into, with the Copyright Office (which Office shall make each such contract available for public inspection); and

(B) the cable system to which the videotape is transferred complies with clause (1)(A), (B), (C)(i), (iii), and (iv), and (D) through (F); and

(C) such system provides a copy of the affidavit required to be made in accordance with clause (1)(D) to each cable system making a previous non-simultaneous transmission of the same videotape.

(3) This subsection shall not be construed to supersede the exclusivity protection provisions of any existing agreement, or any such agreement hereafter entered into, between a cable system and a television broadcast station in the area in which the cable system is located, or a network with which such station is affiliated.

(4) As used in this subsection, the term "videotape," and each of its variant forms, means the reproduction of the images and sounds of a program or programs broadcast by a television broadcast station licensed by the Federal Communications Commission, regardless of the nature of the material objects, such as tapes or films, in which the reproduction is embodied.

(f) *Definitions.* As used in this section, the following terms and their variant forms mean the following:

A "primary transmission" is a transmission made to the public by the transmitting facility whose signals are being received and further transmitted by the secondary transmission service, regardless of where or when the performance or display was first transmitted.

A "secondary transmission" is the further transmitting of a primary transmission simultaneously with the primary transmission, or nonsimultaneously with the primary transmission if by a "cable system" not located in whole or in part within the boundary of the forty-eight contiguous States, Hawaii, or Puerto Rico: *Provided, however,* That a nonsimultaneous further transmission by a cable system located in Hawaii of a primary transmission shall be deemed to be a secondary transmission if the carriage of the television broadcast signal comprising such further transmission is permissible under the rules, regulations, or authorizations of the Federal Communications Commission.

A "cable system" is a facility, located in any State, Territory, Trust Territory, or Possession, that in whole or in part receives signals transmitted or programs broadcast by one or more television broadcast stations licensed by the Federal Communications Commission, and makes secondary transmissions of such signals or programs by wires, cables, or other communications channels to subscribing members of the public who pay for such service. For purposes of determining the royalty fee under subsection (d)(2), two or more cable systems in contiguous communities under common ownership or control or operating from one headend shall be considered as one system.

The "local service area of a primary transmitter," in the case of a television broadcast station, comprises the area in which such station is entitled to insist upon its signal being retransmitted by a cable system pursuant to the rules, regulations, and authorizations of the Federal Communications Commission in effect on April 15, 1976, or in the case of a television broadcast station licensed by an appropriate governmental authority of Canada or Mexico, the area in which it would be entitled to insist upon its signal being retransmitted if it were a television broadcast station subject to such rules, regulations, and authorizations. The "local service area of a primary transmitter," in the case of a radio broadcast station, comprises the primary service area of such station, pursuant to the rules and regulations of the Federal Communications Commission.

A "distant signal equivalent" is the value assigned to the secondary transmission of any nonnetwork television programing carried by a cable system in whole or in part beyond the local service area of the primary transmitter of such programing. It is computed by assigning a value of one to each independent station and a value of one-quarter to each network station and noncommercial educational station for the nonnetwork programing so carried pursuant to the rules, regulations, and authorizations of the Federal Communications Commission. The foregoing values for independent, network, and noncommercial educational stations are subject, however, to the following exceptions and limitations. Where the rules and regulations of the Federal Communications Commission require a cable system to omit the further transmission of a particular program and such rules and regulations also permit the substitution of another program embodying a performance or display of a work in place of the omitted transmission, or where such rules and regulations in effect on the date of enactment of this Act permit a cable system, at its election, to effect such deletion and substitution of a nonlive program or to carry additional programs not transmitted by primary transmitters within whose local service area the cable system is located, no value shall be assigned for the substituted or additional program; where the rules, regulations, or authorizations of the Federal Communications Commission in effect on the date of enactment of this Act permit a cable system, at its election, to omit the further transmission of a particular program and such rules, regulations, or authorizations also permit the substitution of another program embodying a performance or display of a work in place of the omitted transmission, the value assigned for the substituted or additional program shall be, in the case of a live program, the value of one full distant signal equivalent multiplied by a fraction that has as its numerator the number of days in the year in which such substitution occurs and as its denominator the number of days in the year. In the case of a station carried pursuant to the late-night or specialty programing rules of the Federal Communications Commission, or a station carried on a part-time basis where full-time carriage is not possible because the cable system lacks the activated channel capacity to retransmit on a full-time basis all signals which it is authorized to carry, the values for independent, network, and noncommercial educational stations set forth above, as the case may be, shall be multiplied by a fraction which is equal to the ratio of the broadcast hours of such station carried by the cable system to the total broadcast hours of the station.

A "network station" is a television broadcast station that is owned or operated by, or affiliated with, one or more of the television networks in the United States providing nationwide transmissions, and that transmits a substantial part of the programing supplied by such networks for a substantial part of that station's typical broadcast day.

An "independent station" is a commercial television broadcast station other than a network station.

A "noncommercial educational station" is a television station that is a noncommercial educational broadcast station as defined in section 397 of title 47.

46
Indecency in Broadcasting

Pacifica Foundation v. Federal Communications Commission*
556 F.2d 9 (D.C. Cir.)
March 16, 1977

Obscene, indecent, or profane utterances in broadcasting are prohibited by Section 1464 of the U.S. Criminal Code (p. 575) and are not afforded the same protection by the First Amendment to the Constitution (pp. 1-2) and Section 326 of the Communications Act (pp. 542-543) provided to other forms of expression. Civil (as opposed to criminal) sanctions may be invoked by the FCC for violation of Section 1464 under Sections 303 (p. 525), 312 (pp. 535-536) and 503 (p. 566) of the Communications Act. In all probability, profanity on the air is constitutionally protected, although no recent case has tested precisely this question. Clearly, obscenity is not constitutionally protected under present legal standards. Where does this leave indecency?

The FCC first levied a token forfeiture against a radio station that broadcast allegedly indecent speech in the *WUHY-FM* case in 1970 (see p. 310). Because no appeal was taken from this decision, the courts had no opportunity to affirm, reverse, or modify the Commission's determination. Three years later the Commission fined station WGLD-FM of Oak Park, Illinois (a Chicago

*Reprinted with the permission of West Publishing Company.

suburb) $2,000 for airing material characterized by the FCC as "obscene or indecent" [*Sonderling Broadcasting Corp.*, 41 FCC 2d 919 (1973)]. From 10 a.m. to 3 p.m., 5 days a week, the station broadcast a popular call-in show, "Femme Forum," on which a number of topics related to women's interests, including various aspects of sex, were discussed. Perhaps 200 stations throughout America carried similar programs that were available from syndication sources or produced locally. Because of the candor with which sexual matters were treated, the programs were casually referred to as "topless radio." A WGLD-FM program on the topic of oral sex included this exchange:

> Female Listener: . . . of course I had a few hangups at first about—in regard to this, but you know what we did—I have a craving for peanut butter all that [*sic*] time so I used to spread this on my husband's privates and after a while, I mean, I didn't even need the peanut butter any more.
> Announcer: (Laughs) Peanut butter, huh?
> Listener: Right. Oh, we can try anything—you know—any, any of these women that have called and they have, you know, hangups about this, I mean they should try their favorite—you know like—uh. . . .
> Announcer: Whipped cream, marshmallow . . .

Such programming was either softened or whisked off the air following the FCC's announcement of the institution of a "non-public" inquiry to find out whether and to what extent Section 1464 was being violated, the simultaneous passage of a resolution by the National Association of Broadcasters deploring the airing of such content, and a speech to the NAB by FCC Chairman Dean Burch who urged broadcasters to show restraint and good taste in programming lest the government be forced to take action.

WGLD-FM paid the forfeiture. When citizens appealed, the Court of Appeals upheld the Commission's action on the obscenity (but not indecency) finding. The court held that "where a radio call-in show during daytime hours [when the audience may include children] broadcasts explicit discussions of ultimate sexual acts in a titillating context, the Commission does not unconstitutionally infringe upon the public's right to listening alternatives when it determines that the broadcast is obscene." [*Illinois Citizens Committee for Broadcasting* v. *FCC*, 515 F.2d 397 (D.C. Cir. 1975).] Thus the "indecency" question was left unanswered; indeed, even the "obscenity" aspect was not thoroughly resolved, for the issues before the court could have been very different had WGLD-FM itself contested the forfeiture.

Following on the heels of the court's affirmation, the FCC fashioned a definition of "indecency" which it applied to a George Carlin recording aired by radio station WBAI in New York City [*Pacifica Foundation*, 56 FCC 2d 94 (1975)]. Although no forfeiture was imposed by the Commission in this case, the licensee of the noncommercial station appealed the finding that it had broadcast indecent material.

The Court of Appeals overturned the FCC decision by a two-to-one vote. Judge Tamm's narrowly drawn and cogently reasoned opinion for the court is the only one reproduced below. Chief Judge Bazelon's concurring opinion went beyond the majority finding that the FCC's action was contrary to the Communications Act by holding the action unconstitutional as well. Judge Leventhal, author of the court's prior opinion in the "topless radio" case, *supra*, dissented in this case, contending that the Commission's action was legally sound in light of the "compelling state interest" in protecting children from the kind of language used in the Carlin comedy routine. The FCC unsuccessfully sought to have the case reheard by the appellate court, whereupon the Commission petitioned the Supreme Court to review the matter as this book was in press.

Problems will persist in the area of obscenity and indecency on radio, television, and cable. Advertiser-supported media outlets generally manage to avoid violating standards of taste for fear of offending audience members and losing sponsor support. Because noncommercial stations are free of economic ties to advertisers for the most part, they are more likely to test the limits of taste in programming. Hence, those stations that are least able to afford expensive legal battles are the vanguard of those forces tunneling through the shifting sands of free expression in broadcasting. It will be some time before broadcast speech is as protected from inhibiting influences as is intimate, interpersonal dialogue at the informal level. [See *Trustees of the University of Pennsylvania (WXPN(FM))*, 57 FCC 2d 782 (1975); 57 FCC 2d 793 (1976).]

Related Reading: 15, 76, 150, 161, 163, 174, 184, 215, 219, 239.

Tamm, Circuit Judge:

This appeal by Pacifica Foundation (Pacifica) challenges a Federal Communications Commission (FCC or Commission) ruling which purports to ban prospectively the broadcast, whenever children are in the audience, of language which depicts sexual or excretory activities and organs, specifically seven patently offensive words.*

Without deciding the perplexing question of whether the FCC, because of the unique characteristics of radio and television, may prohibit non-obscene speech or speech that would otherwise be constitutionally protected, we find that the challenged ruling is overbroad and carries the FCC beyond protection of the public interest into the forbidden realm of censorship. For the reasons which follow, we reverse the Commission's order.

I. FACTUAL BACKGROUND

On the afternoon of October 30, 1973, Station WBAI, New York, New York (which is licensed to Pacifica), was conducting a general discussion of contemporary society's attitude toward language as part of its regular programming. The WBAI host played a segment from the album, "George Carlin, Occupation: Foole," Little David Records. Immediately prior to broadcast of the Carlin monologue, listeners were advised that it included sensitive language which might be regarded as offensive to some. Those who might be offended were advised to change the station and return to WBAI in fifteen minutes. The monologue consisted of a comedy routine that was almost entirely devoted to the use of seven four-letter words depicting sexual or excretory organs and activities.

On December 3, 1973, the Commission received a complaint from a man in New York stating that, while driving in his car with his young son, he had heard the WBAI broadcast of the Carlin monologue. This was the only complaint lodged with either the FCC or WBAI concerning the Carlin broadcast.

The Commission determined that clarification of its definition of the term "indecent" was in order. As a result, in *Pacifica Foundation,* 56 FCC 2d 94 (1975) (hereinafter *Order*), the Commission defined as indecent, language that describes, in terms patently offensive as measured by contemporary community standards for the broadcast medium, sexual or excretory activities and organs, at times of the day when there is a reasonable risk that children may be in the audience. The Commission found that the seven four-letter words contained in the Carlin monologue depicted sexual or excretory organs and activities in a patently offensive manner, judged by contemporary community standards for the broadcast medium, and accordingly, were indecent. The Commission prohibited them from being broadcast under the authority granted it by 18 U.S.C. § 1464 (1970).[1] As a further rationale for its decision, the Commission cited its

---

*The words are: shit; piss; fuck; cunt; cocksucker; motherfucker; tits. [Ed.]
[1] 18 U.S.C. § 1464 (1970) provides:

Whoever utters any obscene, indecent, or profane language by means of radio communication shall be fined not more than $10,000 or imprisoned not more than two years, or both.

statutory obligation to promote the larger and more effective use of radio in the public interest.[2]

The underlying rationale of the *Order* can be traced to the Commission's view of broadcasting vis-à-vis other modes of communication and expression. According to the Commission, the broadcasting medium carries with it certain unique characteristics which distinguish it from other modes of communication and expression. In the Commission's view the most important characteristic of the broadcast medium is its intrusive nature. Unlike other modes of expression, the television or radio broadcast comes directly into the home without any significant affirmative activity on the part of the listener. *See Eastern Educational Radio (WUHY-FM),* 24 FCC 2d 408 (1970); *Illinois Citizens Committee for Broadcasting* v. *FCC,* 515 F.2d 397 (D.C. Cir. 1975). In the *Order* the FCC concluded this intrusive nature was a critical factor due to four important considerations: (1) children have access to radios and in some cases are unsupervised by parents; (2) radio receivers are in the home, a place where people's privacy interest is entitled to extra deference; (3) unconsenting adults may tune in a station without any warning that offensive language is being or will be broadcast; and (4) there is a scarcity of spectrum space, the use of which the government must therefore license in the public interest. *Order* at 97.

In light of these considerations the Commission felt that questions concerning the broadcast of patently offensive language should be dealt with in a public nuisance context. As a result the Commission determined that the principle of channeling[3] should be borrowed from nuisance law and applied to the broadcasting medium. Rather than prohibit the broadcast of indecent language altogether, the Commission sought to channel it to times of the day when it would offend the fewest number of listeners.

In hopes of avoiding the charge that the *Order* was overbroad, the Commission declared that the channeling was specifically intended to protect children from exposure to language that describes, in terms patently offensive as measured by contemporary community standards for the broadcast medium, sexual or excretory activities and organs, at times of the day when there is a reasonable risk that children may be in the audience. *Order* at 98.

Finally, the Commission did note that when the number of children in the audience is reduced to a minimum, a different standard might conceivably be used. In such an analysis the definition of indecent would remain the same, how-

---

[2] 47 U.S.C. § 303 (1970) provides:

Except as otherwise provided in this Act, the Commission from time to time, as public convenience, necessity or interest requires, shall:

(g) Study new uses for radio, provide for experimental uses of frequencies, and generally encourage the larger and more effective use of radio in the public interest . . . .

[3] The law of nuisance does not say, for example, that no one shall maintain a cement plant; it simply says that no one shall maintain a cement plant in an inappropriate place, such as a residential neighborhood.

ever, the Commission would also consider whether the material had serious literary, artistic, political or scientific value. *Order* at 100.

In concurring statements, Commissioners Reid and Quello felt the *Order* did not go far enough. Commissioner Reid believed indecent language was inappropriate for broadcast at any time. Commissioner Quello was in agreement, commenting that "garbage is garbage" and it should all be prohibited from the airwaves. *Id.* at 102, 103.

Appellant Pacifica argues that section 1464 is unconstitutionally vague unless the term indecent is subsumed by the term obscene as defined in *Miller v. California,* 413 U.S. 15 (1973). Pacifica contends that the Supreme Court, in *Hamling v. United States,* 418 U.S. 87 (1974) and *United States v. 12 200 Ft. Reels of Super 8mm Film,* 413 U.S. 123 (1973), has made it clear that the term indecent, as used in federal criminal statutes, must be construed as referring to material involving the specific types of explicit conduct defined in *Miller v. California,*[4] *supra,* in order for the constitutionality of the statute employing the term to be sustained. Pacifica also cites numerous other federal and state court decisions which have invariably held that the term indecent, as used in criminal statutes, refers to material which appeals to prurient interest as distinguished from material which is merely coarse, rude, vulgar, profane or opprobrious.[5]

Pacifica argues that the Carlin monologue is not obscene because it does not appeal to any prurient interest and because it has literary and political value. Therefore, Pacifica argues it is entitled to constitutional protection in light of *Miller* and *Hamling, supra.* Pacifica concludes that such constitutional protection means that these words may not be prohibited by section 1464. In addition, Pacifica contends that the non-obscene language used in the Carlin monologue does not come within the fighting words prohibition set forth in *Chaplinsky v. New Hampshire,* 315 U.S. 568 (1942).

Finally, Pacifica contends that the FCC standard of indecency, as expressed in the *Order,* is overbroad as it does not assure that programs of serious literary, artistic, political or scientific value will be allowed to air.[6] The amicus brief in this appeal argues that the *Order* is too far-reaching and will have an especially harsh effect on the broadcast of literature depicting minority cultures. In addition, the amicus brief quotes studies,[7] which show that large numbers of children

[4] The *Miller* standard is

(a) whether the average person, applying contemporary community standards would find that the work, taken as a whole, appeals to the prurient interest;
(b) whether the work depicts or describes in a patently offensive way, sexual conduct specifically defined by the applicable state law;
(c) whether the work, taken as a whole, lacks serious literary, artistic, political or scientific value. 413 U.S. at 24.

[5] Pacifica's Brief at 24, n. 23.
[6] *See* App. B. at 28, et seq.
[7] Amicus's Brief at 17 *quoting* Statement of John A. Schneider, Before the House Subcommittee on Communications, July 15, 1975, p. 9.

are in the broadcast audience until 1:30 a.m., as further evidence that the *Order* is overbroad.

One week prior to oral argument in this case the FCC released a memorandum and order seeking to clarify its earlier *Order*. The order of clarification[8] was in response to a petition filed by the Radio Television News Directors Association. In the clarification order, the Commission declared that it never intended to place an absolute prohibition on the broadcast of indecent language but only sought to channel it to times of the day when children would least likely be exposed to it.[9] The clarifying order, in attempting to narrow the scope of the original *Order,* ruled that indecent language could be broadcast in a news or public affairs program or otherwise if it was aired at a time when the number of children in the audience was reduced to a minimum, if sufficient warning were given to unconsenting adults, and if the language in context had serious literary, artistic, political or scientific value.[10] The Commission determined that it would be inequitable to hold a licensee responsible for indecent language broadcast during live coverage of a newsmaking event.[11] The Commission thought it better to trust the licensee to exercise judgment, responsibility and sensitivity to the needs, interest, and tastes of the community.[12]

II. RESOLUTION

Despite the Commission's professed intentions, the direct effect of its *Order* is to inhibit the free and robust exchange of ideas on a wide range of issues and subjects by means of radio and television communications. In promulgating the *Order* the Commission has ignored both the statute which forbids it to censor radio communications[13] and its own previous decisions and orders which leave the question of programming content to the discretion of the licensee.[14]

The Commission claims that its *Order* does not censor indecent language but

[8] Pacifica Foundation, 59 FCC 2d 892, 36 P&F Radio Reg. 2d 1008 (1976).
[9] *Id.*
[10] *Id.*
[11] *Id.*
[12] *Id.*
[13] 47 U.S.C. § 326 (1970) provides:

Nothing in this Act [The Communications Act of 1934] shall be understood or construed to give the Commission the power of censorship over the radio communications or signals transmitted by any radio station, and no regulation or condition shall be promulgated or fixed by the Commission which shall interfere with the right of free speech by means of radio communication.

[14] *See* Sonderling Broadcasting Corp., 41 FCC 2d 777 (1973); Jack Straw Memorial Foundation, 29 FCC 2d 334 (1971); Columbia Broadcasting System, Inc., 21 P&F Radio Reg. 2d 497 (1971); Oliver R. Grace, 22 FCC 2d 667 (1970).

rather channels it to certain times of the day. In fact the *Order* is censorship, regardless of what the Commission chooses to call it. The intent of the Commission is clear. It is to keep language that describes sexual or excretory organs and activities from the airwaves when there is a reasonable risk that children may be in the audience. The Commission expressly states that this language has "no place on radio" and that when children are in the audience a claim that it has literary, artistic, political or scientific value will not redeem it. *Order* at 98.

As the study cited by the amicus curiae, *supra* note 7, illustrates, large numbers of children are in the broadcast audience until 1:30 a.m. The number of children watching television does not fall below one million until 1:00 a.m. As long as such large numbers of children are in the audience the seven words noted in the *Order* may not be broadcast. Whether the broadcast containing such words may have serious artistic, literary, political or scientific value has no bearing on the prohibitive effect of the *Order*. The Commission's action proscribes the uncensored broadcast of many of the great works of literature including Shakespearian plays and contemporary plays which have won critical acclaim, the works of renowned classical and contemporary poets and writers, and passages from the *Bible*.[15]

Section 326 of the Communications Act specifically prohibits the FCC from interfering with licensee discretion in programming. *Writers Guild of America, West, Inc. v. FCC,* 423 F. Supp. 1064 (C.D. Cal. 1976). Such interference is exactly what the *Order* calls for. Therefore it is an action which takes the Commission beyond the limits of the powers which Congress has delegated to it. Congress specifically withheld from the Commission any power to censor broadcasts. *Anti-Defamation League of B'Nai B'Rith v. FCC,* 403 F.2d 169 (D.C. Cir. 1968), *cert. denied,* 394 U.S. 930 (1969); 47 U.S.C. § 326 (1970). An examination of thought or expression in order to prevent publication of objectionable material is censorship. 403 F.2d 169.

In an effort to sustain the validity of its *Order* the Commission labels its prospective ban a channeling mechanism. The label is unimportant, the effect of the *Order* is critical. The effect is that of censorship and that is beyond the mandate of the FCC.

In past decisions the Commission has recognized the ban against censorship and has taken another tack against indecent language. In *Jack Straw Memorial Foundation,* 29 FCC 2d 334 (1971), the Commission determined that the decision whether to broadcast obscene or indecent language was a licensee decision. In this case, the licensee, after careful consideration, broadcast the record, "Murder at Kent State," which contained language which the licensee considered obscene and ordinarily would not have permitted to be broadcast. The trustees and managerial employees decided that in their judgment the use of the particular language was necessary under the circumstances. In its ruling the Commission held that

[15] App. B. at 28–39.

[t] his is a matter of judgment which we conclude the Commission has left to the licensee. In this case, language was not broadcast for shock or sensationalism, but rather for the purpose of presenting a vivid accurate account of a disastrous incident in our recent history. We conclude that on this exercise of judgment, the licensee conformed to standards prescribed by the Commission as well as its own policies regarding suitability.

29 FCC 2d at 354. In *Oliver R. Grace*, 22 FCC 2d 667 (1970), the Commission, recognizing that section 326 of the Communications Act prohibited it from censoring broadcast matter, held that program choice was the responsibility of the licensee; the licensee was required to ascertain and reasonably serve the needs and interests of his community; and the charge that programs are vulgar or presented without due regard for sensitivity, intelligence, and taste, was not properly cognizable by the Commission, in light of the proscription against censorship. *Id.* at 668.

The importance of independent judgment by local licensees has been affirmed again and again by the FCC and the courts.[16] Perhaps the most important ruling for our purpose is the Commission's clarification memorandum regarding the original *Order*. There the Commission recognized that

in some cases, public events likely to produce offensive speech are covered live, and there is no opportunity for journalistic editing. Under these circumstances we believe that it would be inequitable for us to hold a licensee responsible for indecent language.

Pacifica Foundation, 59 FCC 2d 892, 893, n. 1 (1976). Thus the Commission indirectly admitted it had gone too far in banning "indecent" language from the airwaves. The Commission decided it would be better to trust the licensee to exercise judgment, responsibility and sensitivity to the community's needs, interests and tastes. *Id.*

Previously the Commission has readily admitted that its authority in the area of profane, obscene, or indecent language is governed by federal statutes as interpreted by the courts. The FCC has recognized that it must perform its duties in this area without infringing upon constitutional guarantees of freedom of speech and of the press, *Columbia Broadcasting System, Inc.*, 21 P & F Radio Reg. 2d 497 (1971), and without violating the statutory obligations of section 326 of the Communications Act. It must continue to do so.

We do not find it necessary to determine whether the term "indecent" can be more narrowly defined than the term "obscene." The FCC's position is that "indecent" language may be distinguished from "obscene" language in that it

---

[16] *See* Writers Guild of America, West, Inc. v. FCC, 423 F. Supp. 1064 (C.D. Cal. 1976); Report on Broadcast of Violent Indecent and Obscene Material, 51 FCC 2d 418 (1975); Network Programming Inquiry, 39 Fed. Reg. 26372 (1974). En Banc Programming Inquiry, 44 FCC 2303 (1960).

lacks the element of appeal to prurient interest and that when children are in the audience it cannot be redeemed by a claim that it has literary, artistic, political or scientific value. *Order* at 98.

This question has confronted other courts but there have been no definitive resolutions as yet. In *Gagliardo v. United States,* 336 F.2d 720 (9th Cir. 1966), the Ninth Circuit left open the question whether indecent, as used in section 1464, could be defined differently from obscene. Although the question of whether indecent might mean something different from obscene was raised in *Tallman v. United States,* 465 F.2d 282 (7th Cir. 1972), it was not resolved since the case had only been tried on the theory that the defendant had uttered obscene language. The question was considered only tangentially in *United States v. Smith,* 467 F.2d 1126 (7th Cir. 1972), where the court reversed a conviction under section 1464 on the grounds that the jury had not been instructed as to the meaning of the statutory terms profane and indecent, even though the case had been presented to the jury under an indictment charging the defendant with uttering obscene, indecent and profane language. In reversing the conviction, the court did not suggest in what way, if at all, indecent language might differ from obscene language. It is evident therefore that the term indecent has never been authoritatively construed by the courts in connection with section 1464. Since we feel section 326 of the Communications Act is dispositive of this appeal we do not find it necessary to resolve this difficult question.

Unquestionably the Commission's *Order* also raises First Amendment considerations. The Commission recognized that Congress had prohibited it from engaging in censorship or interfering "with the right of free speech by means of radio communication."[17] In the *Order,* the Commission contends that because of its unique qualities the broadcast medium is not subject to the same constitutional standards that may be applied to other less intrusive forms of expression.

There is no doubt that the regulatory authority of the FCC encompasses more than the technical engineering aspects of the broadcast medium. Under its mandate to promote the public interest, the Commission may promulgate rules on a variety of matters, including broadcast programming. However, any such actions by the Commission must be carefully tailored to meet the requirements of the First Amendment, as Congress has explicitly mandated in section 326 of the Communications Act.

The requirements of the First Amendment relating to obscenity are found in *Miller v. California,* 413 U.S. 15 (1973). In *Miller,* the Court set forth a subjective standard by which the trier of fact could determine whether material was obscene. The standard developed by the Court involves: a) whether the average person applying contemporary community standards would find that the work, taken as a whole, appeals to the prurient interest; b) whether the work depicts or describes, in a patently offensive way, sexual conduct specifically defined by

[17]47 U.S.C. § 326 (1970).

the applicable state law; and c) whether the work, taken as a whole, lacks serious literary, artistic, political or scientific value. *Miller,* 413 U.S. at 24.

Applying the *Miller* standard to the language used in the Carlin monologue, it is clear that although the language is crude and vulgar by most standards it is not obscene. The FCC agrees. *Order* at 98. As used, the words do not appeal to the prurient interest.[18] They are merely crude statements and are not used to titillate. Furthermore, the words prohibited by the *Order* may often be connected with programs in the public interest, e.g., plays and live news broadcasts. Thus, these words quite possibly could have literary, political or artistic value. Therefore this non-obscene speech is entitled to First Amendment protection.

The Commission claims an exception from First Amendment requirements in order to carry out its duty to promote the use of radio communications in the public interest. The basis of this claim is that the broadcast medium is unique. Assuming, arguendo, that the FCC has the power to prohibit non-obscene speech from being broadcast, the statute or order instituting such a ban must not be overbroad or vague. *See Young v. American Mini Theatres, Inc.,* 427 U.S. 50 (1976). As will be illustrated, the *Order,* in its application of Section 1464, suffers from overbreadth and vagueness.

In *Erznoznik v. City of Jacksonville,* 422 U.S. 205 (1975), the Court held that rigorous constitutional standards apply when government attempts to regulate expression. Furthermore, when the government, acting as censor, undertakes selectively to shield the public from some kinds of speech on the ground that they are more offensive than others, the First Amendment strictly limits its power. *Id.* at 209. Indeed, when First Amendment freedoms are at stake, the Court has repeatedly emphasized that precision of drafting and clarity of purpose are essential. *Id.* at 217-18.

The FCC's regulation of speech per its *Order* fails to meet the rigorous standards of the Supreme Court. A look at *Erznoznik* will help illustrate why. There a municipal ordinance made it unlawful for a drive-in theater to exhibit any motion picture in which the human male or female buttocks, human female bare breasts or human bare pubic areas were shown. The city attempted to sustain the ordinance as an effort to protect children. The Court held that minors are entitled to First Amendment protection and only in relatively narrow, well-defined circumstances may the government bar public dissemination of protected materials to them. *Erznoznik,* 422 U.S. at 212-13. The Court found the ordinance overbroad in that it sweepingly forbad the display of all films containing any uncovered breasts or buttocks, irrespective of context or pervasiveness. *Id.* at 213. Mr. Justice Powell, writing for the majority, stated that

[s]peech that is neither obscene nor subject to some other legitimate proscription cannot be suppressed solely to protect the young from ideas or images that a legislative body thinks unsuitable for them. 422 U.S. 213-14.

[18]*See* App. A at 10-12.

The situation in this appeal is quite similar to that in *Erznoznik.* The *Order* prohibits the broadcast of seven words at times of the day when there is a reasonable risk that children will be in the audience. Thus, the *Order* sweepingly forbids any broadcast of the seven words irrespective of context or however innocent or educational they may be. For instance, the *Order* would prohibit the broadcast of Shakespeare's *The Tempest* or *Two Gentlemen of Verona.* Certain passages of the *Bible* are also proscribed from broadcast by the *Order.*[19] Clearly every use of these seven words cannot be deemed offensive even as to minors. In this regard the *Order* is overbroad. It is not saved by the attempted clarification, for that order would only permit the words to be broadcast on live news shows or very late at night.[20]

In addition, the *Order* is vague in that it fails to define children. Need a nineteen year old and a seven year old be protected from the same offensive language? The Supreme Court has held that in assessing the requisite capacity of individual choice the age of the minor is a significant factor.[21] The *Order* does not even consider age as a factor, much less a significant one.

The Commission also attempts to justify its *Order* by claiming that, due to the intrusive nature of broadcasting, a captive audience is present. This argument is persuasive when the degree of captivity makes it impractical for the unwilling viewer or auditor to avoid exposure. However, as the Supreme Court noted in *Lehman v. City of Shaker Heights,* 418 U.S. 298, 302 (1974), "[t]he radio can be turned off."

Cohen v. California, 403 U.S. 15 (1971), is also analogous to the present situation. Cohen was convicted of violating California Penal Code Section 415, which prohibits "maliciously and wilfully disturb[ing] the peace or quiet of any neighborhood or person . . . by . . . offensive conduct . . . ." Cohen had walked in a public corridor of the Los Angeles County Courthouse wearing a jacket inscribed with a four-letter word. California argued that the state may act to protect the unwilling or unsuspecting viewers from unavoidable exposure to such language. *Id.* at 21. This reasoning is similar to the FCC's expressed desire to protect the unsuspecting dial scanner from crude, offensive programming. In *Cohen,* the Court held that government control of objectionable speech can be tolerated only when substantial privacy interests are being invaded in an essentially intolerable manner. 403 U.S. at 21. Such an invasion had not occurred in *Cohen,* the Court found, because the offensive expression had occurred in public and because citizens could avoid it easily by averting their eyes. *Id.* Likewise, one can argue an intolerable invasion of privacy would not occur in the broadcast setting. Privacy expectations, even in the home, diminish when listeners

---

[19] In addition, works of Auden, Becket, Lord Byron, Chaucer, Fielding, Greene, Hemingway, Joyce, Knowles, Lawrence, Orwell, Scott, Swift and the Nixon tapes, would not be allowed to air.

[20] Pacifica Foundation, *supra,* note 8.

[21] Rowan v. Post Office Dept., 397 U.S. 728 (1970).

choose to gain access to a public medium.[22] The dial scanner may avoid exposure simply by turning the dial. The Commission itself has recognized that listeners do not possess any right to be free from all unpleasantness.[23] In its effort to shield children from language which is not too rugged for many adults the Commission has taken a step toward reducing the adult population to hearing or viewing only that which is fit for children. The Commission's *Order* is a classic case of burning the house to roast the pig. *See Butler v. Michigan,* 352 U.S. 380, 383 (1957).

As defined by Congress, and refined by the FCC and the courts, public interest has always been understood to require licensees to offer some balance in their program format. *See Renewal of Standard Broadcast and Television Licenses,* 14 F.C.C.2d 1, 8 (1968). Obviously balanced programming requires more than just programs suitable for children. Speech cannot be stifled by the government merely because it would draw an adverse reaction from the majority of the people. *Bazaar v. Fortune,* 476 F.2d 570, 579 (5th Cir.), *modified,* 489 F.2d 225 (1973).

The Commission assumes that absent FCC action, filth will flood the airwaves. Thus the Commission argues that the alternative of turning the dial will not aid the sensitive person in his efforts to avoid filthy language. The *Order* provides no empirical data to substantiate this assumption. Moreover, the assumption ignores the forces of economics and of ratings on the substance of programming. Licensees are businesses and depend on advertising revenues for survival. The corporate profit motive and the connection between advertising revenue and audience size suggest that the dike will hold as long as the community remains actually offended by what it sees or hears.[24] Commentators and commissioners alike have noted that broadcast media require majorities, or at least sizeable pluralities, to pay the bills.[25] If they are correct, and if the Commission truly seeks only to enforce community standards, the market should limit the filth accordingly.[26]

---

[22] *See Filthy Words, The FCC, and the First Amendment: Regulating Broadcast Obscenity,* 61 Va. L. Rev. 579 (1975).

[23] Clarification of Section 76.256 of the Commission's Rules and Regulations, 59 FCC 2d 984 (1976).

[24] *See Filthy Words, supra,* note 18, at 615.

[25] *Id. citing* N. Johnson, How to Talk Back to Your Television Set, 20-21 (1967); N. Minow, Equal Time, The Private Broadcaster and the Public Interest.

[26] *See Filthy Words, supra,* note 18, at 615.

As a final word we take note of a news account which, under the headline "Swearing by British Rock Band Enrages Television Viewers," reported the reaction of the British television audience to a broadcast containing filthy language. According to the report members of a rock band had used a string of obscenities on a London television program which had aired at 6:00 p.m. (The Washington Post, December 3, 1976, Style section, at 7, col. 2) Following the broadcast thousands of angry calls jammed the switchboard at Thames Television Studios and thousands of others were received by the London newspapers in protest of the broadcast. Thames Television broadcast an apology later the same evening and the host of the program planned to make a personal apology on the air the following evening. In this instance it seems rather clear that the London community was offended by what it had heard and that its reaction thereto stemmed any tide of filth that may have been headed its way.

CONCLUSION

As we find that the Commission's *Order* is in violation of its duty to avoid censorship of radio communications under 47 U.S.C. § 326 and that even assuming, arguendo, that the Commission may regulate non-obscene speech, nevertheless its *Order* is overbroad and vague, therefore we must reverse the *Order*. We should continue to trust the licensee to exercise judgment, responsibility, and sensitivity to the community's needs, interests and tastes. To whatever extent we err, or the Commission errs in balancing its duties, it must be in favor of preserving the values of free expression and freedom from governmental interference in matters of taste.

So ordered.

EDITOR'S POSTSCRIPT

On July 3, 1978, the United States Supreme Court reversed the decision of the Court of Appeals by a vote of five to four. Justice John Paul Stevens' opinion for the Court limited the scope of review to the narrow question of whether the FCC's determination that George Carlin's monologue was indecent as broadcast was authorized by law. No decision was rendered on the Commission's prospective ban of indecent language.

Because the FCC did not engage in prior restraint, but only subjected the material to review following its broadcast, no violation of Section 326 of the Communication Act was held to have occurred. Though the Court neither endorsed nor disagreed with the Commission's definition of "indecency," it indicated that broadcast matter lacking prurient appeal (and hence not "obscene" under law) could be termed "indecent" in a civil proceeding if found to be "patently offensive." The Court added that broadcasting enjoys less constitutional protection than other media because it is accessible to impressionable children and because of its "uniquely pervasive presence . . . in the privacy of the home, where the individual's right to be left alone plainly outweighs the First Amendment rights of an intruder." One concurring and two dissenting opinions accompanied the majority views in Case Number 77-528, *FCC* v. *Pacifica Foundation*.

The disparate legal analyses and single-vote majorities by which two tribunals reached divergent conclusions tend to blunt the precedential value of the ultimate decision. It is fair to say that the issue of indecency in broadcasting remains as far from clear legal resolution as ever.

47

The Communications Act of 1934

Public Law 416, 73d Congress
June 19, 1934 (Amended to
January, 1977)

This Act is the organic statute through which Congress currently exercises its jurisdiction over interstate communication by wire and radio. Only those sections most relevant to broadcasting appear in this edited version. Title II, which deals with common carriers such as telegraph and telephone, is entirely omitted.

Comparison of the Communications Act as amended with the Radio Acts of 1912 (Document 3, pp. 5-14) and 1927 (Document 9, pp. 32-48) lends insight into the regulatory evolution that was both a reason for and a reaction to the burgeoning growth of radio and television. Like chickens and eggs, broadcasting and the law have shaped each other with puzzling primacy. Documents 7 (pp. 28-29), 16 (pp. 82-83), and 36 (pp. 356-359) illustrate the roles of three Presidents in prompting Congress to enact statutes influenced by and affecting broadcasting.

The Communications Act is the fundamental embodiment of American public policy in broadcasting. It reiterates the sense of Congress, first expressed in the Radio Act of 1927, that broadcasting in the United States should not be a government operation, a private monopoly, or purely free enterprise with unlimited competition. Instead, Congress opted for private ownership of broadcast stations under licenses issued by a bipartisan commission in "the public interest, convenience, and necessity." Having established basic policy, Congress left it to the Federal Communications Commission (FCC) to implement and elaborate it, reserving to the President the function of appointing commissioners and to the courts the power to review contested Commission decisions. Congress itself retained the right to pass on presidential appointments to the Commission and to oversee the functioning of the licensing agency to which it delegated broad powers.

An example of that "fourth branch of government" not provided for in the Constitution, the FCC performs duties typically associated with the three "traditional" branches, namely, the executive, legislative, and judicial arms of government that are central to the American constitutional system of checks and balances. For this reason administrative bodies like the FCC, Federal Trade Commission, Securities and Exchange Commission, etc., are called "independent regulatory agencies." A commission functions like a government-within-a-government; even though it is ultimately accountable to the other three branches, it uses its own discretion to interpret and apply its statutory standard (the "public interest") within its sphere of congressionally delegated jurisdiction.

This makes the caliber of commissioners a crucial determinant of the quality of regulation, for it is the commissioners who mold an adaptable law through their policy-making, quasi-legislative, and quasi-judicial functions. The President and Congress, who share responsibility for constituting the membership of the FCC, also share a conflict of interest. Their reliance on the good will of networks and stations to develop public sentiment for issues and candidates compromises the ability of these elected officials to adopt strong positions on broadcasting that are reflected by the appointment of commissioners with similarly positive regulatory philosophies. Therefore, the FCC has become a dumping ground for those to whom political favors are owed. In fact, potential nominees to the Commission are most unlikely to gain confirmed appointment if the broadcast industry is opposed. Unless they have previously been broadcasters themselves, most commissioners have little interest and less experience in telecommunications and its control by government for the benefit of the public. Regulatory activists have usually been an endangered species at the FCC.

Agencies like the FCC, left to their own devices, gradually come to equate the public interest with the private interests they regulate. They eventually nurture, protect, and defend the very industries they were established to control. In broadcasting this has formed a regulatory vacuum that citizens groups and the courts have tried to fill in recent years. They have met with a surprising degree of success, considering the fact that their roles must necessarily be reactive rather than active.

Whatever criticisms may be made about the formulation and administration of broadcast law in the United States, it is clear that American broadcasting could never have achieved its amazing accomplishments without the regulatory scheme whose foundation was laid in 1927, reinforced in 1934, and which has been built upon ever since. Recognized miscalculations of the past are rectifiable under democratic trial-and-error processes, as exemplified by the 1967 additions to the Communications Act (pp. 543-560) that made viable a dual commercial–noncommercial system of broadcasting capable of serving pluralistic needs and interests more fully than a monolithic system. Widespread public satisfaction with radio and television lends credence to the contention that America's unique amalgam of private enterprise and the public interest in broadcasting is consistent with public policy as enunciated by the people's elected representatives and their appointees.

Related Reading: 20, 48, 49, 59, 71, 85, 115, 117, 126, 127, 136, 143, 157, 159, 164, 176, 177, 178, 183, 198, 199, 211, 212, 224, 228, 242.

TITLE I
GENERAL PROVISIONS

Purposes of Act: Creation of Federal Communications Commission

Sec. 1.   For the purpose of regulating interstate and foreign commerce in communication by wire and radio so as to make available, so far as possible, to all the people of the United States a rapid, efficient, Nation-wide, and world-wide wire and radio communication service with adequate facilities at reasonable charges, for the purpose of the national defense, for the purpose of promoting safety of life and property through the use of wire and radio communication, and for the purpose of securing a more effective execution of this policy by centralizing authority heretofore granted by law to several agencies and by granting additional authority with respect to interstate and foreign commerce in wire and radio communication, there is hereby created a commission to be known as the "Federal Communications Commission," which shall be constituted as hereinafter provided, and which shall execute and enforce the provisions of this Act.

Application of Act

Sec. 2.   (a)   The provisions of this Act shall apply to all interstate and foreign communication by wire or radio and all interstate and foreign transmission of energy by radio, which originates and/or is received within the United States, and to all persons engaged within the United States in such communication or such transmission of energy by radio, and to the licensing and regulating of all radio stations as hereinafter provided; but it shall not apply to persons engaged in wire or radio communication or transmission in the Canal Zone, or to wire or radio communication or transmission wholly within the Canal Zone.

(b)   Subject to the provisions of section 301, nothing in this Act shall be construed to apply or to give the Commission jurisdiction with respect to (1) charges, classifications, practices, services, facilities, or regulations for or in connection with intrastate communication service by wire or radio of any carrier, or (2) any carrier engaged in interstate or foreign communication solely through physical connection with the facilities of another carrier not directly or indirectly controlling or controlled by, or under direct or indirect common control with such carrier, or (3) any carrier engaged in interstate or foreign communication solely through connection by radio, or by wire and radio, with facilities, located in an adjoining State or in Canada or Mexico (where they adjoin the State in which the carrier is doing business), of another carrier not directly or indirectly controlling or controlled by, or under direct or indirect common control with such carrier, or (4) any carrier to which clause (2) or clause (3) would be applicable except for furnishing interstate mobile radio communication service or radio communication service to mobile stations on land vehicles in Canada or Mexico; except that sections 201 through 205 of this Act, both inclusive, shall, except as otherwise provided therein, apply to carriers described in clauses (2), (3), and (4).

Definitions

Sec. 3.   For the purposes of this Act, unless the context otherwise requires—

(a)   "Wire communication" or "communication by wire" means the transmission of writing, signs, signals, pictures, and sounds of all kinds by aid of wire, cable, or other like connection between the points of origin and reception of such transmission, including all instrumentalities, facilities, apparatus, and services (among other things, the receipt, forwarding, and delivery of communications) incidental to such transmission.

(b)   "Radio communication" or "communication by radio" means the transmission by radio of writing, signs, signals, pictures, and sounds of all kinds, including all instrumentalities, facilities, apparatus, and services (among other things, the receipt, forwarding, and delivery of communications) incidental to such transmission.

(c)   "Licensee" means the holder of a radio station license granted or continued in force under authority of this Act.

(d)   "Transmission of energy by radio" or "radio transmission of energy" includes both such transmission and all instrumentalities, facilities, and services incidental to such transmission.

(e)   "Interstate communication" or "interstate transmission" means communication or transmission (1) from any State, Territory, or possession of the United States (other than the Canal Zone), or the District of Columbia, to any other State, Territory, or possession of the United States (other than the Canal Zone), or the District of Columbia, (2) from or to the United States to or from the Canal Zone, insofar as such communication of transmission takes place within the United States, or (3) between points within the United States but through a foreign country; but shall not, with respect to the provisions of title II of this Act (other than section 223 thereof), include wire or radio communication between points in the same State, Territory, or possession of the United States, or the District of Columbia, through any place outside thereof, if such communication is regulated by a State commission.

(f)   "Foreign communication" or "foreign transmission" means communication or transmission from or to any place in the United States to or from a foreign country, or between a station in the United States and a mobile station located outside the United States.

(g)   "United States" means the several States and Territories, the District of Columbia, and the possessions of the United States, but does not include the Canal Zone.

(h)   "Common carrier" or "carrier" means any person engaged as a common carrier for hire, in interstate or foreign communication by wire or radio or in interstate or foreign radio transmission of energy, except where reference is made to common carriers not subject to this Act; but a person engaged in radio broadcasting shall not, insofar as such person is so engaged, be deemed a common carrier.

(i)   "Person" includes an individual, partnership, association, joint-stock company, trust, or corporation.

(j)   "Corporation" includes any corporation, joint-stock company, or association.

(k)   "Radio station" or "station" means a station equipped to engage in radio communication or radio transmission of energy.

(l)   "Mobile station" means a radio-communication station capable of being moved and which ordinarily does move.

(m)   "Land station" means a station, other than a mobile station, used for radio communication with mobile stations.

(n)   "Mobile service" means the radio-communication service carried on between mobile stations and land stations, and by mobile stations communicating among themselves.

(o)   "Broadcasting" means the dissemination of radio communications intended to be received by the public, directly or by the intermediary of relay stations.

(p)   "Chain broadcasting" means simultaneous broadcasting of an identical program by two or more connected stations.

(q)   "Amateur station" means a radio station operated by a duly authorized person interested in radio technique solely with a personal aim and without pecuniary interest. . . .

(cc)   "Station license," "radio station license," or "license" means that instrument of authorization required by this Act or the rules and regulations of the Commission made pursuant to this Act, for the use or operation of apparatus for transmission of energy, or communications, or signals by radio by whatever name the instrument may be designated by the Commission.

(dd)   "Broadcast station," "broadcasting station," or "radio broadcast station" means a radio station equipped to engage in broadcasting as herein defined.

(ee)   "Construction permit" or "permit for construction" means that instrument of authorization required by this Act or the rules and regulations of the Commission made pursuant to this Act for the construction of a station, or the installation of apparatus, for the transmission of energy, or communications, or signals by radio, by whatever name the instrument may be designated by the Commission. . . .

Provisions relating to the Commission

Sec. 4.   (a)   The Federal Communications Commission (in this Act referred to as the "Commission") shall be composed of seven commissioners appointed by the President, by and with the advice and consent of the Senate, one of whom the President shall designate as chairman.

(b)   Each member of the Commission shall be a citizen of the United States. No member of the Commission or person in its employ shall be financially interested in the manufacture or sale of radio apparatus or of apparatus for wire or radio communication; in communication by wire or radio or in radio transmission of energy; in any company furnishing services or such apparatus to any company engaged in communication by wire or radio or to any company manufacturing or selling apparatus used for communication by wire or radio; or in any company owning stocks, bonds, or other securities of any such company; nor be in the employ of or hold any official relation to any person subject to any of the provisions of this Act, nor own stocks, bonds, or other securities of any corporation subject to any of the provisions of this Act. Such commissioners shall not engage in any other business, vocation, profession, or employment. Any such commissioner serving as such after one year from the date of enactment of the Communications Act Amendments, 1952, shall not for a period of one year following the termination of his service as a commissioner represent any person before the Commission in a professional capacity, except that this restriction shall not apply to any commissioner who has served the full term for which he was appointed. Not more than four members of the Commission shall be members of the same political party.

(c)   The Commissioners first appointed under this Act shall continue in office for the terms of one, two, three, four, five, six, and seven years, respectively, from the date of the taking effect of this Act, the term of each to be designated by the President, but their successors shall be appointed for terms of seven years and until their successors are appointed and have qualified, except that they shall not continue to serve beyond the expiration of the next session of Congress subsequent to the expiration of said fixed term of office; except that any person chosen to fill a vacancy shall be appointed only for the unexpired term of the Commissioner whom he succeeds. No vacancy in the Commission shall impair the right of the remaining commissioners to exercise all the powers of the Commission.

(d)   Each commissioner shall receive an annual salary of $20,000, payable in monthly installments, and the chairman during the period of his service as chairman, shall receive an annual salary of $20,500.*

(e)   The principal office of the Commission shall be in the District of Columbia, where its general sessions shall be held; but whenever the convenience of the public or of the parties may be promoted or delay or expense prevented thereby, the Commission may hold special sessions in any part of the United States.

(f)   (1)   The Commission shall have authority, subject to the provisions of the civil-service laws and the Classification Act of 1949, as amended, to appoint such officers, engineers, accountants, attorneys, inspectors, examiners, and other employees as are necessary in the exercise of its functions.

(2)   Without regard to the civil-service laws, but subject to the Classification Act of 1949, each commissioner may appoint a legal assistant, an engineering assistant, and a secretary, each of whom shall perform such duties as such commissioner shall direct. In addition, the chairman of the Commission may appoint, without regard to the civil-service laws, but subject to the Classification Act of 1949, an administrative assistant who shall perform such duties as the chairman shall direct.

(3)   The Commission shall fix a reasonable rate of extra compen-

*Commissioners currently receive $50,000 annually; the Chairman receives $52,000. [Ed.]

sation for overtime services of engineers in charge and radio engineers of the Field Engineering and Monitoring Bureau of the Federal Communications Commission, who may be required to remain on duty between the hours of 5 o'clock postmeridian and 8 o'clock antemeridian or on Sundays or holidays to perform services in connection with the inspection of ship radio equipment and apparatus for the purposes of part II of title III of this Act or the Great Lakes Agreement, on the basis of one-half day's additional pay for each two hours or fraction thereof of at least one hour that the overtime extends beyond 5 o'clock postmeridian (but not to exceed two and one-half days' pay for the full period from 5 o'clock postmeridian to 8 o'clock antemeridian) and two additional days' pay for Sunday or holiday duty. The said extra compensation for overtime services shall be paid by the master, owner, or agent of such vessel to the local United States collector of customs or his representative, who shall deposit such collection into the Treasury of the United States to an appropriately designated receipt account: *Provided*, That the amounts of such collections received by the said collector of customs or his representatives shall be covered into the Treasury as miscellaneous receipts; and the payments of such extra compensation to the several employees entitled thereto shall be made from the annual appropriations for salaries and expenses of the Commission: *Provided further*, That to the extent that the annual appropriations which are hereby authorized to be made from the general fund of the Treasury are insufficient, there are hereby authorized to be appropriated from the general fund of the Treasury such additional amounts as may be necessary to the extent that the amounts of such receipts are in excess of the amounts appropriated: *Provided further*, That such extra compensation shall be paid if such field employees have been ordered to report for duty and have so reported whether the actual inspection of the radio equipment or apparatus takes place or not: *And provided further*, That in those ports where customary working hours are other than those hereinabove mentioned, the engineers in charge are vested with authority to regulate the hours of such employees so as to agree with prevailing working hours in said ports where inspections are to be made, but nothing contained in this proviso shall be construed in any manner to alter the length of a working day for the engineers in charge and radio engineers or the overtime pay herein fixed.

(g)   The Commission may make such expenditures (including expenditures for rent and personal services at the seat of government and elsewhere, for office supplies, law books, periodicals, and books of reference, for printing and binding, for land for use as sites for radio monitoring stations and related facilities, including living quarters where necessary in remote areas, for the construction of such stations and facilities, and for the improvement, furnishing, equipping, and repairing of such stations and facilities and of laboratories and other related facilities (including construction of minor subsidiary buildings and structures not exceeding $25,000 in any one instance) used in connection with technical research activities), as may be necessary for the execution of the functions vested in the Commission and as from time to time may be appropriated for by Congress. All expenditures of the Commission, including all necessary expenses for transportation incurred by the commissioners or by their employees, under their orders, in making any investigation or upon any official business in any other places than in the city of Washington, shall be allowed and paid on the presentation of itemized vouchers therefor approved by the chairman of the Commission or by such other members or officer thereof as may be designated by the Commission for that purpose.

(h)   Four members of the Commission shall constitute a quorum thereof. The Commission shall have an official seal which shall be judicially noticed.

(i)   The Commission may perform any and all acts, make such rules and regulations, and issue such orders, not inconsistent with this Act, as may be necessary in the execution of its functions.

(j)   The Commission may conduct its proceedings in such manner as will best conduce to the proper dispatch of business and to the ends of justice. No commissioner shall participate in any hearing or proceeding in which he has a pecuniary interest. Any party may appear before the Commission and be heard in person or by attorney. Every vote and official act of the Commission shall be entered of record, and its proceedings shall be public upon the request of any party interested. The Commission is authorized to withhold publication of records or proceedings containing secret information affecting the national defense.

(k)   The Commission shall make an annual report to Congress, copies of which shall be distributed as are other reports transmitted to Congress. Such reports shall contain—

(1)   such information and data collected by the Commission as may be considered of value in the determination of questions connected with the regulation of interstate and foreign wire and radio communication and radio transmission of energy;

(2)   such information and data concerning the functioning of the Commission as will be of value to Congress in appraising the amount and character of the work and accomplishments of the Commission and the adequacy of its staff and equipment: *Provided*, That the first and second annual reports following the date of enactment of the Communications Act Amendments, 1952, shall set forth in detail the number and caption of pending applications requesting approval of transfer of control or assignment of a broadcasting station license, or construction permits for new broadcasting stations, or for increases in power, or for changes of frequency of existing broadcasting stations at the beginning and end of the period covered by such reports;*

(4)   an itemized statement of all funds expended during the preceding year by the Commission, of the sources of such funds, and of the

---

*Subparagraph (3) was repealed by Public Law 86-533, approved June 29, 1960. [Ed.]

authority in this Act or elsewhere under which such expenditures were made; and

(5)   specific recommendations to Congress as to additional legislation which the Commission deems necessary or desirable, including all legislative proposals submitted for approval to the Director of the Bureau of the Budget.

(l)   All reports of investigations made by the Commission shall be entered of record, and a copy thereof shall be furnished to the party who may have complained, and to any common carrier or licensee that may have been complained of.

(m)   The Commission shall provide for the publication of its reports and decisions in such form and manner as may be best adapted for public information and use, and such authorized publications shall be competent evidence of the reports and decisions of the Commission therein contained in all courts of the United States and of the several States without any further proof or authentication thereof.

(n)   Rates of compensation of persons appointed under this section shall be subject to the reduction applicable to officers and employees of the Federal Government generally.

(o)   For the purpose of obtaining maximum effectiveness from the use of radio and wire communications in connection with safety of life and property, the Commission shall investigate and study all phases of the problem and the best methods of obtaining the cooperation and coordination of these systems.

Organization and functioning of the Commission

Sec. 5.   (a)   The member of the Commission designated by the President as chairman shall be the chief executive officer of the Commission. It shall be his duty to preside at all meetings and sessions of the Commission, to represent the Commission in all matters relating to legislation and legislative reports, except that any commissioner may present his own or minority views or supplemental reports, to represent the Commission in all matters requiring conferences or communications with other governmental officers, departments or agencies, and generally to coordinate and organize the work of the Commission in such manner as to promote prompt and efficient disposition of all matters within the jurisdiction of the Commission. In the case of a vacancy in the office of the chairman of the Commission, or the absence or inability of the chairman to serve, the Commission may temporarily designate one of its members to act as chairman until the cause or circumstance requiring such designation shall have been eliminated or corrected.

(b)   Within six months after the enactment of the Communications Act Amendments, 1952, and from time to time thereafter as the Commission may find necessary, the Commission shall organize its staff into (1) integrated bureaus, to function on the basis of the Commission's principal workload operations, and (2) such other divisional organizations as the Commission may deem necessary. Each such integrated bureau shall include such legal, engineering, accounting, administrative, clerical, and other personnel as the Commission may determine to be necessary to perform its functions.*

(d)   (1)   When necessary to the proper functioning of the Commission and the prompt and orderly conduct of its business, the Commission may, by published rule or by order, delegate any of its functions (except functions granted to the Commission by this paragraph and by paragraphs (4), (5), and (6) of this subsection) to a panel of commissioners, an individual commissioner, an employee board, or an individual employee, including functions with respect to hearing, determining, ordering, certifying, reporting, or otherwise acting as to any work, business, or matter; except that in delegating review functions to employees in cases of adjudication (as defined in the Administrative Procedure Act), the delegation in any such case may be made only to an employee board consisting of three or more employees referred to in paragraph (8). Any such rule or order may be adopted, amended, or rescinded only by a vote of a majority of the members of the Commission then holding office. Nothing in this paragraph shall authorize the Commission to provide for the conduct, by any person or persons other than persons referred to in clauses (2) and (3) of section 7(a) of the Administrative Procedure Act, of any hearing to which such section 7(a) applies.

(2)   As used in this subsection (d) the term "order, decision, report, or action" does not include an initial, tentative, or recommended decision to which exceptions may be filed as provided in section 409(b).

(3)   Any order, decision, report, or action made or taken pursuant to any such delegation, unless reviewed as provided in paragraph (4), shall have the same force and effect, and shall be made, evidenced, and enforced in the same manner, as orders, decisions, reports, or other actions of the Commission.

(4)   Any person aggrieved by any such order, decision, report or action may file an application for review by the Commission within such time and in such manner as the Commission shall prescribe, and every such application shall be passed upon by the Commission. The Commission, on its own initiative, may review in whole or in part, at such time and in such manner as it shall determine, any order, decision, report, or action made or taken pursuant to any delegation under paragraph (1).

(5)   In passing upon applications for review, the Commission may grant, in whole or in part, or deny such applications without specifying any

*Subsection 5(c) was repealed by Public Law 87-192, approved August 31, 1961. [Ed.]

reasons therefor. No such application for review shall rely on questions of fact or law upon which the panel of commissioners, individual commissioner, employee board, or individual employee has been afforded no opportunity to pass.

(6)   If the Commission grants the application for review, it may affirm, modify, or set aside the order, decision, report, or action, or it may order a rehearing upon such order, decision, report, or action in accordance with section 405.

(7)   The filing of an application for review under this subsection shall be a condition precedent to judicial review of any order, decision, report, or action made or taken pursuant to a delegation under paragraph (1). The time within which a petition for review must be filed in a proceeding to which section 402(a) applies, or within which an appeal must be taken under section 402(b), shall be computed from the date upon which public notice is given of orders disposing of all applications for review filed in any case.

(8)   The employees to whom the Commission may delegate review functions in any case of adjudication (as defined in the Administrative Procedure Act) shall be qualified, by reason of their training, experience, and competence, to perform such review functions, and shall perform no duties inconsistent with such review functions. Such employees shall be in a grade classification or salary level commensurate with their important duties, and in no event less than the grade classification or salary level of the employee or employees whose actions are to be reviewed. In the performance of such review functions such employees shall be assigned to cases in rotation so far as practicable and shall not be responsible to or subject to the supervision or direction of any officer, employee, or agent engaged in the performance of investigative or prosecuting functions for any agency.

(9)   The secretary and seal of the Commission shall be the secretary and seal of each panel of the Commission, each individual commissioner, and each employee board or individual employee exercising functions delegated pursuant to paragraph (1) of this subsection.

(e)   Meetings of the Commission shall be held at regular intervals, not less frequently than once each calendar month, at which times the functioning of the Commission and the handling of its work load shall be reviewed and such orders shall be entered and other action taken as may be necessary or appropriate to expedite the prompt and orderly conduct of the business of the Commission with the objective of rendering a final decision (1) within three months from the date of filing in all original application, renewal, and transfer cases in which it will not be necessary to hold a hearing, and (2) within six months from the final date of the hearing in all hearing cases; and the Commission shall promptly report to the Congress each such case which has been pending before it more than such three- or six-month period, respectively, stating the reasons therefor.

TITLE III
PROVISIONS RELATING TO RADIO

PART I – GENERAL PROVISIONS

License for radio communication or transmission of energy

Sec. 301. It is the purpose of this Act, among other things, to maintain the control of the United States over all the channels of interstate and foreign radio transmission; and to provide for the use of such channels, but not the ownership thereof, by persons for limited periods of time, under licenses granted by Federal authority, and no such license shall be construed to create any right, beyond the terms, conditions, and periods of the license. No person shall use or operate any apparatus for the transmission of energy or communications or signals by radio (a) from one place in any Territory or possession of the United States or in the District of Columbia to another place in the same Territory, possession, or district; or (b) from any State, Territory, or possession of the United States, or from the District of Columbia to any other State, Territory, or possession of the United States; or (c) from any place in any State, Territory, or possession of the United States, or in the District of Columbia, to any place in any foreign country or to any vessel; or (d) within any State when the effects of such use extend beyond the borders of said State, or when interference is caused by such use or operation with the transmission of such energy, communications, or signals from within said State to any place beyond its borders, or from any place beyond its borders to any place within said State, or with the transmission or reception of such energy, communications, or signals from and/or to places beyond the borders of said State; or (e) upon any vessel or aircraft of the United States; or (f) upon any other mobile stations within the jurisdiction of the United States, except under and in accordance with this Act and with a license in that behalf granted under the provisions of this Act.

Sec. 302. (a) The Commission may, consistent with the public interest, convenience, and necessity, make reasonable regulations governing the interference potential of devices which in their operation are capable of emitting radio frequency energy by radiation, conduction, or other means in sufficient degree to cause harmful interference to radio communications. Such regulations shall be applicable to the manufacture, import, sale, offer for sale, shipment, or use of such devices.

(b) No person shall manufacture, import, sell, offer for sale, ship, or use devices which fail to comply with regulations promulgated pursuant to this section.

(c) The provisions of this section shall not be applicable to carriers transporting such devices without trading in them, to devices manufactured solely for export, to the manufacture, assembly, or installation of devices for its own use by a public utility engaged in providing electric service, or to devices for use by the Government of the United States or any agency thereof. Devices for use by the Government of the United States or any agency thereof shall be developed, procured, or otherwise acquired, including offshore procurement, under United States Government criteria, standards, or specifications designed to achieve the common objective of reducing interference to radio reception, taking into account the unique needs of national defense and security.

General powers of the Commission

Sec. 303.   Except as otherwise provided in this Act, the Commission from time to time, as public convenience, interest, or necessity requires shall—

(a)   Classify radio stations;

(b)   Prescribe the nature of the service to be rendered by each class of licensed stations and each station within any class;

(c)   Assign bands of frequencies to the various classes of stations, and assign frequencies for each individual station and determine the power which each station shall use and the time during which it may operate;

(d)   Determine the location of classes of stations or individual stations;

(e)   Regulate the kind of apparatus to be used with respect to its external effects and the purity and sharpness of the emissions from each station and from the apparatus therein;

(f)   Make such regulations not inconsistent with law as it may deem necessary to prevent interference between stations and to carry out the provisions of this Act: *Provided, however*, that changes in the frequencies, authorized power, or in the times of operation of any station, shall not be made without the consent of the station licensee unless, after a public hearing, the Commission shall determine that such changes will promote public convenience or interest or will serve public necessity, or the provisions of this Act will be more fully complied with;

(g)   Study new uses for radio, provide for experimental uses of frequencies, and generally encourage the larger and more effective use of radio in the public interest;

(h)   Have authority to establish areas or zones to be served by any station;

(i)   Have authority to make special regulations applicable to radio stations engaged in chain broadcasting;

(j)   Have authority to make general rules and regulations requiring stations to keep such records of programs, transmissions of energy, communications, or signals as it may deem desirable;

(k)   Have authority to exclude from the requirements of any regulations in whole or in part any radio station upon railroad rolling stock, or to modify such regulations in its discretion;

(l)   (1)   Have authority to prescribe the qualifications of station operators, to classify them according to the duties to be performed, to fix the forms of such licenses, and to issue them to such citizens or nationals of the United States, or citizens of the Trust Territory of the Pacific Islands presenting valid identity certificates issued by the high Commissioner of such Territory, as the Commission finds qualified, except that in issuing licenses for the operation of radio stations on aircraft the Commission may, if it finds that the public interest will be served thereby, waive the requirement of citizenship in the case of persons holding United States pilot certificates or in the case of persons holding foreign aircraft pilot certificates which are valid in the United States on the basis of reciprocal agreements entered into with foreign governments;

(2)   Notwithstanding paragraph (1) of this subsection, an individual to whom a radio station is licensed under the provisions of this Act may be issued an operator's license to operate that station. . . .

(m)   (1)   Have authority to suspend the license of any operator upon proof sufficient to satisfy the Commission that the licensee—

(A)   Has violated any provision of any Act, treaty, or convention binding on the United States, which the Commission is authorized to administer, or any regulation made by the Commission under any such Act, treaty, or convention; or

(B)   Has failed to carry out a lawful order of the master or person lawfully in charge of the ship or aircraft on which he is employed; or

(C)   Has willfully damaged or permitted radio apparatus or installations to be damaged; or

(D)   Has transmitted superfluous radio communications or signals or communications containing profane or obscene words, language, or meaning, or has knowingly transmitted—

(1)   False or deceptive signals or communications, or

(2)   A call signal or letter which has not been assigned by proper authority to the station he is operating; or

(E)   Has willfully or maliciously interfered with any other radio communications or signals; or

(F)   Has obtained or attempted to obtain, or has assisted another to obtain or attempt to obtain, an operator's license by fraudulent means.

(2)   No order of suspension of any operator's license shall take effect until fifteen days' notice in writing thereof, stating the cause for the proposed suspension, has been given to the operator licensee who may make written application to the Commission at any time within said fifteen days for a hearing upon such order. The notice to the operator licensee shall not be effective until actually received by him, and from that time he shall have fifteen

days in which to mail the said application. In the event that physical conditions prevent mailing of the application at the expiration of the fifteen-day period, the application shall then be mailed as soon as possible thereafter, accompanied by a satisfactory explanation of the delay. Upon receipt by the Commission of such application for hearing, said order of suspension shall be held in abeyance until the conclusion of the hearing which shall be conducted under such rules as the Commission may prescribe. Upon the conclusion of said hearing the Commission may affirm, modify, or revoke said order of suspension.

(n)   Have authority to inspect all radio installations associated with stations required to be licensed by any Act or which are subject to the provisions of any Act, treaty, or convention binding on the United States, to ascertain whether in construction, installation, and operation they conform to the requirements of the rules and regulations of the Commission, the provisions of any Act, the terms of any treaty or convention binding on the United States, and the conditions of the license or other instrument of authorization under which they are constructed, installed, or operated.

(o)   Have authority to designate call letters of all stations;

(p)   Have authority to cause to be published such call letters and such other announcements and data as in the judgment of the Commission may be required for the efficient operation of radio stations subject to the jurisdiction of the United States and for the proper enforcement of this Act;

(q)   Have authority to require the painting and/or illumination of radio towers if and when in its judgment such towers constitute, or there is a reasonable possibility that they may constitute, a menace to air navigation. The permittee or licensee shall maintain the painting and/or illumination of the tower as prescribed by the Commission pursuant to this section. In the event that the tower ceases to be licensed by the Commission for the transmission of radio energy, the owner of the tower shall maintain the prescribed painting and/or illumination of such tower until it is dismantled, and the Commission may require the owner to dismantle and remove the tower when the Administrator of the Federal Aviation Agency determines that there is a reasonable possibility that it may constitute a menace to air navigation.

(r)   Make such rules and regulations and prescribe such restrictions and conditions, not inconsistent with law, as may be necessary to carry out the provisions of this Act, or any international radio or wire communications treaty or convention, or regulations annexed thereto, including any treaty or convention insofar as it relates to the use of radio, to which the United States is or may hereafter become a party.

(s)   Have authority to require that apparatus designed to receive television pictures broadcast simultaneously with sound be capable of adequately receiving all frequencies allocated by the Commission to television broadcasting when such apparatus is shipped in interstate commerce, or is imported from any foreign country into the United States, for sale or resale to the public.

Waiver by licensee

Sec. 304.   No station license shall be granted by the Commission until the applicant therefor shall have signed a waiver of any claim to the use of any particular frequency or of the ether as against the regulatory power of the United States because of the previous use of the same, whether by license or otherwise.

Government-owned stations

Sec. 305.   (a)   Radio stations belonging to and operated by the United States shall not be subject to the provisions of sections 301 and 303 of this Act. All such Government stations shall use such frequencies as shall be assigned to each or to each class by the President. All such stations, except stations on board naval and other Government vessels while at sea or beyond the limits of the continental United States, when transmitting any radio communication or signal other than a communication or signal relating to Government business, shall conform to such rules and regulations designed to prevent interference with other radio stations and the rights of others as the Commission may prescribe.

(b)   Radio stations on board vessels of the United States Maritime Commission or the Inland and Coastwise Waterways Service shall be subject to the provisions of this title.

(c)   All stations owned and operated by the United States, except mobile stations of the Army of the United States, and all other stations on land and sea, shall have special call letters designated by the Commission.

(d)   The provisions of sections 301 and 303 of this Act notwithstanding, the President may, provided he determines it to be consistent with and in the interest of national security, authorize a foreign government, under such terms and conditions as he may prescribe, to construct and operate at the seat of government of the United States a low-power radio station in the fixed service at or near the site of the embassy or legation of such foreign government for transmission of its messages to points outside the United States, but only (1) where he determines that the authorization would be consistent with the national interest of the United States and (2) where such foreign government has provided reciprocal privileges to the United States to construct and operate radio stations within territories subject to its jurisdiction. Foreign government stations authorized pursuant to the provisions of this subsection shall conform to such rules and regulations as the President may prescribe. The authorization of such stations, and the renewal, modification, suspension, revocation, or other termination of such authority shall be in accordance with such procedures as may be established by the President and shall not be subject to the other provisions of this Act or of the Administrative Procedure Act.

Foreign ships

Sec. 306.   Section 301 of this Act shall not apply to any person sending radio communications or signals on a foreign ship while the same is within the jurisdiction of the United States, but such communications or signals shall be transmitted only in accordance with such regulations designed to prevent interference as may be promulgated under the authority of this Act

Allocation of facilities; Terms of licenses

Sec. 307.   (a)   The Commission, if public convenience, interest, or necessity will be served thereby, subject to the limitations of this Act, shall grant to any applicant therefor a station license provided for by this Act.

(b)   In considering applications for licenses, and modifications and renewals thereof, when and insofar as there is demand for the same, the Commission shall make such distribution of licenses, frequencies, hours of operation, and of power among the several States and communities as to provide a fair, efficient, and equitable distribution of radio service to each of the same.

(c)   The Commission shall study the proposal that Congress by statute allocate fixed percentages of radio broadcasting facilities to particular types or kinds of non-profit radio programs or to persons identified with particular types or kinds of non-profit activities, and shall report to Congress, not later than February 1, 1935, its recommendations together with the reasons for the same.

(d)   No license granted for the operation of a broadcasting station shall be for a longer term than three years and no license so granted for any other class of station shall be for a longer term than five years, and any license granted may be revoked as hereinafter provided. Upon the expiration of any license, upon application therefor, a renewal of such license may be granted from time to time for a term of not to exceed three years in the case of broadcasting licenses, and not to exceed five years in the case of other licenses, if the Commission finds that public interest, convenience, and necessity would be served thereby. In order to expedite action on applications for renewal of broadcasting station licenses and in order to avoid needless expense to applicants for such renewals, the Commission shall not require any such applicant to file any information which previously has been furnished to the Commission or which is not directly material to the considerations that affect the granting or denial of such application, but the Commission may require any new or additional facts it deems necessary to make its findings. Pending any hearing and final decision on such an application and the disposition of any petition for rehearing pursuant to section 405, the Commission shall continue such license in effect. Consistently with the foregoing provisions of this subsection, the Commission may by rule prescribe the period or periods for which licenses shall be granted and renewed for particular classes of stations, but the Commission may not adopt or follow any rule which would preclude it, in any case involving a station of a particular class, from granting or renewing a license for a shorter period than that prescribed for stations of such class if, in its judgment, public interest, convenience, or necessity would be served by such action.

(e) No renewal of an existing station license in the broadcast or the common carrier services shall be granted more than thirty days prior to the expiration of the original license.

Applications for licenses;
Conditions in license for foreign communication

Sec. 308. (a) The Commission may grant construction permits and station licenses, or modifications or renewals thereof, only upon written application therefor received by it: *Provided*, That (1) in cases of emergency found by the Commission involving danger to life or property or due to damage to equipment, or (2) during a national emergency proclaimed by the President or declared by the Congress and during the continuance of any war in which the United States is engaged and when such action is necessary for the national defense or security or otherwise in furtherance of the war effort, or (3) in cases of emergency where the Commission finds, in the nonbroadcast services, that it would not be feasible to secure renewal applications from existing licensees or otherwise to follow normal licensing procedure, the Commission may grant construction permits and station licenses, or modifications or renewals thereof, during the emergency so found by the Commission or during the continuance of any such national emergency or war, in such manner and upon such terms and conditions as the Commission shall by regulation prescribe, and without the filing of a formal application, but no authorization so granted shall continue in effect beyond the period of the emergency or war requiring it: *Provided further*, That the Commission may issue by cable, telegraph, or radio a permit for the operation of a station on a vessel of the United States at sea, effective in lieu of a license until said vessel shall return to a port of the continental United States.

(b) All applications for station licenses, or modifications or renewals thereof, shall set forth such facts as the Commission by regulation may prescribe as to the citizenship, character, and financial, technical, and other qualifications of the applicant to operate the station; the ownership and location of the proposed station and of the stations, if any, with which it is proposed to communicate; the frequencies and the power desired to be used; the hours of the day or other periods of time during which it is proposed to operate the station; the purposes for which the station is to be used; and such other information as it may require. The Commission, at any time after the filing of such original application and during the term of any such license, may require from an applicant or licensee further written statements of fact to enable it to determine whether such original application should be granted or denied or such license revoked. Such application and/or such statement of fact shall be signed by the applicant and/or licensee.

(c)   The Commission in granting any license for a station intended or used for commercial communication between the United States or any Territory or possession, continental or insular, subject to the jurisdiction of the United States, and any foreign country, may impose any terms, conditions, or restrictions authorized to be imposed with respect to submarine-cable licenses by section 2 of an Act entitled "An Act relating to the landing and the operation of submarine cables in the United States," approved May 24, 1921.

Action upon applications;
Form of and conditions attached to licenses

Sec. 309.   (a)   Subject to the provisions of this section, the Commission shall determine, in the case of each application filed with it to which section 308 applies, whether the public interest, convenience, and necessity will be served by the granting of such application, and, if the Commission, upon examination of such application and upon consideration of such other matters as the Commission may officially notice, shall find that public interest, convenience, and necessity would be served by the granting thereof, it shall grant such application.

(b)   Except as provided in subsection (c) of this section, no such application—

(1)   for an instrument of authorization in the case of a station in the broadcasting or common carrier services, or

(2)   for an instrument of authorization in the case of a station in any of the following categories:

(A)   fixed point-to-point microwave stations (exclusive of control and relay stations used as integral parts of mobile radio systems),

(B)   industrial radio positioning stations for which frequencies are assigned on an exclusive basis,

(C)   aeronautical en route stations,

(D)   aeronautical advisory stations,

(E)   airdrome control stations,

(F)   aeronautical fixed stations, and

(G)   such other stations or classes of stations, not in the broadcasting or common carrier services, as the Commission shall by rule prescribe, shall be granted by the Commission earlier than thirty days following issuance of public notice by the Commission of the acceptance for filing of such application or of any substantial amendment thereof.

  (c) Subsection (b) of this section shall not apply—

   (1) to any minor amendment of an application to which such subsection is applicable, or

   (2) to any application for—

    (A) a minor change in the facilities of an authorized station,

    (B) consent to an involuntary assignment or transfer under section 310(b) or to an assignment or transfer thereunder which does not involve a substantial change in ownership or control,

    (C) a license under section 319(c) or, pending application for or grant of such license, any special or temporary authorization to permit interim operation to facilitate completion of authorized construction or to provide substantially the same service as would be authorized by such license,

    (D) extension of time to complete construction of authorized facilities,

    (E) an authorization of facilities for remote pickups, studio links and similar facilities for use in the operation of a broadcast station,

    (F) authorizations pursuant to section 325(b) where the programs to be transmitted are special events not of a continuing nature,

    (G) a special temporary authorization for nonbroadcast operation not to exceed thirty days where no application for regular operation is contemplated to be filed or not to exceed sixty days pending the filing of an application for such regular operation, or

    (H) an authorization under any of the proviso clauses of section 308(a).

  (d) (1) Any party in interest may file with the Commission a petition to deny any application (whether as originally filed or as amended) to which subsection (b) of this section applies at any time prior to the day of Commission grant thereof without hearing or the day of formal designation thereof for hearing; except that with respect to any classification of applications, the Commission from time to time by rule may specify a shorter period (no less than thirty days following the issuance of public notice by the Commission of the acceptance for filing of such application or of any substantial amendment thereof), which shorter period shall be reasonably related to the time when the applications would normally be reached for processing. The petitioner shall serve a copy of such petition on the applicant. The petition shall contain specific allegations of fact sufficient to show that the petitioner is a party in interest and that a grant of the application would be prima facie inconsistent with subsection (a). Such allegations of fact shall, except for those of which official notice may be taken, be supported by affidavit of a person or persons with personal knowledge thereof. The applicant shall be given the opportunity to file a reply in which allegations of fact or denials thereof shall similarly be supported by affidavit.

(2)   If the Commission finds on the basis of the application, the pleadings filed, or other matters which it may officially notice that there are no substantial and material questions of fact and that a grant of the application would be consistent with subsection (a), it shall make the grant, deny the petition, and issue a concise statement of the reasons for denying the petition, which statement shall dispose of all substantial issues raised by the petition. If a substantial and material question of fact is presented or if the Commission for any reason is unable to find that grant of the application would be consistent with subsection (a), it shall proceed as provided in subsection (e).

(e)   If, in the case of any application to which subsection (a) of this section applies, a substantial and material question of fact is presented or the Commission for any reason is unable to make the finding specified in such subsection, it shall formally designate the application for hearing on the ground or reasons then obtaining and shall forthwith notify the applicant and all other known parties in interest of such action and the grounds and reasons therefor, specifying with particularity the matters and things in issue but not including issues or requirements phrased generally. When the Commission has so designated an application for hearing, the parties in interest, if any, who are not notified by the Commission of such action may acquire the status of a party to the proceeding thereon by filing a petition for intervention showing the basis for their interest not more than thirty days after publication of the hearing issues or any substantial amendment thereto in the Federal Register. Any hearing subsequently held upon such application shall be a full hearing in which the applicant and all other parties in interest shall be permitted to participate. The burden of proceeding with the introduction of evidence and the burden of proof shall be upon the applicant, except that with respect to any issue presented by a petition to deny or a petition to enlarge the issues, such burdens shall be as determined by the Commission.

(f)   When an application subject to subsection (b) has been filed, the Commission, notwithstanding the requirements of such subsection, may, if the grant of such application is otherwise authorized by law and if it finds that there are extraordinary circumstances requiring emergency operations in the public interest and that delay in the institution of such emergency operations would seriously prejudice the public interest, grant a temporary authorization, accompanied by a statement of its reasons therefor, to permit such emergency operations for a period not exceeding ninety days, and upon making like findings may extend such temporary authorization for one additional period not to exceed ninety days. When any such grant of a temporary authorization is made, the Commission shall give expeditious treatment to any timely filed petition to deny such application and to any petition for rehearing of such grant filed under section 405.

(g)   The Commission is authorized to adopt reasonable classifications of applications and amendments in order to effectuate the purposes of this section.

(h)   Such station licenses as the Commission may grant shall be in such general form as it may prescribe, but each license shall contain, in addition to other provisions, a statement of the following conditions to which such license shall be subject: (1) The station license shall not vest in the licensee any right to operate the station nor any right in the use of the frequencies designated in the license beyond the term thereof nor in any other manner than authorized therein; (2) neither the license nor the right granted thereunder shall be assigned or otherwise transferred in violation of this Act; (3) every license issued under this Act shall be subject in terms to the right of use or control conferred by section 606 of this Act.

Limitation on holding and transfer of licenses

Sec. 310.   (a)   The station license required under this Act shall not be granted to or held by any foreign government or the representative thereof.

(b)   No broadcast or common carrier or aeronautical en route or aeronautical fixed radio station license shall be granted to or held by—

(1)   any alien or the representative of any alien;

(2)   any corporation organized under the laws of any foreign government;

(3)   any corporation of which any officer or director is an alien or of which more than one-fifth of the capital stock is owned of record or voted by aliens or their representatives or by a foreign government or representative thereof or by any corporation organized under the laws of a foreign country,

(4)   any corporation directly or indirectly controlled by any other corporation of which any officer or more than one-fourth of the directors are aliens, or of which more than one-fourth of the capital stock is owned of record or voted by aliens, their representatives, or by a foreign government or representative thereof, or by any corporation organized under the laws of a foreign country, if the Commission finds that the public interest will be served by the refusal or revocation of such license.

(c)   In addition to amateur station licenses which the Commission may issue to aliens pursuant to this Act, the Commission may issue authorizations, under such conditions and terms as it may prescribe, to permit an alien licensed by his government as an amateur radio operator to operate his amateur radio station licensed by his government in the United States, its possessions, and the Commonwealth of Puerto Rico provided there is in effect a bilateral agreement between the United States and the alien's government for such operation on a reciprocal basis by United States amateur radio operators. Other provisions of this Act and of the Administrative Procedure Act shall not be applicable to any request or application for or modification, suspension, or cancellation of any such authorization.

(d)   No construction permit or station license, or any rights thereunder, shall be transferred, assigned, or disposed of in any manner, voluntarily or involuntarily, directly or indirectly, or by transfer of control of any corporation holding such permit or license, to any person except upon application to the Commission and upon finding by the Commission that the public interest, convenience, and necessity will be served thereby. Any such application shall be disposed of as if the proposed transferee or assignee were making application under section 308 of this Act for the permit or license in question; but in acting thereon the Commission may not consider whether the public interest, convenience, and necessity might be served by the transfer, assignment, or disposal of the permit or license to a person other than the proposed transferee or assignee.

Special requirements with respect to certain applications in the broadcasting service

Sec. 311.   (a)   When there is filed with the Commission any application to which section 309(b)(1) applies, for an instrument of authorization for a station in the broadcasting service, the applicant—

(1)   shall give notice of such filing in the principal area which is served or is to be served by the station; and

(2)   if the application is formally designated for hearing in accordance with section 309, shall give notice of such hearing in such area at least ten days before commencement of such hearing.

The Commission shall by rule prescribe the form and content of the notices to be given in compliance with this subsection, and the manner and frequency with which such notices shall be given.

(b)   Hearings referred to in subsection (a) may be held at such places as the Commission shall determine to be appropriate, and in making such determination in any case the Commission shall consider whether the public interest, convenience, or necessity will be served by conducting the hearing at a place in, or in the vicinity of, the principal area to be served by the station involved.

(c)   (1)   If there are pending before the Commission two or more applications for a permit for construction of a broadcasting station, only one of which can be granted, it shall be unlawful, without approval of the Commission, for the applicants or any of them to effectuate an agreement whereby one or more of such applicants withdraws his or their application or applications.

(2)   The request for Commission approval in any such case shall be made in writing jointly by all the parties to the agreement. Such request shall contain or be accompanied by full information with respect to the agreement, set forth in such detail, form, and manner as the Commission shall by rule require.

(3)   The Commission shall approve the agreement only if it determines that the agreement is consistent with the public interest, convenience, or necessity. If the agreement does not contemplate a merger, but contemplates the making of any direct or indirect payment to any party thereto in consideration of his withdrawal of his application, the Commission may determine the agreement to be consistent with the public interest, convenience, or necessity only if the amount or value of such payment, as determined by the Commission, is not in excess of the aggregate amount determined by the Commission to have been legitimately and prudently expended and to be expended by such applicant in connection with preparing, filing, and advocating the granting of his application.

(4)   For the purposes of this subsection an application shall be deemed to be "pending" before the Commission from the time such application is filed with the Commission until an order of the Commission granting or denying it is no longer subject to rehearing by the Commission or to review by any court.

Administrative sanctions

Sec. 312.   (a)   The Commission may revoke any station license or construction permit—

(1)   for false statements knowingly made either in the application or in any statement of fact which may be required pursuant to section 308;

(2)   because of conditions coming to the attention of the Commission which would warrant it in refusing to grant a license or permit on an original application;

(3)   for willful or repeated failure to operate substantially as set forth in the license;

(4)   for willful or repeated violation of, or willful or repeated failure to observe any provision of this Act or any rule or regulation of the Commission authorized by this Act or by a treaty ratified by the United States;

(5)   for violation of or failure to observe any final cease and desist order issued by the Commission under this section;

(6)   for violation of section 1304, 1343, or 1464 of title 18 of the United States Code; or

(7)   for willful or repeated failure to allow reasonable access to or

to permit purchase of reasonable amounts of time for the use of a broadcasting station by a legally qualified candidate for Federal elective office on behalf of his candidacy.

(b)   Where any person (1) has failed to operate substantially as set forth in a license, (2) has violated or failed to observe any of the provisions of this Act, or section 1304, 1343, or 1464 of title 18 of the United States Code, or (3) has violated or failed to observe any rule or regulation of the Commission authorized by this Act or by a treaty ratified by the United States, the Commission may order such person to cease and desist from such action.

(c)   Before revoking a license or permit pursuant to subsection (a), or issuing a cease and desist order pursuant to subsection (b), the Commission shall serve upon the licensee, permittee, or person involved an order to show cause why an order of revocation or a cease and desist order should not be issued. Any such order to show cause shall contain a statement of the matters with respect to which the Commission is inquiring and shall call upon said licensee, permittee, or person to appear before the Commission at a time and place stated in the order, but in no event less than thirty days after the receipt of such order, and give evidence upon the matter specified therein; except that where safety of life or property is involved, the Commission may provide in the order for a shorter period. If after hearing, or a waiver thereof, the Commission determines that an order of revocation or a cease and desist order should issue, it shall issue such order, which shall include a statement of the findings of the Commission and the grounds and reasons therefor and specify the effective date of the order, and shall cause the same to be served on said licensee, permittee, or person.

(d)   In any case where a hearing is conducted pursuant to the provisions of this section, both the burden of proceeding with the introduction of evidence and the burden of proof shall be upon the Commission.

(e)   The provisions of section 9(b) of the Administrative Procedure Act which apply with respect to the institution of any proceeding for the revocation of a license or permit shall apply also with respect to the institution, under this section, of any proceeding for the issuance of a cease and desist order.

Application of antitrust laws;
Refusal of licenses and permits in certain cases

Sec. 313.   (a)   All laws of the United States relating to unlawful restraints and monopolies and to combinations, contracts, or agreements in restraint of trade are hereby declared to be applicable to the manufacture and sale of and to trade in radio apparatus and devices entering into or affecting interstate or foreign commerce and to interstate or foreign radio communications. Whenever in any suit, action, or proceeding, civil or criminal, brought under the provisions of any of said laws or in any proceedings brought to enforce or to review findings and orders of the Federal Trade Commission or other governmental agency in respect of any matters as to which said Commission or other governmental agency is by law authorized to act, any licensee shall be found guilty of the violation of the provisions of such laws or any of them, the court, in addition to the penalties imposed by said laws, may adjudge, order, and/or decree that the license of such licensee shall, as of the date the decree or judgment becomes finally effective or as of such other date as the said decree shall fix, be revoked and that all rights under such license shall thereupon cease: *Provided, however,* That such licensee shall have the same right of appeal or review, as is provided by law in respect of other decrees and judgments of said court.

(b)   The Commission is hereby directed to refuse a station license and/or the permit hereinafter required for the construction of a station to any person (or to any person directly or indirectly controlled by such person) whose license has been revoked by a court under this section.

Preservation of competition in commerce

Sec. 314.   After the effective date of this Act no person engaged directly, or indirectly through any person directly or indirectly controlling or controlled by, or under direct or indirect common control with, such person, or through an agent, or otherwise, in the business of transmitting and/or receiving for hire energy, communications, or signals by radio in accordance with the terms of the license issued under this Act, shall by purchase, lease, construction, or otherwise, directly or indirectly, acquire, own, control, or operate any cable or wire telegraph or telephone line or system between any place in any State, Territory, or possession of the United States or in the District of Columbia, and any place in any foreign country, or shall acquire, own, or control any part of the stock or other capital share or any interest in the physical property and/or other assets of any such cable, wire, telegraph, or telephone line or system, if in either case the purpose is and/or the effect thereof may be to substantially lessen competition or to restrain commerce between any place in any State, Territory, or possession of the United States, or in the District of Columbia, and any place in any foreign country, or unlawfully to create monopoly in any line of commerce; nor shall any person engaged directly, or indirectly through any person directly or indirectly controlling or controlled by, or under direct or indirect common control with, such person, or through an agent, or otherwise, in the business of transmitting and/or receiving for hire messages by any cable, wire, telegraph, or telephone line or system (a) between any place in any State, Territory, or possession of the United States, or in the District of Columbia, and any place in any other State, Territory, or possession of the United States; or (b) between any place in any State, Territory, or possession of the United States, or the

District of Columbia, and any place in any foreign country, by purchase, lease, construction, or otherwise, directly or indirectly acquire, own, control, or operate any station or the apparatus therein, or any system for transmitting and/or receiving radio communications or signals between any place in any State, Territory, or possession of the United States, or in the District of Columbia, and any place in any foreign country, or shall acquire, own, or control any part of the stock or other capital share of any interest in the physical property and/or other assets of any such radio station, apparatus, or system, if in either case, the purpose is and/or the effect thereof may be to substantially lessen competition or to restrain commerce between any place in any State, Territory, or possession of the United States, or in the District of Columbia, and any place in any foreign country, or unlawfully to create monopoly in any line of commerce.

Facilities for candidates for public office

Sec. 315.   (a)   If any licensee shall permit any person who is a legally qualified candidate for any public office to use a broadcasting station, he shall afford equal opportunities to all other such candidates for that office in the use of such broadcasting station: *Provided,* That such licensee shall have no power of censorship over the material broadcast under the provisions of this section. No obligation is imposed under this subsection upon any licensee to allow the use of its station by any such candidate. Appearance by a legally qualified candidate on any—

    (1)   bona fide newscast,

    (2)   bona fide news interview,

    (3)   bona fide news documentary (if the appearance of the candidate is incidental to the presentation of the subject or subjects covered by the news documentary), or

    (4)   on-the-spot coverage of bona fide news events (including but not limited to political conventions and activities incidental thereto),

shall not be deemed to be use of a broadcasting station within the meaning of this subsection. Nothing in the foregoing sentence shall be construed as relieving broadcasters, in connection with the presentation of newscasts, news interviews, news documentaries, and on-the-spot coverage of news events, from the obligation imposed upon them under this Act to operate in the public interest and to afford reasonable opportunity for the discussion of conflicting views on issues of public importance.

    (b)   The charges made for the use of any broadcasting station by any person who is a legally qualified candidate for any public office in connection with his campaign for nomination for election, or election, to such office shall not exceed—

(1)   during the forty-five days preceding the date of a primary or primary runoff election and during the sixty days preceding the date of a general or special election in which such person is a candidate, the lowest unit charge of the station for the same class and amount of time for the same period; and

(2)   at any other time, the charges made for comparable use of such station by other users thereof.

(c)   For the purposes of this section—

(1)   the term "broadcasting station" includes a community antenna television system; and

(2)   the terms "licensee" and "station licensee" when used with respect to a community antenna television system mean the operator of such system.

(d)   The Commission shall prescribe appropriate rules and regulations to carry out the provisions of this section.

Modification by Commission of construction permits or licenses

Sec. 316.   (a)   Any station license or construction permit may be modified by the Commission either for a limited time or for the duration of the term thereof, if in the judgment of the Commission such action will promote the public interest, convenience, and necessity, or the provisions of this Act or of any treaty ratified by the United States will be more fully complied with. No such order of modification shall become final until the holder of the license or permit shall have been notified in writing of the proposed action and the grounds and reasons therefor, and shall have been given reasonable opportunity, in no event less than thirty days, to show cause by public hearing, if requested, why such order of modification should not issue: *Provided*, That where safety of life or property is involved, the Commission may by order provide for a shorter period of notice.

(b)   In any case where a hearing is conducted pursuant to the provisions of this section, both the burden of proceeding with the introduction of evidence and the burden of proof shall be upon the Commission.

Announcement with respect to certain matter broadcast

Sec. 317.   (a)   (1)   All matter broadcast by any radio station for which any money, service or other valuable consideration is directly or indirectly paid, or promised to or charged or accepted by, the station so broadcasting, from any person, shall, at the time the same is so broadcast, be announced as paid for or furnished, as the case may be, by such person: *Provided*, That "service or other valuable consideration" shall not include any service or property furnished without charge or at a nominal charge for use on, or in connection with, a broadcast unless it is so furnished in consideration for an identification in a broadcast of any person, product, service, trademark, or brand name beyond an identification which is reasonably related to the use of such service or property on the broadcast.

(2)   Nothing in this section shall preclude the Commission from requiring that an appropriate announcement shall be made at the time of the broadcast in the case of any political program or any program involving the discussion of any controversial issue for which any films, records, transcriptions, talent, scripts, or other material or service of any kind have been furnished, without charge or at a nominal charge, directly or indirectly, as an inducement to the broadcast of such program.

(b)   In any case where a report has been made to a radio station, as required by section 508 of this Act, of circumstances which would have required an announcement under this section had the consideration been received by such radio station, an appropriate announcement shall be made by such radio station.

(c)   The licensee of each radio station shall exercise reasonable diligence to obtain from its employees, and from other persons with whom it deals directly in connection with any program or program matter for broadcast, information to enable such licensee to make the announcement required by this section.

(d)   The Commission may waive the requirement of an announcement as provided in this section in any case or class of cases with respect to which it determines that the public interest, convenience, or necessity does not require the broadcasting of such announcement.

(e)   The Commission shall prescribe appropriate rules and regulations to carry out the provisions of this section.

Operation of transmitting apparatus

Sec. 318.   The actual operation of all transmitting apparatus in any radio station for which a station license is required by this Act shall be carried on only by a person holding an operator's license issued hereunder, and no person shall operate any such apparatus in such station except under and in accordance with an operator's license issued to him by the Commission: *Provided, however,* That the Commission if it shall find that the public interest, convenience, or necessity will be served thereby may waive or modify the foregoing provisions of this section for the operation of any station except (1) stations for which licensed operators are required by international agreement, (2) stations for which licensed operators are required for safety purposes, (3) stations engaged in broadcasting (other than those engaged primarily in the function of rebroadcasting the signals of broadcast stations) and (4) stations operated as common carriers on frequencies below thirty thousand kilocycles: *Provided further*, That the Commission shall have power to make special regulations governing the granting of licenses for the use of automatic radio devices and for the operation of such devices.

Construction permits

Sec. 319.   (a)   No license shall be issued under the authority of this Act for the operation of any station the construction of which is begun or is continued after this Act takes effect, unless a permit for its construction has been granted by the Commission. The application for a construction permit shall set forth such facts as the Commission by regulation may prescribe as to the citizenship, character, and the financial, technical, and other ability of the applicant to construct and operate the station, the ownership and location of the proposed station and of the station or stations with which it is proposed to communicate, the frequencies desired to be used, the hours of the day or other periods of time during which it is proposed to operate the station, the purpose for which the station is to be used, the type of transmitting apparatus to be used, the power to be used, the date upon which the station is expected to be completed and in operation, and such other information as the Commission may require. Such application shall be signed by the applicant.

(b)   Such permit for construction shall show specifically the earliest and latest dates between which the actual operation of such station is expected to begin, and shall provide that said permit will be automatically forfeited if the station is not ready for operation within the time specified or within such further time as the Commission may allow, unless prevented by causes not under the control of the grantee.

(c)   Upon the completion of any station for the construction or continued construction of which a permit has been granted, and upon it being made to appear to the Commission that all the terms, conditions, and obligations set forth in the application and permit have been fully met, and that no cause or circumstance arising or first coming to the knowledge of the Commission since the granting of the permit would, in the judgment of the Commission, make the operation of such station against the public interest, the Commission shall issue a license to the lawful holder of said permit for the operation of said station. Said license shall conform generally to the terms of said permit. The provisions of section 309(a), (b), (c), (d), (e), (f), and (g) shall not apply with respect to any station license the issuance of which is provided for and governed by the provisions of this subsection.

(d)   A permit for construction shall not be required for Government stations, amateur stations, or mobile stations. With respect to stations or classes of stations other than Government stations, amateur stations, mobile stations, and broadcasting stations, the Commission may waive the requirement of a permit for construction if it finds that the public interest, convenience, or necessity would be served thereby: *Provided, however,* That such waiver shall apply only to stations whose construction is begun subsequent to the effective date of the waiver. If the Commission finds that the public interest, convenience, and necessity would be served thereby, it may waive the requirement of a permit for construction of a station that is engaged solely in rebroadcasting television signals if such station was constructed on or before the date of enactment of this sentence.

False distress signals; Rebroadcasting; Studios of foreign stations

Sec. 325.   (a)   No person within the jurisdiction of the United States shall knowingly utter or transmit, or cause to be uttered or transmitted, any false or fraudulent signal of distress, or communication relating thereto, nor shall any broadcasting station rebroadcast the program or any part thereof of another broadcasting station without the express authority of the originating station.

(b)   No person shall be permitted to locate, use, or maintain a radio broadcast studio or other place or apparatus from which or whereby sound waves are converted into electrical energy, or mechanical or physical reproduction of sound waves produced, and caused to be transmitted or delivered to a radio station in a foreign country for the purpose of being broadcast from any radio station there having a power output of sufficient intensity and/or being so located geographically that its emissions may be received consistently in the United States, without first obtaining a permit from the Commission upon proper application therefor.

(c)   Such application shall contain such information as the Commission may by regulation prescribe, and the granting or refusal thereof shall be subject to the requirements of section 309 hereof with respect to applications for station licenses or renewal or modification thereof, and the license or permission so granted shall be revocable for false statements in the application so required or when the Commission, after hearings, shall find its continuation no longer in the public interest.

Censorship

Sec. 326.   Nothing in this Act shall be understood or construed to give the Commission the power of censorship over the radio communications or signals transmitted by any radio station, and no regulation or condition shall be promulgated or fixed by the Commission which shall interfere with the right of free speech by means of radio communication.

Prohibition against shipment of certain television receivers

Sec. 330. (a) No person shall ship in interstate commerce, or import from any foreign country into the United States, for sale or resale to the public, apparatus described in paragraph (s) of section 303 unless it complies with rules prescribed by the Commission pursuant to the authority granted by that paragraph: *Provided*, That this section shall not apply to carriers transporting such apparatus without trading in it.

(b) For the purposes of this section and section 303(s)–

(1) The term "interstate commerce" means (A) commerce between any State, the District of Columbia, the Commonwealth of Puerto Rico, or any possession of the United States and any place outside thereof which is within the United States, (B) commerce between points in the same State, the District of Columbia, the Commonwealth of Puerto Rico, or any possession of the United States but through any place outside thereof, or (C) commerce wholly within the District of Columbia or any possession of the United States

(2) The term "United States" means the several States, the District of Columbia, the Commonwealth of Puerto Rico, and the possessions of the United States, but does not include the Canal Zone.*

PART IV—ASSISTANCE FOR NONCOMMERCIAL EDUCATIONAL BROADCASTING FACILITIES: TELECOMMUNICATIONS DEMONSTRATIONS; CORPORATION FOR PUBLIC BROADCASTING

SUBPART A
ASSISTANCE FOR NONCOMMERCIAL
EDUCATIONAL BROADCASTING FACILITIES
AND TELECOMMUNICATIONS DEMONSTRATIONS

Declaration of purpose

Sec. 390. The purposes of this subpart are (1) to assist (through matching grants) in the construction of noncommercial educational television or radio broadcasting facilities, and (2) to demonstrate (through grants or contracts) the

*Parts II and III of Title III relating to maritime uses of radio are omitted. [Ed.]

use of telecommunications technologies for the distribution and dissemination of health, education, and other public or social service information.

Authorization of appropriations

Sec. 391.   There are authorized to be appropriated $7,500,000 for the period July 1, 1976, through September 30, 1976, and $30,000,000 for the fiscal year ending September 30, 1977, to assist (through matching grants) in the construction of noncommercial educational television or radio broadcasting facilities as provided in this subpart. Sums appropriated under this section for any fiscal year or period shall remain available for payment of grants for projects for which applications approved under section 392 of this title have been submitted under such section within one year after the last day of such fiscal year or period.

Grants for construction

Sec. 392.   (a)   For each project for the construction of noncommercial educational television or radio broadcasting facilities there shall be submitted to the Secretary an application for a grant containing such information with respect to such project as the Secretary may by regulation require, including the total cost of such project and the amount of the Federal grant requested for such project, and providing assurance satisfactory to the Secretary—

(1)   that the applicant is (A) an agency or officer responsible for the supervision of public elementary or secondary education or public higher education within that State, or within a political subdivision thereof, (B) in the case of a project for television facilities, the State noncommercial educational television agency or, in the case of a project for radio facilities, the State educational radio agency, (C) a public or private nonprofit college or university or other educational or cultural institution which is affiliated with an eligible college or university, (D) (i) in the case of a project for televison facilities, a nonprofit foundation, corporation, or association which is organized primarily to engage in or encourage noncommercial educational television broadcasting and is eligible to receive a license from the Federal Communications Commission for a noncommercial educational television broadcasting station pursuant to the rules and regulations of the Commission in effect on April 12, 1962, or (ii) in the case of a project for radio facilities, a nonprofit foundation, corporation, or association which is organized primarily to engage in or encourage noncommercial educational radio broadcasting and is eligible to receive a license from the Federal Communications Commission; or meets the requirements of clause (i) and is also organized to engage in or encourage such radio broadcasting and is eligible for such a license for such a radio station, or

(E) a municipality which owns and operates a broadcasting facility transmitting only noncommercial programs;

(2)   that the operation of such educational broadcasting facilities will be under the control of the applicant or a person qualified under paragraph (1) to be such an applicant;

(3)   that necessary funds to construct, operate, and maintain such educational broadcasting facilities will be available when needed;

(4)   that such broadcasting facilities will be used only for educational purposes; and

(5)   that, in the case of an application with respect to radio broadcasting facilities, there has been comprehensive planning for educational broadcasting facilities and services in the area the applicant proposes to serve and the applicant has participated in such planning, and the applicant will make the most efficient use of the frequency assignment.

(b)   The total of the grants made under this part from the appropriation for any fiscal year for the construction of noncommercial educational television broadcasting facilities and noncommercial educational radio broadcasting facilities in any State may not exceed 8½ per centum of such appropriation.

Notice to State educational television and radio agencies

(c)   (1)   In order to assure proper coordination of construction of noncommercial educational television broadcasting facilities within each State which has established a State educational television agency, each applicant for a grant under this section for a project for construction of such facilities in such State, other than such agency, shall notify such agency of each application for such a grant which is submitted by it to the Secretary, and the Secretary shall advise such agency with respect to the disposition of each such application.

(2)   In order to assure proper coordination of construction of noncommercial educational radio broadcasting facilities within each State which has established a State educational radio agency, each applicant for a grant under this section for a project for construction of such facilities in such State, other than such agency, shall notify such agency of each application for such a grant which is submitted by it to the Secretary, and the Secretary shall advise such agency with respect to the disposition of each such application.

Criteria for approval by Secretary

(d)   (1)   The Secretary shall base his determinations of whether to approve applications for television grants under this section and the amount of such grants on criteria set forth in regulations and designed to achieve (A) a strengthening of the capability of existing noncommercial educational television stations to provide local services; (B) the adaptation of existing noncommercial educational television facilities to broaden educational uses; and (C) extension of noncommercial educational television services, with due consideration to equitable geographic coverage throughout the United States.

(2)   The Secretary shall base his determination of whether to approve applications for radio grants under this section and the amount of such grants on criteria set forth in regulations and designed to achieve (A) extension of noncommercial educational radio services with due consideration to equitable geographic coverage throughout the United States; (B) a strengthening of the capability of existing noncommercial educational radio stations to provide local service; and (C) the provision of multiple radio stations in major population centers to broaden services for special interest, minority, and educational uses.

(e)   Upon approving any application under this section with respect to any project, the Secretary shall make a grant to the applicant in the amount determined by him, but not exceeding 75 per centum of the amount determined by the Secretary to be the reasonable and necessary cost of such project. The Secretary shall pay such amount from the sum available therefor, in advance or by way or reimbursement, and in such installments consistent with construction progress, as he may determine.

(f)   If, within ten years after completion of any project for construction of educational television or radio broadcasting facilities with respect to which a grant has been made under this section—

(1)   the applicant or other owner of such facilities ceases to be an agency, officer, institution, foundation, corporation, or association described in subsection (a)(1) of this section, or

(2)   such facilities cease to be used for noncommercial educational television purposes or noncommercial educational radio purposes, as the case may be (unless the Secretary determines, in accordance with regulations, that there is good cause for releasing the applicant or other owner from the obligation so to do),

the United States shall be entitled to recover from the applicant or other owner of such facilities the amount bearing the same ratio to the then value (as determined by agreement of the parties or by action brought in the United States district court for the district in which such facilities are situated) of such facilities, as the amount of the Federal participation bore to the cost of construction of such facilities.

Telecommunications demonstrations—purpose; grants and contracts

Sec. 392a.   (a)   It is the purpose of this section to promote the development of nonbroadcast telecommunications facilities and services for the transmission, distribution and delivery of health, education, and public or social service information. The Secretary is authorized, upon receipt of an application in such form and containing such information as he may by regulation require, to make grants to, and enter into contracts with public and private nonprofit agencies, organizations, and institutions for the purpose of carrying out telecommunications demonstrations.

Application approval

(b)   The Secretary may approve an application submitted under subsection (a) of this section if he determines—

(1)   that the project for which application is made will demonstrate innovative methods or techniques of utilizing nonbroadcast telecommunications equipment or facilities to satisfy the purpose of this section;

(2)   that demonstrations and related activities assisted under this section will remain under the administration and control of the applicant;

(3)   that the applicant has the managerial and technical capability to carry out the project for which the application is made; and

(4)   that the facilities and equipment acquired or developed pursuant to the application will be used substantially for the transmission, distribution, and delivery of health, education, or public or social service information.

Amount of grant or contract; payment

(c)   Upon approving any application under this section with respect to any project, the Secretary shall make a grant to or enter into a contract with the applicant in an amount determined by the Secretary not to exceed the reasonable and necessary cost of such project. The Secretary shall pay such amount from the sum available therefor, in advance or by way of reimbursement, and in such installments consistent with established practice, as he may determine.

Uses of funds

(d)   Funds made available pursuant to this section shall not be available for the construction, remodeling, or repair of structures to house the facilities or equipment acquired or developed with such funds, except that such funds may be used for minor remodeling which is necessary for and incident to the installation of such facilities or equipment.

Nonbroadcast telecommunications facilities

(e)   For purposes of this section, the term "nonbroadcast telecommunications facilities" includes, but is not limited to, cable television systems, communications satellite systems and related terminal equipment, and other methods of transmitting, emitting, or receiving images and sounds or intelligence by means of wire, radio, optical, electromagnetic or other means.

Duration of funding of demonstrations

(f)   The funding of any demonstration pursuant to this section shall continue for not more than three years from the date of the original grant or contract.

Summary and evaluation

(g)   The Secretary shall require that the recipient of a grant or contract under this section submit a summary and evaluation of the results of the demonstration at least annually for each year in which funds are received pursuant to this section.

Authorization of appropriations

(h)   There are authorized to be appropriated $1,000,000 for the fiscal year ending September 30, 1977, and $250,000 for the period July 1, 1976, through September 30, 1976, to carry out the provisions of this section. Sums appropriated under this subsection for any fiscal year or period shall remain available for payment of grants or contracts for projects for which applications approved under this section have been submitted within one year after the last day of such fiscal year or period.

Records

Sec. 393. (a) Each recipient of assistance under this subpart shall keep such records as may be reasonably necessary to enable the Secretary to carry out his functions under this subpart, including records which fully disclose the amount and the disposition by such recipient of the proceeds of such assistance, the total cost of the project or undertaking in connection with which such assistance is given or used, and the amount and nature of that portion of the cost of the project or undertaking supplied by other sources, and such other records as will facilitate an effective audit.

(b)   The Secretary and the Comptroller General of the United States, or any of their duly authorized representatives, shall have access for the purpose of audit and examination to any books, documents, papers, and records of the recipient that are pertinent to assistance received under this subpart.

Rules and regulations

Sec. 394.   The Secretary is authorized to make such rules and regulations as may be necessary to carry out this subpart, including regulations relating to the order of priority in approving applications for projects under section 392 or to determining the amounts of grants for such projects.

Assistance by Commission; coordination with Commission and Corporation

Sec. 395.   The Federal Communications Commission is authorized to provide such assistance in carrying out the provisions of this subpart as may be requested by the Secretary. The Secretary shall provide for close coordination with the Federal Communications Commission in the administration of his functions under this subpart which are of interest to or affect the functions of the Commission. The Secretary shall provide for close coordination with the Corporation for Public Broadcasting in the administration of his functions under this subpart which are of interest to or affect the functions of the Corporation.

SUBPART B
CORPORATION FOR PUBLIC BROADCASTING

Congressional declaration of policy

Sec. 396.   (a)   The Congress hereby finds and declares—
(1)   that it is in the public interest to encourage the growth and development of noncommercial educational radio and television broadcasting, including the use of such media for instructional purposes;
(2)   that expansion and development of noncommercial educational radio and television broadcasting and of diversity of its programing depend on freedom, imagination, and initiative on both the local and national levels;

(3)   that the encouragement and support of noncommercial educational radio and television broadcasting, while matters of importance for private and local development, are also of appropriate and important concern to the Federal Government;

(4)   that it furthers the general welfare to encourage noncommercial educational radio and television broadcast programing which will be responsive to the interests of people both in particular localities and throughout the United States, and which will constitute an expression of diversity and excellence;

(5)   that it is necessary and appropriate for the Federal Government to complement, assist, and support a national policy that will most effectively make noncommercial educational radio and television service available to all the citizens of the United States;

(6)   that a private corporation should be created to facilitate the development of educational radio and television broadcasting and to afford maximum protection to such broadcasting from extraneous interference and control.

Corporation established

(b)   There is authorized to be established a nonprofit corporation, to be known as the "Corporation for Public Broadcasting," which will not be an agency or establishment of the United States Government. The Corporation shall be subject to the provisions of this section, and, to the extent consistent with this section, to the District of Columbia Nonprofit Corporation Act.

Board of Directors

(c)   (1)   The Corporation shall have a Board of Directors (hereinafter in this section referred to as the "Board"), consisting of fifteen members appointed by the President, by and with the advice and consent of the Senate. Not more than eight members of the Board may be members of the same political party.

(2)   The members of the Board (A) shall be selected from among citizens of the United States (not regular fulltime employees of the United States) who are eminent in such fields as education, cultural and civic affairs, or the arts, including radio and television; (B) shall be selected so as to provide as nearly as practicable a broad representation of various regions of the country, various professions and occupations, and various kinds of talent and experience appropriate to the functions and responsibilities of the Corporation.

(3)   The members of the initial Board of Directors shall serve as

incorporators and shall take whatever actions are necessary to establish the Corporation under the District of Columbia Nonprofit Corporation Act.

(4)   The term of office of each member of the Board shall be six years; except that (A) any member appointed to fill a vacancy occurring prior to the expiration of the term for which his predecessor was appointed shall be appointed for the remainder of such term; and (B) the terms of office of members first taking office shall begin on the date of incorporation and shall expire, as designated at the time of their appointment, five at the end of two years, five at the end of four years, and five at the end of six years. No member shall be eligible to serve in excess of two consecutive terms of six years each. Notwithstanding the preceding provisions of this paragraph, a member whose term has expired may serve until his successor has qualified.

(5)   Any vacancy in the Board shall not affect its power, but shall be filled in the manner in which the original appointments were made.

Election of Chairman; compensation

(d)   (1)   The President shall designate one of the members first appointed to the Board as Chairman; thereafter the members of the Board shall annually elect one of their number as Chairman. The members of the Board shall also elect one or more of them as a Vice Chairman or Vice Chairmen.

(2)   The members of the Board shall not, by reason of such membership, be deemed to be employees of the United States. They shall, while attending meetings of the Board or while engaged in duties related to such meetings or in other activities of the Board pursuant to this subpart be entitled to receive compensation at the rate of $100 per day including travel time, and while away from their homes or regular places of business they may be allowed travel expenses, including per diem in lieu of subsistence, equal to that authorized by law (5 U.S.C. 5703) for persons in the Government service employed intermittently.

Officers and employees

(e)   (1)   The Corporation shall have a President, and such other officers as may be named and appointed by the Board for terms and at rates of compensation fixed by the Board. No individual other than a citizen of the United States may be an officer of the Corporation. No officer of the Corporation, other than the Chairman and any Vice Chairman, may receive any salary or other compensation from any source other than the Corporation during the period of his employment by the Corporation. All officers shall serve at the pleasure of the Board.

(2)   Except as provided in the second sentence of subsection (c)(1) of this section, no political test or qualification shall be used in selecting, appointing, promoting, or taking other personnel actions with respect to officers, agents, and employees of the Corporation.

Nonprofit and nonpolitical nature of the Corporation

(f)   (1)   The Corporation shall have no power to issue any shares of stock, or to declare or pay any dividends.

(2)   No part of the income or assets of the Corporation shall inure to the benefit of any director, officer, employee, or any other individual except as salary or reasonable compensation for services.

(3)   The Corporation may not contribute to or otherwise support any political party or candidate for elective public office.

Purposes and activities of the Corporation

(g)   (1)   In order to achieve the objectives and to carry out the purposes of this subpart, as set out in subsection (a), the Corporation is authorized to—

(A)   facilitate the full development of educational broadcasting in which programs of high quality, obtained from diverse sources, will be made available to noncommercial educational television or radio broadcast stations, with strict adherence to objectivity and balance in all programs or series of programs of a controversial nature;

(B)   assist in the establishment and development of one or more systems of interconnection to be used for the distribution of educational television or radio programs so that all noncommercial educational television or radio broadcast stations that wish to may broadcast the programs at times chosen by the stations;

(C)   assist in the establishment and development of one or more systems of noncommercial educational television or radio broadcast stations throughout the United States;

(D)   carry out its purposes and functions and engage in its activities in ways that will most effectively assure the maximum freedom of the noncommercial educational television or radio broadcast systems and local stations from interference with or control of program content or other activities.

(2)   Included in the activities of the Corporation authorized for accomplishment of the purposes set forth in subsection (a) of this section, are, among others not specifically named—

(A)   to obtain grants from and to make contracts with

individuals and with private, State, and Federal agencies, organizations, and institutions;

(B)   to contract with or make grants to program production entities, individuals, and selected noncommercial educational broadcast stations for the production of, and otherwise to procure, educational television or radio programs for national or regional distribution to noncommercial educational broadcast stations;

(C)   to make payments to existing and new noncommercial educational broadcast stations to aid in financing local educational television or radio programing costs of such stations, particularly innovative approaches thereto, and other costs of operation of such stations;

(D)   to establish and maintain a library and archives of noncommercial educational television or radio programs and related materials and develop public awareness of and disseminate information about noncommercial educational television or radio broadcasting by various means, including the publication of a journal;

(E)   to arrange, by grant or contract with appropriate public or private agencies, organizations, or institutions, for interconnection facilities suitable for distribution and transmission of educational television or radio programs to noncommercial educational broadcast stations;

(F)   to hire or accept the voluntary services of consultants, experts, advisory boards, and panels to aid the Corporation in carrying out the purposes of this section;

(G)   to encourage the creation of new noncommercial educational broadcast stations in order to enhance such service on a local, State, regional, and national basis;

(H)   conduct (directly or through grants or contracts) research, demonstrations, or training in matters related to noncommercial educational television or radio broadcasting and the use of nonbroadcast communications technologies for the dissemination of educational television or radio programs.

(3)   To carry out the foregoing purposes and engage in the foregoing activities, the Corporation shall have the usual powers conferred upon a nonprofit corporation by the District of Columbia Nonprofit Corporation Act, except that the Corporation may not own or operate any television or radio broadcast station, system, or network, community antenna television system, or interconnection or program production facility.

Authorization for free or reduced rate interconnection service

(h)   Nothing in the Communications Act of 1934, as amended, or in any other provision of law shall be construed to prevent United States communications common carriers from rendering free or reduced rate communications interconnection services for noncommercial educational television or radio services, subject to such rules and regulations as the Federal Communications Commission may prescribe.

Report to Congress

(i)   The Corporation shall submit an annual report for the preceding fiscal year ending June 30 to the President for transmittal to the Congress on or before the 31st day of December of each year. The report shall include a comprehensive and detailed report of the Corporation's operations, activities, financial condition, and accomplishments under this section and may include such recommendations as the Corporation deems appropriate. The officers and directors of the Corporation shall be available to testify before appropriate committees of the Congress with respect to such report, the report of any audit made by the Comptroller General pursuant to subsection (l) of this section, or any other matter which any such committee may determine.

Right to repeal, alter, or amend

(j)   The right to repeal, alter, or amend this section at any time is expressly reserved.

Financing

(k)   (1)   There is authorized to be appropriated for expenses of the Corporation $50,000,000 for the fiscal year ending June 30, 1974, and $60,000,000 for the fiscal year ending June 30, 1975.

(2)   In addition to the sums authorized to be appropriated by paragraph (1) of this subsection, there are authorized to be appropriated for payment to the Corporation for each fiscal year during the period July 1, 1970, to June 30, 1975, amounts equal to the amount of total grants, donations, bequests, or other contributions (including money and the fair market value of any property) from non-Federal sources received by the Corporation under section 396 (g) (2) (A) of this Act during such fiscal year; except that the amount appropriated pursuant to this paragraph for any fiscal year may not exceed $5,000,000.

(3)   There is hereby established in the Treasury a fund which shall

be known as the "Public Broadcasting Fund" administered by the Secretary of the Treasury. There are authorized to be appropriated to such fund for each of the fiscal years during the period beginning July 1, 1975, and ending September 30, 1980, an amount equal to 40 per centum of the total amount of non-Federal financial support received by public broadcasting entities during the fiscal year second preceding each such fiscal year, and for the period July 1, 1976, through September 30, 1976, an amount equal to 10 per centum of the total amount of non-Federal financial support received by public broadcasting entities during the fiscal year ending June 30, 1975; except that the amount so appropriated shall not exceed $88,000,000 for the fiscal year ending June 30, 1976; $22,000,000 for the period July 1, 1976, through September 30, 1976; $103,000,000 for the fiscal year ending September 30, 1977; $121,000,000 for the fiscal year ending September 30, 1978; $140,000,000 for the fiscal year ending September 30, 1979; and $160,000,000 for the fiscal year ending September 30, 1980.

(4) The funds authorized by this subsection shall be used solely for the expenses of the Corporation. The Corporation shall determine the amount of non-Federal financial support received by public broadcasting entities during each of the fiscal years indicated in paragraph (3) of this subsection for the purpose of determining the amount of each authorization, and shall certify such amount to the Secretary of the Treasury. Upon receipt of such certification, the Secretary of the Treasury shall disburse to the Corporation, from such funds as may be appropriated to the Public Broadcasting Fund, the amount authorized for each of the fiscal years and for the period July 1, 1976, through September 30, 1976, pursuant to the provisions of this subsection.

(5) The Corporation shall reserve for distribution among the licensees and permittees of noncommercial educational broadcast stations that are on-the-air an amount equal to not less than 40 per centum of the funds disbursed to the Corporation from the Public Broadcasting Fund during the period July 1, 1975, through September 30, 1976, and in each fiscal year in which the amount disbursed is $88,000,000 or more, but less than $121,000,000; not less than 45 per centum in each fiscal year in which the amount disbursed is $121,-000,000 or more, but less than $160,000,000; and not less than 50 per centum in each fiscal year in which the amount disbursed is $160,000,000.

(6) The Corporation shall, after consultation with licensees and permittees of noncommercial educational broadcast stations that are on-the-air, establish, and review annually, criteria and conditions regarding the distribution of funds reserved pursuant to paragraph (5) of this subsection, as set forth below:

(A) The total amount of funds shall be divided into two portions, one to be distributed among radio stations, and one to be distributed among television stations. The Corporation shall make a basic grant from the portion reserved for television stations to each licensee and permittee of a noncommercial educational television station that is on-the-air. The balance of the portion reserved for television stations and the total portion reserved for radio stations shall be distributed to licensees and permittees of such stations in accordance with eligibility criteria that promote the public interest in noncommercial educational broadcasting, and on the basis of a formula designed to—

(i)   provide for the financial need and requirements of stations in relation to the communities and audiences such stations undertake to serve;

(ii)   maintain existing, and stimulate new, sources of non-Federal financial support for stations by providing incentives for increases in such support; and

(iii)   assure that each eligible licensee and permittee of a noncommercial educational radio station receives a basic grant.

(B)   No distribution of funds pursuant to this subsection shall exceed, in any fiscal year, one-half of a licensee's or permittee's total non-Federal financial support during the fiscal year second preceding the fiscal year in which such distribution is made.

(7)   Funds distributed pursuant to this subsection may be used at the discretion of stations for purposes related to the provision of educational television and radio programing, including but not limited to the following: producing, acquiring, broadcasting, or otherwise disseminating educational television or radio programs; procuring national or regional program distribution services that make educational television or radio programs available for broadcast or other dissemination at times chosen by stations; acquiring, replacing, and maintaining facilities, and real property used with facilities, for the production, broadcast, or other dissemination of educational television and radio programs; developing and using nonbroadcast communications technologies for educational television or radio programing purposes.

Records and audit

(l)   (1)   (A)   The accounts of the Corporation shall be audited annually in accordance with generally accepted auditing standards by independent certified public accountants or independent licensed public accountants certified or licensed by a regulatory authority of a State or other political subdivision of the United States. The audits shall be conducted at the place or places where the accounts of the Corporation are normally kept. All books, accounts, financial records, reports, files, and all other papers, things, or property belonging to or in use by the Corporation and necessary to facilitate the audits shall be made available to the person or persons conducting the audits; and full facilities for verifying transactions with the balances or securities held by depositories, fiscal agents and custodians shall be afforded to such person or persons.

(B)   The report of each such independent audit shall be

included in the annual report required by subsection (i) of this section. The audit report shall set forth the scope of the audit and include such statements as are necessary to present fairly the Corporation's assets and liabilities, surplus or deficit, with an analysis of the changes therein during the year, supplemented in reasonable detail by a statement of the Corporation's income and expenses during the year, and a statement of the sources and application of funds, together with the independent auditor's opinion of those statements.

(2) (A) The financial transactions of the Corporation for any fiscal year during which Federal funds are available to finance any portion of its operations may be audited by the General Accounting Office in accordance with the principles and procedures applicable to commercial corporate transactions and under such rules and regulations as may be prescribed by the Comptroller General of the United States. Any such audit shall be conducted at the place or places where accounts of the Corporation are normally kept. The representative of the General Accounting Office shall have access to all books, accounts, records, reports, files, and all other papers, things, or property belonging to or in use by the Corporation pertaining to its financial transactions and necessary to facilitate the audit, and they shall be afforded full facilities for verifying transactions with the balances or securities held by depositories, fiscal agents, and custodians. All such books, accounts, records, reports, files, papers and property of the Corporation shall remain in possession and custody of the Corporation.

(B) A report of each such audit shall be made by the Comptroller General to the Congress. The report to the Congress shall contain such comments and information as the Comptroller General may deem necessary to inform Congress of the financial operations and condition of the Corporation, together with such recommendations with respect thereto as he may deem advisable. The report shall also show specifically any program, expenditure, or other financial transaction or undertaking observed in the course of the audit, which, in the opinion of the Comptroller General, has been carried on or made without authority of law. A copy of each report shall be furnished to the President, to the Secretary, and to the Corporation at the time submitted to the Congress.

(3) (A) Each recipient of assistance by grant or contract, other than a fixed price contract awarded pursuant to competitive bidding procedures, under this section shall keep such records as may be reasonably necessary to fully disclose the amount and the disposition by such recipient of the proceeds of such assistance, the total cost of the project or undertaking in connection with which such assistance is given or used, and the amount and nature of that portion of the cost of the project or undertaking supplied by other sources, and such other records as will facilitate an effective audit.

(B) The Corporation or any of its duly authorized representatives, shall have access for the purpose of audit and examination to any books, documents, papers, and records of the recipient that are pertinent to assistance received under this section. The Comptroller General of the United States or any of his duly authorized representatives shall also have access thereto for such purpose during any fiscal year for which Federal funds are available to the Corporation.

SUBPART C
GENERAL

Definitions

Sec. 397.   For the purposes of sections 390–399 of this title—

(1)   The term "State" includes the District of Columbia, the Commonwealth of Puerto Rico, the Virgin Islands, Guam, American Samoa, and the Trust Territory of the Pacific Islands.

(2)   The term "construction," as applied to educational television broadcasting facilities or educational radio broadcasting facilities, means the acquisition and installation of transmission and reception apparatus (including towers, microwave equipment, boosters, translators, repeaters, mobile equipment, video recording equipment, nonvideo recording equipment, radio subcarrier receivers, and satellite transceivers) necessary for television broadcasting or radio broadcasting, as the case may be, including apparatus which may incidentally be used for transmitting closed circuit television or radio programs, but such term does not include the construction or repair of structures to house such apparatus. In the case of apparatus, the acquisition and installation of which is so included, such term also includes planning therefor.

(3)   The term "Secretary" means the Secretary of Health, Education, and Welfare.

(4)   The terms "State educational television agency" and "State educational radio agency" mean, with respect to television broadcasting and radio broadcasting, respectively, (A) a board or commission established by State law for the purpose of promoting such broadcasting within a State, (B) a board or commission appointed by the Governor of a State for such purpose if such appointment is not inconsistent with State law, or (C) a State officer or agency responsible for the supervision of public elementary or secondary education or public higher education within the State which has been designated by the Governor to assume responsibility for the promotion of such broadcasting; and, in the case of the District of Columbia, the term "Governor" means the Board of Commissioners of the District of Columbia and, in the case of the Trust Territory of the Pacific Islands, means the High Commissioner thereof.

(5)   The term "nonprofit" as applied to any foundation, corporation, or association, means a foundation, corporation, or association, no part of the net earnings of which inures, or may lawfully inure, to the benefit of any private shareholder or individual.

(6) The term "Corporation" means the Corporation authorized to be established by subpart B of this part.

(7) The term "noncommercial educational broadcast station" means a television or radio broadcast station, which (A) under the rules and regulations of the Federal Communications Commission in effect on the date of enactment of the Public Broadcasting Act of 1967, is eligible to be licensed or is licensed by the Commission as a noncommercial educational radio or television broadcast station and which is owned and operated by a public agency or nonprofit private foundation, corporation, or association or (B) is owned and operated by a municipality and which transmits only noncommercial programs for educational purposes.

(8) The term "interconnection" means the use of microwave equipment, boosters, translators, repeaters, communication space satellites, or other apparatus or equipment for the transmission and distribution of television or radio programs to noncommercial educational television or radio broadcast stations.

(9) The term "educational television or radio programs" means programs which are primarily designed for educational or cultural purposes.

(10) The term "non-Federal financial support" means the total value of cash and the fair market value of property and services (except for personal services of volunteers) received—

(A) as gifts, grants, bequests, donations, or other contributions for the construction or operation of noncommercial educational broadcast stations, or for the production, acquisition, distribution, or dissemination of educational television or radio programs, and related activities, from any source other than (i) the United States or any agency or establishment thereof, or (ii) any public broadcasting entity; or

(B) as gifts, grants, donations, contributions, or payments from any State, any agency or political subdivision of a State, or any educational institution, for the construction or operation of noncommercial educational broadcast stations or for the production, acquisition, distribution, or dissemination of educational television or radio programs, or payments in exchange for services or materials respecting the provision of educational or instructional television or radio programs.

(11) The term "public broadcasting entity" means the Corporation, any licensee or permittee of a noncommercial educational broadcast station, or any nonprofit institution engaged primarily in the production, acquisition, distribution, or dissemination of educational television or radio programs.

Federal interference or control prohibited

Sec. 398.   Nothing contained in this part shall be deemed (1) to amend any other provision of, or requirement under this Act; or (2) to authorize any department, agency, officer, or employee of the United States to exercise any direction, supervision, or control over educational television or radio broadcasting, or over the Corporation or any of its grantees or contractors, or over the charter or bylaws of the Corporation, or over the curriculum, program of instruction, or personnel of any educational institution, school system, or educational broadcasting station or system.

Editorializing and support of political candidates prohibited; recording of certain programs

Sec. 399.   (a)   No noncommercial educational broadcasting station may engage in editorializing or may support or oppose any candidate for political office.

(b)   (1)   Except as provided in paragraph (2), each licensee which receives assistance under sections 390 to 399 of this title after August 6, 1973 shall retain an audio recording of each of its broadcasts of any program in which any issue of public importance is discussed. Each such recording shall be retained for the sixty-day period beginning on the date on which the licensee broadcasts such program.

(2)   The requirements of paragraph (1) shall not apply with respect to a licensee's broadcast of a program if an entity designated by the licensee retains an audio recording of each of the licensee's broadcasts of such a program for the period prescribed by paragraph (1).

(3)   Each licensee and entity designated by a licensee under paragraph (2) which retains a recording under paragraph (1) or (2) shall, in the period during which such recording is required under such paragraph to be retained, make a copy of such recording available—

(A)   to the Commission upon its request, and

(B)   to any other person upon payment to the licensee or designated entity (as the case may be) of its reasonable cost of making such copy.

(4)   The Commission shall by rule prescribe—

(A)   the manner in which recordings required by this subsection shall be kept, and

(B)   the conditions under which they shall be available to persons other than the Commission,

giving due regard to the goals of eliminating unnecessary expense and effort and minimizing administrative burdens.

(5)   From amounts appropriated pursuant to section 391 of this title after June 5, 1976, the Secretary may make a grant to any licensee of a noncommercial educational broadcast station who received assistance under this part of the full amount necessary to acquire equipment to permit such licensee to comply with paragraph (1) of this subsection.

TITLE IV
PROCEDURAL AND ADMINISTRATIVE PROVISIONS

Jurisdiction to enforce Act and orders of Commission

Sec. 401.   (a)   The district courts of the United States shall have jurisdiction, upon application of the Attorney General of the United States at the request of the Commission, alleging a failure to comply with or a violation of any of the provisions of this Act by any person, to issue a writ or writs of mandamus commanding such person to comply with the provisions of this Act.

(b)   If any person fails or neglects to obey any order of the Commission other than for the payment of money, while the same is in effect, the Commission or any party injured thereby, or the United States, by its Attorney General, may apply to the appropriate district court of the United States for the enforcement of such order. If, after hearing, that court determines that the order was regularly made and duly served, and that the person is in disobedience of the same, the court shall enforce obedience to such order by a writ of injunction or other proper process, mandatory or otherwise, to restrain such person or the officers, agents, or representatives of such person, from further disobedience of such order, or to enjoin upon It or them obedience to the same.

(c)   Upon the request of the Commission it shall be the duty of any United States attorney to whom the Commission may apply to institute in the proper court and to prosecute under the direction of the Attorney General of the United States all necessary proceedings for the enforcement of the provisions of this Act and for the punishment of all violations thereof, and the costs and expenses of such prosecutions shall be paid out of the appropriations for the expenses of the courts of the United States.

Proceedings to enjoin, set aside, annul, or suspend orders of the Commission

Sec. 402.   (a)   Any proceeding to enjoin, set aside, annul, or suspend any order of the Commission under this Act (except those appealable under subsection (b) of this section) shall be brought as provided by and in the manner prescribed in Public Law 901, Eighty-first Congress, approved December 29, 1950.

(b)   Appeals may be taken from decisions and orders of the Commission to the United States Court of Appeals for the District of Columbia in any of the following cases:

(1)   By any applicant for a construction permit or station license, whose application is denied by the Commission.

(2)   By any applicant for the renewal or modification of any such instrument of authorization whose application is denied by the Commission.

(3)   By any party to an application for authority to transfer, assign, or dispose of any such instrument of authorization, or any rights thereunder, whose application is denied by the Commission.

(4)   By any applicant for the permit required by section 325 of this Act whose application has been denied by the Commission, or by any permittee under said section whose permit has been revoked by the Commission.

(5)   By the holder of any construction permit or station license which has been modified or revoked by the Commission.

(6)   By any other person who is aggrieved or whose interests are adversely affected by any order of the Commission granting or denying any application described in paragraphs (1), (2), (3), and (4) hereof.

(7)   By any person upon whom an order to cease and desist has been served under section 312 of this Act.

(8)   By any radio operator whose license has been suspended by the Commission.

(c)   Such appeal shall be taken by filing a notice of appeal with the court within thirty days from the date upon which public notice is given of the decision or order complained of. Such notice of appeal shall contain a concise statement of the nature of the proceedings as to which the appeal is taken; a concise statement of the reasons on which the applicant intends to rely, separately stated and numbered; and proof of service of a true copy of said notice and statement upon the Commission. Upon filing of such notice, the court shall have jurisdiction of the proceedings and of the questions determined therein and shall have power, by order, directed to the Commission or any other party to the appeal, to grant such temporary relief as it may deem just and proper. Orders granting temporary relief may be either affirmative or negative in their scope and application so as to permit either the maintenance of the status quo in the matter in which the appeal is taken or the restoration of a position or status terminated or adversely affected by the order appealed from and shall, unless otherwise ordered by the court, be effective pending hearing and determination of said appeal and compliance by the Commission with the final judgment of the court rendered in said appeal.

(d)   Upon the filing of any such notice of appeal the Commission shall, not later than five days after the date of service upon it, notify each person shown by the records of the Commission to be interested in said appeal of the filing and pendency of the same and shall thereafter permit any such person to inspect and make copies of said notice and statement of reasons therefor at the office of the Commission in the city of Washington. Within thirty days after the filing of an appeal, the Commission shall file with the court the record upon which the order complained of was entered, as provided in Section 2112 of Title 28, United States Code.

(e)   Within thirty days after the filing of any such appeal any interested person may intervene and participate in the proceedings had upon said appeal by filing with the court a notice of intention to intervene and a verified statement showing the nature of the interest of such party, together with proof of service of true copies of said notice and statement, both upon appellant and upon the Commission. Any person who would be aggrieved or whose interest would be adversely affected by a reversal or modification of the order of the Commission complained of shall be considered an interested party.

(f) The record and briefs upon which any such appeal shall be heard and determined by the court shall contain such information and material, and shall be prepared within such time and in such manner as the court may by rule prescribe.

(g) At the earliest convenient time the court shall hear and determine the appeal upon the record before it in the manner prescribed by section 10(e) of the Administrative Procedure Act.

(h) In the event that the court shall render a decision and enter an order reversing the order of the Commission, it shall remand the case to the Commission to carry out the judgment of the court and it shall be the duty of the Commission, in the absence of the proceedings to review such judgment, to forthwith give effect thereto, and unless otherwise ordered by the court, to do so upon the basis of the proceedings already had and the record upon which said appeal was heard and determined.

(i) The court may, in its discretion, enter judgment for costs in favor of or against an appellant, or other interested parties intervening in said appeal, but not against the Commission, depending upon the nature of the issues involved upon said appeal and the outcome thereof.

(j) The court's judgment shall be final, subject, however, to review by the Supreme Court of the United States upon writ of certiorari on petition therefor under section 1254 of title 28 of the United States Code, by the appellant, by the Commission, or by any interested party intervening in the appeal, or by certification by the court pursuant to the provisions of that section.

Inquiry by Commission on its own motion

Sec. 403. The Commission shall have full authority and power at any time to institute an inquiry, on its own motion, in any case and as to any matter or thing concerning which complaint is authorized to be made, to or before the Commission by any provision of this Act, or concerning which any question may arise under any of the provisions of this Act, or relating to the enforcement of any of the provisions of this Act. The Commission shall have the same powers and authority to proceed with any inquiry instituted on its own motion as though it had been appealed to by complaint or petition under any of the provisions of this Act, including the power to make and enforce any order or orders in the case, or relating to the matter or thing concerning which the inquiry is had, excepting orders for the payment of money.

Reports of investigations

Sec. 404.   Whenever an investigation shall be made by the Commission it shall be its duty to make a report in writing in respect thereto, which shall state the conclusions of the Commission, together with its decision, order, or requirements in the premises; and in case damages are awarded such report shall include the findings of fact on which the award is made.

Rehearings

Sec. 405.   After an order, decision, report, or action has been made or taken in any proceeding by the Commission, or by any designated authority within the Commission pursuant to a delegation under section 5(d)(1), any party thereto, or any other person aggrieved or whose interests are adversely affected thereby, may petition for rehearing only to the authority making or taking the order, decision, report, or action; and it shall be lawful for such authority, whether it be the Commission or other authority designated under section 5(d)(1), in its discretion, to grant such a rehearing if sufficient reason therefor be made to appear. A petition for rehearing must be filed within thirty days from the date upon which public notice is given of the order, decision, report, or action complained of. No such application shall excuse any person from complying with or obeying any order, decision, report, or action of the Commission, or operate in any manner to stay or postpone the enforcement thereof, without the special order of the Commission. The filing of a petition for rehearing shall not be a condition precedent to judicial review of any such order, decision, report, or action, except where the party seeking such review (1) was not a party to the proceedings resulting in such order, decision, report, or action, or (2) relies on questions of fact or law upon which the Commission, or designated authority within the Commission, has been afforded no opportunity to pass. The Commission, or designated authority within the Commission, shall enter an order, with a concise statement of the reasons therefor, denying a petition for rehearing or granting such petition, in whole or in part, and ordering such further proceedings as may be appropriate: *Provided*, That in any case where such petition relates to an instrument of authorization granted without a hearing, the Commission, or designated authority within the Commission, shall take such action within ninety days of the filing of such petition. Rehearings shall be governed by such general rules as the Commission may establish, except that no evidence other than newly discovered evidence, evidence which has become available only since the original taking of evidence, or evidence which the Commission or designated authority within the Commission believes should have been taken in the original proceeding shall be taken on any rehearing. The time within which a petition for review must be filed in a proceeding to which section 402(a) applies, or within which an appeal must be taken under section 402(b) in any case, shall be computed from the date upon which public notice is given of orders disposing of all petitions for rehearing filed with the Commission in such proceeding or case, but any order, decision, report, or action made or taken after such rehearing reversing, changing, or modifying the original order shall be subject to the same provisions with respect to rehearing as an original order.

TITLE V
PENAL PROVISIONS – FORFEITURES

General penalty

Sec. 501.   Any person who willfully and knowingly does or causes or suffers to be done any act, matter, or thing, in this Act prohibited or declared to be unlawful, or who willfully or knowingly omits or fails to do any act, matter, or thing in this Act required to be done, or willfully and knowingly causes or suffers such omission or failure, shall, upon conviction thereof, be punished for such offense, for which no penalty (other than a forfeiture) is provided in this Act, by a fine of not more than $10,000 or by imprisonment for a term not exceeding one year, or both; except that any person, having been once convicted of an offense punishable under this section, who is subsequently convicted of violating any provision of this Act punishable under this section, shall be punished by a fine of not more than $10,000 or by imprisonment for a term not exceeding two years, or both.

Sec. 502.   Any person who willfully and knowingly violates any rule, regulation, restriction, or condition made or imposed by the Commission under authority of this Act, or any rule, regulation, restriction, or condition made or imposed by any international radio or wire communications treaty or convention, or regulations annexed thereto, to which the United States is or may hereafter become a party, shall, in addition to any other penalties provided by law, be punished, upon conviction thereof, by a fine of not more than $500 for each and every day during which such offense occurs.

Sec. 503.   (a)   Any person who shall deliver messages for interstate or foreign transmission to any carrier, or for whom, as sender or receiver, any such carrier shall transmit any interstate or foreign wire or radio communication, who shall knowingly by employee, agent, officer, or otherwise, directly or indirectly, by or through any means or device whatsoever, receive or accept from such common carrier any sum of money or any other valuable consideration as a rebate or offset against the regular charges for transmission of such messages as fixed by the schedules of charges provided for in this Act, shall in addition to any other penalty provided by this Act forfeit to the United States a sum of money three times the amount of money so received or accepted and three times the value of any other consideration so received or accepted, to be ascertained by the trial court; and in the trial of said action all such rebates or other considerations so received or accepted, for a period of six years prior to the commencement of the action, may be included therein, and the amount recovered shall be three times the total amount of money, or three times the total value of such consideration, so received or accepted, or both, as the case may be.

(b)   (1)   Any licensee or permittee of a broadcast station who—

(A)   willfully or repeatedly fails to operate such station substantially as set forth in his license or permit,

(B)   willfully or repeatedly fails to observe any of the provisions of this Act or of any rule or regulation of the Commission prescribed under authority of this Act or under authority of any treaty ratified by the United States,

(C)   fails to observe any final cease and desist order issued by the Commission,

(D)   violates section 317(c) or section 509(a)(4) of this Act, or

(E)   violates section 1304, 1343, or 1464 of title 18 of the United States Code,

shall forfeit to the United States a sum not to exceed $1,000. Each day during which such violation occurs shall constitute a separate offense. Such forfeiture shall be in addition to any other penalty provided by this Act

(2)   No forfeiture liability under paragraph (1) of this subsection (b) shall attach unless a written notice of apparent liability shall have been issued by the Commission and such notice has been received by the licensee or permittee or the Commission shall have sent such notice by registered or certified mail to the last known address of the licensee or permittee. A licensee or permittee so notified shall be granted an opportunity to show in writing, within such reasonable period as the Commission shall by regulations prescribe, why he should not be held liable. A notice issued under this paragraph shall not be valid unless it sets forth the date, facts, and nature of the act or omission with which the licensee or permittee is charged and specifically identifies the particular provision or provisions of the law, rule, or regulation or the license, permit, or cease and desist order involved.

(3)   No forfeiture liability under paragraph (1) of this subsection (b) shall attach for any violation occurring more than one year prior to the date of issuance of the notice of apparent liability and in no event shall the forfeiture

imposed for the acts or omission set forth in any notice of apparent liability exceed $10,000.

Provisions relating to forfeitures

Sec. 504. (a) The forfeitures provided for in this Act shall be payable into the Treasury of the United States, and shall be recoverable in a civil suit in the name of the United States brought in the district where the person or carrier has its principal operating office or in any district through which the line or system of the carrier runs: *Provided,* That any suit for the recovery of a forfeiture imposed pursuant to the provisions of this Act shall be a trial de novo: *Provided further,* That in the case of forfeiture by a ship, said forfeiture may also be recoverable by way of libel in any district in which such ship shall arrive or depart. Such forfeitures shall be in addition to any other general or specific penalties herein provided. It shall be the duty of the various district attorneys, under the direction of the Attorney General of the United States, to prosecute for the recovery of forfeitures under this Act. The costs and expenses of such prosecutions shall be paid from the appropriation for the expenses of the courts of the United States.

(b) The forfeitures imposed by parts II and III of title III and section 503(b), section 507, and section 510 of this Act shall be subject to remission or mitigation by the Commission, upon application therefor, under such regulations and methods of ascertaining the facts as may seem to it advisable, and, if suit has been instituted, the Attorney General, upon request of the Commission, shall direct the discontinuance of any prosecution to recover such forfeitures: *Provided, however,* That no forfeiture shall be remitted or mitigated after determination by a court of competent jurisdiction.

(c) In any case where the Commission issues a notice of apparent liability looking toward the imposition of a forfeiture under this Act, that fact shall not be used, in any other proceeding before the Commission, to the prejudice of the person to whom such notice was issued, unless (i) the forfeiture has been paid, or (ii) a court of competent jurisdiction has ordered payment of such forfeiture, and such order has become final.

Venue of offenses

Sec. 505. The trial of any offense under this Act shall be in the district in which it is committed; or if the offense is committed upon the high seas, or out of the jurisdiction of any particular State or district, the trial shall be in the district where the offender may be found or into which he shall be first brought. Whenever the offense is begun in one jurisdiction and completed in another it may be dealt with, inquired of, tried, determined, and punished in either jurisdiction in the same manner as if the offense had been actually and wholly committed therein.

Coercive practices affecting broadcasting

Sec. 506.   (a)   It shall be unlawful, by the use or express or implied threat of the use of force, violence, intimidation, or duress, or by the use or express or implied threat of the use of other means, to coerce, compel or constrain or attempt to coerce, compel, or constrain a licensee—

(1)   to employ or agree to employ, in connection with the conduct of the broadcasting business of such licensee, any person or persons in excess of the number of employees needed by such licensee to perform actual services; or

(2)   to pay or give or agree to pay or give any money or other thing of value in lieu of giving, or on account of failure to give, employment to any person or persons, in connection with the conduct of the broadcasting business of such licensee, in excess of the number of employees needed by such licensee to perform actual services; or

(3)   to pay or agree to pay more than once for services performed in connection with the conduct of the broadcasting business of such licensee; or

(4)   to pay or give or agree to pay or give any money or other thing of value for services, in connection with the conduct of the broadcasting business of such licensee, which are not to be performed; or

(5)   to refrain, or agree to refrain, from broadcasting or from permitting the broadcasting of a noncommercial educational or cultural program in connection with which the participants receive no money or other thing of value for their services, other than their actual expenses, and such licensee neither pays nor gives any money or other thing of value for the privilege of broadcasting such program nor receives any money or other thing of value on account of the broadcasting of such program; or

(6)   to refrain, or agree to refrain, from broadcasting or permitting the broadcasting of any radio communication originating outside the United States.

(b)   It shall be unlawful, by the use or express or implied threat of the use of force, violence, intimidation or duress, or by the use or express or implied threat of the use of other means, to coerce, compel or constrain or attempt to coerce, compel or constrain a licensee or any other person—

(1)   to pay or agree to pay any exaction for the privilege of, or on account of, producing, preparing, manufacturing, selling, buying, renting, operating, using, or maintaining recordings, transcriptions, or mechanical, chemical, or electrical reproductions, or any other articles, equipment, machines, or materials, used or intended to be used in broadcasting or in the production, preparation, performance, or presentation of a program or programs for broadcasting; or

(2)　to accede to or impose any restriction upon such production, preparation, manufacture, sale, purchase, rental, operation, use, or maintenance, if such restriction is for the purpose of preventing or limiting the use of such articles, equipment, machines, or materials in broadcasting or in the production, preparation, performance, or presentation of a program or programs for broadcasting; or

(3)　to pay or agree to pay any exaction on account of the broadcasting, by means of recordings or transcriptions, of a program previously broadcast, payment having been made, or agreed to be made, for the services actually rendered in the performance of such program.

(c)　The provisions of subsection (a) or (b) of this section shall not be held to make unlawful the enforcement or attempted enforcement, by means lawfully employed, of any contract right heretofore or hereafter existing or of any legal obligation heretofore or hereafter incurred or assumed.

(d)　Whoever willfully violates any provision of subsection (a) or (b) of this section shall, upon conviction thereof, be punished by imprisonment for not more than one year or by a fine of not more than $1,000, or both.

(e)　As used in this section the term "licensee" includes the owner or owners, and the person or persons having control or management, of the radio station in respect of which a station license was granted.

Disclosure of certain payments

Sec. 508.　(a)　Subject to subsection (d), any employee of a radio station who accepts or agrees to accept from any person (other than such station), or any person (other than such station) who pays or agrees to pay such employee, any money, service or other valuable consideration for the broadcast of any matter over such station shall, in advance of such broadcast, disclose the fact of such acceptance or agreement to such station.

(b)　Subject to subsection (d), any person who, in connection with the production or preparation of any program or program matter which is intended for broadcasting over any radio station, accepts or agrees to accept, or pays or agrees to pay, any money, service or other valuable consideration for the inclusion of any matter as a part of such program or program matter, shall, in advance of such broadcast, disclose the fact of such acceptance or payment or agreement to the payee's employer, or to the person for whom such program or program matter is being produced, or to the licensee of such station over which such program is broadcast.

(c)　Subject to subsection (d), any person who supplies to any other person any program or program matter which is intended for broadcasting over any radio station shall, in advance of such broadcast, disclose to such other person any information of which he has knowledge, or which has been disclosed to him, as to any money, service or other valuable consideration which any person has paid or accepted, or has agreed to pay or accept, for the inclusion of any matter as a part of such program or program matter.

(d)   The provisions of this section requiring the disclosure of information shall not apply in any case where, because of a waiver made by the Commission under section 317(d), an announcement is not required to be made under section 317.

(e)   The inclusion in the program of the announcement required by section 317 shall constitute the disclosure required by this section.

(f)   The term "service or other valuable consideration" as used in this section shall not include any service or property furnished without charge or at a nominal charge for use on, or in connection with, a broadcast, or for use on a program which is intended for broadcasting over any radio station, unless it is so furnished in consideration for an identification in such broadcast or in such program of any person, product, service, trademark, or brand name beyond an identification which is reasonably related to the use of such service or property in such broadcast or such program.

(g)   Any person who violates any provision of this section shall, for each such violation, be fined not more than $10,000 or imprisoned not more than one year, or both.

Prohibited practices in case of contests of intellectual knowledge, intellectual skill, or chance

Sec. 509.   (a)   It shall be unlawful for any person, with intent to deceive the listening or viewing public—

(1)   To supply to any contestant in a purportedly bona fide contest of intellectual knowledge or intellectual skill any special and secret assistance whereby the outcome of such contest will be in whole or in part prearranged or predetermined.

(2)   By means of persuasion, bribery, intimidation, or otherwise, to induce or cause any contestant in a purportedly bona fide contest of intellectual knowledge or intellectual skill to refrain in any manner from using or displaying his knowledge or skill in such contest, whereby the outcome thereof will be in whole or in part prearranged or predetermined.

(3)   To engage in any artifice or scheme for the purpose of prearranging or predetermining in whole or in part the outcome of a purportedly bona fide contest of intellectual knowledge, intellectual skill, or chance.

(4)   To produce or participate in the production for broadcasting of, to broadcast or participate in the broadcasting of, to offer to a licensee for broadcasting, or to sponsor, any radio program, knowing or having reasonable ground for believing that, in connection with a purportedly bona fide contest of

intellectual knowledge, intellectual skill, or chance constituting any part of such program, any person has done or is going to do any act or thing referred to in paragraph (1), (2), or (3) of this subsection.

(5) To conspire with any other person or persons to do any act or thing prohibited by paragraph (1), (2), (3), or (4) of this subsection, if one or more of such persons do any act to effect the object of such conspiracy.

(b) For the purposes of this section—

(1) The term "contest" means any contest broadcast by a radio station in connection with which any money or any other thing of value is offered as a prize or prizes to be paid or presented by the program sponsor or by any other person or persons, as announced in the course of the broadcast.

(2) The term "the listening or viewing public" means those members of the public who, with the aid of radio receiving sets, listen to or view programs broadcast by radio stations.

(c) Whoever violates subsection (a) shall be fined not more than $10,000 or imprisoned not more than one year, or both.

TITLE VI
MISCELLANEOUS PROVISIONS

War emergency — Powers of President

Sec. 606. (a) During the continuance of a war in which the United States is engaged, the President is authorized, if he finds it necessary for the national defense and security, to direct that such communications as in his judgment may be essential to the national defense and security shall have preference or priority with any carrier subject to this Act. He may give these directions at and for such times as he may determine, and may modify, change, suspend, or annul them and for any such purpose he is hereby authorized to issue orders directly, or through such person or persons as he designates for the purpose, or through the Commission. Any carrier complying with any such order or direction for preference or priority herein authorized shall be exempt from any and all provisions in existing law imposing civil or criminal penalties, obligations, or liabilities upon carriers by reason of giving preference or priority in compliance with such order or direction.

(b) It shall be unlawful for any person during any war in which the United States is engaged to knowingly or willfully, by physical force or intimidation by threats of physical force, obstruct or retard or aid in obstructing or retarding interstate or foreign communication by radio or wire. The President is hereby authorized, whenever in his judgment the public interest requires, to employ the armed forces of the United States to prevent any such obstruction or retardation of communication: *Provided*, That nothing in this section shall be construed to repeal, modify, or affect either section 6 or section 20 of the Act entitled "An Act to supplement existing laws against unlawful restraints and monopolies, and for other purposes," approved October 15, 1914.

(c)   Upon proclamation by the President that there exists war or a threat of war, or a state of public peril or disaster or other national emergency, or in order to preserve the neutrality of the United States, the President, if he deems it necessary in the interest of national security, or defense, may suspend or amend, for such time as he may see fit, the rules and regulations applicable to any or all stations or devices capable of emitting electromagnetic radiations within the jurisdiction of the United States as prescribed by the Commission, and may cause the closing of any station for radio communication, or any device capable of emitting electromagnetic radiations between 10 kilocycles and 100,000 megacycles, which is suitable for use as a navigational aid beyond five miles, and the removal therefrom of its apparatus and equipment, or he may authorize the use or control of any such station or device and/or its apparatus and equipment, by any department of the Government under such regulations as he may prescribe upon just compensation to the owners. The authority granted to the President, under this subsection, to cause the closing of any station or device and the removal therefrom of its apparatus and equipment, or to authorize the use or control of any station or device and/or its apparatus and equipment, may be exercised in the Canal Zone.

(d)   Upon proclamation by the President that there exists a state or threat of war involving the United States, the President, if he deems it necessary in the interest of the national security and defense, may, during a period ending not later than six months after the termination of such state or threat of war and not later than such earlier date as the Congress by concurrent resolution may designate, (1) suspend or amend the rules and regulations applicable to any or all facilities or stations for wire communication within the jurisdiction of the United States as prescribed by the Commission, (2) cause the closing of any facility or station for wire communication and the removal therefrom of its apparatus and equipment, or (3) authorize the use or control of any such facility or station and its apparatus and equipment by any department of the Government under such regulations as he may prescribe, upon just compensation to the owners.

(e)   The President shall ascertain the just compensation for such use or control and certify the amount ascertained to Congress for appropriation and payment to the person entitled thereto. If the amount so certified is unsatisfactory to the person entitled thereto, such person shall be paid only 75 per centum of the amount and shall be entitled to sue the United States to recover such further sum as added to such payment of 75 per centum will make such amount as will be just compensation for the use and control. Such suit shall be brought in the manner provided by paragraph 20 of section 24, or by section 145, of the Judicial Code, as amended.

(f)   Nothing in subsection (c) or (d) shall be construed to amend, repeal, impair, or affect existing laws or powers of the States in relation to taxation or the lawful police regulations of the several States, except wherein such laws, powers, or regulations may affect the transmission of Government communications, or the issue of stocks and bonds by any communication system or systems.

(g)   Nothing in subsection (c) or (d) shall be construed to authorize the President to make any amendment to the rules and regulations of the Commission which the Commission would not be authorized by law to make; and nothing in subsection (d) shall be construed to authorize the President to take any action the force and effect of which shall continue beyond the date after which taking of such action would not have been authorized.

(h)   Any person who willfully does or causes or suffers to be done any act prohibited pursuant to the exercise of the President's authority under this section, or who willfully fails to do any act which he is required to do pursuant to the exercise of the President's authority under this section, or who willfully causes or suffers such failure, shall, upon conviction thereof, be punished for such offense by a fine of not more than $1,000 or by imprisonment for not more than one year, or both, and, if a firm, partnership, association, or corporation, by fine of not more than $5,000, except that any person who commits such an offense with intent to injure the United States, or with intent to secure an advantage to any foreign nation, shall, upon conviction thereof, be punished by a fine of not more than $20,000 or by imprisonment for not more than 20 years, or both.

48

The Criminal Code

Title 18, United States Code

These selected sections of the U.S. Criminal Code pertaining to broadcasting supplement the provisions of the Communications Act of 1934 as amended. Section 1464 of the Code was originally incorporated in the Communications Act itself as part of Section 326; see Section 29 of the Radio Act of 1927 (p. 46) for the exact wording of the ban as it existed until 1948.

Section 1304 of the Code was also part of the Communications Act (Section 316) prior to 1948. The spread of state-sponsored lotteries prompted passage of Section 1307 of the Criminal Code which, as of January 2, 1975, makes Section 1304 inapplicable to "an advertisement, list of prizes, or information concerning a lottery conducted by a State acting under authority of State law . . . broadcast by a radio or television station licensed to a location in that State or an adjacent State which conducts such a lottery. . . ."

Related Reading: 30, 239.

§ 1304.　Broadcasting lottery information

Whoever broadcasts by means of any radio station for which a license is required by any law of the United States, or whoever, operating any such station, knowingly permits the broadcasting of, any advertisement of or information concerning any lottery, gift enterprise, or similar scheme, offering prizes dependent in whole or in part upon lot or chance, or any list of the prizes drawn or awarded by means of any such lottery, gift enterprise, or scheme, whether said list contains any part or all of such prizes, shall be fined not more than $1,000 or imprisoned not more than one year, or both.

Each day's broadcasting shall constitute a separate offense.

(Codified June 25, 1948, Ch. 645, 62 Stat. 763.)

§ 1343.   Fraud by wire, radio, or television

Whoever, having devised or intending to devise any scheme or artifice to defraud, or for obtaining money or property by means of false or fraudulent pretenses, representations, or promises, transmits or causes to be transmitted by means of wire, radio, or television communication in interstate or foreign commerce, any writings, signs, signals, pictures, or sounds for the purpose of executing such scheme or artifice, shall be fined not more than $1,000 or imprisoned not more than five years, or both.

(Codified July 16, 1952, Ch. 879, sec. 18(a), 66 Stat. 722; amended July 11, 1956, Ch. 561, 70 Stat. 523.)

§ 1464.   Broadcasting obscene language

Whoever utters any obscene, indecent, or profane language by means of radio communication shall be fined not more than $10,000 or imprisoned not more than two years, or both.

(Codified June 25, 1948, Ch. 645, 62 Stat. 769.)

49

The NAB TV Code*

19th Edition
June, 1976 (Amended through
September, 1977)

Broadcasters first subjected themselves to voluntary self-regulation through their trade association, the National Association of Broadcasters (NAB), in 1929 (see Document 12, pp. 63–66). During the past half-century self-regulation in broadcasting has become pervasive and complex, as comparison of this Television Code with the 1929 Code and Standards demonstrates.

The current TV Code is a product of the gradual evolution of broadcasting as a governmentally regulated mass medium and business. The values reflected in the TV Code parallel those expressed in the companion NAB Radio Code, a copy of which may be obtained from:

The Code Authority
National Association of Broadcasters
1771 N Street, N.W.
Washington, D.C. 20036

The TV Code is divided into two major parts: program standards and advertising standards. The programming guidelines are more generally phrased and open to individual interpretation than the advertising rules, most of which are relatively specific and unequivocal. Although most commercial television stations and the three national networks subscribe to the Code, more than one-third of the stations do not. Reasons for not subscribing vary. Some

*Reprinted with the permission of the Code Authority, National Association of Broadcasters.

telecasters have developed their own self-regulatory structures whose provisions and enforceability, they feel, are superior to those of the NAB. Other broadcasters are unable to subscribe to the Code in good faith, for they know they cannot adhere to the Code's advertising time limitations; such stations operate in markets capable of providing only marginal advertising revenues. They cannot afford what Sydney Head aptly calls the "luxury of integrity."

The broadcasters who support the Code do so for many reasons. Many feel that the Code embodies a realistic ethical approach to responsible broadcasting with which they agree and by which they can abide. Others use the Code as a convenient excuse not to develop their own standards. Code subscribers find some security by belonging—there is "safety in numbers." All TV licensees are aware that if they don't regulate themselves, somebody else will regulate them. Self-regulation by trade association is more palatable to the industry as an instrument of content control than government decrees.

But while the Code can be perceived as an indication of enlightened collective responsibility in broadcasting, it is not without problems, of which lax enforcement is only one. The NAB TV Code is, for the most part, a defensive gesture rather than a mark of true professionalism. It is used as a kind of window dressing to show off to civic groups, legislators, and the FCC whenever increased external control of broadcasting is threatened. Without federal saber rattling, the Codes have been swords rusting in their scabbards.

Broadcasters successfully fought off an attempt by the FCC in 1963–1964 to adopt the NAB Radio and TV Codes' commercial time standards as Commission regulations. Nevertheless, broadcasters have been much less reluctant to enact code provisions in order to allay governmental intervention in such areas as cigarette commercials (see p. 360) and advertising standards applicable to children's television programming.

In 1975 this characteristic industry response to government "jawboning" became regulatory incest when the NAB adopted the "family viewing time" provisions found in the last three paragraphs of Section I of the TV Code below. Influential legislators had been urging the FCC to "do something" about what was widely regarded as excessive sex and violence on television. Commission staff members and FCC Chairman Richard Wiley discussed this problem privately with TV network executives on a number of occasions, after which the family viewing time standards were promulgated as part of the Code. The following year, however, a federal district court ruled that family viewing time was a violation of the First Amendment because it was adopted by the industry under threat of government action at the urging of the FCC. The court went on to say, "NAB attempts to enforce the family viewing policy in any way would violate the First Amendment," as does the delegation of programming authority regarding family viewing matters by the networks to the NAB. "The networks are required to independently program. . . " [*Writers Guild of America, West, Inc.* v. *FCC*, 423 F.Supp. 1064, 1161 (C.D. Cal. 1976)]. This case was being appealed as this volume went to press.* Its outcome, perhaps ultimately to be decided by the Supreme Court, will have incalculable impact on the future of institutionalized collective self-regulation in broadcasting.

Related Reading: 28, 31, 55, 101, 132, 139, 144, 148, 154, 171, 179, 185, 225.

PREAMBLE

Television is seen and heard in nearly every American home. These homes include children and adults of all ages, embrace all races and all varieties of philosophic or religious conviction and reach those of every educational background. Television broadcasters must take this pluralistic audience into account in programming their stations. They are obligated to bring their positive responsibility for professionalism and reasoned judgment to bear upon all those involved in the development, production and selection of programs.

The free, competitive American system of broadcasting which offers programs of entertainment, news, general information, education and culture is supported and made possible by revenues from advertising. While television broadcasters are responsible for the programming and advertising on their stations, the advertisers who use television to convey their commercial messages also have a responsibility to the viewing audience. Their advertising messages should be presented in an honest, responsible and tasteful manner. Advertisers should also support the endeavors of broadcasters to offer a diversity of programs that meet the needs and expectations of the total viewing audience.

The viewer also has a responsibility to help broadcasters serve the public. All viewers should make their criticisms and positive suggestions about programming and advertising known to the broadcast licensee. Parents particularly should

* *In Writers Guild of America* v. *American Broadcasting Co.,* 609 F. 2d 355 (9th Cir. 1979), the district courts' decision was vacated and remanded to permit the FCC to exercise primary jurisdiction over the complaints against it, whereupon appeal was taken to the Supreme Court on procedural grounds.

oversee the viewing habits of their children, encouraging them to watch programs that will enrich their experience and broaden their intellectual horizons.

PROGRAM STANDARDS

I. Principles governing program content

It is in the interest of television as a vital medium to encourage programs that are innovative, reflect a high degree of creative skill, deal with significant moral and social issues and present challenging concepts and other subject matter that relate to the world in which the viewer lives.

Television programs should not only reflect the influence of the established institutions that shape our values and culture, but also expose the dynamics of social change which bear upon our lives.

To achieve these goals, television broadcasters should be conversant with the general and specific needs, interests and aspirations of all the segments of the communities they serve. They should affirmatively seek out responsible representatives of all parts of their communities so that they may structure a broad range of programs that will inform, enlighten, and entertain the total audience.

Broadcasters should also develop programs directed toward advancing the cultural and educational aspects of their communities.

To assure that broadcasters have the freedom to program fully and responsibly, none of the provisions of this Code should be construed as preventing or impeding broadcast of the broad range of material necessary to help broadcasters fulfill their obligations to operate in the public interest.

The challenge to the broadcaster is to determine how suitably to present the complexities of human behavior. For television, this requires exceptional awareness of considerations peculiar to the medium.

Accordingly, in selecting program subjects and themes, great care must be exercised to be sure that treatment and presentation are made in good faith and not for the purpose of sensationalism or to shock or exploit the audience or appeal to prurient interests or morbid curiosity.

Additionally, entertainment programming inappropriate for viewing by a general family audience should not be broadcast during the first hour of network entertainment programming in prime time and in the immediately preceding hour. In the occasional case when an entertainment program in this time period is deemed to be inappropriate for such an audience, advisories should be used to alert viewers. Advisories should also be used when programs in later prime time periods contain material that might be disturbing to significant segments of the audience.

These advisories should be presented in audio and video form at the beginning of the program and when deemed appropriate at a later point in the program. Advisories should also be used responsibly in promotional material in advance of the program. When using an advisory, the broadcaster should attempt to notify publishers of television program listings.

Special care should be taken with respect to the content and treatment of audience advisories so that they do not disserve their intended purpose by containing material that is promotional, sensational or exploitative. Promotional announcements for programs that include advisories should be scheduled on a basis consistent with the purpose of the advisory.

II. Responsibility toward children

Broadcasters have a special responsibility to children. Programs designed primarily for children should take into account the range of interests and needs of children from instructional and cultural material to a wide variety of entertainment material. In their totality, programs should contribute to the sound, balanced development of children to help them achieve a sense of the world at large and informed adjustments to their society.

In the course of a child's development, numerous social factors and forces, including television, affect the ability of the child to make the transition to adult society.

The child's training and experience during the formative years should include positive sets of values which will allow the child to become a responsible adult, capable of coping with the challenges of maturity.

Children should also be exposed, at the appropriate times, to a reasonable range of the realities which exist in the world sufficient to help them make the transition to adulthood.

Because children are allowed to watch programs designed primarily for adults, broadcasters should take this practice into account in the presentation of material in such programs when children may constitute a substantial segment of the audience.

All the standards set forth in this section apply to both program and commercial material designed and intended for viewing by children.

III. Community responsibility

1. Television broadcasters and their staffs occupy positions of unique responsibility in their communities and should conscientiously endeavor to be acquainted fully with the community's needs and characteristics in order better to serve the welfare of its citizens.

2. Requests for time for the placement of public service announcements or programs should be carefully reviewed with respect to the character and reputation of the group, campaign or organization involved, the public interest content of the message, and the manner of its presentation.

IV. Special program standards

1. Violence, physical or psychological, may only be projected in responsibly handled contexts, not used exploitatively. Programs involving violence should present the consequences of it to its victims and perpetrators.

Presentation of the details of violence should avoid the excessive, the gratuitous and the instructional.

The use of violence for its own sake and the detailed dwelling upon brutality or physical agony, by sight or by sound, are not permissible.

The depiction of conflict, when presented in programs designed primarily for children, should be handled with sensitivity.

2. The treatment of criminal activities should always convey their social and human effects.

The presentation of techniques of crime in such detail as to be instructional or invite imitation shall be avoided.

3. Narcotic addiction shall not be presented except as a destructive habit. The use of illegal drugs or the abuse of legal drugs shall not be encouraged or shown as socially acceptable.

4. The use of gambling devices or scenes necessary to the development of plot or as appropriate background is acceptable only when presented with discretion and in moderation, and in a manner which would not excite interest in, or foster, betting nor be instructional in nature.

5. Telecasts of actual sports programs at which on-the-scene betting is permitted by law shall be presented in a manner in keeping with federal, state and local laws, and should concentrate on the subject as a public sporting event.

6. Special precautions must be taken to avoid demeaning or ridiculing members of the audience who suffer from physical or mental afflictions or deformities.

7. Special sensitivity is necessary in the use of material relating to sex, race, color, age, creed, religious functionaries or rites, or national or ethnic derivation.

8. Subscribers shall not broadcast any material which they determine to be obscene, profane or indecent.

Above and beyond the requirements of law, broadcasters must consider the family atmosphere in which many of their programs are viewed.

There shall be no graphic portrayal of sexual acts by sight or sound. The portrayal of implied sexual acts must be essential to the plot and presented in a responsible and tasteful manner.

Subscribers are obligated to bring positive responsibility and reasoned judgment to bear upon all those involved in the development, production and selection of programs.

9. The presentation of marriage, the family and similarly important human relationships, and material with sexual connotations, shall not be treated exploitatively or irresponsibly, but with sensitivity. Costuming and movements of all performers shall be handled in a similar fashion.

10. The use of liquor and the depiction of smoking in program content shall be deemphasized. When shown, they should be consistent with plot and character development.

11. The creation of a state of hypnosis by act or detailed demonstration on camera is prohibited, and hypnosis as a form of "parlor game" antics to create humorous situations within a comedy setting is forbidden.

12. Program material pertaining to fortune-telling, occultism, astrology, phrenology, palm-reading, numerology, mind-reading, character-reading, and the like is unacceptable if it encourages people to regard such fields as providing commonly accepted appraisals of life.

13. Professional advice, diagnosis and treatment will be presented in conformity with law and recognized professional standards.

14. Any technique whereby an attempt is made to convey information to the viewer by transmitting messages below the threshold of normal awareness is not permitted.

15. The use of animals, consistent with plot and character delineation, shall be in conformity with accepted standards of humane treatment.

16. Quiz and similar programs that are presented as contests of knowledge, information, skill or luck must, in fact, be genuine contests; and the results must not be controlled by collusion with or between contestants, or by any other action which will favor one contestant against any other.

17. The broadcaster shall be constantly alert to prevent inclusion of elements within a program dictated by factors other than the requirements of the program itself. The acceptance of cash payments or other considerations in return for including scenic properties, the choice and identification of prizes, the selection of music and other creative program elements and inclusion of any identification of commercial products or services, their trade names or advertising slogan within the program are prohibited except in accordance with Sections 317 and 508 of the Communications Act.

18. Contests may not constitute a lottery.

19. No program shall be presented in a manner which through artifice or simulation would mislead the audience as to any material fact. Each broadcaster must exercise reasonable judgment to determine whether a particular method of presentation would constitute a material deception, or would be accepted by the audience as normal theatrical illusion.

20. A television broadcaster should not present fictional events or other non-news material as authentic news telecasts or announcements, nor permit drama-

tizations in any program which would give the false impression that the dramatized material constitutes news.

21. The standards of this Code covering program content are also understood to include, wherever applicable, the standards contained in the advertising section of the Code.

V. Treatment of news and public events

General

Television Code standards relating to the treatment of news and public events are, because of constitutional considerations, intended to be exhortatory. The standards set forth hereunder encourage high standards of professionalism in broadcast journalism. They are not to be interpreted as turning over to others the broadcaster's responsibility as to judgments necessary in news and public events programming.

News

1. A television station's news schedule should be adequate and well-balanced.

2. News reporting should be factual, fair and without bias.

3. A television broadcaster should exercise particular discrimination in the acceptance, placement and presentation of advertising in news programs so that such advertising should be clearly distinguishable from the news content.

4. At all times, pictorial and verbal material for both news and comment should conform to other sections of these standards, wherever such sections are reasonably applicable.

5. Good taste should prevail in the selection and handling of news:

Morbid, sensational or alarming details not essential to the factual report, especially in connection with stories of crime or sex, should be avoided. News should be telecast in such a manner as to avoid panic and unnecessary alarm.

6. Commentary and analysis should be clearly identified as such.

7. Pictorial material should be chosen with care and not presented in a misleading manner.

8. All news interview programs should be governed by accepted standards of ethical journalism, under which the interviewer selects the questions to be asked. Where there is advance agreement materially restricting an important or newsworthy area of questioning, the interviewer will state on the program that such limitation has been agreed upon. Such disclosure should be made if the per-

son being interviewed requires that questions be submitted in advance or participates in editing a recording of the interview prior to its use on the air.

9. A television broadcaster should exercise due care in the supervision of content, format, and presentation of newscasts originated by his/her station, and in the selection of newscasters, commentators, and analysts.

Public events

1. A television broadcaster has an affirmative responsibility at all times to be informed of public events, and to provide coverage consonant with the ends of an informed and enlightened citizenry.

2. The treatment of such events by a television broadcaster should provide adequate and informed coverage.

VI. Controversial public issues

1. Television provides a valuable forum for the expression of responsible views on public issues of a controversial nature. The television broadcaster should seek out and develop with accountable individuals, groups and organizations, programs relating to controversial public issues of import to his/her fellow citizens; and to give fair representation to opposing sides of issues which materially affect the life or welfare of a substantial segment of the public.

2. Requests by individuals, groups or organizations for time to discuss their views on controversial public issues should be considered on the basis of their individual merits, and in the light of the contribution which the use requested would make to the public interest, and to a well-balanced program structure.

3. Programs devoted to the discussion of controversial public issues should be identified as such. They should not be presented in a manner which would mislead listeners or viewers to believe that the program is purely of an entertainment, news, or other character.

4. Broadcasts in which stations express their own opinions about issues of general public interest should be clearly identified as editorials. They should be unmistakably identified as statements of station opinion and should be appropriately distinguished from news and other program material.

VII. Political telecasts

1. Political telecasts should be clearly identified as such. They should not be presented by a television broadcaster in a manner which would mislead listeners or viewers to believe that the program is of any other character.

(Ref.: Communications Act of 1934, as amended, Secs. 315 and 317, and FCC Rules and Regulations, Secs. 3.654, 3.657, 3.663, as discussed in NAB's "Political Broadcast Catechism & The Fairness Doctrine.")

VIII. Religious programs

1. It is the responsibility of a television broadcaster to make available to the community appropriate opportunity for religious presentations.

2. Programs reach audiences of all creeds simultaneously. Therefore, both the advocates of broad or ecumenical religious precepts, and the exponents of specific doctrines, are urged to present their positions in a manner conducive to viewer enlightenment on the role of religion in society.

3. In the allocation of time for telecasts of religious programs the television station should use its best efforts to apportion such time fairly among responsible individuals, groups and organizations.

ADVERTISING STANDARDS

IX. General advertising standards

1. This Code establishes basic standards for all television broadcasting. The principles of acceptability and good taste within the Program Standards section govern the presentation of advertising where applicable. In addition, the Code establishes in this section special standards which apply to television advertising.

2. Commercial television broadcasters make their facilities available for the advertising of products and services and accept commercial presentations for such advertising. However, television broadcasters should, in recognition of their responsibility to the public, refuse the facilities of their stations to an advertiser where they have good reason to doubt the integrity of the advertiser, the truth of the advertising representations, or the compliance of the advertiser with the spirit and purpose of all applicable legal requirements.

3. Identification of sponsorship must be made in all sponsored programs in accordance with the requirements of the Communications Act of 1934, as amended, and the Rules and Regulations of the Federal Communications Commission

4. Representations which disregard normal safety precautions shall be avoided. Children shall not be represented, except under proper adult supervision, as

being in contact with or demonstrating a product recognized as potentially dangerous to them.

5. In consideration of the customs and attitudes of the communities served, each television broadcaster should refuse his/her facilities to the advertisement of products and services, or the use of advertising scripts, which the station has good reason to believe would be objectionable to a substantial and responsible segment of the community. These standards should be applied with judgment and flexibility, taking into consideration the characteristics of the medium, its home and family audience, and the form and content of the particular presentation.

6. The advertising of hard liquor (distilled spirits) is not acceptable.

7. The advertising of beer and wines is acceptable only when presented in the best of good taste and discretion, and is acceptable only subject to federal and local laws.

8. Advertising by institutions or enterprises which in their offers of instruction imply promises of employment or make exaggerated claims for the opportunities awaiting those who enroll for courses is generally unacceptable.

9. The advertising of firearms/ammunition is acceptable provided it promotes the product only as sporting equipment and conforms to recognized standards of safety as well as all applicable laws and regulations. Advertisements of firearms/ammunition by mail order are unacceptable. The advertising of fireworks is unacceptable.

10. The advertising of fortune-telling, occultism, astrology, phrenology, palm-reading, numerology, mind-reading, character-reading or subjects of a like nature is not permitted.

11. Because all products of a personal nature create special problems, acceptability of such products should be determined with especial emphasis on ethics and the canons of good taste. Such advertising of personal products as is accepted must be presented in a restrained and obviously inoffensive manner.

12. The advertising of tip sheets and other publications seeking to advertise for the purpose of giving odds or promoting betting is unacceptable.

The lawful advertising of government organizations which conduct legalized lotteries is acceptable provided such advertising does not unduly exhort the public to bet.

The advertising of private or governmental organizations which conduct legalized betting on sporting contests is acceptable provided such advertising is limited to institutional type announcements which do not exhort the public to bet.

13. An advertiser who markets more than one product should not be permitted to use advertising copy devoted to an acceptable product for purposes of publicizing the brand name or other identification of a product which is not acceptable.

14. "Bait-switch" advertising, whereby goods or services which the advertiser has no intention of selling are offered merely to lure the customer into purchasing higher-priced substitutes, is not acceptable.

15. Personal endorsements (testimonials) shall be genuine and reflect personal experience. They shall contain no statement that cannot be supported if presented in the advertiser's own words.

X. Presentation of advertising

1. Advertising messages should be presented with courtesy and good taste; disturbing or annoying material should be avoided; every effort should be made to keep the advertising message in harmony with the content and general tone of the program in which it appears.

2. The role and capability of television to market sponsors' products are well recognized. In turn, this fact dictates that great care be exercised by the broadcaster to prevent the presentation of false, misleading or deceptive advertising. While it is entirely appropriate to present a product in a favorable light and atmosphere, the presentation must not, by copy or demonstration, involve a material deception as to the characteristics, performance or appearance of the product.

Broadcast advertisers are responsible for making available, at the request of the Code Authority, documentation adequate to support the validity and truthfulness of claims, demonstrations and testimonials contained in their commercial messages.

3. The broadcaster and the advertiser should exercise special caution with the content and presentation of television commercials placed in or near programs designed for children. Exploitation of children should be avoided. Commercials directed to children should in no way mislead as to the product's performance and usefulness.

Commercials, whether live, film or tape, within programs initially designed primarily for children under 12 years of age shall be clearly separated from program material by an appropriate device.

Trade name identification or other merchandising practices involving the gratuitous naming of products is discouraged in programs designed primarily for children.

Appeals involving matters of health which should be determined by physicians should not be directed primarily to children.

4. No children's program personality or cartoon character shall be utilized to deliver commercial messages within or adjacent to the programs in which such a personality or cartoon character regularly appears. This provision shall also apply to lead-ins to commercials when such lead-ins contain sell copy or imply endorsement of the product by program personalities or cartoon characters.

5. Appeals to help fictitious characters in television programs by purchasing the advertiser's product or service or sending for a premium should not be

permitted, and such fictitious characters should not be introduced into the advertising message for such purposes.

6. Commercials for services or over-the-counter products involving health considerations are of intimate and far-reaching importance to the consumer. The following principles should apply to such advertising:

a. Physicians, dentists or nurses or actors representing physicians, dentists or nurses, shall not be employed directly or by implication. These restrictions also apply to persons professionally engaged in medical services (e.g., physical therapists, pharmacists, dental assistants, nurses' aides).

b. Visual representations of laboratory settings may be employed, provided they bear a direct relationship to bona fide research which has been conducted for the product or service. (*See Television Code, X, 11*) In such cases, laboratory technicians shall be identified as such and shall not be employed as spokespersons or in any other way speak on behalf of the product.

c. Institutional announcements not intended to sell a specific product or service to the consumer and public service announcements by non-profit organizations may be presented by accredited physicians, dentists or nurses, subject to approval by the broadcaster. An accredited professional is one who has met required qualifications and has been licensed in his/her resident state.

7. Advertising should offer a product or service on its positive merits and refrain from discrediting, disparaging or unfairly attacking competitors, competing products, other industries, professions or institutions.

8. A sponsor's advertising messages should be confined within the framework of the sponsor's program structure. A television broadcaster should avoid the use of commercial announcements which are divorced from the program either by preceding the introduction of the program (as in the case of so-called "cow-catcher" announcements) or by following the apparent sign-off of the program (as in the case of so-called trailer or "hitch-hike" announcements). To this end, the program itself should be announced and clearly identified, both audio and video, before the sponsor's advertising material is first used, and should be signed off, both audio and video, after the sponsor's advertising material is last used.

9. Since advertising by television is a dynamic technique, a television broadcaster should keep under surveillance new advertising devices so that the spirit and purpose of these standards are fulfilled.

10. A charge for television time to churches and religious bodies is not recommended.

11. Reference to the results of bona fide research, surveys or tests relating to the product to be advertised shall not be presented in a manner so as to create an impression of fact beyond that established by the work that has been conducted.

XI. Advertising of medical products

1. The advertising of medical products presents considerations of intimate and far-reaching importance to consumers because of the direct bearing on their health.

2. Because of the personal nature of the advertising of medical products, claims that a product will effect a cure and the indiscriminate use of such words as "safe," "without risk," harmless," or terms of similar meaning should not be accepted in the advertising of medical products on television stations.

3. A television broadcaster should not accept advertising material which in his/her opinion offensively describes or dramatizes distress or morbid situations involving ailments, by spoken word, sound or visual effects.

XII. Contests

1. Contests shall be conducted with fairness to all entrants, and shall comply with all pertinent laws and regulations. Care should be taken to avoid the concurrent use of the three elements which together constitute a lottery—prize, chance and consideration.

2. All contest details, including rules, eligibility requirements, opening and termination dates should be clearly and completely announced and/or shown, or easily accessible to the viewing public, and the winners' names should be released and prizes awarded as soon as possible after the close of the contest.

3. When advertising is accepted which requests contestants to submit items of product identification or other evidence of purchase of products, reasonable facsimiles thereof should be made acceptable unless the award is based upon skill and not upon chance.

4. All copy pertaining to any contest (except that which is required by law) associated with the exploitation or sale of the sponsor's product or service, and all references to prizes or gifts offered in such connection should be considered a part of and included in the total time allowances as herein provided. (*See Television Code, XIV*)

XIII. Premiums and offers

1. Full details of proposed offers should be required by the television broadcaster for investigation and approved before the first announcement of the offer is made to the public.

2. A final date for the termination of an offer should be announced as far in advance as possible.

3. Before accepting for telecast offers involving a monetary consideration, a television broadcaster should be satisfied as to the integrity of the advertiser and the advertiser's willingness to honor complaints indicating dissatisfaction with the premium by returning the monetary consideration.

4. There should be no misleading descriptions or visual representations of any premiums or gifts which would distort or enlarge their value in the minds of the viewers.

5. Assurances should be obtained from the advertiser that premiums offered are not harmful to person or property.

6. Premiums should not be approved which appeal to superstition on the basis of "luck-bearing" powers or otherwise.

XIV. Time standards for non-program material*

In order that the time for non-program material and its placement shall best serve the viewer, the following standards are set forth in accordance with sound television practice:

1. Non-Program Material Definition:

Non-program material, in both prime and all other time, includes billboards, commercials and promotional announcements.

Non-program material also includes:

a. In programs of 90 minutes in length or less, credits in excess of 30 seconds per program, except in feature films, shall be counted against the allowable time for non-program material. In no event should credits exceed 40 seconds in such programs.

The 40 second limitation on credits shall not apply, however, in any situation governed by a contract entered into before October 1, 1971.

b. In programs longer than 90 minutes, credits in excess of 50 seconds per program, except in feature films, shall be counted against the allowable time for non-program material. In no event should credits exceed 60 seconds in such programs.

Public service announcements and promotional announcements for the same program are excluded from this definition.

2. Allowable Time for Non-Program Material:

a. In prime time on network affiliated stations, non-program material shall not exceed 9 minutes 30 seconds in any 60-minute period.

*See Time Standards for Independent Stations, pp. 592–593.

Prime time is a continuous period of not less than 3 consecutive hours per broadcast day as designated by the station between the hours of 6:00 P.M. and midnight.

b. In all other time, non-program material shall not exceed 16 minutes in any 60-minute period.

c. Children's Programming Time—Defined as those hours other than prime time in which programs initially designed primarily for children under 12 years of age are scheduled.

Within this time period on Saturday and Sunday, non-program material shall not exceed 9 minutes 30 seconds in any 60-minute period.

Within this time period on Monday through Friday, non-program material shall not exceed 12 minutes in any 60-minute period.

3. Program Interruptions:

a. Definition: A program interruption is any occurrence of non-program material within the main body of the program.

b. In prime time, the number of program interruptions shall not exceed 2 within any 30-minute program, or 4 within any 60-minute program.

Programs longer than 60 minutes shall be prorated at 2 interruptions per half-hour.

The number of interruptions in 60-minute variety shows shall not exceed 5.

c. In all other time, the number of interruptions shall not exceed 4 within any 30-minute program period.

d. In children's weekend programming time, as above defined in 2c, the number of program interruptions shall not exceed 2 within any 30-minute program or 4 within any 60-minute program.

e. In both prime time and all other time, the following interruption standard shall apply within programs of 15 minutes or less in length:

5-minute program—1 interruption;
10-minute program—2 interruptions;
15-minute program—2 interruptions.

f. News, weather, sports and special events programs are exempt from the interruption standard because of the nature of such programs.

4. No more than 4 non-program material announcements shall be scheduled consecutively within programs, and no more than 3 non-program material announcements shall be scheduled consecutively during station breaks. The consecutive non-program material limitation shall not apply to a single sponsor who wishes to further reduce the number of interruptions in the program.

5. A multiple product announcement is one in which 2 or more products or services are presented within the framework of a single announcement. A multiple product announcement shall not be scheduled in a unit of time less than 60 seconds, except where integrated so as to appear to the viewer as a single message. A multiple product announcement shall be considered integrated and counted as a single announcement if:

a. the products or services are related and interwoven within the framework of the announcement (related products or services shall be defined as those having a common character, purpose and use); and

b. the voice(s), setting, background and continuity are used consistently throughout so as to appear to the viewer as a single message.

Multiple product announcements of 60 seconds in length or longer not meeting this definition of integration shall be counted as 2 or more announcements under this section of the Code. This provision shall not apply to retail or service establishments.

6. [Deleted on June 29, 1977.—Ed.]

7. Reasonable and limited identification of prizes and donors' names where the presentation of contest awards or prizes is a necessary part of program content shall not be included as non-program material as defined above.

8. Programs presenting women's/men's service features, shopping guides, fashion shows, demonstrations and similar material provide a special service to the public in which certain material normally classified as non-program is an informative and necessary part of the program content. Because of this, the time standards may be waived by the Code Authority to a reasonable extent on a case-by-case basis.

9. Gratuitous references in a program to a non-sponsor's product or service should be avoided except for normal guest identification.

10. Stationary backdrops or properties in television presentations showing the sponsor's name or product, the name of the sponsor's product, trade-mark or slogan should be used only incidentally and should not obtrude on program interest or entertainment.

Time standards for independent stations

1. Non-program elements shall be considered as all-inclusive, with the exception of required credits, legally required station identifications, and "bumpers." Promotion spots and public service announcements, as well as commercials, are to be considered non-program elements.

2. The allowed time for non-program elements, as defined above, shall not

exceed seven minutes in a 30-minute period or multiples thereof in prime time (prime time is defined as any three contiguous hours between 6:00 P.M. and midnight, local time), or eight minutes in a 30-minute period or multiples thereof during all other times.

3. Where a station does not carry a commercial in a station break between programs, the number of program interruptions shall not exceed four within any 30-minute program, or seven within any 60-minute program, or 10 within any 90-minute program, or 13 in any 120-minute program. Stations which do carry commercials in station breaks between programs shall limit the number of program interruptions to three within any 30-minute program, or six within any 60-minute program, or nine within any 90-minute program, or 12 in any 120-minute program. News, weather, sports, and special events are exempted because of format.

4. Not more than four non-program material announcements as defined above shall be scheduled consecutively. An exception may be made only in the case of a program 60 minutes or more in length, when no more than seven non-program elements may be scheduled consecutively by stations who wish to reduce the number of program interruptions.

5. The conditions of paragraphs three and four shall not apply to live sports programs where the program format dictates and limits the number of program interruptions.

Legal Citation and Glossary

Because legal citations are incomprehensible to the uninitiated, this explanation is intended for readers who wish to explore sources cited throughout the text. A legal citation is a kind of shorthand, like map coordinates or the symbols used in a chemical formula, enabling one to find the material to which reference is made. Once you know the system, using citations becomes easy.

A complete citation begins with the name of the case, usually in italics. For example, the name of the case in Document 41 (pp. 407–425) is *Columbia Broadcasting System, Inc.* v. *Democratic National Committee.* (The "v." between the two parties in a case is unitalicized and is a standard legal abbreviation for "versus.") The case name is followed by a comma, after which appears a series of numbers and letters constituting a citation to a published source of the decision called a "reporter." The citation for the above case is 412 U.S. 94 (1973). "U.S." means the reporter cited is *United States Reports,* the official government version of United States Supreme Court decisions published by the Government Printing Office. The number immediately preceding the letters, "412," stands for the volume in which the decision is found. The number directly after the letters indicates the first page of the decision. And the number in parentheses following the page denotes the year in which the case was decided. The complete citation for this case is: *Columbia Broadcasting System, Inc.* v. *Democratic National Committee,* 412 U.S. 94 (1973). You could examine the full text of this case, which was decided in 1973, by asking your library for volume 412 of *United States Reports* and turning to page 94. (If you read through all of the concurring and dissenting opinions, you would find yourself at

page 204. Some decisions are even longer, but most are con-
iderably shorter than this example.)

The following reporters and their abbreviations are the most
frequently encountered in broadcast law citations:

Abbreviation	Name of Reporter
FCC (or F.C.C.)	*Federal Communications Commission Reports*
F. (or Fed.)	*Federal Reporter*
F.Supp.	*Federal Supplement*
Ops. Att'y Gen (or Op.)	*Opinions of the Attorney General*
R.R. (or Radio Reg.)	*Radio Regulation* (Pike and Fischer)
S.Ct. (or Sup. Ct.)	*Supreme Court Reporter*
U.S. App. D.C.	*U.S. Court of Appeals, District of Columbia*
U.S.	*United States Reports*
L.Ed.	*U.S. Supreme Court Reports, Lawyer's Edition*

*Indicates the official government reporter published by the
Government Printing Office. Privately published reporters are
used more widely than the "official" reporter in some instances,
and they are frequently cited as alternates to the official reporter.

A citation followed by the notation "2d" means the decision
is found in the second series of the indicated reporter. For example, 506 F.2d 246 (Document 43) refers to a decision that
begins on page 246 of volume 506 of *Federal Reporter*, second
series. F., FCC, and R.R. are presently in their second series. An
entry such as 57 FCC 2d 418, 441 (Document 44) indicates a
specific page (441 in this example) of a document that starts on
an earlier page (namely, page 418 of volume 57 of *Federal Communications Commission Reports*, second series).

Citations are also made to sources of legal documents other
than decisions, such as laws, regulations, etc. C.F.R. indicates the
Code of Federal Regulations, Title 47 of which embodies the
rules and regulations of the Federal Communications Commission. Proposed and enacted FCC rules appear in the daily *Federal
Register,* abbreviated Fed. Reg. or FR. Acts of Congress are
found in *Statutes at Large* (Stat.), the *United States Code* (U.S.C.),
or the *United States Code Annotated* (U.S.C.A.). FCC Ann. Rep.

refers to the *Annual Reports* of the Federal Communications Commission. The *Congressional Record* (Cong. Rec.) contains transcripts of debates on the floor of the Senate and House of Representatives. Records of hearings before congressional committees are separately published by the Government Printing Office. Miscellaneous reports of congressional committees and other legislative documents, including presidential messages to Congress, are compiled in serial sets for each house of Congress.

For further guidance concerning legal notation consult the latest edition of *A Uniform System of Citation* published by the Harvard Law Review Association, Cambridge, Massachusetts 02138. Another useful supplementary source is Joseph M. Foley's article, "Broadcast Regulation Research: A Primer for Non-Lawyers," in the *Journal of Broadcasting*, 17, No. 2 (Spring 1973), pp. 147–157.

Legal terminology, too, poses obstacles for people who want to understand the language of broadcast regulation. The FCC, courts, and Congress are, for the most part, bodies of lawyers dealing with other lawyers. They frequently use "legalese," a para-language fully comprehensible only to Latin scholars, bureaucrats, and law school graduates. While the use of specialized jargon is not intended to impede the transfer of meaning to lay persons, unfortunately this is often its effect.

Because law is far too important a matter to be left only to lawyers, the user of this book must make a special effort to understand legalese. Any standard law dictionary (*Black's,* for example) will serve to define legal terms, as will Daniel Oran's highly portable and recommended *Law Dictionary for Non-Lawyers* (St. Paul, Minn.: West Publishing Company, 1975). Below is a glossary of many of the specialized legal terms appearing in this volume.

GLOSSARY

ad hoc   temporary, for a specific circumstance; case-by-case.

administrative law judge   presiding officer at FCC hearings who takes and weighs evidence and issues a preliminary decision subject to modification by the Commission itself; formerly called "hearing examiner" or simply "examiner."

arguendo   for argument's sake.

bona fide(s)   in good faith; genuine; free of intent to deceive or of knowledge of fraud.

certiorari (abbreviated *cert.*)   an appeal, typically to the U.S. Supreme Court; if the Court grants a petition for writ of *certiorari*, case records are transmitted by the lower court (such as the Court of Appeals) to the High Court for "certification," meaning review.

de minimus   insignificant; small; trifling.

dicta (plural of *dictum*)   see *obiter dicta.*

en banc (or **in banc**)   a session which the entire membership of a court or the FCC meets together.

et seq.   abbreviation for *et sequens;* and (the) following.

examiner   see **administrative law judge**.

ex parte   one-sided; contact with a decision-making authority by one party to a proceeding without the other parties present.

ex rel.   in relation to; on behalf of.

id., Id.   same as *ibid.* or *ibidem;* something already cited or referred to.

infra   below; following; opposite of *supra.*

in haec verba   in these words.

in re   in the matter of; used frequently in administrative case titles or whenever "versus" would be inappropriate.

inter alia   in addition to other things.

obiter dicta   the portions of a decision that are tangential (or even irrelevant) to the legal determination; not legally binding; opposite of *ratio decidendi.*

prima facie   at first glance; sufficient to satisfy the initial burden of proof and, if uncontradicted, to determine the outcome of a proceeding.

pro forma   according to form; a formality.

pro tanto   for so much; to such (an) extent.

ratio decidendi   the portions of a decision that are central to the resolution of a case; having the weight of precedent; opposite of *obiter dicta.*

remand   to send back to a lower body; an appellate court oftens returns a reversed case to the body that issued the improper decision with instructions to rectify the errors causing reversal.

seriatim   one at a time; in order; each in turn.

sine qua non   the essence; an indispensable part.

standing   the right to participate in a legal proceeding, typically restricted to those having a substantial stake in the outcome.

stare decisis   the judicial doctrine that legal precedent will be adhered to in subsequent cases raising similar issues unless there are powerful reasons not to do so.

statute   an enacted bill; a law passed by the legislature.

stay order   an enforceable command issued by a court to prevent something from taking place, either temporarily or permanently.

sua sponte   spontaneously, as when the FCC or a court acts on its own initiative instead of in response to a petition or motion of a party to a proceeding.

supra   above; preceding; opposite of *infra.*

ultra vires   beyond the scope; exceeding permissible authority.

vel non   or not.

Bibliography

The entries in this selective bibliography are numbered to correspond to the **Related Reading** references given at the end of the introductory remarks for each of the preceding documents. Entry numbers 47, 79, 99, and 216a are basic broadcasting textbooks. Entries 71, 80, 81, 90, 116, 158, and 221 are legal texts. Comprehensive histories of broadcasting are 2, 8, 9, 10, 11, 137, 215a, and 241.

Students of historical, regulatory, and public policy aspects of broadcasting who want the latest data in their field should consult *Broadcasting* magazine (for weekly news reports), *Journal of Broadcasting* and *Journal of Communication* (for scholarly articles on historical and issue oriented facets of mass telecommunications), and the *Index to Legal Periodicals* (for monthly listings and annual compilations of law review coverage found under the "Radio" heading). *Mass Media Booknotes* is the most convenient monthly survey of newly published books in the field. For current subscription rates and a sample copy, write to:

Dr. Christopher H. Sterling
Editor, *Mass Media Booknotes*
School of Communications and Theater
Temple University
Philadelphia, Pennsylvania   19122

1. Appelman, Daniel, "The OTP and Reorganizational Alternatives," *Public Telecommunications Review*, 5, No. 1 (January/February 1977), 44-51. [Revised and extended in *Telecommunications Policy*, 1, No. 3 (June 1977), 221-229.]

2. Archer, Gleason L., *History of Radio to 1926*. New York; American Historical Society, 1938. (Reprinted New York: Arno Press, 1971.)

3. Baird, Frank L., "Program Regulation on the New Frontier," *Journal of Broadcasting,* 11, No. 3 (Summer 1967), 231–243.

4. Baker, W. J., *A History of the Marconi Company.* New York: St. Martin's Press, 1972.

5. Baldwin, Thomas F., and Stuart H. Surlin, "A Study of Broadcast Station License Application Exhibits on Ascertainment of Community Needs," *Journal of Broadcasting,* 14, No. 2 (Spring 1970), 157–170.

6. Banning, William P., *Commercial Broadcasting Pioneer: The WEAF Experiment, 1922-1926.* Cambridge, Mass.: Harvard University Press, 1946.

7. Barber, Oren G., "Competition, Free Speech, and FCC Radio Network Regulations," *George Washington Law Review,* 12 (December 1943), 34–53.

8. Barnouw, Erik, *The Golden Web: A History of Broadcasting in the United States, Vol. II—1933-1953.* New York: Oxford University Press, 1968.

9. Barnouw, Erik, *The Image Empire: A History of Broadcasting in the United States, Vol. III—from 1953.* New York: Oxford University Press, 1970.

10. Barnouw, Erik, *A Tower in Babel: A History of Broadcasting in the United States, Vol. I—to 1933.* New York: Oxford University Press, 1966.

11. Barnouw, Erik, *Tube of Plenty: The Development of American Television.* New York: Oxford University Press, 1975.

12. Barron, Jerome A., "Access to the Press—A New First Amendment Right," *Harvard Law Review,* 80 (1967), 1641–1678.

13. Barron, Jerome A., *Freedom of the Press for Whom? The Right of Access to Mass Media.* Bloomington, Indiana: Indiana University Press, 1973.

14. Barth, Alan, ed., *Rights in Conflict: Report of the Twentieth Century Fund Task Force on Justice, Publicity, and the First Amendment.* New York: McGraw-Hill, 1976.

15. Barton, Richard L., "The Lingering Legacy of Pacifica: Broadcasters' Freedom of Silence," *Journalism Quarterly,* 53, No. 3 (Autumn 1976), 429–433.

16. Bazelon, David L., "FCC Regulation of the Telecommunications Press," *Duke Law Journal,* 1975, No. 2 (May 1975), 213–251.

17. Bennett, Robert W., *A Lawyer's Sourcebook: Representing the Audience in Broadcast Proceedings.* New York: Office of Communication of the United Church of Christ, 1974.

18. Bensman, Marvin R., "Regulation of Broadcasting by the Department of Commerce, 1921-1927," pp. 544–555, 682–683 of Lichty and Topping, eds., *American Broadcasting* (see entry number 137).

19. Bensman, Marvin R., "The Zenith-WJAZ Case and the Chaos of 1926-27," *Journal of Broadcasting,* 14, No. 4 (Fall 1970), 423–440.

20. Bernstein, Marver H., *Regulating Business by Independent Commission.* Princeton, N.J.: Princeton University Press, 1955.

21. Blake, Jonathan D., "Red Lion Broadcasting Co. v. FCC: Fairness and the Emperor's New Clothes," *Federal Communications Bar Journal,* 23, No. 2 (1969), 75-92.

22. Blakely, Robert J., *The People's Instrument: A Philosophy for Public Television.* Washington, D.C.: Public Affairs Press, 1971.

23. Bliss, Edward, Jr., ed., *In Search of Light: The Broadcasts of Edward R. Murrow, 1938-1961.* New York: Alfred A. Knopf, 1967.

24. Bluem, A. William, *Documentary in American Television.* New York: Hastings House, 1965.

25. Botein, Michael, "New Copyright Act and Cable Television—A Signal of Change," *Bulletin of the Copyright Society of the U.S.A.,* 24 (October 1976), 1-17.

26. Branscomb, Anne W., "The Cable Fable: Will It Come True?," *Journal of Communication,* 25, No. 1 (Winter 1975), 44-56.

27. Brenner, Daniel L., "Toward a New Balance in License Renewals," *Journal of Broadcasting,* 17, No. 1 (Winter 1972-1973), 63-76.

28. Brenner, Daniel L., "The Limits of Broadcast Self-Regulation Under the First Amendment," *Stanford Law Review,* 27, No. 6 (July 1975), 1527-1562. [Reprinted in *Federal Communications Bar Journal,* 28, No. 1 (1975), 1-62.]

29. *Broadcasting and the Bill of Rights.* Washington, D.C.: National Association of Broadcasters, 1947.

30. *Broadcasting and the Federal Lottery Laws,* 5th ed. Washington D.C.: National Association of Broadcasters, 1974.

31. Brown, Les, "Westinghouse's McGannon Hits TV Industry Code," *The New York Times,* April 9, 1976, p. 74.

32. Burke, John E., "The Public Broadcasting Act of 1967—Parts I-III," *Educational Broadcasting Review,* 6 (1972), 105-119, 178-192, 251-266.

33. Cabinet Committee on Cable Communications, *Cable: Report to the President.* Washington, D.C.: Government Printing Office, 1974.

34. *Cable Communications and the States: A Sourcebook for Legislative Decision-Makers.* Albany: New York State Senate, 1975.

35. Caldwell, Louis G., "Freedom of Speech and Radio Broadcasting," *The Annals of the American Academy of Political and Social Science,* 177 (January 1935), 179-207. (Reprinted in *Radio: Selected A.A.P.S.S. Surveys, 1929-1941.* New York: Arno Press, 1971.)

36. Caldwell, O. H., "The Administration of Federal Radio Legislation," *The Annals of the American Academy of Political and Social Science,* 142 (supplement, March 1929), 45-56. (Reprinted in *Radio: Selected A.A.P.S.S. Surveys, 1929-1941.* New York: Arno Press, 1971.)

37. Cantril, Hadley, *The Invasion from Mars: A Study in the Psychology of Panic.* Princeton, N.J.: Princeton University Press, 1940. (Reprinted New York: Harper & Row, 1966.)

38. Carlson, Robert A., "1951: A Pivotal Year for ETV," *Educational Broadcasting Review,* 1, No. 2 (December 1967), 47–54.

39. Carnegie Commission on Educational Television, *Public Television: A Program for Action.* New York: Harper & Row, 1967.

40. Carson, Gerald, *The Roguish World of Doctor Brinkley.* New York: Holt, Rinehart and Winston, 1960.

41. Cater, Douglass, and Michael J. Nyhan, eds., *The Future of Public Broadcasting.* New York: Praeger, 1976.

42. *Catholic University Law Review,* 24, No. 4 (Summer 1975), 677–898. (The entire issue deals with "Developing Legal Issues in Cable Communications.")

43. Chayes, Abram, et al., *Satellite Broadcasting.* London: Oxford University Press, 1973.

44. Chazen, Leonard, and Leonard Ross, "Federal Regulation of Cable Television: The Visible Hand," *Harvard Law Review,* 83 (1970), 1820–1841.

45. Chester, Edward W., *Radio, Television and American Politics.* New York: Sheed and Ward, 1969.

46. Chester, Giraud, "The Press–Radio War: 1933–1935," *Public Opinion Quarterly,* 13 (Summer 1949), 252–264.

47. Chester, Giraud, Garnet R. Garrison, and Edgar E. Willis, *Television and Radio,* 5th ed. Englewood Cliffs, N.J.: Prentice-Hall, 1978.

48. Chisman, Forrest P., "Public Interest and FCC Policy Making," *Journal of Communication,* 27, No. 1 (Winter 1977), 77–84.

49. Coase, R. H., "The Federal Communications Commission," *Journal of Law and Economics,* 2 (October 1959), 1–40.

50. *Code of Professional Responsibility and Code of Judicial Conduct.* Chicago: American Bar Association, 1975.

51. Cogley, John, *Report on Blacklisting: Radio–Television,* Vol. II. New York: Fund for the Republic, 1956. (Reprinted New York: Arno Press, 1971.)

52. Cole, John P., Jr., "Community Antenna Television, The Broadcaster Establishment, and the Federal Regulator," *American University Law Review,* 16 (June 1965), 125–145.

53. Comanor, William S., and Bridger M. Mitchell, "The Costs of Planning: The FCC and Cable Television," *Journal of Law and Economics,* 15 (April 1972), 177–206.

54. Commission on Campaign Costs in the Electronic Era, *Voters' Time.* New York: Twentieth Century Fund, 1969.

55. Committee for Economic Development, *Broadcasting and Cable Television: Policies for Diversity and Change.* New York: Committee for Economic Development, 1975.

56. *Control of the Direct Broadcast Satellite: Values in Conflict.* Palo Alto, Calif.: Aspen Institute Program on Communications and Society, 1974.

57. Crandall, Robert W., "The Economic Effect of Television Network Program 'Ownership,'" *Journal of Law and Economics,* 14 (October 1971), 385–412.

58. Culbert, David Holbrook, *News for Everyman: Radio and Foreign Affairs in Thirties America.* Westport, Conn.: Greenwood Press, 1976.

59. Cushman, Robert E., *The Independent Regulatory Commissions.* New York: Oxford University Press, 1941. (Reprinted New York: Octagon Books, 1972.)

60. Danna, Sammy R., "The Rise of Radio News" and "The Press–Radio War," *Freedom of Information Center Reports 211* and *213,* reprinted with abridgment in pp. 338–350, 674–675 of Lichty and Topping, eds., *American Broadcasting* (see entry number 137).

61. Davis, Stephen. *The Law of Radio Communication.* New York: McGraw-Hill, 1927.

62. Dill, Clarence C., "Radio and the Press: A Contrary View," *The Annals of the American Academy of Political and Social Science,* 177 (January 1935), 170–175. (Reprinted in *Radio: Selected A.A.P.S.S. Surveys, 1929 1941.* New York: Arno Press, 1971.)

63. Doerfer, John C., "Community Antenna Television Systems," *Federal Communications Bar Journal,* 14 (1955), 4–14.

64. Dreher, Carl, "How the Wasteland Began: The Early Days of Radio," *The Atlantic,* 217 (February 1966), 53–58.

65. Dunlap, Orrin E., Jr., *Communications in Space,* 3rd ed. New York: Harper & Row, 1970.

66. Dunn, Delmer D., *Financing Presidential Campaigns.* Washington, D.C.: The Brookings Institution, 1972.

67. Dunning, John, *Tune in Yesterday: The Ultimate Encyclopedia of Old-Time Radio.* Englewood Cliffs, N.J.: Prentice-Hall, 1976.

68. "Electronic Journalism and First Amendment Problems: Recommendations of Communications Law Committee, Section on Science and Technology, American Bar Association," *Federal Communications Bar Journal,* 29, No. 1 (1976), 1–61.

69. Emery, Edwin, *The Press and America: An Interpretative History of the Mass Media,* 3rd ed. Englewood Cliffs, N.J.: Prentice-Hall, 1972.

70. Emery, Michael C., "The Munich Crisis Broadcasts: Radio News Comes of Age," *Journalism Quarterly,* 42 (1965), 576–580.

71. Emery, Walter B., *Broadcasting and Government: Responsibilities and Regulations,* rev. ed. East Lansing, Mich.: Michigan State University Press, 1971.

72. Emery, Walter B., *National and International Systems of Broadcasting: Their History, Operation and Control.* East Lansing, Mich.: Michigan State University Press, 1969.

73. Esplin, Fred C., "Looking Back: Clay Whitehead's OTP," *Public Telecommunications Review,* 3, No. 2 (March/April 1975), 17-22.

74. Fang, Irving, E., and John W. Whelan, Jr., "Survey of Television Editorials and Ombudsman Segments," *Journal of Broadcasting,* 17, No. 3 (Summer 1973), 363-371.

75. Federal Communications Commission, *Report on Chain Broadcasting.* Washington, D.C.: Government Printing Office, 1941. (Reprinted New York: Arno Press, 1974.)

76. Feldman, Charles, and Stanley Tickton, "Obscene/Indecent Programming: Regulation of Ambiguity," *Journal of Broadcasting,* 20, No. 2 (Spring 1976), 273-282.

77. Foley, Joseph M., "Ascertaining Ascertainment: Impact of the FCC Primer on TV Renewal Applications," *Journal of Broadcasting,* 16, No. 4 (Fall 1972), 387-406.

78. Ford, Frederick W., "The Meaning of the 'Public Interest, Convenience or Necessity,'" *Journal of Broadcasting,* 5, No. 3 (Summer 1961), 205-218.

79. Foster, Eugene S., *Understanding Broadcasting.* Reading, Mass.: Addison-Wesley, 1978.

80. Francois, William E., *Mass Media Law and Regulation.* Columbus, Ohio: Grid, 1975.

81. Franklin, Marc A., *Cases and Materials on Mass Media Law.* Mineola, N.Y.: Foundation Press, 1977.

82. Friendly, Alfred, and Ronald L. Goldfarb, *Crime and Publicity.* New York: Twentieth Century Fund, 1967.

83. Friendly, Fred W., *Due to Circumstances Beyond Our Control . . . .* New York: Random House, 1967.

84. Friendly, Fred W., *The Good Guys, the Bad Guys and the First Amendment: Free Speech vs. Fairness in Broadcasting.* New York: Random House, 1976.

85. Friendly, Henry J., *The Federal Administrative Agencies: The Need for Better Definition of Standards.* Cambridge, Mass.: Harvard University Press, 1962.

86. Frost, S. E., Jr., *Education's Own Stations.* Chicago: University of Chicago Press, 1937. (Reprinted New York: Arno Press, 1971.)

87. Galloway, Jonathan, *The Politics and Technology of Satellite Communications.* Lexington, Mass.: Lexington Books, 1972.

88. Geller, Henry, "The Comparative Renewal Process in Television: Problems and Suggested Solutions," *Virginia Law Review,* 61, No. 3 (April 1975), 471-514.

89. Gillmor, Donald M., *Free Press and Fair Trial.* Washington, D.C.: Public Affairs Press, 1967.

90. Gillmor, Donald M., and Jerome A. Barron, *Mass Communication Law: Cases and Comment,* 2nd ed. St. Paul, Minn.: West Publishing Co., 1974.

91. Goldin, Hyman H., " 'Spare the Golden Goose'—the Aftermath of WHDH in FCC License Renewal Policy," *Harvard Law Review,* 83 (1970), 1014-1036.

92. Grundfest, Joseph, "Participation in FCC Licensing," *Journal of Communication,* 27, No. 1 (Winter 1977), 85-88.

93. Guback, Thomas H., "Political Broadcasting and Public Policy," *Journal of Broadcasting,* 12, No. 3 (Summer 1968), 191-211.

94. Guimary, Donald L., *Citizens Groups and Broadcasting.* New York: Praeger, 1975.

95. Gumpert, Gary, and Dan F. Hahn, "An Historical and Organizational Perspective of the Office of Telecommunications Policy," *Educational Broadcasting Review,* 6 (1972), 309-314.

96. Hall, W. Clayton, Jr., and Robert Bomi D. Batlivala, "The Prime-Time Rule: A Misadventure in Broadcast Regulation?", *Journal of Broadcasting,* 17, No. 2 (Spring 1973), 215-222.

97. Hamburg, Morton I., "Use of Broadcasting Facilities: A Matter of Fairness," *New York Law Forum,* 21, No. 2 (Fall 1975), 209-230.

98. Harris, E. H., "Radio and the Press," *The Annals of the American Academy of Political and Social Science,* 177 (January 1935), 163-169. (Reprinted in *Radio: Selected A.A.P.S.S. Surveys, 1929-1941.* New York: Arno Press, 1971.)

99. Head, Sydney W., *Broadcasting in America,* 3rd ed. Boston: Houghton Mifflin, 1976.

100. Heighton, Elizabeth J., and Don R. Cunningham, *Advertising in the Broadcast Media.* Belmont, Calif.: Wadsworth, 1976.

101. Helffrich, Stockton, "The Radio and Television Codes and the Public Interest," *Journal of Broadcasting,* 14, No. 3 (Summer 1970), 267-274.

102. Herman W. Land Associates, Inc., *The Hidden Medium: A Status Report on Educational Radio in the United States.* Washington, D.C.: National Association of Educational Broadcasters, 1967.

103. Hesbacher, Peter, et al., "Radio Format Strategies," *Journal of Communication*, 26, No. 1 (Winter 1976), 110–119.

104. Hightower, Paul, "Canon 35 Remains Same Despite Courtroom Tests," *Journalism Quarterly*, 52, No. 3 (Autumn 1975), 546–548.

105. Hoffer, Thomas W., and Gerald A. Butterfield, "The Right to Reply: A Florida First Amendment Aberration," *Journalism Quarterly*, 53, No. 1 (Spring 1976), 111–116.

106. Holt, Darrel, "The Origin of 'Public Interest' in Broadcasting," *Educational Broadcasting Review*, 1, No. 1 (October 1967), 15–19.

107. Hoover, Herbert, *The Memoirs of Herbert Hoover: The Cabinet and the Presidency, 1920-1933,* pp. 139–148. New York: Macmillan, 1952.

108. Hyde, Rosel H., "FCC Policy and Procedures Relating to Hearings on Broadcast Applications in Which a New Applicant Seeks to Displace a Licensee Seeking Renewal," *Duke Law Journal,* 1975, No. 2 (May 1975), 253–278.

109. Jaffe, Louis L., "The Editorial Responsibility of the Broadcaster: Reflections on Fairness and Access," *Harvard Law Review,* 85 (1972), 768–792.

110. Jaffe, Louis L., "WHDH: The FCC and Broadcasting License Renewals," *Harvard Law Review,* 82 (1969), 1693–1702.

111. Jansky, C. M., Jr., "The Contribution of Herbert Hoover to Broadcasting," *Journal of Broadcasting,* 1, No. 3 (Summer 1957), 241–249.

112. Jennings, Ralph M., and Pamela Richard, *How to Protect Your Rights in Television and Radio.* New York: Office of Communication of the United Church of Christ, 1974.

113. Johnson, Nicholas, "Freedom to Create: The Implications of Antitrust Policy for Television Programming Content," *Law and the Social Order* (1970), 337–377.

114. Johnson, Nicholas, *How to Talk Back to Your Television Set.* Boston: Atlantic-Little, Brown, 1970.

115. Johnson, Nicholas, and John Jay Dystel, "A Day in the Life: The Federal Communications Commission," *Yale Law Journal,* 82, No. 8 (July 1973), 1575–1634.

116. Jones, William K., *Cases and Materials on Electronic Mass Media: Radio, Television and Cable.* Mineola, N.Y.: Foundation Press, 1976.

117. Kahn, Frank J., "Economic Injury and the Public Interest," *Federal Communications Bar Journal,* 23, No. 3 (1969), 182–201.

118. Kahn, Frank J., "The Quasi-Utility Basis for Broadcast Regulation," *Journal of Broadcasting,* 18, No. 3 (Summer 1974), 259–276.

119. Kahn, Frank J., "Regulation of Intramedium 'Economic Injury' by the

FCC," *Journal of Broadcasting,* 13, No. 3 (Summer 1969), 221-240.

120. Katzman, Natan, *Program Decisions in Public Television.* Washington, D.C.: National Association of Educational Broadcasters, 1976.

121. Kendrick, Alexander, *Prime Time: The Life of Edward R. Murrow.* Boston: Little, Brown, 1969.

122. Kinsley, Michael, *Outer Space and Inner Sanctums: Government, Business, and Satellite Communication.* New York: John Wiley & Sons, 1976.

123. Kittross, John M., ed., *Documents in American Telecommunications Policy,* Vol. 1. New York: Arno Press, 1977.

124. Kittross, John M., and Kenneth Harwood, eds., *Free and Fair: Courtroom Access and the Fairness Doctrine.* Philadelphia: Association for Professional Broadcasting Education, 1970.

125. Koch, Howard, *The Panic Broadcast: Portrait of an Event.* Boston: Little, Brown, 1970.

126. Kohlmeier, Louis M., Jr., *The Regulators: Watchdog Agencies and the Public Interest.* New York: Harper & Row, 1969.

127. Krasnow, Erwin G., and Lawrence D. Longley, *The Politics of Broadcast Regulation.* New York: St. Martin's Press, 1973.

128. Kraus, Sidney, ed., *The Great Debates.* Bloomington: Indiana University Press, 1962.

129. Kubin, Karen J., "Antitrust Implications of Network Television Programming," *Hastings Law Journal,* 27 (May 1976), 1207-1229.

130. Le Duc, Don R., *Cable Television and the FCC: A Crisis in Media Control.* Philadelphia: Temple University Press, 1973.

131. Le Duc, Don R., and Thomas A. McCain, "The Federal Radio Commission in Federal Court: Origins of Broadcast Regulatory Doctrines," *Journal of Broadcasting,* 14, No. 4 (Fall 1970), 393-410.

132. Lee, Robert E., "Self-Regulation or Censorship," *Educational Broadcasting Review,* 3, No. 5 (October 1969), 17-20.

133. Legal Advisory Committee on Fair Trial and Free Press, *Fair Trial/Free Press: Voluntary Agreements.* Chicago: American Bar Association, 1974.

134. Legal Advisory Committee on Fair Trial and Free Press, *The Rights of Fair Trial and Free Press.* Chicago: American Bar Association, 1969.

135. Leone, Richard C., "Public Interest Advocacy and the Regulatory Process," *The Annals of the American Academy of Political and Social Science,* 400 (March 1972), 46-58.

136. Lichty, Lawrence W., "The Impact of FRC and FCC Commissioners' Backgrounds on the Regulation of Broadcasting," *Journal of Broadcasting,* 6, No. 2 (Spring 1962), 97-110.

137. Lichty, Lawrence W., and Malachi C. Topping, eds., *American Broadcasting: A Sourcebook on the History of Radio and Television.* New York: Hastings House, 1975.

138. Lindsey, Michael K., "Public Broadcasting: Editorial Restraints and the First Amendment," *Federal Communications Bar Journal,* 28, No. 1 (1975), 63–100.

139. Linton, Bruce A., *Self-Regulation in Broadcasting: A Three-Part College-Level Study Guide.* Washington, D.C.: National Association of Broadcasters, 1967.

140. Lott, George E., Jr., "The Press-Radio War of the 1930s," *Journal of Broadcasting,* 14, No. 3 (Summer 1970), 275–286.

141. Lynd, Robert D., "Banzhaf v. FCC: Public Interest and the Fairness Doctrine," *Federal Communications Bar Journal,* 23, No. 1 (1969), 39–56.

142. Lyons, Eugene, *David Sarnoff.* New York: Harper & Row, 1966.

143. MacAvoy, Paul W., ed., *The Crisis of the Regulatory Commissions.* New York: Norton, 1970.

144. Mackey, David R., "The Development of the National Association of Broadcasters," *Journal of Broadcasting,* 1, No. 4 (Fall 1957), 305–325.

145. Macy, John, Jr., *To Irrigate a Wasteland: The Struggle to Shape a Public Television System in the United States.* Berkeley: University of California Press, 1974.

146. Mayer, Martin, "The Challengers," *TV Guide,* February 3, 1973, 5–13; February 10, 1973, 33–40; February 17, 1973, 18–21.

147. McDaniel, Drew, and Lewis A. Day, "INTELSAT and Communist Nations' Policy on Communications Satellites," *Journal of Broadcasting,* 18, No. 3 (Summer 1974), 311–321.

148. McGannon, Donald H., "Is the TV Code a Fraud?", *TV Guide,* January 22, 1977, 11–13.

149. McGranery, Regina C., "Exemptions from the Section 315 Equal Time Standard: A Proposal for Presidential Elections," *Federal Communications Bar Journal,* 24, No. 2 (1970–1971), 177–205.

150. McKinney, Eleanor, ed., *The Exacting Ear: The Story of Listener-Sponsored Radio.* New York: Random House, 1966.

151. Meyer, Richard J., " 'The Blue Book,' " *Journal of Broadcasting,* 6, No. 3 (Summer 1962), 197–207.

152. Meyer, Richard J., "Reaction to the 'Blue Book,' " *Journal of Broadcasting,* 6, No. 4 (Fall 1962), 295–312.

153. *Miami Herald v. Tornillo: The Trial of the First Amendment.* Columbia, Missouri: Freedom of Information Center, 1975.

154. Miller, Neville, "Self-Regulation in American Radio," *The Annals of the American Academy of Political and Social Science,* 213 (January 1941), 93-96. (Reprinted in *Radio: Selected A.A.P.S.S. Surveys, 1929-1941.* New York: Arno Press, 1971.)

155. Minasian, Jora R., "The Political Economy of Broadcasting in the 1920's," *Journal of Law and Economics,* 12 (October 1960), 391-403.

156. Minow, Newton N., *Equal Time: The Private Broadcaster and the Public Interest,* ed., Lawrence Laurent. New York: Atheneum, 1964.

157. Mosco, Vincent, *Reforming Regulation: The FCC and Innovations in the Broadcasting Market.* Cambridge, Mass.: Harvard University Program on Information Technologies and Public Policy, 1976.

158. Nelson, Harold L., and Dwight L. Teeter, Jr., *Law of Mass Communications: Freedom and Control of Print and Broadcast Media,* 2nd ed. Mineola, N.Y.: Foundation Press, 1973.

159. Noll, Roger G., Merton J. Peck, and John J. McGowan, *Economic Aspects of Television Regulation.* Washington, D.C.: The Brookings Institution, 1973.

160. "Note: Federal Regulation of Radio Broadcasting—Standards and Procedures for Regulating Format Changes in the Public Interest," *Rutgers Law Review,* 28 (1975), 966-985.

161. "Note: Filthy Words, the FCC, and the First Amendment: Regulating Broadcast Obscenity," *Virginia Law Review,* 61, No. 3 (April 1975), 579-642.

162. "Note: Judicial Review of FCC Program Diversity Regulations" [by Francis S. Blake], *Columbia Law Review,* 75, No. 2 (March 1975), 401-440.

163. "Note: Offensive Speech and the FCC," *Yale Law Journal,* 79 (June 1970), 1343-1368.

164. Owen, Bruce M., *Economics and Freedom of Expression: Media Structure and the First Amendment.* Cambridge, Mass.: Ballinger, 1975.

165. Owen, Bruce M., Jack H. Beebe, and Willard G. Manning, Jr., *Television Economics.* Lexington, Mass.: Lexington Books, 1974.

166. Padden, Preston R., "The Emerging Role of Citizens' Groups in Broadcast Regulation," *Federal Communications Bar Journal,* 25, No. 2 (1972), 82-110.

167. Palmer, John C., Jr., James R. Smith, and Edwin L. Wade, "Note: Community Antenna Television: Survey of a Regulatory Problem," *Georgetown Law Journal,* 52 (Fall 1963), 136-176.

168. Park, Rolla Edward, ed., *The Role of Analysis in Regulatory Decision-making: The Case of Cable Television.* Lexington, Mass.: Lexington Books, 1973.

169. Pepper, Robert, "The Interconnection Connection: The Formation of PBS," *Public Telecommunications Review,* 4, No. 1 (January/February 1976), 6-26.

170. Phillips, Mary Alice Mayer, *CATV: A History of Community Antenna Television.* Evanston, Ill.: Northwestern University Press, 1972.

171. Pierson, W. Theodore, "The Active Eyebrow—A Changing Style for Censorship," *Television Quarterly,* 1, No. 1 (February 1962), 14-21.

172. Policy Review and Development Division, Cable Television Bureau, *Regulatory Developments in Cable Television.* Washington, D.C.: Federal Communications Commission, 1976.

173. Porter, William E., *Assault on the Media: The Nixon Years.* Ann Arbor: University of Michigan Press, 1976.

174. Post, Steve, *Playing in the FM Band: A Personal Account of Free Radio.* New York: Viking Press, 1974.

175. Powledge, Fred, *The Engineering of Restraint: The Nixon Administration and the Press.* Washington, D.C.: Public Affairs Press, 1971.

176. President's Advisory Council on Executive Organization, *A New Regulatory Framework: Report on Selected Independent Regulatory Agencies.* Washington, D.C.: Government Printing Office, 1971.

177. President's Communications Policy Board, *Telecommunications: A Program for Progress.* Washington, D.C.: Government Printing Office, 1951.

178. President's Task Force on Communications Policy, *Final Report.* Washington, D.C.: Government Printing Office, 1969.

179. Preston, Ivan L., *The Great American Blow-up: Puffery in Advertising and Selling.* Madison, Wisconsin: University of Wisconsin Press, 1975.

180. Price, Monroe E., "Requiem for the Wired Nation: Cable Rulemaking at the FCC," *Virginia Law Review,* 61, No. 3 (April 1975), 541-577.

181. Proxmire, William, "Abandon the Fairness Doctrine!" *TV Guide,* April 12, 1975, 11-12.

182. Quinlan, Sterling, *The Hundred Million Dollar Lunch: The Broadcasting Industry's Own Watergate.* Chicago: Philip O'Hara, Inc., 1974.

183. "Remarks on the Fortieth Anniversary of the Federal Communications Commission," *Federal Communications Bar Journal,* 27, No. 2 (1974), 109-160.

184. *The Report of the Commission on Obscenity and Pornography.* New York: Bantam, 1970.

185. Rintels, David W., " 'Why We Fought the Family Viewing Hour,' " *The New York Times,* November 21, 1976, p. D31.

186. Robinson, Thomas P., *Radio Networks and the Federal Government.* New York: Columbia University Press, 1943.

187. Rosenbloom, Joel, "Authority of the Federal Communications Commission," in *Freedom and Responsibility in Broadcasting,* ed., John E. Coons. Evanston, Ill.: Northwestern University Press, 1961.

188. Ross, Leonard, *Economic and Legal Foundations of Cable Television.* Beverly Hills: Sage, 1974.

189. Rowland, Willard D., Jr., " 'Public Involvement': The Anatomy of a Myth," *Public Telecommunications Review,* 3, No. 3 (May/June 1975), 6-21.

190. Sanders, Keith P., "The Collapse of the Press-Radio News Bureau," *Journalism Quarterly,* 44 (1967), 549-552.

191. Sarno, Edward F., Jr., "The National Radio Conferences," *Journal of Broadcasting,* 13, No. 2 (Spring 1969), 189-202.

192. Sarnoff, David, *Looking Ahead: The Papers of David Sarnoff.* New York: McGraw-Hill, 1968.

193. Scalia, Antonin, "Don't Go Near the Water," *Federal Communications Bar Journal,* 25, No. 2 (1972), 111-120.

194. Schement, Jorge Reina, et al., "The Anatomy of a License Challenge," *Journal of Communication,* 27, No. 1 (Winter 1977), 89-94.

195. Schmeckebier, Lawrence F., *The Federal Radio Commission: Its History, Activities and Organization.* Washington, D.C.: The Brookings Institution, 1932.

196. Schmidt, Benno C., Jr., *Freedom of the Press vs. Public Access.* New York: Praeger, 1976.

197. Schwartz, Bernard, "Comparative Television and the Chancellor's Foot," *Georgetown Law Review,* 47 (Summer 1959), 655-699.

198. Schwartz, Bernard, *The Professor and the Commissions.* New York: Knopf, 1959.

199. Schwartz, Bernard, ed., *The Economic Regulation of Business and Industry: A Legislative History of U.S. Regulatory Agencies,* Vols. III and IV. New York: Chelsea House, 1973. (The two volumes include congressional debates leading to passage of the Radio Act of 1927 and Communications Act of 1934, respectively.)

200. Shapiro, Andrew O., *Media Access: Your Rights to Express Your Views on Radio and Television.* Boston: Little, Brown, 1976.

201. Shayon, Robert Lewis, *Parties in Interest: A Citizens Guide to Improving Television and Radio.* New York: Office of Communication of the United Church of Christ, 1974.

202. Shelby, Maurice E., Jr., "John R. Brinkley: His Contribution to Broadcasting," pp. 560-568, 683-685 of Lichty and Topping, eds., *American Broadcasting* (see entry number 137).

203. Siebert, Frederick S., Theodore Peterson, and Wilbur Schramm, *Four Theories of the Press.* Urbana, Ill.: University of Illinois Press, 1956.

204. Siepmann, Charles A., *Radio's Second Chance*. Boston: Little, Brown, 1946.

205. Simmons, Steven J., "Commercial Advertising and the Fairness Doctrine: The New F.C.C. Policy in Perspective," *Columbia Law Review*, 75, No. 6 (October 1975), 1083-1120.

206. Sloan Commission on Cable Communications, *On the Cable: The Television of Abundance*. New York: McGraw-Hill, 1971.

207. Smith, Robert R., and Paul T. Prince, "WHDH: The Unconscionable Delay," *Journal of Broadcasting*, 18, No. 1 (Winter 1974), 85-96.

208. Spalding, John W., "1928: Radio Becomes a Mass Advertising Medium," *Journal of Broadcasting*, 8, No. 1 (Winter 1963-1964), 31-44.

209. Sparkes, Vernone, "Local Regulatory Agencies for Cable Television," *Journal of Broadcasting*, 19, No. 2 (Spring 1975), 221-233.

210. Special Committee on Radio and Television of the Association of the Bar of the City of New York, *Freedom of the Press and Fair Trial: Final Report with Recommendations*. New York: Columbia University Press, 1967.

211. Sperry, Robert, "A Selected Bibliography of Works on the Federal Communications Commission," *Journal of Broadcasting*, 12, No. 1 (Winter 1967-1968), 83-93. [A 1967-1969 supplement is found in *Journal of Broadcasting*, 14, No. 3 (Summer 1970), 377-389.]

212. Sperry, Robert, "A Selected Bibliography of Works on the FCC and OTP: 1970-1973," *Journal of Broadcasting*, 19, No. 1 (Winter 1975), 55-113.

213. Spievack, Edwin B., "Presidential Assault on Telecommunications," *Federal Communications Bar Journal*, 23, No. 3 (1969), 155-181.

214. Stanton, Frank, "The Case for Political Debates on TV," *The New York Times Magazine*, January 19, 1964, pp. 16, 68-70.

215. Stebbins, Gene R., "Pacifica's Battle for Free Expression," *Educational Broadcasting Review*, 4, No. 3 (June 1970), 19-28.

215a. Sterling, Christopher H., and John M. Kittross, *Stay Tuned: A Concise History of American Broadcasting*. Belmont, Calif.: Wadsworth, 1978.

216. Summers, Harrison B., comp., *Radio Censorship*. New York: H. W. Wilson, 1939. (Reprinted New York: Arno Press, 1971.)

216a. Summers, Harrison B., Robert E. Summers, and John H. Pennybacker, *Broadcasting and the Public*, 2nd ed. Belmont, Calif.: Wadsworth, 1978.

217. Tate, Charles, ed., *Cable Television in the Cities: Community Control, Public Access, and Minority Ownership*. Washington, D.C.: Urban Institute, 1972.

218. Taylor, Reese H., Jr., "The Case for State Regulation of CATV Distribution Systems," *Federal Communications Bar Journal*, 23, No. 2 (1969), 110-121.

219. *Technical Report of the Commission on Obscenity and Pornography,* Vol. II: Legal Analysis. Washington, D.C.: Government Printing Office, 1971.

220. Tomlinson, John D., *The International Control of Radiocommunications.* Geneva, Switzerland: University of Geneva, 1938. (Reprinted New York: Kraus Reprint Co., 1972.)

221. Toohey, Daniel W., Richard D. Marks, and Arnold P. Lutzker, *Legal Problems in Broadcasting: Identification and Analysis of Selected Issues.* Lincoln, Neb.: Great Plains National Instructional Television Library, 1974.

222. Tressel, George W., et al., *The Future of Educational Telecommunication.* Lexington, Mass.: Lexington Books, 1975.

223. United States Congress, House, Committee on Interstate and Foreign Commerce, *Cable Television: Promise Versus Regulatory Performance* (report of the staff of the Subcommittee on Communications). Washington, D.C.: Government Printing Office, 1976.

224. United States Congress, House, Committee on Interstate and Foreign Commerce, *Regulation of Broadcasting: Half a Century of Government Regulation of Broadcasting and the Need for Further Legislative Action,* study for the Committee [by Robert S. McMahon], 85th Congress, 2d Session, on H. Res. 99. Washington, D.C.: Government Printing Office, 1958.

225. United States Congress, House, Committee on Interstate and Foreign Commerce, *Regulation of Radio and Television Cigarette Advertisements,* hearing before the Committee, 91st Congress, 1st Session, on Self-Regulation by the Broadcasting Industry of Radio and Television Cigarette Advertisements, June 10, 1969. Washington, D.C.: Government Printing Office, 1969.

226. United States Congress, House, Committee on Judiciary, *Copyright Law Revision,* hearings before the Subcommittee on Courts, Civil Liberties, and the Administration of Justice, on H.R. 2223, May 7–December 4, 1975, Parts 1–3. Washington, D.C.: Government Printing Office, 1976.

227. United States Congress, Senate, Committee on Commerce, *Amend Communications Act of 1934,* hearings before Communications Subcommittee, 91st Congress, 1st Session, on S. 2004, Part I, August 5–7, 1969; Part II, December 1–5, 1969. Washington, D.C.: Government Printing Office, 1969.

228. United States Congress, Senate, Committee on Commerce, *Appointments to the Regulatory Agencies: The Federal Communications Commission and the Federal Trade Commission (1949–1974)* [by James M. Graham and Victor H. Kramer]. Washington, D.C.: Government Printing Office, 1976.

229. United States Congress, Senate, Committee on Commerce, *Fairness Doctrine,* hearings before Subcommittee on Communications, 94th Congress, 1st Session, on S. 2, . . . April 28–May 6, 1975. Washington, D.C.: Government Printing Office, 1975.

230. United States Congress, Senate, Committee on Commerce, *The FCC's Actions and the Broadcasters' Operations in Connection with the Commis-*

sion's Fairness Doctrine, staff report for the Subcommittee on Communications [by Robert Lowe], 90th Congress, 2d Session. Washington, D.C.: Government Printing Office, 1968.

231. United States Congress, Senate, Committee on Commerce, *The Public Television Act of 1967,* hearings before Subcommittee on Communications, 90th Congress, 1st Session, on S. 1160, April 11-14, 25-28, 1967. Washington, D.C.: Government Printing Office, 1967.

232. United States Congress, Senate, Committee on Commerce, *Waiver of Equal Time Law and the 1976 Presidential Debates,* hearing, 94th Congress, 2d Session, August 24, 1976. Washington, D.C.: Government Printing Office, 1976.

233. United States Congress, Senate, Subcommittee on Freedom of Communications of the Subcommittee on Communications of the Committee on Commerce, *Final Report Pursuant to S. Res. 305, 86th Congress,* Parts I-VI, 87th Congress, 1st and 2d Sessions. Washington, D.C.: Government Printing Office, 1961-1962.

234. "Universal Copyright Convention and the Problem of Community Antenna Television," *Ohio Northern University Law Review,* 3 (1975), 535-549.

235. Voorhees, John, "Development of New Public Interest Standards in the *Format Change Cases,*" *Catholic University Law Review,* 25 (Winter 1976), 364-379.

236. Warren, Albert, "Cable TV, Problem Child: What It Will Be When It Grows Up," *TV Guide,* December 4, 1976, 18-20.

237. Warren, Albert, "What's 26 Years Old and Still Has Growing Pains?", *TV Guide,* November 27, 1976, 4-8.

238. Weinberg, Meyer, *TV in America: The Morality of Hard Cash.* New York: Ballantine, 1962.

239. Wesolowski, James Walter, "Obscene, Indecent, or Profane Broadcast Language as Construed by the Federal Courts," *Journal of Broadcasting,* 13, No. 2 (Spring 1969), 203-219.

240. White, Anthony G., comp., *Copyrights: A Selective Bibliography* (Exchange Bibliography No. 686). Monticello, Ill.: Council of Planning Librarians, 1974.

241. White, Llewellyn, *The American Radio.* Chicago: University of Chicago Press, 1947. (Reprinted New York: Arno Press, 1971.)

242. Williams, Wenmouth, Jr., "Impact of Commissioner Background on FCC Decisions: 1962-1975," *Journal of Broadcasting,* 20, No. 2 (Spring 1976), 239-260.

243. Wolfe, G. Joseph, "Norman Baker and KTNT," *Journal of Broadcasting,* 12, No. 4 (Fall 1968), 389-399.

244. Wood, Donald N., and Donald G. Wylie, *Educational Telecommunications.* Belmont, Calif.: Wadsworth, 1977.

245. Woodby, Kathleen R., and F. Leslie Smith, "The Cigarette Commercial Ban: A Pattern for Change," *Quarterly Journal of Speech,* 60, No. 4 (December 1974), 431–441.

246. Wyckoff, Gene, *The Image Candidates.* New York: Macmillan, 1968.

247. Yaeger, Murray R., "The Evolution of SEE IT NOW," *Journal of Broadcasting,* 1, No. 4 (Fall 1957), 337–344.

Index

to Legal Decisions

(Page references to texts of decisions appear in **boldface** type.)

General Index